THE ASSEMBLY PROGRAMMING MASTER BOOK

LIMITED WARRANTY AND DISCLAIMER OF LIABILITY

THE CD-ROM THAT ACCOMPANIES THE BOOK MAY BE USED ON A SINGLE PC ONLY. THE LICENSE DOES NOT PERMIT THE USE ON A NETWORK (OF ANY KIND). YOU FURTHER AGREE THAT THIS LICENSE GRANTS PERMISSION TO USE THE PRODUCTS CONTAINED HEREIN, BUT DOES NOT GIVE YOU RIGHT OF OWNERSHIP TO ANY OF THE CONTENT OR PRODUCT CONTAINED ON THIS CD-ROM. USE OF THIRD-PARTY SOFTWARE CONTAINED ON THIS CD-ROM IS LIMITED TO AND SUBJECT TO LICENSING TERMS FOR THE RESPECTIVE PRODUCTS.

FIREWALL MEDIA (AN IMPRINT OF LAXMI PUBLICATIONS PVT. LTD.) OR CHARLES RIVER MEDIA, INC. ("CRM") AND/OR ANYONE WHO HAS BEEN INVOLVED IN THE WRITING, CREATION, OR PRODUCTION OF THE ACCOMPANYING CODE ("THE SOFTWARE") OR THE THIRD-PARTY PRODUCTS CONTAINED ON THE CD-ROM OR TEXTUAL MATERIAL IN THE BOOK, CANNOT AND DO NOT WARRANT THE PERFORMANCE OR RESULTS THAT MAY BE OBTAINED BY USING THE SOFTWARE OR CONTENTS OF THE BOOK. THE AUTHOR AND PUBLISHER HAVE USED THEIR BEST EFFORTS TO ENSURE THE ACCURACY AND FUNCTIONALITY OF THE TEXTUAL MATERIAL AND PROGRAMS CONTAINED HEREIN. WE HOWEVER, MAKE NO WARRANTY OF ANY KIND, EXPRESS OR IMPLIED, REGARDING THE PERFORMANCE OF THESE PROGRAMS OR CONTENTS. THE SOFTWARE IS SOLD "AS IS" WITHOUT WARRANTY (EXCEPT FOR DEFECTIVE MATERIALS USED IN MANUFACTURING THE DISK OR DUE TO FAULTY WORKMANSHIP).

THE AUTHOR, THE PUBLISHER, DEVELOPERS OF THIRD-PARTY SOFTWARE, AND ANYONE INVOLVED IN THE PRODUCTION AND MANUFACTURING OF THIS WORK SHALL NOT BE LIABLE FOR DAMAGES OF ANY KIND ARISING OUT OF THE USE OF (OR THE INABILITY TO USE) THE PROGRAMS, SOURCE CODE, OR TEXTUAL MATERIAL CONTAINED IN THIS PUBLICATION. THIS INCLUDES, BUT IS NOT LIMITED TO, LOSS OF REVENUE OR PROFIT, OR OTHER INCIDENTAL OR CONSEQUENTIAL DAMAGES ARISING OUT OF THE USE OF THE PRODUCT.

THE SOLE REMEDY IN THE EVENT OF A CLAIM OF ANY KIND IS EXPRESSLY LIMITED TO REPLACEMENT OF THE BOOK AND/OR CD-ROM, AND ONLY AT THE DISCRETION OF CRM OR FIREWALL MEDIA (AN IMPRINT OF LAXMI PUBLICATIONS PVT. LTD.).

THE USE OF "IMPLIED WARRANTY" AND CERTAIN "EXCLUSIONS" VARIES FROM STATE TO STATE, AND MAY NOT APPLY TO THE PURCHASER OF THIS PRODUCT.

THE ASSEMBLY PROGRAMMING MASTER BOOK

Vlad Pirogov

FIREWALL MEDIA
(An Imprint of Laxmi Publications Pvt.Ltd.)
An ISO 9001:2015 Company

BENGALURU • CHENNAI • GUWAHATI • HYDERABAD
KOCHI • KOLKATA • LUCKNOW • RANCHI
NEW DELHI

THE ASSEMBLY PROGRAMMING MASTER BOOK

Vlad Pirogov. *The Assembly Programming Master Book*

Printed and bound in India

First Edition : 2006, *Reprint :*2008, 2014, 2018, 2020, 2022; *Edition* : 2026

FAS-2836-899-ASSEMBLY PROG MASTER BOOK

ISBN: 81-7008-817-8

Price: ₹ 899.00

Branches

✆	Bengaluru	080-26 75 69 30
✆	Chennai	044-24 34 47 26
✆	Guwahati	0361-254 36 69
✆	Hyderabad	040-27 55 53 83
✆	Kochi	0484-405 13 03
✆	Kolkata	033-40 04 77 79
✆	Lucknow	0522-430 36 13
✆	Ranchi	0651-224 24 64

PUBLISHED IN INDIA BY

FIREWALL MEDIA
(An Imprint of Laxmi Publications Pvt.Ltd.)
An ISO 9001:2015 Company
113, GOLDEN HOUSE, GURUDWARA ROAD, DARYAGANJ,
NEW DELHI - 110002, INDIA

Corporate Office : B-33, Sector-5, Noida,
Gautambuddha Nagar (U.P.) - 201 301, INDIA
Telephone : +91-120-44 46 900
www.laxmipublications.com
info@laxmipublications.com

C—R/026/08
Printed at: Sanjeev Offset Printers, Delhi-110051.

Contents

Introduction

Writing programs in Assembly language for a long time meant writing programs for MS-DOS. The arrival of the Windows 95 operating system has changed the position of the Assembly language programming. In a certain respect, Assembly programming didn't recover its lost position till now. By writing this book, I aim to encourage programmers to pay attention to this interesting field of programming and recover the Assembly language position.

There are lots of books concentrating on the topic of Assembly programming in general and Windows programming using the Assembly language in particular. However, I have done a considerable job revising, improving, and refining such materials. These revisions relate not only to Assembly language but also to the new capabilities of contemporary operating systems of the Windows NT family, including Windows 2000, Windows XP, and Windows Server 2003. For example, the book includes special chapters concentrating on file management, the development of services, and kernel-mode drivers.

I'd also like to mention that all examples included in this book were tested under operating systems of the Windows NT family. Therefore, although I did my best, I cannot guarantee that all examples will work under Windows 9*x* and Windows Millennium Edition (ME). The same relates to processors: all examples were tested on computers equipped with Pentium III and Pentium IV.

When developing programs presented in this book, I used two assemblers — Microsoft Assembler (MASM) and Turbo Assembler (TASM). Recently, Borland sold the TASM assembler to Paradigm, and now this product is available under another name — PASM. However, because TASM remains popular among programmers writing in Assembly language, I still use the TASM term and, whenever possible, develop programs oriented toward both compilers.

In many respects, this book reflects my point of view on programming and a methodic of teaching programming. This relates to the Assembly macro tools. In my opinion, they substantially hide the beauty of the Assembly language and its capabilities. I think that when explaining programming as a technology and describing programming style, using macro tools makes you forget that programming for many individuals is an art. These two sides of programming often come into conflict. However, this relates to specific philosophical aspects; therefore, this topic will not be covered in this book.

So, why do you need the Assembly language when programming for Windows? After all, there is C language to speak nothing of other high-level programming languages. The simplest and the most convincing answer to this question is that Assembly language is the processor's language; consequently, it will exist as long as processors exist. Other conclusive proof of the importance of Assembly language is that it is needed for optimizing program code, developing drivers, translators, programming some peripheral devices, etc. Finally, programming in Assembly language gives you a sense of power over the computer, and striving for power is a basic human instinct.

As relates to the Windows,[i] programming in Assembly language for this operating system is much easier that programming for MS-DOS, however strange this might seem to most programmers. In this book, I try to prove that programming in Assembly language is no more difficult that doing the same thing using high-level languages such as C language. Furthermore, you'll get compact, efficient, and fast code using Assembly language. Unfortunately, when working with high-level languages, most programmers lose certain algorithmic skills, and the implications of this process are ongoing. Honestly, improving your professional skills alone makes the Assembly language worth studying.

The book also includes material that can be considered hackish. I pay special attention to the methods and tools of analyzing and correcting program code. To those who insist that this practice is illegal and immoral, I would argue that because hackers exist, you should know their methods of work. This knowledge will be useful for most programmers.

It is necessary to mention that contemporary literature on Windows programming has one common drawback. Authors quickly migrated from describing programming API to covering visual components of specific languages. The books concentrating on pure Windows programming using API functions only are not numerous. Happy exceptions from this rule are some books listed in the *Bibliography* [4, 10, 13]. In this book, I try to follow the approach adopted by the authors of these books and to cover many topics that are not covered in sufficient detail in the existing literature,

[i] When speaking about Windows, I mean several operating systems of this family: Windows 9*x*/ME, Windows NT, and Windows 2000/XP. When necessary, I will specify which operating system is meant.

such as programming for networks, using multitasking, writing virtual device drivers, and file processing.

As a rule, most books on programming tend to take one of two extreme positions: they concentrate either on describing the programming language in as much detail as possible or on describing the capabilities of programming for a specific operating system. My goal was to avoid such extremities and achieve the golden mean. Therefore, this book is neither a detailed manual on Assembly programming nor a manual on Windows programming. It pays equal attention to both topics — Assembly language and Windows programming.

The main principles that I tried to observe when writing this book are as follows:

- I have provided detailed and comprehensive descriptions of the topics under consideration. As I already mentioned, I am not a fan of macro tools. However, the main goal of this book — writing Assembly programs that can be translated using both MASM and TASM — requires you to know macro tools, among other things. Therefore, these tools play a subordinated role in this book, although there is a chapter that provides a detailed description of directives and macro tools of the Assembly language.
- To make the materials as useful as possible, I provide all programs in two versions (for MASM and for TASM) or I supply detailed comments explaining how to migrate to another assembler. As a basis, I have taken MASM version 7.0, TASM32.EXE version 5.0, and TLINK32.EXE version 1.6.71. To compile and build the examples, I recommend that you also use these (or later) versions of MASM and TASM.
- The book explains Assembly programming step by step, starting with simple programs and continuing to topics related to system programming. Therefore, it might be considered a teaching course on Windows programming. It is highly desirable (although not required) that you be acquainted with the C programming language. Knowing at least the basics of the Assembly language will be a benefit. If you do not have previous knowledge in these fields, I recommend that you read other books beforehand [1, 4, 11]. Detailed explanations of the microprocessor commands can be found in additional books [1, 3, 7, 8, 9].
- Good knowledge of the Assembly language helps you to easily understand and navigate the program code. Hackers are usually good programmers in Assembly language. The aspects of code analysis are not frequently covered in computing literature. However, sound knowledge in this field will be helpful for every programmer, especially those involved in developing protection mechanisms.
- If you are only beginning to program in the Assembly language, I recommend that you start with a careful study of the opening chapters, which provide detailed descriptions of the structure of a typical Windows program.

PART I: BASICS OF 32-BIT PROGRAMMING FOR WINDOWS

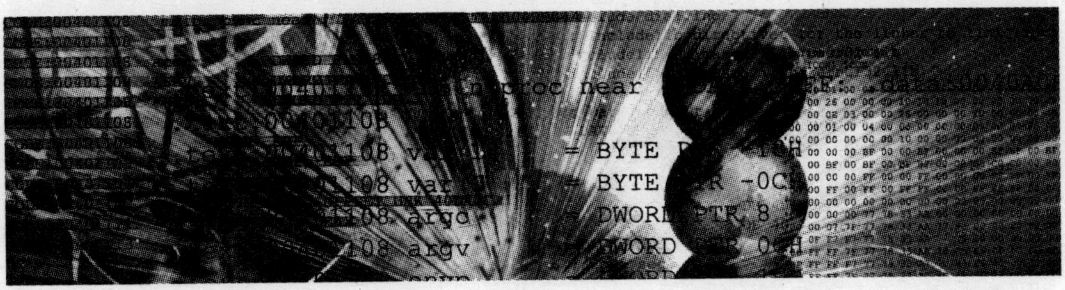

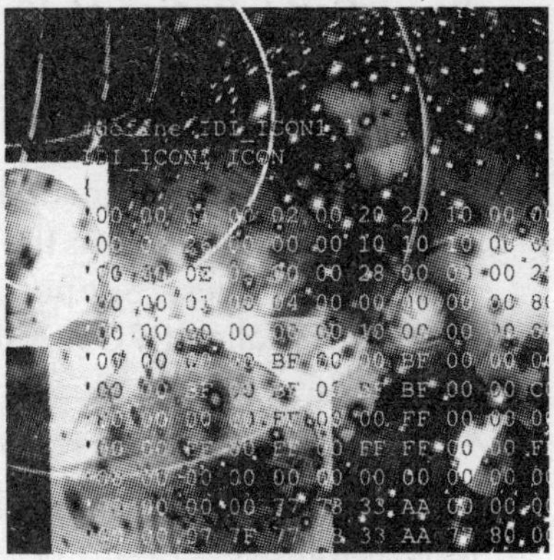

Chapter 1

Windows Programming Tools

In this chapter, I provide a brief introduction to Assembly language programming tools. This chapter is intended for beginners; therefore, experienced programmers can skip it.

First, note that the title of this chapter is deceptive because compiling technologies for MS-DOS and for Windows have much in common. However, programming for MS-DOS is gradually becoming a thing of the past.

The First Assembly Program and Its Translation

Fig. 1.1 shows the scheme of translating the module in Assembly language.

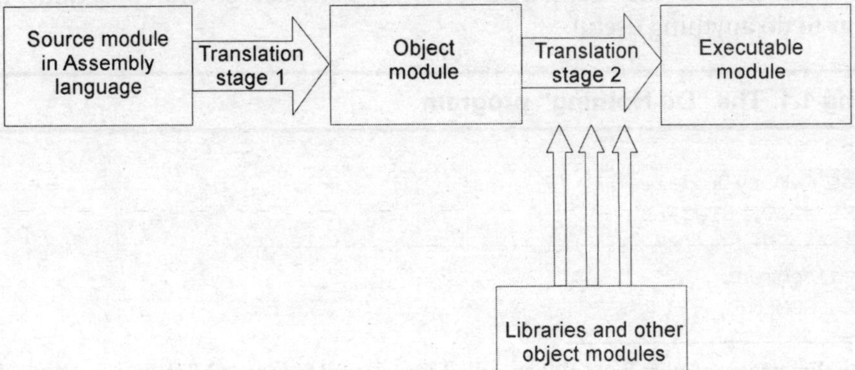

Fig. 1.1. Scheme of translating an Assembly module

Two main programs correspond to the two stages of translation in Fig. 1.1: the ML.EXE assembler[i] and the LINK.EXE linker (or TASM32.EXE and TLINK32.EXE in Turbo Assembler). Suppose that the source file of your program written in Assembly language is called PROG.ASM. Without diving into details, the first stage of translation will look as follows:

```
c:\masm32\bin\ml /c /coff PROG.ASM
```

As a result of this step, the PROG.OBJ module will appear. The second stage will look as follows:

```
c:\masm32\bin\Link /SUBSYSTEM:WINDOWS PROG.OBJ
```

As a result of this step, you'll get the executable module: PROG.EXE. You can easily guess that `/c` and `/coff` are command-line options of the ML.EXE program and `/SUBSYSTEM:WINDOWS` is the command-line option for LINK.EXE.

Other command-line options of these programs will be covered in more detail in *Chapter 5*.

The more I think about this two-pass scheme of translation, the more perfect it seems. The format of the resulting module depends on the operating system. Having specified the requirements for the structure of the object module, you get the following possibilities:

- Employ ready-to-use object modules
- Link programs written using different programming languages

The main advantage here, however, is the possibility of expanding the object module standard for different operating systems. This means that you'd be able to use modules written for different operating systems.[ii]

To understand the translation process, consider several programs that don't appear to do anything useful.

Listing 1.1. The "Do Nothing" program

```
.586P
; Flat memory model
.MODEL FLAT, STDCALL
;-----------------------------------------------------
; Data segment
_DATA SEGMENT
```

[i] Traditionally, programmers have always called translators for assembly languages *assemblers* rather than *compilers*.

[ii] This portability is limited, though, because the coordination of system calls in different operating systems can cause considerable difficulties.

```
_DATA ENDS
; Code segment
_TEXT SEGMENT
START:
     RET   ; Exit
_TEXT ENDS
END START
```

The example of a "Do Nothing" program is presented in Listing 1.1. I'll call this program PROG1. Note for future reference that microprocessor commands and macroassembler directives will be written in CAPITAL LETTERS.

Thus, to get the executable module, issue the following commands[i]:

```
ML /c /coff PROG1.ASM
LINK /SUBSYSTEM:WINDOWS PROG1.OBJ
```

Or, for Turbo Assembler, issue the following:

```
TASM32 /ml PROG1.ASM
TLINK32 -aa PROG1.OBJ
```

For the moment, take the translation examples for granted and continue your investigations.

Quite often, it is convenient to split the source code into several parts and join them at the first stage of translation. This can be achieved using the INCLUDE directive. For example, one file might contain the program code, and the constants and data (such as variable definitions) — along with the prototypes of external procedures — might be placed into separate files. Such files often have the INC filename extension.

Listing 1.2 illustrates this approach.

Listing 1.2. Using the INCLUDE directive

```
; The CONS.INC file
CONS1 EQU 1000
CONS2 EQU 2000
CONS3 EQU 3000
CONS4 EQU 4000
CONS5 EQU 5000
CONS6 EQU 6000
CONS7 EQU 7000
```

[i] If names of modules being compiled and linked contain blanks, then the names of these modules have to be enclosed by quotation marks:

```
ML /c /coff "MY FIRST PROGRAM.ASM"
```

```
CONS8  EQU 8000
CONS9  EQU 9000
CONS10 EQU 10000
CONS11 EQU 11000
CONS12 EQU 12000

; The DAT.INC file
DAT1   DWORD 0
DAT2   DWORD 0
DAT3   DWORD 0
DAT4   DWORD 0
DAT5   DWORD 0
DAT6   DWORD 0
DAT7   DWORD 0
DAT8   DWORD 0
DAT9   DWORD 0
DAT10  DWORD 0
DAT11  DWORD 0
DAT12  DWORD 0
; The PROG1.ASM file
.586P
; Flat memory model
.MODEL FLAT, STDCALL
; Include the file with constants
INCLUDE CONS.INC
;-----------------------------------------------
; Data segment
_DATA SEGMENT
; Include the data file
INCLUDE DAT.INC
_DATA ENDS
; Code segment
_TEXT SEGMENT
START:
    MOV   EAX, CONS1
    SHL   EAX, 1 ; Multiply by 2
    MOV   DAT1, EAX
;------------------------------------
    MOV   EAX, CONS2
    SHL   EAX, 2 ; Multiply by 4
    MOV   DAT2, EAX
;------------------------------------
    MOV   EAX, CONS3
    ADD   EAX, 1000 ; Add 1000
```

```
    MOV   DAT3, EAX
;-----------------------------------
    MOV   EAX, CONS4
    ADD   EAX, 2000 ; Add 2000
    MOV   DAT4, EAX
;-----------------------------------
    MOV   EAX, CONS5
    SUB   EAX, 3000 ; Subtract 3000
    MOV   DAT5, EAX
;-----------------------------------
    MOV   EAX, CONS6
    SUB   EAX, 4000 ; Subtract 4000
    MOV   DAT6, EAX
;-----------------------------------
    MOV   EAX, CONS7
    MOV   EDX, 3
    IMUL  EDX ; Multiply by 3
    MOV   DAT7, EAX
;-----------------------------------
    MOV   EAX, CONS8
    MOV   EDX, 7 ; Multiply by 7
    IMUL  EDX
    MOV   DAT8, EAX
;-----------------------------------
    MOV   EAX, CONS9
    MOV   EBX, 3 ; Divide by 3
    MOV   EDX, 0
    IDIV  EBX
    MOV   DAT9, EAX
;-----------------------------------
    MOV   EAX, CONS10
    MOV   EBX, 7 ; Divide by 7
    MOV   EDX, 0
    IDIV  EBX
    MOV   DAT10, EAX
;-----------------------------------
    MOV   EAX, CONS11
    SHR   EAX, 1 ; Divide by 2
    MOV   DAT11, EAX
;-----------------------------------
    MOV   EAX, CONS12
    SHR   EAX, 2 ; Divide by 4
    MOV   DAT12, EAX
```

```
;---------------------------------------
    RET         ; Exit
_TEXT ENDS
END START
```

The example program in Listing 1.2, like the other programs provided in this chapter, is senseless. However, it demonstrates the convenience of using the `INCLUDE` directive. I'd like to remind you not to concentrate your attention on the obvious microprocessor commands. I'd only like to draw your attention to the `IDIV` command.

In this case, the `IDIV` command carries out the division operation over the operand residing in the `EDX:EAX` register pair. By resetting `EDX` to zero, you specify that the entire operand is in `EAX`.

Program translation is carried out as specified earlier for MASM and TASM.

> ***Data Types***
>
> NOTE
>
> In this book, you'll mainly encounter three simple data types: byte, word, and double word. The following standard notation is widely used: byte — `BYTE` or `DB`, word — `WORD` or `DW`, and double word — `DWORD` or `DD`. The choice of notation (e.g., `DB` in one case or `BYTE` in another) is imposed only by my desire to demonstrate various language capabilities and diversify the description.

Object Modules

Now, I'll proceed with an explanation of the need to connect other object modules and libraries at the second stage of translation. First, it is necessary to mention that no matter how many object modules are linked, only one of them is the main module. The general idea is straightforward: this is the module, from which the program execution starts. This is the only difference between it and other modules. Also, agree that the main module will always contain the `START` label at the starting point of the segment. It is specified after the `END` directive because the translator must know the program's entry point to specify it in the header of the module to be loaded.

As a rule, all procedures that will be called from modules are placed into `INCLUDE` modules. Consider such a module in Listing 1.3.

Listing 1.3. The PROG2.ASM module containing PROC1 procedure that will be called from the main module

```
.586P
; The PROG2.ASM module
; Flat memory model
.MODEL FLAT, STDCALL
```

```
PUBLIC PROC1
_TEXT SEGMENT
PROC1 PROC
    MOV EAX, 1000
    RET
PROC1 ENDP
_TEXT ENDS
END
```

First, notice that no label is specified after the END directive. Clearly, this is not the main module and its procedures will be called from other modules.

The second important aspect, to which I'd like to draw your attention, is that the procedure to be called must be declared as PUBLIC. Its name will be saved in the object module; later, it can be linked to calls from other modules.

Thus, you can issue the following command:

```
ML /coff /c PROG1.ASM
```

As a result, the PROG2.OBJ module will be created.

Now, carry out a small investigation. View the object module using some simple viewer, such as the built-in viewer of the Far.exe file manager. The following will be easily noticed: Instead of the PROC1 name, you'll see the name _PROC1@0. Now, pay attention, because the characters that I describe here are of special importance! First, the leading underscore (_) reflects the ANSI standard, which requires all public names (i.e., the names available to several modules) to add the underscore automatically. In this case, the assembler will act automatically; therefore, you don't need to worry about this.

The situation with the @0 suffix is somewhat more complicated. First, what does it mean? The digit that follows the @ character specifies the number of bytes that need to be passed to the stack as parameters when the procedure is called. In this case, the assembler thinks that the procedure doesn't require parameters. This was done for the convenience of using the INVOKE directive that will be described later. Now, try to construct the main module, PROG1.ASM.

Listing 1.4. The PROG1.ASM module, calling a procedure from PROG2.ASM

```
.586P
; Flat memory model
.MODEL FLAT, STDCALL
;-----------------------------------------------------
; Prototype of the external procedure
EXTERN    PROC1@0:NEAR
; Data segment
_DATA SEGMENT
```

```
_DATA ENDS
; Code segment
_TEXT SEGMENT
START:
    CALL PROC1@0
    RET    ; Exit
_TEXT ENDS
END START
```

Obviously, the procedure called from another module is declared as EXTERN. Furthermore, instead of the name PROC1, you must use the name PROC1@0. For the moment, nothing can be done about it. A question related to the NEAR type can arise. In MS-DOS, the NEAR type meant that the procedure call (or unconditional jump) would take place within the same segment. The FAR type meant that procedure (or jump) would be called from another segment. Since Windows implements the so-called flat memory model, the entire memory can be interpreted as one large segment. Thus, the use of the NEAR type is logical.

Issue the following command:

```
ML /coff /c PROG1.ASM
```

As a result, you'll get the PROG1.OBJ object module. Now you can combine these modules to get the PROG1.EXE executable program:

```
LINK /SUBSYSTEM:WINDOWS PROG1.OBJ PROG2.OBJ
```

When linking several modules, the main module must be specified first followed by the other modules in an arbitrary order.

The INVOKE Directive

Now, consider the INVOKE directive. This is a convenient command. However, for reasons that will be clarified later, I'll use it in my programs only occasionally.

Its convenience is, first, that you don't need to add the @N suffix. Second, this directive takes care of loading the passed parameters into the stack. The following sequence of commands is not used:

```
PUSH par1
PUSH par2
PUSH par3
PUSH par4
CALL NAME_PROC@N ; N — Number of bytes sent to the stack
```

Instead, the following is used:

```
INVOKE NAME_PROC, par4, par3, par2, par1
```

Here, the role of the parameter can be played by a register, a direct value, or an address. Besides this, for an address it is possible to use both the `OFFSET` operator and the `ADDR` operator.

Modify the PROG1.ASM module (the PROG2.ASM module doesn't need to be modified) as shown in Listing 1.5.

Listing 1.5. Using the INVOKE directive

```
.586P
; Flat memory model
.MODEL FLAT, STDCALL
;----------------------------------------
; Prototype of the external procedure
PROC1 PROTO
; Data segment
_DATA SEGMENT
_DATA ENDS
; Code segment
_TEXT SEGMENT
START:
    INVOKE PROC1
    RET    ; Exit
_TEXT ENDS
END START
```

As can be easily seen, the external procedure is now declared using the `PROTO` directive. This directive allows parameters to be specified when necessary. For example, consider the following line:

```
PROC1 PROTO :DWORD, :WORD
```

This means that the procedure needs two parameters having lengths of 4 and 2 bytes, respectively (6 bytes total, indicated as `@6`).

As I mentioned earlier, I'll rarely use the `INVOKE` directive. Now, I'll clarify the first reason that I avoid this option: I'm an advocate of the purity of Assembly language. Consequently, any use of macros makes me feel uncomfortable. In my opinion, beginner programmers mustn't let themselves be carried away by macro tools; otherwise, they'll never feel the beauty of this language. As for the second reason, I'll clarify it later.

The scheme presented in Fig. 1.1 shows that it is possible to link both object modules and libraries. If there are several object modules, this will cause some inconvenience. Because of this, object modules are combined into libraries. Using the `INCLUDELIB` directive is the most convenient and the easiest way to link the library using MASM.

The `INCLUDELIB` directive will be stored in the object code for further use by the LINK.EXE program.

However, how can you create a library from object modules? For this purpose, there is a special program called librarian. Assume that you need to create the LIB1.LIB library consisting of a single module — PROG2.OBJ. To achieve this, issue the following command:

```
LIB /OUT:LIB1.LIB PROG2.OBJ
```

If it is necessary to add another module to the library (MODUL.OBJ), simply execute the following command:

```
LIB LIB1.LIB MODUL.OBJ
```

Here are two more useful examples of using the librarian:

- `LIB /LIST LIB1.LIB` — Produces the list of library modules
- `LIB /REMOVE:MODUL.OBJ LIB1.LIB` — Removes the specified module, MODUL.OBJ, from the LIB1.LIB library

Now, return to the example. Instead of the object module, you are now using the LIB1.LIB library. The modified text of the PROG1.ASM program is shown in Listing 1.6.

Listing 1.6. Using the library

```
.586P
; Flat memory model
.MODEL FLAT, STDCALL
;--------------------------------------------------
; Prototype of the external procedure
EXTERN    PROC1@0:NEAR
;--------------------------------------------------
INCLUDELIB LIB1.LIB
;--------------------------------------------------
; Data segment
_DATA SEGMENT
_DATA ENDS
; Code segment
_TEXT SEGMENT
START:
    CALL PROC1@0
    RET  ; Exit
_TEXT ENDS
END START
```

Data in the Object Module

Now, it is time to consider an important aspect of using data (variables) defined in another object module. Here, everything will be clear if you have carefully read the preceding material. The PROG2.ASM and PROG1.ASM modules demonstrating the technique of using external variables[i] are provided in Listings 1.7 and 1.8.

Listing 1.7. The module containing the ALT variable used in another module, PROG1.ASM

```
.586P
; The PROG2.ASM module
; Flat memory model
.MODEL FLAT, STDCALL
PUBLIC PROC1
PUBLIC ALT
; Data segment
_DATA SEGMENT
    ALT DWORD 0
_DATA ENDS
_TEXT SEGMENT
PROC1 PROC
    MOV EAX, ALT
    ADD EAX, 10
    RET
PROC1 ENDP
_TEXT ENDS
END
```

Listing 1.8. The module using the ALT variable defined in another module, PROG2.ASM

```
.586P
; The PROG1.ASM
; Flat memory model
.MODEL FLAT, STDCALL
;----------------------------------------
; Prototype of the external procedure
EXTERN   PROC1@0:NEAR
; External variable
```

[i] The term "external variable" is used by analogy with the term "external procedure."

```
EXTERN    ALT:DWORD
; Data segment
_DATA SEGMENT
_DATA ENDS
; Code segment
_TEXT SEGMENT
START:
     MOV  ALT, 10
     CALL PROC1@0
     MOV  EAX, ALT
     RET    ; Exit
_TEXT ENDS
END START
```

Note that in contrast to external procedures, external variables don't require the suffix @N because the variable size is known.

Translation Using TASM

Now, it is time to test all the programs presented in this chapter by translating them using TASM.

The situation is easy for the programs shown in Listings 1.1 and 1.2. To translate them, it is sufficient to execute the following commands:

```
TASM32 /ml PROG1.ASM
TLINK32 -aa PROG1.OBJ
```

Now, proceed with translation of the PROG2.ASM and PROG1.ASM modules provided in Listings 1.3 and 1.4, respectively. Object modules are created without difficulties. Viewing the PROG2.OBJ module, you'll notice that the external procedure is represented by a simple name — PROC1. Consequently, the only thing that you should do is replace the PROC1@0 name with PROC1 in the PROG1.ASM module. Further linking of the modules also is straightforward:

```
TLINK32 -aa PROG1.OBJ PROG2.OBJ
```

For working with libraries, TASM provides a librarian — TLIB.EXE. Issuing the following command creates a library from the PROG2.OBJ module:

```
TLIB LIB1.LIB + PROG2.OBJ
```

As a result, the library named LIB1.LIB will appear on the disk. It is necessary to link the PROG1.OBJ module to this library:

```
TLINK32 -aa PROG1, PROG1, PROG1, LIB1
```

As a result, you'll get the PROG1.EXE executable module.

You should pay close attention to the TLINK32 command-line option. In the most general form, it looks as follows:[i]

```
TLINK32 -aa OBJFILES, EXEFILE, MAPFILE, LIBFILES
```

- `OBJFILES` — One or more object files (separated by blanks); the main module must be specified first.
- `EXEFILE` — An executable file.
- `MAPFILE` — A MAP file containing information on the module structure.
- `LIBFILES` — One or more libraries (separated by blanks).

In TASM, there is no `INVOKE` directive; therefore, I'll avoid using it later.[ii]

When introducing this book, I declared my intention to reconcile two assemblers. Since the differences between them mainly lie in directives and macro commands (see *Chapter 5*), a simple idea suggests itself, namely, that it is possible to achieve compatibility by simply avoiding such directives and macro commands. The basis of the Windows program is formed by API calls (see *Chapter 2*). As you know already, the difference in calls to the external procedure is that the names for MASM have `@N` suffix. Here, it is impossible to do without macro definitions. These aspects will be considered in due time.

The Simplified Segmentation Mode

Both MASM and TASM support so-called simplified segmentation. I am backing the classical structure of an Assembly language program. However, I must admit that simplified segmentation is a convenient method, especially when programming for Windows.

The main idea of simplified segmentation is as follows: The starting point of the code segment is determined by the `.CODE` directive, and the `.DATA` directive[iii] specifies the starting point of the data segment. Both directives can occur several times in the source code of the program. The translator then assembles the code and data together as appropriate. The main goal of such an approach is the possibility of placing the data in the source code of the program as close as possible to the lines of code that use them. Such a possibility was in due time implemented in C++. In my opinion, it results in inconvenience when reading the code. Furthermore, although I don't pretend to be an aesthete, I don't feel comfortable when I see data mixed with the code.

Listing 1.9 illustrates the use of the simplified segmentation mode.

---

[i] Note that this form is slightly simplified.

[ii] My opinion is that nothing can be better than manually loading parameters into the stack.

[iii] There also is a special directive for the stack — namely, the `.STACK` directive. However, I will use it rarely.

Listing 1.9. A program that uses simplified segmentation

```
.586P
; Flat memory model
.MODEL FLAT, STDCALL
;--------------------------------------------------------
; Data segment
.DATA
    SUM DWORD 0
; Code segment
.CODE
    START:
; Data segment
.DATA
    A    DWORD 100
; Code segment
.CODE
    MOV EAX, A
; Data segment
.DATA
    B    DWORD 200
; Code segment
.CODE
    ADD EAX, B
    MOV SUM, EAX
    RET    ; Exit
END START
```

NOTE

Commands such as `.DATA` and `.CODE` can be used within the code segment defined in a traditional way. This is convenient for creating useful macro definitions (these will be covered in more detail in *Chapter 12*).

Utilities for Working with Assembler

In concluding this chapter, I provide a brief overview of other programs often used when programming in Assembly language. Later, I will describe some of these programs in more detail; others will never be mentioned.

Editors

Although I never use specialized editors for writing Assembly programs myself, for completeness I'll briefly describe two of them. I'll start with the QEDITOR.EXE program supplied with MASM32. The editor, as well as all companion utilities, is written in Assembly language. After analyzing their size and functional capabilities, you'll be impressed. For example, the editor is only 27 KB, and the utility used for viewing reports on the results of translation is only 6 KB long. This editor is suitable for working with small, single-module applications. However, it isn't convenient for working with several modules. The operation of this editor is based on interaction with various utilities using batch files. For example, program translation is carried out by the ASSMBL.BAT batch file, which uses the ML.EXE assembler and directs the result into the ASMBL.TXT text file. To view this file, it is necessary to use the THEGUN.EXE utility. Linking is carried out in a similar way.

The DUMPPE.EXE utility is used for disassembling executable modules, and the results of its operation are sent to the DISASM.TXT file. Other operations are carried out in the same way. You can easily customize these operations by editing the appropriate batch file. When necessary, it is possible to replace the utilities being used (e.g., it is possible to replace ML.EXE by TASM32.EXE).

The second editor, to which I'd like to draw your attention, is the Easy Assembler Shell (EAS.EXE). This editor, or shell, as its name implies, allows you to create, compile, and link sophisticated projects, which comprise ASM, OBJ, RC, RES, and DEF files. This program can work with TASM and MASM, as well as with other utilities (debuggers, resource editors, etc.). Compilers and linkers can be customized for a specific operating mode directly from the shell by specifying the required command-line options for these utilities.

Debuggers

Debuggers allow programs to be executed in a step-by-step mode. In *Part IV* of this book, I cover debuggers and disassemblers in more detail. The list of the most popular debuggers[i] includes CodeView (Microsoft), Turbo Debugger (Borland), and Ice.

Disassemblers

Disassemblers convert the executable module into Assembly language code. An example of the simplest disassembler is the DUMPPE.EXE program, which operates in the command-line mode. Listing 1.10 provides an example of the results produced by DUMPPE.EXE.

---

[i] The DEBUG.EXE program is still supplied with the Windows operating system; however, this debugger does not support the new format of executable files.

This example illustrates the result produced by disassembling the program provided in Listing 1.4. Can you recognize the program?

Listing 1.10. The results of disassembling a program using DUMPPE.EXE

```
knla.exe                         (hex)           (dec)
.EXE size (bytes)                490             1168
Minimum load size (bytes)        450             1104
Overlay number                   0               0
Initial CS:IP                    0000:0000
Initial SS:SP                    0000:00B8       184
Minimum allocation (para)        0               0
Maximum allocation (para)        FFFF            65535
Header size (para)               4               4
Relocation table offset          40              64
Relocation entries               0               0
Portable executable starts at    a8
Signature                        00004550 (PE)
Machine                          014C (Intel 386)
Sections                         0001
Time date stamp                  3AE6D1B1 Wed Apr 25 19:31:29 2001
Symbol table                     00000000
Number of symbols                00000000
Optional header size             00E0
Characteristics                  010F
Relocation information stripped
Executable image
Line numbers stripped
Local symbols stripped
32-bit word machine
Magic                            010B
Linker version                   5.12
Size of code                     00000200
Size of initialized data         00000000
Size of uninitialized data       00000000
Address of entry point           00001000
Base of code                     00001000
Base of data                     00002000
Image base                       00400000
Section alignment                00001000
File alignment                   00000200
Operating system version         4.00
Image version                    0.00
```

```
Subsystem version            4.00
Reserved                     00000000
Image size                   00002000
Header size                  00000200
Checksum                     00000000
Subsystem                    0002 (Windows)
DLL characteristics          0000
Size of stack reserve        00100000
Size of stack commit         00001000
Size of heap reserve         00100000
Size of heap commit          00001000
Loader flags                 00000000
Number of directories        00000010
Directory name               VirtAddr  VirtSize
---------------------------- --------  --------
Export                       00000000  00000000
Import                       00000000  00000000
Resource                     00000000  00000000
Exception                    00000000  00000000
Security                     00000000  00000000
Base relocation              00000000  00000000
Debug                        00000000  00000000
Description/architecture     00000000  00000000
Machine value (MIPS GP)      00000000  00000000
Thread storage               00000000  00000000
Load configuration           00000000  00000000
Bound import                 00000000  00000000
Import address table         00000000  00000000
Delay import                 00000000  00000000
COM runtime descriptor       00000000  00000000
(reserved)                   00000000  00000000
Section table
-------------
Virtual address        0001000
Virtual size           00000E
Raw data offset        000200
Raw data size          0000200
Relocation offset      000000
Relocation count       000
Line number offset     0000000
Line number count      000
Characteristics        0000020
```

```
Code
Executable
Readable
Disassembly
00401000 start:
00401000 E803000000 call  fn_00401008
00401005 C3         ret
00401006 CC         int   3
00401007 CC         int   3
00401008 fn_00401008:
00401008 B8E8030000 mov   eax,3E8h
0040100D C3         ret
```

I'd also like to mention the W32Dasm disassembler, which will be covered in detail in the last part of this book, and the well-known Ida Pro disassembler. In *Part IV*, I will consider both disassemblers in detail, as well as the techniques of efficiently using them.

Hex Editors

Hex editors allow you to view and edit executable modules in hex format. There are lots of programs of this type available. Furthermore, the most popular debuggers and disassemblers have built-in hex editors. Here, I'll only mention the HIEW.EXE program, which is popular with hackers. This program allows executable modules to be loaded both in hex format and in the form of Assembly code. Besides simply viewing these modules, HIEW.EXE allows you to edit them.

Resource Compilers

Both the MASM32 and the TASM32 assembler have a built-in resource compiler, which will be described in *Chapter 9*. These are the RC.EXE and BRC32.EXE programs, respectively.

Resource Editors

As a rule, I use the resource editor supplied as part of Borland C++ 5.0 or the one supplied along with Visual Studio.NET. Simple resources can be created using practically any text editor. The resource language will be covered in more detail in *Chapters 9* and *10.*

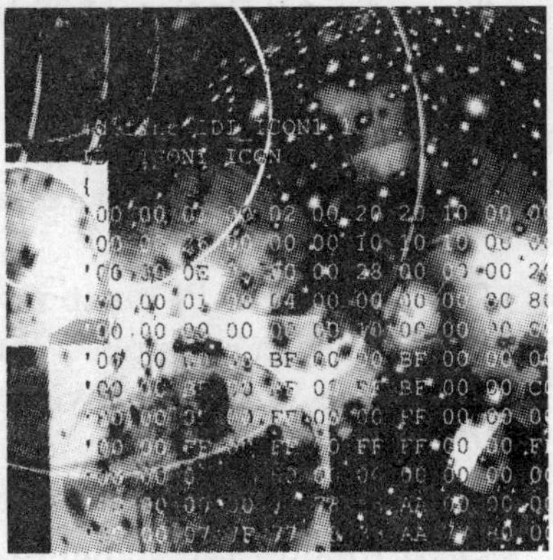

Chapter 2

Windows Programming Basics

In this chapter, I cover the two aspects most important for everyone who is going to start programming for Windows in Assembly language. These are application programming interface (API) function calls and possible structures of Windows programs.[i] There are several types of program structures, conventionally classified as follows:[ii]

- Classical structure — The structure with one main window.
- Dialog structure — The main window is a dialog box.
- Console application — The main window is the console window (either created or inherited).
- Nonwindowing structure — A Windows application that has no main window.[iii]
- Services — Specialized programs that play a specific role in the operating system.
- Drivers — Specialized programs for controlling peripheral devices.

In this chapter, the main attention will be concentrated on the first (classical) program structure.

Well, let me start by explaining several fundamental concepts of Windows programming. Those of you who already have some experience in the field of Windows programming can skip this material.

- Windows programming is based on the calls to API functions. The number of such functions is about 2,000. Most of your program will consist of such calls. All interaction

---

[i] Not to be confused with the structure of executable modules.

[ii] I developed this classification.

[iii] As will be shown later, console applications also can have dialogs.

with peripheral devices and operating system resources will be carried out using these functions.

- The list of API functions and their descriptions can be found in the WIN32.HLP file, which is supplied, for example, with the Borland C++ compiler.
- In the Windows environment, the main element of the program is its window. For every window, a special message-processing procedure[i] must be defined. More information on this topic will be provided later.
- A window can contain various controls: command buttons, drop-down lists, edit fields, etc. Principally, these controls also represent windows with special properties. All events related to the window controls and to the window itself dispatch messages to the window procedure.
- Windows uses flat memory addressing. In other words, the entire memory space can be considered one segment. For the programmer writing programs in Assembly language, this means that the address of any memory cell will be defined by the content of a single 32-bit register (e.g., `EBX`).
- As a consequence of the previous statement, there are practically no limitations to the size of the data, code, or stack (the size of the local variables). Segments now play another role in the program text. They allow you to specify certain properties for individual code sections: protection against writing, general access, etc.
- Windows is a multitasking environment. Every task has its own address space and its own message queue. Furthermore, multitasking is possible within a single task — every procedure can be executed as a separate task.

Now, after explaining some theoretical aspects, it is time to proceed with considering some programming examples.

Calling API Functions

To begin with, consider how to call API functions. You can open the help file and choose any API function; for now, choose `MessageBox`:

```
int MessageBox(HWND hWnd, LPCTSTR lpText, LPCTSTR lpCaption, UINT uType);
```

This function displays a message box with one or more command buttons that allow you to close it:

`hWnd` — The descriptor (handle) of the message box window.
`lpText` — The text that will be displayed in this message box.

---

[i] Based on the terminology once adopted in MS-DOS, such a procedure must be called the "interrupt procedure." Windows, however, uses different terminology. Such procedures, called by the operating system itself, are `CALLBACK` procedures.

`lpCaption` — The window header text.
`uType` — The window type; in particular, it allows you to define the number of command buttons.

Now, consider the parameter types. All parameters are 32-bit integer numbers:

`HWND` — 32-bit integer
`LPCTSTR` — 32-bit pointer to the string
`UINT` — 32-bit integer

For a reason that will be explained later, you will have to add the `A` suffix to function names. Besides this, when using MASM, it is necessary to add the `@16` suffix to the function names. Thus, the call to the previously described function will look as follows:

```
CALL MessageBoxA@16
```

What about parameters? They must have been loaded beforehand into the stack using `PUSH` commands. Memorize a simple rule: *from left to right, and from bottom to top.* Thus, assume that the window descriptor is located by the address `HW`, the strings are located by the addresses `STR1` and `STR2`, and the message box type is a constant. The simplest type has the zero value and is called `MB_OK`. Thus, you'll have the following:

```
MB_OK  equ 0
.
.
STR1       DB "Invalid entry! ", 0
STR2       DB "Error message.", 0
HW         DWORD ?
.
.
PUSH       MB_OK
PUSH       OFFSET STR1
PUSH       OFFSET STR2
PUSH       HW
CALL       MessageBoxA@16
```

As you can see, everything is easy and straightforward, as if you were calling this function from a program written in C or Pascal. The result returned by any function is usually an integer number returned into the `EAX` register.

Strings deserve to be considered separately. Generally, when speaking about strings, one usually means a string address (or pointer). In most cases, it is assumed that the string is terminated by the character with the code 0. However, one of the parameters of an API function often specifies the string length (in documentation often called the buffer) defined by another parameter. You should bear this in mind, because it might happen that the returned string won't be terminated by zero, and zero is required to use that string in another function. If this possibility is not taken into account, this might result in phantom errors in your program (i.e., such errors that appear or disappear like ghosts).

NOTE

Microsoft declares that when returning from an API function, the registers `EBX`, `EBP`, `ESP`, `ESI`, and `EDI` must be preserved. The function value is normally returned into the `EAX` register. The contents of other registers are not guaranteed to be preserved.

C structures can be easily reproduced in Assembly language using a similar approach. For example, consider the following structure defining a system message:

```
typedef struct tagMSG {   //Msg
    HWND hwnd;
    UINT message;
    WPARAM wParam;
    LPARAM lParam;
    DWORD time;
    POINT pt;
} MSG;
```

This message, supplied with detailed comments, will appear in one of the examples provided later. In Assembly language, this structure will appear as follows:

```
MSGSTRUCT STRUC
    MSHWND          DD ?
    MSMESSAGE       DD ?
    MSWPARAM        DD ?
    MSLPARAM        DD ?
    MSTIME          DD ?
    MSPT            DD ?
MSGSTRUCT ENDS
```

As you can see, in Assembly language everything looks even simpler. To tell the truth, the only thing difficult to understand is why Microsoft has muddled everything to such an extent with its attitude about variable types.

NOTE

When calling an API function, an error can occur related either to invalid input parameters or to the impossibility of obtaining the desired results because of a specific system condition. In such cases, the contents returned in the `EAX` register serve as an indicator. Unfortunately, for different functions, these values might be different. Most frequently this is 0, but it also can be −1 or any other nonzero value. In this relationship, recall that 0 in most programming languages is the synonym of the `FALSE` value, and the `TRUE` value is mapped to 1. In any particular case, I recommend that you consult the documentation. Using the `GetLastError` function, it is possible to get the code of the error that occurred last. This will explain why the API function couldn't complete successfully. Examples using the `GetLastError` function will be provided later. For decoding error codes, it is convenient to use the ERRLOOK.EXE program supplied as part of Microsoft Visual Studio.NET.

The Program Structure

Now, investigate the entire program structure. As I have already mentioned, in this chapter I describe the classical structure of a Windows application. In every program of this type, there is the main window and, consequently, the main window procedure. Generally, the following sections can be distinguished in the program code:

- Window class registration
- Creation of the main window
- Message-processing loop
- Main window procedure

Naturally, the program might have other sections. However, the listed sections are always present, and they make up the main program skeleton. Consider them one by one.

The Window Class Registration

Window class registration is carried out using the `RegisterClassA` function, which accepts the only parameter — the pointer to the `WNDCLASS` structure containing all information about the window (see the example later in this chapter).

Creating a Window

Based on the registered window class, it is possible to create an instance of the window using the `CreateWindowExA` (or `CreateWindowA`) function. As can be easily noticed, this is similar to the object-oriented programming paradigm.

The Message-Processing Loop

Being written in C, this loop might appear as follows:

```
while (GetMessage (&msg, NULL, 0, 0))
{
```

```
    // Allow keyboard use by translating virtual key messages
    // into alphanumeric key messages
    TranslateMessage(&msg);
    // Return control to Windows and pass the message
    // to the window procedure
    DispatchMessage(&msg);
    }
```

The GetMessage() function "traps" the next message, pulling it from the message queue and placing it into the MSG structure. If there are no messages in the queue, the function waits for a message to arrive. Instead of the GetMessage function, the PostMessage with the same set of parameters is frequently used. The difference between GetMessage and PostMessage lies in that the latter does not wait for the message if there are no messages in the queue. The PostMessage function is often used to optimize program operation.

As relates to the TranslateMessage function, it covers the WM_KEYDOWN and WM_KEYUP messages, which are translated into WM_CHAR and WM_DEDCHAR and into WM_SYSKEYDOWN and WM_SYSKEYUP messages that are further converted into WM_SYSCHAR and WM_SYSDEADCHAR. The idea of translation isn't simple replacement. Rather, the function sends additional messages. For example, if you press and release an alphanumeric key, the window will first receive the WM_KEYDOWN message, the WM_KEYUP message will be the next, and the WM_CHAR message will be the last to arrive. As can be easily seen, the exit from the loop takes place only when the GetMessage function returns 0. This is possible only when the exit message arrives (the WM_QUIT message as shown in the example later in this chapter). Thus, the waiting loop plays a double role: First, the messages intended for a specific window are processed in a certain way, and second, the loop waits for the message instructing it to exit the program.

The Main Window Procedure

Here is the prototype of the window function[i] written in C:

```
LRESULT CALLBACK WindowFunc(HWND hwnd, UINT message,
                            WPARAM wParam, LPARAM lParam)
```

Leaving alone the type of the function's return value,[ii] pay special attention to the parameters passed to it. Here they are with brief explanations:

hwnd — window identifier
message — message identifier

[i] I'd like to point out once again that in this book, the terms "procedure" and "function" are synonyms.
[ii] You'll never need it.

`wParam` and `lParam` — parameters clarifying the message goal (for each message, different parameters may play different roles or play no role at all)

As you probably have guessed, all four parameters are of the `DWORD` type. And now, consider the "skeleton" of this function written in Assembly language.

Listing 2.1. The "skeleton" of window procedure

```
WNDPROC   PROC
  PUSH  EBP
  MOV   EBP, ESP ; Now EBP points to the top of the stack
  PUSH  EBX
  PUSH  ESI
  PUSH  EDI
  PUSH  DWORD PTR [EBP+14H] ; LPARAM (lParam)
  PUSH  DWORD PTR [EBP+10H] ; WPARAM (wParam)
  PUSH  DWORD PTR [EBP+0CH] ; MES (message)
  PUSH  DWORD PTR [EBP+08H] ; HWND (hwnd)
  CALL  DefWindowProcA@16
  POP   EDI
  POP   ESI
  POP   EBX
  POP   EBP
  RET   16
WNDPROC   ENDP
```

Now, let me comment the fragment provided in Listing 2.1:

`RET 16` — Exit and pop four parameters from the stack ($16 = 4 \times 4$)

Access to parameters is carried out using the `EBP` register:

```
DWORD PTR [EBP+14H] ; LPARAM (lParam)
DWORD PTR [EBP+10H] ; WPARAM (wParam)
DWORD PTR [EBP+0CH] ; MES (message) - Message code
DWORD PTR [EBP+08H] ; HWND (hwnd) - Window descriptor
```

The `DefWindowProc` function is called for the messages that are not handled in the window function. As you can see in this example, no messages arriving to the window function are processed. I have guaranteed that the contents of the following four registers have been preserved: `EBX`, `EBP`, `ESI`, and `EDI`. This is a requirement specified in the documentation, although I usually try to guarantee that no registers change.

Examples of Simple Windows Programs

Now, consider some examples. Listing 2.2 presents a simple program. I recommend that you study it carefully, since it will become a foundation for all materials that you will consider further. The window that appears when this program is started is shown in Fig. 2.1.

Pay special attention to the `INCLUDELIB` directives. MASM32 provides lots of libraries. For this example, you needed two of them: user32.lib and kernel32.lib.

Now, you need to define the constants and the library procedures.

All these definitions can be found in `INCLUDE` files supplied with MASM32. I will not use standard `INCLUDE` files for two reasons: by avoiding this approach, it is much easier to grasp the idea of programming and it simplifies the migration from MASM to TASM.

You must clearly understand the method of window procedure operation because it defines the entire Windows programming paradigm. The aim of this procedure is to ensure the correct reaction of the application to all incoming messages. Let me explain the operation of the application in detail. To begin with, note that unhandled messages must be returned to the system using the `DefWindowProcA` function. You must handle four messages: `WM_CREATE`, `WM_DESTROY`, `WM_LBUTTONDOWN`, and `WM_RBUTTONDOWN`. In terms of object-oriented programming, the `WM_CREATE` and `WM_DESTROY` messages play the roles of constructor and destructor, respectively. They arrive to the window function when the window is created or destroyed. If you click the small button with the `x` in the top right corner of the window, the `WM_DESTROY` message will arrive to the window function. After that, the `PostQuitMessage` function will be executed, and the `WM_QUIT` message will be sent to the function. This message will cause the message-handling loop to terminate. Then, the `ExitProcess` function will execute. This, in turn, will delete the application from the memory.

I'd like to draw your attention to the `_ERR` label. The jump to this label takes place if an error occurs. Here, it is possible to place an appropriate error message.

Listing 2.2. An example of a simple Windows application (MASM32)

```
.386P
; Flat memory model
.MODEL FLAT, stdcall
; Constants
; The message arrives when the window is closed
WM_DESTROY          equ 2
; The message arrives when the window is created
WM_CREATE           equ 1
; The message arrives if the left mouse button is clicked
```

```
; somewhere in the window area
WM_LBUTTONDOWN        equ 201h
; The message arrives if the right mouse button is clicked
; somewhere in the window area
WM_RBUTTONDOWN        equ 204h
; Window properties
CS_VREDRAW            equ 1h
CS_HREDRAW            equ 2h
CS_GLOBALCLASS        equ 4000h
WS_OVERLAPPEDWINDOW   equ 000CF0000H
Style                 equ CS_HREDRAW+CS_VREDRAW+CS_GLOBALCLASS
; Standard icon identifier
IDI_APPLICATION       equ 32512
; Cursor identifier
IDC_CROSS             equ 32515
; Normal mode of displaying the window
SW_SHOWNORMAL         equ 1
; Prototypes of external procedures
EXTERN  MessageBoxA@16:NEAR
EXTERN  CreateWindowExA@48:NEAR
EXTERN  DefWindowProcA@16:NEAR
EXTERN  DispatchMessageA@4:NEAR
EXTERN  ExitProcess@4:NEAR
EXTERN  GetMessageA@16:NEAR
EXTERN  GetModuleHandleA@4:NEAR
EXTERN  LoadCursorA@8:NEAR
EXTERN  LoadIconA@8:NEAR
EXTERN  PostQuitMessage@4:NEAR
EXTERN  RegisterClassA@4:NEAR
EXTERN  ShowWindow@8:NEAR
EXTERN  TranslateMessage@4:NEAR
EXTERN  UpdateWindow@4:NEAR
; Directives for linking libraries
includelib c:\masm32\lib\user32.lib
includelib c:\masm32\lib\kernel32.lib
;-------------------------------------------
; Structures
; Message structure
MSGSTRUCT STRUC
    MSHWND        DD    ? ; Identifier of the window
                          ; that received the message
    MSMESSAGE     DD    ? ; Message identifier
    MSWPARAM      DD    ? ; Auxiliary information about the message
```

```
    MSLPARAM        DD    ? ; Auxiliary information about the message
    MSTIME          DD    ? ; Time of sending the message
    MSPT            DD    ? ; Cursor position at the time of sending
                            ; the message
MSGSTRUCT ENDS
;---------
WNDCLASS STRUC
    CLSSTYLE        DD    ? ; Window style
    CLWNDPROC       DD    ? ; Pointer to the window procedure
    CLSCEXTRA       DD    ? ; Information on auxiliary bytes for
                            ; this structure
    CLWNDEXTRA      DD    ? ; Information on auxiliary bytes for the window
    CLSHINSTANCE    DD    ? ; Application descriptor
    CLSHICON        DD    ? ; Window icon descriptor
    CLSHCURSOR      DD    ? ; Window cursor descriptor
    CLBKGROUND      DD    ? ; Window brush descriptor
    CLMENUNAME      DD    ? ; Menu identifier
    CLNAME          DD    ? ; Specifies the window class name
WNDCLASS ENDS
; Data segment
_DATA SEGMENT
    NEWHWND         DD 0
    MSG             MSGSTRUCT <?>
    WC              WNDCLASS  <?>
    HINST           DD 0 ; Here, the application descriptor is stored
    TITLENAME       DB 'Simple example of a 32-bit application', 0
    CLASSNAME       DB 'CLASS32', 0
    CAP             DB 'Message', 0
    MES1            DB 'You have clicked the left mouse button', 0
    MES2            DB 'Exit. Bye!', 0
_DATA ENDS
; Code segment
_TEXT SEGMENT
START:
; Get application descriptor
    PUSH  0
    CALL  GetModuleHandleA@4
    MOV   [HINST], EAX
REG_CLASS:
; Fill window structure
; Style
    MOV   [WC.CLSSTYLE], style
; Message-handling procedure
```

```
    MOV    [WC.CLWNDPROC], OFFSET WNDPROC
    MOV    [WC.CLSCEXTRA], 0
    MOV    [WC.CLWNDEXTRA], 0
    MOV    EAX, [HINST]
    MOV    [WC.CLSHINSTANCE], EAX
;---------- Window icon
    PUSH   IDI_APPLICATION
    PUSH   0
    CALL   LoadIconA@8
    MOV    [WC.CLSHICON], EAX
;---------- Window cursor
    PUSH   IDC_CROSS
    PUSH   0
    CALL   LoadCursorA@8
    MOV    [WC.CLSHCURSOR], EAX
;----------
    MOV    [WC.CLBKGROUND], 17 ; Window color
    MOV    DWORD PTR [WC.CLMENUNAME], 0
    MOV    DWORD PTR [WC.CLNAME], OFFSET CLASSNAME
    PUSH   OFFSET WC
    CALL   RegisterClassA@4
; Create a window of the registered class
    PUSH   0
    PUSH   [HINST]
    PUSH   0
    PUSH   0
    PUSH   400      ; DY — Window height
    PUSH   400      ; DX — Window width
    PUSH   100      ; Y — Coordinate of the window's top left corner
    PUSH   100      ; X — Coordinate of the window's top left corner
    PUSH   WS_OVERLAPPEDWINDOW
    PUSH   OFFSET TITLENAME ; Window name
    PUSH   OFFSET CLASSNAME ; Class name
    PUSH   0
    CALL   CreateWindowExA@48
; Check for errors
    CMP    EAX, 0
    JZ     _ERR
    MOV    [NEWHWND], EAX ; Window descriptor
;-----------------------------------
    PUSH   SW_SHOWNORMAL
    PUSH   [NEWHWND]
    CALL   ShowWindow@8 ; Display the newly created window
```

```
;-----------------------------------
    PUSH   [NEWHWND]
    CALL   UpdateWindow@4 ; Redraw the visible part of the window
; WM_PAINT message
; Message-handling loop
MSG_LOOP:
    PUSH   0
    PUSH   0
    PUSH   0
    PUSH   OFFSET MSG
    CALL   GetMessageA@16
    CMP    EAX, 0
    JE     END_LOOP
    PUSH   OFFSET MSG
    CALL   TranslateMessage@4
    PUSH   OFFSET MSG
    CALL   DispatchMessageA@4
    JMP    MSG_LOOP
END_LOOP:
; Exit the program (close the process)
    PUSH   [MSG.MSWPARAM]
    CALL   ExitProcess@4
_ERR:
    JMP    END_LOOP
;-------------------------------------------------------------
; Window procedure
; Position of parameters in the stack
; [EBP+014H] LPARAM
; [EBP+10H] WAPARAM
; [EBP+0CH] MES
; [EBP+8] HWND
WNDPROC PROC
    PUSH   EBP
    MOV    EBP, ESP
    PUSH   EBX
    PUSH   ESI
    PUSH   EDI
    CMP    DWORD PTR [EBP+0CH], WM_DESTROY
    JE     WMDESTROY
    CMP    DWORD PTR [EBP+0CH], WM_CREATE
    JE     WMCREATE
    CMP    DWORD PTR [EBP+0CH], WM_LBUTTONDOWN ; Left button
    JE     LBUTTON
```

```
    CMP   DWORD PTR [EBP+0CH], WM_RBUTTONDOWN ; Right button
    JE    RBUTTON
    JMP   DEFWNDPROC
; Clicking the right mouse button closes the window
RBUTTON:
    JMP   WMDESTROY
; Clicking the left mouse button
LBUTTON:
; Displaying the message
    PUSH  0 ; MB_OK
    PUSH  OFFSET CAP
    PUSH  OFFSET MES1
    PUSH  DWORD PTR [EBP+08H]
    CALL   MessageBoxA@16
    MOV    EAX, 0
    JMP    FINISH
WMCREATE:
    MOV    EAX, 0
    JMP    FINISH
DEFWNDPROC:
    PUSH   DWORD PTR [EBP+14H]
    PUSH   DWORD PTR [EBP+10H]
    PUSH   DWORD PTR [EBP+0CH]
    PUSH   DWORD PTR [EBP+08H]
    CALL   DefWindowProcA@16
    JMP    FINISH
WMDESTROY:
    PUSH   0            ; MB_OK
    PUSH   OFFSET CAP
    PUSH   OFFSET MES2
    PUSH   DWORD PTR [EBP+08H] ; Window descriptor
    CALL   MessageBoxA@16
    PUSH   0
    CALL   PostQuitMessage@4        ; WM_QUIT message
    MOV    EAX, 0
FINISH:
    POP    EDI
    POP    ESI
    POP    EBX
    POP    EBP
    RET    16
WNDPROC  ENDP
_TEXT ENDS
END START
```

Fig. 2.1. Window of the program presented in Listing 2.2

How To Do It Using TASM32

After considering the program shown in Listing 2.2, you might ask a reasonable question — how do I implement the same program in TASM? Only minor changes are required to achieve this: Instead of using the user32.lib and kernel32.lib libraries, it is necessary to link the import32.lib library, delete the `@N` suffix from all names of library procedures, and issue the following commands:

```
tasm32 /ml prog.asm
tlink32 -aa prog.obj
```

Listing 2.3. An easy example of a Windows application (TASM32)

```
.586P
; Flat memory model
.MODEL FLAT, stdcall
; Constants
; Message arrives when the window is closed
WM_DESTROY          equ 2
```

```
; Message arrives when the window is created
WM_CREATE          equ 1
; Message when left-clicking the mouse in the window area
WM_LBUTTONDOWN     equ 201h
; Message when right-clicking the mouse in the window area
WM_RBUTTONDOWN     equ 204h
; Window properties
CS_VREDRAW         equ 1h
CS_HREDRAW         equ 2h
CS_GLOBALCLASS     equ 4000h
WS_OVERLAPPEDWINDOW equ 000CF0000H
Style              equ CS_HREDRAW+CS_VREDRAW+CS_GLOBALCLASS
; Identifier of the standard icon
IDI_APPLICATION    equ 32512
; Cursor identifier
IDC_CROSS          equ 32515
; Normal mode of displaying the window
SW_SHOWNORMAL      equ 1
; Prototypes of external procedures
EXTERN  MessageBoxA:NEAR
EXTERN  CreateWindowExA:NEAR
EXTERN  DefWindowProcA:NEAR
EXTERN  DispatchMessageA:NEAR
EXTERN  ExitProcess:NEAR
EXTERN  GetMessageA:NEAR
EXTERN  GetModuleHandleA:NEAR
EXTERN  LoadCursorA:NEAR
EXTERN  LoadIconA:NEAR
EXTERN  PostQuitMessage:NEAR
EXTERN  RegisterClassA:NEAR
EXTERN  ShowWindow:NEAR
EXTERN  TranslateMessage:NEAR
EXTERN  UpdateWindow:NEAR
; Directives for the linker to link libraries
includelib c:\tasm32\lib\import32.lib
;----------------------------------------------
; Structures
; Message structure
MSGSTRUCT STRUC
    MSHWND     DD ? ; Identifier of the window that received the message
    MSMESSAGE  DD ? ; Message identifier
```

```
    MSWPARAM   DD ? ; Auxiliary information about the message
    MSLPARAM   DD ? ; Auxiliary information about the message
    MSTIME     DD ? ; Time when the message was sent
    MSPT       DD ? ; Cursor position at the time of sending the message
MSGSTRUCT ENDS
;---------
WNDCLASS STRUC
    CLSSTYLE          DD ? ; Window style
    CLWNDPROC         DD ? ; Pointer to the window structure
    CLSCEXTRA         DD ? ; Information on the auxiliary bytes
                           ; for this structure
    CLWNDEXTRA        DD ? ; Information on the auxiliary bytes
                           ; for the window
    CLSHINSTANCE      DD ? ; Application descriptor
    CLSHICON          DD ? ; Window icon identifier
    CLSHCURSOR        DD ? ; Window cursor identifier
    CLBKGROUND        DD ? ; Window brush identifier
    CLMENUNAME        DD ? ; Menu identifier
    CLNAME            DD ? ; Specifies the window class name
WNDCLASS ENDS
; Data segment
_DATA SEGMENT
    NEWHWND   DD 0
    MSG       MSGSTRUCT <?>
    WC        WNDCLASS  <?>
    HINST     DD 0 ; Here, the application descriptor is stored
    TITLENAME DB 'A simple example of a 32-bit application', 0
    CLASSNAME DB 'CLASS32', 0
    CAP       DB 'Message', 0
    MES1      DB 'You have clicked the left mouse button', 0
    MES2      DB 'Exit. Bye!', 0
_DATA ENDS
; Code segment
_TEXT SEGMENT
START:
; Get the application descriptor
    PUSH  0
    CALL  GetModuleHandleA
    MOV   [HINST], EAX
REG_CLASS:
; Fill the window structure
```

```
; Style
   MOV   [WC.CLSSTYLE], style
; Message-handling procedure
   MOV   [WC.CLWNDPROC], OFFSET WNDPROC
   MOV   [WC.CLSCSEXTRA], 0
   MOV   [WC.CLNDEXTRA], 0
   MOV   EAX, [HINST]
   MOV   [WC.CLSHINSTANCE], EAX
;---------- Window icon
   PUSH  IDI_APPLICATION
   PUSH  0
   CALL  LoadIconA
   MOV   [WC.CLSHICON], EAX
;---------- Window cursor
   PUSH  IDC_CROSS
   PUSH  0
   CALL  LoadCursorA
   MOV   [WC.CLSHCURSOR], EAX
;----------
   MOV   [WC.CLBCKGROUND], 17 ; Window color
   MOV   DWORD PTR [WC.CLMENUNAME], 0
   MOV   DWORD PTR [WC.CLNAME], OFFSET CLASSNAME
   PUSH  OFFSET WC
   CALL  RegisterClassA
; Create the window of the registered class
   PUSH  0
   PUSH  [HINST]
   PUSH  0
   PUSH  0
   PUSH  400  ; DY — Window height
   PUSH  400  ; DX — Window width
   PUSH  100  ; Y — Coordinate of the window's top left corner
   PUSH  100  ; X — Coordinate of the window's top left corner
   PUSH  WS_OVERLAPPEDWINDOW
   PUSH  OFFSET TITLENAME ; Window name
   PUSH  OFFSET CLASSNAME ; Window class
   PUSH  0
   CALL  CreateWindowExA
; Checking for errors
   CMP   EAX, 0
   JZ    _ERR
```

```
    MOV   [NEWHWND], EAX
    PUSH  SW_SHOWNORMAL
    PUSH  [NEWHWND]
    CALL  ShowWindow ; Show the newly-created window
    PUSH  [NEWHWND]
    CALL  UpdateWindow ; Redraw the visible part
                       ; of the window, the WM_PAINT message
; Message-handling loop
MSG_LOOP:
    PUSH  0
    PUSH  0
    PUSH  0
    PUSH  OFFSET MSG
    CALL  GetMessageA
    CMP   EAX, 0
    JE    END_LOOP
    PUSH  OFFSET MSG
    CALL  TranslateMessage
    PUSH  OFFSET MSG
    CALL  DispatchMessageA
    JMP   MSG_LOOP
END_LOOP:
; Exit the program (close the process)
    PUSH  [MSG.MSWPARAM]
    CALL  ExitProcess
_ERR:
    JMP   END_LOOP
;--------------------- Window procedure
; Position of the parameters in the stack
; [EBP+014H]  LPARAM
; [EBP+10H]   WAPARAM
; [EBP+0CH]   MES
; [EBP+8]     HWND
WNDPROC PROC
    PUSH  EBP
    MOV   EBP, ESP
    PUSH  EBX
    PUSH  ESI
    PUSH  EDI
    CMP   DWORD PTR [EBP+0CH], WM_DESTROY
    JE    WMDESTROY
    CMP   DWORD PTR [EBP+0CH], WM_CREATE
```

```
        JE    WMCREATE
        CMP   DWORD PTR [EBP+0CH], WM_LBUTTONDOWN ; Left button
        JE    LBUTTON
        CMP   DWORD PTR [EBP+0CH], WM_RBUTTONDOWN ; Right button
        JE    RBUTTON
        JMP   DEFWNDPROC
; Right-clicking the mouse closes the window
RBUTTON:
        JMP  WMDESTROY
; Left-clicking the mouse
LBUTTON:
; Displaying the message
        PUSH  0  ; MB_OK
        PUSH  OFFSET CAP
        PUSH  OFFSET MES1
        PUSH  DWORD PTR [EBP+08H]
        CALL  MessageBoxA
        MOV   EAX, 0
        JMP   FINISH
WMCREATE:
        MOV   EAX, 0
        JMP   FINISH
DEFWNDPROC:
        PUSH  DWORD PTR [EBP+14H]
        PUSH  DWORD PTR [EBP+10H]
        PUSH  DWORD PTR [EBP+0CH]
        PUSH  DWORD PTR [EBP+08H]
        CALL  DefWindowProcA
        JMP   FINISH
WMDESTROY:
        PUSH  0           ; MB_OK
        PUSH  OFFSET CAP
        PUSH  OFFSET MES2
        PUSH  DWORD PTR [EBP+08H] ; Window descriptor
        CALL  MessageBoxA
        PUSH  0
        CALL  PostQuitMessage ; WM_QUIT message
        MOV   EAX, 0
FINISH:
        POP   EDI
        POP   ESI
```

```
        POP    EBX
        POP    EBP
        RET    16
WNDPROC ENDP
_TEXT ENDS
END START
```

By the way, note that the executable module translated using TASM32 is always longer than the similar module translated using MASM32.

Note how window properties are specified. Descriptions of these properties can be found in the help system for the `CreateWindow` function. Principally, the selection of the required window properties and their combinations is a tedious task. This is one of the reasons why the resources became an integral part of the executable module. The concept of resources will be covered in detail in *Chapters 9* and *10.*

The examples provided here show that the window procedure must correctly react to the received messages. Later, you'll discover that the window procedure itself can send messages to the application, other windows, and to its own window.[i]

Some API functions have the `A` suffix. API functions have two prototypes: the ones with the `A` suffix support ANSI, and the ones with the `W` suffix support Unicode.

Passing Parameters Using the Stack

Here, I'd like to explain in more detail the process of passing parameters using the stack. This isn't the only method of passing parameters; however, parameters to API functions are passed using this method. Therefore, it deserves special attention. Fig. 2.2 shows the stack before and after the procedure call.

Fig. 2.2 demonstrates the standard entry to the procedure used in high-level programming languages such as C and Pascal. When entering the procedure, the following standard sequence of commands is executed:

```
PUSH   EBP
MOV    EBP, ESP
SUB    ESP, N ; N — Number of bytes for local variables
```

The address of the first parameter is defined as `[EBP+8H]`, which you have used several times. The address of the first local variable, if it is reserved, is defined as `[EBP - 4]` (with the `DWORD` variable in mind). When programming in Assembly language, local variables are not convenient; therefore, do not reserve space for them

[i] `PostQuit` is an example illustrating a message sent to the procedure's own window.

(see *Chapters 11* and *12*). At the end of the procedure, the following commands can be found:

```
MOV ESP, EBP
POP EBP
RET M
```

Here, M is the stack volume taken for passing parameters.

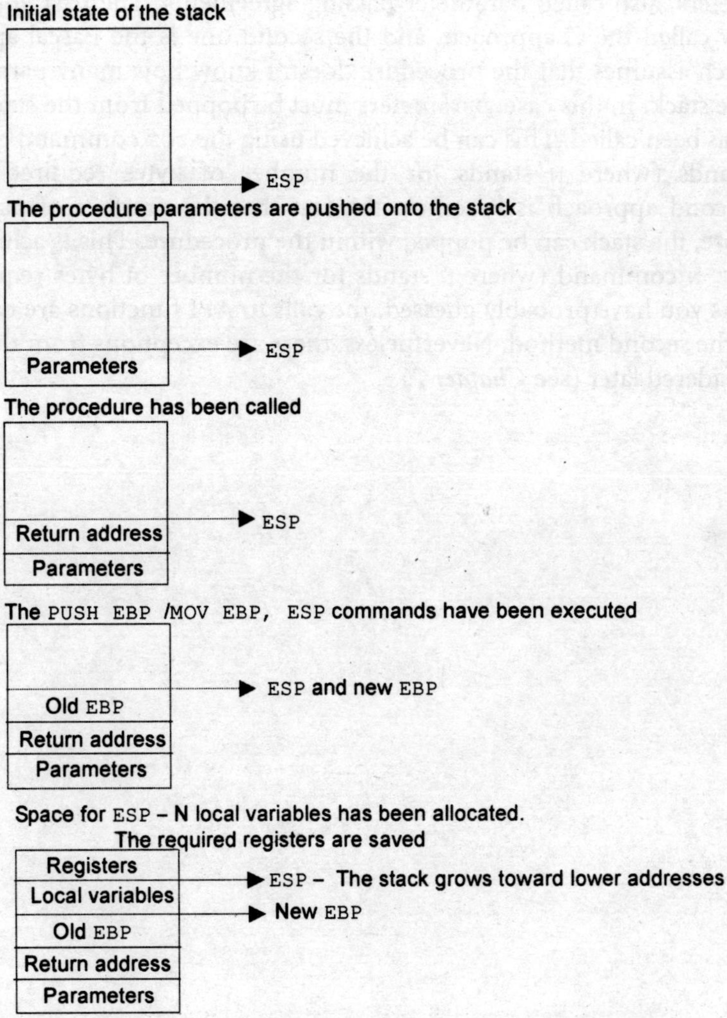

Fig. 2.2. Method of passing parameters to the procedure (the stack grows in the direction of the lower addresses)

The same result can be achieved using the `ENTER N, 0 (PUSH EBP\MOV EBP, ESP\SUB ESP)` command at the starting point of the procedure and the `LEAVE (MOV ESP, EBP\POP EBP)` at its end. These commands were first introduced for Intel's 286 processor. They gave the possibility of optimizing the translated code, especially when dealing with large modules developed using high-level programming languages.

It is necessary to mention another aspect related to the structure of the procedure and the methods used for calling it. There are two main approaches to passing parameters, also called parameter passing agreements. The first approach is conventionally called the C approach, and the second one is the Pascal approach. The first approach assumes that the procedure doesn't know how many parameters are placed into the stack. In this case, parameters must be popped from the stack after the procedure has been called. This can be achieved using the `POP` command or the `ADD ESP, N` commands (where `N` stands for the number of bytes required for parameters). The second approach is based on the fact that the number of parameters is fixed; therefore, the stack can be popped within the procedure. This is achieved by executing the `RET N` command (where `N` stands for the number of bytes required for parameters). As you have probably guessed, the calls to API functions are carried out according to the second method. Nevertheless, there are exceptions from this rule, which will be considered later (see *Chapter 7*).

Chapter 3

Simple Programs Written in Assembly Language

This chapter is dedicated to simple examples intended to demonstrate the techniques of creating windows and their elements, a topic covered in *Chapter 2.*

Principles of Building Windowing Applications

I'll formulate several general statements that later will help you to easily manipulate windows and create powerful, flexible, and high-performance applications.

- The properties of a specific window are set when calling the `CreateWindow` function by setting the `Style` parameters. The constants specifying the window properties are set in special files, which are included at the compile time. Since function properties are defined by the value of the specific bit of the constant, the combination of properties is nothing but the sum of bit constants (obtained using the `OR` command). In contrast to recommendations for software developers, most constants are defined directly in programs. Among other aspects, this ensures your psychological comfort because your program will be self-sufficient.
- The window is created on the basis of the registered class. It can contain various controls, such as command buttons, edit fields, lists, and scroll bars. All these elements can be created as windows characterized by predefined properties (e.g., for buttons, this might be the `BUTTON` class; for edit fields, this might be the `EDIT` class; and for the lists, this might be the `LISTBOX` class).

- The system communicates with the window — and, consequently, with the application — by exchanging messages. These messages must be processed by the window procedure. Windows programming in many respects represents the programming of message processing. Messages are also generated by the system if some visual events take place in respect to the window or some of its controls.[i] The list of such events might include moving a window, changing its size, clicking a button, selecting some of the list elements, and moving the mouse cursor. All these events are obvious, since the program must react to such events anyway.
- The message has its assigned code (designate it as `MES` in your program) and two parameters (`WPARAM` and `LPARAM`). For each message code, there is a macro name, although it is just an integer value. The `WM_CREATE` message arrives only once, when the window is created; `WM_PAINT` is sent to the window when it has to be redrawn;[ii] `WM_RBUTTONDOWN` is generated if you right-click the mouse when placing the cursor somewhere in the window area; etc. Message parameters can play some role intended to clarify their sense, or they may not play a role. For example, the `WM_COMMAND` message is generated if something happens to the window controls. In this case, parameter values allow you to detect the window element and what happened to it. (`LPARAM` is the element descriptor; the most significant word of `WPARAM` specifies the event; and the least significant `WPARAM` word usually stands for the resource identifier. See *Part II.*) Thus, it is possible to say that the `WM_COMMAND` message is the message from a window element.
- The message can be generated both by the system and by the program. For example, it is possible to send the command message to some of the window controls (to add an element to the list, to pass a string to the edit field, and so on). Sometimes, messages are sent to implement some programming technique. For example, it is possible to construct custom messages so that the program carries out specific operations when receiving such messages. Naturally, such messages must be handled either in the window procedure of some window or in the message-processing loop. This approach is convenient because it allows you to execute looping algorithms so that possible changes to the window would be displayed immediately at execution.

---

[i] It is possible to classify all window elements as controls (e.g., buttons or checkboxes) or controllable elements (e.g., edit fields). However, all window elements generally are called controls.

[ii] Although the window procedure is called with the appropriate values of its parameters, now and further on I will say that the message is sent to the window.

A Window with a Button

Consider the first example. When you start this program, a window with an **Exit** button will appear. As you clearly understand, pressing this button terminates the program.

The most important thing here is how the program is informed that the button has been clicked. Everything is simple: First, it is necessary to check the WM_COMMAND message; then, you must check LPARAM containing the window descriptor (the unique number, called handle). The button is created in the form of the window. In this case, for the button, it is sufficient to define an event.[i]

Pay special attention to the button that you are creating. This combination of properties is the most typical but is not the only possible one. For example, if you want a button to contain an icon, you'll have to specify the BS_ICON (or BS_BITMAP) property for it.

Listing 3.1. A window with an Exit button

```
; The button.inc file
; Constants
; The message that arrives when the window is closed
WM_DESTROY          equ 2
; The message that arrives when the window is opened
WM_CREATE           equ 1
; The message that arrives when the user
; clicks the left mouse button in the window area
WM_LBUTTONDOWN      equ 201h
WM_COMMAND          equ 111h
; Window properties
CS_VREDRAW          equ 1h
CS_HREDRAW          equ 2h
CS_GLOBALCLASS      equ 4000h
WS_OVERLAPPEDWINDOW equ 000CF0000H
STYLE               equ CS_HREDRAW+CS_VREDRAW+CS_GLOBALCLASS
BS_DEFPUSHBUTTON    equ 1h
WS_VISIBLE          equ 10000000h
WS_CHILD            equ 40000000h
STYLBTN             equ WS_CHILD+BS_DEFPUSHBUTTON+WS_VISIBLE
```

[i] Honestly, I am not proceeding properly here. After making sure that the button generated an event, you ought to determine what kind of event it was by checking the most significant word of WPARAM (the BN_CLICKED = 0 event). However, without going into particulars, I'd like to note that in most examples you consider here it is not necessary to do this for a button.

```
; Standard icon identifier
IDI_APPLICATION        equ 32512
; Cursor identifier
IDC_ARROW              equ 32512
; Normal mode of displaying the window
SW_SHOWNORMAL          equ 1
; Prototypes of external procedures
EXTERN  MessageBoxA@16:NEAR
EXTERN  CreateWindowExA@48:NEAR
EXTERN  DefWindowProcA@16:NEAR
EXTERN  DispatchMessageA@4:NEAR
EXTERN  ExitProcess@4:NEAR
EXTERN  GetMessageA@16:NEAR
EXTERN  GetModuleHandleA@4:NEAR
EXTERN  LoadCursorA@8:NEAR
EXTERN  LoadIconA@8:NEAR
EXTERN  PostQuitMessage@4:NEAR
EXTERN  RegisterClassA@4:NEAR
EXTERN  ShowWindow@8:NEAR
EXTERN  TranslateMessage@4:NEAR
EXTERN  UpdateWindow@4:NEAR
; Structure
; Message structure
MSGSTRUCT STRUC
    MSHWND          DD ?
    MSMESSAGE       DD ?
    MSWPARAM        DD ?
    MSLPARAM        DD ?
    MSTIME          DD ?
    MSPT            DD ?
MSGSTRUCT ENDS
;---- Window class structure
WNDCLASS STRUC
    CLSSTYLE        DD ?
    CLWNDPROC       DD ?
    CLSCBCLSEX      DD ?
    CLSCBWNDEX      DD ?
    CLSHINST        DD ?
    CLSHICON        DD ?
    CLSHCURSOR      DD ?
    CLBKGROUND      DD ?
    CLMENNAME       DD ?
    CLNAME          DD ?
```

```
WNDCLASS ENDS
; The button.asm file
.586P
; Flat memory model
.MODEL FLAT, stdcall
include button.inc
; Directives for the linker to link libraries
includelib c:\masm32\lib\user32.lib
includelib c:\masm32\lib\kernel32.lib
;------------------------------------------------
; Data segment
_DATA SEGMENT DWORD PUBLIC USE32 'DATA'
    NEWHWND        DD 0
    MSG            MSGSTRUCT <?>
    WC             WNDCLASS  <?>
    HINST          DD 0 ; Application descriptor
    TITLENAME      DB 'The example - Exit button', 0
    CLASSNAME      DB 'CLASS32', 0
    CPBUT          DB 'Exit', 0 ; Exit
    CLSBUTN        DB 'BUTTON', 0
    HWNDBTN        DWORD 0
    CAP            DB 'Message', 0
    MES            DB 'Program termination', 0
_DATA ENDS
; Code segment
_TEXT SEGMENT DWORD PUBLIC USE32 'CODE'
START:
; Get the application descriptor
    PUSH   0
    CALL   GetModuleHandleA@4
    MOV    [HINST], EAX
REG_CLASS:
; Fill the window structure
; Style
    MOV    [WC.CLSSTYLE], STYLE
; Message handling procedure
    MOV    [WC.CLWNDPROC], OFFSET WNDPROC
    MOV    [WC.CLSCBCLSEX], 0
    MOV    [WC.CLSCBWNDEX], 0
    MOV    EAX, [HINST]
    MOV    [WC.CLSHINST], EAX
;---------- Window icon
    PUSH   IDI_APPLICATION
```

```
    PUSH    0
    CALL    LoadIconA@8
    MOV     [WC.CLSHICON], EAX
;---------- Window cursor
    PUSH    IDC_ARROW
    PUSH    0
    CALL    LoadCursorA@8
    MOV     [WC.CLSHCURSOR], EAX
;----------
    MOV     [WC.CLBKGROUND], 17 ; Window color
    MOV     DWORD PTR [WC.CLMENNAME], 0
    MOV     DWORD PTR [WC.CLNAME], OFFSET CLASSNAME
    PUSH    OFFSET WC
    CALL    RegisterClassA@4
; Create a window of the registered class
    PUSH    0
    PUSH    [HINST]
    PUSH    0
    PUSH    0
    PUSH    400     ; DY — Window height
    PUSH    400     ; DX — Window width
    PUSH    100     ; Y — Coordinate of the top left corner
    PUSH    100     ; X — Coordinate of the top right corner
    PUSH    WS_OVERLAPPEDWINDOW
    PUSH    OFFSET TITLENAME ; Window name
    PUSH    OFFSET CLASSNAME ; Class name
    PUSH    0
    CALL    CreateWindowExA@48
; Check for error
    CMP     EAX,0
    JZ      _ERR
    MOV     [NEWHWND], EAX ; Window descriptor
;-----------------------------------
    PUSH    SW_SHOWNORMAL
    PUSH    [NEWHWND]
    CALL    ShowWindow@8 ; Show newly-created window
;-----------------------------------
    PUSH    [NEWHWND]
    CALL    UpdateWindow@4 ; The command for redrawing the visible
                           ; part of the window, the WM_PAINT message
; Message-processing loop
MSG_LOOP:
    PUSH    0
```

```
    PUSH    0
    PUSH    0
    PUSH    OFFSET MSG
    CALL    GetMessageA@16
    CMP     EAX, 0
    JE      END_LOOP
    PUSH    OFFSET MSG
    CALL    TranslateMessage@4
    PUSH    OFFSET MSG
    CALL    DispatchMessageA@4
    JMP     MSG_LOOP
END_LOOP:
; Exit the program (close the process)
    PUSH    [MSG.MSWPARAM]
    CALL    ExitProcess@4
_ERR:
    JMP     END_LOOP
;----------------------------------------------------- Window procedure
; Position of parameters in the stack
;  [EBP+014H]  ; LPARAM
;  [EBP+10H]   ; WAPARAM
;  [EBP+0CH]   ; MES
;  [EBP+8]     ; HWND
WNDPROC     PROC
    PUSH    EBP
    MOV     EBP, ESP
    PUSH    EBX
    PUSH    ESI
    PUSH    EDI
    CMP     DWORD PTR [EBP+0CH], WM_DESTROY
    JE      WMDESTROY
    CMP     DWORD PTR [EBP+0CH], WM_CREATE
    JE      WMCREATE
    CMP     DWORD PTR [EBP+0CH], WM_COMMAND
    JE      WMCOMMND
    JMP     DEFWNDPROC
WMCOMMND:
    MOV     EAX, HWNDBTN
    CMP     DWORD PTR [EBP+14H], EAX ; Hasn't the user clicked the button?
    JE      WMDESTROY
    MOV     EAX, 0
    JMP     FINISH
WMCREATE:
```

```
; Create the button window
    PUSH    0
    PUSH    [HINST]
    PUSH    0
    PUSH    DWORD PTR [EBP+08H]
    PUSH    20    ;  DY
    PUSH    60    ;  DX
    PUSH    10    ;  Y
    PUSH    10    ;  X
    PUSH    STYLBTN
    PUSH    OFFSET CPBUT    ; Window name
    PUSH    OFFSET CLSBUTN ; Window class
    PUSH    0
    CALL    CreateWindowExA@48
    MOV     HWNDBTN, EAX ; Save the button descriptor
    MOV     EAX, 0
    JMP     FINISH
DEFWNDPROC:
    PUSH    DWORD PTR [EBP+14H]
    PUSH    DWORD PTR [EBP+10H]
    PUSH    DWORD PTR [EBP+0CH]
    PUSH    DWORD PTR [EBP+08H]
    CALL    DefWindowProcA@16
    JMP     FINISH
WMDESTROY:
    PUSH    0          ; MB_OK
    PUSH    OFFSET CAP
    PUSH    OFFSET MES
    PUSH    DWORD PTR [EBP+08H] ; Window descriptor
    CALL    MessageBoxA@16
    PUSH    0
    CALL    PostQuitMessage@4 ; WM_QUIT message
    MOV     EAX, 0
FINISH:
    POP     EDI
    POP     ESI
    POP     EBX
    POP     EBP
    RET     16
WNDPROC     ENDP
_TEXT ENDS
END START
```

A Window with an Edit Field

The second example relates to the Edit field. The program is shown in Listing 3.2, and the result of its operation is shown in Fig. 3.1. When the **Exit** button is clicked, the program displays the message box with the edited string.

Notice how the message is sent to the window control. Mainly, two functions are used for this purpose: `SendMessage` and `PostMessage`. The difference between these two functions is that the first one calls window procedure with the appropriate parameters and waits until it returns the control; the second function places the message into the queue and returns the control immediately.

Listing 3.2. A window with an edit field

```
; The edit.inc file
; Constants
WM_SETFOCUS          equ 7h
; The message that arrives when the window is closed
WM_DESTROY           equ 2
; The message that arrives when the window is created
WM_CREATE            equ 1
; The message that arrives when something happens
; to the window controls
WM_COMMAND           equ 111h
; The message that allows you to send the string to the window
WM_SETTEXT           equ 0Ch
; The message that allows you to receive the string
WM_GETTEXT           equ 0Dh
; Window properties
CS_VREDRAW           equ 1h
CS_HREDRAW           equ 2h
CS_GLOBALCLASS       equ 4000h
WS_TABSTOP           equ 10000h
WS_SYSMENU           equ 80000h
WS_OVERLAPPEDWINDOW  equ 0+WS_TABSTOP+WS_SYSMENU
STYLE                equ CS_HREDRAW+CS_VREDRAW+CS_GLOBALCLASS
CS_HREDRAW           equ 2h
BS_DEFPUSHBUTTON     equ 1h
WS_VISIBLE           equ 10000000h
WS_CHILD             equ 40000000h
WS_BORDER            equ 800000h
STYLBTN              equ WS_CHILD+BS_DEFPUSHBUTTON+WS_VISIBLE+WS_TABSTOP
STYLEDT              equ WS_CHILD+WS_VISIBLE+WS_BORDER+WS_TABSTOP
```

```
; Standard icon identifier
IDI_APPLICATION        equ 32512
; Cursor identifier
IDC_ARROW              equ 32512
; Window display mode - normal
SW_SHOWNORMAL          equ 1
; Prototypes of external procedures
EXTERN  SetFocus@4:NEAR
EXTERN  SendMessageA@16:NEAR
EXTERN  MessageBoxA@16:NEAR
EXTERN  CreateWindowExA@48:NEAR
EXTERN  DefWindowProcA@16:NEAR
EXTERN  DispatchMessageA@4:NEAR
EXTERN  ExitProcess@4:NEAR
EXTERN  GetMessageA@16:NEAR
EXTERN  GetModuleHandleA@4:NEAR
EXTERN  LoadCursorA@8:NEAR
EXTERN  LoadIconA@8:NEAR
EXTERN  PostQuitMessage@4:NEAR
EXTERN  RegisterClassA@4:NEAR
EXTERN  ShowWindow@8:NEAR
EXTERN  TranslateMessage@4:NEAR
EXTERN  UpdateWindow@4:NEAR
; Structures
; Message structure
MSGSTRUCT STRUC
    MSHWND      DD ?
    MSMESSAGE   DD ?
    MSWPARAM    DD ?
    MSLPARAM    DD ?
    MSTIME      DD ?
    MSPT        DD ?
MSGSTRUCT ENDS
;---- Window class structure
WNDCLASS STRUC
    CLSSTYLE    DD ?
    CLWNDPROC   DD ?
    CLSCBCLSEX  DD ?
    CLSCBWNDEX  DD ?
    CLSHINST    DD ?
    CLSHICON    DD ?
    CLSHCURSOR  DD ?
    CLBKGROUND  DD ?
    CLMENNAME   DD ?
```

```
    CLNAME      DD ?
WNDCLASS ENDS

; The edit.asm file
.586P
; Flat memory model
.MODEL FLAT, stdcall
include edit.inc
; Directives for the linker to link libraries
includelib c:\masm32\lib\user32.lib
includelib c:\masm32\lib\kernel32.lib
;------------------------------------------------
; Data segment
_DATA SEGMENT DWORD PUBLIC USE32 'DATA'
    NEWHWND     DD 0
    MSG         MSGSTRUCT <?>
    WC          WNDCLASS  <?>
    HINST       DD 0 ; Application descriptor
    TITLENAME   DB 'Application example - Edit window', 0
    CLASSNAME   DB 'CLASS32', 0
    CPBUT       DB 'Exit', 0 ; Exit
    CPEDT       DB ' ', 0
    CLSBUTN     DB 'BUTTON', 0
    CLSEDIT     DB 'EDIT', 0
    HWNDBTN     DWORD 0
    HWNDEDT     DWORD 0
    CAP         DB 'Message', 0
    MES         DB 'Program termination', 0
    TEXT        DB 'Edit string', 0
                DB 50 DUP(0) ; Buffer continuation
_DATA ENDS
; Code segment
_TEXT SEGMENT DWORD PUBLIC USE32 'CODE'
START:
; Get the application descriptor
    PUSH    0
    CALL    GetModuleHandleA@4
    MOV     [HINST], EAX
REG_CLASS:
; Fill the window structure
; Style
    MOV     [WC.CLSSTYLE], STYLE
; Message-handling procedure
    MOV     [WC.CLWNDPROC], OFFSET WNDPROC
```

```
    MOV       [WC.CLSCBCLSEX], 0
    MOV       [WC.CLSCBWNDEX], 0
    MOV       EAX, [HINST]
    MOV       [WC.CLSHINST], EAX
;---------- Window icon
    PUSH      IDI_APPLICATION
    PUSH      0
    CALL      LoadIconA@8
    MOV       [WC.CLSHICON], EAX
;---------- Window cursor
    PUSH      IDC_ARROW
    PUSH      0
    CALL      LoadCursorA@8
    MOV       [WC.CLSHCURSOR], EAX
;----------
    MOV       [WC.CLBKGROUND], 17 ; Window color
    MOV       DWORD PTR [WC.CLMENNAME], 0
    MOV       DWORD PTR [WC.CLNAME], OFFSET CLASSNAME
    PUSH      OFFSET WC
    CALL      RegisterClassA@4
; Create a window of the registered class
    PUSH      0
    PUSH      [HINST]
    PUSH      0
    PUSH      0
    PUSH      150     ; DY — Window height
    PUSH      400     ; DX — Window width
    PUSH      100     ; Y — Coordinate of the top left corner
    PUSH      100     ; X — Coordinate of the top left corner
    PUSH      WS_OVERLAPPEDWINDOW
    PUSH      OFFSET TITLENAME ; Window title
    PUSH      OFFSET CLASSNAME ; Class name
    PUSH      0
    CALL      CreateWindowExA@48
; Check for error
    CMP       EAX, 0
    JZ        _ERR
    MOV       [NEWHWND], EAX ; Window descriptor
;----------------------------------
    PUSH      SW_SHOWNORMAL
    PUSH      [NEWHWND]
    CALL      ShowWindow@8 ; Show newly-created window
;----------------------------------
    PUSH      [NEWHWND]
```

```
    CALL     UpdateWindow@4 ; Command to redraw the visible
                            ; part of the window, the WM_PAINT message
; Message-handling loop
MSG_LOOP:
    PUSH     0
    PUSH     0
    PUSH     0
    PUSH     OFFSET MSG
    CALL     GetMessageA@16
    CMP      EAX, 0
    JE       END_LOOP
    PUSH     OFFSET MSG
    CALL     TranslateMessage@4
    PUSH     OFFSET MSG
    CALL     DispatchMessageA@4
    JMP      MSG_LOOP
END_LOOP:
; Exit the program (close the process)
    PUSH     [MSG.MSWPARAM]
    CALL     ExitProcess@4
_ERR:
    JMP      END_LOOP
;------------------------------ Window procedure
; Position of parameters in the stack
; [EBP+014H]  ; LPARAM
; [EBP+10H]   ; WAPARAM
; [EBP+0CH]   ; MES
; [EBP+8]     ; HWND
WNDPROC    PROC
    PUSH     EBP
    MOV      EBP, ESP
    PUSH     EBX
    PUSH     ESI
    PUSH     EDI
    CMP      DWORD PTR [EBP+0CH], WM_DESTROY
    JE       WMDESTROY
    CMP      DWORD PTR [EBP+0CH], WM_CREATE
    JE       WMCREATE
    CMP      DWORD PTR [EBP+0CH], WM_COMMAND
    JE       WMCOMMND
    JMP      DEFWNDPROC
WMCOMMND:
    MOV      EAX, HWNDBTN
```

```
    CMP     DWORD PTR [EBP+14H], EAX
    JNE     NODESTROY
; Get the edited string
    PUSH    OFFSET TEXT
    PUSH    150
    PUSH    WM_GETTEXT
    PUSH    HWNDEDT
    CALL    SendMessageA@16
; Display the edited string
    PUSH    0
    PUSH    OFFSET CAP
    PUSH    OFFSET TEXT
    PUSH    DWORD PTR [EBP+08H] ; Window descriptor
    CALL    MessageBoxA@16
; Exit
    JMP   WMDESTROY
NODESTROY:
    MOV     EAX, 0
    JMP     FINISH
WMCREATE:
; Create the button window
    PUSH    0
    PUSH    [HINST]
    PUSH    0
    PUSH    DWORD PTR [EBP+08H]
    PUSH    20    ; DY
    PUSH    60    ; DX
    PUSH    10    ; Y
    PUSH    10    ; X
    PUSH    STYLBTN
    PUSH    OFFSET CPBUT    ; Window name
    PUSH    OFFSET CLSBUTN ; Class name
    PUSH    0
    CALL    CreateWindowExA@48
    MOV     HWNDBTN,EAX ; Save the button descriptors
; Create the edit window
    PUSH    0
    PUSH    [HINST]
    PUSH    0
    PUSH    DWORD PTR [EBP+08H]
    PUSH    20    ; DY
    PUSH    350   ; DX
    PUSH    50    ; Y
    PUSH    10    ; X
```

```
    PUSH    STYLEDT
    PUSH    OFFSET CPEDT   ; Window name
    PUSH    OFFSET CLSEDIT ; Class name
    PUSH    0
    CALL    CreateWindowExA@48
    MOV     HWNDEDT, EAX
;--------- Place the string into the edit field
    PUSH    OFFSET TEXT
    PUSH    0
    PUSH    WM_SETTEXT
    PUSH    HWNDEDT
    CALL    SendMessageA@16
;--------- Set the focus to the edit window
    PUSH    HWNDEDT
    CALL    SetFocus@4
;-------------------------------------------
    MOV     EAX, 0
    JMP     FINISH
DEFWNDPROC:
    PUSH    DWORD PTR [EBP+14H]
    PUSH    DWORD PTR [EBP+10H]
    PUSH    DWORD PTR [EBP+0CH]
    PUSH    DWORD PTR [EBP+08H]
    CALL    DefWindowProcA@16
    JMP    FINISH
WMDESTROY:
    PUSH    0          ; MB_OK
    PUSH    OFFSET CAP
    PUSH    OFFSET MES
    PUSH    DWORD PTR [EBP+08H] ; Window descriptor
    CALL    MessageBoxA@16
    PUSH    0
    CALL    PostQuitMessage@4 ; WM_QUIT message
    MOV     EAX, 0
FINISH:
    POP     EDI
    POP     ESI
    POP     EBX
    POP     EBP
    RET     16
WNDPROC  ENDP
_TEXT ENDS
END START
```

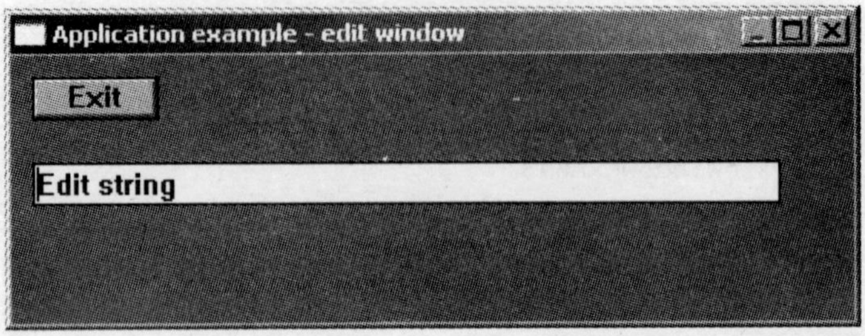

Fig. 3.1. Running the program with the edit field (see Listing 3.2)

A Window with a List

The last example in this chapter demonstrates the operation of a program with a drop-down list. When creating a list, it is filled with the names of different colors. If you double-click a specific color, the message box displaying the name of this color will appear.

The steps that occur after you double-click a specific list element are as follows: the event related to the list is detected first, then the most significant word of `WPARAM` is used, to determine which event took place. This task is carried out by the `[EBP+10H]` parameter, namely, by its most significant part — `[EBP+12H]`.

Although I have no opportunity to cover the properties of various controls in detail, I'll outline the basic idea of a control such as a list. Each element of the list has a set of attributes that can be used to locate it within the list: an ordinal number, a unique number, and an element name. The unique number is especially important because it allows the element to be identified uniquely.

Listing 3.3. A window with a simple list

```
; The lst.inc file
; Constants
WM_SETFOCUS          equ 7h
; The message that arrives when the window is closed
WM_DESTROY           equ 2
; The message that arrives when the window is created
WM_CREATE            equ 1
; The message that arrives when something happens
; to the window controls
WM_COMMAND           equ 111h
; The message that allows you to send the string to the control
WM_SETTEXT           equ 0Ch
```

```
; The message that allows you to receive the string
WM_GETTEXT           equ 0Dh
; The command message for adding strings
LB_ADDSTRING         equ 180h
LB_GETTEXT           equ 189h
LB_GETCURSEL         equ 188h
LBN_DBLCLK           equ 2
; Window properties
CS_VREDRAW           equ 1h
CS_HREDRAW           equ 2h
CS_GLOBALCLASS       equ 4000h
WS_TABSTOP           equ 10000h
WS_SYSMENU           equ 80000h
WS_THICKFRAME        equ 40000h
WS_OVERLAPPEDWINDOW  equ WS_TABSTOP+WS_SYSMENU
STYLE                equ CS_HREDRAW+CS_VREDRAW+CS_GLOBALCLASS
CS_HREDRAW           equ 2h
BS_DEFPUSHBUTTON     equ 1h
WS_VISIBLE           equ 10000000h
WS_CHILD             equ 40000000h
WS_BORDER            equ 800000h
WS_VSCROLL           equ 200000h
LBS_NOTIFY           equ 1h
STYLBTN              equ WS_CHILD + BS_DEFPUSHBUTTON +
                         WS_VISIBLE + WS_TABSTOP
STYLLST              equ WS_THICKFRAME + WS_CHILD + WS_VISIBLE +
                         WS_BORDER + WS_TABSTOP + WS_VSCROLL + LBS_NOTIFY
; Standard icon identifier
IDI_APPLICATION      equ 32512
; Cursor identifier
IDC_ARROW            equ 32512
; Normal window display mode
SW_SHOWNORMAL        equ 1
; Prototypes of external procedures
EXTERN  SetFocus@4:NEAR
EXTERN  SendMessageA@16:NEAR
EXTERN  MessageBoxA@16:NEAR
EXTERN  CreateWindowExA@48:NEAR
EXTERN  DefWindowProcA@16:NEAR
EXTERN  DispatchMessageA@4:NEAR
EXTERN  ExitProcess@4:NEAR
EXTERN  GetMessageA@16:NEAR
EXTERN  GetModuleHandleA@4:NEAR
```

```
EXTERN  LoadCursorA@8:NEAR
EXTERN  LoadIconA@8:NEAR
EXTERN  PostQuitMessage@4:NEAR
EXTERN  RegisterClassA@4:NEAR
EXTERN  ShowWindow@8:NEAR
EXTERN  TranslateMessage@4:NEAR
EXTERN  UpdateWindow@4:NEAR
; Structures
; Message structure
MSGSTRUCT STRUC
    MSHWND      DD ?
    MSMESSAGE   DD ?
    MSWPARAM    DD ?
    MSLPARAM    DD ?
    MSTIME      DD ?
    MSPT        DD ?
MSGSTRUCT ENDS
;---- Window class structure
WNDCLASS STRUC
    CLSSTYLE    DD ?
    CLWNDPROC   DD ?
    CLSCBCLSEX  DD ?
    CLSCBWNDEX  DD ?
    CLSHINST    DD ?
    CLSHICON    DD ?
    CLSHCURSOR  DD ?
    CLBKGROUND  DD ?
    CLMENNAME   DD ?
    CLNAME      DD ?
WNDCLASS ENDS

; The list.asm file
.586P
; Flat memory model
.MODEL FLAT, stdcall
include list.inc
; Directives for the linker to link libraries
includelib c:\masm32\lib\user32.lib
includelib c:\masm32\lib\kernel32.lib
;-------------------------------------------------
; Data segment
_DATA SEGMENT DWORD PUBLIC USE32 'DATA'
    NEWHWND     DD 0
```

```
    MSG         MSGSTRUCT <?>
    WC          WNDCLASS  <?>
    HINST       DD 0 ; Application descriptor
    TITLENAME   DB 'The example of the LISTBOX window', 0
    CLASSNAME   DB 'CLASS32', 0
    CPBUT       DB 'Exit', 0 ; Exit
    CPLST       DB ' ', 0
    CLSBUTN     DB 'BUTTON', 0
    CLSLIST     DB 'LISTBOX', 0
    HWNDBTN     DWORD 0
    HWNDLST     DWORD 0
    CAP         DB 'Message', 0
    CAP1        DB 'Chosen', 0
    MES         DB 'Program termination', 0
; Array of strings
STR1      DB 'Red', 0
STR2      DB 'Green', 0
STR3      DB 'Blue', 0
STR4      DB 'Yellow', 0
STR5      DB 'Black', 0
STR6      DB 'White', 0
; Pointers to strings
PS     DWORD OFFSET STR1
       DWORD OFFSET STR2
       DWORD OFFSET STR3
       DWORD OFFSET STR4
       DWORD OFFSET STR5
       DWORD OFFSET STR6
BUF   DB 30 dup(0)
_DATA ENDS
; Code segment
_TEXT SEGMENT DWORD PUBLIC USE32 'CODE'
START:
; Get the application descriptor
    PUSH   0
    CALL   GetModuleHandleA@4
    MOV    [HINST], EAX
REG_CLASS:
; Fill the window structure
; Style
    MOV    [WC.CLSSTYLE], STYLE
; Message-handling procedure
    MOV    [WC.CLWNDPROC], OFFSET WNDPROC
```

```
    MOV    [WC.CLSCBCLSEX], 0
    MOV    [WC.CLSCBWNDEX], 0
    MOV    EAX, [HINST]
    MOV    [WC.CLSHINST], EAX
;---------- Window icon
    PUSH   IDI_APPLICATION
    PUSH   0
    CALL   LoadIconA@8
    MOV    [WC.CLSHICON], EAX
;---------- Window cursor
    PUSH   IDC_ARROW
    PUSH   0
    CALL   LoadCursorA@8
    MOV    [WC.CLSHCURSOR], EAX
;----------
    MOV    [WC.CLBKGROUND], 17 ; Window color
    MOV    DWORD PTR [WC.CLMENNAME], 0
    MOV    DWORD PTR [WC.CLNAME], OFFSET CLASSNAME
    PUSH   OFFSET WC
    CALL   RegisterClassA@4
; Create a window of the registered class
    PUSH   0
    PUSH   [HINST]
    PUSH   0
    PUSH   0
    PUSH   200     ; DY - Window height
    PUSH   250     ; DX - Window width
    PUSH   100     ; Y - Coordinate of the top left corner
    PUSH   100     ; X - Coordinate of the top left corner
    PUSH   WS_OVERLAPPEDWINDOW
    PUSH   OFFSET TITLENAME ; Window title
    PUSH   OFFSET CLASSNAME ; Class name
    PUSH   0
    CALL   CreateWindowExA@48
; Check for error
    CMP    EAX, 0
    JZ     _ERR
    MOV    [NEWHWND], EAX ; Window descriptor
;----------------------------------
    PUSH   SW_SHOWNORMAL
    PUSH   [NEWHWND]
    CALL   ShowWindow@8 ; Display the newly created window
;----------------------------------
```

```
    PUSH    [NEWHWND]
    CALL    UpdateWindow@4 ; Command to redraw the visible part
                           ; of the window, the WM_PAINT message
; Message-handling loop
MSG_LOOP:
    PUSH    0
    PUSH    0
    PUSH    0
    PUSH    OFFSET MSG
    CALL    GetMessageA@16
    CMP     EAX, 0
    JE      END_LOOP
    PUSH    OFFSET MSG
    CALL    TranslateMessage@4
    PUSH    OFFSET MSG
    CALL    DispatchMessageA@4
    JMP     MSG_LOOP
END_LOOP:
; Exit the program (close the process)
    PUSH    [MSG.MSWPARAM]
    CALL    ExitProcess@4
_ERR:
    JMP     END_LOOP
;-----------------------------------------------
; Window procedure
; Position of parameters in the stack
;   [EBP+014H]  ; LPARAM
;   [EBP+10H]   ; WAPARAM
;   [EBP+0CH]   ; MES
;   [EBP+8]     ; HWND
WNDPROC  PROC
    PUSH  EBP
    MOV   EBP, ESP
    PUSH  EBX
    PUSH  ESI
    PUSH  EDI
    CMP   DWORD PTR [EBP+0CH], WM_DESTROY
    JE    WMDESTROY
    CMP   DWORD PTR [EBP+0CH], WM_CREATE
    JE    WMCREATE
    CMP   DWORD PTR [EBP+0CH], WM_COMMAND
    JE    WMCOMMND
    JMP   DEFWNDPROC
```

```
WMCOMMND:
    MOV    EAX, HWNDBTN
    CMP    DWORD PTR [EBP+14H], EAX ; Button?
; Exit?
    JE     WMDESTROY
    MOV    EAX, HWNDLST
    CMP    DWORD PTR [EBP+14H], EAX ; List?
    JNE    NOLIST
; Working with the list
    CMP    WORD PTR [EBP+12H], LBN_DBLCLK
    JNE    NOLIST
; There was a double-click
; Now determine the chosen line
; First index
    PUSH   0
    PUSH   0
    PUSH   LB_GETCURSEL
    PUSH   HWNDLST
    CALL  SendMessageA@16
; Now text
    PUSH   OFFSET BUF
    PUSH   EAX
    PUSH   LB_GETTEXT
    PUSH   HWNDLST
    CALL   SendMessageA@16
; Specify, what has been chosen
    PUSH   0
    PUSH   OFFSET CAP1
    PUSH   OFFSET BUF
    PUSH   DWORD PTR [EBP+08H]
    CALL   MessageBoxA@16
NOLIST:
    MOV    EAX, 0
    JMP    FINISH
WMCREATE:
; Create the button window
    PUSH   0
    PUSH   [HINST]
    PUSH   0
    PUSH   DWORD PTR [EBP+08H]
    PUSH   20     ; DY
    PUSH   60     ; DX
    PUSH   10     ; Y
```

```
    PUSH   10    ; X
    PUSH   STYLBTN
    PUSH   OFFSET CPBUT    ; Window name
    PUSH   OFFSET CLSBUTN ; Class name
    PUSH   0
    CALL   CreateWindowExA@48
    MOV    HWNDBTN, EAX ; Save the button descriptor
;-------------------------------------------
; Create the LISTBOX window
    PUSH   0
    PUSH   [HINST]
    PUSH   0
    PUSH   DWORD PTR [EBP+08H]
    PUSH   90    ; DY
    PUSH   150   ; DX
    PUSH   50    ; Y
    PUSH   10    ; X
    PUSH   STYLLST
    PUSH   OFFSET CPLST    ; Window name
    PUSH   OFFSET CLSLIST ; Class name
    PUSH   0
    CALL   CreateWindowExA@48
    MOV    HWNDLST, EAX
; Fill the list
    PUSH   PS
    PUSH   0
    PUSH   LB_ADDSTRING
    PUSH   HWNDLST
    CALL   SendMessageA@16
    PUSH   PS+4
    PUSH   0
    PUSH   LB_ADDSTRING
    PUSH   HWNDLST
    CALL   SendMessageA@16
    PUSH   PS+8
    PUSH   0
    PUSH   LB_ADDSTRING
    PUSH   HWNDLST
    CALL   SendMessageA@16
    PUSH   PS+12
    PUSH   0
    PUSH   LB_ADDSTRING
    PUSH   HWNDLST
```

```
    CALL    SendMessageA@16
    PUSH    PS+16
    PUSH    0
    PUSH    LB_ADDSTRING
    PUSH    HWNDLST
    CALL    SendMessageA@16
    PUSH    PS+20
    PUSH    0
    PUSH    LB_ADDSTRING
    PUSH    HWNDLST
    CALL    SendMessageA@16
    MOV     EAX, 0
    JMP     FINISH
DEFWNDPROC:
    PUSH    DWORD PTR [EBP+14H]
    PUSH    DWORD PTR [EBP+10H]
    PUSH    DWORD PTR [EBP+0CH]
    PUSH    DWORD PTR [EBP+08H]
    CALL    DefWindowProcA@16
    JMP     FINISH
WMDESTROY:
    PUSH    0           ; MB_OK
    PUSH    OFFSET CAP
    PUSH    OFFSET MES
    PUSH    DWORD PTR [EBP+08H]  ; Window descriptor
    CALL    MessageBoxA@16
    PUSH    0
    CALL    PostQuitMessage@4 ; WM_QUIT message
    MOV     EAX, 0
FINISH:
    POP     EDI
    POP     ESI
    POP     EBX
    POP     EBP
    RET     16
WNDPROC  ENDP
_TEXT ENDS
END START
```

I'd like to mention one important topic. In the course of program execution, various interesting and unusual events may occur to the window. For example, the user may drag the window over the screen, resize it as desired, and finally open other windows that overlap the current one.

In such situations, the system sends the `WM_PAINT` message to the window. The same message is sent to the window when executing some functions related to redrawing the window, such as the `UpdateWindow` function. If the `WM_PAINT` message is not processed by the window procedure but is returned to the system by the `DefWindowProc` function, the system redraws the window (under any conditions) and redraws the window contents. However, only child windows are related to window contents, such as buttons, lists, and other controls. In the next chapters, I will describe various methods of putting text and graphical information into the window. To ensure that the information is preserved in the window, you must process the `WM_PAINT` message.

To conclude, note that the examples provided in this chapter are written to be compiled using MASM32. To use them with TASM32, as mentioned previously, it is sufficient to remove the `@N` suffix from all names of API functions and to use the IMPORT32.LIB library instead of USER32.LIB and KERNEL32.LIB.

Child Windows and Owned Windows

Later, you will see many times that windows have numerous attributes. In addition, windows can be related to each other in a certain way. In other words, every window can have a parent window and several child windows. A window that has no parent is called a top-level window. All examples considered previously demonstrated top-level windows. Elements located in the window (buttons, lists, etc.) are child windows. In addition to child windows, there are owned windows. An owned window has an owner but is not a child window to it. Examples of owned windows are so-called pop-up windows used for building various dialog panels. The main difference between a dialog box and an owned window is that the child window can be moved only within an area limited by the area of the parent window and an owned window can be moved anywhere within the screen area. The behavior of the parent window influences the behavior of its child and owned windows:

- When the parent window is minimized or maximized, all its child and owned windows are also hidden or restored.
- When the parent window is moved, all its child windows move with it (this doesn't relate to owned windows).
- When the parent window is destroyed, all its child and owned windows are destroyed.

Child windows with the common parent window can overlap. The order, in which such windows are displayed, is called Z-order and can be regulated using special API functions, such as `SetWindowPos`, `DeferWindowPos`, and `GetNextWindow`. Later, I won't concentrate on this topic.

Listing 3.4 shows a program that demonstrates the properties of child and owned windows (Fig. 3.2). When this program is started, its main window appears. When the user clicks the mouse within its client area, two windows appear: the child window and the owned window. To better understand their properties, I recommend that you experiment with these windows.

Listing 3.4. A program that creates a main window and two secondary windows

```
.586P
; Flat memory model
.MODEL FLAT, stdcall
;-----------------------------------------------
; Constants
; The message that arrives when the window is closed
WM_DESTROY          equ 2
; The message that arrives when the window is created
WM_CREATE           equ 1
; The message that arrives when the user clicks the left mouse
; button in the client area of the window
WM_LBUTTONDOWN      equ 201h
; Window properties
CS_VREDRAW          equ 1h
CS_HREDRAW          equ 2h
CS_GLOBALCLASS      equ 4000h
WS_OVERLAPPEDWINDOW equ 000CF0000H
WS_POPUP            equ 80000000h
WS_CHILD            equ 40000000h
STYLE               equ CS_HREDRAW+CS_VREDRAW+CS_GLOBALCLASS
BS_DEFPUSHBUTTON    equ 1h
WS_VISIBLE          equ 10000000h
WS_CHILD            equ 40000000h
STYLBTN             equ WS_CHILD+BS_DEFPUSHBUTTON+WS_VISIBLE
; Standard icon identifier
IDI_APPLICATION     equ 32512
; Cursor identifier
IDC_ARROW           equ 32512
; Window display mode — normal
SW_SHOWNORMAL       equ 1
; Prototypes of external procedures
EXTERN MessageBoxA@16:NEAR
EXTERN CreateWindowExA@48:NEAR
EXTERN DefWindowProcA@16:NEAR
EXTERN DispatchMessageA@4:NEAR
```

```
EXTERN ExitProcess@4:NEAR
EXTERN GetMessageA@16:NEAR
EXTERN GetModuleHandleA@4:NEAR
EXTERN LoadCursorA@8:NEAR
EXTERN LoadIconA@8:NEAR
EXTERN PostQuitMessage@4:NEAR
EXTERN RegisterClassA@4:NEAR
EXTERN ShowWindow@8:NEAR
EXTERN TranslateMessage@4:NEAR
EXTERN UpdateWindow@4:NEAR
; Structures
; Message structure
MSGSTRUCT STRUC
 MSHWND       DD ?
 MSMESSAGE    DD ?
 MSWPARAM     DD ?
 MSLPARAM     DD ?
 MSTIME       DD ?
 MSPT         DD ?
MSGSTRUCT ENDS
;---- Window class structure
WNDCLASS STRUC
 CLSSTYLE     DD ?
 CLWNDPROC    DD ?
 CLSCBCLSEX   DD ?
 CLSCBWNDEX   DD ?
 CLSHINST     DD ?
 CLSHICON     DD ?
 CLSHCURSOR   DD ?
 CLBKGROUND   DD ?
 CLMENNAME    DD ?
 CLNAME       DD ?
WNDCLASS ENDS
;------------------------------------------------------
; INCLUDELIB directives for the linker to link libraries
includelib c:\masm32\lib\user32.lib
includelib c:\masm32\lib\kernel32.lib
;------------------------------------------------------
; Data segment
_DATA SEGMENT
 NEWHWND   DD 0
 MSG       MSGSTRUCT <?>
 WC        WNDCLASS  <?>
 HINST     DD 0 ; Application descriptor
```

```
TITLENAME     DB 'Child and owned windows', 0
TITLENAMED    DB 'Child window', 0
TITLENAMEO    DB 'Owned window', 0
CLASSNAME     DB 'CLASS32', 0
CLASSNAMED    DB 'CLASS321', 0
CLASSNAMEO    DB 'CLASS322', 0
_DATA ENDS
; Code segment
_TEXT SEGMENT
START:
; Get the application descriptor
  PUSH 0
  CALL GetModuleHandleA@4
  MOV  [HINST], EAX
REG_CLASS:
; Fragment in which the main window is registered
; Style
  MOV  [WC.CLSSTYLE], STYLE
; Message-handling procedure
  MOV  [WC.CLWNDPROC], OFFSET WNDPROC
  MOV  [WC.CLSCBCLSEX], 0
  MOV  [WC.CLSCBWNDEX], 0
  MOV  EAX, [HINST]
  MOV  [WC.CLSHINST], EAX
;---------- Window icon
  PUSH IDI_APPLICATION
  PUSH 0
  CALL LoadIconA@8
  MOV  [WC.CLSHICON], EAX
;---------- Window cursor
  PUSH IDC_ARROW
  PUSH 0
  CALL LoadCursorA@8
  MOV  [WC.CLSHCURSOR], EAX
;---------- Registration of the main window
  MOV  [WC.CLBKGROUND], 17 ; Window color
  MOV  DWORD PTR [WC.CLMENNAME], 0
  MOV  DWORD PTR [WC.CLNAME], OFFSET CLASSNAME
  PUSH OFFSET WC
  CALL RegisterClassA@4
; Fragment in which the child window is registered
; Style
  MOV  [WC.CLSSTYLE], STYLE
; Message-handling procedure
```

```
MOV   [WC.CLWNDPROC], OFFSET WNDPROCD
MOV   [WC.CLSCBCLSEX], 0
MOV   [WC.CLSCBWNDEX], 0
MOV   EAX, [HINST]
MOV   [WC.CLSHINST], EAX
;----------
MOV   [WC.CLBKGROUND], 2 ; Window color
MOV   DWORD PTR [WC.CLMENNAME], 0
MOV   DWORD PTR [WC.CLNAME], OFFSET CLASSNAMED
PUSH  OFFSET WC
CALL  RegisterClassA@4
; Fragment in which the owned window is registered
; Style
MOV   [WC.CLSSTYLE],STYLE
; Message-handling procedure
MOV   [WC.CLWNDPROC], OFFSET WNDPROCO
MOV   [WC.CLSCBCLSEX], 0
MOV   [WC.CLSCBWNDEX], 0
MOV   EAX, [HINST]
MOV   [WC.CLSHINST], EAX
;----------
MOV   [WC.CLBKGROUND], 1 ; Window color
MOV   DWORD PTR [WC.CLMENNAME], 0
MOV   DWORD PTR [WC.CLNAME], OFFSET CLASSNAMEO
PUSH  OFFSET WC
CALL  RegisterClassA@4
; Create a window of the registered class
PUSH  0
PUSH  [HINST]
PUSH  0
PUSH  0
PUSH  400   ; DY — Window height
PUSH  600   ; DX — Window width
PUSH  100   ; Y — Coordinate of the top left corner
PUSH  100   ; X — Coordinate of the top left corner
PUSH  WS_OVERLAPPEDWINDOW
PUSH  OFFSET TITLENAME ; Window name
PUSH  OFFSET CLASSNAME ; Window class
PUSH  0
CALL  CreateWindowExA@48
; Check for error
CMP   EAX, 0
JZ    _ERR
MOV   [NEWHWND], EAX ; Window descriptor
```

```
;-----------------------------------
  PUSH  SW_SHOWNORMAL
  PUSH  [NEWHWND]
  CALL  ShowWindow@8 ; Show the newly created window
;-----------------------------------
  PUSH  [NEWHWND]
  CALL  UpdateWindow@4
; Redraw the visible part of the window, the WM_PAINT message
; Message-processing loop
MSG_LOOP:
   PUSH  0
   PUSH  0
   PUSH  0
   PUSH  OFFSET MSG
   CALL  GetMessageA@16
   CMP   EAX, 0
   JE    END_LOOP
   PUSH  OFFSET MSG
   CALL  TranslateMessage@4
   PUSH  OFFSET MSG
   CALL  DispatchMessageA@4
   JMP   MSG_LOOP
END_LOOP:
; Exit the program (close the process)
   PUSH  [MSG.MSWPARAM]
   CALL  ExitProcess@4
_ERR:
   JMP   END_LOOP


;***********************************
; Main window procedure
; Position of parameters in the stack
; [EBP+014H]  ; LPARAM
; [EBP+10H]   ; WAPARAM
; [EBP+0CH]   ; MES
; [EBP+8]     ; HWND
WNDPROC     PROC
   PUSH  EBP
   MOV   EBP, ESP
   PUSH  EBX
   PUSH  ESI
   PUSH  EDI
   CMP   DWORD PTR [EBP+0CH], WM_DESTROY
```

```
   JE    WMDESTROY
   CMP   DWORD PTR [EBP+0CH], WM_CREATE
   JE    WMCREATE
   CMP   DWORD PTR [EBP+0CH], WM_LBUTTONDOWN
   JE    LB
   JMP   DEFWNDPROC
WMCREATE:
   MOV   EAX, 0
   JMP   FINISH
LB:
; Create the child window
   PUSH  0
   PUSH  [HINST]
   PUSH  0
   PUSH  DWORD PTR [EBP+08H]
   PUSH  200  ; DY — Window height
   PUSH  200  ; DX — Window width
   PUSH  50   ; Y — Coordinate of the top left corner
   PUSH  50   ; X — Coordinate of the top left corner
   PUSH  WS_CHILD OR WS_VISIBLE OR WS_OVERLAPPEDWINDOW
   PUSH  OFFSET TITLENAMED ; Window name
   PUSH  OFFSET CLASSNAMED ; Window class
   PUSH  0
   CALL  CreateWindowExA@48
; Create an owned window
   PUSH  0
   PUSH  [HINST]
   PUSH  0
   PUSH  DWORD PTR [EBP+08H]
   PUSH  200   ; DY — Window height
   PUSH  200   ; DX — Window width
   PUSH  150   ; Y — Coordinate of the top left corner
   PUSH  250   ; X — Coordinate of the top left corner
   PUSH  WS_POPUP OR WS_VISIBLE OR WS_OVERLAPPEDWINDOW
   PUSH  OFFSET TITLENAMEO ; Window name
   PUSH  OFFSET CLASSNAMEO ; Window class
   PUSH  0
   CALL  CreateWindowExA@48
DEFWNDPROC:
   PUSH  DWORD PTR [EBP+14H]
   PUSH  DWORD PTR [EBP+10H]
   PUSH  DWORD PTR [EBP+0CH]
   PUSH  DWORD PTR [EBP+08H]
   CALL  DefWindowProcA@16
```

```
    JMP   FINISH
WMDESTROY:
    PUSH  0
    CALL  PostQuitMessage@4 ; WM_QUIT message
    MOV   EAX, 0
FINISH:
    POP   EDI
    POP   ESI
    POP   EBX
    POP   EBP
    RET   16
WNDPROC ENDP
;*************************************
; Child window procedure
; Position of parameters in the stack
; [EBP+014H]   ; LPARAM
; [EBP+10H]    ; WAPARAM
; [EBP+0CH]    ; MES
; [EBP+8]      ; HWND
WNDPROCD       PROC
    PUSH EBP
    MOV   EBP, ESP
    PUSH EBX
    PUSH ESI
    PUSH EDI
    CMP   DWORD PTR [EBP+0CH], WM_DESTROY
    JE    WMDESTROY
    CMP   DWORD PTR [EBP+0CH], WM_CREATE
    JE    WMCREATE
    JMP   DEFWNDPROC
WMCREATE:
    JMP   FINISH
DEFWNDPROC:
    PUSH  DWORD PTR [EBP+14H]
    PUSH  DWORD PTR [EBP+10H]
    PUSH  DWORD PTR [EBP+0CH]
    PUSH  DWORD PTR [EBP+08H]
    CALL  DefWindowProcA@16
    JMP   FINISH
WMDESTROY:
    MOV   EAX, 0
FINISH:
    POP   EDI
    POP   ESI
```

```
    POP   EBX
    POP   EBP
    RET   16
WNDPROCD   ENDP

;************************************
; Procedure of the owned window
; Position of parameters in the stack
;  [EBP+014H]  ; LPARAM
;  [EBP+10H]   ; WAPARAM
;  [EBP+0CH]   ; MES
;  [EBP+8]     ; HWND
WNDPROCO   PROC
    PUSH EBP
    MOV   EBP, ESP
    PUSH EBX
    PUSH ESI
    PUSH EDI
 CMP DWORD PTR [EBP+0CH], WM_DESTROY
    JE    WMDESTROY
    CMP   DWORD PTR [EBP+0CH], WM_CREATE
    JE    WMCREATE
    JMP   DEFWNDPROC
WMCREATE:
 JMP FINISH
DEFWNDPROC:
    PUSH  DWORD PTR [EBP+14H]
    PUSH  DWORD PTR [EBP+10H]
    PUSH  DWORD PTR [EBP+0CH]
    PUSH  DWORD PTR [EBP+08H]
    CALL  DefWindowProcA@16
    JMP   FINISH
WMDESTROY:
    MOV   EAX, 0
FINISH:
    POP   EDI
    POP   ESI
    POP   EBX
    POP   EBP
    RET   16
WNDPROCO   ENDP

_TEXT ENDS
END START
```

It is necessary to mention that to translate the program presented in Listing 3.4 using TASM, in addition to the changes that are common and already known to you, it is necessary to add the `@@` prefix (the locality indicator) to the names of matching labels from different procedures and to insert the `LOCALS` directive in the beginning of the program. MASM automatically considers all labels encountered within the procedure as local. In TASM, however, the situation is more complicated. More information on local labels will be provided in *Chapters 11* and *12*.

Note that for each of the three windows, a separate message-handling procedure is defined. Message-handling procedures for the child and owned windows do not contain a `PostQuitMessage` command. This is natural, because closing a child or owned window must not initiate program termination. In all other respects, the contents of the window procedures for this window can be the same as for the main (or top-level) window. They can contain controls, have headers, process any messages, and so on.

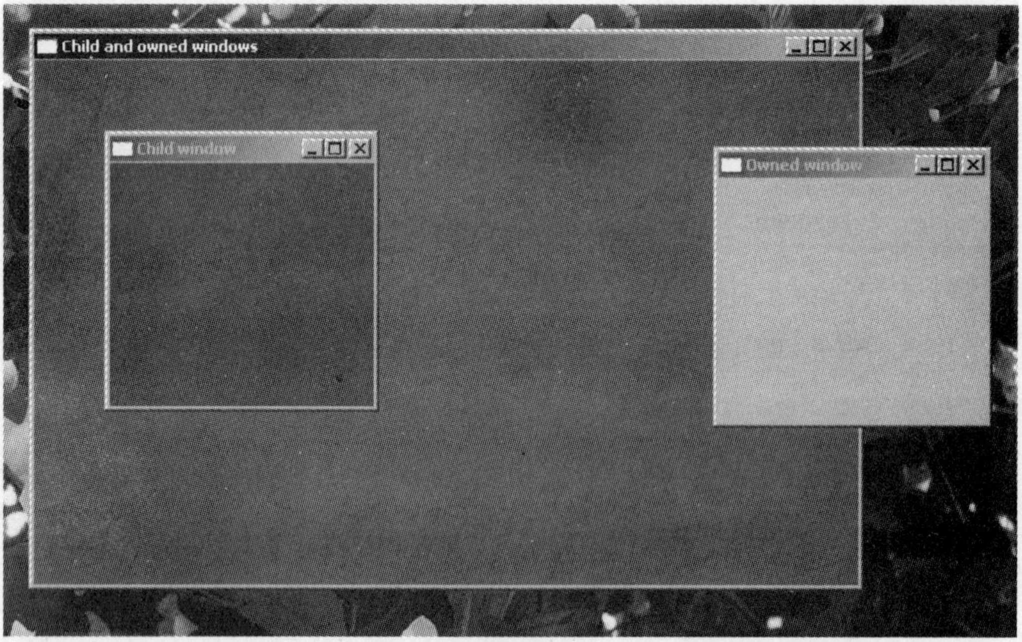

Fig. 3.2. Main window with one child window and one owned window (see Listing 3.4)

Chapter 4

16-Bit Programming Overview

History deserves to be learned! Although this chapter presents information of only historical interest, and although those who remember Windows 3.1 are few in number, I won't delete it even from future editions of my book. This chapter contains material that is valuable from a historical point of view. As a rule, when providing basic information about Windows programming in Assembly language, most authors start by describing 16-bit programming. In my opinion, it is obsolete and can no longer serve as an introduction to Windows programming.[i] Since it is extremely unlikely that you'll need to develop a 16-bit application, I'll limit myself to providing a simple example. If you are interested in this topic, I recommend that you read other books [1, 7] in addition to this chapter.

The Idea of 16-Bit Windows Programming

Let me start by considering the differences between 16-bit and 32-bit Assembly programming. You'll discover that programming has become considerably easier over time.

- In contrast to the Windows 9*x* model, the memory model in Windows 3.1*x* was segmented. Accordingly, in the program, the data, the stack, and the code relate to different segments.[ii] As with MS-DOS, the DS register pointed to the data segment and CS pointed to the code segment.

---

[i] As you'll see for yourself, 16-bit programming is slightly more difficult than 32-bit programming.

[ii] I hope that you remember that in 32-bit model division of data and code into segments is a matter of convention.

- In the 16-bit model, addressing is accomplished according to the segment/offset method. Accordingly, the address is defined by two 16-bit components. For example, to load the address of variable `M` into the stack, you'll need at least two commands: `PUSH DS/PUSH OFFSET M`. At the same time, the segment address must be loaded into the cell with the address higher than that of the offset (the stack grows in the direction of lower addresses).
- For developing 16-bit applications, MASM 6.1 is the most convenient tool. Because this chapter provides only a historical overview, I won't concentrate attention on the development of 16-bit applications using Turbo Assembler. For linking the applications, you will use the LIBW.LIB library supplied with MASM 6.1. A feature of API calls, in this case, is the inverse order of loading parameters into the stack, as compared to all examples considered previously. In this chapter, and only here, I will use the following principle: *from left to right — from top to bottom.*
- After starting the program, it is necessary to initialize startup. For this purpose, it is necessary to call the following API functions: `INITTASK`, `WAITEVENT`, and `INITAPP`.
  - `INITTASK` initializes registers, the command line, and memory. This function doesn't require any parameters and is the first one to be called. Return values of registers are as follows: `AX = 1` (0 = error), `CX` = the stack size, `DI` = the unique number for the current task, `DX` = `NCMDSHOW` (described later), `ES` = the segment address (selector) `PSP`, `ES:BX` = the command line address, and `SI` = the unique number of the previous copy of the same application started earlier. In Windows 3.1, when starting an application, only a part of the registers is loaded into the memory each time and a part of the segments is the common resource. This was the way to economize on the memory. The developers of Windows 95 abandoned this approach. Every task running in the system is isolated and independent. In Windows 95, `SI` is always zero. Furthermore, this procedure fills the reserved header of the data segment.
  - `WAITEVENT` checks whether there are events intended for the specified application. If there is such an event in the queue, it is removed from the queue. The call looks as follows:

```
PUSH AX ; AX - Application number
        ; If it is set to 0, this is the current application
CALL WAITEVENT
```

  - `INITAPP` initializes the event queue for the current application. The call looks as follows:

```
PUSH DI ; Unique number of the task
CALL INITAPP
```

In case of an error, this function returns 0; otherwise, it returns a nonzero value.

- Some parameters of the API functions of a 16-bit application have a size of 2 bytes. In particular, the `WPARAM` and `HWND` parameters of the window procedure are 2 bytes long. When you need to operate with 4-byte parameters, they must be processed in two passes.
- Consider the last difference: the data segment in the program start must contain the reserved 16-byte block.
- An interesting fact is that in a 16-bit application, you can use normal MS-DOS interrupts by means of `INT 21H`. You only have to bear in mind which functions make sense with Windows.

An Example of 16-bit Windows Application

To illustrate the idea explained in the preceding section, I'll provide a simple program. Program translation is carried out using MASM 6.1:

```
ML /c prog.asm
LINK prog, prog, , libw
```

The question about the DEF file can be ignored.

Listing 4.1. An example of a 16-bit application

```
.286
.DOSSEG ; Segment order according to the agreement with Microsoft
DGROUP GROUP  DATA, STA
     ASSUME CS:CODE, DS:DGROUP
; Prototypes of external procedures
EXTRN INITTASK:FAR
EXTRN INITAPP:FAR
EXTRN WAITEVENT:FAR
EXTRN DOS3CALL:FAR
EXTRN REGISTERCLASS:FAR
EXTRN LOADCURSOR:FAR
EXTRN GETSTOCKOBJECT:FAR
EXTRN GETMESSAGE:FAR
EXTRN TRANSLATEMESSAGE:FAR
EXTRN DISPATCHMESSAGE:FAR
EXTRN CREATEWINDOW:FAR
EXTRN CREATEWINDOWEX:FAR
EXTRN UPDATEWINDOW:FAR
EXTRN SHOWWINDOW:FAR
EXTRN POSTQUITMESSAGE:FAR
EXTRN DEFWINDOWPROC:FAR
```

```
; Templates
WNDCL           STRUCT
    STYLE           DW 0 ; Window class style
    LPFNWNDPROC     DD 0 ; Pointer to the handler procedure
    CBCLSEXTRA      DW 0
    CBWNDEXTRA      DW 0
    HINSTANCE       DW 0
    HICON           DW 0
    HCURSOR         DW 0
    HBRBACKGROUND   DW 0
    LPSZMENUNAME    DD 0 ; Pointer to the string
    LPSZCLASSNAME   DD 0 ; Pointer to the string
WNDCL           ENDS
;
MESSA           STRUCT
    HWND            DW ?
    MESSAGE         DW ?
    WPARAM          DW ?
    LPARAM          DD ?
    TIME            DW ?
    X               DW ?
    Y               DW ?
MESSA           ENDS
; Stack segment
STA SEGMENT STACK 'STACK'
    DW 2000 DUP(?)
STA ENDS
; Data segment
DATA SEGMENT WORD 'DATA'
; The 16 bits at the starting point provide the reserve
; required for a 16-bit application to correctly
; operate in the Windows environment
    DWORD 0
    WORD 5
    WORD 5 DUP (0)
    HPREV   DW ?
    HINST   DW ?
    LPSZCMD DD ?
    CMDSHOW DW ?
; Structure for creating a class
    WNDCLASS        WNDCL <>
; Message structure
    MSG             MESSA <>
```

```
; Window class name
   CLASS_NAME   DB 'HELLO', 0
; Window header
   APP_NAME     DB '16-bit program', 0
; Cursor type
   CURSOR  EQU 00007F00H
; Window style
   STYLE        EQU 000CF0000H
; Window parameters
   XSTART       DW 100
   YSTART       DW 100
   DXCLIENT     DW 300
   DYCLIENT     DW 200
DATA ENDS
; Code segment
CODE SEGMENT WORD 'CODE'
_BEGIN:
; I. Initial code
   CALL  INITTASK                   ; Initialize the task
   OR    AX, AX                     ; CX - Stack boundaries
   JZ    _ERR
   MOV   HPREV, SI                  ; Number of the previous application
   MOV   HINST, DI                  ; Number for the new task
   MOV   WORD PTR LPSZCMD, BX       ; ES:BX - Address
   MOV   WORD PTR LPSZCMD+2, ES     ; of the command line
   MOV   CMDSHOW, DX                ; Screen parameter
   PUSH  0                          ; Current task
   CALL  WAITEVENT                  ; Clear the event queue
   PUSH  HINST
   CALL  INITAPP                    ; Initialize applications
   OR    AX, AX
   JZ    _ERR
   CALL  MAIN                       ; Start the main procedure
_TO_OS:
   MOV   AH, 4CH
   INT   21H                        ; Exit the program
_ERR:
; Here, it is possible to place the error message
   JMP   SHORT _TO_OS
; Main procedure
;*****************************************************
MAIN PROC
; II. Registering the window class
; Window style NULL - Standard window
   MOV   WNDCLASS.STYLE, 0
```

```
; Handler procedure
    LEA     BX, WNDPROC
    MOV     WORD PTR WNDCLASS.LPFNWNDPROC, BX
    MOV     BX, CS
    MOV     WORD PTR WNDCLASS.LPFNWNDPROC+2, BX
;------------------------------
; Reserved bytes terminating the structure being reserved
    MOV     WNDCLASS.CBCLSEXTRA, 0
; Reserved bytes terminating the structure for each window
    MOV     WNDCLASS.CBWNDEXTRA, 0
; The window icon is missing
    MOV     WNDCLASS.HICON, 0
; The number of the task being started
    MOV     AX, HINST
    MOV     WNDCLASS.HINSTANCE, AX
; Get the standard cursor number
    PUSH    0
    PUSH    DS
    PUSH    CURSOR
    CALL    LOADCURSOR
    MOV     WNDCLASS.HCURSOR, AX
; Get the number of the standard object
    PUSH    0     ; WHITE_BRUSH
    CALL    GETSTOCKOBJECT
; Background color
    MOV     WNDCLASS.HBRBACKGROUND, AX
; Menu name from the resource file  (NULL if missing)
    MOV     WORD PTR WNDCLASS.LPSZMENUNAME, 0
    MOV     WORD PTR WNDCLASS.LPSZMENUNAME+2, 0
; Pointer to the string containing the class name
    LEA     BX, CLASS_NAME
    MOV     WORD PTR WNDCLASS.LPSZCLASSNAME, BX
    MOV     WORD PTR WNDCLASS.LPSZCLASSNAME+2, DS
; Call the registration procedure
    PUSH    DS                ; Pointer to
    LEA     DI, WNDCLASS
    PUSH    DI                ; WNDCLASS structures
    CALL    REGISTERCLASS
    CMP     AX, 0
    JNZ     _OK1
; Registration error
    RET    ; Error in the course of registration
_OK1:
; III. Creating the window
```

```
; Address of the window class name string
    PUSH    DS
    LEA     BX, CLAS_NAME
    PUSH    BX
; Address of the window header string
    PUSH    DS
    LEA     BX, APP_NAME
    PUSH    BX
; Window style
    MOV     BX, HIGHWORD STYLE
    PUSH    BX
    MOV     BX, LOWWORD STYLE
    PUSH    BX
; X coordinate of the window's top left corner
    PUSH    XSTART
; Y coordinate of the window's top left corner
    PUSH    YSTART
; Window width
    PUSH    DXCLIENT
; Window height
    PUSH    DYCLIENT
; Number of the parent window
    PUSH    0
; Number (identifier) of the window menu
    PUSH    0 ; NULL
; Task number
    PUSH    HINST
; Address of the block of window parameters (none)
    PUSH    0
    PUSH    0
    CALL    CREATEWINDOW
    CMP     AX, 0
    JNZ     NO_NULL
; Window creation error
    RET   ; Error when creating a window
; Set the window visibility state (window or icon)
; according to the CMDSHOW parameter and its display
NO_NULL:
    MOV     SI, AX
    PUSH    SI
    PUSH    CMDSHOW
    CALL    SHOWWINDOW
; Send the command to redraw the window area
; (WM_PAINT command)
```

```
; The message is sent to the window directly
    PUSH    SI
    CALL    UPDATEWINDOW
; IV. Waiting loop
    LOOP1:
; Retrieve the message from the queue
    PUSH    DS
    LEA     BX, MSG     ; Pointer to the message structure
    PUSH    BX
    PUSH    0
    PUSH    0
    PUSH    0
    CALL    GETMESSAGE
; Check whether the "exit" message has been received
    CMP     AX, 0
    JZ      NO_LOOP1
; Convert all received messages to the ANSI standard
    PUSH    DS
    LEA     BX, MSG
    PUSH    BX
    CALL    TRANSLATEMESSAGE
; Instruct Windows to pass this message
; to the appropriate window
    PUSH    DS
    LEA     BX, MSG
    PUSH    BX
    CALL    DISPATCHMESSAGE
; Close the message-processing loop
    JMP     SHORT LOOP1
NO_LOOP1:
    RET
MAIN    ENDP
; Procedure for the specified window class
; Windows passes the following parameters to this procedure:
; HWND - Window descriptor, WORD type
; MES - Message number, WORD type
; WPARAM - Additional information, WORD type
; LPARAM - Additional information, DWORD type
WNDPROC PROC
    PUSH    BP
    MOV     BP, SP
    MOV     AX, [BP+0CH]  ; MES - Message number
    CMP     AX, 2         ; Is this the WM_DESTROY message?
    JNZ     NEXT
```

```
; Pass the message about application termination
; This message will be received by the message-handling
; loop, and the application will thus be terminated
    PUSH     0
    CALL     POSTQUITMESSAGE
    JMP      _QUIT
NEXT:
; Pass the message further to Windows
; This means that everything that wasn't processed
; by the procedure is provided to Windows for processing
    PUSH     [BP+0EH]    ; HWND
    PUSH     [BP+0CH]    ; MES — Message number
    PUSH     [BP+0AH]    ; WPARAM
    PUSH     [BP+8]      ; HIGHWORD LPARAM
    PUSH     [BP+6]      ; LOWWORD LPARAM
    CALL     DEFWINDOWPROC
; ******************************************************
_QUIT:
    POP      BP
; The call to the window procedure is always FAR;  therefore, you use RETF
    RETF     10       ; Clear the stack from the parameters
WNDPROC ENDP
CODE    ENDS
END     _BEGIN
```

That's all. The compiled and linked program will start both in older versions of the operating system and in all newer versions of operating systems from the Windows family. I'd only like to draw your attention to the .DOSSEG directive. This directive specifies a certain order of segments in the EXE file. This order is as follows: The starting segment is the segment of the CODE class, it is followed by segments of classes other than CODE that do not belong to the group of segments (GROUP), then there are segments grouped using the GROUP directive. At the same time, the segments not from the BSS and STACK classes go first, then come the segments of the BSS class (if any), and the last segment is the segment of the STACK class.

For Assembly language, Windows 95 was a significant advance. Obviously, Assembly language programming became considerably easier.

Now, say good-bye to 16-bit programming. You'll never encounter it again in this book.

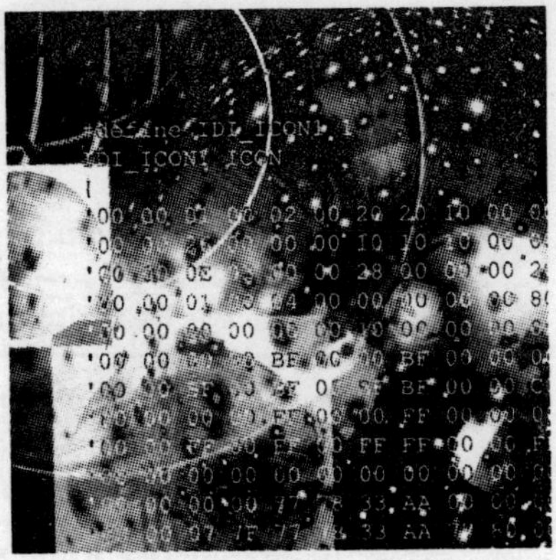

Chapter 5

MASM and TASM Assemblers

In this chapter, I describe two competing products, MASM and TASM, and their advantages, drawbacks, common features, and differences. In the late 1980s, when I first started to work on an IBM PC, the first question that I asked more experienced colleagues was about Assembly language. Before that time, I was involved in programming for different computers, which mainly had limited resources. Naturally, Assembly language was the main language for such computers.[i] I started to work with MASM version 2, as far as I recall. Surprisingly, I started to write database applications using it. My project was not accomplished, but I have grown to love Assembly language. Some time later, I encountered Turbo Assembler 1.0. It operated considerably faster than MASM.

Later, I had to use both assemblers alternately. As you probably guessed, the first love was stronger. Nevertheless, now I must seriously tell you, which of the two products is best suited for writing Windows applications.

Command-Line Options of ML.EXE and TASM32.EXE

I'll start with reference information about the command-line options of ML.EXE (Table 5.1) and TASM32.EXE (Table. 5.2). First consider the ML.EXE translator.

---

[i] For example, at one time Yamaha PCs were widely used in education. Those PCs had only 64 KB (later 128 KB) of RAM. Naturally, writing programs in high-level programming languages such as Pascal for such a PC was an impermissible luxury.

Table 5.1. Command-line parameters of the ML.EXE program

Parameter	Description
`/?`	Display help.
`/AT`	Create a COM file. Naturally, this option is not needed when programming for Windows.
`/Bl<linker>`	Use the alternative linker. The linker is supposed to start automatically.
`/c`	Compile without linking.
`/Cp`	Preserve the case of user identifiers. This can be used for additional control.
`/Cu`	Toggle all user identifiers to uppercase.
`/Cx`	Preserve the case in all user identifiers declared as `PUBLIC` or `EXTERNAL`.
`/coff`	Generate object modules in the common object file format (COFF). This is a required option.
`/D<name> = [string]`	Define a text macro. This is useful for debugging with conditional compiling.
`/EP`	Output the preprocessed listing (program code with `INCLUDE` files) to `stdout`.
`/F<hex>`	Set the stack size (bytes). The default value is 1 MB.
`/Fe<file>`	Define a name for the resulting executable file name. This makes sense when used without the `/c` option.
`/Fl<file>`	Generate a listing file.
`/Fm<file>`	Generate a map file. This makes sense when used without the `/c` option.
`/Fo<file>`	Set the object file name.
`/Fpi`	Include the 80x87 coprocessor emulation code. This option became obsolete with the arrival of the i486 processor.
`/Fr`	Generate limited browser information.
`/FR`	Generate full browser information.
`/G<c|d|z>`	Use a Pascal, C, or `Stdcall` calling convention.
`/H<number>`	Set the maximum length of external names.
`/I<name>`	Add the path for the `INCLUDE` files. Up to 10 `/I` options are allowed.
`/link<opt>`	Linker command-line options. This makes sense when used without the `/c` option.

continues

Table 5.1 *Continued*

Parameter	Description
`/nologo`	Do not display the compiler logo text.
`/Sa`	Maximize the listing format.
`/Sc`	Include timings in the listing.
`/Sf`	Generate a first-pass listing.
`/Sl<number>`	Set the listing line width.
`/Sn`	Suppress a symbol-table listing.
`/Sp<number>`	Set the listing page length.
`/Ss<string>`	Set listing subtitle text.
`/St<string>`	Set listing title text.
`/Sx`	Include fragments of conditional compiling in the listing.
`/Ta<file>`	Assemble files with a filename extension other than ASM.
`/W<number>`	Set the list of compile-time events that should be interpreted as warnings.
`/WX`	Interpret warnings as errors.
`/w`	This is the same as `/W0` or `/WX`.
`/X`	Ignore the path set by the `INCLUDE` environment variable.
`/Zd`	Debug information. This comprises only line numbers.
`/Zf`	Declare all names as `PUBLIC`.
`/Zi`	Include full debug information.
`/Zm`	Enable the compatibility mode with MASM 5.01.
`/Zp<n>`	Set structure alignment.
`/Zs`	Perform a syntax check only.

Table 5.2. Command-line parameters of the TASM32.EXE program

Parameter	Description
`/?` or `/h`	Display a help screen.
`/a`	Order segments in the object file alphabetically.

continues

Table 5.2 *Continued*

Parameter	Description
`/s`	Order segments in the object file sequentially.
`/d<name>=[string]`	Define a text macro. This is convenient for debugging using conditional compiling.
`/e`	Generate the 80x87 coprocessor emulation code.
`/r`	Resolve coprocessor instructions.
`/i<string>`	Set the path for `INCLUDE` files. The syntax is similar to that of the `PATH` command.
`/j<dir>`	Define the assembler startup directive.
`/kh<number>`	Specifies the maximum number of identifiers. The default value is 16,384.
`/l`	Generate a listing file.
`/la`	Generate a listing file and show high-level interface code inserted by the assembler.
`/ml`	Treat all identifiers as case sensitive.
`/mx`	Treat `PUBLIC` and `EXTERNAL` identifiers as case sensitive.
`/mu`	Interpret all characters in identifiers as uppercase.
`/mv<number>`	Set the maximum identifier length.
`/m<number>`	Set the number of translator passes. The default value is 1.
`/n`	Suppress the symbol table in the listing file.
`/os, /o, /op, /oi`	The object code type: Choose from standard, overlay, Pharlap, and IBM.
`/p`	Check for impure protected-mode code (e.g., the code with side effects).
`/q`	Remove all redundant information (e.g., all information not necessary for linking) from the object code.
`/t`	Suppress all messages on successful assembling.
`/w0, /w1, /w2.`	The level of message verbosity: Do not generate messages or generate messages.
`/w+<xxx>` `/w-<xxx>`	Generate (+) or do not generate (–) messages of class `xxx`.
`/x`	Include false conditional assembling messages in the listing.

continues

Table 5.2 *Continued*

Parameter	Description
/z	Display the source line containing an error along with error messages.
/zi	Include debug information in the object code.
/zd	Include line numbers in the object code.
/zn	Do not include debug information in the object code.

To start assembling using MASM32 or TASM32, it is possible to use a special batch file. This is a normal text file that lists all command-line options. For example, instead of the `MASM32 /ml /c mt.asm` command line, it is possible to create a text file containing the following commands:

```
/c mt.asm
```

Name the file MT.CMD, and issue the following command:

```
ml @mt.cmd.
```

TASM32 works with batch files in a similar way.

Command-Line Options of LINK.EXE and TLINK32.EXE

Descriptions of the command-line options of the MASM linker (LINK.EXE) are provided in Table 5.3.

Table 5.3. Command-line parameters of the LINK.EXE (32-bit) program

Parameter	Description
/ALIGN:number	Define the section alignment for the flat memory model. The default value is 4096.
/BASE:{address|@filename, key}	Define the base address (loading address). For an EXE file, the default value is 0x400000; for a DLL file, it is 0x10000000.
/COMMENT: ["]*comment*["]	Define the comment placed into headers of EXE and DLL files.
/DEBUG	Create debug information for EXE and DLL files. The debug information is placed into a PDB file.

continues

Table 5.3 *Continued*

Parameter	Description
`/DEBUGTYPE:{CV|COFF|BOTH}`	`CV` indicates the debug information in the Microsoft format. `COFF` indicates the debug information in COFF. `BOTH` means that both types of debug information are created.
`/DEF:filename`	Define the DEF file.
`/DEFAULTLIB:library`	Add one library to the list of used libraries.
`/DLL`	Create a DLL file.
`/DRIVER[:{UPONLY|WDM}]`	Used for building an NT driver (kernel mode driver).
`/ENTRY:symbol`	Define the starting address for EXE and DLL files.
`/EXETYPE:DYNAMIC`	This option is used when creating VXD drivers.
`/EXPORT:`*`entryname`*`[=`*`internalname`*`] [,@ordinal[,NONAME]][,DATA]`	This option allows you to export a function from your program, making it available to other programs. In this case, an `import` library will be created.
`/FIXED[:NO]`	Fix the base address specified in the `/BASE` option.
`/FORCE[:{MULTIPLE|UNRESOLVED}]`	This option allows you to create an executable file even if the external name is not found or several definitions are available.
`/GPSIZE:number`	Define the size of general variables for MIPS and Alpha platforms.
`/HEAP:reserve[,commit]`	Define the heap (`HEAP`) size in bytes. The default value is 1 MB.
`/IMPLIB:filename`	Define the name of the `import` library. It is necessary to create one.
`/INCLUDE:symbol`	Add a name to the name table.
`/INCREMENTAL:{YES|NO}`	If the `/INCREMENTAL:YES` option is set, then additional information will be added to the EXE file, allowing you to quickly recompile that file. By default, this information will not be added into the file.
`/LARGEADDRESSAWARE[:NO]`	Specify that the application operates with addresses larger than 2 GB.

continues

Table 5.3 *Continued*

Parameter	Description
/LIBPATH:dir	Define the library that will be sought first by the compiler.
/MACHINE:{ALPHA|ARM|IX86|MIPS|MIPS16|MIPSR41XX|PPC|SH3|SH4}	Define the target platform. In most cases, there is no need to do so.
/MAP[:filename]	Instruct the linker to create a MAP file.
/MAPINFO:{EXPORTS|FIXUPS|LINES}	Instruct the linker to include appropriate information in the MAP file.
/MERGE:from=to	Instruct the linker to merge the `from` section to the `to` section and assign it the name `to`.
/NODEFAULTLIB[:library]	Ignore all libraries or a specific library.
/NOENTRY	This is required to create a DLL file.
/NOLOGO	Do not display the linker's logo message.
/OPT:{ICF[,iterations]|NOICF|NOREF|NOWIN98|REF|WIN98}	Define the linker's optimization method.
/ORDER:@filename	Optimize the program by inserting specific initialized data (COMDAT).
/OUT:filename	Define the output file.
/PDB:{filename|NONE}	Define the name of the file containing debug information.
/PDBTYPE:{CON[SOLIDATE]|SEPT[YPES]}	Define the type of the PDB file.
/PROFILE	This is used for working with the profiler.
/RELEASE	Place the checksum into the output file.
/SECTION:name,[E][R][W][S][D][K][L][P][X]	This option allows you to change the section attribute.
/STACK:reserve[,commit]	Define the size of the allocated stack. `Commit` defines the memory size interpreted by the operating system.
/STUB:filename	Define the STUB file that starts under MS-DOS.
/SUBSYSTEM:{NATIVE|WINDOWS|CONSOLE|WINDOWSCE|POSIX}[,#[.##]]	Set the method of starting the resulting EXE file: `CONSOLE` starts using console application, `WINDOWS` uses the normal Windows application, `NATIVE` uses Windows NT applications, and `PCSIX` uses the application for the Windows NT POSIX subsystem.

continues

Table 5.3 *Continued*

Parameter	Description
/SWAPRUN:{CD|NET}	Instruct the operating system to copy the output file into the swap file (Windows NT).
/VERBOSE[:LIB]	This indicates the verbose mode of the linking process.
/VERSION:#[.#]	Place version information into the EXE header.
/VXD	Create a VXD driver.
/WARN[:*warninglevel*]	Specify the number of possible linker warnings.
/WS:AGGRESSIVE	Decrease the execution speed of the target application (Windows NT). The operating system removes this application from the memory when it runs idle.

In Borland C software products, starting from 1997, there were two programs for linking object files: TLINK32.EXE (Table 5.4) and ILINK32.EXE. Command-line options of these programs were practically the same. ILINK32.EXE is an incremental linker. It saves information about the preceding linking operations, which allows you to considerably speed up the entire process of repeated compiling operations. Recently, the TLINK32.EXE program was removed from the distribution set. Later in this book, I won't note the difference between these two programs. Options marked with the plus sign (+) have appeared in the newer versions of ILINK32.EXE, and options marked by the minus sign (–) have been removed. In newer versions, the slash (/) is used instead of the dash (-) to separate an option.

Table 5.4. Command-line parameters of the TLINK32.EXE program

Parameter	Description
-m	Create a MAP file with information about the segments and two listings with PUBLIC names (in alphabetic and sequential order).
-s	Include detailed information about the segments in the MAP file.
-M	Include abbreviated identifier names in the MAP file.
-c	Distinguish uppercase and lowercase letters in PUBLIC and EXTERNAL names.
-E*nn*	Specify the maximum number of errors. If this number is exceeded, the linking process stops.

continues

Table 5.4 *Continued*

Parameter	Description
`-P-`	Do not pack segments. This makes sense for 16-bit applications only (`-P` = allow).
`-b:`*xxxx*	Specify the base address. The default value is 400000H (+).
`-B:`*xxxx*	This is similar to the `-b` option but doesn't create a tuning table. Using the `-b` and `-B` keys may somewhat improve program performance.
`-w`*xxx*	This indicates possible warnings. For example, `-w-stk` warns you to ignore the lack of stack segment.
`-T`*xx*	Type of the output file may be as follows:
`-Tp`*x* `PE image` (x: e=EXE, d=DLL)	• `-Tpe` — Create an EXE file. • `-Tpd` — Create a DLL file. • `-Tpp` — Create a batch file (+).
`-a`*x*	• `-ap` — Create a console application. • `-aa` — Create a standard Windows application (GUI). • `-ad` — Create a 32-bit Windows driver (+).
`-r`	Instruct the compiler to display information about the linking progress.
`-Vd.d`	Place the expected Windows version into the EXE header.
`-Ud.d`	Place the program version into the EXE file header (+).
`-o`	Import by function number (–).
`-Ao:`*nnnn*	Define the alignment value (multiple of 2 and minimum value of 16).
`-Af:`*nnnn*	This is the alignment file.
`-Sc:`*xxxx*	Define the stack size.
`-S:`*xxxx*	Define the reserve stack size. The minimum value is 4 KB.
`-Hc:`*xxxx*	Define the special heap size.
`-H:`*xxxx*	Define the reserve heap size.
`-n`	This means that there is no default library (–).
`-v`	Include full debug information in the executable file. For the selective inclusion of debug information in individual files, use `-v+` and `-v-`.
`-j`	Define the search path for OBJ files.

continues

Table 5.4 *Continued*

Parameter	Description
`-L`	Define the path to the LIB library.
`-x`	Do not create a MAP file.
`-Rr`	This allows you to replace or delete resources (+).
`-d`	Set the DLL loading delay. It will be loaded only when the main procedure is called (+).
`-Dxxxx`	Place a special descriptor into the PE header.
`-GC`	Place a string or strings into the PE header—for example, `-GC"Hello!"` (+).
`-GD`	Generate a Delphi-compatible resource file (+).
`-GF`	Set one of the following flags for the loadable module: • `SWAPNET` — Instruct the operating system to place a loadable module into the swap file and load it from there if the swap file resides on a network drive. • `SWAPCD` — This is similar to the previous flag but is intended for removable devices. • `UNIPROCESSOR` — This application mustn't start in the multi-processor system. • `LARGEADDRESSAWARE` — This application uses addresses larger than 4 GB. • `AGGRESSIVE` — The operating system removes any idle application from the memory (+).
`-Gk`	In case of error, this instructs the linker to leave the files that otherwise would be deleted (+).
`-Gl`	Generate a LIB file (+).
`-Gpr`	Create a run-time package (+).
`-Gpd`	Create a compile-time package (+).
`-Gn`	Disable incremental compiling (+).
`-GS:string`	`-GS:string = [ECIRWSDKP]`. This adds flags to the existing section flags (+).
`-Gz`	Place the executable module checksum into the PE header.

Similar to assemblers, LINK.EXE and TLINK32.EXE can work with batch files. For example, assume that your command line appears as follows:

```
link /windows:console mt.obj
```

Instead of this command line, you can create a text file named MTL.CMD containing the following:

```
/subsystem:console
Mt.obj
```

Having completed this, issue the following command:

```
link @mtl.cmd
```

TLINK32.EXE works in a similar way.

At first glance, it is difficult to detect any differences that would make you prefer MASM32 or TASM32. However, consider the following:

- MASM32 has slightly more reach capabilities. In this case, I mean command-line options.
- TASM32 is no longer supported as a standalone product. Because of this, MASM has beaten its competitor in the number of examples, the extent of its libraries, the amount of documentation, etc.
- TASM32 carries out a more complicated algorithm for calling API functions, which makes the executable modules built using TASM32 larger than those built using MASM32.

To conclude this chapter, I'd like to provide some easy examples.

Including Debug Information in the Executable File

If any debug information was included in the executable file, then the debugger from that manufacturer allows you to work simultaneously with the program source code and with the disassembled code. This feature is convenient for high-level languages. For Assembly programs, this is a powerful debugging tool.

Suppose that the source code of your program is stored in the PROG.ASM file. To include the debug information into the executable module, use the following command-line options:

MASM

```
ML /c /coff / /Zd /Zi prog.asm
LINK /subsystem:windows /debug prog.obj
```

In this case, in addition to the PROG.EXE file, the PROG.PDB file will be created and saved on the hard disk. Now, to debug the program, you'll have to start the Microsoft's 32-bit debugger — Code View.

TASM

```
TASM32 /ml /zi prog.asm
TLINK32 -aa -v prog.obj
```

As a result of running the linker with these command-line options, the debug information will be included into the PROG.EXE executable module. For debugging of this module, use the 32-bit Turbo Debugger — TD32.EXE. Fig. 5.1 shows the debugger window with the program being debugged. As can be seen from this illustration, the window displays both the program source code and its disassembled code. More detailed information on debuggers will be provided in the last part of this book.

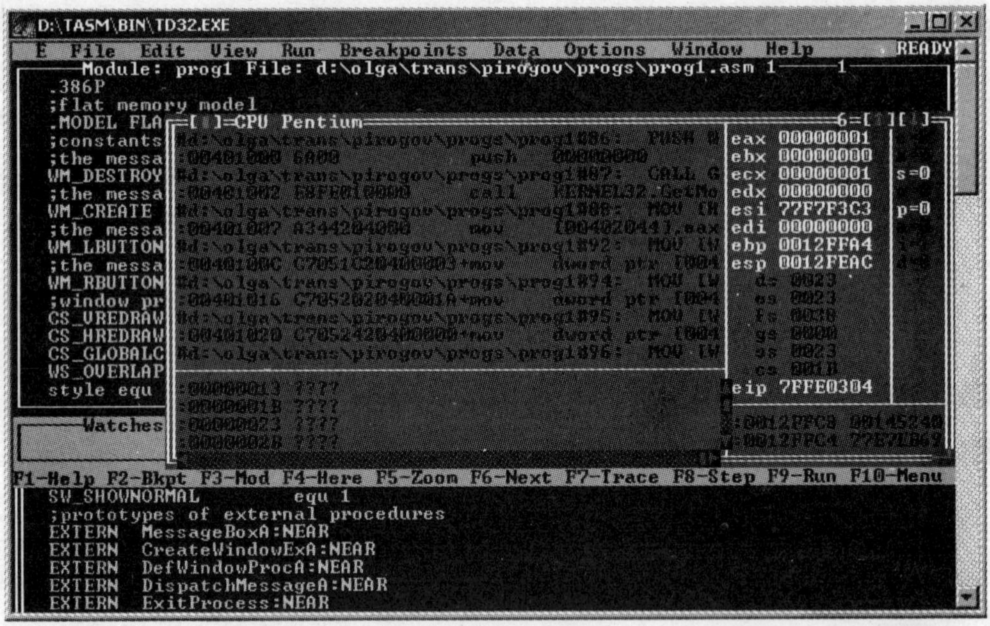

Fig. 5.1. The TD32.EXE program window with the program being debugged

Developing Console Applications and GUI Applications

Console applications will be covered in more detail later in this book. For the moment, it is sufficient to mention that these are applications operating in the text mode. At the same time, they are fully functional 32-bit programs. The structure of a typical console application will be covered in *Chapter 8*. For now, it is essential to mention only that to generate a console application using TLINK32.EXE, it is necessary to use the `-ap` command-line option instead of `-aa`. As for the linker supplied as part of the MASM32 product, it is necessary to use `/subsystem:console` instead of `/subsystem:windows`.

Automatic Linking

The ML.EXE translator provides the convenient feature of automatically starting the linker. As a rule, this feature is ignored using the `/c` command-line option. If this option isn't used, the ML compiler will try to start the LINK.EXE program. To correctly compile and link the program, it is necessary to specify the required options of the linker. Thus, the entire command line would appear as follows:

```
ML /coff prog.asm /LINK /subsystem:windows
```

Very convenient, isn't it?

Self-Translating Program

There exists one interesting technique that allows you to format the program source code to make it possible to start it as a BAT file, which would immediately assemble and link the program. This technique is possible because the command processor ignores the semicolon character (;). At the same time, the assembler uses this character for marking the comments. Thus, you can always mask the OS commands from the assembler's view. Listing 5.1 is a skeleton for such a program. Do not forget that the file must have the BAT filename extension. For this example, name your program M.BAT.

Listing 5.1. A self-assembling and self-linking program

```
; goto masm

; Program code here

.
.
.

END START

; ml /c /coff M.BAT
; link /subsysytem:windows M.OBJ
```

That's all. Of course, this is a trifle; however, the art of programming consists of such small details.

PART II: WINDOWS PROGRAMMING

Chapter 6

Text Encoding in Windows

Encoding is exceedingly important. Even as long ago as Windows was still under construction and there were only vague rumors about it, I often had to convert text information. Once upon a time I even had to write a special driver for a printer that refused to understand standard encoding.

Encoding Text Information

The American National Standards Institute (ANSI) has introduced the American Standard Code for Information Interchange (ASCII). In the ASCII standard, there are two code tables — basic and extended. The basic table includes codes from 0 to 127, and extended table adds the values from 128 to 255. The starting 32 codes of the ASCII table are reserved for use by hardware manufacturers. They are so-called control codes. Codes from 32 to 127 are used for English alphabetic characters, digits, punctuation marks, and other characters.

The extended table was intended for encoding national language characters. Here, there is no common standard. The International Standards Organization (ISO) standard provides encoding for national language characters; however, in each country, there are also national standards that are used more frequently. For example, in Russia, there are several encoding methods pretending to play the role of a standard. Thus, to encode Cyrillic characters, Microsoft has introduced Windows code page 1251. KOI8 encoding was inherited from the Soviet Union. DOS encoding, or CP-866, is generally used by Windows for displaying text information in the console window.[i]

[i] One of the most important tasks of the console window was displaying MS-DOS programs.

Single-byte encoding doesn't allow two or more alphabets to be used simultaneously. Furthermore, some national alphabets cannot be encoded using single-byte numbers. Currently, a more universal encoding system is used, which is based on representing characters using two-byte numbers. This universal encoding system is known as Unicode. Note that despite obvious advantages of such an approach, two-byte encoding became popular only recently. The reason is straightforward: additional resources are required to use Unicode. This relates both to the RAM, since all text strings have a double length, and to the CPU resources.

OEM and ANSI

Windows uses two types of encoding.

- Encoding used for the output of text information into graphical windows. It is known as ANSI encoding.
- Encoding used for output into console windows. It is also called original equipment manufacturers (OEM) encoding.

I'd like to point out once again that, principally, any encoding system can play the role of ANSI or OEM. The important point here is that Windows uses different code tables for output into GUI windows and for output into console windows. As mentioned previously, code layout for the codes from 0 to 127 is the same for different encodings. Consequently, a problem might arise if the information that you are going to output will contain text in national languages other than English. Windows provides various means of converting text strings from one encoding system to another encoding system. Most frequently, API functions such as `OemToChar` and `CharToOem` are used for this purpose. Consider these functions in more detail, since I'll use them extensively later in this book. In C notation, these functions appear as follows:

```
BOOL OemToChar(
      LPCSTR lpszSrc,
      LPTSTR lpszDst
)

BOOL CharToOem(
      LPCTSTR lpszSrc,
      LPSTR lpszDst
)
```

The `OemToChar` function converts the string from encoding used for console output into encoding used for GUI output. The `CharToOem` function carries out the inverse operation. The first argument of both functions is the address of the buffer, where the converted string will be copied. The second argument is the address of the string that has to be converted.

Unicode

Operating systems of the Windows NT family, starting from Windows 2000, have fully migrated to Unicode. However, most programmers haven't even noticed this event. This is because all operations with Unicode are internal for Windows. As relates to output parameters, such as strings for the `MessageBox` function, Windows continues to accept them in ANSI encoding. When such a function is called, the operating system converts the input ANSI string into a two-byte string and then works with the result. If the function must return the string value, the string must be converted from Unicode to ANSI. Additionally, for all functions that accept or return strings, there are "twins" with the same name, complemented by the trailing `W` — functions such as `MessageBoxW` or `CharToOemW`. These functions operate with Unicode strings. The resources, which will be covered later, are also stored in the Unicode format. Consequently, all functions that store and retrieve the resource information also convert it prior to accomplishing their tasks.

One of the most interesting functions is `IsTextUnicode`, which checks the information stored in the current buffer and determines whether or not it is presented in the Unicode format. The function is statistic, which means that it correctly determines whether the given text is in the Unicode format with a certain level of probability. Consider this function in more detail:

```
BOOL IsTextUnicode(
          CONST VOID* pBuffer,
          int cb,
          LPINT lpi
          )
```

The function returns a nonzero value if it successfully recognizes Unicode format; otherwise, it returns zero.

- The first parameter of this function is the address of the buffer containing text information that has to be checked.
- The second parameter contains the length of the buffer being checked.
- The third parameter is the pointer to the memory area that must contain instructions about which tests must be carried out. If the memory area contains 0, this means that it is necessary to carry out all tests. For example, the value `IS_TEXT_UNICODE_ASCII16` equal to 1 means that the text being tested must be presented in the Unicode format and contain characters of a national alphabet.

Other values of constants can be found in the WINDOWS.INC file supplied with the MASM32 product. The most important point here is that all constants contain bits that don't overlap, which means that the memory area, to which the third argument of this function points, can contain combinations of these constants. An example illustrating the use of this function will be provided later.

Now, consider how conversions from ANSI to Unicode and from Unicode to ANSI are carried out. Two functions are intended for this purpose, `MultiByteToWideChar` and `WideCharToMultiByte`. Consider these functions in more detail.

The `MultiByteToWideChar` function is used for converting ANSI strings to Unicode strings:

```
int MultiByteToWideChar(
  UINT CodePage,
  DWORD dwFlags,
  LPCSTR lpMultiByteStr,
  int cbMultiByte,
  LPWSTR lpWideCharStr,
  int cchWideChar
)
```

- The first parameter specifies the number of the codepage of the source string. For example, the `CP_ACP = 0` constant corresponds to ASCII.
- The second parameter is the flag that regulates the conversion of letters with diacritical signs. Usually this parameter is assumed to be zero.
- The third parameter points to the string being converted.
- The fourth parameter must be equal to the length of the string being converted. If this parameter is set to 1, the function must determine the string length on its own.
- The fifth parameter points to the buffer intended to store the converted string.
- The sixth parameter specifies the maximum size of the buffer that will store the converted string.

If the function completes successfully, it returns the size of the converted string. If the sixth parameter is set to 0, the function won't carry out the conversion. Instead, it will return the buffer size required to store the converted string:

```
int WideCharToMultiByte(
  UINT CodePage,
  DWORD dwFlags,
  LPCWSTR lpWideCharStr,
  int cchWideChar,
  LPSTR lpMultiByteStr,
```

```
  int cbMultiByte,
  LPCSTR lpDefaultChar,
  LPBOOL lpUsedDefaultChar
)
```

- The first parameter specifies the codepage for the resulting string.
- The second parameter is the flag that regulates the conversion of letters with diacritical signs. Usually this parameter is assumed to be zero.
- The third parameter is the address of the string being converted.
- The fourth parameter is the length of the string being converted (in characters). If this parameter is set to 1, then the function must determine the string length on its own.
- The fifth parameter is the address of the buffer that will store the resulting ANSI string.
- The sixth parameter determines the maximum size of the buffer that would store the converted string.
- The seventh parameter is the default address of the symbol. If the function encounters the symbol missing from the specified codepage, it replaces the missing character with the one pointed to by the specified parameter. Usually, this parameter is assumed to be 0 (or `NULL`).
- The eighth parameter points to the memory area, in which the function places either 0 or 1, depending on whether or not it succeeded to convert all the symbols in the source string.

Listing 6.1 is the code fragment that converts the source string from ANSI to Unicode.

Listing 6.1. The fragment that carries out ANSI to UNICODE conversion

```
.
.
; The string to be converted
STR1 DB "Console application", 0
; The buffer for copying the converted string
BUF  DB 200 DUP(0)
.
.
.

PUSH   200            ; Maximum buffer length
PUSH   OFFSET BUF     ; Buffer address
```

```
PUSH  -1              ; Define the string length automatically
PUSH  OFFSET STR1     ; String address
PUSH  0               ; Flag
PUSH  0               ; CP_ACP — ANSI encoding
CALL MultiByteToWideChar@24
; Now it is possible to work with the Unicode string BUF.
...
```

Regarding the provided fragment, it should be pointed out that it would be better to proceed as follows:

1. Start the `MultiByteToWideChar` function with the sixth parameter set to 0. The function would return the size of the buffer for storing the converted string (in bytes).
2. Allocate memory for that buffer.
3. Convert the string by calling the `MultiByteToWideChar` function and specifying the sixth parameter.
4. Work with the string.
5. Release the memory block allocated to the buffer.

Chapter 12 contains an interesting macro that simplifies the conversion of the string from ASCII to Unicode.

Finally, I'd like to point out that there is a convenient technique of specifying the string that will be interpreted as Unicode directly in the program. For example, you could choose not to specify the string in a traditional manner, for example, as follows:

```
STR1 DB "MASM 7.0",0
```

Instead, it can be written as follows:

```
STR1 DW 'M','A','S','M','7','.','0',0
```

After that, you can comfortably use the `MessageBoxW` function instead of `MessageBoxA`.

Chapter 7

Examples of Simple Programs

Examples are essential for studying programming. I also learned on the examples. In this chapter, I start with a detailed description of the `WM_PAINT` message. In *Chapter 3*, you considered this message but didn't use it. This was because the program window contained only controls — no text information or graphics. Now, I am going to correct this situation. Besides the `WM_PAINT` message, you will also consider various problems related to Windows programming.

Outputting Text into a Window

Listing 7.1 contains an example of a simple Windows program. If you only start to develop Windows applications, you'll find lots of new ideas in this listing. Therefore, start with a detailed description of this program.

- In this program, the colors of the window background and text are defined on the basis of combinations of three colors: red, green, and blue. The color is set by a 32-bit number. The first byte specifies the intensity of red, the second byte specifies the intensity of green, and the third byte specifies the intensity of blue. The last byte is set to zero. The mechanism of generating this number is illustrated by the definition of the `RGBW` constant.
- Window background color is set by defining a brush through the `CreateSolidBrush` function. A brush is a bitmap used by the system for filling solid areas.
- Because the `WM_PAINT` message is sent by the system when redrawing window, the contents of the program window must be redrawn when receiving this message.

This program outputs only one text string. To output this information into the window, it is first necessary to get the window context (also known as device context). From a programmer's point of view, this device context is simply a number used for ensuring communication between a program and its window. As a rule, the device context is defined by calling the `GetDC` function. When receiving the `WM_PAINT` message, the program acquires the device context by calling the `BeginPaint` function. The argument of this function is the pointer to the special structure `PAINTSTR`; however, the fields of this structure are not used in this program.

- I hope that you have already guessed on the basis of the program listing — text output is carried out using the `OutText` function. Before calling this function, you define the background and foreground colors by calling the `SetBkColor` and `SetTextColor` functions. Background color, naturally, is the same as window color.
- Now, it is necessary to pay attention to the coordinate system. Its center is in the top left corner of the window, the Y-axis is directed downward, and the X-axis is directed rightward. This variant is commonly adopted for graphical screens.
- Another important aspect relates to text output into the window. The length of the string that must be displayed in the window is one of parameters of the `OutText` function. At this point, there are several important aspects that should be noted. There are several methods of determining the output string length (minus the trailing 0). For example, you can use the `SIZEOF` or `LENGTHOF` operators of a macroassembler. However, Turbo Assembler lacks these operators. It is possible to resolve this discrepancy by placing a label in the end of the string or by using obsolete `LENGTH` and `SIZE` directives. However, I hope that you have already grasped the idea that to ensure compatibility and portability between MASM32 and TASM32, it is wise to avoid using macros. Moreover, because you are using string definitions according to C language conventions, it would be natural to define string functions (*see the note at the end of this chapter*). In this example, I have defined the function that returns the string length. Don't be confused because this function returns the result into the `EBX` register. It is simply more convenient. Besides, functions have another important advantage over macro tools, namely, they get the string length at run time instead of compile time.

Now, to ensure that this program can be compiled using Turbo Assembler, it is necessary to carry out the same manipulations as before, namely, to delete all `@N` suffixes and to include the IMPORT32.LIB library.

Listing 7.1. The simplest program that performs text output

```
; The TEXT1.INC file
; Constants
; The message arrives when the window is closed
WM_DESTROY        equ 2
; The message arrives when the window is created
WM_CREATE         equ 1
; The message arrives when the window must be redrawn
WM_PAINT          equ 0Fh
; Window properties
CS_VREDRAW        equ 1h
CS_HREDRAW        equ 2h
CS_GLOBALCLASS    equ 4000h
WS_OVERLAPPEDWINDOW equ 000CF0000H
stylcl            equ CS_HREDRAW+CS_VREDRAW+CS_GLOBALCLASS
DX0               equ 300
DY0               equ 200
; Color components
RED               equ 50
GREEN             equ 50
BLUE              equ 255
RGBW              equ (RED or (GREEN shl 8)) or (BLUE shl 16)
RGBT              equ 255 ; Red
; Standard icon identifier
IDI_APPLICATION   equ 32512
; Cursor identifier
IDC_CROSS         equ 32515
; Normal display mode
SW_SHOWNORMAL     equ 1
; Prototypes of external procedures
EXTERN  CreateWindowExA@48:NEAR
EXTERN  DefWindowProcA@16:NEAR
EXTERN  DispatchMessageA@4:NEAR
EXTERN  ExitProcess@4:NEAR
EXTERN  GetMessageA@16:NEAR
EXTERN  GetModuleHandleA@4:NEAR
EXTERN  LoadCursorA@8:NEAR
EXTERN  LoadIconA@8:NEAR
EXTERN  PostQuitMessage@4:NEAR
EXTERN  RegisterClassA@4:NEAR
EXTERN  ShowWindow@8:NEAR
EXTERN  TranslateMessage@4:NEAR
```

```
EXTERN   UpdateWindow@4:NEAR
EXTERN   BeginPaint@8:NEAR
EXTERN   EndPaint@8:NEAR
EXTERN   TextOutA@20:NEAR
EXTERN   GetStockObject@4:NEAR
EXTERN   CreateSolidBrush@4:NEAR
EXTERN   SetBkColor@8:NEAR
EXTERN   SetTextColor@8:NEAR
; Structures
; Message structure
MSGSTRUCT STRUC
        MSHWND          DD ? ; Identifier of the window
                             ; that receives the message
        MSMESSAGE       DD ? ; Message identifier
        MSWPARAM        DD ? ; Additional information about the message
        MSLPARAM        DD ? ; Additional information about the message

        MSTIME          DD ? ; Time the message was sent
        MSPT            DD ? ; Cursor position when this message was sent
MSGSTRUCT ENDS
;---------
WNDCLASS  STRUC
        CLSSTYLE          DD ? ; Window style
        CLSLPFNWNDPROC    DD ? ; Pointer to the window procedure
        CLSCBCLSEXTRA     DD ? ; Information about auxiliary bytes
                               ; for this structure
        CLSCBWNDEXTRA     DD ? ; Information about auxiliary bytes
                               ; for the window
        CLSHINSTANCE      DD ? ; Application descriptor
        CLSHICON          DD ? ; Window icon identifier
        CLSHCURSOR        DD ? ; Window cursor identifier
        CLSHBRBACKGROUND  DD ? ; Window brush identifier
        MENNAME           DD ? ; Identifier of the menu name
        CLSNAME           DD ? ; Specifies the name for the window class
WNDCLASS  ENDS
;---
PAINTSTR  STRUC
    hdc     DWORD 0
    fErase  DWORD 0
    left    DWORD 0
    top     DWORD 0
    right   DWORD 0
    bottom  DWORD 0
```

```
    fRes     DWORD 0
    fIncUp   DWORD 0
    Reserv   DB 32 dup(0)
PAINTSTR        ENDS
; The TEXT1.ASM file
.586P
; Flat memory model
.MODEL FLAT, stdcall
;---------------------------------------------------
include text1.inc
; Connecting libraries
includelib c:\masm32\lib\user32.lib
includelib c:\masm32\lib\kernel32.lib
includelib c:\masm32\lib\gdi32.lib
;---------------------------------------------------
; Data segment
_DATA SEGMENT
        NEWHWND         DD 0
        MSG             MSGSTRUCT       <?>
        WC              WNDCLASS        <?>
        PNT             PAINTSTR        <?>
        HINST           DD 0
        TITLENAME       DB 'Window text', 0
        NAM             DB 'CLASS32', 0
        XT              DWORD 30
        YT              DWORD 30
        TEXT            DB 'Text in the window is red', 0
_DATA   ENDS
; Code segment
_TEXT   SEGMENT
START:
; Get the application descriptor
        PUSH  0
        CALL  GetModuleHandleA@4
        MOV   [HINST], EAX
REG_CLASS:
; Fill the window structure
; Style
        MOV   [WC.CLSSTYLE], stylcl
; Message-handling procedure
        MOV   [WC.CLSLPFNWNDPROC], OFFSET WNDPROC
        MOV   [WC.CLSCBCLSEXTRA], 0
        MOV   [WC.CLSCBWNDEXTRA], 0
```

```
        MOV   EAX,[HINST]
        MOV   [WC.CLSHINSTANCE], EAX
; Window icon
        PUSH  IDI_APPLICATION
        PUSH  0
        CALL  LoadIconA@8
        MOV   [WC.CLSHICON], EAX
;---------- Window cursor
        PUSH  IDC_CROSS
        PUSH  0
        CALL  LoadCursorA@8
        MOV   [WC.CLSHCURSOR], EAX
;----------
        PUSH  RGBW ; Brush color
        CALL  CreateSolidBrush@4 ; Create a brush
        MOV   [WC.CLSHBRBACKGROUND], EAX
        MOV   DWORD PTR [WC.MENNAME], 0
        MOV   DWORD PTR [WC.CLSNAME], OFFSET NAM
        PUSH  OFFSET WC
        CALL  RegisterClassA@4
; Create a window of the registered class
        PUSH  0
        PUSH  [HINST]
        PUSH  0
        PUSH  0
        PUSH  DY0        ; DY0 — Window height
        PUSH  DX0        ; DX0 — Window width
        PUSH  100        ; The Y coordinate
        PUSH  100        ; The X coordinate
        PUSH  WS_OVERLAPPEDWINDOW
        PUSH  OFFSET TITLENAME ; Window name
        PUSH  OFFSET NAM    ; Class name
        PUSH  0
        CALL  CreateWindowExA@48
; Error check
        CMP   EAX, 0
        JZ    _ERR
        MOV   [NEWHWND], EAX ; Window descriptor
;-----------------------------------
        PUSH  SW_SHOWNORMAL
        PUSH  [NEWHWND]
        CALL  ShowWindow@8 ; Show the window that you have just created
;-----------------------------------
```

```
        PUSH  [NEWHWND]
        CALL  UpdateWindow@4 ; Redraw the visible part of the window
; Message-processing loop
MSG_LOOP:
        PUSH  0
        PUSH  0
        PUSH  0
        PUSH  OFFSET MSG
        CALL  GetMessageA@16
        CMP   AX, 0
        JE    END_LOOP
        PUSH  OFFSET MSG
        CALL  TranslateMessage@4
        PUSH  OFFSET MSG
        CALL  DispatchMessageA@4
        JMP   MSG_LOOP
END_LOOP:
; Exit the program (terminate the process)
        PUSH  [MSG.MSWPARAM]
        CALL  ExitProcess@4
_ERR:
        JMP  END_LOOP
; Window procedure
; Parameters in the stack
;  [EBP+014H]  ; LPARAM
;  [EBP+10H]   ; WAPARAM
;  [EBP+0CH]   ; MES
;  [EBP+8]     ; HWND
WNDPROC    PROC
        PUSH  EBP
        MOV   EBP, ESP
        PUSH  EBX
        PUSH  ESI
        PUSH  EDI
        CMP   DWORD PTR [EBP+0CH], WM_DESTROY
        JE    WMDESTROY
        CMP   DWORD PTR [EBP+0CH], WM_CREATE
        JE    WMCREATE
        CMP   DWORD PTR [EBP+0CH], WM_PAINT
        JE    WMPAINT
        JMP   DEFWNDPROC
WMPAINT:
;----------------
```

```
        PUSH  OFFSET PNT
        PUSH  DWORD PTR [EBP+08H]
        CALL  BeginPaint@8
        PUSH  EAX ; Save the context (descriptor)
;----------------Background color = window color
        PUSH  RGBW
        PUSH  EAX
        CALL  SetBkColor@8
;----------------Context
        POP   EAX
        PUSH  EAX
;----------------Text color (red)
        PUSH  RGBT
        PUSH  EAX
        CALL  SetTextColor@8
;----------------Context
        POP   EAX
;----------------Display text
        PUSH  OFFSET TEXT
        CALL  LENSTR
        PUSH  EBX ; string length
        PUSH  OFFSET TEXT ; String address
        PUSH  YT  ; Y
        PUSH  XT  ; X
        PUSH  EAX ; Window context
        CALL  TextOutA@20
;----------------Close
        PUSH  OFFSET PNT
        PUSH  DWORD PTR [EBP+08H]
        CALL  EndPaint@8
        MOV   EAX, 0
        JMP   FINISH
WMCREATE:
        MOV   EAX, 0
        JMP   FINISH
DEFWNDPROC:
        PUSH  DWORD PTR [EBP+14H]
        PUSH  DWORD PTR [EBP+10H]
        PUSH  DWORD PTR [EBP+0CH]
        PUSH  DWORD PTR [EBP+08H]
        CALL  DefWindowProcA@16
        JMP   FINISH
WMDESTROY:
```

```
        PUSH  0
        CALL  PostQuitMessage@4 ; WM_QUIT
        MOV   EAX, 0
FINISH:
        POP   EDI
        POP   ESI
        POP   EBX
        POP   EBP
        RET   16
WNDPROC ENDP
;----------- Function -------------------------
; String length [EBP+08H] — Pointer to the string
LENSTR PROC
        PUSH  EBP
        MOV   EBP, ESP
        PUSH  ESI
        MOV   ESI, DWORD PTR [EBP+8]
        XOR   EBX, EBX
LBL1:
        CMP   BYTE PTR [ESI], 0
        JZ    LBL2
        INC   EBX
        INC   ESI
        JMP   LBL1
LBL2:
        POP   ESI
        POP   EBP
        RET   4
LENSTR ENDP
_TEXT ENDS
END START
```

Now consider another example illustrating text output into the window. Now your task is more complicated. Aim at ensuring that the text string always remains in the middle of the window no matter what happens to it. To achieve it, you'll need to know the window size in pixels and the string length. The string length in pixels is defined using the `GetTextExtentPoint32` function; to determine the window size, use the `GetWindowRect` function. When doing so, you'll need structures such as `SIZET` and `RECT`. I hope you understand how to determine the string position if its length and window size are given. I'll only mention again that it's necessary to take into account the height of the window header.

Listing 7.2. Keeping the text string in the center of the window

```
; The TEXT2.INC file
; Constants
; The message arrives when the window is closed
WM_DESTROY          equ 2
; The message arrives when the window is created
WM_CREATE           equ 1
; The message arrives when the window is redrawn
WM_PAINT            equ 0Fh
; Window properties
CS_VREDRAW          equ 1h
CS_HREDRAW          equ 2h
CS_GLOBALCLASS      equ 4000h
WS_OVERLAPPEDWINDOW equ 000CF0000H
stylcl              equ CS_HREDRAW+CS_VREDRAW+CS_GLOBALCLASS
DX0                 equ 300
DY0                 equ 200
; Color components
RED                 equ 80
GREEN               equ 80
BLUE                equ 255
RGBW                equ (RED or (GREEN shl 8)) or (BLUE shl 16)
RGBT                equ 00FF00H ; Green
; Standard icon identifier
IDI_APPLICATION     equ 32512
; Cursor identifier
IDC_CROSS           equ 32515
; Window display mode is normal
SW_SHOWNORMAL       equ 1
; Prototypes of external procedures
EXTERN  CreateWindowExA@48:NEAR
EXTERN  DefWindowProcA@16:NEAR
EXTERN  DispatchMessageA@4:NEAR
EXTERN  ExitProcess@4:NEAR
EXTERN  GetMessageA@16:NEAR
EXTERN  GetModuleHandleA@4:NEAR
EXTERN  LoadCursorA@8:NEAR
EXTERN  LoadIconA@8:NEAR
EXTERN  PostQuitMessage@4:NEAR
EXTERN  RegisterClassA@4:NEAR
EXTERN  ShowWindow@8:NEAR
EXTERN  TranslateMessage@4:NEAR
```

```
EXTERN  UpdateWindow@4:NEAR
EXTERN  BeginPaint@8:NEAR
EXTERN  EndPaint@8:NEAR
EXTERN  TextOutA@20:NEAR
EXTERN  GetStockObject@4:NEAR
EXTERN  CreateSolidBrush@4:NEAR
EXTERN  SetBkColor@8:NEAR
EXTERN  SetTextColor@8:NEAR
EXTERN  GetTextExtentPoint32A@16:NEAR
EXTERN  GetWindowRect@8:NEAR
; Structures
; Message structure
MSGSTRUCT STRUC
        MSHWND          DD ? ; Identifier of the window
                             ; that receives the message
        MSMESSAGE       DD ? ; Message identifier
        MSWPARAM        DD ? ; Additional information about the message
        MSLPARAM        DD ? ; Additional information about the message
        MSTIME          DD ? ; Message sending time
        MSPT            DD ? ; Cursor position when the message was sent
MSGSTRUCT ENDS
;---------
WNDCLASS STRUC
        CLSSTYLE          DD ? ; Window style
        CLSLPFNWNDPROC    DD ? ; Pointer to the window procedure
        CLSCBCLSEXTRA     DD ? ; Information about additional bytes for
                               ; this structure
        CLSCBWNDEXTRA     DD ? ; Information about additional bytes
                               ; for the window
        CLSHINSTANCE      DD ? ; Application descriptor
        CLSHICON          DD ? ; Window icon identifier
        CLSHCURSOR        DD ? ; Window cursor identifier
        CLSHBRBACKGROUND  DD ? ; Window brush identifier
        MENNAME           DD ? ; Menu identifier name
        CLSNAME           DD ? ; Specifies the window class name
WNDCLASS ENDS
;----------
PAINTSTR STRUC
        hdc     DWORD 0
        fErase  DWORD 0
        left    DWORD 0
        top     DWORD 0
        right   DWORD 0
```

```
        bottom  DWORD 0
        fRes    DWORD 0
        fIncUp  DWORD 0
        Reserv  DB 32 dup(0)
PAINTSTR ENDS
;------------
SIZET STRUC
        X1      DWORD ?
        Y1      DWORD ?
SIZET ENDS
RECT STRUC
        L       DWORD ? ; X — Abscissa of the top left corner
        T       DWORD ? ; Y — Ordinate of the top left corner
        R       DWORD ? ; X — Abscissa of the bottom right corner
        B       DWORD ? ; Y — Ordinate of the bottom right corner
RECT ENDS

; The TEXT2.ASM file
.586P
; Flat memory model
.MODEL FLAT, stdcall
;-----------------------------------------------
include text2.inc
; Directive to the linker to include libraries
c:\masm32\lib\user32.lib
includelib c:\masm32\lib\kernel32.lib
includelib c:\masm32\lib\gdi32.lib
;-----------------------------------------------

; Data segment
_DATA SEGMENT
        NEWHWND DD 0
        MSG     MSGSTRUCT <?>
        WC      WNDCLASS  <?>
        PNT     PAINTSTR  <?>
        SZT     SIZET     <?>
        RCT     RECT      <?>
        HINST   DD 0
        TITLENAME DB 'Text in the window', 0
        NAM     DB 'CLASS32', 0
        XT      DWORD ?
        YT      DWORD ?
        TEXT    DB 'Text displayed in the window is green', 0
```

```
        CONT    DWORD ?
_DATA   ENDS
; Code segment
_TEXT SEGMENT
START:
; Get the application descriptor
        PUSH  0
        CALL  GetModuleHandleA@4
        MOV   [HINST], EAX
REG_CLASS:
; Fill the window structure
; Style
        MOV   [WC.CLSSTYLE], stylcl
; Message-handling procedure
        MOV   [WC.CLSLPFNWNDPROC], OFFSET WNDPROC
        MOV   [WC.CLSCBCLSEXTRA], 0
        MOV   [WC.CLSCBWNDEXTRA], 0
        MOV   EAX,[HINST]
        MOV   [WC.CLSHINSTANCE], EAX
;---------- Window icon
        PUSH  IDI_APPLICATION
        PUSH  0
        CALL  LoadIconA@8
        MOV   [WC.CLSHICON], EAX
;---------- Window cursor
        PUSH  IDC_CROSS
        PUSH  0
        CALL  LoadCursorA@8
        MOV  [WC.CLSHCURSOR], EAX
;----------
        PUSH  RGBW ; Brush color
        CALL  CreateSolidBrush@4 ; Create a brush
        MOV   [WC.CLSHBRBACKGROUND], EAX
        MOV   DWORD PTR [WC.MENNAME], 0
        MOV   DWORD PTR [WC.CLSNAME], OFFSET NAM
        PUSH  OFFSET WC
        CALL  RegisterClassA@4
; Create a window of the registered class
        PUSH  0
        PUSH  [HINST]
        PUSH  0
        PUSH  0
        PUSH  DY0        ; DY0 — Window height
```

```
        PUSH  DX0          ; DX0 - Window width
        PUSH  100          ; The Y coordinate
        PUSH  100          ; The X coordinate
        PUSH  WS_OVERLAPPEDWINDOW
        PUSH  OFFSET TITLENAME ; Window name
        PUSH  OFFSET NAM       ; Class name
        PUSH  0
        CALL  CreateWindowExA@48
; Check for error
        CMP   EAX, 0
        JZ    _ERR
        MOV   [NEWHWND], EAX ; Window descriptor
;-----------------------------------
        PUSH  SW_SHOWNORMAL
        PUSH  [NEWHWND]
        CALL  ShowWindow@8 ; Display the newly created window
;-----------------------------------
        PUSH  [NEWHWND]
        CALL  UpdateWindow@4 ; Redraw the visible part of the window
                             ; Message processing
MSG_LOOP:
        PUSH  0
        PUSH  0
        PUSH  0
        PUSH  OFFSET MSG
        CALL  GetMessageA@16
        CMP   AX, 0
        JE    END_LOOP
        PUSH  OFFSET MSG
        CALL  TranslateMessage@4
        PUSH  OFFSET MSG
        CALL  DispatchMessageA@4
        JMP   MSG_LOOP
END_LOOP:
; Exit the program (close the process)
        PUSH  [MSG.MSWPARAM]
        CALL  ExitProcess@4
_ERR:
        JMP   END_LOOP
;---------------------------------------------------; Window procedure
; Positions of the parameters in the stack
; [EBP+014H]  ; LPARAM
; [EBP+10H]   ; WAPARAM
```

```
; [EBP+0CH]   ; MES
; [EBP+8]     ; HWND
WNDPROC    PROC
        PUSH  EBP
        MOV   EBP, ESP
        PUSH  EBX
        PUSH  ESI
        PUSH  EDI
        CMP   DWORD PTR [EBP+0CH], WM_DESTROY
        JE    WMDESTROY
        CMP   DWORD PTR [EBP+0CH], WM_CREATE
        JE    WMCREATE
        CMP   DWORD PTR [EBP+0CH], WM_PAINT
        JE    WMPAINT
        JMP   DEFWNDPROC
WMPAINT:
;----------------
        PUSH  OFFSET PNT
        PUSH  DWORD PTR [EBP+08H]
        CALL  BeginPaint@8
        MOV   CONT, EAX ; Save the context (descriptor)
;----------------Background color = window color
        PUSH  RGBW
        PUSH  EAX
        CALL  SetBkColor@8
;----------------Text color (red)
        PUSH  RGBT
        PUSH  CONT
        CALL  SetTextColor@8
; Compute text length in pixels
        PUSH  OFFSET TEXT
        CALL  LENSTR
        PUSH  EBX ; Save the string length
        PUSH  OFFSET SZT
        PUSH  EBX
        PUSH  OFFSET TEXT
        PUSH  CONT
        CALL  GetTextExtentPoint32A@16
;---------------- Window size
        PUSH  OFFSET RCT
        PUSH  DWORD PTR [EBP+8]
        CALL  GetWindowRect@8
;---------------- Compute coordinates
```

```
        MOV   EAX, RCT.R
        SUB   EAX, RCT.L
        SUB   EAX, SZT.X1
        SHR   EAX, 1 ; Text in the middle
        MOV   XT, EAX
        MOV   EAX, RCT.B
        SUB   EAX, RCT.T
        SHR   EAX, 1
        SUB   EAX, 25 ; Take the window header into account
        MOV   YT, EAX
;---------------- Display text
; String length in the stack
        PUSH  OFFSET TEXT
        PUSH  YT
        PUSH  XT
        PUSH  CONT
        CALL  TextOutA@20
;---------------- Close context
        PUSH  OFFSET PNT
        PUSH  DWORD PTR [EBP+08H]
        CALL  EndPaint@8
        MOV   EAX, 0
        JMP   FINISH
WMCREATE:
        MOV   EAX, 0
        JMP   FINISH
DEFWNDPROC:
        PUSH  DWORD PTR [EBP+14H]
        PUSH  DWORD PTR [EBP+10H]
        PUSH  DWORD PTR [EBP+0CH]
        PUSH  DWORD PTR [EBP+08H]
        CALL  DefWindowProcA@16
        JMP   FINISH
WMDESTROY:
        PUSH  0
        CALL  PostQuitMessage@4 ; WM_QUIT
        MOV   EAX, 0
FINISH:
        POP   EDI
        POP   ESI
        POP   EBX
        POP   EBP
        RET   16
```

```
WNDPROC      ENDP
; String length
; String pointer is in the word located by the [EBP+8] address
LENSTR PROC
        PUSH  EBP
        MOV   EBP, ESP
        PUSH  ESI
        MOV   ESI, DWORD PTR [EBP+8]
        XOR   EBX, EBX
LBL1:
        CMP   BYTE PTR [ESI], 0
        JZ    LBL2
        INC   EBX
        INC   ESI
        JMP   LBL1
LBL2:
        POP   ESI
        POP   EBP
        RET   4
LENSTR ENDP
_TEXT ENDS
END START
```

I can't help admiring the possibilities that an assembler provides to programmers. You can pass parameters through the stack or, if desired, through registers. If you want to, you can save the registers' procedure beginning; if you don't want it, you can do without it. Assembler code can be improved beyond any perceivable limits of perfection. By the way, for the fans of string commands, I'll provide another procedure for determining the string length based on the SCAS microprocessor command. This command allows you to search for the required element (byte — SCASB, word — SCASW, and double word — SCASD) within a string.

```
; String length — [EBP+08H]
LENSTR PROC
        PUSH  EBP
        MOV   EBP, ESP
        PUSH  EAX
;--------------------
        CLD
        MOV   EDI, DWORD PTR [EBP+08H]
        MOV   EBX, EDI
        MOV   ECX, 100 ; Limit the string length
```

```
        XOR     AL, AL
        REPNE   SCASB ; Find symbol 0
        SUB     EDI, EBX ; String length, including 0
        MOV     EBX, EDI
        DEC     EBX ; String length is saved here
;--------------------
        POP     EAX
        POP     EBP
        RET     4
        LENSTR  ENDP
```

Choosing Font

Now, consider how to display text information with different types of fonts. The `CreateFontIndirect` function is the most convenient for specifying the font format. This function accepts the pointer to the `LOGFONT` structure as the parameter. Although the function name starts from `Create`, in this case, I am referring to modifying the existing font according to the specified parameters rather than to creating a new one. There is another function called `CreateFont` that, in my opinion, is less convenient for using in Assembly language programming. If you'd like, you could experiment with this function on your own. The selection of the required font is carried out using the `SelectObject` function.

For now, start with a detailed description of the fields of the `LOGFONT` structure:

```
LOGFONT STRUC
LfHeight          DWORD ?
LfWidth           DWORD ?
LfEscapement      DWORD ?
LfOrientation     DWORD ?
LfWeight          DWORD ?
LfItalic          DB ?
LfUnderline       DB ?
LfStrikeOut       DB ?
LfCharSet         DB ?
LfOutPrecision    DB ?
LfClipPrecision   DB ?
LfQuality         DB ?
LfPitchAndFamily  DB ?
LfFaceName        DB 32 DUP (0)
LOGFONT ENDS
```

Here:

- `LfHeight` — Defines the font height in logical units; if this value is set to 0, then the height value is taken by default.
- `LfWidth` — Defines the font width in logical units; if this value is set to 0, then the font width value is taken by default.
- `LfEscapement` — Angle of the text inclination in relation to the horizontal axis (counterclockwise) in tenths of a degree.
- `LfOrientation` — Same as the previous parameter but in relation to an individual symbol (ignored in Windows 9*x*).
- `LfWeight` — Specifies the font weight (0–900).
- `LfItalic` — In italics, if set to 1.
- `LfUnderline` — If 1, characters are underlined.
- `LfStrikeOut` — If 1, a line is drawn through the characters.
- `LfCharSet` — Specifies the set of font characters, usually defined by the `ANSI_CHARSET (=0)` constant.
- `LfOutPrecision` — The flag of the font precision; it specifies the precision of correspondence between the newly-created font and its predefined parameters. Possible values are as follows:
  - `OUT_DEFAULT_PRECIS = 0`
  - `OUT_STRING_PRECIS = 1`
  - `OUT_CHARACTER_PRECIS = 2`
  - `OUT_STROKE_PRECIS = 3`
  - `OUT_TT_PRECIS = 4`
  - `OUT_DEVICE_PRECIS = 5`
  - `OUT_RASTER_PRECIS = 6`
  - `OUT_TT_ONLY_PRECIS = 7`
  - `OUT_OUTLINE_PRECIS = 8`
  - `OUT_SCREEN_OUTLINE_PRECIS = 9`
- `LfClipPrecision` — The flag of font-clipping precision; defines how to clip font parts that do not fit within the visible area. Possible values are as follows:
  - `CLIP_DEFAULT_PRECIS = 0`
  - `CLIP_CHARACTER_PRECIS = 1`
  - `CLIP_STROKE_PRECIS = 2`
  - `CLIP_MASK = 0fH`
  - `CLIP_LH_ANGLES = (1 SHL 4)`

- `CLIP_TT_ALWAYS = (2 SHL 4)`
- `CLIP_EMBEDDED = (8 SHL 4)`

❒ `LfQuality` — The font quality flag; it defines the correspondence between the logical font and the font allowed for this device. Possible values are as follows:

- `DEFAULT_QUALITY = 0`
- `DRAFT_QUALITY = 1`
- `PROOF_QUALITY = 2`

❒ `LfPitchAndFamily` — Defines the font type and family. Possible values are defined by the `OR` combination of the two groups of constants as follows:

- `DEFAULT_PITCH = 0`
- `FIXED_PITCH = 1`
- `VARIABLE_PITCH = 2`

and

- `FF_DONTCARE = 0`
- `FF_ROMAN = (1 SHL 4)`
- `FF_SWISS = (2 SHL 4)`
- `FF_MODERN = (3 SHL 4)`
- `FF_SCRIPT = (4 SHL 4)`
- `FF_DECORATIVE = (5 SHL 4)`

❒ `LfFaceName` — Contains the font name. The length of the name cannot exceed 32 characters.

Consider the example illustrating how to specify a custom font. The result of executing this program is shown in Fig. 7.1. However, since the main part of this listing is the same as similar parts of all previous programs, I provide here only the required fragments. First, consider the fragment that executes when the `WM_PAINT` message arrives (Listing 7.3).

Listing 7.3. Program fragment that outputs text using a custom font (see Fig. 7.1)

```
WMPAINT:
;------- Define the context
        PUSH OFFSET PNT
        PUSH DWORD PTR [EBP+08H]
        CALL BeginPaint@8
        MOV  CONT, EAX ; Save the context (descriptor)
;------- Background color = window color
        PUSH RGBW
```

```
        PUSH  EAX
        CALL  SetBkColor@8
;------- Text color (red)
        PUSH  RGBT
        PUSH  CONT
        CALL  SetTextColor@8
;------ Coordinates are defined here
        MOV   XT, 120
        MOV   YT, 140
;------ Specify (create) font
        MOV   lg.lfHeight, 12         ; Font height
        MOV   lg.lfWidth, 9           ; Font width
        MOV   lg.lfEscapement, 900    ; Orientation
        MOV   lg.lfOrientation, 0     ; Vertical
        MOV   lg.lfWeight, 400        ; Font line weight
        MOV   lg.lfItalic, 0          ; Italic
        MOV   lg.lfUnderline, 0       ; Underline
        MOV   lg.lfStrikeOut, 0       ; Strikethrough
        MOV   lg.lfCharSet, 0         ; Font set
        MOV   lg.lfOutPrecision, 0
        MOV   lg.lfClipPrecision, 0
        MOV   lg.lfQuality, 2
        MOV   lg.lfPitchAndFamily ,0
        PUSH OFFSET lg
; Specify the font name
        PUSH  OFFSET NFONT
        PUSH  OFFSET lg.LfFaceName
        CALL  COPYSTR
        CALL  CreateFontIndirectA@4
;------ Select the newly created object
        PUSH  EAX
        PUSH  CONT
        CALL  SelectObject@8
        PUSH  EAX
;------ Compute the text length in pixels
        PUSH  OFFSET TEXT
        CALL  LENSTR
;------------- Text output ---------------
        PUSH  EBX
        PUSH  OFFSET TEXT
        PUSH  YT
        PUSH  XT
        PUSH  CONT
        CALL  TextOutA@20
```

```
; Delete the "FONT" object
; Identifier is in the stack already
CALL DeleteObject@4
;---------------- Close the context
        PUSH   OFFSET PNT
        PUSH   DWORD PTR [EBP+08H]
        CALL   EndPaint@8
        MOV    EAX, 0
        JMP    FINISH
```

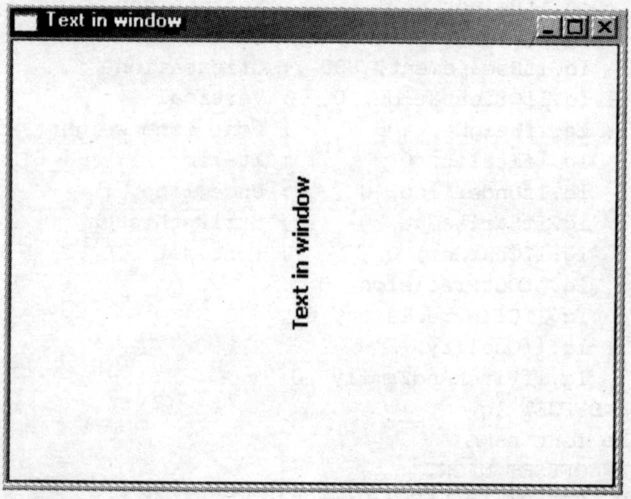

Fig. 7.1. Text output at a 90-degree angle

As can be seen in this fragment, the font is created according to the following scheme: First, it is necessary to create the font using the `CreateFontIndirect` function. Then, you must select the font using the `SelectObject` function, display the text using the specified font, and delete the object (font) created earlier. The `LfFaceName` field of the `LOGFONT` structure must contain the font name. If there is no such font, then the default font will be used. The font name is specified in the `NFONT` string, and you copy it into the `LfFaceName` field using the `COPYSTR` function whose source code is provided in Listing 7.4.

Listing 7.4. Copying one string into another

```
; The procedure of copying one string into another
; The target string [EBP+08H]
; The source string [EBP+0CH]
COPYSTR PROC
```

```
        PUSH EBP
        MOV  EBP, ESP
        MOV  ESI, DWORD PTR [EBP+0CH]
        MOV  EDI, DWORD PTR [EBP+08H]
L1:
        MOV  AL, BYTE PTR [ESI]
        MOV  BYTE PTR [EDI], AL
        CMP  AL, 0
        JE   L2
        INC  ESI
        INC  EDI
        JMP  L1
L2:
        POP  EBP
        RET  8
COPYSTR ENDP
```

This procedure doesn't account for the length of the target string. The best approach is to account for the length by including another parameter — the maximum number of characters that can be copied. I recommend that you do this on your own.

To conclude this section, consider one important topic. When considering all previous examples, this question was unlikely to arise. The reason for this is straightforward: All output took place only when receiving the `WM_PAINT` message. In real-world programs, information output into the window can take place as a result of different events and various procedures. Furthermore, if the window contains lots of information, then direct output of this information using the `TextOut` function will be slow. To display the window contents, it is necessary to store it somewhere. Thus, the problem of temporary storage of window information (not only text) arises.

Those who have some experience with MS-DOS programming will recall that MS-DOS had a similar problem. This problem was solved by outputting all information into the background video page. After that, the background page was copied into the visible page. This produced an impression of instantaneous display of the information. Both RAM and video memory can be used as a background page.

Similar to this approach, a virtual window can be created under the Windows operating system, and all information can be output is into this window. Then, after the arrival of the `WM_PAINT` message, the contents of the virtual window are copied into the real one.

Generally, the procedure is as follows:

1. When a window is created, the following occurs:
   - A compatible device context is created. For this purpose, the `CreateCompatibleDC` function is used. The obtained context must be saved.

- The bit map compatible with this context is created. This is achieved using the `CreateCompatibleBitmap` function.
- The brush of the color matching the color of the main window is created.
- The bit template is created through the bitmap operation using the chosen brush. This is achieved using the `PatBlt` function.

2. All information is output into the virtual window; then, the command to redraw a window is issued. These operations are carried out by the `InvalidateRect` function.
3. When the `WM_PAINT` message is received, the contents of the virtual window is copied into the real window using the `BitBlt` function.

The practical application of this theory will be considered in the next section.

Graphical Images

This section is dedicated to graphics. Because the basics of Windows graphics are easily understood, I'll offer one simple example illustrating the output of graphical images. However, it is first necessary to explain several basic concepts:

- The coordinate system for the output of graphic images is the same as for text output. Coordinates are measured in logical units that, by default, coincide with pixels. If desired, this proportion can be changed.
- Drawing color can be created using three methods. When the `SetPixel` function is used, the color of a given point is specified. For lines, it is necessary to specify the pen color. To specify the color of graphic objects, it is necessary to specify the brush color.
- The pen is created using the `CreatePen` function, and the brush is created using the `CreateSolidBrush` function, which you have used already. To create a colored picture, it is possible to create several pens and brushes beforehand and then choose the required ones when necessary using the `SelectObject` function, which you have also used already.
- The following API functions can be used for drawing:
  - `SetPixel` — Set the specified pixel color.
  - `LineTo` — Draw a line from the current point to the point having the specified coordinates. This point, in its turn, becomes the current point.
  - `MoveToEx` — Change the current point.
  - `Arc` — Draw an arc.
  - `Rectangle` — Draw a rectangle.

- `RoundRect` — Draw a rectangle with rounded corners.
- `Ellipse`, `Pie` — Draw ellipses and elliptical sectors.

- If a brush color set when drawing a closed figure was different from the background color, the closed figure will be filled with this color.
- To set the proportion between logical units and pixels, the `SetMapMode` function is used.
- To specify the input area, it is possible to use the `SetViewportExtEx` function. The `SetViewportOrgEx` function can be used to specify the starting point of the input area.

After providing this introductory information, it is time to demonstrate the program. It is simple but still implements the basic principles of working with graphics.

After you click the left mouse button for the first time, the horizontal line will be drawn. When you click the mouse button a second time, an inclined line will be drawn; the third click draws a colored rectangle. The source code of this program is provided in Listing 7.5, and the result of its execution is shown in Fig. 7.2.

Listing 7.5. A simple program demonstrating how to work with graphics

```
; The GRAPH1.INC file
; Constants
; The message arrives when the window is closed
WM_DESTROY         equ 2
; The message arrives when the window is created
WM_CREATE          equ 1
; The message arrives when you click the left mouse button in the window
area
WM_LBUTTONDOWN     equ 201h
; The message arrives when the window is redrawn
WM_PAINT           equ 0Fh
; Window properties
CS_VREDRAW         equ 1h
CS_HREDRAW         equ 2h
CS_GLOBALCLASS     equ 4000h
WS_OVERLAPPEDWINDOW equ 000CF0000H
stylcl             equ CS_HREDRAW+CS_VREDRAW+CS_GLOBALCLASS
DX0                equ 600

DY0                equ 400
; Color components
RGBW               equ (50 or (50 shl 8)) or (255 shl 16) ; Window color
RGBR               equ 150 ; Region color
RGBL               equ 0 ; Line color
```

```
RGBP   equ 255 or (100 shl 8) ; Point color
; Identifier of the standard icon
IDI_APPLICATION equ 32512
; Cursor identifier
IDC_CROSS       equ 32515
; Window display mode
SW_SHOWNORMAL   equ 1
; Prototypes of external procedures
EXTERN      CreateWindowExA@48:NEAR
EXTERN      DefWindowProcA@16:NEAR
EXTERN      DispatchMessageA@4:NEAR
EXTERN      ExitProcess@4:NEAR
EXTERN      GetMessageA@16:NEAR
EXTERN      GetModuleHandleA@4:NEAR
EXTERN      LoadCursorA@8:NEAR
EXTERN      LoadIconA@8:NEAR
EXTERN      PostQuitMessage@4:NEAR
EXTERN      RegisterClassA@4:NEAR
EXTERN      ShowWindow@8:NEAR
EXTERN      TranslateMessage@4:NEAR
EXTERN      UpdateWindow@4:NEAR
EXTERN      BeginPaint@8:NEAR
EXTERN      EndPaint@8:NEAR
EXTERN      GetStockObject@4:NEAR
EXTERN      CreateSolidBrush@4:NEAR
EXTERN      GetSystemMetrics@4:NEAR
EXTERN      GetDC@4:NEAR
EXTERN      CreateCompatibleDC@4:NEAR
EXTERN      SelectObject@8:NEAR
EXTERN      CreateCompatibleBitmap@12:NEAR
EXTERN      PatBlt@24:NEAR
EXTERN      BitBlt@36:NEAR
EXTERN      ReleaseDC@8:NEAR
EXTERN      DeleteObject@4:NEAR
EXTERN      InvalidateRect@12:NEAR
EXTERN      GetStockObject@4:NEAR
EXTERN      DeleteDC@4:NEAR
EXTERN      CreatePen@12:NEAR
EXTERN      SetPixel@16:NEAR
EXTERN      LineTo@12:NEAR
EXTERN      MoveToEx@16:NEAR
EXTERN      Rectangle@20:NEAR
; Structures
```

```
; Message structure
MSGSTRUCT STRUC
        MSHWND     DD ? ; Identifier of the window
                        ; that receives the message
        MSMESSAGE  DD ? ; Message identifier
        MSWPARAM   DD ? ; Additional information about the message
        MSLPARAM   DD ? ; Additional information about the message
        MSTIME     DD ? ; Message sending time
        MSPT       DD ? ; Cursor position when the message was sent
MSGSTRUCT ENDS
;---------
WNDCLASS STRUC
        CLSSTYLE          DD ? ; Window style
        CLSLPFNWNDPROC    DD ? ; Pointer to the window procedure
        CLSCBCLSEXTRA     DD ? ; Information about additional bytes
                               ; for this structure
        CLSCBWNDEXTRA     DD ? ; Information about additional bytes
                               ; for the window
        CLSHINSTANCE      DD ? ; Application descriptor
        CLSHICON          DD ? ; Window icon identifier
        CLSHCURSOR        DD ? ; Window cursor identifier
        CLSHBRBACKGROUND  DD ? ; Window brush identifier
        MENNAME           DD ? ; Menu name identifier
        CLSNAME           DD ? ; Specifies the window class name
WNDCLASS ENDS
;---
PAINTSTR STRUC
    hdc     DD 0
    fErase  DD 0
    left    DD 0
    top     DD 0
    right   DD 0
    bottom  DD 0
    fRes    DD 0
    fIncUp  DD 0
    Reserv  DB 32 dup(0)
PAINTSTR ENDS
;----
RECT STRUC
    L   DD ? ; X — Top left corner
    T   DD ? ; Y — Top left corner
    R   DD ? ; X — Bottom right corner
    B   DD ? ; Y — Bottom right corner
```

```
RECT ENDS

; The GRAPH.ASM file
.586P
; Flat memory model
.MODEL FLAT, stdcall
;------------------------------------------------
include graph1.inc
; Include libraries
includelib c:\masm32\lib\user32.lib
includelib c:\masm32\lib\kernel32.lib
includelib c:\masm32\lib\gdi32.lib
;------------------------------------------------
; Data segment
_DATA SEGMENT
        NEWHWND DWORD 0
        MSG     MSGSTRUCT <?>
        WC      WNDCLASS  <?>
        PNT     PAINTSTR  <?>
        HINST   DWORD 0
        TITLENAME BYTE 'Graphics in a window', 0
        NAM     BYTE 'CLASS32', 0
        XT      DWORD 30
        YT      DWORD 30
        XM      DWORD ?
        YM      DWORD ?
        HDC     DWORD ?
        MEMDC   DWORD ?
        HPEN    DWORD ?
        HBRUSH  DWORD ?
        P       DWORD 0 ; Output indicator
        XP      DWORD ?
        YP      DWORD ?
_DATA ENDS
; Code segment
_TEXT SEGMENT
START:
; Get application descriptor
        PUSH  0
        CALL  GetModuleHandleA@4
        MOV   [HINST], EAX
REG_CLASS:
; Fill window structure
```

```
; Style
        MOV    [WC.CLSSTYLE], stylcl
; Message-handling procedure
        MOV    [WC.CLSLPFNWNDPROC], OFFSET WNDPROC
        MOV    [WC.CLSCBCLSEXTRA], 0
        MOV    [WC.CLSCBWNDEXTRA], 0
        MOV    EAX,[HINST]
        MOV    [WC.CLSHINSTANCE], EAX
;---------- Window icon
        PUSH   IDI_APPLICATION
        PUSH   0
        CALL   LoadIconA@8
        MOV    [WC.CLSHICON], EAX
;---------- Window cursor
        PUSH   IDC_CROSS
        PUSH   0
        CALL   LoadCursorA@8
        MOV    [WC.CLSHCURSOR], EAX
;----------
    PUSH   RGBW ; Brush color
    CALL   CreateSolidBrush@4 ; Create a brush
        MOV    [WC.CLSHBRBACKGROUND], EAX
        MOV    DWORD PTR [WC.MENNAME], 0
        MOV    DWORD PTR [WC.CLSNAME], OFFSET NAM
        PUSH   OFFSET WC
        CALL   RegisterClassA@4
; Create a window of the registered class
        PUSH   0
        PUSH   [HINST]
        PUSH   0
        PUSH   0
        PUSH   DY0         ; DY0 — Window height
        PUSH   DX0         ; DX0 — Window width
        PUSH   100         ; The Y coordinate
        PUSH   100         ; The X coordinate
        PUSH   WS_OVERLAPPEDWINDOW
        PUSH   OFFSET TITLENAME ; Window name
        PUSH   OFFSET NAM       ; Class name
        PUSH   0
        CALL   CreateWindowExA@48
; Check for error
        CMP    EAX, 0
        JZ     _ERR
```

```
        MOV   [NEWHWND], EAX ; Window descriptor
;-----------------------------------
        PUSH  SW_SHOWNORMAL
        PUSH  [NEWHWND]
        CALL  ShowWindow@8 ; Show the newly created window
;-----------------------------------
        PUSH  [NEWHWND]
        CALL  UpdateWindow@4 ; Redraw the visible part of a window
; Message-handling loop
MSG_LOOP:
        PUSH  0
        PUSH  0
        PUSH  0
        PUSH  OFFSET MSG
        CALL  GetMessageA@16
        CMP   AX, 0
        JE    END_LOOP
        PUSH  OFFSET MSG
        CALL  TranslateMessage@4
        PUSH  OFFSET MSG
        CALL  DispatchMessageA@4
        JMP   MSG_LOOP
END_LOOP:
; Exit the program (close the process)
        PUSH  [MSG.MSWPARAM]
        CALL  ExitProcess@4
_ERR:
        JMP   END_LOOP
;----------------------------------------------------------
; Window procedure
; Placement of parameters in the stack
; [EBP+014H]   ; LPARAM
; [EBP+10H]    ; WAPARAM
; [EBP+0CH]    ; MES
; [EBP+8]      ; HWND
WNDPROC    PROC
        PUSH  EBP
        MOV   EBP, ESP
        PUSH  EBX
        PUSH  ESI
        PUSH  EDI
        CMP   DWORD PTR [EBP+0CH], WM_DESTROY
        JE    WMDESTROY
```

```
        CMP   DWORD PTR [EBP+0CH], WM_CREATE
        JE    WMCREATE
        CMP   DWORD PTR [EBP+0CH], WM_PAINT
        JE    WMPAINT
        CMP   DWORD PTR [EBP+0CH], WM_LBUTTONDOWN
        JE    LBUTTON
        JMP   DEFWNDPROC
LBUTTON:
        CMP   P, 0
        JNE   F1
; Line (horizontal)
        MOV   YP, 50 ; Y
        MOV   XP, 10 ; X
        MOV   ECX, 200
LL:
        PUSH  ECX
        PUSH  RGBP
        PUSH  YP
        PUSH  XP
        PUSH  MEMDC
        CALL  SetPixel@16
        INC   XP
        POP   ECX
        LOOP  LL
        INC   P
        JMP   F3
F1:
        CMP   P, 1
        JNE   F2
; Set the current coordinates to the end of the previous line
        PUSH  0
        PUSH  YP
        PUSH  XP
        PUSH  MEMDC
        CALL  MoveToEx@16
; Line drawn by a pen
        PUSH  300
        PUSH  550
        PUSH  MEMDC
        CALL  LineTo@12
        INC   P
        JMP   F3
```

```
F2:
        CMP   P, 2
        JNE   FIN
; Closed rectangle
; Select a brush for filling the closed area
        PUSH  HBRUSH
        PUSH  MEMDC
        CALL  SelectObject@8
; Draw a filled rectangle
; If you do not choose a brush,
; the rectangle will not be filled
        PUSH  350
        PUSH  400
        PUSH  200
        PUSH  200
        PUSH  MEMDC
        CALL  Rectangle@20
        INC   P
F3:
; Issue a command to redraw the window
        PUSH  0
        PUSH  OFFSET RECT
        PUSH  DWORD PTR [EBP+08H]
        CALL  InvalidateRect@12
FIN:
        MOV   EAX, 0
        JMP   FINISH
WMPAINT:
        PUSH  OFFSET PNT
        PUSH  DWORD PTR [EBP+08H]
        CALL  BeginPaint@8
        MOV   HDC, EAX  ; Save the context (descriptor)
; Copy the virtual window to the real one
        PUSH  0CC0020h ; SRCCOPY = display the image as is
        PUSH  0        ; Y - Coordinate of the source
        PUSH  0        ; X - Coordinate of the source
        PUSH  MEMDC    ; Source context
        PUSH  YM       ; Height
        PUSH  XM       ; Width
        PUSH  0        ; Y - Where
        PUSH  0        ; X - Where
        PUSH  HDC      ; Context - Where
        CALL  BitBlt@36
```

```
;---------------- Close the window context
        PUSH  OFFSET PNT
        PUSH  DWORD PTR [EBP+08H]
        CALL  EndPaint@8
        MOV   EAX, 0
        JMP   FINISH
WMCREATE:
; Screen size
        PUSH  0 ; X
        CALL  GetSystemMetrics@4
        MOV   XM,EAX
        PUSH  1 ; Y
        CALL  GetSystemMetrics@4
        MOV   YM, EAX
; Open the window context
        PUSH  DWORD PTR [EBP+08H]
        CALL  GetDC@4
        MOV   HDC, EAX
; Create the device context compatible with this window
        PUSH  EAX
        CALL  CreateCompatibleDC@4
        MOV   MEMDC,EAX
; Create a bitmap compatible to the hdc context in memory
        PUSH  YM
        PUSH  XM
        PUSH  HDC
        CALL  CreateCompatibleBitmap@12
; Choose the bitmap in this context
        PUSH  EAX
        PUSH  MEMDC
        CALL  SelectObject@8
; Brush color
        PUSH  RGBW
        CALL  CreateSolidBrush@4 ; Create a brush
; Choose the brush in the given context
        PUSH  EAX
        PUSH  MEMDC
        CALL  SelectObject@8
; Fill the rectangular area
        PUSH  0F00021h ; PATCOPY = Fill with the specified color
        PUSH  YM
        PUSH  XM
        PUSH  0
```

```
        PUSH  0
        PUSH  MEMDC
        CALL  PatBlt@24
; Create a pen and a brush for drawing
        PUSH  RGBR
        CALL  CreateSolidBrush@4 ; Create a brush
        MOV   HBRUSH,EAX
; Specify the pen
        PUSH  RGBR ; Color
        PUSH  0    ; Thickness = 1
        PUSH  0    ; Solid line
        CALL CreatePen@12
        MOV   HPEN,EAX
; Delete the context
        PUSH  HDC
        PUSH  DWORD PTR [EBP+08H]
        CALL  ReleaseDC@8
        MOV   EAX, 0
        JMP   FINISH
DEFWNDPROC:
        PUSH  DWORD PTR [EBP+14H]
        PUSH  DWORD PTR [EBP+10H]
        PUSH  DWORD PTR [EBP+0CH]
        PUSH  DWORD PTR [EBP+08H]
        CALL  DefWindowProcA@16
        JMP   FINISH
WMDESTROY:
; Delete the pen
        PUSH  HPEN
        CALL  DeleteDC@4
; Delete the brush
        PUSH  HBRUSH
        CALL  DeleteDC@4
; Delete the virtual window
        PUSH  MEMDC
        CALL  DeleteDC@4
; Exit
        PUSH  0
        CALL  PostQuitMessage@4 ; WM_QUIT
        MOV   EAX, 0
FINISH:
        POP   EDI
        POP   ESI
```

```
        POP  EBX
        POP  EBP
        RET  16
WNDPROC     ENDP
_TEXT ENDS
END START
```

Fig. 7.2. The result of executing the program in Listing 7.5

My explanation of graphical output would be incomplete without considering the topic of manipulating bitmap images. Consider the sequence of actions that need to be carried out for output of a bitmap image. Practical examples of graphics output will be provided in later chapters.

1. Load the bitmap image and store its descriptor.
2. Get the device handle for the memory area, in which the image will be stored.
3. Select the image in the given context.
4. Copy the image to the screen using the `BitBlt` function.

Using resources is a convenient way of working with bitmap images. Resources can be generated directly within the program or loaded from a file.

These topics will be covered later.

NOTE

To a professional in the field of Windows programming, it might seem strange that I write custom string functions instead of using the available API functions. Yes, such functions exist. And the reason I neglect them is straightforward. First, my book is intended not only for advanced programmers but also for beginners that are just starting to master programming in the Assembly language. Second, as I mentioned in the Introduction, this book is an attempt to create some symbiosis of Assembly language and Windows programming. By following this principle, you will not always solve problems using only API functions. However, because I understand the importance of string API functions, I'll provide examples of their use in due time.

Chapter 8

Console Applications

What are console applications? They are indispensable tools for those who love to work with command line. The most beloved and famous console application is Far Manager (Far.exe). When working with such applications, at first glance it might seem that you are working with an MS-DOS program. However, the reason behind the popularity of console applications isn't any special love for the text mode. Quite often, there is no special need in graphical user interface; moreover, you as the programmer often have no time to implement it. At the same time, your program must do something useful, for example, process large volumes of information. In this situation, console applications are helpful. Later, you'll see that console applications are compact, not only in the compiled form but also in the text variant. The most important point is that a console application has the same possibilities of accessing Windows resources, by calling API functions, as any normal Graphic User Interface (GUI) application.

In this book, I use MASM32 6.14 and TASM32 5.0 for assembling and linking console applications. Here, everything is quite simple.

For MASM:

```
ml /c /coff cons1.asm
link /subsystem:console cons1.obj
```

For TASM32:

```
TASM32 /ml cons1.asm
tlink32 /ap cons1.exe
```

As before, I specify the libraries using the `INCLUDELIB` directive. Listings 8.1 and 8.2 present variants of a simple console application for MASM and TASM, respectively.

For text output, I'll use the `WriteConsoleA` API function, which receives the following parameters (counted from left to right):

- First parameter — Descriptor of the output buffer of the console, which can be obtained using the `GetStdHandle` function
- Second parameter — Pointer to the buffer that contains the text for output
- Third parameter — Number of characters for output
- Fourth parameter — Pointer to the `DWORD` variable that will store the number of characters actually displayed on the console
- Fifth parameter — Reserved; should be zero

Note that the buffer that contains the text for output mustn't necessarily be terminated with zero, because this function accepts the number of characters for output as one of its parameters. It is only necessary to agree that you won't confuse the input or output buffers of the console and the buffers created within the program, including the ones created especially for exchanging data with console buffers.

Listing 8.1. A simple console application for MASM32

```
.586P
; Flat memory model
.MODEL FLAT, stdcall
; Constants
STD_OUTPUT_HANDLE equ -11
; Prototypes of external procedures
EXTERN  GetStdHandle@4:NEAR
EXTERN  WriteConsoleA@20:NEAR
EXTERN  ExitProcess@4:NEAR
; Directives for the linker to link libraries
includelib c:\masm32\lib\user32.lib
includelib c:\masm32\lib\kernel32.lib
;-----------------------------------------------
; Data segment
_DATA SEGMENT
; DOS-encoded string
        STR1 DB "Console application",0
        LENS DD ? ; Number of output characters
        RES DD ?
_DATA ENDS
; Code segment
_TEXT SEGMENT
START:
; Get the output handle
```

```
        PUSH  STD_OUTPUT_HANDLE
        CALL  GetStdHandle@4
; String length
        PUSH  OFFSET STR1
        CALL  LENSTR
; Output the string
        PUSH  OFFSET RES    ; Reserved
        PUSH  OFFSET LENS   ; Symbols displayed
        PUSH  EBX           ; String length
        PUSH  OFFSET STR1   ; String address
        PUSH  EAX           ; Output handle
        CALL  WriteConsoleA@20
        PUSH  0
        CALL  ExitProcess@4
; String — [EBP+08H]
; Length in EBX
LENSTR PROC
        PUSH  EBP
        MOV   EBP, ESP
        PUSH  EAX
;--------------------
        CLD
        MOV   EDI, DWORD PTR [EBP+08H]
        MOV   EBX, EDI
        MOV   ECX, 100 ; Limit the string length
        XOR   AL, AL
        REPNE SCASB ; Find the 0 character
        SUB   EDI, EBX ; String length including 0
        MOV   EBX, EDI
        DEC   EBX
;--------------------
        POP   EAX
        POP   EBP
        RET   4
LENSTR ENDP
_TEXT ENDS
END START
```

Listing 8.2. A simple console application for TASM32

```
.586P
; Flat memory model
.MODEL FLAT, stdcall
```

```
; Constants
STD_OUTPUT_HANDLE equ -11
; Prototypes of external procedures
EXTERN  GetStdHandle:NEAR
EXTERN  WriteConsoleA:NEAR
EXTERN  ExitProcess:NEAR
; Directives for the linker to link libraries
includelib c:\tasm32\lib\import32.lib
;--------------------------------------------------
; Data segment
_DATA SEGMENT
; DOS-encoded string
STR1 DB "Console application", 0
LENS DD ? ; Number of displayed characters
RES  DD ?
_DATA ENDS
; Code segment
_TEXT SEGMENT
START:
; Get the output handle
        PUSH  STD_OUTPUT_HANDLE
        CALL  GetStdHandle
; String length
        PUSH  OFFSET STR1
        CALL  LENSTR
; Display the string
        PUSH  OFFSET RES   ; Reserved
        PUSH  OFFSET LENS  ; Characters displayed
        PUSH  EBX          ; String length
        PUSH  OFFSET STR1  ; String address
        PUSH  EAX          ; Output handle
        CALL  WriteConsoleA
        PUSH  0
        CALL  ExitProcess
; String — [EBP+08H]
; Length in   EBX
LENSTR PROC
        PUSH  EBP
        MOV   EBP, ESP
        PUSH  EAX
;--------------------
        CLD
```

```
        MOV    EDI, DWORD PTR [EBP+08H]
        MOV    EBX, EDI
        MOV    ECX, 100 ; Limit the string length
        XOR    AL, AL
        REPNE SCASB ; Find the 0 character
        SUB    EDI, EBX ; String length including 0
        MOV    EBX, EDI
        DEC    EBX
;-------------------
        POP EAX
        POP EBP
        RET 4
LENSTR ENDP
_TEXT ENDS
END START
```

It should be mentioned that because information is output into the console window, all string constants must be DOS-encoded (or, to be more precise, OEM-encoded; see *Chapter 6*). Otherwise, this information must be dynamically converted in the course of program execution. Later, I'll explain how to convert programmatically.

Now, I will explain the previously provided programs. When they are started from a command line (e.g., from the Far.exe command line), the "Console application" string will be displayed. When these programs are started as normal Windows applications (e.g., from the My Computer folder), the console window appears for a couple of seconds and then is closed. Why does this happen? Console applications can create their own consoles. If an application creates a console, all input and output uses that console. If the application doesn't create its own console, two kinds of situations are possible. If this application was started from another console, it inherits that console. If, however, the application was started from Windows GUI, Windows creates a console for that application, and this console closes immediately after the application completes its operation.

Creating a Console

Consider several simple console functions and their use.

Working with inherited console isn't always convenient. To create a new console, the `AllocConsole` function is used. When the program terminates, all automatically allocated consoles are released. However, this can be forced using the `FreeConsole` function. To obtain the console descriptor, the `GetStdHandle` function is used, which you have already encountered. This function accepts one of the following three constants as an argument:

```
STD_INPUT_HANDLE   equ -10 ; For input
STD_OUTPUT_HANDLE  equ -11 ; For output
STD_ERROR_HANDLE   equ -12 ; For an error message
```

It is necessary to mention that a process can have only one console; therefore, execution of the `FreeConsole` function is required when the program starts. If the program is started from another console, it inherits that console. Thus, it is impossible to create a new console until the process detaches itself from its current (inherited) console by executing the `FreeConsole` function.

For reading data from the console buffer, the `ReadConsole` function is used. The values of parameters accepted by this function (from left to right) are as follows:[i]

- First — Descriptor of the input buffer
- Second — Address of the buffer, in which the information for input is loaded
- Third — Length of that buffer
- Fourth — Number of symbols actually read
- Fifth — Reserved

To set the cursor position within the console, use the `SetConsoleCursorPosition` function, which accepts the following parameters:

- First — Descriptor of the console's input buffer
- Second — The `COORD` structure, written as follows:

```
COORD STRUC
    X WORD ?
    Y WORD ?
COORD ENDS
```

I'd like to mention again that the second parameter isn't the pointer to the structure (which usually is the case); on the contrary, it is the structure itself. Actually, for an assembler, this is simply a double word (`DWORD`), for which the least significant word stands for the X-coordinate and most significant word stands for the Y-coordinate.

The color of characters to be displayed can be set by the `SetConsoleTextAttribute` function. The first parameter of this function is the descriptor of the console's output buffer, and the second parameter specifies the foreground and background colors.

---

[i] As you probably understand, for an assembler, practically all parameters have the `DWORD` type. By their meaning, however, they are either addresses or values. Therefore, it is much easier to list them by specifying their meaning rather than writing a function in C notation.

Actual color is obtained by combining (via the sum or the logical OR operation) two or more of the constants listed after this paragraph. Note that in addition to the possibility of creating combinations of color and intensity, it is possible to combine different colors (see Listing 8.3).

```
FOREGROUND_BLUE          equ 1h ; Blue foreground letters
FOREGROUND_GREEN         equ 2h ; Green foreground letters
FOREGROUND_RED           equ 4h ; Red foreground letters
FOREGROUND_INTENSITY     equ 8h ; Foreground intensity
BACKGROUND_BLUE          equ 10h ; Blue background
BACKGROUND_GREEN         equ 20h ; Green background
BACKGROUND_RED           equ 40h ; Red background
BACKGROUND_INTENSITY     equ 80h ; Increased background intensity
```

To define the console window header, the SetConsoleTitle function is used. This function accepts the only parameter that represents the address of a zero-terminated string. At this point, it is necessary to point out that in contrast to output into the console window, where DOS-encoding was needed, here you need Windows encoding. To solve this problem and never return to it again, consider how this goal can be achieved using Windows functionality.

In Windows, there is a special function called CharToOem, which you considered in *Chapter 6*. The first parameter of this function is the pointer to the string that needs to be converted, and the second parameter is the pointer to the string that would store the result. Note that the result can be placed into the string being converted. Thus, the encoding problem will be solved. Later, in console applications, I will use this function without special mention.

You have considered only a small number of console functions, the total number of which is about 50. However, there is no need to describe them all. Some of them will be mentioned later; however, I hope that if you are interested, you can find information on other console functions on your own and use them according to the examples and explanations provided in the book. I'd only like to mention that most console functions typically return nonzero values if they terminate normally. In the case of an error, a zero value will be placed into the EAX register.

Well, it is time to proceed with examples.

Listing 8.3. Creating a console

```
.586P
; Flat memory model
.MODEL FLAT, stdcall
; Constants
STD_OUTPUT_HANDLE equ -11
STD_INPUT_HANDLE equ -10
```

```
; Color attributes
FOREGROUND_BLUE   equ 1h ; Blue foreground
FOREGROUND_GREEN  equ 2h ; Green foreground
FOREGROUND_RED    equ 4h ; Red foreground
FOREGROUND_INTENSITY equ 8h ; Increased foreground intensity
BACKGROUND_BLUE   equ 10h ; Blue background
BACKGROUND_GREEN  equ 20h ; Green background
BACKGROUND_RED    equ 40h ; Red background
BACKGROUND_INTENSITY equ 80h ; Increased background intensity
COL1 = 2h+8h ; Color of the text being displayed
COL2 = 1h+2h+8h ; Second color of the text being displayed
; Prototypes of external procedures
EXTERN  GetStdHandle@4:NEAR
EXTERN  WriteConsoleA@20:NEAR
EXTERN  SetConsoleCursorPosition@8:NEAR
EXTERN  SetConsoleTitleA@4:NEAR
EXTERN  FreeConsole@0:NEAR
EXTERN  AllocConsole@0:NEAR
EXTERN  CharToOemA@8:NEAR
EXTERN  SetConsoleCursorPosition@8:NEAR
EXTERN  SetConsoleTextAttribute@8:NEAR
EXTERN  ReadConsoleA@20:NEAR
EXTERN  SetConsoleScreenBufferSize@8:NEAR
EXTERN  ExitProcess@4:NEAR
; Directives for the linker to include libraries
includelib c:\masm32\lib\user32.lib
includelib c:\masm32\lib\kernel32.lib
;-----------------------------------------------
COOR  STRUC
X  WORD ?
Y  WORD ?
COOR  ENDS
; Data segment
_DATA SEGMENT
    HANDL  DWORD ?
    HANDL1 DWORD ?
    STR1   DB "Enter a string:", 13, 10, 0
    STR2   DB "A simple example of a console application", 0
    BUF    DB 200 dup(?)
    LENS   DWORD ? ; Number of displayed symbols
    CRD    COOR <?>
_DATA ENDS
; Code segment
```

```
_TEXT SEGMENT
START:
; Convert the string
    PUSH  OFFSET STR1
    PUSH  OFFSET STR1
    CALL  CharToOemA@8
; Create a console
; First, release the existing console
    CALL  FreeConsole@0
    CALL  AllocConsole@0
; Get the HANDL1 input handle
    PUSH  STD_INPUT_HANDLE
    CALL  GetStdHandle@4
    MOV   HANDL1, EAX
; Get the HANDL output handle
    PUSH  STD_OUTPUT_HANDLE
    CALL  GetStdHandle@4
    MOV   HANDL, EAX
; Set the new size of the console window
    MOV   CRD.X, 100
    MOV   CRD.Y, 25
    PUSH  CRD
    PUSH  EAX
    CALL  SetConsoleScreenBufferSize@8
; Specify the console window header
    PUSH  OFFSET STR2
    CALL  SetConsoleTitleA@4
; Set the cursor position
    MOV   CRD.X, 0
    MOV   CRD.Y, 10
    PUSH  CRD
    PUSH  HANDL
    CALL SetConsoleCursorPosition@8
; Set the color attributes of the text being displayed
    PUSH  COL1
    PUSH  HANDL
    CALL  SetConsoleTextAttribute@8
; Output the string
    PUSH  OFFSET STR1
    CALL  LENSTR ; EBX contains the string length
    PUSH  0
    PUSH  OFFSET LENS
    PUSH  EBX
```

```
    PUSH  OFFSET STR1
    PUSH  HANDL
    CALL  WriteConsoleA@20
; Wait for string input
    PUSH  0
    PUSH  OFFSET LENS
    PUSH  200
    PUSH  OFFSET BUF
    PUSH  HANDL1
    CALL  ReadConsoleA@20
; Display the entered string
; First, specify the color attributes of the displayed text
    PUSH  COL2
    PUSH  HANDL
    CALL  SetConsoleTextAttribute@8
;-----------------------------------------
    PUSH  0
    PUSH  OFFSET LENS
    PUSH  [LENS] ; Length of the entered string
    PUSH  OFFSET BUF
    PUSH  HANDL
    CALL  WriteConsoleA@20
; A small delay
    MOV ECX,01FFFFFFH
L1:
    LOOP  L1
; Close the console
    CALL  FreeConsole@0
    CALL  ExitProcess@4
; String — [EBP+08H]
; Length is in EBX
LENSTR PROC
    ENTER  0, 0
    PUSH  EAX
;--------------------
    CLD
    MOV   EDI, DWORD PTR [EBP+08H]
    MOV   EBX, EDI
    MOV   ECX, 100 ; Limit the string length
    XOR   AL, AL
    REPNE SCASB ; Find the 0 character
    SUB   EDI, EBX ; String length including 0
    MOV   EBX, EDI
```

```
    DEC   EBX
;--------------------
    POP   EAX
    LEAVE
    RET   4
LENSTR ENDP
_TEXT ENDS
END START
```

Listing 8.3 contains two functions in addition to the ones that I have described. These are the `SetConsoleCursorPosition` and `SetConsoleScreenBufferSize` functions. The `SetConsoleCursorPosition` function is used to set the cursor position. With this function, everything is clear and obvious. The `SetConsoleScreenBufferSize` function is less self-evident. It sets the size of the console window buffer. This cannot decrease the size of an already existing buffer (the existing window); it can only increase it.

Note that in the `LENSTR` function you are now using the `ENTER – LEAVE` pair of commands (see *Chapter 2*) instead of traditional combinations, such as `PUSH BP/ MOV BP, SP/ SUB SP,N – MOV SP, BP/ POP BP`. Honestly, the `ENTER – LEAVE` pair doesn't provide any particular advantage. It's simply time to extend your available fund of commands.

Processing Keyboard and Mouse Events

This section is dedicated to descriptions of the keyboard and mouse events in console applications. These capabilities make console applications flexible and powerful, considerably extending the range of tasks that can be carried out in this mode.

Before proceeding any further, however, consider one unusual but useful API function. This is the `wsprintfA` function. I specially emphasize that this is an API function, which is provided to applications by the operating system. This function is an analogue of the `sprintf` built-in C function. Its first parameter is the pointer to the buffer, into which the result of formatting is loaded. The second argument is the pointer to the format string (e.g., `"Numbers: %lu, %lu"`). Then follow the pointers to parameters (or parameters themselves if they are numeric). The number of parameters is limited only by the contents of the format string. Now, the most important point must be considered: Because the number of parameters is undefined, you have to clear the stack on your own. The example illustrating the use of this function will be provided later. It is also necessary to mention that for the IMPORT32.LIB (TASM32) library, the prototype of this function will be `_wsprintfA` instead of `wsprintfA`. Finally, note that if the function has completed successfully, then the length of the copied string will be returned into `EAX`.

The `ReadConsoleInput` function serves as a basis for getting information about the keyboard and mouse in the console mode. Parameters of this function are briefly described here:

- First — Descriptor of the console's input buffer
- Second — The pointer to the structure (or an array of structures) containing information about the events that occurred in this console (later, I will cover this structure in more detail)
- Third — The number of received records (structures)
- Fourth — The pointer to the double word containing the number of records actually received

Now consider the structure containing information about the console event in more detail. First, I'd like to note that in C this structure is defined using the `UNION` data type (data types will be covered in detail in *Chapter 12*). In my opinion, frequent use of this word obscures its actual meaning. Therefore, when describing this structure, I will do without the `STRUCT` and `UNION` keywords. Also, note that this block of data starts with the double word whose least significant word defines the event type. Depending on the value of this word, all further bytes (18 at most) will be interpreted in a specific way. If you are already acquainted with various structures used in C and macroassembler, you must now understand why `UNION` is relevant here.

However, let's return to the event type. The total number of events reserved by the system is five:

```
KEY_EVENT                 equ 1h ; Keyboard event
MOUSE_EVENT               equ 2h ; Mouse event
WINDOW_BUFFER_SIZE_EVENT  equ 4h ; Window size has changed
MENU_EVENT                equ 8h ; Reserved
FOCUS_EVENT               equ 10h ; Reserved
```

Now, it is time to describe the values of other bytes of this structure depending on the event that took place. The description of the `KEY_EVENT` event is provided in Table 8.1.

Table 8.1. The KEY_EVENT event

Offset	Length	Value
+4	4	The field value is greater than zero when a key is pressed.
+8	2	This shows the number of repetitions when a key is held.
+10	2	This field holds the virtual code of the key.
+12	2	Here is the scan code of the key.

continues

Table 8.1 *Continued*

Offset	Length	Value
+14	2	For the `ReadConsoleInputA` function, the least significant byte is equal to the ASCII code of the key. For the `ReadConsoleInputW` function, the word contains the Unicode code of the key.
+16	4	This contains the status of the control keys. It can represent the sum of the following constants: • `RIGHT_ALT_PRESSED equ 1h` • `LEFT_ALT_PRESSED equ 2h` • `RIGHT_CTRL_PRESSED equ 4h` • `LEFT_CTRL_PRESSED equ 8h` • `SHIFT_PRESSED equ 10h` • `NUMLOCK_ON equ 20h` • `SCROLLLOCK_ON equ 40h` • `CAPSLOCK_ON equ 80h` • `ENHANCED_KEY equ 100h` The meaning of these constants is obvious.

The description of the `MOUSE_EVENT` event is provided in Table 8.2.

Table 8.2. The MOUSE_EVENT event

Offset	Length	Value
+4	4	The least significant word is the X-coordinate of the mouse, and the most significant word is the Y-coordinate.
+8	4	This field describes the state of the mouse buttons. The first bit corresponds to the left button, the second bit corresponds to the right button, and the third bit corresponds to the third button. (Recall that bit numbering starts from zero.) If a bit is set to one, this means that the key is pressed.
+12	4	This shows the state of control keys, similar to the field of the previous table.
+16	4	This field can contain the following values: • `MOUSE_MOV equ 1h ; The mouse was moved` • `DOUBLE_CL equ 2h ; There was a double-click`

Consider the `WINDOW_BUFFER_SIZE_EVENT` event.

The double word containing the new size of the console window resides by the offset +4. The least significant word is the X-size, and the most significant word is the Y-size. Note that when you are dealing with a console window, all size and coordinate values are given in "symbolic" units.

As relates to the last two events, the most significant word is the one located by the offset +4. Listing 8.4 provides a simple example illustrating the processing of console events.

Listing 8.4. Processing keyboard and mouse events for a console application

```
.586P
; Flat memory model
.MODEL FLAT, stdcall
; Constants
STD_OUTPUT_HANDLE  equ -11
STD_INPUT_HANDLE   equ -10
; Event type
KEY_EV             equ 1h
MOUSE_EV           equ 2h
; Constants - Keyboard status
RIGHT_ALT_PRESSED  equ 1h
LEFT_ALT_PRESSED   equ 2h
RIGHT_CTRL_PRESSED equ 4h
LEFT_CTRL_PRESSED  equ 8h
SHIFT_PRESSED      equ 10h
NUMLOCK_ON         equ 20h
SCROLLLOCK_ON      equ 40h
CAPSLOCK_ON        equ 80h
ENHANCED_KEY       equ 100h
; Prototypes of external procedures
EXTERN  wsprintfA:NEAR
EXTERN  GetStdHandle@4:NEAR
EXTERN  WriteConsoleA@20:NEAR
EXTERN  SetConsoleCursorPosition@8:NEAR
EXTERN  SetConsoleTitleA@4:NEAR
EXTERN  FreeConsole@0:NEAR
EXTERN  AllocConsole@0:NEAR
EXTERN  CharToOemA@8:NEAR
EXTERN  SetConsoleTextAttribute@8:NEAR
EXTERN  ReadConsoleInputA@16:NEAR
EXTERN  ExitProcess@4:NEAR
; INCLUDELIB directives
```

```
includelib c:\masm32\lib\user32.lib
includelib c:\masm32\lib\kernel32.lib
;-------------------------------------------
; Structure for defining events
COOR  STRUC
X  WORD ?
Y  WORD ?
COOR  ENDS
; Data segment
_DATA SEGMENT
HANDL DWORD ?
HANDL1 DWORD ?
        TITL DB "Processing mouse events", 0
        BUF  DB 200 dup(?)
        LENS DWORD ? ; Number of displayed characters
        CO   DWORD ?
        FORM DB "Coordinates: %u %u "
        CRD  COOR <?>
        STR1 DB "Press ESC to exit", 0
        MOUS_KEY WORD 9 dup(?)
_DATA ENDS
; Code segment
_TEXT SEGMENT
START:
; Create a console
; First, release the existing console
    CALL  FreeConsole@0
    CALL  AllocConsole@0
; Get the HANDL1 input handle
    PUSH  STD_INPUT_HANDLE
    CALL  GetStdHandle@4
    MOV   HANDL1, EAX
; Get the HANDL output handle
    PUSH  STD_OUTPUT_HANDLE
    CALL  GetStdHandle@4
    MOV   HANDL, EAX
; Create the console window header
    PUSH  OFFSET TITL
    CALL  SetConsoleTitleA@4
;******************************
; String reencoding
    PUSH  OFFSET STR1
    PUSH  OFFSET STR1
```

```
    CALL   CharToOemA@8
; String length
    PUSH   OFFSET STR1
    CALL   LENSTR
; Display the string
    PUSH   0
    PUSH   OFFSET LENS
    PUSH   EBX
    PUSH   OFFSET STR1
    PUSH   HANDL
    CALL   WriteConsoleA@20
; Waiting loop — Mouse move or double-click
LOO:
; Cursor coordinates
    MOV   CRD.X, 0
    MOV   CRD.Y, 10
    PUSH  CRD
    PUSH  HANDL
    CALL SetConsoleCursorPosition@8
; Read one record about the event
    PUSH  OFFSET CO
    PUSH  1
    PUSH  OFFSET MOUS_KEY
    PUSH  HANDL1
    CALL  ReadConsoleInputA@16
; Check events from the mouse
    CMP   WORD PTR MOUS_KEY, MOUSE_EV
    JNE   LOO1
; Convert the mouse coordinates to a string
    MOV   AX, WORD PTR MOUS_KEY+6 ; Y-mouse
; Copy and res et the most significant bits to zero
    MOVZX EAX, AX
    PUSH EAX
    MOV   AX, WORD PTR MOUS_KEY+4 ; X-mouse
; Copy and reset the most significant bits to zero
    MOVZX EAX, AX
    PUSH  EAX
    PUSH  OFFSET FORM
    PUSH  OFFSET BUF
    CALL  wsprintfA
; Restore the stack
    ADD   ESP, 16
; Convert the output string
```

```
    PUSH   OFFSET BUF
    PUSH   OFFSET BUF
    CALL   CharToOemA@8
; String length
    PUSH   OFFSET BUF
    CALL   LENSTR
; Display the cursor coordinates
    PUSH   0
    PUSH   OFFSET LENS
    PUSH   EBX
    PUSH   OFFSET BUF
    PUSH   HANDL
    CALL   WriteConsoleA@20
    JMP    LOO ; Jump to the starting point of the loop
LOO1:
; Check for keyboard events
    CMP   WORD PTR MOUS_KEY, KEY_EV
    JNE   LOO
; There was a keyboard event; which one?
    CMP   BYTE PTR MOUS_KEY+14, 27
    JNE   LOO
;******************************
; Close the console
    CALL  FreeConsole@0
    PUSH  0
    CALL  ExitProcess@4
    RET
; The procedure for determining the string length
; String — [EBP+08H]
; Length in EBX
LENSTR  PROC
    ENTER 0, 0
    PUSH  EAX
    CLD
    MOV   EDI, DWORD PTR [EBP+08H]
    MOV   EBX, EDI
    MOV   ECX, 100 ; Limit the string length
    XOR   AL, AL
    REPNE SCASB ; Find the 0 character
    SUB   EDI, EBX ; String length including 0
    MOV   EBX, EDI
    DEC   EBX
    POP   EAX
```

```
    LEAVE
    RET    4
LENSTR ENDP
_TEXT ENDS
END START
```

Consider this program in more detail.

First, consider the wsprintfA function. As I have already mentioned, this is an unusual function.

- It has an unlimited number of parameters. The first two parameters are required. The first parameter is the pointer to the buffer, into which the resulting string will be copied. The next parameter is the pointer to the format string. The format string can contain text and the format of the parameters for output. The fields containing information about the parameters start from the % character. The format of these fields is practically the same as the format of the fields used in standard C library functions, such as printf and sprintf. The only exception is the lack of real numbers in the format for the wsprintf function. There is no need to consider this format in detail. It is only necessary to note that every field in the format string corresponds to a parameter (starting from the third one). For example, in the program under consideration, the format string appeared as follows: "Coordinates: %u %u". This means that two numeric parameters of the WORD type will be pushed into the stack. In fact, you will have pushed into the stack two double words, having previously reset the most significant words to zero. For such an operation, it is expedient to use the MOVZX microprocessor command, which copies the second operand into the first so that the bits of the most significant word are filled with zeroes. If the parameters were double words, then instead of the %u field you would use %lu. If the field of the format string defines a string parameter, for example, "%S", then the pointer to that string must be pushed into the stack (which is natural).[i]
- Because the function has no information about the number of parameters that can be passed to it, the developers decided not to complicate the code of the function and left the task of clearing the stack to the programmer's discretion.[ii] The stack is released by the ADD ESP, N command, where N is the number of bytes to be deleted.

[i] I can't help mentioning that in some publications on Assembly language, I have encountered information that says all parameters for this function pushed into the stack are pointers. As you can see, this statement is generally incorrect.

[ii] Naturally, the C compiler carries out this task automatically.

Now, turn your attention to the `ReadConsoleInputA` function. To the information already provided about it, I'll only add that if the event buffer is empty, the function will wait until any event occurs to the console window and will return the control only after such an event. Besides this, you can specify that the function should return not one but two or more records on the events that occurred to the console window. In this case, several information records will be pushed into the stack. However, I won't concentrate on this aspect.

As usual, I'd like to explain how to compile this program using TASM32. As before, it is necessary to remove all `@N` entries, specify the IMPORT32.LIB library in the `INCLUDELIB` directive, and replace `wsprintfA` with `_wsprintfA`.

The Timer in a Console Application

In the last section of this chapter, I'll consider an aspect rarely covered in programming literature — timers in console applications. It should be pointed out that, by doing so, I am rushing slightly ahead, because I consider timers in console applications before timers in GUI applications.

The main method of creating a timer is by using the `SetTimer` function. Later, I'll cover this function in more detail. There are two modes for setting a timer. The first mode is the one in which the last function parameter is zero. In this case, the current window (or, to be more precise, its function) will receive the `WM_TIMER` message with a predefined time period defined by the third parameter. When operating in the second mode, the last parameter will point to the function that will be called with the predefined periodicity. However, this function isn't suitable for a console application, because the `WM_TIMER` message is dispatched to a window by the `DispatchMessage` function employed in the message-processing loop. This, the use of this function for console applications is problematic.

For console applications, it is expedient to use the `timeSetEvent` function, the parameters of which are briefly outlined here:

- First parameter — Timer delay (from your viewpoint, this time is the same as the period between two timer calls)
- Second parameter — Timer precision (the priority of message sending)
- Third parameter — Address of the procedure being called
- Fourth parameter — Address sent to the procedure
- Fifth parameter— Type of the procedure call: one time or periodic

If the function has completed successfully, then the timer identifier will be returned into `EAX`.

The calling procedure itself receives the following five parameters:

- First parameter — Timer identifier
- Second parameter — Not used
- Third parameter — `Dat` (see the description of the `timeSetEvent` function)
- Fourth and fifth parameters — Not used

To remove the timer, use the `timeKillEvent` function that receives the timer identifier as its parameter.

Listing 8.5. A timer in the console mode

```
.586P
; Flat memory model
.MODEL FLAT, stdcall
; Constants
STD_OUTPUT_HANDLE        equ -11
STD_INPUT_HANDLE         equ -10
TIME_PERIODIC            equ 1   ; Type of the timer call
; Color attributes
FOREGROUND_BLUE          equ 1h  ; Blue foreground color
FOREGROUND_GREEN         equ 2h  ; Green foreground color
FOREGROUND_RED           equ 4h  ; Red foreground color
FOREGROUND_INTENSITY     equ 8h  ; Increased intensity
BACKGROUND_BLUE          equ 10h ; Blue background color
BACKGROUND_GREEN         equ 20h ; Green background color
BACKGROUND_RED           equ 40h ; Red background color
BACKGROUND_INTENSITY     equ 80h ; Increased intensity
COL1 = 2h+8h ; Color of the displayed text
; Prototypes of external procedures
EXTERN  wsprintfA:NEAR
EXTERN  GetStdHandle@4:NEAR
EXTERN  WriteConsoleA@20:NEAR
EXTERN  SetConsoleCursorPosition@8:NEAR
EXTERN  SetConsoleTitleA@4:NEAR
EXTERN  FreeConsole@0:NEAR
EXTERN  AllocConsole@0:NEAR
EXTERN  CharToOemA@8:NEAR
EXTERN  SetConsoleCursorPosition@8:NEAR
EXTERN  SetConsoleTextAttribute@8:NEAR
EXTERN  ReadConsoleA@20:NEAR
EXTERN  timeSetEvent@20:NEAR
EXTERN  timeKillEvent@4:NEAR
```

```
EXTERN  ExitProcess@4:NEAR
; INCLUDELIB directives for the linker
includelib c:\masm32\lib\user32.lib
includelib c:\masm32\lib\kernel32.lib
includelib c:\masm32\lib\winmm.lib
;----------------------------------------------
COOR  STRUC
X  WORD ?
Y  WORD ?
COOR  ENDS
; Data segment
_DATA SEGMENT
    HANDL  DWORD ?
    HANDL1 DWORD ?
    STR2   DB "Example of a timer in a console application", 0
    STR3   DB 100 dup(0)
    FORM   DB "Number of timer calls: %lu", 0
    BUF    DB 200 dup(?)
    NUM    DWORD 0
    LENS   DWORD ? ; Number of displayed characters
    CRD    COOR <?>
    ID     DWORD ? ; Timer identifier
    HWND   DWORD ?
_DATA ENDS
; Code segment
_TEXT SEGMENT
START:
; Create a console
; First, release the existing console
    CALL  FreeConsole@0
    CALL  AllocConsole@0
; Get the HANDL1 input handle
    PUSH  STD_INPUT_HANDLE
    CALL  GetStdHandle@4
    MOV   HANDL1, EAX
; Get the HANDL output handle
    PUSH  STD_OUTPUT_HANDLE
    CALL  GetStdHandle@4
    MOV   HANDL, EAX
; Specify the console window header
    PUSH  OFFSET STR2
    CALL  SetConsoleTitleA@4
; Specify the color attributes for the output text
```

```
    PUSH  COL1
    PUSH  HANDL
    CALL  SetConsoleTextAttribute@8
; Set the timer
    PUSH  TIME_PERIODIC ; Periodic call
    PUSH  0
    PUSH  OFFSET TIME   ; Procedure being called by the timer
    PUSH  0             ; Precision of the timer call
    PUSH  1000          ; Calls per second
    CALL  timeSetEvent@20
    MOV   ID, EAX
; Wait for the string input
    PUSH  0
    PUSH  OFFSET LENS
    PUSH  200
    PUSH  OFFSET BUF
    PUSH  HANDL1
    CALL  ReadConsoleA@20
; Close the timer
    PUSH  ID
    CALL  timeKillEvent@4
; Close the console
    CALL  FreeConsole@0
    PUSH  0
    CALL  ExitProcess@4
; String — [EBP+08H]
; Length in EBX
LENSTR    PROC
    ENTER 0, 0
    PUSH  EAX
;--------------------
    CLD
    MOV   EDI, DWORD PTR [EBP+08H]
    MOV   EBX, EDI
    MOV   ECX, 100 ; Limit the string length
    XOR   AL, AL
    REPNE SCASB ; Find the 0 character
    SUB   EDI, EBX ; String length including 0
    MOV   EBX, EDI
    DEC   EBX
;--------------------
    POP   EAX
    LEAVE
```

```
    RET     4
LENSTR ENDP
; Procedure called by the timer
TIME  PROC
    PUSHA ; Save all registers
; Set the cursor position
    MOV   CRD.X, 0
    MOV   CRD.Y, 10
    PUSH  CRD
    PUSH  HANDL
    CALL  SetConsoleCursorPosition@8
; Fill the STR3 string
    PUSH  NUM
    PUSH  OFFSET FORM
    PUSH  OFFSET STR3
    CALL  wsprintfA
    ADD   ESP, 12 ; Restore the stack
; Reencode the STR3 string
    PUSH  OFFSET STR3
    PUSH  OFFSET STR3
    CALL  CharToOemA@8
; Display the string with the timer call number
    PUSH  OFFSET STR3
    CALL  LENSTR
    PUSH  0
    PUSH  OFFSET LENS
    PUSH  EBX
    PUSH  OFFSET STR3
    PUSH  HANDL
    CALL  WriteConsoleA@20
    INC   NUM
    POPA
    RET 20 ; Exit and release the stack
TIME  ENDP
_TEXT ENDS
END START
```

The program presented in Listing 8.5 will output the counter value into the window. This value will be incremented by one once per second.

This chapter was opened with considerations about the command line; however, until now, I haven't explained how to work with the command line. Well, everything is easy here. There is an API function called `GetCommandLine`, which returns the pointer to the command string. This function operates similarly both for console applications and for GUI applications. The program presented in Listing 8.6 prints the command-line parameters. As you may have guessed, the first parameter is the program's full name.

Listing 8.6. Working with the command-line parameters

```
; The program for the output of the command-line parameters
.586P
; Flat memory model
.MODEL FLAT, stdcall
; Constants
STD_OUTPUT_HANDLE equ -11
; Prototypes of external procedures
EXTERN  GetStdHandle@4:NEAR
EXTERN  WriteConsoleA@20:NEAR
EXTERN  ExitProcess@4:NEAR
EXTERN  GetCommandLineA@0:NEAR
; Include directives for the linker
includelib c:\masm32\lib\user32.lib
includelib c:\masm32\lib\kernel32.lib
;-----------------------------------------------
; Data segment
_DATA SEGMENT
    BUF   DB  100 dup(0)
    LENS  DWORD ? ; Number of displayed characters
    NUM   DWORD ?
    CNT   DWORD ?
    HANDL DWORD ?
_DATA ENDS
; Code segment
_TEXT SEGMENT
START:
; Get the HANDLE output handle
    PUSH STD_OUTPUT_HANDLE
    CALL GetStdHandle@4
    MOV HANDL, EAX
; Get the number of parameters
    CALL NUMPAR
    MOV NUM, EAX
    MOV CNT, 0
;-----------------------------
; Output the command-line parameters
```

```
LL1:
    MOV   EDI, CNT
    CMP   NUM, EDI
    JE    LL2
; Parameter number
    INC   EDI
    MOV   CNT, EDI
; Get the parameter number EDI
    LEA   EBX, BUF
    CALL  GETPAR
; Get the parameter length
    PUSH  OFFSET BUF
    CALL  LENSTR
; Line feed in the end
    MOV   BYTE PTR [BUF+EBX], 13
    MOV   BYTE PTR [BUF+EBX+1], 10
    MOV   BYTE PTR [BUF+EBX+2], 0
    ADD   EBX, 2
; String output
    PUSH  0
    PUSH  OFFSET LENS
    PUSH  EBX
    PUSH  OFFSET BUF
    PUSH  HANDL
    CALL  WriteConsoleA@20
    JMP   LL1
LL2:
    PUSH  0
    CALL  ExitProcess@4
; String - [EBP+08H]
; Length in EBX
LENSTR PROC
    PUSH  EBP
    MOV   EBP, ESP
    PUSH  EAX
;---------------------
    CLD
    MOV   EDI, DWORD PTR [EBP+08H]
    MOV   EBX, EDI
    MOV   ECX, 100 ; Limit the string length
    XOR   AL, AL
    REPNE SCASB ; Find the 0 character
    SUB   EDI, EBX ; String length including 0
```

```
    MOV   EBX, EDI
    DEC   EBX
;--------------------
    POP   EAX
    POP   EBP
    RET   4
LENSTR ENDP
; Define the number of parameters (→ EAX)
NUMPAR PROC
    CALL  GetCommandLineA@0
    MOV   ESI, EAX ; Pointer to the string
    XOR   ECX, ECX ; Counter
    MOV   EDX, 1   ; Indicator
L1:
    CMP   BYTE PTR [ESI], 0
    JE    L4
    CMP   BYTE PTR [ESI], 32
    JE    L3
    ADD   ECX, EDX ; Parameter number
    MOV   EDX, 0
    JMP   L2
L3:
    OR    EDX, 1
L2:
    INC   ESI
    JMP   L1
L4:
    MOV   EAX, ECX
    RET
NUMPAR ENDP
; Get the parameter
; EBX — Points to the buffer in which the parameter will be loaded
; Zero-terminated string is loaded into the buffer
; EDI — Parameter number
GETPAR PROC
    CALL  GetCommandLineA@0
    MOV   ESI, EAX ; Pointer to the string
    XOR   ECX, ECX ; Counter
    MOV   EDX, 1   ; Indicator
L1:
    CMP   BYTE PTR [ESI], 0
    JE    L4
    CMP   BYTE PTR [ESI], 32
```

```
    JE   L3
    ADD  ECX, EDX ; Parameter number
    MOV  EDX, 0
    JMP  L2
L3:
    OR   EDX, 1
L2:
    CMP  ECX, EDI
    JNE  L5
    MOV  AL, BYTE PTR [ESI]
    MOV  BYTE PTR [EBX], AL
    INC  EBX
L5:
    INC  ESI
    JMP  L1
L4:
    MOV  BYTE PTR [EBX], 0
    RET
GETPAR ENDP
_TEXT ENDS
END START
```

I strongly recommend that you make sure you understand the working algorithms of the `NUMPAR` and `GETPAR` procedures.

Note that to assemble and link the program from Listing 8.6 using TASM, in addition to the standard modifications that you know already, it is necessary to add the `@@` locality prefix for matching labels and add the `LOCALS` directive to the start of the program.

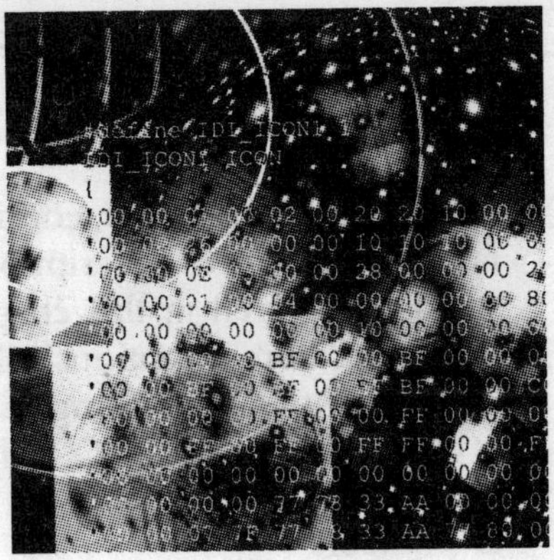

Chapter 9

The Concept of Resource— Resource Editors and Compilers

The Windows operating system includes the concept of resource. The resource is a certain (often) visual element with predefined properties that is stored in the executable file separate from data and code and that requires separate functions to be displayed. The use of resources provides two noticeable advantages:

1. Resources are loaded only when they are accessed. This allows economic memory use.
2. Resource properties are automatically supported by the system and do not require the programmer to write supplementary code.

Descriptions of resources are stored separately from the program in a text file with the RC filename extension. RC files must be compiled into RES files using special resource compilers. The resources are included into executable files by the linker. In MASM32, there is the RC.EXE resource compiler; and in TASM32, the same task is delegated to the BRCC32.EXE program.

The Resource Description Language

In this section, I cover the resource description language. Knowing this language, it is possible to do without a special resource editor. There are lots of resource-editing tools available.[i] Probably because of this, most books on programming pay little or no attention to the resource description language. In contrast to this approach, I won't

---

[i] Personally, I prefer to use either the resource editor from the Visual Studio.NET product or any simple text editor.

even touch the resource-editing applications. Instead, I'll cover the structure and syntax of the resource description language in as much detail as possible. Note that the standard covered in this chapter will be interpreted the same way by both resource compilers. Rare exceptions will be considered separately.

Start with a brief listing of the most widely used resources:

- Icons
- Cursors
- Bitmaps
- Strings
- Dialogs
- Menus
- Accelerators

This list contains the most popular resources. It is only necessary to bear in mind that resources such as dialogs can include controls, which also must be defined within the framework of the window description. However, this topic will be covered later in this chapter.

Icons

Icons can be either described within the resource file or stored separately in files with the ICO filename extension. Consider the latter case. Suppose that you have a resource file called RESU.RC:

```
#define IDI_ICON1 1
IDI_ICON1 ICON "Cdrom01.ico"
```

As you can see, this file contains only two lines. The first line defines the icon identifier, and the second one associates this identifier to the CDROM01.ICO file. The `DEFINE` operator is the C preprocessor directive. As you'll see later, the resource description language is similar to C. Compile the resource file called RESU.RC by issuing the following command: `RC resu.rc`. The new object file, RESU.RES, will appear on the disk. When linking the program, specify this file in the command line as follows:

```
LINK /subsystem:windows resu.obj resu.res
```

A question might arise: How do you use this resource in the program? The answer to this question is straightforward: Suppose that you need to set a new icon for the window. Here is a fragment of the program that sets a standard icon for the main window:

```
PUSH  IDI_APPLICATION
PUSH  0
CALL  LoadIconA@8
MOV   [WC.CLSHICON], EAX
```

And here is the program fragment for setting the icon specified in the resource file:

```
PUSH    1          ; Icon identifier (see the RESU.RC file)
PUSH    [HINST]    ; Process identifier
CALL    LoadIconA@8
MOV     [WC.CLSHICON], EAX
```

The BRCC32.EXE resource compiler (included with TASM32) allows the icon to be included in the project code. In this case, the project will appear as shown in Listing 9.1.

Listing 9.1. A resource file with an icon code

```
#define IDI_ICON1 1
IDI_ICON1 ICON
{
'00 00 01 00 02 00 20 20 10 00 00 00 00 00 E8 02'
'00 00 26 00 00 00 10 10 10 00 00 00 00 00 28 01'
'00 00 0E 03 00 00 28 00 00 00 20 00 00 00 40 00'
'00 00 01 00 04 00 00 00 00 00 80 02 00 00 00 00'
'00 00 00 00 00 00 10 00 00 00 00 00 00 00 00 00'
'00 00 00 00 BF 00 00 BF 00 00 00 BF BF 00 BF 00'
'00 00 BF 00 BF 00 BF BF 00 00 C0 C0 C0 00 80 80'
'80 00 00 00 FF 00 00 FF 00 00 00 FF FF 00 FF 00'
'00 00 FF 00 FF 00 FF FF 00 00 FF FF FF 00 00 00'
'00 00 00 00 00 00 00 00 00 00 00 00 00 00 00 00'
'00 00 00 00 77 78 33 AA 00 00 00 00 00 00 00 00'
'00 00 07 7F 77 78 33 AA 77 80 00 00 00 00 00 00'
'00 0F F7 F7 77 78 33 AA 77 C8 60 00 00 00 00 00'
'00 FF FF 7F 77 78 33 AA 78 C6 66 00 00 00 00 00'
'0F FF FF F7 77 78 38 A7 7C 86 66 60 00 00 00 00'
'77 FF FF 7F 77 78 37 A7 8C 66 66 77 00 00 00 07'
'87 7F FF F7 F7 78 37 A7 C8 66 67 77 70 00 00 08'
'78 77 FF FF 77 78 3A A8 C6 66 77 77 E0 00 00 87'
'87 87 7F FF F7 78 3A AC 86 67 77 EE EE 00 00 78'
'78 78 77 FF 7F 78 3A 8C 66 77 EE EE BB 00 07 87'
'87 87 87 7F F7 78 3A C8 67 7E EB BB BA A0 08 78'
'78 78 78 77 F8 88 88 C6 7E BB BB AA AA A0 07 87'
'87 87 87 87 88 00 00 88 BB BA AA A3 33 30 08 78'
'78 78 78 78 80 8F F8 08 33 33 33 DD DD D0 08 88'
'88 88 88 88 80 FF FF 08 5D 5D 5D 5D 5D 50 05 D5'
'D5 D5 D5 D5 80 FF FF 08 88 88 88 88 88 80 0D DD'
'DD 33 33 33 80 8F F8 08 87 87 87 87 87 80 03 33'
```

```
'3A AA AB BB 88 00 00 88 78 78 78 78 78 70 0A AA'
'AA BB BB E7 6C 88 88 8F 77 87 87 87 87 80 0A AB'
'BB BE E7 76 8C A3 87 7F F7 78 78 78 78 70 00 BB'
'EE EE 77 66 C8 A3 87 F7 FF 77 87 87 87 00 00 EE'
'EE 77 76 68 CA A3 87 7F FF F7 78 78 78 00 00 0E'
'77 77 66 6C 8A A3 87 77 FF FF 77 87 80 00 00 07'
'77 76 66 8C 7A 73 87 7F 7F FF F7 78 70 00 00 00'
'77 66 66 C8 7A 73 87 77 F7 FF FF 77 00 00 00 00'
'06 66 68 C7 7A 83 87 77 7F FF FF F0 00 00 00 00'
'00 66 6C 87 AA 33 87 77 F7 FF FF 00 00 00 00 00'
'00 06 8C 77 AA 33 87 77 7F 7F F0 00 00 00 00 00'
'00 00 08 77 AA 33 87 77 F7 70 00 00 00 00 00 00'
'00 00 00 00 AA 33 87 77 00 00 00 00 00 00 00 00'
'00 00 00 00 00 00 00 00 00 00 00 00 00 00 FF F0'
'0F FF FF 80 01 FF FE 00 00 7F FC 00 00 3F F8 00'
'00 1F F0 00 00 0F E0 00 00 07 C0 00 00 03 C0 00'
'00 03 80 00 00 01 80 00 00 01 00 00 00 00 00 00'
'00 00 00 00 00 00 00 00 00 00 00 00 00 00 00 00'
'00 00 00 00 00 00 00 00 00 00 00 00 00 00 00 00'
'00 00 80 00 00 01 80 00 00 01 C0 00 00 03 C0 00'
'00 03 E0 00 00 07 F0 00 00 0F F8 00 00 1F FC 00'
'00 3F FE 00 00 7F FF 80 01 FF FF F0 0F FF 28 00'
'00 00 10 00 00 00 20 00 00 00 01 00 04 00 00 00'
'00 00 C0 00 00 00 00 00 00 00 00 00 00 00 00 00'
'00 00 00 00 00 00 00 00 00 00 00 00 80 00 00 80'
'00 00 00 80 80 00 80 00 00 00 80 00 80 00 80 80'
'00 00 80 80 80 00 C0 C0 C0 00 00 00 FF 00 00 FF'
'00 00 00 FF FF 00 FF 00 00 00 FF 00 FF 00 FF FF'
'00 00 FF FF FF 00 00 00 00 00 00 00 00 00 00 00'
'08 87 3A 80 00 00 00 0F F8 87 32 CC 60 00 00 08'
'F8 87 32 C6 68 00 00 87 8F 87 2C 66 86 00 08 78'
'78 87 2C 68 AA A0 07 87 87 70 08 2A A2 20 08 78'
'78 0F F0 11 15 50 05 51 11 0F F0 87 87 80 02 2A'
'A2 80 08 78 78 70 0A AA 86 C2 78 87 87 80 00 68'
'66 C2 78 F8 78 00 00 86 6C 23 78 8F 88 00 00 06'
'CC 23 78 8F F0 00 00 00 08 A3 78 80 00 00 00 00'
'00 00 00 00 00 00 F8 1F 00 00 E0 07 00 00 C0 03'
'00 00 80 01 00 00 80 01 00 00 00 00 00 00 00 00'
'00 00 00 00 00 00 00 00 00 00 00 00 00 00 00 00'
'00 00 80 01 00 00 80 01 00 00 C0 03 00 00 E0 07'
'00 00 F8 1F 00 00'
}
```

Cursors

The approach here is identical to the one used with icons. I'll just provide the resource file, where both a cursor and an icon are defined.

```
#define IDI_ICON1 1
#define IDI_CUR1 2

IDI_ICON1 ICON "Cdrom01.ico"
IDI_CUR1 CURSOR "4way01.cur"
```

Here is a fragment of a program that calls both the cursor and the icon:

```
;----------- Window icon
    PUSH  1 ; Icon identifier
    PUSH  [HINST]
    CALL  LoadIconA@8
    MOV   [WC.CLSHICON], EAX
;----------- Window cursor
    PUSH  2 ; Cursor identifier
    PUSH  [HINST]
    CALL  LoadCursorA@8
    MOV   [WC.CLSHCURSOR], EAX
```

Similar to icons, the BRCC32.EXE program is capable of processing cursor definitions included into the code of the resource file.

Bitmaps

The situation here is similar to the previous two ones. Here is an example of the resource file defining a bitmap (BMP) image:

```
#define BIT1 1
BIT1 BITMAP "PIR2.BMP"
```

Strings

To specify one or more strings, the `STRINGTABLE` keyword is used. Provided in this section is a fragment of the resource file specifying two strings. To load the string into your program, use the `LoadString` function (used later in this chapter). The strings specified in the resource file can play the role of constants.

```
#define STR1 1
#define STR2 2
STRINGTABLE
```

```
{
STR1, "Message"
STR2, "Version 1.01"
}
```

Dialogs

Dialogs are the most complicated resource elements. In contrast to the resources that you considered previously, no identifier is specified for a dialog. The dialog is accessed by its name (a string).

```
#define WS_SYSMENU          0x00080000L
#define WS_MINIMIZEBOX      0x00020000L
#define WS_MAXIMIZEBOX      0x00010000L
DIAL1 DIALOG 0, 0, 240, 120
STYLE WS_SYSMENU | WS_MINIMIZEBOX | WS_MAXIMIZEBOX
CAPTION "Example of a dialog"
FONT 8, "Arial"
{
}
```

As you can see, the dialog definition starts with the line containing the `DIALOG` keyword. The same line specifies the size and position of the dialog. Further lines specify other properties of the dialog. Then, there are braces. In this case, these braces do not enclose anything. This means that the window doesn't contain any controls. The types of dialog and other elements are defined by the constants placed at the start of the file. These constants are standard and, according to the C/C++ rules, are stored in the RESOURCE.H file. As before, I'll define all constants directly in the resource file. I'd like you to note that the constants are defined according to the C language notation.

Before I explain the example provided in Listing 9.2, consider the specific features of working with dialogs. A dialog is similar to a normal window. Like any normal window, it has the window procedure. The dialog procedure has the same parameters as a normal window procedure. However, significantly fewer messages arrive to the dialog procedure. At the same time, the messages accepted by a dialog are essentially the same as messages of a normal window. The only difference is that instead of the `WM_CREATE` message, the `WM_INITDIALOG` message arrives. The dialog procedure can return either zero or nonzero values. A nonzero value must be returned when the dialog procedure handles the message delivered to it; if it delegates message processing to the system, it must return zero.

The differences in the behavior of a dialog and that of a normal window can be easily explained. If you create a normal window, all properties of that window are defined by the following factors: class properties defined when creating a window and procedure reaction to specific messages. When creating a dialog, all its properties are specified in resources. Some of these properties are set when the `CreateWindow` function is implicitly called during a call to the function that creates a dialog (`DialogBox`, `DialogBoxParam`, etc.). Other properties depend on the behavior of the internal function generated by the system when creating the dialog. If something happens to the dialog, the message first arrives to the internal procedure, and then the dialog procedure that you have created in the program is called. If the procedure returns 0, then the internal procedure continues processing this message; otherwise, the internal procedure doesn't handle the message. Thus, since I have briefly covered the mechanisms regulating the dialog box operation, consider the program presented in Listing 9.2. A brief explanation will be provided after the listing.

Listing 9.2. The use of simple resources

```
// The DIAL.RC file
// Constant definitions
#define WS_SYSMENU       0x00080000L
#define WS_MINIMIZEBOX   0x00020000L
#define WS_MAXIMIZEBOX   0x00010000L

// Identifiers
#define STR1 1
#define STR2 2
#define IDI_ICON1 3
// Defining an icon
IDI_ICON1 ICON "ico1.ico"
// Defining a dialog
DIAL1 DIALOG 0, 0, 240, 120
STYLE WS_SYSMENU | WS_MINIMIZEBOX | WS_MAXIMIZEBOX
CAPTION "Example of a dialog"
FONT 8, "Arial"
{
}
// Strings definitions
STRINGTABLE
{
    STR1, "Message"
    STR2, "Program version 1.00"
}
; The DIAL.INC file
; Constants
; The message arrives when the window is closed
```

```
WM_CLOSE       equ 10h
WM_INITDIALOG equ 110h
WM_SETICON     equ 80h
; Prototypes of external procedures
EXTERN     MessageBoxA@16:NEAR
EXTERN     ExitProcess@4:NEAR
EXTERN     GetModuleHandleA@4:NEAR
EXTERN     DialogBoxParamA@20:NEAR
EXTERN     EndDialog@8:NEAR
EXTERN     LoadStringA@16:NEAR
EXTERN     LoadIconA@8:NEAR
EXTERN     SendMessageA@16:NEAR
; Structures
; Message structure
MSGSTRUCT STRUC
        MSHWND      DD ?
        MSMESSAGE   DD ?
        MSWPARAM    DD ?
        MSLPARAM    DD ?
        MSTIME      DD ?
        MSPT        DD ?
MSGSTRUCT ENDS
; The DIAL.ASM file
.586P
; Flat memory model
.MODEL FLAT, stdcall
include dial.inc
; Includelib directives for the linker to link libraries
includelib c:\masm32\lib\user32.lib
includelib c:\masm32\lib\kernel32.lib
;-----------------------------------------------------
; Data segment
_DATA SEGMENT
        MSG     MSGSTRUCT <?>
        HINST   DD 0 ; Application descriptor
        PA      DB "DIAL1", 0
        BUF1    DB 40 dup (0)
        BUF2    DB 40 dup (0)
_DATA ENDS
; Code segment
_TEXT SEGMENT
START:
; Get the application handle
```

```
    PUSH  0
    CALL  GetModuleHandleA@4
    MOV   [HINST], EAX
;---------------------------------
; Load the string
    PUSH  40
    PUSH  OFFSET BUF1
    PUSH  1
    PUSH  [HINST]
    CALL  LoadStringA@16
; Load the string
    PUSH  40
    PUSH  OFFSET BUF2
    PUSH  2
    PUSH  [HINST]
    CALL  LoadStringA@16
;---------------------------------
    PUSH  0          ; MB_OK
    PUSH  OFFSET BUF1
    PUSH  OFFSET BUF2
    PUSH  0
    CALL  MessageBoxA@16
; Create the dialog
    PUSH  0
    PUSH  OFFSET WNDPROC ; Window procedure
    PUSH  0
    PUSH  OFFSET PA    ; Resource name (DIAL1)
    PUSH  [HINST]
    CALL  DialogBoxParamA@20
    CMP   EAX, -1
    JNE   KOL
KOL:
;----------------------------------
    PUSH  0
    CALL  ExitProcess@4
;----------------------------------
; Dialog procedure
; Position of parameters in the stack
; [EBP+014H]  ; LPARAM
; [EBP+10H]   ; WAPARAM
; [EBP+0CH]   ; MES
; [EBP+8]     ; HWND
WNDPROC PROC
```

```
    PUSH  EBP
    MOV   EBP, ESP
    PUSH  EBX
    PUSH  ESI
    PUSH  EDI
;----------------
    CMP   DWORD PTR [EBP+0CH], WM_CLOSE
    JNE   L1
    PUSH  0
    PUSH  DWORD PTR [EBP+08H]
    CALL  EndDialog@8
    JMP   FINISH
L1:
    CMP   DWORD PTR [EBP+0CH], WM_INITDIALOG
    JNE   FINISH
; Load the icon
    PUSH  3   ; Icon identifier
    PUSH  [HINST] ; Process identifier
    CALL  LoadIconA@8
; Set the icon
    PUSH  EAX
    PUSH  0   ; Icon type (small)
    PUSH  WM_SETICON
    PUSH  DWORD PTR [EBP+08H]
    CALL  SendMessageA@16
FINISH:
    POP   EDI
    POP   ESI
    POP   EBX
    POP   EBP
    MOV   EAX, 0
    RET   16
WNDPROC ENDP
_TEXT ENDS
END START
```

Now consider how this program works.

- The resource file structure must be clear to you because earlier you considered all resources used there in detail. I'd only note that the resource file contains several elements. All resources, except the dialog box, must have identifiers. For the dialog, this role is played by its name, which in this case appears as `DIAL1`.

- Before opening the dialog, the program demonstrates how to work with such resources as strings. As you can see, everything is straightforward here. First, it is necessary to load the string into the buffer using the `LoadString` function; after accomplishing this, it is possible to work with it as with any normal string.
- The dialog call is self-evident, so I'll proceed with a description of the dialog procedure. Start with the `WM_INITDIALOG` message. This message, similar to the `WM_CREATE` message for a standard window, arrives only once: when the window is created. This is convenient for carrying out certain operations at the start of program execution (e.g., initialization). You'll use this possibility to define the dialog icon. First, it is necessary to load the icon; then, send the `WM_SETICON` message, which sets the icon for this window. The second message that you must process is `WM_CLOSE`. This message arrives when a user clicks the "x" button in the top right corner of the window. Having received this message, the program executes the `EndDialog` function, which removes the dialog from the memory, exits the `DialogBoxParamA` function, and finally closes the program.

As mentioned earlier, the dialog procedure must return a nonzero value if it handles the current message. As shown in this example, principally, this isn't always necessary. From now on, I'll concentrate your attention on those cases, in which this is required.

Menus

Menus also can be specified in resource files. Like dialogs, menus in programs are identified by their names (strings). Menus can be specified both in normal windows and in dialogs. For a normal window, when registering a class, it is sufficient to replace the following string:

```
MOV  DWORD PTR [WC.CLMENNAME], 0
```

Replace this string with the following:

```
MOV  DWORD PTR [WC.CLMENNAME], OFFSET MENS
```

Here, `MENS` is the name assigned to the menu in the resource file.

For dialogs, menus are set using another method, which, naturally, is also suitable for a normal window. First, the menu is loaded using the `LoadMenu` function; then, it is set using the `SetMenu` function.

Now, consider this in more detail. Consider the structure of the resource file containing a menu definition. Here is the text of the file containing a menu definition:

```
MENUP MENU
{
POPUP "&First item"
```

```
{
  MENUITEM "&First", 1
  MENUITEM "S&econd", 2
  POPUP "Subme&nu"
  {
    MENUITEM "Tent&h item", 6
  }
}
POPUP "&Second item"
{
  MENUITEM "Th&ird", 3
  MENUITEM "F&ourth", 4
}
MENUITEM "E&xit", 5
}
```

Carefully look at the menu text. As you can see, menu items have identifiers that the program can use to determine which menu item was chosen. Also note that a drop-down menu can contain a submenu.

Listing 9.3 provides an example of a program that demonstrates the use of a menu with a dialog box.

Listing 9.3. A program with a menu

```
// The MENU.RC file
// Definitions of constants
#define WS_SYSMENU      0x00080000L
#define WS_MINIMIZEBOX  0x00020000L
#define WS_MAXIMIZEBOX  0x00010000L
#define WS_POPUP        0x80000000L
#define WS_CAPTION      0x00C00000L
MENUP MENU
{
POPUP "&First item"
{
  MENUITEM "&", 1
  MENUITEM "&Second", 2
}
POPUP "&Second item"
{
  MENUITEM "&Third", 3
  MENUITEM "F&ourth", 4
  POPUP "Another sub&menu"
  {
```

```
    MENUITEM "Te&nth subitem", 6
  }
}
MENUITEM "E&xit", 5
}
// Identifiers
#define IDI_ICON1 100
// Defining the icon
IDI_ICON1 ICON "ico1.ico"
// Defining the dialog box
DIAL1 DIALOG 0, 0, 240, 120
STYLE WS_POPUP | WS_CAPTION | WS_SYSMENU | WS_MINIMIZEBOX
               | WS_MAXIMIZEBOX
CAPTION "An example dialog box"
FONT 8, "Arial"
{
}
```

```
; The MENU.INC file
; Constants
; The message arrives when the window is closed
WM_CLOSE        equ 10h
WM_INITDIALOG   equ 110h
WM_SETICON      equ 80h
WM_COMMAND      equ 111h
; Prototypes of external procedures
EXTERN      MessageBoxA@16:NEAR

EXTERN      ExitProcess@4:NEAR
EXTERN      GetModuleHandleA@4:NEAR
EXTERN      DialogBoxParamA@20:NEAR
EXTERN      EndDialog@8:NEAR
EXTERN      LoadStringA@16:NEAR
EXTERN      LoadIconA@8:NEAR
EXTERN      LoadMenuA@8:NEAR
EXTERN      SendMessageA@16:NEAR
EXTERN      SetMenu@8:NEAR
; Structures
; Message structure
MSGSTRUCT STRUC
        MSHWND      DD ?
        MSMESSAGE   DD ?
        MSWPARAM    DD ?
```

```
        MSLPARAM    DD ?
        MSTIME      DD ?
        MSPT        DD ?
MSGSTRUCT ENDS

; The MENU.ASM file
.586P
; Flat memory model
.MODEL FLAT, stdcall
include menu.inc
; INCLUDELIB directives for the linker
includelib c:\masm32\lib\user32.lib
includelib c:\masm32\lib\kernel32.lib
;------------------------------------------------
; Data segment
_DATA SEGMENT
        MSG       MSGSTRUCT <?>
        HINST     DD 0 ; Application descriptor
        PA        DB "DIAL1", 0
        PMENU     DB "MENUP", 0
        STR1      DB "Exit the program", 0
        STR2      DB "Message", 0
_DATA ENDS
; Code segment
_TEXT SEGMENT
START:
; Get the application descriptor
    PUSH  0
    CALL  GetModuleHandleA@4
    MOV   [HINST], EAX
;--------------------------------
    PUSH  0

    PUSH  OFFSET WNDPROC
    PUSH  0
    PUSH  OFFSET PA
    PUSH  [HINST]
    CALL  DialogBoxParamA@20
    CMP   EAX, -1
    JNE   KOL
KOL:
    PUSH  0
    CALL  ExitProcess@4
```

```
; Window procedure
; Parameter positions in the stack
; [EBP+014H]  LPARAM
; [EBP+10H]   WAPARAM
; [EBP+0CH]   MES
; [EBP+8]     HWND
WNDPROC PROC
    PUSH  EBP
    MOV   EBP, ESP
    PUSH  EBX
    PUSH  ESI
    PUSH  EDI
;-----------------
    CMP   DWORD PTR [EBP+0CH], WM_CLOSE
    JNE   L1
; Close the dialog
    PUSH  0
    PUSH  DWORD PTR [EBP+08H]
    CALL  EndDialog@8
    JMP   FINISH
L1:
    CMP   DWORD PTR [EBP+0CH], WM_INITDIALOG
    JNE   L2
; Load the icon
    PUSH  100  ; Icon identifier
    PUSH  [HINST]; Process identifier
    CALL LoadIconA@8
; Set the icon
    PUSH  EAX
    PUSH  0  ; Icon type (small)
    PUSH  WM_SETICON
    PUSH  DWORD PTR [EBP+08H]
    CALL  SendMessageA@16
; Load the menu
    PUSH  OFFSET PMENU
    PUSH  [HINST]
    CALL  LoadMenuA@8
; Set the menu
    PUSH  EAX
    PUSH  DWORD PTR [EBP+08H]
    CALL  SetMenu@8
    JMP   FINISH
L2:
; Checking whether something has happened to the
```

```
; controls in the dialog
; In this case, there is only one
; control - the menu
    CMP   DWORD PTR [EBP+0CH], WM_COMMAND
    JNE   FINISH
; Determining the identifier
; In this case, this is the menu item identifier
    CMP   WORD PTR [EBP+10H], 5
    JNE   FINISH
; Message
    PUSH  0          ; MB_OK
    PUSH  OFFSET STR2
    PUSH  OFFSET STR1
    PUSH  0
    CALL  MessageBoxA@16
; Close the dialog
    PUSH  0
    PUSH  DWORD PTR [EBP+08H]
    CALL  EndDialog@8
FINISH:
    MOV   EAX, 0
    POP   EDI
    POP   ESI
    POP   EBX
    POP   EBP
    RET   16
WNDPROC ENDP
_TEXT ENDS
END START
```

It is necessary to provide a small comment about the program from Listing 9.3. First, pay attention to the transparent analogy between the dialog and the menu. In both cases, the resource is defined by its name instead of its identifier. Furthermore, both the dialog and the menu contain elements defined by identifiers, which have been specified in the resource file and placed into the least significant word of the WPARAM parameter.

In Listing 9.3, you load the menu programmatically. It is possible to use a different approach: Specify the menu in dialog options as follows:

```
// Dialog definition
DIAL1 DIALOG 0, 0, 240, 120
STYLE WS_POPUP | WS_CAPTION | WS_SYSMENU | WS_MINIMIZEBOX |
                WS_MAXIMIZEBOX
```

```
MENU MENUP
CAPTION "Dialog example"
FONT 8, "Arial"
{
}
```

This is sufficient to automatically load and display the menu.

Recall that in *Chapter 3* an example was provided, in which a button was created as a child window. The event related to clicking this button was identified by the content of the LPARAM of the button descriptor. As you can see, the element of the dialog can be identified both by the resource descriptor and by the resource identifier.

Now, return to the menu. Menu items can contain additional parameters that define additional properties of those items. The resource compiler recognizes the following properties:

- CHECKED — The item is selected with a checkmark.
- GRAYED — The element is unavailable (and displayed in gray).
- HELP — The element has an associated help string. Resource editors create an additional string resource. The string identifier matches that of the menu item.
- MENUBARBREAK — For a horizontal menu item, this means that starting from it, all further horizontal menu items are located in a new line. For a vertical item, this means that all further items start from a new column. The items are separated by a line delimiter.
- MENUBREAK — This is similar to the previous property, but no separating line is present.
- INACTIVE — This menu item doesn't work.
- SEPARATOR — This item creates a separator in the menu but doesn't provide an identifier.

To conclude the menu description, I'll note that Windows provides a range of functions that can be used to change menu properties (e.g., to add or remove items or to modify their properties). In the next chapter, I'll provide several examples of functions from this group.

Accelerators

At first glance, this topic seems easy. However, as you'll see later, it generates a lot of questions. An accelerator allows you to select a menu item using keyboard shortcuts (e.g., by pressing predefined key combinations). This feature is convenient. The accelerator table is the resource whose name must match the name of the menu (resource), for which it defines shortcuts. Provided here is an example of such a table. This example defines an accelerator for the MENUP menu item that has the identifier 4.

```
MENUP ACCELERATORS
{
VK_F5, 4, VIRTKEY
}
```

Here is the general format of the accelerator table:

```
Name ACCELERATORS
{
Key 1, Menu item identifier (1) [,type][,parameter]
Key 2, Menu item identifier (2) [,type][,parameter]
Key 3, Menu item identifier (3) [,type][,parameter]
...
Key N, Menu item identifier  (N) [,type][,parameter]
}
```

Consider the preceding format. *Key* is either a character enclosed in quotation marks or ASCII character code or a virtual key. If a character code is used, then the type is specified as ASCII. If a virtual key is used, then the type is defined as VIRTUAL. All names (macro names) of virtual keys can be found in INCLUDE files (WINDOWS.H). As usual, I'll define all macro names directly in the program.

The parameter can take one of the following values: NOINVERT, ALT, CONTROL, or SHIFT. The NOINVERT value means that the menu item selected using accelerator isn't highlighted. The values ALT, SHIFT, and CONTROL mean that the corresponding control key must be pressed with the key defined by accelerator. Furthermore, if the key is enclosed in quotation marks, then pressing the CONTROL key is designated by the ^ sign: "^A".

Now, look at the working mechanism of accelerators. To ensure that accelerators work, it is necessary to satisfy the following conditions:

- Accelerator table must be loaded. For this purpose, use the LoadAccelerators function.
- Messages arriving from accelerator must be converted into the WM_COMMAND message. Here, the TranslateAccelerator function will be useful.

Now, concentrate your attention on the second condition. The TranslateAccelerator function converts WM_KEYDOWN and WM_SYSKEYDOWN into WM_COMMAND and WM_SYSCOMMAND messages, respectively. In this case, the distinguishing feature of accelerator is that the most significant word of WPARAM must contain 1. The least significant word, as you recall, must contain the identifier of the menu item. A question might arise: Why do you need two messages, WM_COMMAND and WM_SYSCOMMAND? The WM_SYSCOMMAND message is generated to the items of the system menu or window menu (Fig. 9.1).

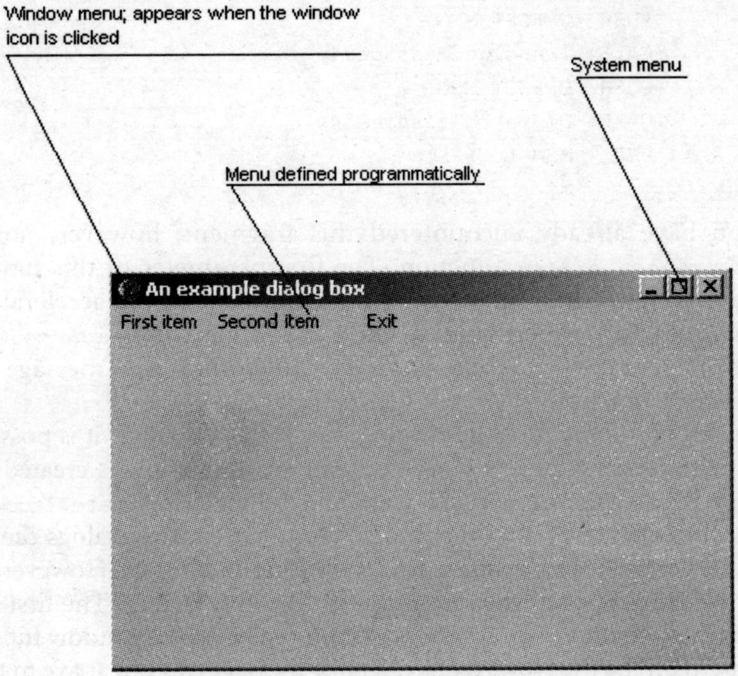

Fig. 9.1. Window menu

The `TranslateAccelerator` function returns a nonzero value if accelerator translation was carried out; otherwise, it returns zero. Thus, it is natural to include the call to this function in the message-processing loop. The fragment provided here illustrates this:

```
MSG_LOOP:
        PUSH   0
        PUSH   0
        PUSH   0
        PUSH   OFFSET MSG
        CALL   GetMessageA@16
        CMP    EAX, 0
        JE     END_LOOP
        PUSH   OFFSET MSG
        PUSH   [ACC]
        PUSH   [NEWHWND]
        CALL   TranslateAcceleratorA@12
        CMP    EAX, 0
```

```
        JNE   MSG_LOOP
        PUSH  OFFSET MSG
        CALL  TranslateMessage@4
        PUSH  OFFSET MSG
        CALL  DispatchMessageA@4
        JMP   MSG_LOOP
END_LOOP:
```

You have already encountered this fragment; however, now it includes the `TranslateAccelerator` function. The first parameter of this function is the application descriptor; it is followed by the descriptor of the accelerators table (`[ACC]`), which is obtained when loading the table using the `LoadAccelerators` function. The third parameter is the address containing the message received by the `GetMessage` function.

At this point, the most interesting things start, because it is possible to say that the message-processing loop is used when the main window is created in a standard way (e.g., by registering the window class and calling the `CreateWindow` function). However, in this chapter, I am describing dialogs. Of course, dialogs can be generated by a standard window, and in this case, everything is normal. However, what should you do in the simplest case when dealing with the only dialog? The first idea that comes to mind is to place the `TranslateAccelerator` call into the window function and carry out translation on the fly. However, accelerator messages do not arrive to this function.

At this point, you run into at the new material: modal and modeless windows.

Modeless Dialogs

Until now, you worked with modal dialogs. The main property of such dialogs is that when they are called the program must wait until such a window is closed. However, after calling such windows, the program would continue execution. A modeless window allows the user to switch to other windows. Modeless dialogs are characterized by the following properties:

- Modeless dialogs are created using the `CreateDialog` function.
- Modeless dialogs are destroyed by the `DestroyWindow` function.
- For a modeless dialog to appear on the screen, it must have the `WS_VISIBLE` property, or the dialog creation command must be followed by the `ShowWindow` function.

Listing 9.4 illustrates a program that demonstrates a modeless dialog with a menu and ensures the processing of the accelerator messages.

Listing 9.4. Modeless dialog with a menu and the processing of accelerator messages

```
// The MENU1.RC file
// Definitions of constants
#define WS_SYSMENU      0x00080000L
#define WS_MINIMIZEBOX 0x00020000L
#define WS_MAXIMIZEBOX 0x00010000L
#define WS_POPUP        0x80000000L
#define VK_F5           0x74
#define st WS_SYSMENU | WS_MINIMIZEBOX | WS_MAXIMIZEBOX
MENUP MENU
{
POPUP "&First item"
{
  MENUITEM "&First", 1
  MENUITEM "S&econd", 2, HELP
  MENUITEM "What?", 8
}
POPUP "&Second item"
{
  MENUITEM "Thi&rd", 3
  MENUITEM "Fo&urth", 4
  MENUITEM SEPARATOR
  POPUP "Another subme&nu"
{
MENUITEM "Tenth ite&m", 6
}
}
MENUITEM "E&xit", 5
}
// Identifiers
#define IDI_ICON1 100
// Defining an icon
IDI_ICON1 ICON "ico1.ico"
// Defining the dialog
DIAL1 DIALOG 0, 0, 240, 120
STYLE WS_POPUP | st
CAPTION "An example of modeless dialog"
FONT 8, "Arial"
{
}
MENUP ACCELERATORS
```

```
{
VK_F5, 4, VIRTKEY, ALT
}

; The MENU1.INC file
; Constants
; The message arrives when the window is closed
WM_CLOSE        equ 10h
WM_INITDIALOG   equ 110h
WM_SETICON      equ 80h
WM_COMMAND      equ 111h
; Prototypes of external procedures
EXTERN      ShowWindow@8:NEAR
EXTERN      MessageBoxA@16:NEAR
EXTERN      ExitProcess@4:NEAR
EXTERN      GetModuleHandleA@4:NEAR
EXTERN      LoadIconA@8:NEAR
EXTERN      LoadMenuA@8:NEAR
EXTERN      SendMessageA@16:NEAR
EXTERN      SetMenu@8:NEAR
EXTERN      LoadAcceleratorsA@8:NEAR
EXTERN      TranslateAcceleratorA@12:NEAR
EXTERN      GetMessageA@16:NEAR
EXTERN      DispatchMessageA@4:NEAR
EXTERN      PostQuitMessage@4:NEAR
EXTERN      CreateDialogParamA@20:NEAR
EXTERN      DestroyWindow@4:NEAR
EXTERN      TranslateMessage@4:NEAR
; Structures
; Message structure
MSGSTRUCT STRUC
        MSHWND          DD ?
        MSMESSAGE       DD ?
        MSWPARAM        DD ?
        MSLPARAM        DD ?
        MSTIME          DD ?
        MSPT            DD ?
MSGSTRUCT ENDS

; The MENU1.ASM file
.586P
; Flat memory model
.MODEL FLAT, stdcall
include menu1.inc
```

```
; INCLUDELIB directives for the linker
includelib c:\masm32\lib\user32.lib
includelib c:\masm32\lib\kernel32.lib
; Data segment
_DATA SEGMENT
        NEWHWND         DD 0
        MSG             MSGSTRUCT <?>
        HINST           DD 0 ; Application descriptor
        PA              DB "DIAL1", 0
        PMENU           DB "MENUP", 0
        STR1            DB "Exit the program", 0
        STR2            DB "Message", 0
        STR3            DB "Fourth item selected", 0
        ACC             DWORD ?
_DATA ENDS
; Code segment
_TEXT SEGMENT
START:
; Get the application descriptor
        PUSH  0
        CALL  GetModuleHandleA@4
        MOV   [HINST], EAX
; Load the accelerators
        PUSH  OFFSET PMENU
        PUSH  [HINST]
        CALL  LoadAcceleratorsA@8
        MOV   ACC, EAX ; Store the table descriptor
; Create the modeless dialog
        PUSH  0
        PUSH  OFFSET WNDPROC
        PUSH  0
        PUSH  OFFSET PA
        PUSH  [HINST]
        CALL  CreateDialogParamA@20
; Show the modeless dialog
        MOV   NEWHWND,EAX
        PUSH  1 ; SW_SHOWNORMAL
        PUSH  [NEWHWND]
        CALL  ShowWindow@8 ; Show the newly created window
; Message-processing loop
MSG_LOOP:
        PUSH  0
        PUSH  0
        PUSH  0
```

```
        PUSH   OFFSET MSG
        CALL   GetMessageA@16
        CMP    EAX, 0
        JE     END_LOOP
; Translate the accelerator message
        PUSH   OFFSET MSG
        PUSH   [ACC]
        PUSH   [NEWHWND]
CALL TranslateAcceleratorA@12
        CMP    EAX, 0
        JNE    MSG_LOOP
        PUSH   OFFSET MSG
        CALL   TranslateMessage@4
        PUSH   OFFSET MSG
        CALL   DispatchMessageA@4
        JMP    MSG_LOOP
END_LOOP:
        PUSH   0
        CALL   ExitProcess@4
; Window procedure
; Position of parameters in the stack
; [EBP+014H]   LPARAM
; [EBP+10H]    WAPARAM
; [EBP+0CH]    MES
; [EBP+8]      HWND
WNDPROC PROC
        PUSH   EBP
        MOV    EBP, ESP
        PUSH   EBX
        PUSH   ESI
        PUSH   EDI
;----------------
        CMP    DWORD PTR [EBP+0CH], WM_CLOSE
        JNE    L1
; Close the dialog
        JMP    L5
L1:
        CMP    DWORD PTR [EBP+0CH], WM_INITDIALOG
        JNE    L3
; Load the icon
        PUSH   100  ; Icon identifier
        PUSH   [HINST] ; Process identifier
        CALL   LoadIconA@8
; Set the icon
```

```
        PUSH  EAX
        PUSH  0  ; Icon type (small)
        PUSH  WM_SETICON
        PUSH  DWORD PTR [EBP+08H]
        CALL  SendMessageA@16
; Load the menu
        PUSH  OFFSET PMENU
        PUSH  [HINST]
        CALL  LoadMenuA@8
; Set the menu
        PUSH  EAX
        PUSH  DWORD PTR [EBP+08H]
        CALL  SetMenu@8
;--------------------------------
        MOV   EAX, 1 ; Return a nonzero value
        JMP   FIN
; Checking whether or not something happened
; to the dialog controls
L3:
        CMP   DWORD PTR [EBP+0CH], WM_COMMAND
        JE    L6
        JMP   FINISH
; Defining identifier
; In this case, this is the menu item identifier
L6:
        CMP   WORD PTR [EBP+10H], 4
        JNE   L4
        PUSH  0          ; MB_OK
        PUSH  OFFSET STR2
        PUSH  OFFSET STR3
        PUSH  0
        CALL  MessageBoxA@16
        JMP   FINISH
L4:
        CMP   WORD PTR [EBP+10H], 5
        JNE   FINISH
; Message
        PUSH  0          ; MB_OK
        PUSH  OFFSET STR2
        PUSH  OFFSET STR1
        PUSH  0
        CALL  MessageBoxA@16
; Close the modeless dialog
```

```
L5:
        PUSH   DWORD PTR [EBP+08H]
        CALL   DestroyWindow@4
; Send the message to exit
; the message-processing loop
        PUSH   0
        CALL   PostQuitMessage@4 ; The WM_QUIT message
FINISH:
        MOV    EAX, 0
FIN:
        POP    EDI
        POP    ESI
        POP    EBX
        POP    EBP
        RET    16
WNDPROC ENDP
_TEXT ENDS
END START
```

Some comments are needed to explain the program provided in Listing 9.4.

A modeless dialog is specified in the resource file just as modal one would be specified. Because I didn't specify the `WS_VISIBLE` property when describing window properties, to make the dialog visible, it is necessary to use the `ShowWindow` function.

To exit the program in this case, it is necessary not only to remove the dialog from memory using the `DestroyWindow` function but also to exit the message-processing loop. The latter is achieved by calling the `PostQuitMessage` function.

To conclude, it is necessary to mention that I didn't cover the following types of resources:

- The resource containing unstructured data

  ```
  name RCDATA
  BEGIN
    raw-data
  ...
  END
  ```

- The `VERSIONINFO` resource

  ```
  ID VERSIONINFO
  BEGIN
    block-statement
  ...
  END
  ```

Both of these resources are rarely used in comparison to other types of resources. Therefore, I won't concentrate your attention on them.

Assembling and Linking Using TASM32

When working with resources using TASM32, some specific features must be taken into account. First, resource compilers can have specific language constructs that are not supported by other compilers. However, this isn't the only problem. There is another difference. Assume that the program name is DIAL.ASM, and the resource file has the name DIAL.RC. Then, the commands for compiling and building the executable module in TASM32 will appear as follows:

```
TASM32 /ml DIAL.ASM
BRCC32 DIAL.RC
TLINK32 DIAL.OBJ,,,,,DIAL.RES
```

As a result, the DIAL.EXE program will be created. If the program displays a dialog instead of the standard window, then probably (but not necessarily) you'll notice that its style corresponds to the Windows 3.1 style. For MASM32, this isn't the case. The problem can be solved if you add `DS_3DLOOK` equal to 0x0004L into the window style. The Help file states that the `DS_3DLOOK` style must be set automatically for dialogs. The reason of this is specific features of BRCC32.EXE operation. As far as I know, there are no other significant differences between the resource compilers of MASM32 and TASM32.

Chapter 10

Examples of Programs That Use Resources

Examples are essential for mastering the art of programming. It is impossible to study programming only on the basis of theory. Programming is closer to art. It is a way of self-actualization.

The topic of resource usage in Windows programming is important; therefore, it deserves a separate chapter. Here, I provide three more sophisticated programs illustrating the use of resources and supply detailed explanations.

A Dynamic Menu

You probably have already noticed that in many programs, menus can dynamically change during program execution: Some items are added or removed, one menu appears as the built-in menu of another one, etc. An example illustrating the simplest manipulations with a menu is provided in Listing 10.1.

The program opens a window with a menu and a command button. When the user clicks the button, another menu replaces the current one. If the button is clicked again, the menu disappears. Repeatedly clicking the button displays the first menu, the second menu, and so on, cyclically. Additionally, the first menu contains the item that, when chosen, produces the same result as clicking the button. Finally, for this menu item there is an accelerator key — <F5>. When scrolling the menu, the titles of menu items and popup menus are displayed in the window header. This, briefly, is the way of the program's operation. The mechanisms according to which the program works are described in detail after Listing 10.1.

Listing 10.1. An example of manipulations with the menu

```
// The MENU2.RC file

// Virtual key - <F5>
#define VK_F5   0x74


//********* MENUP **********

MENUP MENU
 {
 POPUP "&First item"
  {
  MENUITEM "&First", 1
  MENUITEM "S&econd", 2
  }

 POPUP "&Second item"
  {
  MENUITEM "Thir&d", 3
  MENUITEM "Fou&rth\tF5", 4
  MENUITEM SEPARATOR
  POPUP "Another submen&u"
  {
  MENUITEM "Additional &item", 6
  }

  }

 MENUITEM "E&xit", 5
 }
//********* MENUC **********
MENUC MENU
 {
 POPUP "Set 1"
  {
  MENUITEM "White", 101
  MENUITEM "Gray", 102
  MENUITEM "Black", 103
```

```
 }
 POPUP "Set 2"
 {
 MENUITEM "Red", 104
 MENUITEM "Blue", 105
 MENUITEM "Green", 106
 }
}

// Accelerator table
// One accelerator is defined
// for calling an item from the MENUP menu
MENUP ACCELERATORS
{
 VK_F5, 4, VIRTKEY, NOINVERT
}

; The MENU2.INC file
; Constants
; The message arrives when the window is closed
WM_DESTROY           equ 2
; The message arrives when the window is created
WM_CREATE            equ 1
; The message arrives when the user clicks the
; left mouse button in the window
WM_COMMAND           equ 111h
WM_MENUSELECT        equ 11Fh
WM_SETTEXT           equ 0Ch
MIIM_TYPE            equ 10h
MF_STRING            equ 0h
MF_POPUP             equ 10h
; Window properties
CS_VREDRAW           equ 1h
CS_HREDRAW           equ 2h
CS_GLOBALCLASS       equ 4000h
WS_OVERLAPPEDWINDOW  equ 000CF0000H
STYLE                equ CS_HREDRAW+CS_VREDRAW+CS_GLOBALCLASS
BS_DEFPUSHBUTTON     equ 1h
WS_VISIBLE           equ 10000000h
WS_CHILD             equ 40000000h
STYLBTN              equ WS_CHILD+BS_DEFPUSHBUTTON+WS_VISIBLE
; Standard icon identifier
IDI_APPLICATION      equ 32512
```

```
; Cursor identifier
IDC_ARROW             equ 32512
; Window display mode — Normal
SW_SHOWNORMAL         equ 1
SW_HIDE               equ 0
SW_SHOWMINIMIZED      equ 2
; Prototypes of external procedures
EXTERN  wsprintfA:NEAR
EXTERN  GetMenuItemInfoA@16:NEAR
EXTERN  LoadMenuA@8:NEAR
EXTERN  SendMessageA@16:NEAR
EXTERN  MessageBoxA@16:NEAR
EXTERN  CreateWindowExA@48:NEAR
EXTERN  DefWindowProcA@16:NEAR
EXTERN  DispatchMessageA@4:NEAR
EXTERN  ExitProcess@4:NEAR
EXTERN  GetMessageA@16:NEAR
EXTERN  GetModuleHandleA@4:NEAR
EXTERN  LoadCursorA@8:NEAR
EXTERN  LoadIconA@8:NEAR
EXTERN  PostQuitMessage@4:NEAR
EXTERN  RegisterClassA@4:NEAR
EXTERN  ShowWindow@8:NEAR
EXTERN  TranslateMessage@4:NEAR
EXTERN  UpdateWindow@4:NEAR
EXTERN  TranslateAcceleratorA@12:NEAR
EXTERN  LoadAcceleratorsA@8:NEAR
EXTERN  GetMenu@4:NEAR
EXTERN  DestroyMenu@4:NEAR
EXTERN  SetMenu@8:NEAR
; Structures
; Message structure
MSGSTRUCT STRUC
 MSHWND     DD ?
 MSMESSAGE DD ?
 MSWPARAM  DD ?
 MSLPARAM  DD ?
 MSTIME    DD ?
 MSPT      DD ?
MSGSTRUCT ENDS
;---- Window class structure
WNDCLASS STRUC
 CLSSTYLE  DD ?
```

```
  CLWNDPROC      DD ?
  CLSCBCLSEX     DD ?
  CLSCBWNDEX     DD ?
  CLSHINST       DD ?
  CLSHICON       DD ?
  CLSHCURSOR     DD ?
  CLBKGROUND     DD ?
  CLMENNAME      DD ?
  CLNAME         DD ?
WNDCLASS ENDS
MENINFO STRUCT
  CbSize         DD ?
  FMask          DD ?
  FType          DD ?
  FState         DD ?
  WID            DD ?
  HSubMenu       DD ?
  HbmpChecked    DD ?
  HbmpUnchecked DD ?
  DwItemData     DD ?
  DwTypeData     DD ?
  Cch            DD ?
MENINFO ENDS

; The MENU2.ASM file
.586P
; Flat memory model
.MODEL FLAT, stdcall
include menu2.inc
; INCLUDELIB directives for the linker to link libraries
includelib c:\masm32\lib\user32.lib
includelib c:\masm32\lib\kernel32.lib
;-----------------------------------------------
; Data segment
_DATA SEGMENT
 SPACE      DB 30 dup(32), 0
 MENI       MENINFO  <0>
 NEWHWND    DD 0
 MSG        MSGSTRUCT <?>
 WC         WNDCLASS  <?>
 HINST      DD 0 ; Application descriptor
 CLASSNAME DB 'CLASS32', 0
 CPBUT      DB 'BUTTON', 0 ; Exit
```

```
 CLSBUTN    DB 'BUTTON', 0
 HWNDBTN    DD 0
 CAP        DB 'Message', 0
 MES        DB 'Exit the program', 0
 MEN        DB 'MENUP', 0
 MENC       DB 'MENUC', 0
 ACC        DD ?
 HMENU      DD ?
 PRIZN      DD ?
 BUFER      DB 100 DUP(0)
_DATA ENDS
; Code segment
_TEXT SEGMENT
START:
; Initialize the counter
   MOV   PRIZN,2
; Get the application descriptor
   PUSH  0
   CALL  GetModuleHandleA@4
   MOV   [HINST], EAX
REG_CLASS:
; Fill the window structure
; Style
   MOV   [WC.CLSSTYLE], STYLE
; Message-handling procedure
   MOV   [WC.CLWNDPROC], OFFSET WNDPROC
   MOV   [WC.CLSCBCLSEX], 0
   MOV   [WC.CLSCBWNDEX], 0
   MOV   EAX, [HINST]
   MOV   [WC.CLSHINST], EAX
;---------- Window icon
   PUSH  IDI_APPLICATION
   PUSH  0
   CALL  LoadIconA@8
   MOV   [WC.CLSHICON], EAX
;---------- Window cursor
   PUSH  IDC_ARROW
   PUSH  0
   CALL  LoadCursorA@8
   MOV   [WC.CLSHCURSOR], EAX
;----------
   MOV   [WC.CLBKGROUND], 17 ; Window color
   MOV   DWORD PTR [WC.CLMENNAME], OFFSET MEN
```

```
    MOV   DWORD PTR [WC.CLNAME], OFFSET CLASSNAME
    PUSH  OFFSET WC
    CALL  RegisterClassA@4
; Create a window of the registered class
    PUSH  0
    PUSH  [HINST]
    PUSH  0
    PUSH  0
    PUSH  400    ; DY — Window height
    PUSH  400    ; DX — Window width
    PUSH  100    ; Y
    PUSH  100    ; X
    PUSH  WS_OVERLAPPEDWINDOW
    PUSH  OFFSET SPACE ; Window name
    PUSH  OFFSET CLASSNAME ; Class name
    PUSH  0
    CALL  CreateWindowExA@48
; Check for errors
    CMP   EAX,0
    JZ    _ERR
    MOV   [NEWHWND], EAX ; Window descriptor
; Determine the menu identifier
    PUSH  EAX
    CALL  GetMenu@4
    MOV   HMENU,EAX
; Load the accelerators
    PUSH  OFFSET MEN
    PUSH  [HINST]
    CALL  LoadAcceleratorsA@8
    MOV   ACC, EAX
;-----------------------------------
    PUSH  SW_SHOWNORMAL
    PUSH  [NEWHWND]
    CALL  ShowWindow@8 ; Show the newly-created window
;-----------------------------------
    PUSH  [NEWHWND]
    CALL  UpdateWindow@4  ; Redraw the visible part of the
                          ; window, the WM_PAINT message
; Message-processing loop
MSG_LOOP:
    PUSH  0
    PUSH  0
    PUSH  0
```

```
  PUSH  OFFSET MSG
  CALL  GetMessageA@16
  CMP   EAX, 0
  JE    END_LOOP
  PUSH  OFFSET MSG
  PUSH  [ACC]
  PUSH  [NEWHWND]
  CALL  TranslateAcceleratorA@12
  CMP   EAX, 0
  JNE   MSG_LOOP
  PUSH  OFFSET MSG
  CALL  TranslateMessage@4
  PUSH  OFFSET MSG
  CALL  DispatchMessageA@4
  JMP   MSG_LOOP
END_LOOP:
; Exit the program (close the process)
  PUSH  [MSG.MSWPARAM]
  CALL  ExitProcess@4
_ERR:
  JMP   END_LOOP
;----------------------------------
; Window procedure
; Position of parameters in the stack
; [EBP+014H]  ; LPARAM
; [EBP+10H]   ; WAPARAM
; [EBP+0CH]   ; MES
; [EBP+8]     ; HWND
WNDPROC  PROC
  PUSH  EBP
  MOV   EBP, ESP
  PUSH  EBX
  PUSH  ESI
  PUSH  EDI
; The WM_DESTROY message — When closing the window
  CMP   DWORD PTR [EBP+0CH], WM_DESTROY
  JE    WMDESTROY
; The WM_CREATE message — When creating the window
  CMP   DWORD PTR [EBP+0CH], WM_CREATE
  JE    WMCREATE
; The WM_COMMAND message — In case events
; that happen to the window elements
  CMP   DWORD PTR [EBP+0CH], WM_COMMAND
```

```
   JE    WMCOMMND
; The WM_MENUSELECT message - Menu-related events
   CMP   DWORD PTR [EBP+0CH], WM_MENUSELECT
   JE    WMMENUSELECT
; Returning all other messages
   JMP   DEFWNDPROC
WMMENUSELECT:
; Skipping the first event when accessing the menu
   CMP   WORD PTR [EBP+14H], 0
   JE    FINISH
; Checking what has been activated - menu item
; or popup menu header
   MOV   EDX,0
   TEST  WORD PTR [EBP+12H], MF_POPUP
   SETNE DL
; Filling the structure for function call
; GetMenuItemInfo
   MOVZX EAX, WORD PTR [EBP+10H] ; Identifier
   MOV   MENI.cbSize, 48
   MOV   MENI.fMask, MIIM_TYPE
   MOV   MENI.fType, MF_STRING
   MOV   EBX, DWORD PTR [EBP+14H]
   MOV   MENI.hSubMenu, EBX
   MOV   MENI.dwTypeData, OFFSET BUFER
   MOV   MENI.cch, 100
; Get information about the chosen menu item
   PUSH  OFFSET MENI
   PUSH  EDX
   PUSH  EAX
   PUSH  DWORD PTR [EBP+14H]
   CALL  GetMenuItemInfoA@16
; Check the result of function execution
   CMP   EAX, 0
   JE    FINISH
; Display the menu item name
   PUSH  MENI.dwTypeData
   PUSH  0
   PUSH  WM_SETTEXT
   PUSH  DWORD PTR [EBP+08H]
   CALL  SendMessageA@16
   MOV   EAX, 0
   JMP   FINISH
WMCOMMND:
```

```
    MOV   EAX, HWNDBTN
  ; Check whether the button has been pressed
    CMP   DWORD PTR [EBP+14H], EAX
    JE    YES_BUT
  ; Check whether the Exit menu item of MENUC has been chosen
    CMP   WORD PTR [EBP+10H], 5
    JE    WMDESTROY
  ; Check whether the menu item with the identifier 5 has been chosen
    CMP   WORD PTR [EBP+10H], 4
    JNE   LOO
  JMP YES_BUT
  LOO:
    MOV   EAX, 0
    JMP   FINISH
  YES_BUT:
  ; Button-click handling
  ; First, erase the name in the header
    PUSH  OFFSET SPACE
    PUSH  0
    PUSH  WM_SETTEXT
    PUSH  DWORD PTR [EBP+08H]
    CALL  SendMessageA@16
  ; Check whether the menu has been loaded
    CMP   PRIZN, 0
    JE    L1
    CMP   RIZN, 1
    JE    L2
  ; Load MENC
    PUSH  OFFSET MENC
    PUSH  [HINST]
    CALL  LoadMenuA@8
  ; Set the menu
    MOV   HMENU, EAX
    PUSH  EAX
    PUSH  DWORD PTR [EBP+08H]
    CALL  SetMenu@8
  ; Set the identifier
    MOV   PRIZN, 0
    MOV   EAX, 0
    JMP   FINISH
  L2:
  ; Load  MENUP
    PUSH  OFFSET MEN
```

```
  PUSH  [HINST]
  CALL  LoadMenuA@8
; Set the menu
  MOV   HMENU, EAX
  PUSH  EAX
  PUSH  DWORD PTR [EBP+08H]
  CALL  SetMenu@8
; Set the indicator
  MOV   PRIZN, 2
  MOV   EAX, 0
  JMP   FINISH
L1:
; Delete the menu
  PUSH  HMENU
  CALL  DestroyMenu@4
; Refresh the window contents
  PUSH  SW_SHOWMINIMIZED
  PUSH  DWORD PTR [EBP+08H]
  CALL  ShowWindow@8
  PUSH  SW_SHOWNORMAL
  PUSH  DWORD PTR [EBP+08H]
  CALL  ShowWindow@8
  MOV   PRIZN, 1
  MOV   EAX, 0
  JMP   FINISH
WMCREATE:
; Create a window button
  PUSH  0
  PUSH  [HINST]
  PUSH  0
  PUSH  DWORD PTR [EBP+08H]
  PUSH  20 ; DY
  PUSH  60 ; DX
  PUSH  10 ; Y
  PUSH  10 ; X
  PUSH  STYLBTN
; Window name (button label)
  PUSH  OFFSET CPBUT
  PUSH  OFFSET CLSBUTN ; Class name
  PUSH  0
  CALL  CreateWindowExA@48
  MOV   HWNDBTN, EAX ; Store the button descriptor
  MOV   EAX, 0
```

```
   JMP   FINISH
DEFWNDPROC:
   PUSH  DWORD PTR [EBP+14H]
   PUSH  DWORD PTR [EBP+10H]
   PUSH  DWORD PTR [EBP+0CH]
   PUSH  DWORD PTR [EBP+08H]
   CALL  DefWindowProcA@16
   JMP   FINISH
WMDESTROY:
   PUSH  0            ; MB_OK
   PUSH  OFFSET CAP
   PUSH  OFFSET MES
   PUSH  DWORD PTR [EBP+08H]  ; Window descriptor
   CALL  MessageBoxA@16
   PUSH  0
   CALL  PostQuitMessage@4 ; The WM_QUIT message
   MOV   EAX, 0
FINISH:
   POP   EDI
   POP   ESI
   POP   EBX
   POP   EBP
   RET   16
WNDPROC ENDP
_TEXT ENDS
END START
```

The program provided in Listing 10.1 implements several mechanisms that I need to describe. First, note that the program uses three resources: two menus and one accelerator table (see the resource file).

- First, I'd like to draw your attention to the `PRIZN` variable. It stores the menu status: 2 means the `MENUP` menu has been loaded; 1 means no menu; and 0 means the initial menu, `MENUC`, has been loaded. The initial state is ensured by specifying the menu when registering the window class:

  ```
  MOV   DWORD PTR [WC.CLMENNAME], OFFSET MEN
  ```

- The second aspect that deserves attention is the button. The mechanism used for detecting button-clicking events has already been considered, so I won't concentrate on it any more. One of the events that can take place as a result of the button-clicking events is menu removal. The menu is removed using the `DestroyMenu` function. After removing the menu, it is necessary to refresh the window by calling the ShowWindow function twice.

- Another event that takes place when the button is clicked is menu change. The menu will be changed automatically if you load and install a new menu.
- Choosing one of the items of the MENUP menu also changes the menu. Here, everything should be clear to you, because the same section of the program is accessed like in case of the button click.
- An interesting situation arises with the accelerator. The accelerator key is <F5>. When this key is pressed, the same message is generated as when choosing the "fourth" item of the MENUP menu. The important point is that the same message will be generated when MENUC is loaded and when no menu is displayed. Because the procedure processes the message in either case, the <F5> key will also work in either case.
- Now, consider how the name of the chosen menu item is determined. The central role in this mechanism is delegated to the WM_MENUSELECT message. This message arrives any time a menu item is selected. It is important to note that when you activate the menu, the WM_MENUSELECT message will be the first to arrive. This message has the LPARAM value that defines the menu identifier as zero. This is achieved by the following lines of code:

```
CMP     WORD PTR [EBP+14H], 0
JE      FINISH
```

- When receiving the WM_MENUSELECT message, the least significant word of the WPARAM parameter can contain either the identifier of the menu item or the number of the header of the popup menu. This is the key point. You must know this information, because the header string of the popup menu item and the string of the menu item are obtained differently. To define what has been chosen, it is possible to use the most significant word of WPARAM. For this purpose, use the MF_POPUP constant: `TEST WORD PTR [EBP+12H], MF_POPUP`. Note how convenient the SETNE command is here.
- Furthermore, to get the name string, use the GetMenuItemInfo function. The third parameter of this function can be either 0 or 1. If 0 is chosen, then the second parameter is the menu item identifier. If 1 is chosen, then the second parameter is the identifier of the popup menu header. The fourth parameter is the pointer to the structure that will be filled as a result of function execution. However, some fields of this structure must be filled beforehand. I draw your attention to the dwTypeData field, which must contain the pointer to the buffer containing the required string. The cch field must contain the length of that buffer. However,

for the function to interpret the dwTypeData and cch fields exactly as the pointer to the buffer and the buffer length, the fields fMask and fType must be filled properly (see Listing 10.1). Finally, the cbSize field must contain the length of the entire structure.

- Having received the required information (e.g., the menu item name string), send the WM_SETTEXT message using the SendMessage function. This message gives the command to set the window header.

Hotkeys

Well, I'll continue this description of resources. Now, I'd like to explain you an interesting technique that can be used when working with edit fields. When working with visual programming environments such as Visual Basic and Delphi, you probably noticed that edit fields can be programmed so that they allow only a predefined set of characters to be entered. For this purpose, it is necessary to specify certain field properties. For example, in Delphi, this property is called EditMask. I assume that you'd like to know how to implement such behavior using API functions only.

A standard window gets WM_KEYDOWN, WM_KEYUP, or their distillation, WM_CHAR, when a key is pressed (if it is active). However, in this case, you are dealing with the dialog and not with the standard window. Dialogs do not get such messages. It only remains to hope that the messages are sent in response to events that happen to the edit field. Unfortunately, here you'll also be disappointed. This element receives only two messages out of those that might be of any interest. These are EN_UPDATE and EN_CHANGE messages. Both messages arrive when any change has been made to the edit field. However, the EN_UPDATE message arrives when the changes have not been displayed on the screen yet, and the EN_CHANGE message is delivered after such changes. You'll have to first receive the contents of the edit field, determine which character was the last to be supplied there, and, if this is an invalid character, delete it from the string and send the string into the edit field. An additional problem relates to the cursor position and repeated delivery of the EN_UPDATE message. Would you proceed this way? Well, I never would!

There is another approach, much more elegant and convenient: using the hotkey concept. Limit yourself only to the programmatic properties of hotkeys — that is, the properties that every programmer must know to use hotkeys in programs.

The hotkey can be defined for every virtual key — that is, for every key defined using the macro constant with the VK prefix. For normal alphanumeric keys, the values of these constants coincide to ASCII codes. It is also possible to use combinations with control keys, such as <Alt>, <Ctrl>, and <Shift>. After the hotkey for a given window is defined, the WM_HOTKEY message arrives at the window function any time such a key or combination is pressed. By message parameters, it is possible to determine, which hotkey has been pressed. The important point is that the hotkey definition is global, which means that it will work even if other windows, possibly belonging to other applications, are active. This requires the programmer to work carefully, because pressing hotkeys can block normal operation of other applications. In other words, it is necessary to trace when the given window is active and when it is inactive. For this purpose, the `WM_ACTIVATE` and `WM_ACTIVATEAPP` messages can be helpful. The first message always arrives at the window function when the window is activated or deactivated. The first time this message arrives is when the window is created. After receiving this message, it makes sense to register hotkeys. The second message always arrives at the window function when the window loses the focus — in other words, when another window is activated. Respectively, when this message arrives, it is necessary to cancel registration of these hotkeys.

For working with hotkeys, the following two functions are mainly used: `RegisterHotKey` and `UnregisterHotKey`. The `RegisterHotKey` function has the following parameters:

- First parameter — Window descriptor
- Second parameter — Hotkey identifier
- Third parameter — Modifier defining whether a control key is pressed
- Fourth parameter — Virtual code of the key

The `UnregisterHotKey` function has only two parameters:

- First parameter — Window descriptor
- Second parameter — Window identifier

If you have defined a hotkey, it stops to participate in any events and becomes locked. The only method that it is possible to use to determine whether this hotkey has been pressed is the `WM_HOTKEY` message.

Consider a simple example of a dialog box that contains two edit fields and an **Exit** button. Formulate the following goal: The first edit field must accept only digits from 0 to 9. The second edit field must accept all characters. A possible mechanism of using hotkeys with `WM_ACTIVATE` and `WM_ACTIVATEAPP` messages was considered previously. Clearly, in this case, such events will be of no help. Here, the situation is more complicated, and you need to use the messages related to the same edit field. These are the `EN_SETFOCUS` and `EN_KILLFOCUS` messages, passed using `WM_COMMAND`. The program demonstrating this mechanism, supplied with comments, is provided in Listing 10.2. The `EN_SETFOCUS` message informs the program that the edit window was activated, and the `EN_KILLFOCUS` message informs the program that the edit field was deactivated.

Listing 10.2. The use of hotkeys with a dialog box

```
// The DIAL1.RC file
// Constant definitions
// Window styles
#define WS_SYSMENU          0x00080000L
#define WS_MINIMIZEBOX      0x00020000L
#define WS_MAXIMIZEBOX      0x00010000L
// Text in the edit field is aligned on the left
#define ES_LEFT             0x0000L
// Style of all window elements
#define WS_CHILD            0x40000000L
// Window elements initially must be visible
#define WS_VISIBLE          0x10000000L
// Border around the element
#define WS_BORDER           0x00800000L
// Elements can be sequentially activated using the <Tab> key
#define WS_TABSTOP          0x00010000L
// Left-align the string
#define SS_LEFT             0x00000000L
// Button style
#define BS_PUSHBUTTON       0x00000000L
// Center button text
#define BS_CENTER           0x00000300L
#define DS_LOCALEDIT        0x20L


// Dialog definition
DIAL1 DIALOG 0, 0, 240, 120
STYLE WS_SYSMENU | WS_MINIMIZEBOX | WS_MAXIMIZEBOX
CAPTION "Dialog example"
FONT 8, "Arial"
{
// Edit field, identifier 1
 CONTROL "", 1, "edit", ES_LEFT | WS_CHILD
 | WS_VISIBLE | WS_BORDER | WS_TABSTOP, 24, 20, 128, 12
// Another edit field, identifier 2
 CONTROL "", 2, "edit", ES_LEFT | WS_CHILD
 | WS_VISIBLE | WS_BORDER | WS_TABSTOP, 24, 52, 127, 12
// Text, identifier 3
 CONTROL "String 1", 3, "static", SS_LEFT
 | WS_CHILD | WS_VISIBLE, 164, 22, 60, 8
// More text, identifier 4
```

```
CONTROL "String 2", 4, "static", SS_LEFT
 | WS_CHILD | WS_VISIBLE, 163, 54, 60, 8
// Button, identifier 5
CONTROL "Exit", 5, "button", BS_PUSHBUTTON
 | BS_CENTER | WS_CHILD | WS_VISIBLE | WS_TABSTOP,
 180, 76, 50, 14
}

; The DIAL1.INC file
; Constants
; The message arrives when the window is closed
WM_CLOSE       equ 10h
WM_INITDIALOG  equ 110h
WM_COMMAND     equ 111h
WM_SETTEXT     equ 0Ch
WM_HOTKEY      equ 312h
EN_SETFOCUS    equ 100h
EN_KILLFOCUS   equ 200h
; Prototypes of external procedures
EXTERN     UnregisterHotKey@8:NEAR
EXTERN     RegisterHotKey@16:NEAR
EXTERN     MessageBoxA@16:NEAR
EXTERN     ExitProcess@4:NEAR
EXTERN     GetModuleHandleA@4:NEAR
EXTERN     DialogBoxParamA@20:NEAR
EXTERN     EndDialog@8:NEAR
EXTERN     SendMessageA@16:NEAR
EXTERN     GetDlgItem@8:NEAR
EXTERN     MessageBoxA@16:NEAR
; Structures
; Message structure
MSGSTRUCT STRUC
 MSHWND     DWORD ?
 MSMESSAGE  DWORD ?
 MSWPARAM   DWORD ?
 MSLPARAM   DWORD ?
 MSTIME     DWORD ?
 MSPT       DWORD ?
MSGSTRUCT ENDS


; The DIAL.ASM file
.586P
; Flat memory model
```

```
.MODEL FLAT, stdcall
include dial1.inc
; INCLUDELIB directives for the linker to link libraries
includelib c:\masm32\lib\user32.lib
includelib c:\masm32\lib\kernel32.lib
;------------------------------------------------
; Data segment
_DATA SEGMENT
MSG MSGSTRUCT <?>
HINST DD 0     ; Application descriptor
PA  DB "DIAL1", 0
STR1 DB "Invalid character!", 0
STR2 DB "Error!", 0
; Table for creating hotkeys
TAB DB   32,  33,  34,  35,  36,  37,  38,  39,  40
DB  41,  42,  43,  44,  45,  46,  47,  58,  59,  60
DB  61,  62,  63,  64,  65,  66,  67,  68,  69,  70
DB  71,  72,  73,  74,  75,  76,  77,  78,  79,  80
DB  81,  82,  83,  84,  85,  86,  87,  88,  89,  90
DB  91,  92,  93,  94,  95,  96,  97,  98,  99, 100
DB 101, 102, 103, 104, 105, 106, 107, 108, 109, 110
DB 111, 112, 113, 114, 115, 116, 117, 118, 119, 120
DB 121, 122, 123, 124, 125, 126, 127, 128, 129, 130
DB 131, 132, 133, 134, 135, 136, 137, 138, 139, 140
DB 141, 142, 143, 144, 145, 146, 147, 148, 149, 150
DB 151, 152, 153, 154, 155, 156, 157, 158, 159, 160
DB 161, 162, 163, 164, 165, 166, 167, 168, 169, 170
DB 171, 172, 173, 174, 175, 176, 177, 178, 179, 180
DB 181, 182, 183, 184, 185, 186, 187, 188, 189, 190
DB 191, 192, 193, 194, 195, 196, 197, 198, 199, 200
DB 201, 202, 203, 204, 205, 206, 207, 208, 209, 210
DB 211, 212, 213, 214, 215, 216, 217, 218, 219, 220
DB 221, 222, 223, 224, 225, 226, 227, 228, 229, 230
DB 231, 232, 233, 234, 235, 236, 237, 238, 239, 240
DB 241, 242, 243, 244, 245, 246, 247, 248, 249, 250
DB 251, 252, 253, 254, 255

_DATA ENDS
; Code segment
_TEXT SEGMENT
START:
; Get the application descriptor
   PUSH  0
   CALL  GetModuleHandleA@4
```

```
   MOV    [HINST], EAX
;-----------------------------------
   PUSH   0
   PUSH   OFFSET WNDPROC
   PUSH   0
   PUSH   OFFSET PA
   PUSH   [HINST]
   CALL   DialogBoxParamA@20
   CMP    EAX, -1
   JNE    KOL
KOL:
;-----------------------------------
   PUSH   0
   CALL   ExitProcess@4
;-----------------------------------
; Window procedure
; Position of parameters in the stack
; [EBP+014H]  ; LPARAM
; [EBP+10H]   ; WAPARAM
; [EBP+0CH]   ; MES
; [EBP+8]  ; HWND
WNDPROC     PROC
   PUSH   EBP
   MOV    EBP, ESP
   PUSH   EBX
   PUSH   ESI
   PUSH   EDI
;-----------------------------------
   CMP    DWORD PTR [EBP+0CH], WM_CLOSE
   JNE    L1
   PUSH   0
   PUSH   DWORD PTR [EBP+08H]
   CALL   EndDialog@8
   MOV    EAX, 1
   JMP    FIN
L1:
   CMP    DWORD PTR [EBP+0CH], WM_INITDIALOG
   JNE    L2
; If needed, fill edit fields here
;
;
   MOV    EAX, 1
   JMP    FIN
L2:
```

```
   CMP   DWORD PTR [EBP+0CH], WM_COMMAND
   JNE   L5
; Exit button?
   CMP   WORD PTR [EBP+10H], 5
   JNE   L3
   PUSH  0
   PUSH  DWORD PTR [EBP+08H]
   CALL  EndDialog@8
   MOV   EAX, 1
   JMP   FIN
L3:
   CMP   WORD PTR [EBP+10H], 1
   JNE   FINISH
; Message-processing block for the first edit field
   CMP   WORD PTR [EBP+12H], EN_KILLFOCUS
   JNE   L4
; Edit field with an identifier
; 1 loses focus
   MOV   EBX,  0
; Unregister all hotkeys
   L33:
   MOVZX EAX, BYTE PTR [TAB+EBX]
   PUSH  EAX
   PUSH  DWORD PTR [EBP+08H]
   CALL  UnregisterHotKey@8
   INC   EBX
   CMP   EBX,  214
   JNE   L33
   MOV   EAX, 1
   JMP   FIN
L4:
   CMP   WORD PTR [EBP+12H], EN_SETFOCUS
   JNE   FINISH
; Edit field with an identifier
; 1 gains focus
   MOV   EBX, 0
; Registering hotkeys
L44:
   MOVZX EAX, BYTE PTR [TAB+EBX]
   PUSH  EAX
   PUSH  0
   PUSH  EAX
   PUSH  DWORD PTR [EBP+08H]
   CALL  RegisterHotKey@16
```

```
   INC  EBX
   CMP  EBX, 214
   JNE  L44
   MOV  EAX, 1
   JMP  FIN
L5:
   CMP  DWORD PTR [EBP+0CH], WM_HOTKEY
   JNE  FINISH
; Reaction to invalid character
   PUSH 0        ; MB_OK
   PUSH OFFSET STR2
   PUSH OFFSET STR1
   PUSH DWORD PTR [EBP+08H] ; Window descriptor
   CALL MessageBoxA@16
FINISH:
   MOV  EAX, 0
FIN:
   POP  EDI
   POP  ESI
   POP  EBX
   POP  EBP
   RET  16
WNDPROC ENDP
_TEXT ENDS
END START
```

The following is comment related to the program presented in Listing 10.2:

1. It is most important to understand when the first edit field loses and gains the focus. First, it is necessary to determine that the message has arrived from the edit field with identifier 1. Then, you need to determine which message has arrived — `EN_SETFOCUS` or `EN_KILLFOCUS`. In the first case, you register the hotkeys; in the latter case, you unregister them.
2. In the data area, specify the hotkey table. The `RegisterHotKey` function has the following parameters:
   - First parameter — Window identifier
   - Second parameter — Hotkey identifier
   - Third parameter — Hotkey-pressing flag
   - Fourth parameter — Virtual code of the key

In Listing 10.2, the key virtual code and hotkey identifier match. Naturally, you have a wide field for improvement. For example, it is possible to exclude the arrow keys from the processing. I suggest that you carry out this task on your own.

Managing Lists

This section considers the processing of a dialog with two lists. The right list is filled by double-clicking elements from the first list. Alternatively, to move an item from the left list to the right list, press the <Insert> key. You must also take into account the possibility that a user will double-click the same element twice. Principally, there is nothing difficult here. The comments to this situation will be provided after Listing 10.3. However, I'd like to explain one important element, the list, and draw your attention to some important aspects of working with it.

The means for managing lists can be classified into two groups — messages and properties.[i] The properties are specified in the resource file. For example, setting the `LBS_SORT` property automatically sorts the list contents any time a new element is added to the list. One of the most important properties is `LBS_WANTKEYBOARDINPUT`. If this property is set, the application receives the `WM_VKEYTOITEM` message when the user presses any key, provided that this list is activated. You can choose either independent processing (the <Page Up> key) or standard processing. If standard processing is not needed, the dialog function must return a negative value.

Listing 10.3. A program working with two lists

```
//The DIALLST.RC file
//Constant definitions
#define WS_SYSMENU             0x00080000L
#define WS_MINIMIZEBOX         0x00020000L
#define WS_MAXIMIZEBOX         0x00010000L
#define WS_VISIBLE             0x10000000L
#define WS_TABSTOP             0x00010000L
#define WS_VSCROLL             0x00200000L
#define WS_THICKFRAME          0x00040000L
#define LBS_NOTIFY             0x0001L
#define LBS_SORT               0x0002L
#define LBS_WANTKEYBOARDINPUT  0x0400L
```

[i] The same is true for all elements in a dialog box. Don't you think that this is similar to objects in properties in object-oriented programming? However, if you dive deeper, you'll discover that a considerable part of the properties will once again be reduced to message processing (see comments about the program presented in Listing 10.3).

```
// Identifiers
#define LIST1     101
#define LIST2     102
#define IDI_ICON1 3

// Define an icon
IDI_ICON1 ICON "ico1.ico"

// Dialog definition
DIAL1 DIALOG 0, 0, 210, 110
STYLE WS_SYSMENU | WS_MINIMIZEBOX | WS_MAXIMIZEBOX
CAPTION "First dialog box example"
FONT 8, "Arial"
{
 CONTROL "ListBox1", LIST1, "listbox", WS_VISIBLE |
 WS_TABSTOP | WS_VSCROLL | WS_THICKFRAME |
 LBS_NOTIFY|LBS_WANTKEYBOARDINPUT,
 16, 16, 70, 75
 CONTROL "ListBox2", LIST2, "listbox", WS_VISIBLE |
 WS_TABSTOP | WS_VSCROLL | WS_THICKFRAME |LBS_NOTIFY |
 LBS_SORT, 116, 16, 70, 75
}
```

```
; The DIALLST.INC file
; Constants
; The message arrives when the window is closed
WM_CLOSE          equ 10h
WM_INITDIALOG     equ 110h
WM_SETICON        equ 80h
WM_COMMAND        equ 111h
WM_VKEYTOITEM     equ 2Eh
LB_ADDSTRING      equ 180h
LBN_DBLCLK        equ 2
LB_GETCURSEL      equ 188h
LB_GETTEXT        equ 189h
LB_FINDSTRING     equ 18Fh
VK_INSERT         equ 2Dh

; Prototypes of external procedures
EXTERN     ExitProcess@4:NEAR
```

```
EXTERN     GetModuleHandleA@4:NEAR
EXTERN     DialogBoxParamA@20:NEAR
EXTERN     EndDialog@8:NEAR
EXTERN     LoadIconA@8:NEAR
EXTERN     SendMessageA@16:NEAR
EXTERN     SendDlgItemMessageA@20:NEAR
EXTERN     MessageBoxA@16:NEAR
; Structures
; Message structure
MSGSTRUCT STRUC
 MSHWND    DD ?
 MSMESSAGE DD ?
 MSWPARAM  DD ?
 MSLPARAM  DD ?
 MSTIME    DD ?
 MSPT      DD ?
MSGSTRUCT ENDS


; The DIALLST.ASM file
.586P
; Flat memory model
.MODEL FLAT, stdcall
include diallst.inc
; INCLUDELIB directives for the linker to link libraries
includelib c:\masm32\lib\user32.lib
includelib c:\masm32\lib\kernel32.lib
;------------------------------------------------
; Data segment
_DATA SEGMENT
 MSG    MSGSTRUCT <?>
 HINST     DD 0 ; Application descriptor
 PA     DB "DIAL1", 0
 BUFER     DB 100 DUP(0)
 STR1      DB "First", 0
 STR2      DB "Second", 0
 STR3      DB "Third", 0
 STR4      DB "Fourth", 0
 STR5      DB "Fifth", 0
 STR6      DB "Sixth", 0
 STR7      DB "Seventh", 0
 STR8      DB "Eighth", 0
 STR9      DB "Nineth", 0
```

```
STR10      DB "Tenth", 0
STR11      DB "Eleventh", 0
STR12      DB "Twelveth", 0
STR13      DB "Thirteenth", 0
STR14      DB "Fouteenth", 0
STR15      DB "Fifteenth", 0
INDEX      DD OFFSET STR1
       DD OFFSET STR2
       DD OFFSET STR3
       DD OFFSET STR4
       DD OFFSET STR5
       DD OFFSET STR6
       DD OFFSET STR7
       DD OFFSET STR8
       DD OFFSET STR9
       DD OFFSET STR10
       DD OFFSET STR11
       DD OFFSET STR12
       DD OFFSET STR13
       DD OFFSET STR14
       DD OFFSET STR15
_DATA ENDS
; Code segment
_TEXT SEGMENT
START:
; Get the application descriptor
   PUSH  0
   CALL  GetModuleHandleA@4
   MOV   [HINST], EAX
;---------------------------------
   PUSH  0
   PUSH  OFFSET WNDPROC
   PUSH  0
   PUSH  OFFSET PA
   PUSH  [HINST]
   CALL  DialogBoxParamA@20
   CMP   EAX, -1
   JNE   KOL
; Error message
KOL:
;----------------------------------
   PUSH  0
   CALL  ExitProcess@4
```

```
;--------------------------------
; Window procedure
; Position of parameters in the stack
; [EBP+014H]       ; LPARAM
; [EBP+10H]        ; WAPARAM
; [EBP+0CH]        ; MES
; [EBP+8]          ; HWND
WNDPROC      PROC
   PUSH  EBP
   MOV   EBP, ESP
   PUSH  EBX
   PUSH  ESI
   PUSH  EDI
; ---------------------------------------
   CMP   DWORD PTR [EBP+0CH], WM_CLOSE
   JNE   L1
   PUSH  0
   PUSH  DWORD PTR [EBP+08H]
   CALL  EndDialog@8
   JMP   FINISH
L1:
   CMP   DWORD PTR [EBP+0CH],WM_INITDIALOG
   JNE   L2
; Load the icon
   PUSH  3  ; Icon identifier
   PUSH  [HINST] ; Process identifier
CALL LoadIconA@8
; Set the icon
   PUSH  EAX
   PUSH  0 ; Icon type (small)
   PUSH  WM_SETICON
   PUSH  DWORD PTR [EBP+08H]
   CALL  SendMessageA@16
; Fill  the left list
   MOV   ECX, 15
   MOV   ESI, 0
LO1:
   PUSH  ECX ; Save the loop variable
   PUSH  INDEX[ESI]
   PUSH  0
   PUSH  LB_ADDSTRING
   PUSH  101
   PUSH  DWORD PTR [EBP+08H]
```

```
    CALL  SendDlgItemMessageA@20
    ADD   ESI, 4
    POP   ECX
    LOOP  L01
    JMP   FINISH
L2:
    CMP   DWORD PTR [EBP+0CH], WM_COMMAND
    JNE   L3
; Is there a message from the left list?
CMP WORD PTR [EBP+10H], 101
    JNE   FINISH
; Wasn't there a double-click event?
    CMP   WORD PTR [EBP+12H], LBN_DBLCLK
    JNE   FINISH
; There was a double-click; now, determine on which item
; Get the index of the chosen item
L4:
    PUSH  0
    PUSH  0
    PUSH  LB_GETCURSEL
    PUSH  101
    PUSH  DWORD PTR [EBP+08H]
    CALL  SendDlgItemMessageA@20
; Copy the list item into the buffer
    PUSH  OFFSET BUFER
    PUSH  EAX ; Record index
    PUSH  LB_GETTEXT
    PUSH  101
    PUSH  DWORD PTR [EBP+08H]
    CALL  SendDlgItemMessageA@20
; Determine whether this element is in the right list
    PUSH  OFFSET BUFER
    PUSH  -1 ; Search the entire list
    PUSH  LB_FINDSTRING
    PUSH  102
    PUSH  DWORD PTR [EBP+08H]
    CALL  SendDlgItemMessageA@20
    CMP   EAX, -1
    JNE   FINISH ; The element was found
; If the item was not found, it can be added
    PUSH  OFFSET BUFER
    PUSH  0
    PUSH  LB_ADDSTRING
```

```
    PUSH  102
    PUSH  DWORD PTR [EBP+08H]
    CALL  SendDlgItemMessageA@20
    MOV   EAX, -1
    JMP   FIN
L3:
; Check whether a key has been pressed
    CMP   DWORD PTR [EBP+0CH], WM_VKEYTOITEM
    JNE   FINISH
    CMP   WORD PTR [EBP+10H], VK_INSERT
    JE    L4
    MOV   EAX, -1
JMP FIN
FINISH:
    MOV   EAX, 0
FIN:
    POP   EDI
    POP   ESI
    POP   EBX
    POP   EBP
    RET   16
WNDPROC    ENDP
_TEXT ENDS
END START
```

The program in Listing 10.3 requires some comments.

- First, pay attention to the `SendDlgItemMessage` function. This function is more convenient for sending messages to elements of a dialog box than the `SendMessage` function, because the item in it is identified by the number specified in the resource file instead of a descriptor, which it is necessary to determine beforehand.
- Have a look at the resource file, and you'll see that the right list is assigned the `LBS_SORT` property. If this property is assigned to the list, then this list remains ordered after an element is added to it using the `LB_ADDSTRING` message. The `LBS_SORT` property costs significant overhead for the Windows operating system. By sending the `WM_COMPAREITEM` message, the operating system determines the required position for the new list item and then inserts the new item by sending the `LB_INSERTSTRING` message.
- It is also necessary to draw your attention to the loop that fills the left list. You must store the `ECX` register in the stack. Well, isn't it quite natural when

organizing a loop using the LOOP command? I would oppose this statement and declare that this isn't obvious. Unfortunately, available documentation on API functions and Windows messages doesn't state which processor registers are saved and which aren't saved for a specific API function. All this information has to be discovered experimentally. The only known fact is that the EBX, EBP, EDI, and ESI registers must not change. The WM_VKEYTOITEM message arrives when the user presses any key if that the list is activated. For this feature to work, the list must be assigned the LBS_WANTKEYBOARDINPUT property. Because this property is set only for the left list, you don't need to check from which list the message arrived.

Windows XP-Style Programming

In the Windows XP operating system, as can be easily noticed, the window style and the design of controls have changed. Still, if desired, you can return to the classic Windows style by setting this property (Fig. 10.1).

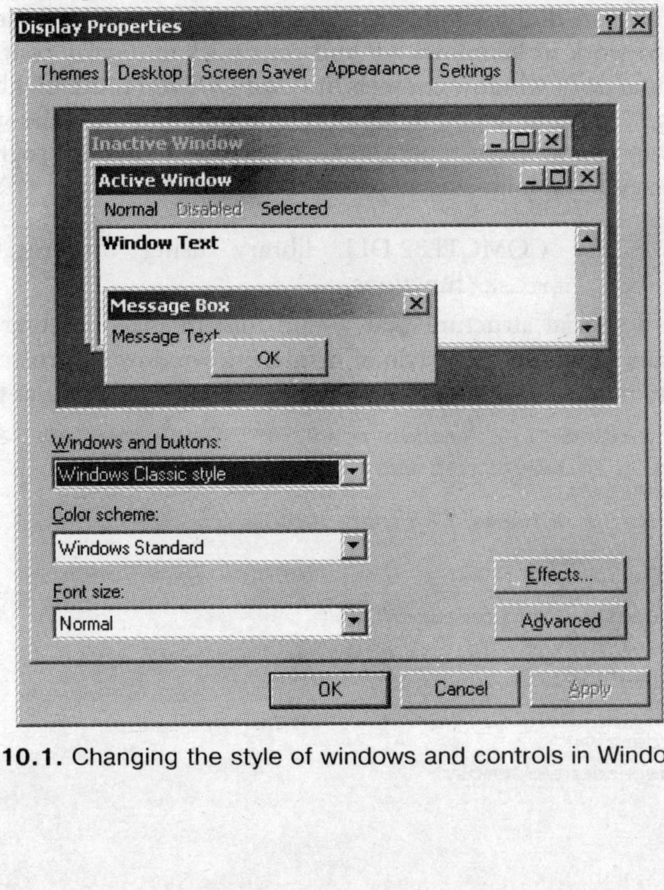

Fig. 10.1. Changing the style of windows and controls in Windows XP

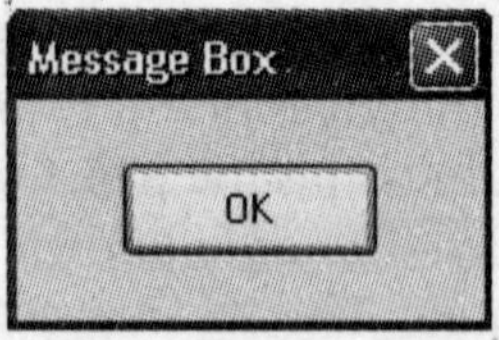

Fig. 10.2. Window and button styles

It is necessary to distinguish window appearance and control style (Fig. 10.2).

In contrast to window style, which is automatically formed by the operating system, the style of controls must be defined by the programmer. Because of this, all window controls of the programs written before the release of Windows XP have the old style. However, even if you program under Windows XP, the new style won't appear automatically if you are not using Delphi or C Builder. To achieve this goal, it is necessary to use an appropriate technology. This technology is the one that I'll describe now.

The USER32.DLL library was always responsible for displaying window controls. Consequently, you always include the `INCLUDELIB …USER32.LIB` directive into your programs to gain the possibility of controlling these window elements. This library continues to work in Windows XP and continues to display controls in the old style. For the new style of window controls, it is the COMCTL32.DLL library responsible for supporting it. In other words, to support window controls in the style of Windows XP, it is necessary to add the `INLUDELIB COMCTL32.LIB` into your programs. This, however, is not sufficient. The following steps are also required:

1. Initialize the COMCTL32.DLL library using the `InitCommonControls` or `InitCommonControlsEx` functions.
2. Create a special structure that would inform the operating system about your intention to use the new style of displaying window controls. This structure must be written in extensible markup language (XML). Its text is as follows:

```
<?xml version="1.0" encoding="UTF-8" standalone="yes"?>
<assembly xmlns="urn:schemas-microsoft-com:asm.v1"
manifestVersion="1.0">
<description>Windows XP program</description>
<assemblyIdentity
    version="1.0.0.0"
    processorArchitecture="X86"
    name="m.exe"
    type="win32"
/>
<dependency>
    <dependentAssembly>
```

```
        <assemblyIdentity
            type="win32"
            name="Microsoft.Windows.Common-Controls"
            version="6.0.0.0"
            processorArchitecture="X86"
            publicKeyToken="6595b64144ccf1df"
            language="*"
        />
    </dependentAssembly>
</dependency>
</assembly>
```

Pay special attention to the `version="6.0.0.0"` line. It informs the operating system that it is necessary to use the functions of COMCTL32.DLL library version 6.0. The `name="m.exe"` string specifies the name of your program.

I think that you'll immediately ask: How is it possible to integrate this text into my programs? In fact, there are two ways of doing so:

- If the text of your program is named, say, M.ASM, and the program, accordingly, is named M.EXE, then the XML code must be inserted into the file called M.EXE.MANIFEST. This file must be located in the same directory as the executable module M.EXE. This will be enough to display window controls in the new style. However, this is not always convenient, because the file with the manifest filename extension can be accidentally deleted or corrupted. Therefore, another, more reliable method is preferable.
- XML text can be included in the resource file. This is achieved by inserting the following string into the beginning of the file `"1 24 "m.xml""`. It is supposed that the XML code is located in the M.XML file. The resource compiler RC.EXE will compile this text into the object module; from there, it will be copied into the executable module.

At this point, I complete the theoretical considerations. You can start writing programs with elements in the Windows XP style right now (Listing 10.4 and Fig. 10.3).

Listing 10.4. A simple program presenting a window with elements in the Windows XP style

```
// The M.RC file
// Constant definitions
// Window styles
1   24      "m.xml"
```

```
#define WS_VSCROLL        200000h
#define CBS_DROPDOWNLIST 3h
#define WS_OVERLAPPED     0h
#define WS_CAPTION        0C00000h
#define IDC_COMBOBOX1     101
#define WS_SYSMENU        0x00080000L
#define WS_MINIMIZEBOX    0x00020000L
#define WS_MAXIMIZEBOX    0x00010000L
// Style of all window elements
#define WS_CHILD          0x40000000L
// Window elements must
// be initially visible
#define WS_VISIBLE        0x10000000L
// Using the <Tab> key,
// it is possible to sequentially initialize
// the button style
#define BS_PUSHBUTTON     0x00000000L
// Center the button text
#define BS_CENTER         0x00000300L
#define DS_LOCALEDIT      0x20L

// Dialog definition
DIAL1 DIALOG 0, 0, 240, 80
STYLE WS_OVERLAPPED | WS_CAPTION | WS_SYSMENU | WS_MINIMIZEBOX |
WS_MAXIMIZEBOX
CAPTION "Dialog example"
FONT 8, "Arial"
{
 CONTROL "Exit", 5, "button", BS_PUSHBUTTON | BS_CENTER | WS_CHILD |
WS_VISIBLE, 180, 30, 50, 14
 CONTROL "ComboBox1", IDC_COMBOBOX1, "combobox", CBS_DROPDOWNLIST |
WS_CHILD | WS_VISIBLE | WS_VSCROLL, 24, 30, 124, 16
}

.586P
; Flat memory model
.MODEL FLAT, stdcall
; INCLUDELIB directives for linking libraries
includelib d:\masm32\lib\comctl32.lib
includelib d:\masm32\lib\user32.lib
includelib d:\masm32\lib\kernel32.lib
;-----------------------------------------------
; Constants
```

```
; The message arrives when the window is closed
WM_CLOSE      equ 10h
WM_INITDIALOG equ 110h
WM_COMMAND    equ 111h
; Prototypes of external procedures
EXTERN     InitCommonControls@0:NEAR
EXTERN     UnregisterHotKey@8:NEAR
EXTERN     RegisterHotKey@16:NEAR
EXTERN     MessageBoxA@16:NEAR
EXTERN     ExitProcess@4:NEAR
EXTERN     GetModuleHandleA@4:NEAR
EXTERN     DialogBoxParamA@20:NEAR
EXTERN     EndDialog@8:NEAR
EXTERN     SendMessageA@16:NEAR
EXTERN     GetDlgItem@8:NEAR
EXTERN     MessageBoxA@16:NEAR
; Data segment
_DATA SEGMENT
HINST DD 0    ; Application descriptor
PA   DB "DIAL1", 0
STR1 DB "Invalid character!", 0
STR2 DB "Error!", 0

_DATA ENDS
; Code segment
_TEXT SEGMENT
START:
   CALL  InitCommonControls@0
; Get the application descriptor
   PUSH  0
   CALL  GetModuleHandleA@4
   MOV   [HINST], EAX
;--------------------------------
   PUSH  0
   PUSH  OFFSET WNDPROC
   PUSH  0
   PUSH  OFFSET PA
   PUSH  [HINST]
   CALL  DialogBoxParamA@20
   CMP   EAX, -1
   JNE   KOL
KOL:
;--------------------------------
```

```
   PUSH  0
   CALL  ExitProcess@4
;-------------------------------
; Window procedure
; Position of parameters in the stack
; [EBP+014H]   ; LPARAM
; [EBP+10H]    ; WAPARAM
; [EBP+0CH]    ; MES
; [EBP+8]      ; HWND
WNDPROC      PROC
   PUSH EBP
   MOV  EBP, ESP
   PUSH EBX
   PUSH ESI
   PUSH EDI
;-------------------------------
   CMP  DWORD PTR [EBP+0CH], WM_CLOSE
   JNE  L1
   PUSH 0
   PUSH DWORD PTR [EBP+08H]
   CALL EndDialog@8
   MOV  EAX, 1
   JMP  FIN
L1:
   CMP  DWORD PTR [EBP+0CH], WM_INITDIALOG
   JNE  L2
   MOV  EAX,  1
   JMP  FIN
L2:
   CMP  DWORD PTR [EBP+0CH], WM_COMMAND
   JNE  FINISH
; Exit button?
   CMP  WORD PTR [EBP+10H], 5
   JNE  FINISH
   PUSH 0
   PUSH DWORD PTR [EBP+08H]
   CALL EndDialog@8
   MOV  EAX, 1
   JMP  FIN
FINISH:
   MOV  EAX, 0
FIN:
   POP  EDI
```

```
    POP   ESI
    POP   EBX
    POP   EBP
    RET   16
WNDPROC ENDP
_TEXT ENDS
END START
```

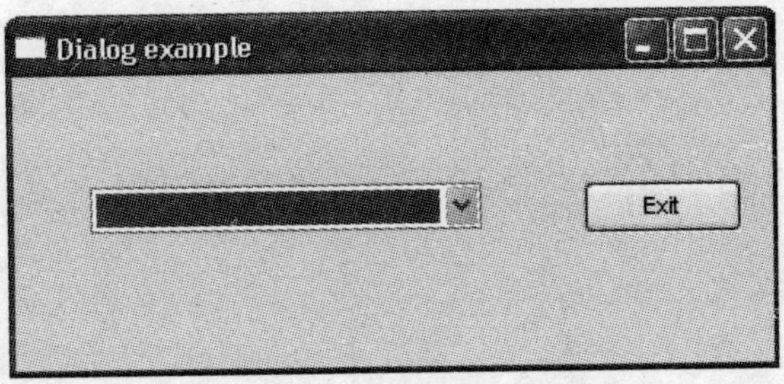

Fig. 10.3. Window created by the program in Listing 10.4

Because I only wanted to demonstrate the possibilities of using new styles of displaying elements, the program is elementary. The window contains only two elements: a button and a combobox. I'd like to emphasize again that window style has no relation to the theory. On the contrary, it is automatically formed by the operating system.

To assemble and link the program, issue the following commands:

```
ML /c /coff "m.asm"
RC "m.rc"
LINK /SUBSYSTEM:WINDOWS "m.obj" "m.res"
```

The use of TASM32 isn't considered here.

Chapter 11

Working with Files

All information is stored in files. File management is a vital component of practically any program. Beginners pay excessive attention to the design — windows, toolbars, and nonstandard buttons. Unfortunately, they often neglect file operations. However, files must be paid the attention they require — actually, mastering operations over files is the key to mastery of programming.

With the arrival of large and fast hard disks, the importance of files has grown considerably. Using API functions for file management can make your program more efficient and ensure its high performance. Most programs presented in this chapter are console applications. This is because console applications are the most suitable for demonstrating file processing. File processing is the method of hiding from users and programmers all the events that take place when information is read from or written to the storage media. Operating systems of the Windows NT family work with two types of file systems — File Allocation Table 32 (FAT32) and the New Technology File System (NTFS). FAT32 is the direct descendant of the two file systems, FAT12 and FAT16. It has inherited most of their drawbacks. Microsoft continues to support this file system for backward compatibility with previous versions of its file systems, although in future versions of Windows, FAT32 support will be reduced to the capability of reading files from FAT volumes. On the contrary, NTFS is generally considered as one of the most perfect file systems. In the following few sections, I will cover the basic concepts of these file systems, which are required for efficient programming.

File Characteristics

When providing descriptions of file characteristics, I'll base them on the parameters that API functions manipulate. The types of file systems and their structure will be covered later. First, I'll list and briefly describe the main file attributes. Most of them are present in NTFS, and a considerable part is also present in FAT32.

File Attributes

The attribute is an integer of the `DWORD` type. It defines how the operating system treats the file.

- `FILE_ATTRIBUTE_READONLY equ 1h` — The "read only" attribute. Applications can only read this file. Accordingly, any attempt at writing to this file will cause an error.
- `FILE_ATTRIBUTE_HIDDEN equ 2h` — The "hidden file" attribute. The file with this attribute will not be displayed when viewing the directory using "standard" tools (see the *File Search* section later in this chapter).
- `FILE_ATTRIBUTE_SYSTEM equ 4h` — The "system file" attribute. If this attribute is set, the file either belongs to the operating system or is used by the system in exclusive mode.
- `FILE_ATTRIBUTE_DIRECTORY equ 10h` — The "directory" attribute. The operating system treats a file with this attribute in a special way. It considers such files as directories, namely, lists of files composed of 32-byte records. Normal files cannot be converted into directories. To create a directory, use the `CreateDirectory` function.
- `FILE_ATTRIBUTE_ARCHIVE equ 20h` — Since the time of MS-DOS, this attribute has been set for files that were not archived using the `BACKUP` or `XCOPY` operation. For programming purposes, this attribute is equivalent to the zero value.
- `FILE_ATTRIBUTE_DEVICE equ 40h` — Reserved for future use.
- `FILE_ATTRIBUTE_NORMAL equ 80h` — This attribute means that no other attributes are set for the file.
- `FILE_ATTRIBUTE_TEMPORARY equ 100h` — This attribute means that the file is intended for temporary data storage. After the file is closed, the system must delete it. The system stores the main part of such a file in memory.
- `FILE_ATTRIBUTE_SPARSE_FILE equ 200h` — This attribute allows you to use distributed (or sparse) files. The logical length of such files can significantly exceed the disk space taken by the file. This attribute first appeared in NTFS 5.0.
- `FILE_ATTRIBUTE_REPARSE_POINT equ 400h` — This attribute was introduced in Windows 2000. It is used for extending the functional capabilities of the file system. Reparse points (described later in this chapter) allow NTFS-based hierarchical

storage management (HSM) technology to be implemented. This technology allows you to considerably extend the framework of available disk space by using remote storage media. The system operates with such storage media automatically. This attribute was first introduced with NTFS 5.0.

- `FILE_ATTRIBUTE_COMPRESSED equ 800h` — If this attribute is set, the file has been compressed by the system. For directories, the presence of this attribute means that all newly created files in such a directory must be compressed by default.
- `FILE_ATTRIBUTE_OFFLINE equ 1000h` — If this attribute is set, the information stored in this file is unavailable. Perhaps, this file resides on a storage device that is offline (not connected).
- `FILE_ATTRIBUTE_NOT_CONTENT_INDEXED equ 2000h` — The presence of this attribute means that the file cannot be indexed by the Windows indexing service.
- `FILE_ATTRIBUTE_ENCRYPTED equ 4000h` — The file is encrypted. This attribute first appeared in NTFS 5.0, which provides the possibility of file encryption (more details will be provided later in this chapter).

File attributes can be changed using the `SetFileAttributes` function. To read file attributes, use the `GetFileAttributes` function. The values of the following attributes can be set only using the `DeviceIoControl` function:

- `FILE_ATTRIBUTE_COMPRESSED`
- `FILE_ATTRIBUTE_DEVICE`
- `FILE_ATTRIBUTE_DIRECTORY`
- `FILE_ATTRIBUTE_ENCRYPTED`
- `FILE_ATTRIBUTE_REPARSE_POINT`
- `FILE_ATTRIBUTE_SPARSE_FILE`

Note that if the operating system doesn't impose any limitations on the possibility of changing file attributes, then the attributes themselves lose sense. For example, if the read-only attribute can be removed any time, then any user will be able to do with the file whatever he or she pleases.

The file has three time characteristics: creation time, last modification time, and last access time. The time is counted in nanoseconds, starting from 12 p.m., January 1, 1600, and is stored in two 32-bit values that can be represented by the following structure:

```
FILETIME STRUC
   dwLowDateTime DW ?
   dwLowHighTime DW ?
FILETIME ENDS
```

It is necessary to point out that time is stored in universal coordinates and must be converted to the local time (this is achieved using the `FileTimeToLocalFileTime` function). To get all three time values, use the `GetFileTime` function. For output and manipulations with the file, it is expedient to invent a more convenient structure than two 32-bit values. There is such a structure — `SYSTIME`. It has the following format:

```
SYSTIME STRUC
  wYear           DW ?
  wMonth          DW ?
  wDayOfWeek      DW ?
  wDay            DW ?
  wHour           DW ?
  wMinute         DW ?
  wSecund         DW ?
  wMilliseconds   DW ?
SYSTIME ENDS
```

For converting the structure obtained using the `GetFileTime` function into the `SYSTIME` structure, use the `FileTimeToSystemTime` API function.

To set the time characteristics of a file, the `SetFileTime` function is used. For defining the time, it is convenient to use the `SYSTIME` structure and then convert it into the `SetFileTime` format using the `SystemTimeToFileTime` function. Later in this chapter, I'll provide an example illustrating how to obtain time characteristics of the file (see Listing 11.6).

File length in bytes is usually stored in two 32-bit values or in one 64-bit value. If 32-bit values are designated as `l1` (least significant part) and `l2` (most significant part), then a 64-bit value will be obtained according to the following formula: `l2*0FFFFH+l1`. The file size can be obtained using the `GetFileSize` function. This function returns the least significant part of the file length, which is enough in most cases. The second argument of this function is the pointer to the most significant part of the file length. However, the `GetFileSizeEx` function is more convenient for determining the file length. The second argument of this function is the address of the following structure:

```
FSIZE STRUC
  LOWPART  DW ?
  HIGHPART DW ?
FSISE ENDS
```

This structure is the one that gets the file length.

It is necessary to note that functions able to be used for obtaining file characteristics receive the file descriptor as their first argument. In other words, to get these characteristics, it is first necessary to open the file (see the description of the `CreateFile` function later in this chapter). An alternative method of receiving these parameters is using the `FindFirstFile` function (see the *File Search* section later in this chapter).

In addition to the previously described characteristics, the file, naturally, has a name. Note that it is necessary to distinguish between the long name and the short name of the file. Also, it is necessary to distinguish the fully qualified pathname (with all long names) and the abbreviated pathname (in which all long names are replaced by abbreviated ones). An abbreviated pathname is needed because some older programs interpret blank characters as parameter delimiters. To convert the long name into the short one, use the `GetShortPathName` function, which is capable of converting both names and paths. The inverse operation can be carried out using the `GetFullPathName` function.

In this book, I don't even touch direct disk access. However, you may still ask about the structure of the directory records. This is quite natural because, with the migration from FAT (MS-DOS) to FAT32[i] (Windows 95), there appeared the possibility of storing long filenames. In addition to the time and date of modification, there appeared such characteristics as time and date of creation and last access. Where are all these characteristics stored? This question will be answered in the next section.

The FAT32 File System

To answer the question in the preceding section, recall that the directory in FAT file systems[ii] is divided into 32-byte records. Table 11.1 outlines the structure of the FAT32 record. Blank records are the ones containing 0 bytes or starting from the `E5H` code (for deleted records). For files with short names (8 bytes for the name and 3 bytes for the filename extension), 32 bytes are allocated. The byte located by offset +11 (see Table 11.2) contains the file attribute. If the file attribute is equal to `0FH`, then the system considers the filename to be long. Long names are encoded as Unicode and are written in reverse order before short names, which means that one or more records with a long name must be followed by a record with a short name containing the ~ character in the seventh position. The ~ character is followed by digits starting from 1. The digits are needed to distinguish the short names of the files, to which the first six characters of a long name match. Here, the record with a short name contains all the other information about the file. As you can see, the algorithm of directory viewing with detection of information about the file is easy. Now, consider the structure of the directory record containing the short filename. In MS-DOS, bytes from 12 to 21 were

[i] Initially, Windows 95 worked with FAT16; however, support for long filenames was also provided.
[ii] FAT is one of the elements, upon which file systems of MS-DOS and Windows 9*x* are based. Because of this, such file systems are called FAT systems.

not used by the system. The new system has found an application for them. Table 11.1 describes the new structure of the directory record.

Table 11.1. Structure of the FAT32 directory record

Offset	Size	Contents
(+0)	8	Name of the file or the directory aligned by the left boundary and padded with blank characters
(+8)	3	Filename extension aligned by the left boundary and padded with blank characters
(+11)	1	File attribute
(+12)	2	Used by operating systems of the Windows NT family; ensures that case-sensitive filenames are displayed correctly
(+14)	2	Creation time
(+16)	2	Creation date
(+18)	2	Access date
(+20)	2	Two most significant bytes of the number of the first cluster of the file
(+22)	2	File modification time
(+24)	2	File modification date
(+26)	2	Two least significant bytes of the first cluster of the file
(+28)	4	File size in bytes

As you can see, now all bytes of the 32-byte record are used. This is just more evidence that initially, the MS-DOS file system was designed inefficiently. In particular, it relates to the file length. As can be easily noticed, only 4 bytes are allocated for storing the file length. How do you find the file length if it requires more than 4 bytes? In this case, it is necessary to consider that the directory stores only the least significant bytes of the length, and the full length can be determined by the FAT. However, no one would argue that this is an obvious drawback. The `GetFileSize` function also looks strange because it returns the four least significant bytes of the file length; most significant bytes are returned in the second parameter.

As I have already mentioned, the record with a short filename and file characteristics can be preceded by one or more records with long names. Table 11.2 outlines the structure of such a record.

Table 11.2. Structure of a directory record with a long name

Offset	Size	Contents
(+0)	1	Ordinal number of the long filename fragment. Only 6 bits are used. In the last fragment, the ordinal number is increased by 64 (6th bit is set to 1).
(+1)	10	Five characters of the long filename in Unicode (10 bytes).
(+11)	1	The attribute field. It must be always set to `0FH`. Old MS-DOS programs ignore such directory entries; therefore, they see only short filenames.*
(+12)	1	The byte must be zero.
(+13)	1	The checksum. It was intended for avoiding collisions that might occur when simultaneously running MS-DOS and Windows applications. The program might arise when an MS-DOS application deletes a file with a long name and creates a new file, overwriting the record of the deleted file. In this case, Windows will have to determine that the long filename has no relation to the short filename. Now, this field is obsolete.
(+14)	12	Six symbols of long filename in Unicode.
(+26)	2	Two 0 bytes.
(+28)	4	Two characters of the long filename in Unicode.

* I wonder if the developers of MS-DOS and FAT had foreseen the possibility of using this attribute in such a way.

From Table 11.2, it follows that the maximum length of the filename can be 819 characters (63 × 13 = 819); however, the system won't allow you to set a filename length exceeding 260 characters.

In addition to directories, the file system also contains the FAT — the table, using which the operating system traces file allocation in the data area. The directory record stores the starting cluster of the file and the file length in bytes. Knowing the cluster size (information about the sector size and the number of sectors in the cluster), it is possible to determine how many clusters are required for storing the file. However, this is not enough, because the file can be stored in several nonadjacent chains of clusters. FAT is located directly after the reserved sectors at the beginning. The number of these sectors is specified in the boot sector. The size of the FAT element is 4 bytes.[i] The first two FAT elements are reserved. The first byte is always set to `F8H`. The other 3 bytes can be used at the discretion of the operating system and are undocumented.

[i] Naturally, I mean FAT32. In FAT16, the FAT element size is 2 bytes. In the FAT12 file system, which is used in file systems for diskettes, the FAT element length is 12 bits.

Thus, the first meaningful table element of the table has the number 2 and corresponds to the cluster in the file area — the numbers of elements and clusters match. Their possible values are as follows:

- 0 — The cluster is free.
- 1 — The cluster is damaged.
- `0FFFFFF8h` – `0FFFFFFFh` — The cluster is the last in the chain of file clusters.
- Other values determine the number of the next cluster in the chain for a given file. The four most significant bits do not participate in cluster numbering. Thus, the maximum cluster number is 268,435,455.

This table structure allows the operating system to easily find all clusters of any given file using the chain of elements.

The New Technology File System

NTFS is an advanced and sophisticated file system developed independently of FAT. In my opinion, this is one of the most advanced and perfect file systems. Because of this, I'll cover its structure in detail.

Similar to FAT, NTFS also stores files as chains of clusters. Clusters in NTFS can range in size from 512 bytes to 64 KB. The standard (default) cluster size is 4 KB. The main structure in NTFS is the Master File Table (MFT) file. It is necessary to point out that according to the general NTFS concept, NTFS doesn't contain anything but files. The length of filename is limited to 255 characters, and the maximum pathname length cannot exceed 32,767 characters.

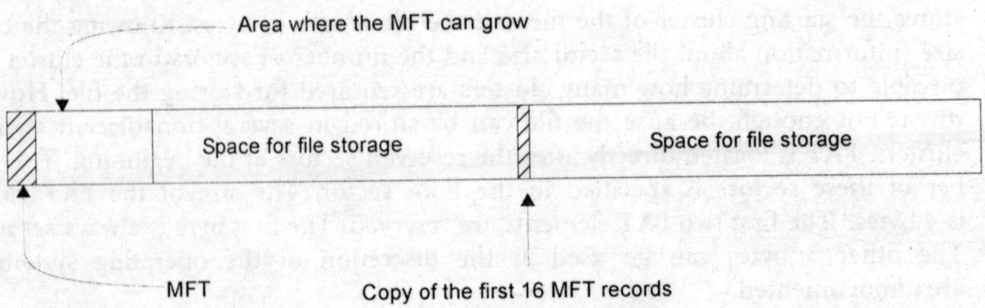

Fig. 11.1. General structure of an NTFS volume

For MFT, the main NTFS file, an area in the beginning of the volume is allocated (the boot sector contains the number of the first MFT cluster). However, because MFT is also a file, this file can be located anywhere. To avoid fragmenting this file (although it can be fragmented), a disk space that is 12% of the entire volume space is allocated for it beforehand. If necessary, the operating system can increase or decrease this area and then return it to its initial state. By its meaning, this is not a system area and therefore is included in the total value of the available disk space.

The MFT file contains records about each file in the system. The MFT record size is 1 KB. If one record is not sufficient for describing a file, other records are added. The first 16 files, whose records are located in the beginning of MFT, are system files. The names of these files start with the `$` character. Table 11.3 provides information about these files. Note that the first record (numbering starts from 0) of the MFT file contains information about the MFT file itself.[i]

Table 11.3. NTFS metafiles

Record No. in MFT	Name of system file	Comment
0	`$MFT`	Master file table.
1	`$MFTMIRR`	The copy of the first 16 records of the MFT. In a normal situation, this file resides directly in the middle of the volume.
2	`$LOGFILE`	Log file for system recovery. According to this file, the operating system can recover the file system of a damaged volume with a high level of probability.
3	`$VOLUME`	The volume file (volume label, file system version, size, etc.).
4	`$ATTRDEF`	This file contains the list of standard volume attributes.
5	`$.`	Root directory. As any file, it can be increased or decreased in size. Note that all system files are located in this directory.
6	`$BITMAP`	This file contains the bitmap for finding available space in the volume.
7	`$BOOT`	The bootstrap file.
8	`$BADCLUS`	The file that lists bad clusters.
9	`$SECURE`	Security information.
10	`$UPCASE`	Uppercase and lowercase mapping for the volume.
11	`$QUOTA`	The directory that contains files used for disk quotes.
12–15		Reserved records.

[i] Certainly, this is an elegant solution that allows a certain information redundancy. Under some conditions, this allows you to recover the damaged file system.

Now, consider the MFT file record. Every record consists of a header followed by a header attribute and its value. Each header contains the checksum; the file ordinal number, which is increased when the record is used for another file; the file access counter; the number of bytes used in the record; and other fields. The record header is followed by the header of the first attribute and the value of this attribute. Then comes the header of the second attribute, and so on. If the attribute is large enough, it is stored in a separate file (nonresident attribute). The important point is that if the volume of data stored in the file is small, they are stored in the MFT record.

Table 11.4 lists the attributes.

Table 11.4. Attributes of the MFT records

Attribute	Description
Standard information (information attribute)	Information about the owner, security data, hard links counter, and bit attributes (read only, archive, etc.).
Filename	Filename in the Unicode format.
Security descriptor	This attribute has become obsolete; the $EXTENDEDSECURE attribute has replaced it.
List of attributes	Location of additional MFT records, used when the attributes do not fit within a single record.
Object identifier	64-bit file identifier unique for this volume.
Reparse point	For creating hierarchical storage; this attribute instructs the procedure that processes the filename to carry out additional operations.
Volume name	Used in $VOLUME.
Information about the volume	Volume version (used in $VOLUME).
Root index	For directories.
Index layout	For large directories implemented as B-trees instead of normal lists.
Bit array	For large directories.
Data flow of the registration utility	Controls data registration in the $LOGFILE file.
Data	Flow of the file data; the header of this attribute is followed by the list of clusters, where the data reside, or the data themselves if their volume doesn't exceed hundreds of bytes.

Thus, in NTFS, files are nothing but sets of attributes. Attributes are represented in the form of the byte flow. As you can see, one of the attributes is the data stored in the file, or the data flow. The file system allows you to add new attributes to the file, which can contain additional information.

NTFS implements many interesting technical solutions. One of these advanced innovations was already mentioned: a small file can entirely reside in a single MFT record. Another approach assumes that the operating system, when writing a file, always tries to carry out this operation to make as many cluster chains (sections, in which disk clusters follow each other directly) as possible. Groups of file clusters are described by special structures — records placed into MFT records.[i] For example, a file made up of a single chain of clusters is described by one such record. The same can be said about a file that consists of a small number of cluster chains. Cluster chains within a record are described by the following pair of values: cluster offset from the starting position and the number of clusters. The record header specifies the offset of the first cluster from the starting point of the file and the offset of the first cluster that goes beyond the limits of the current record.

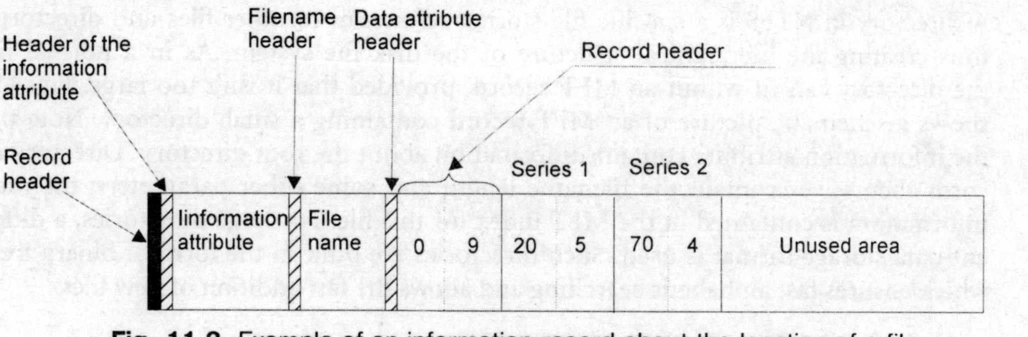

Fig. 11.2. Example of an information record about the location of a file that consists of nine clusters

Fig. 11.2 shows a schematic illustration of an MFT record for a file that consists of nine clusters. The record header specifies the offset of the first cluster of the file and the first cluster that doesn't fit within this record. This header is followed by two pairs of numbers that specify the continuous sequences of clusters. The first element of the pair is the offset of the cluster from the starting point of the disk space and the second

---

[i] Do not confuse MFT file records and file records describing positions of the file clusters on the disk.

element is the number of clusters in a chain. Such pairs are also called a series. As you can see, in this case, the file consists of two continuous chains and is specified by two series. Note that the numeric values defining the number of clusters and the cluster offset are 64-bit values in NTFS.

What will happen if the file is fragmented so that all its chains cannot be described by a single MFT record? In this case, several MFT records are used. At the same time, they may not necessarily have numbers differing from each other by 1. To interrelate these records, a base record is used. In the first MFT record that starts this file, the base record precedes the record containing the descriptor of cluster chains. It also has the header followed by a list of the numbers of MFT records, which contain information about location of the file data on the disk. All other MFT records have the same structure as shown in Fig. 11.2. A question might arise: What if the base record cannot fit within a single MFT record? In this case, it is placed into the separate file. According to the NTFS terminology, this makes the record nonresident.

Now, consider some other specific features of NTFS.

Directories in NTFS

A directory in NTFS is a specific file storing references to other files and directories, thus creating the hierarchical structure of the disk file system. As in a normal file, the directory can fit within an MFT record, provided that it isn't too large. Fig. 11.3 shows a schematic picture of an MFT record containing a small directory. Note that the information attribute contains information about the root directory. Directory records themselves contain the filename length and some other parameters; the main information is contained in the MFT index for this file. For large directories, a different data storage format is used. Such directories are built in the form of binary trees, which ensures fast alphabetic searching and allows the fast addition of new files.

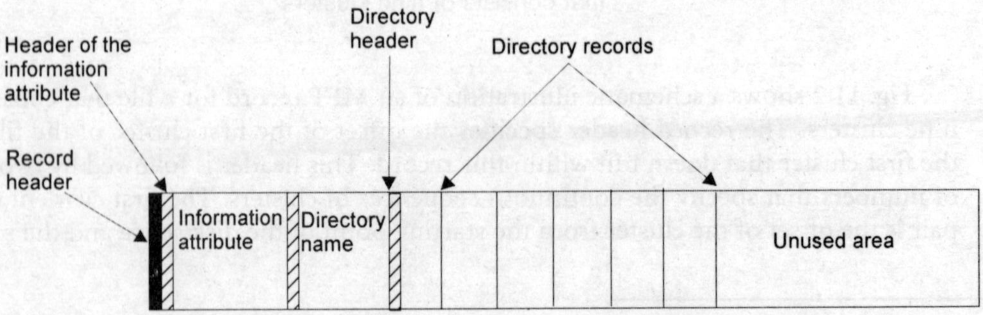

Fig. 11.3. Small directory entirely fits within an MFT record

NTFS File Compression

NTFS allows files to be stored in a compressed form. The compression mechanism is interesting and deserves a special mention. Compression is carried out in 16-cluster blocks. When writing data, the operating system tries to compress the first 16 clusters of a record, then the next 16-cluster bunch, etc. If the system fails to compress the block, it is written "as is." Suppose that you are compressing a 16-cluster block. Assume that the offset of the first cluster is 50 and that you succeeded in achieving a 25% level of compression. This means that instead of 16 clusters you now have only 12. For simplicity, assume that the clusters are sequential, thus forming a chain. A compressed cluster chain in the MFT record will be represented by two pairs of numbers, (50,12) and (0,4), instead of one pair — (50,16). The second pair is needed for the operating system to recognize, which of the chains was compressed. As you can see, file compression mechanism is easy and built into the file system.

The standard method of determining the file system applied in the current partition is to use the `GetVolumeInformation` function. I won't describe this function in detail but will mention that its seventh parameter (out of eight) is the buffer, into which the file system type will be loaded after this function is called.

Reparse Points

A reparse point allows you to extend NTFS functionality. Reparse points were introduced into the NTFS version intended for use with Windows 2000. The developers made provision for several types of reparse points, including volume mount points, NTFS directory attachment points, and HSM reparse points.

- Volume mount points allow a volume to be bound to the directory without assigning a drive letter to that volume. Thus, several volumes can be joined and assigned a single drive letter. For example, assume that the mount point is C:\TEMP, and the D: volume is mounted to it. After that, all directories of that volume will be available through the mount point: C:\TEMP\ARH, C:\TEMP\PROGRAM, etc. When the user attempts to access, say, the C:\TEMP\PROGRAM\FC.EXE file, the system detects the mount point for the TEMP directory connected to the D: volume and then accesses the PROGRAM directory on that volume.
- Directory connection points are similar to mount points. However, this mechanism is used for mounting directories instead of volumes. For instance, if you return to the previous example, you can connect the PROGRAM directory to the TEMP directory and access the FC.EXE file in a similar way: C:\TEMP\PROGRAM\FC.EXE.

- In HSM, reparse points move rarely used files to the backup storage medium. When doing so, the file contents are deleted and replaced with reparse points. The reparse point data contain all information needed for the HSM system to find the file on the backup media. When the user accesses the file, the system processes its reparse point and determines that the file has been moved to the backup medium (and determines where it resides). After that, the system starts the mechanism for retrieving the file from the backup storage medium. After the file has been moved successfully, the reparse point is deleted automatically, and the file access procedure is repeated.

If the reparse point is related to a file or directory, NTFS creates a `$Reparse` attribute for it. This attribute stores the code and the reparse point data. Because of this mechanism, NTFS easily detects all reparse points on the volume.

File Searching

For searching files, Windows provides two functions: `FindFirstFile` and `FindNextFile`. These resemble similar functions of the MS-DOS. Like in MS-DOS, in Windows these functions operate in coordination. When the search is successful, the first function returns some number or identifier then used by the second function to continue the search.

The first parameter of the `FindFirstFile` function is the pointer for the search string. The second parameter is the pointer to the structure that receives information about the files found. The `FindNextFile` received the identifier obtained by the first function as its first parameter, and its second parameter is the pointer to the structure. The example illustrating the use of this structure is presented in Listing 11.1.

Similar functions existed in MS-DOS. The difference between Windows file-searching functions and the respective MS-DOS functions lies in that only the search mask (*.*, *.exe, etc.) is specified in the input. If the file was found, then by the return structure containing all information about that file, it is possible to decide whether the file found is the one you required. In MS-DOS, for file search, it was necessary to additionally specify the file attribute.

The program in Listing 11.1 searches for files in the specified directory. The program can accept one or two parameters or can have no parameters. If two parameters are used, then the first parameter is interpreted as the search directory. The program accounts for the presence of a trailing backslash (allowed options are C:, C:\, C:\WINDOWS\, C:\WINDOWS\SYSTEM, etc.). The second parameter (in the program, it has the number 3 because the first parameter is the command line), if present, specifies the search mask. If this parameter is missing, *.* will be the default mask. Finally, if no parameters are specified, then the program searches the current directory using the "*.*" mask. Note that you can easily extend this program and make a useful utility out of it. I hope that you will do this on your own. Comments about this program are provided after the listing.

Listing 11.1. A simple program that searches for files and displays the list of found files

```
; The FILES.ASM file
.586P
; Flat memory model
.MODEL FLAT, stdcall
; Constants
STD_OUTPUT_HANDLE equ -11
STD_INPUT_HANDLE  equ -10
; Prototypes of external procedures
EXTERN  wsprintfA:NEAR
EXTERN  CharToOemA@8:NEAR
EXTERN  GetStdHandle@4:NEAR
EXTERN  WriteConsoleA@20:NEAR
EXTERN  ReadConsoleA@20:NEAR
EXTERN  ExitProcess@4:NEAR
EXTERN  GetCommandLineA@0:NEAR
EXTERN  lstrcatA@8:NEAR
EXTERN  FindFirstFileA@8:NEAR
EXTERN  FindNextFileA@8:NEAR
EXTERN  FindClose@4:NEAR
;-----------------------------------------------
; The structure for file searching
; using the FindFirstFile and FindNextFile functions
_FIND STRUC
; File attribute
  ATR         DWORD ?
; File creation time
  CRTIME      DWORD ?
  DWORD ?
; File access time
  ACTIME      DWORD ?
  DWORD ?
; File modification time
  WRTIME      DWORD ?
DWORD ?
; File size
  SIZEH       DWORD ? ; Most significant part
```

```
   SIZEL  DWORD ? ; Least significant part
; Reserved
   DWORD  ?
   DWORD  ?
; Long filename
   NAM    DB 260 DUP(0)
; Short filename
   ANAM   DB 14 DUP(0)
_FIND ENDS
;-----------------------------------------------
; INCLUDELIB directives for linking libraries
includelib c:\masm32\lib\user32.lib
includelib c:\masm32\lib\kernel32.lib
;-----------------------------------------------
; Data segment
_DATA SEGMENT
   BUF     DB  0
   DB      100 dup(0)
   LENS    DWORD ? ; Number of displayed characters
   HANDL   DWORD ?
   HANDL1  DWORD ?
   MASKA   DB "*.*", 0
   AP      DB "\", 0
   FIN     _FIND <0>
   TEXT    DB "Press <ENTER> to continue", 13, 10, 0
   BUFIN   DB 10 DUP(0)
   FINDH DWORD ?
   NUM     DB 0
   NUMF    DWORD 0 ; Files counter
   NUMD    DWORD 0 ; Directories counter
   FORM    DB "Files found: %lu", 0
   FORM1   DB "Directories found: %lu", 0
   BUFER   DB 100 DUP(?)
   DIR     DB " <DIR>", 0
   PAR     DB 0 ; Number of parameters
_DATA ENDS
; Code segment
_TEXT    SEGMENT
START:
; Get the output handle
   PUSH    STD_OUTPUT_HANDLE
   CALL    GetStdHandle@4
   MOV     HANDL, EAX
```

```
; Get the input handle HANDL1
  PUSH   STD_INPUT_HANDLE
  CALL   GetStdHandle@4
  MOV    HANDL1, EAX
; Convert strings for output
  PUSH   OFFSET TEXT
  PUSH   OFFSET TEXT
  CALL   CharToOemA@8
  PUSH   OFFSET FORM
  PUSH   OFFSET FORM
  CALL   CharToOemA@8
  PUSH   OFFSET FORM1
  PUSH   OFFSET FORM1
  CALL   CharToOemA@8
; Get the number of parameters
  CALL   NUMPAR
  MOV    PAR, AL
; Search the current directory if only one parameter is passed
  CMP    EAX, 1
  JE     NO_PAR
;-------------------------------------
; Get the parameter with EDI number
  MOV    EDI, 2
  LEA    EBX, BUF
  CALL   GETPAR
  PUSH   OFFSET BUF
  CALL   LENSTR
; Add the trailing backslash if it is missing
  CMP    BYTE PTR [BUF+EBX-1], "\"
  JE     NO_PAR
  PUSH   OFFSET AP
  PUSH   OFFSET BUF
  CALL   lstrcatA@8
; Is there a parameter specifying the search mask?
  CMP    PAR, 3
  JB     NO_PAR
; Get the search mask
  MOV    EDI, 3
  LEA    EBX, MASKA
  CALL   GETPAR
NO_PAR:
;-------------------------------------
  CALL   FIND
```

```
; Display the number of files
   PUSH  NUMF
   PUSH  OFFSET FORM
   PUSH  OFFSET BUFER
   CALL  wsprintfA
   LEA   EAX, BUFER
   MOV   EDI, 1
   CALL  WRITE
; Display the number of directories
   PUSH  NUMD
   PUSH  OFFSET FORM1
   PUSH  OFFSET BUFER
   CALL  wsprintfA
   LEA   EAX, BUFER
   MOV   EDI, 1
   CALL  WRITE
_END:
   PUSH  0
   CALL  ExitProcess@4
;************************
; Procedures
;************************
; Display a string (terminated by a line feed character)
; EAX — To the string beginning
; EDX — With or without a line feed
WRITE PROC
; Get the parameter length
   PUSH  EAX
   CALL  LENSTR
   MOV   ESI, EAX
   CMP   EDI, 1
   JNE   NO_ENT
;Terminated by the line feed
   MOV   BYTE PTR [EBX+ESI], 13
   MOV   BYTE PTR [EBX+ESI+1], 10
   MOV   BYTE PTR [EBX+ESI+2], 0
   ADD   EBX, 2
NO_ENT:
; String output
   PUSH  0
   PUSH  OFFSET LENS
   PUSH  EBX
   PUSH  EAX
```

```
    PUSH    HANDL
    CALL    WriteConsoleA@20
    RET
WRITE    ENDP
; Procedure for determining the string length
; String in [EBP+08H]
; Length in EBX
LENSTR    PROC
    PUSH    EBP
    MOV     EBP, ESP
    PUSH    EAX
    PUSH    EDI
;--------------------
    CLD
    MOV     EDI, DWORD PTR [EBP+08H]
    MOV     EBX, EDI
    MOV     ECX, 100 ; Limit the string length
    XOR     AL, AL
    REPNE   SCASB ; Find the 0 character
    SUB     EDI, EBX ; String length including the 0 character
    MOV     EBX, EDI
    DEC     EBX
;--------------------
    POP     EDI
    POP     EAX
    POP     EBP
RET 4
LENSTR ENDP
; Procedure for determining the number of parameters
; in the string
; Determine the number of parameters (->EAX)
NUMPAR PROC
    CALL    GetCommandLineA@0
    MOV     ESI, EAX ; Pointer to the string
    XOR     ECX, ECX ; Counter
    MOV     EDX, 1 ; Indication
L1:
    CMP     BYTE PTR [ESI], 0
    JE      L4
    CMP     BYTE PTR [ESI], 32
    JE      L3
    ADD     ECX, EDX ; Parameter number
    MOV     EDX, 0
```

```
   JMP  L2
L3:
   OR   EDX, 1
L2:
   INC  ESI
   JMP  L1
L4:
   MOV  EAX, ECX
   RET
NUMPAR ENDP
; Get the parameter from the command line
; EBX — Points to the buffer where the parameter
; will be loaded
; Zero-terminated string is loaded into the buffer
; EDI — Number of the parameter
GETPAR PROC
   CALL  GetCommandLineA@0
   MOV   ESI, EAX ; Pointer to the string
   XOR   ECX, ECX ; Counter
   MOV   EDX, 1 ; Indicator
L1:
   CMP   BYTE PTR [ESI], 0
   JE    L4
   CMP   BYTE PTR [ESI], 32
   JE    L3
   ADD   ECX, EDX ; Number of the parameter
   MOV   EDX, 0
   JMP   L2
L3:
   OR    EDX, 1
L2:
   CMP   ECX, EDI
   JNE   L5
   MOV   AL, BYTE PTR [ESI]
   MOV   BYTE PTR [EBX], AL
   INC   EBX
L5:
   INC   ESI
   JMP   L1
L4:
   MOV   BYTE PTR [EBX], 0
   RET
GETPAR   ENDP
```

```
; Searching for files in a directory and their output
; Directory name in BUF
  FIND  PROC
; Path with a mask
  PUSH  OFFSET MASKA
  PUSH  OFFSET BUF
  CALL  lstrcatA@8
; The search starts here
  PUSH  OFFSET FIN
  PUSH  OFFSET BUF
  CALL  FindFirstFileA@8
  CMP   EAX, -1
  JE    _ERR
; Save the search descriptor
  MOV   FINDH, EAX
LF:
; Exclude "." and ".." "files"
  CMP   BYTE PTR FIN.NAM, "."
  JE    _NO
; Is this a directory?
  TEST  BYTE PTR FIN.ATR, 10H
  JE    NO_DIR
  PUSH  OFFSET DIR
  PUSH  OFFSET FIN.NAM
  CALL  lstrcatA@8
  INC   NUMD
  DEC   NUMF
NO_DIR:
; Convert the string
  PUSH  OFFSET FIN.NAM
  PUSH  OFFSET FIN.NAM
  CALL  CharToOemA@8
; Results output
  LEA   EAX, FIN.NAM
  MOV   EDI, 1
  CALL  WRITE
; Increase the counters
  INC   NUMF
  INC   NUM
; Page end?
  CMP   NUM, 22
  JNE   _NO
  MOV   NUM, 0
```

```
; Wait for the input string
   MOV   EDI, 0
   LEA   EAX, TEXT
   CALL  WRITE
   PUSH  0
   PUSH  OFFSET LENS
   PUSH  10
   PUSH  OFFSET BUFIN
   PUSH  HANDL1
   CALL  ReadConsoleA@20
_NO:
; Continue the search
   PUSH  OFFSET FIN
   PUSH  FINDH
   CALL  FindNextFileA@8
   CMP   EAX, 0
   JNE   LF
; Terminate the search
   PUSH  FINDH
   CALL  FindClose@4
_ERR:
   RET
   FIND  ENDP
_TEXT    ENDS
END START
```

The program in Listing 11.1 is simple. The only new feature that you'd find here is working with the `FindFirstFile` and `FindNextFile` functions. Procedures used for working with command-line parameters were encountered before. Information is output into the current console; this feature, too, has been encountered before. To get the console descriptor, the `GetStdHandle` function is used. The `WRITE` procedure simplifies the code sections responsible for screen output. Earlier, I promised that string API functions will be the paid attention they deserve. In this program, I have kept my word. Along with custom string procedures, this program makes use of the `lstrcat` string function, which concatenates strings. As relates to the command-line parameter, note that if the directory name contains blanks, the filename must be specified in abbreviated form, for example, C:\PROGRA~1 instead of C:\PROGRAM FILES. The reason is straightforward, because blanks serve as parameter delimiters. To solve the problem correctly, it is necessary to introduce a special delimiter for parameters, for example, - or /.

The program in Listing 11.1 searches either the current directory or the specified directory. If this program was written in a high-level programming language, such as C, it could be easily modified so that it would search the directory tree. Only the `FIND` procedure, which must be called recursively, would require a minor modification. As can be seen, this ease is because of the presence of local variables in high-level languages. Well, try to implement the same thing basing on materials presented in *Chapter 2*. Is it possible to achieve the same goal without using local variables?

NOTE

The length of the first parameter of the `FindFirstFile` API function cannot exceed the value of the `MAX_PATH` constant, which is equal to 260. If you need to use longer strings, it is necessary to use the Unicode version of this function (which has the `W` suffix). In this case, the string length can reach 32,000 characters. However, do not forget to convert the string into Unicode format and precede it with the `\\?\` prefix.

The program presented in Listing 11.2 is similar to the previous program. However, it searches the entire directory tree, starting from the specified directory. This is one of the most complicated programs presented in this book. Therefore, I strongly recommend that you study it carefully. I hope that you'll be able to improve it. I'd like to give you some directions, with which you can work. The second command-line parameter allows you to specify the search mask. For example, if you specify the `*.EXE` option, not only files but also directories will be searched by this mask. This is an obvious drawback that is the first candidate for elimination.

The directory tree can be easily searched recursively; however, for this purpose, you need local variables.[i] The meaning of using a local variable in a recursive algorithm is that part of data must be preserved when returning from the procedure.

In the program under consideration, for simplicity, I abandoned the `LENSTR` procedure and decided to use the `lstrlen` API function instead. In addition, I improved the output to display the fully qualified filename on the screen.

Listing 11.2. Example program that recursively searches the directory tree

```
; The FILES.ASM file
.586P
; Flat memory model
.MODEL FLAT, stdcall
; Constants
STD_OUTPUT_HANDLE  equ -11
STD_INPUT_HANDLE   equ -10
; Prototypes of external procedures
EXTERN    wsprintfA:NEAR
```

---

[i] Naturally, it is possible to do without local variables. For example, it is possible to store the data in a global array and access the required elements of this array depending on the recursion level.

```
EXTERN   CharToOemA@8:NEAR
EXTERN   GetStdHandle@4:NEAR
EXTERN   WriteConsoleA@20:NEAR
EXTERN   ReadConsoleA@20:NEAR
EXTERN   ExitProcess@4:NEAR
EXTERN   GetCommandLineA@0:NEAR
EXTERN   lstrcatA@8:NEAR
EXTERN   lstrcpyA@8:NEAR
EXTERN   lstrlenA@4:NEAR
EXTERN   FindFirstFileA@8:NEAR
EXTERN   FindNextFileA@8:NEAR
EXTERN   FindClose@4:NEAR
;-----------------------------------------------
; The structure for file search
; using the FindFirstFile and FindNextFile functions
_FIND STRUC
; File attribute
  ATR      DWORD ?
; File creation time
  CRTIME   DWORD ?
           DWORD ?
; File access time
  ACTIME   DWORD ?
           DWORD ?
; File modification time
  WRTIME   DWORD ?
           DWORD ?
; File size
  SIZEH    DWORD ?
  SIZEL    DWORD ?
; Reserved
           DWORD ?
           DWORD ?
; Long filename
  NAM      DB 260 DUP(0)
; Short filename
  ANAM     DB 14 DUP(0)
_FIND ENDS
;-----------------------------------------------
; INCLUDELIB directives for the linker
includelib c:\masm32\lib\user32.lib
includelib c:\masm32\lib\kernel32.lib
;-----------------------------------------------
```

```
; Data segment
_DATA SEGMENT
        BUF     DB     0
                DB     100 dup(0)
        LENS    DWORD ? ; Number of output characters
        HANDL   DWORD ?
        HANDL1  DWORD ?
        MASKA   DB "*.*"
                DB 50 DUP(0)
        AP      DB "\", 0
        FIN     _FIND <0>
        TEXT    DB "Press <Enter> to continue", 13, 10, 0
        BUFIN   DB 10 DUP(0) ; Output buffer
        NUM     DB 0
        NUMF    DWORD 0 ; Files counter
        NUMD    DWORD 0 ; Directories counter
        FORM    DB "Number of files found: %lu", 0
        FORM1   DB "Number of directories found: %lu", 0
        DIRN    DB " <DIR>", 0
        PAR     DWORD 0
        PRIZN   DB 0
_DATA ENDS
; Code segment
_TEXT  SEGMENT
START:
; Get the output handle
       PUSH   STD_OUTPUT_HANDLE
       CALL   GetStdHandle@4
       MOV    HANDL, EAX
; Get the input handle HANDL1
       PUSH   STD_INPUT_HANDLE
       CALL   GetStdHandle@4
       MOV    HANDL1, EAX
; Convert strings for output
       PUSH   OFFSET TEXT
       PUSH   OFFSET TEXT
       CALL   CharToOemA@8
       PUSH   OFFSET FORM
       PUSH   OFFSET FORM
       CALL   CharToOemA@8
       PUSH   OFFSET FORM1
       PUSH   OFFSET FORM1
       CALL   CharToOemA@8
```

```
; Get the number of parameters
        CALL  NUMPAR
        MOV   PAR, EAX
; If there is only one parameter, search the current directory
        CMP   EAX, 1
        JE    NO_PAR
;-------------------------------------
; Get the parameter with the EDI number
        MOV   EDI, 2
        LEA   EBX, BUF
        CALL  GETPAR
        CMP   PAR, 3
        JB    NO_PAR
; Get the search mask
        MOV   EDI, 3
        LEA   EBX, MASKA
        CALL  GETPAR
NO_PAR:
;-------------------------------------
        PUSH  OFFSET BUF
        CALL  FIND
; Output the number of files
        PUSH  NUMF
        PUSH  OFFSET FORM
        PUSH  OFFSET BUF
        CALL  wsprintfA
        LEA   EAX, BUF
        MOV   EDI, 1
        CALL  WRITE
;++++++++++++++++
; Output the number of directories
        PUSH  NUMD
        PUSH  OFFSET FORM1
        PUSH  OFFSET BUF
        CALL  wsprintfA
        LEA   EAX, BUF
        MOV   EDI, 1
        CALL  WRITE
_END:
        PUSH  0
        CALL  ExitProcess@4

; Procedures
```

```
;****************************************
; Output the string (terminated with line feed)
; EAX — To the beginning of the string
; EDX — With or without line feed
  WRITE  PROC
; Get the parameter length
        PUSH  EAX
        PUSH  EAX
        CALL  lstrlenA@4
        MOV   ESI, EAX
        POP   EBX
        CMP   EDI, 1
        JNE   NO_ENT
; Line feed in the end
        MOV   BYTE PTR [EBX+ESI], 13
        MOV   BYTE PTR [EBX+ESI+1], 10
        MOV   BYTE PTR [EBX+ESI+2], 0
        ADD   EAX,2
NO_ENT:
; String output
        PUSH  0
        PUSH  OFFSET LENS
        PUSH  EAX
        PUSH  EBX
        PUSH  HANDL
        CALL  WriteConsoleA@20
        RET
WRITE   ENDP
; Procedure for determining the number of parameters
; Determine the number of parameters (->EAX)
NUMPAR  PROC
        CALL  GetCommandLineA@0
        MOV   ESI, EAX ; Pointer to the string
        XOR   ECX, ECX ; Counter
        MOV   EDX, 1   ; Indicator
L1:
        CMP   BYTE PTR [ESI], 0
        JE    L4
        CMP   BYTE PTR [ESI], 32
        JE    L3
        ADD   ECX, EDX  ; Parameter number
        MOV   EDX, 0
        JMP   L2
```

```
L3:
        OR    EDX, 1
L2:
        INC   ESI
        JMP   L1
L4:
        MOV   EAX, ECX
        RET
NUMPAR  ENDP
; Get the parameter from the command line
; EBX - Points to the buffer, in which to load the parameter
; Zero-terminated string is loaded into the buffer
; EDI - Parameter number
GETPAR PROC
        CALL  GetCommandLineA@0
        MOV   ESI, EAX ; Pointer to the string
        XOR   ECX, ECX ; Counter
        MOV   EDX, 1   ; Indicator
L1:
        CMP   BYTE PTR [ESI], 0
        JE    L4
        CMP   BYTE PTR [ESI], 32
        JE    L3
        ADD   ECX, EDX  ; Parameter number
        MOV   EDX, 0
        JMP   L2
L3:
        OR    EDX, 1
L2:
        CMP   ECX, EDI
        JNE   L5
        MOV   AL, BYTE PTR [ESI]
        MOV   BYTE PTR [EBX], AL
        INC   EBX
L5:
        INC   ESI
        JMP   L1
L4:
        MOV   BYTE PTR [EBX], 0
        RET
GETPAR ENDP
;-----------------------------------
; Searching files in the directory and sending them for output
```

```
FINDH   EQU   [EBP-4]   ; Search descriptor
DIRS    EQU   [EBP-304] ; Fully qualified filename
DIRSS   EQU   [EBP-604] ; For storing the directory
DIRV    EQU   [EBP-904] ; For temporary storage
DIR     EQU   [EBP+8]   ; Parameter — Directory name
FIND    PROC
        PUSH  EBP
        MOV   EBP, ESP
        SUB   ESP, 904
; Initializing local variables
        MOV   ECX, 300
        MOV   AL, 0
        MOV   EDI, 0
CLR:
        MOV   BYTE PTR DIRS+[EDI], AL
        MOV   BYTE PTR DIRSS+[EDI], AL
        MOV   BYTE PTR DIRV+[EDI], AL
        INC   EDI
        LOOP  CLR
; Determine the path length
        PUSH  DIR
        CALL  lstrlenA@4
        MOV   EBX, EAX
        MOV   EDI, DIR
        CMP   BYTE PTR [EDI], 0
        JE    _OK
; Add the trailing backslash if it is missing
        CMP   BYTE PTR [EDI+EBX-1], "\"
        JE    _OK
        PUSH  OFFSET AP
        PUSH  DIR
        CALL  lstrcatA@8
_OK:
; Store the directory
        PUSH  DIR
        LEA   EAX, DIRSS
        PUSH  EAX
        CALL  lstrcpyA@8
; Path with the mask
        PUSH  OFFSET MASKA
        PUSH  DIR
        CALL  lstrcatA@8
; Search starts here
```

```
        PUSH  OFFSET FIN
        PUSH  DWORD PTR DIR
        CALL  FindFirstFileA@8
        CMP   EAX, -1
        JE    _ERR
; Save the search descriptor
        MOV   FINDH, EAX
LF:
; Exclude the "files" "." and ".."
        CMP   BYTE PTR FIN.NAM, "."
        JE    _FF
;------------------
        LEA   EAX, DIRSS
        PUSH  EAX
        LEA   EAX, DIRS
        PUSH  EAX
        CALL  lstrcpyA@8
;------------------
        PUSH  OFFSET FIN.NAM
        LEA   EAX, DIRS
        PUSH  EAX
        CALL  lstrcatA@8
; Is this a directory?
        TEST  BYTE PTR FIN.ATR, 10H
        JE    NO_DIR
; Add to the <DIR> string
        PUSH  OFFSET DIRN
        LEA   EAX, DIRS
        PUSH  EAX
        CALL  lstrcatA@8
; Increase the counters
        INC   NUMD
        DEC   NUMF
; Set the directory attribute
        MOV   PRIZN, 1
; Display the directory name
        LEA   EAX, DIRS
        PUSH  EAX
        CALL  OUTF
        JMP   _NO
NO_DIR:
; Display the filename
        LEA   EAX, DIRS
        PUSH  EAX
```

```
        CALL  OUTF
; Indicator of the file (not a directory)
        MOV   PRIZN, 0
_NO:
        CMP   PRIZN, 0
        JZ    _F
; Directory, preparing a recursive call
        LEA   EAX, DIRSS
        PUSH  EAX
        LEA   EAX, DIRV
        PUSH  EAX
        CALL  lstrcpyA@8
        PUSH  OFFSET FIN.NAM
        LEA   EAX, DIRV
        PUSH  EAX
        CALL  lstrcatA@8
; Calling
        LEA   EAX, DIRV
        PUSH  EAX
        CALL  FIND
; Continue the search
_F:
        INC   NUMF
_FF:
        PUSH  OFFSET FIN
        PUSH  FINDH
        CALL  FindNextFileA@8
        CMP   EAX, 0
        JNE   LF
; Close the search descriptor
        PUSH  FINDH
        CALL  FindClose@4
_ERR:
        MOV   ESP, EBP
        POP   EBP
        RET   4
FIND    ENDP
;--------------------------
; Page output of the names of found files
STRN    EQU   [EBP+8]
OUTF    PROC
        PUSH  EBP
        MOV   EBP, ESP
; Convert the string
```

```
        PUSH   STRN
        PUSH   STRN
        CALL   CharToOemA@8
; Output of the results
        MOV    EAX, STRN
        MOV    EDI, 1
        CALL   WRITE
        INC    NUM
; End of page?
        CMP    NUM, 22
        JNE    NO
        MOV    NUM, 0
; Wait for string input
        MOV    EDI, 0
        LEA    EAX, TEXT
        CALL   WRITE
        PUSH   0
        PUSH   OFFSET LENS
        PUSH   10
        PUSH   OFFSET BUFIN
        PUSH   HANDL1
        CALL   ReadConsoleA@20
NO:
        POP    EBP
        RET    4
OUTF    ENDP
_TEXT ENDS
END START
```

Now, it is necessary to explain the role of local variables in the FIND procedure. The FINDH variable stores the search descriptor for the current directory. The FIND procedure can be called recursively even if the search in the current directory hasn't been accomplished yet. Consequently, after returning from a recursive call, the search must continue. This can be ensured only with the old value of the descriptor. A local variable ensures this possibility, because it is destroyed only when returning to the lower level (to the parent directory).

The DIRSS variable plays a similar role. It stores the current directory. This is important because the fully qualified filename is formed using this variable.

The DIRS and DIRV variables play an auxiliary role. Principally, they could be replaced by global variables. In this respect, bear in mind that, although global variables are undesirable in recursive algorithms from the efficiency point of view, the smaller is the space required for local variables, the better.

Here is another aspect that I want to explain: For passing the directory name when calling the procedure, the `DIRV` variable is used. Why can't you use the `DIRSS` variable for the same purpose? The point is that instead of the referenced value, the pointer is passed to the procedure. Consequently, any modifications to the `DIR` parameter will result in similar changes to the `DIRSS` variable at the lower level of recursion. Naturally, this isn't the goal.

The Program Translation Using TASM

The main problem with translating the programs presented in Listings 11.1 and 11.2 relates to local labels. A local label is a label that works within the limits of a certain block of the program. In this case, such a block is the procedure. MASM automatically distinguishes labels located within the limit of a specific procedure and interprets them as local labels. Therefore, no problems arise when labels with the same names are encountered within different procedures. TASM uses a slightly different approach: By default, labels are considered global. Thus, local labels must be preceded by the `@@` prefix. Furthermore, it is necessary to insert the `LOCALS` directive in the starting point of the procedure. Having inserted the `LOCALS` directive and marked the required labels as local, you'll easily convert the program to the format acceptable by TASM. Also, do not forget about converting `wsprintfA` to `_wsprintfA`.

Techniques of Working with Binary Files

Manipulations over external files[i] are based on several API functions, the most important and sophisticated of which is the `CreateFile` function. I will cover this function in detail in *Chapter 13*. Here, practical information will be provided that is needed to start using this function in your programs. Note, however, that using this function it is possible not only to create or open files but also to manipulate with such objects as pipes, consoles, disk devices, and communication resources (see *Chapter 13* for more details). The function distinguishes the device by the name structure. For example, a name like C:\CONFIG.SYS defines a file, and a name like `CONOUT$` defines the output buffer of the current console.

Listings 11.3 and 11.4 present two simple but important programs. Both programs output the contents of the text file[ii] whose name is displayed as a command-line option in the current console. In the first case, you get the descriptor of the current con-

[i] By external files I mean files located on an external device.

[ii] Actually, they output the contents of any file, but this method of file output into the console makes sense only for text files.

sole in a standard way. In the second case, you open the console as a file and output information there as you would do when outputting information to a file. Pay attention to the role of the buffer, into which the file contents are read. Experiment with the buffer size. For example, try to output a large text file to it. An interesting point is that the structure of the text file is not taken into account in both programs because for such input and output this is not needed. Later in this chapter, I will describe the text file structure.

Listing 11.3. Text output from a file to a console (first method)

```
; The FILES1.ASM file
.586P
; Flat memory model
.MODEL FLAT, stdcall
; Constants
STD_OUTPUT_HANDLE equ -11
GENERIC_READ      equ 80000000h
GENERIC_WRITE     equ 40000000h
GEN = GENERIC_READ or GENERIC_WRITE
SHARE = 0
OPEN_EXISTING   equ 3
; Prototypes of external procedures
EXTERN  GetStdHandle@4:NEAR
EXTERN  WriteConsoleA@20:NEAR
EXTERN  ExitProcess@4:NEAR
EXTERN  GetCommandLineA@0:NEAR
EXTERN  CreateFileA@28:NEAR
EXTERN  CloseHandle@4:NEAR
EXTERN  ReadFile@20:NEAR
;------------------------------------------------
; INCLUDELIB directives for the linker
includelib c:\masm32\lib\user32.lib
includelib c:\masm32\lib\kernel32.lib
;------------------------------------------------
; Data segment
_DATA SEGMENT
HANDL DWORD ?
HFILE DWORD ?
BUF   DB 100 DUP(0)
BUFER DB 300 DUP(0)
NUMB  DWORD ?
NUMW  DWORD ?
_DATA ENDS
```

```
; Code segment
_TEXT SEGMENT
START:
; Get the output handle
    PUSH  STD_OUTPUT_HANDLE
    CALL  GetStdHandle@4
    MOV   HANDL, EAX
; Get the number of parameters
    CALL  NUMPAR
    CMP   EAX, 1
    JE    NO_PAR
;-------------------------------------
; Get the parameter with the EDI number
    MOV   EDI, 2
    LEA   EBX, BUF
    CALL  GETPAR
; Open file
    PUSH  0              ; Must be 0
    PUSH  0              ; File attribute (if creating a file)
    PUSH  OPEN_EXISTING  ; How to open
    PUSH  0              ; The pointer to the security attribute
    PUSH  0              ; Common access mode
    PUSH  GEN            ; Access mode
    PUSH  OFFSET BUF      ; Filename
    CALL  CreateFileA@28
    CMP   EAX, -1
    JE    NO_PAR
    MOV   HFILE, EAX
LOO:
; Read into buffer
    PUSH  0
    PUSH  OFFSET NUMB
    PUSH  300
    PUSH  OFFSET BUFER
    PUSH  HFILE
    CALL  ReadFile@20
; Output the buffer contents to the console
    PUSH  0
    PUSH  OFFSET NUMW
    PUSH  NUMB
    PUSH  OFFSET BUFER
    PUSH  HANDL
    CALL  WriteConsoleA@20
```

```
; Check whether the last bytes have been read
    CMP   NUMB, 300
    JE    LOO
; Close the file
    PUSH  HFILE
    CALL  CloseHandle@4
; End of program
NO_PAR:
    PUSH  0
    CALL  ExitProcess@4
; Procedures
; Procedure for defining the number of parameters in the string
; Determine the number of parameters (->EAX)
NUMPAR PROC
    CALL  GetCommandLineA@0
    MOV   ESI, EAX ; Pointer to the string
    XOR   ECX, ECX ; Counter
    MOV   EDX, 1   ; Indicator
L1:
    CMP   BYTE PTR [ESI], 0
    JE    L4
    CMP   BYTE PTR [ESI], 32
    JE    L3
    ADD   ECX, EDX ; Parameter number
    MOV   EDX, 0
    JMP   L2
L3:
    OR    EDX, 1
L2:
    INC   ESI
    JMP   L1
L4:
    MOV   EAX,ECX
    RET
NUMPAR ENDP
; Get the parameter from the command line
; EBX — Points to the buffer, in which to load the parameter
; Zero-terminated string will be placed into the buffer
; EDI — Parameter number
GETPAR PROC
    CALL  GetCommandLineA@0
    MOV   ESI, EAX ; Pointer to the string
    XOR   ECX, ECX ; Counter
```

```
    MOV   EDX, 1 ; Indicator
L1:
    CMP   BYTE PTR [ESI], 0
    JE    L4
    CMP   BYTE PTR [ESI], 32
    JE    L3
    ADD   ECX, EDX ; Parameter number
    MOV   EDX, 0
    JMP   L2
L3:
    OR    EDX, 1
L2:
    CMP   ECX, EDI
    JNE   L5
    MOV   AL, BYTE PTR [ESI]
    MOV   BYTE PTR [EBX], AL
    INC   EBX
L5:
    INC   ESI
    JMP   L1
L4:
    MOV   BYTE PTR [EBX], 0
    RET
GETPAR ENDP
_TEXT ENDS
END START
```

Listing 11.4. Output of the contents of a text file into a console (second method)

```
; The FILES2.ASM file
.586P
; Flat memory model
.MODEL FLAT, stdcall
; Constants
STD_OUTPUT_HANDLE equ -11
GENERIC_READ     equ 80000000h
GENERIC_WRITE    equ 40000000h
GEN = GENERIC_READ or GENERIC_WRITE
SHARE = 0
OPEN_EXISTING    equ 3
; Prototypes of external procedures
EXTERN  ExitProcess@4:NEAR
```

```
EXTERN  GetCommandLineA@0:NEAR
EXTERN  CreateFileA@28:NEAR
EXTERN  CloseHandle@4:NEAR
EXTERN  ReadFile@20:NEAR
EXTERN  WriteFile@20:NEAR
;------------------------------------------------
; INCLUDELIB directives for the linker
includelib c:\masm32\lib\user32.lib
includelib c:\masm32\lib\kernel32.lib
;------------------------------------------------
; Data segment
_DATA SEGMENT
HANDL  DWORD ?
HFILE  DWORD ?
BUF    DB 100 DUP(0)
BUFER  DB 300 DUP(0)
NUMB   DWORD ?
NUMW   DWORD ?
NAMEOUT DB "CONOUT$"
_DATA ENDS
; Code segment
_TEXT SEGMENT
START:
; Get the output handle (console as a file)
    PUSH  0
    PUSH  0
    PUSH  OPEN_EXISTING
    PUSH  0
    PUSH  0
    PUSH  GEN
    PUSH  OFFSET NAMEOUT
    CALL  CreateFileA@28
    MOV   HANDL, EAX
; Get the number of parameters
    CALL  NUMPAR
    CMP   EAX, 1
    JE    NO_PAR
;-------------------------------------
; Get the parameter with the EDI number
    MOV   EDI, 2
    LEA   EBX, BUF
    CALL  GETPAR
; Open the file
```

```
    PUSH  0
    PUSH  0
    PUSH  OPEN_EXISTING
    PUSH  0
    PUSH  0
    PUSH  GEN
    PUSH  OFFSET BUF
    CALL  CreateFileA@28
    CMP   EAX, -1
    JE    NO_PAR
    MOV   HFILE, EAX
LOO:
; Read into the buffer
    PUSH  0
    PUSH  OFFSET NUMB
    PUSH  300
    PUSH  OFFSET BUFER
    PUSH  HFILE
    CALL  ReadFile@20
; Output to the console as to a file
    PUSH  0
    PUSH  OFFSET NUMW
    PUSH  NUMB
    PUSH  OFFSET BUFER
    PUSH  HANDL
    CALL  WriteFile@20
    CMP   NUMB, 300
    JE    LOO
; Close the file
    PUSH  HFILE
    CALL  CloseHandle@4
; End of program operation
NO_PAR:
    PUSH  0
    CALL  ExitProcess@4
; Procedures
; Procedure for determining the number of parameters in the string
; Determine the number of parameters (->EAX)
NUMPAR PROC
    CALL  GetCommandLineA@0
    MOV   ESI, EAX ; Pointer to the string
    XOR   ECX, ECX ; Counter
    MOV   EDX, 1   ; Indicator
```

```
L1:
    CMP   BYTE PTR [ESI], 0
    JE    L4
    CMP   BYTE PTR [ESI], 32
    JE    L3
    ADD   ECX, EDX ; Parameter number
    MOV   EDX, 0
    JMP   L2
L3:
    OR    EDX, 1
L2:
    INC   ESI
    JMP   L1
L4:
    MOV   EAX, ECX
    RET
NUMPAR ENDP
; Get the parameter from the command line
; EBX - Points to the buffer, in which the parameter will be loaded
; Zero-terminated string is loaded into the buffer
; EDI - Parameter number
GETPAR PROC
    CALL  GetCommandLineA@0
    MOV   ESI, EAX ; Pointer to the string
    XOR   ECX, ECX ; Counter
    MOV   EDX, 1   ; Indicator
L1:
    CMP   BYTE PTR [ESI], 0
    JE    L4
    CMP   BYTE PTR [ESI], 32
    JE    L3
    ADD   ECX, EDX ; Parameter number
    MOV   EDX, 0
    JMP   L2
L3:
    OR    EDX, 1
L2:
    CMP   ECX, EDI
    JNE   L5
    MOV   AL, BYTE PTR [ESI]
    MOV   BYTE PTR [EBX], AL
    INC   EBX
L5:
```

```
    INC    ESI
    JMP    L1
L4:
    MOV    BYTE PTR [EBX], 0
    RET
GETPAR ENDP
_TEXT ENDS
END START
```

Now, consider the text file structure in more detail. When working with a high-level programming language, certain algorithmic skills are lost. In particular, this relates to working with text files. Assembly language, on the contrary, doesn't allow you to relax. Consider possible variants of working with text files.

The main characteristic of a text file is that such files consist of strings that have different lengths. Strings are separated by delimiters. Most frequently, the role of the delimiter is delegated to a sequence of two codes — `13` and `10`. Other variants are also possible. For example, some MS-DOS text editors separated strings by only one code — `13`.

Reading data from text files string by string can be implemented using four approaches:

- Byte-by-byte reading from a file. When a delimiter is encountered, carry out an operation over the string read, and proceed with reading the next string. When doing so, naturally, it is necessary to account for the possible lack of the delimiter character in the end of the file. If you think that this method is too slow, I'd point out that Windows implements an efficient disk-caching algorithm. Therefore, the situation is not as bad as it seems.
- Reading data into a small buffer that can hold at least one text line. Having read the line, find the end-of-line character and carry out some operation over the string. Then, access the file and move the pointer to the start of the next line. Finally, repeat the operation.
- Reading data into the buffer of arbitrary length. After completing the read operation, search for all strings loaded into the buffer and carry out some operations over them. In this case, it is highly probable that one of the strings won't fit entirely into the buffer. You must take this situation into account.
- Reading data into the buffer capable of holding the entire file. This is a particular case of the third approach. From the programming point of view, it is the easiest to implement.

The program presented in Listing 11.5 implements the third approach.

Listing 11.5. An example illustrating the processing of a text file

```
; The FILES2.ASM file
.586P
; Flat memory model
.MODEL FLAT, stdcall
; Constants
STD_OUTPUT_HANDLE equ -11
GENERIC_READ       equ 80000000h
GENERIC_WRITE      equ 40000000h
GEN = GENERIC_READ or GENERIC_WRITE
SHARE = 0
OPEN_EXISTING    equ 3
; Prototypes of external procedures
EXTERN  ExitProcess@4:NEAR
EXTERN  GetCommandLineA@0:NEAR
EXTERN  CreateFileA@28:NEAR
EXTERN  CloseHandle@4:NEAR
EXTERN  ReadFile@20:NEAR
EXTERN  WriteFile@20:NEAR
EXTERN  CharToOemA@8:NEAR
;------------------------------------------------
; INCLUDELIB directives for the linker
includelib c:\masm32\lib\user32.lib
includelib c:\masm32\lib\kernel32.lib
;------------------------------------------------
; Data segment
_DATA SEGMENT
HANDL   DWORD ? ; Console descriptor
HFILE   DWORD ? ; File descriptor
BUF     DB 100 DUP(0)   ; Buffer for parameters
BUFER   DB 1000 DUP(0) ; Buffer for the file
NAMEOUT DB "CONOUT$"
INDS    DD 0 ; Number of the character in the string
INDB    DD 0 ; Number of the character in the buffer
NUMB    DD ?
NUMC    DD ?
PRIZN   DD 0
STROKA  DB 300 DUP(0)
_DATA ENDS
; Code segment
_TEXT SEGMENT
START:
```

```
; Get the output handle HANDLE (console as file)
     PUSH  0
     PUSH  0
     PUSH  OPEN_EXISTING
     PUSH  0
     PUSH  0
     PUSH  GEN
     PUSH  OFFSET NAMEOUT
     CALL  CreateFileA@28
     MOV   HANDL, EAX
; Get the number of parameters
     CALL  NUMPAR
     CMP   EAX, 1
     JE    NO_PAR
;-------------------------------------
; Get the parameter with the EDI number
     MOV   EDI, 2
     LEA   EBX, BUF
     CALL  GETPAR
; Open the file
     PUSH  0
     PUSH  0
     PUSH  OPEN_EXISTING
     PUSH  0
     PUSH  0
     PUSH  GEN
     PUSH  OFFSET BUF
     CALL  CreateFileA@28
     CMP   EAX, -1
     JE    NO_PAR
     MOV   HFILE, EAX
;++++++++++++++++++++++++++++++
LOO:
; Read 1000 bytes
     PUSH  0
     PUSH  OFFSET NUMB
     PUSH  1000
     PUSH  OFFSET BUFER
     PUSH  HFILE
     CALL  ReadFile@20
     MOV   INDB, 0
; Check whether the bytes are in the buffer
     CMP   NUMB, 0
```

```
    JZ     _CLOSE
; Fill the string
LOO1:
    MOV    EDI, INDS
    MOV    ESI, INDB
    MOV    AL, BYTE PTR BUFER[ESI]
    CMP    AL, 13 ; Check whether the end-of-line character has been encountered
    JE     _ENDSTR
    MOV    BYTE PTR STROKA[EDI], AL
    INC    ESI
    INC    EDI
    MOV    INDS, EDI
    MOV    INDB, ESI
    CMP    NUMB, ESI ; Check for the buffer end
    JNBE   LOO1
; Buffer end
    MOV    INDS, EDI
    MOV    INDB, ESI
    JMP    LOO
_ENDSTR:
; Carry out some operation with the string
    CALL   OUTST
; Reset the string to zero
    MOV    INDS, 0
; Go to another string in the buffer
    ADD    INDB, 2
; Has the buffer end been reached?
    MOV    ESI, INDB
    CMP    NUMB, ESI
    JAE    LOO1
    JMP    LOO
;++++++++++++++++++++++++++++++
_CLOSE:
; Check whether the string is empty
    CMP    INDS, 0
    JZ     CONT
; Carry out some operation over the string
    CALL   OUTST
CONT:
; Close the files
    PUSH   HFILE
    CALL   CloseHandle@4
; End of program operation
```

```
NO_PAR:
    PUSH  0
    CALL  ExitProcess@4
; Procedures
; The procedure for determining the number of parameters in the string
; Determine the number of parameters (->EAX)
NUMPAR PROC
    CALL  GetCommandLineA@0
    MOV   ESI, EAX ; Pointer to the string
    XOR   ECX, ECX ; Counter
    MOV   EDX, 1 ; Indicator
L1:
    CMP   BYTE PTR [ESI], 0
    JE    L4
    CMP   BYTE PTR [ESI], 32
    JE    L3
    ADD   ECX, EDX ; Parameter number
    MOV   EDX, 0
    JMP   L2
L3:
    OR    EDX, 1
L2:
    INC   ESI
    JMP   L1
L4:
    MOV   EAX, ECX
    RET
NUMPAR ENDP
; Get the parameter from the command line
; EBX - Points to the buffer, in which the parameter will be loaded
; Zero-terminated string is loaded into the buffer
; EDI - Parameter number
GETPAR PROC
    CALL  GetCommandLineA@0
    MOV   ESI, EAX ; Pointer to the string
    XOR   ECX, ECX ; Counter
    MOV   EDX, 1   ; Indicator
L1:
    CMP   BYTE PTR [ESI], 0
    JE    L4
    CMP   BYTE PTR [ESI], 32
    JE    L3
    ADD   ECX, EDX ; Parameter number
```

```
    MOV   EDX, 0
    JMP   L2
L3:
    OR    EDX, 1
L2:
    CMP   ECX, EDI
    JNE   L5
    MOV   AL, BYTE PTR [ESI]
    MOV   BYTE PTR [EBX], AL
    INC   EBX
L5:
    INC   ESI
    JMP   L1
L4:
    MOV   BYTE PTR [EBX], 0
    RET
GETPAR ENDP
; Output the string with the delimiter into the console
OUTST PROC
    MOV   EBX, INDS
    MOV   BYTE PTR STROKA[EBX], 0
    PUSH  OFFSET STROKA
    PUSH  OFFSET STROKA
    CALL  CharToOemA@8
; String is terminated by the delimiter
    MOV   BYTE PTR STROKA[EBX], 6
    INC   INDS
;Output string
    PUSH  0
    PUSH  OFFSET NUMC
    PUSH  INDS
    PUSH  OFFSET STROKA
    PUSH  HANDL
    CALL  WriteFile@20
    RET
OUTST ENDP
_TEXT ENDS
END START
```

The program presented in Listing 11.5 demonstrates one of the possible algorithms for processing text files — line-by-line reading of the text file. The program fragment responsible for reading and analyzing the text file is between the `LOO` label and the CONT label. Carefully consider the algorithms, and you'll decide that high-level language will never stimulate writing such algorithms. Consequently, the Assembly language stimulates your intellectual capabilities.

How To Obtain Time Attributes of a File

Now I will demonstrate how to obtain time attributes of a file using the GetFileTime function mentioned earlier in this chapter.

Listing 11.6. Obtaining time attributes of a file

```
.586P
; Flat memory model
.MODEL FLAT, stdcall
; Constants
STD_OUTPUT_HANDLE equ -11
GENERIC_READ      equ 80000000h
GENERIC_WRITE     equ 40000000h
GEN = GENERIC_READ or GENERIC_WRITE
OPEN_EXISTING   equ 3
; Prototypes of external procedures
EXTERN  CreateFileA@28:NEAR
EXTERN  lstrlenA@4:NEAR
EXTERN  GetStdHandle@4:NEAR
EXTERN  WriteConsoleA@20:NEAR
EXTERN  ExitProcess@4:NEAR
EXTERN  CloseHandle@4:NEAR
EXTERN  GetFileTime@16:NEAR
EXTERN  FileTimeToLocalFileTime@8:NEAR
EXTERN  FileTimeToSystemTime@8:NEAR
EXTERN  wsprintfA:NEAR
; Structures
; The FILETIME structure
FILETIME STRUC
  LOTIME    DD 0
  HITIME    DD 0
  FILETIME  ENDS
SYSTIME STRUC
  Y    DW 0   ; Year
  M    DW 0   ; Month
  DWE  DW 0   ; Day of week
  D    DW 0   ; Day of month
```

```
  H   DW 0   ; Hour
  MI  DW 0   ; Minute
  S   DW 0   ; Second
  MS  DW 0   ; Thousandths of a second
SYSTIME ENDS

; INCLUDELIB directives for the linker
includelib c:\masm32\lib\user32.lib
includelib c:\masm32\lib\kernel32.lib
;-----------------------------------------------------
; Data segment
_DATA SEGMENT
LENS    DD ? ; String length will be placed here
HANDL   DD ? ; Descriptor of the output console
HFILE   DD ? ; Descriptor of the file being opened
ERRS    DB 'Error!', 0 ; Error message
PATH    DB 'e:\backup3.pst', 0 ; Path to the file
FTMCR   FILETIME <0> ; For creation time
FTMAC   FILETIME <0> ; For access time
FTMWR   FILETIME <0> ; For modification time
LOCALS1 FILETIME <0> ; For local time
FORM    DB "Write time: Sec %lu Min %lu Hou %lu Day %lu Mon %lu Yea %lu", 0
SST     SYSTIME  <0> ; System time format
BUF     DB  60 DUP(0); Buffer for the formatted string
TEXT1   DB  'File: ', 0
_DATA ENDS
; Code segment
_TEXT SEGMENT
START:
; Get the output handle
    PUSH  STD_OUTPUT_HANDLE
    CALL  GetStdHandle@4
    MOV   HANDL, EAX
; Open the file
    PUSH  0             ; Must be 0
    PUSH  0             ; File attribute (if creating)
    PUSH  OPEN_EXISTING ; How to open
    PUSH  0             ; Pointer to the attribute
    PUSH  0             ; Generic access mode
    PUSH  GEN            ; Access mode
    PUSH  OFFSET PATH    ; Filename
    CALL  CreateFileA@28
; Check whether the file has been opened
```

```
    CMP     EAX, -1
    JNE     CONT
; Error message and exit
    LEA     EAX, ERRS
    MOV     EDI, 1
    CALL    WRITE
    JMP     EXI
CONT:
    MOV     HFILE, EAX
; Get the file time
    PUSH    OFFSET FTMWR
    PUSH    OFFSET FTMAC
    PUSH    OFFSET FTMCR
    PUSH    HFILE
    CALL    GetFileTime@16
; Convert the file time to local time
    PUSH    OFFSET LOCALS1
    PUSH    OFFSET FTMWR
    CALL    FileTimeToLocalFileTime@8
; Format to the system time format
    PUSH    OFFSET SST
    PUSH    OFFSET LOCALS1
    CALL    FileTimeToSystemTime@8
; Convert the string
    MOV     AX, SST.Y
    MOVZX   EAX, AX
    PUSH    EAX
    MOV     AX, SST.M
    MOVZX   EAX, AX
    PUSH    EAX
    MOV     AX, SST.D
    MOVZX   EAX, AX
    PUSH    EAX
    MOV     AX, SST.H
    MOVZX   EAX, AX
    PUSH    EAX
    MOV     AX, SST.MI
    MOVZX   EAX, AX
    PUSH    EAX
    MOV     AX, SST.S
    MOVZX   EAX, AX
    PUSH    EAX
    PUSH    OFFSET FORM
```

```
    PUSH   OFFSET BUF
    CALL   wsprintfA
; Release the stack
    ADD    ESP, 32
; Output information
    LEA    EAX, TEXT1
    MOV    EDI, 0
    CALL   WRITE
    LEA    EAX, PATH
    MOV    EDI, 1
    CALL   WRITE
    LEA    EAX, BUF
    MOV    EDI, 1
    CALL   WRITE
; Close the file
CLOSE:
    PUSH   HFILE
    CALL   CloseHandle@4
; Exit
    EXI:
    PUSH   0
    CALL   ExitProcess@4
; Output the string (terminated by the line feed)
; EAX — To the start of the string
; EDI — With or without line feed
WRITE   PROC
; Get the parameter length
    PUSH   EAX
    PUSH   EAX
    CALL   lstrlenA@4
    MOV    ESI, EAX
    POP    EBX
    CMP    EDI, 1
    JNE    NO_ENT
; Line feed in the end
    MOV    BYTE PTR [EBX+ESI], 13
    MOV    BYTE PTR [EBX+ESI+1], 10
    MOV    BYTE PTR [EBX+ESI+2], 0
    ADD    EAX, 2
    NO_ENT:
; String output
    PUSH   0
    PUSH   OFFSET LENS
```

```
    PUSH   EAX
    PUSH   EBX
    PUSH   HANDL
    CALL   WriteConsoleA@20
    RET
WRITE   ENDP
_TEXT ENDS
END START
```

As a result of execution of this program, the string with the filename and the string containing its last modification date in the "second minute hour day month year" format will be sent for output to the current console. Principally, this program is simple and doesn't need any comments. The only thing that I'd like to point out is the use of the `wsprintfA` function, because only it can cause any difficulties if you have read the book up to this chapter.

To translate this program using TASM32, proceed in a normal way:

1. Remove all `@N` suffixes.
2. Replace `wsprintfA` with `_wsprintfA`.
3. Include the IMPORT32.LIB library.

PART III: MORE SOPHISTICATED EXAMPLES OF WINDOWS PROGRAMMING

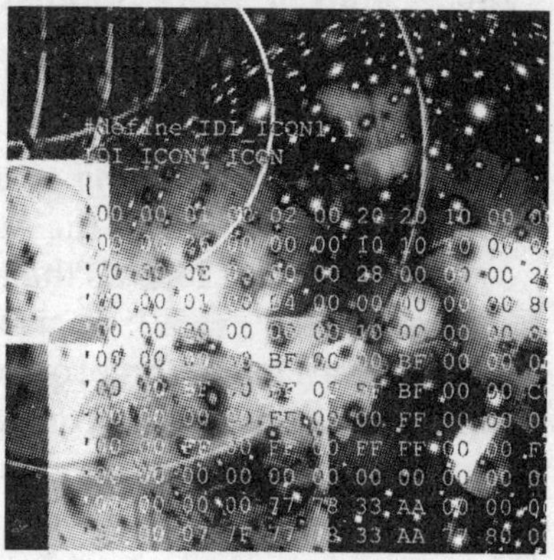

Chapter 12

Assembly Language Macro Tools and Directives

Well, you have finally made it to macros, although I tried to delay this moment as long as I could. The main part of this chapter can be classified as reference material. Why do I provide reference information in the middle of the book instead of the opening chapters? I am convinced that reference material in the first chapters may take away any interest you have in reading a book. Most material provided in this chapter is already known to you; consequently, you won't encounter any difficulties understanding it. Furthermore, the macros being considered here, in my opinion, prevent beginner programmers from feeling the beauty of the Assembly language. I have one practical goal: I want you to write programs that can be translated using both MASM and TASM.

Labels

A label followed by a colon defines the address of the command that follows the label.

The `LABEL` directive allows you to explicitly define the label type. The value of the label defined in this way is equal to the address of command or data that immediately follows it. For example: `LABEL L1 DWORD`.

The expression *NAME* `PROC` defines the label, to which the jump is usually carried out by `CALL`. The block of code starting from such a label is called a procedure. The jump to such a label can also be carried out using the `JMP` command, and the `CALL` command can be used for jumping to an ordinary label. This, of course, serves as proof of the power and flexibility of the Assembly language.

The line that follows the label can contain the data reservation directive, for example, `ERR DB 'Error'` or `NUM DWORD 0`. With a high-level language, you determine a global variable when proceeding in such a way. With Assembly language, there is no difference between the command and the data. Therefore, there also is no difference between the label defining a command and the label defining data. Since I have mentioned data, let me list their main types:

- `BYTE` (`DB`) — 1 byte
- `WORD` (`DW`) — 2 bytes
- `DWORD` (`DD`) — 4 bytes
- `FWORD` (`DF`) — 6 bytes
- `QWORD` (`DQ`) — 8 bytes
- `TBYTE` (`DT`) — 10 bytes

In terms of high-level languages, the `EQU` directive is used for defining constants. For example: `MES EQU "ERROR!"`, `LAB EQU 145H`. Using the `EQU` directive, it is possible to assign a value to the label only once. To the right of the `EQU` directive, an expression using arithmetical, logical, and bit operations can be placed. They are as follows: +, –, *, /, `MOD` (the remainder from the division), `AND`, `OR`, `NOT`, `XOR`, `SHR`, and `SHL`. Comparison operations also can be used, for example, `EQ`, `GE`, `GT`, `LE`, `LT`, and `NE`. The expression containing a comparison operation is considered Boolean. It takes the value of 0 if the logical condition is not satisfied; otherwise, it takes the value 1. Using the = directive, it is possible to assign integer values only; however, it is also possible to reassign values. Note that the expression can be a command operand: `MOV EAX, 16*16-1`. To assign purely string constants, use angle brackets, for example, `err equ <Incorrect procedure call>`.

Assignment using the = operator is less universal and can be used for assigning numeric values.

The `$` label always defines the current address.

In MASM, the labels within a procedure are automatically considered local. Consequently, label names in procedures can be duplicated. In TASM, all labels by default are interpreted as global. To make labels within a procedure local, precede them with the `@@` prefix and insert the `LOCALS` directive in the start of the program (see *Chapter 11*).

Often it is required that the data block in a program starts at the boundary that is a multiple of a specific number of bytes. This is achieved by the `ALIGN` directive. This keyword is followed by the required number of bytes. For example: `ALIGN 4`, `ALIGN 16`. The following is a fragment of a program containing a code segment, in which this directive is used:

```
_DATA SEGMENT
PATH   DB "C:\1.TXT"
HANDLE DD ?
ALIGN  4
```

```
BUF     DB 1000 DUP (0)
...
_DATA ENDS
```

The `ALIGN 4` directive used here ensures that the buffer designated by the `BUF` label will always start from a boundary that is a multiple of 4 bytes.

Structures

The `STRUC` directive allows you to join several dissimilar data values of different types. These data items are called structure fields. First, it is necessary to define the structure template using the `STRUC` keyword; then, using the < > directive, it is possible to define any number of structures. Consider the following example:

```
STRUC COMPLEX
   RE  DD ?
   IM  DD ?
STRUC ENDS
   ...
; In data segment
COMP1 COMPLEX <?>
COMP2 COMPLEX <0>
; Initialization by zero
```

Access to the structure fields is carried out by reference points, for example, `MOV COMP1.RE, EAX`.

NOTE

For working with string constants, MASM32 and TASM32 provide a large set of string macros: `CATSTR`, `INSTR`, and so on. However, we are not going to practice macro programming in Assembly language, therefore, we won' t consider these possibilities.

Unions

Unions are similar to structures. They also consist of individual records. However, there is one significant difference: The length of the union instance in memory is equal to the length of its longest field. All fields will start with the same address — the one, in which the union will start. The sense of a union is that the same memory area can be considered in the context of the same data type.

An example of a union appears as follows:

```
EXTCHAR   UNION
   ascii      DB ?
   extascii   DW ?
EXTCHAR ENDS
```

This union is an extended definition of the ASCII code. To use a union in your program, it is necessary to define the union in a way similar to defining structures.

```
   ; In data segment
   easc EXTCHAR <0>
```

Now, you will have a 2-byte structure. Access to the entire word is carried out through the `extascii` field: `MOV easc.extascii, AX`. Access to the least significant byte of the word is through the `ascii` field: `MOV easc.ascii, AL`.

A Convenient Method of Working with Structures

There is one convenient method of working with structures and unions that deserves a special mention. It is based on the `ASSUME` directive. Actually, I make practically no use of this directive in this book. When programming for MS-DOS, this directive is mainly used to inform the assembler that the segment register points to the current segment. However, this directive can be used with more than segment registers. Here is the fragment that illustrates such a technique.

```
COMPLEX STRUC
        RE   DD ?
        IM   DD ?
COMPLEX ENDS
.
.
.
; In data segment
COMP COMPLEX <0>
; In code segment
      MOV     EBX, OFFSET COMP
      ASSUME EBX:PTR COMPLEX
      MOV     [EBX].RE, 10
      MOV     [EBX].IM, 10
      ASSUME EBX:NOTHING
```

Actually, the `MOV [EBX].RE, 10` command is equivalent to `MOV DWORD PTR [EBX], 10`, and the `MOV [EBX].IM, 10` command is equivalent to `MOV DWORD PTR [EBX+4], 10`. You likely will agree that this is very convenient.

Conditional Assembling

Conditional assembling provides the possibility of bypassing specific program fragments when assembling. There are the following types of conditional assembling:

A)

```
IF expression
...

ENDIF
```

B)

```
IF expression
...

ELSE
...

ENDIF
```

C)

```
IF expression 1
...

ELSEIF expression 2
...

ELSEIF expression 3
...

ELSE
...

ENDIF
```

The expression is considered to be satisfied if the expression takes a nonzero value; otherwise, the condition is not satisfied.

MASM and TASM support several special-purpose directives for conditional assembling.

A)

```
IFE expression
...
```

```
    ELSEIFE
    ...
    ENDIFE
```

B) The `IF1` and `IF2` operators check the first and the second pass of assembling.

C) The `IFDEF` operator checks whether a symbolic name is defined in the program; `IFDEFN` is an inverse operator.

There are other types of `IF` operators. The required information can be found in any reference on Assembly language.

D) There is the large set of directives starting with `.ERR`. For example, `.ERRE` will cause the assembling process stop and will display an error message if the condition takes the value 0.

Conditional assembling will be used in the end of this chapter to write the example program that can be translated using both MASM and TASM.

Procedure Calls

You have become acquainted with the simplified method of calling procedures in MASM. This is the `INVOKE` directive. The procedure must be defined beforehand using the `PROTO` keyword, for example:

```
MessageBoxA PROTO :DWORD,:DWORD,:DWORD,:DWORD

...

invoke MessageBox, h, ADDR TheMsg, ADDR TitleW, MB_OK
```

Here, `h` is the descriptor of the window, from which the message is called, `TheMsg` is the message string, `TitleW` is the window header, and `MB_OK` is the message type. `ADDR` in this case is synonymous to `OFFSET`.

The TASM syntax also has a simplified call.

```
EXTERN MESSAGEBOX:PROC
...
call MessageBox PASCAL, h, ADDR TheMsg, ADDR TitleW, MB_OK
```

Here, `PASCAL` is the call type, or, to be more precise, the order of parameters. It is also possible to use the `C` parameter; then the order of parameters will be inverted.

Macro Repetitions

Macro repetition specifies the repetition of a directive specified several times. For this purpose, the REPT directive is used, for example:

```
A EQU 10
  REPT 100
  DB A
ENDM
```

This will generate 100 DB 10 directives. It is convenient to use the = operator with this directive, because it allows you to change the variable value multiple times, for example, using expressions like A = A + 5.

The IRP directive has the following format:

```
IRP parameter,<list>
...
ENDM
```

The block will be called the number of times corresponding to the number of parameters in the list. For example:

```
IRP   REG, <EAX, EBX, ECX, EDX, ESI, EDI>
PUSH  REG
ENDM
```

This will generate the following lines of code:

```
PUSH  EAX
PUSH  EBX
PUSH  ECX
PUSH  EDX
PUSH  ESI
PUSH  EDI
```

The IRPC directive is as follows:

```
IRPC  parameter, cstring
Operators
ENDM
```

For example:

```
IRPC  CHAR, azklg
CMP   AL, '&CHAR&'
JZ    EndC
ENDM
EndC:
```

This fragment is the equivalent of the following sequence:

```
    CMP  AL, 'a'
    JZ   EndC
    CMP  AL, 'z'
    JZ   EndC
    CMP  AL, 'k'
    JZ   EndC
    CMP  AL, 'l'
    JZ   EndC
    CMP  AL, 'g'
    JZ   EndC
EndC:
```

The `&` character in the latter example is used to specify that the parameter of the repeat block must be computed even within the quotation marks. The `&` character stands for the macro operation that works within the repeat block, because repeat blocks are one of the types of macro commands.

Macro Definitions

The general format of a macro definition appears as follows:

```
Name MACRO parameters
  ...

  ENDM
```

Having defined the block once, it is possible to use it multiple times in the program. Depending on the values of the parameters, the section being replaced can take different values. If the specified section is presumed to be reused multiple times — for example, within a loop — then the macro definition provides indisputable advantages in comparison to a procedure because it speeds up the code execution, for example:

```
EXC MACRO par1, par2
    PUSH  par1
    POP   par2
    ENDM
```

This macro definition will exchange contents between parameters. For example, `EXC EAX, EBX` is equivalent to `PUSH EAX\POP EAX`, `EXC MEM1, ESI` is equivalent to `PUSH MEM1\POP ESI`, and so on. Note that if the first parameter is a number, this will load this number into the second operand.

The problem of labels is important with respect to macro definitions. If you use normal labels in macro definitions, then a collision would occur if you use that macro definition more than once. This collision can be avoided by declaring local labels. To achieve this, the LOCAL keyword is used, for example:

```
EXC MACRO par1, par2
    LOCAL EXI
    CMP   par1, par2
    JE    EXI
    PUSH  par1
    POP   par2
EXI:
ENDM
```

This macro definition can be reused as many times as needed, because the assembler will generate a unique label in the course of each substitution.

To exit a macro definition (to stop its generation), the EXITM directive is used. This directive will be useful if you are using conditional constructs, such as IF...ENDIF, in your macro definition.

Now, consider another example of a useful macro.

```
ustring MACRO quoted_text, ptr_buf
   LOCAL asc_txt
      .data
      asc_txt db quoted_text, 0
      .code
      invoke MultiByteToWideChar, CP_ACP, 0,
      OFFSET asc_txt, -1, OFFSET ptr_buf, LENGTHOF ptr_buf
      ENDM
```

This macro converts the specified ASCII string into the Unicode string and loads it into the buffer pointed to by ptr_buf. In a more general form, this macro will appear as follows:

```
ustring MACRO quoted_text, ptr_buf
LOCAL asc_txt
.data
   asc_txt db quoted_text, 0
.code
   PUSH  LENGTHOF ptr_buf
   PUSH  OFFSET BUF ; Buffer address
   PUSH  -1
   PUSH  OFFSET asc_txt
   PUSH  0
   PUSH  0
   CALL  MultiByteToWideChar@24
ENDM
```

For example, consider the following code fragment:

```
ustring "Hello!", buf ; Buf — In data segment
PUSH  0
PUSH  OFFSET buf
PUSH  OFFSET buf
PUSH  0
CALL  MessageBoxW@16 ; Output of the Unicode string
```

It is convenient; do you agree?

Some Other Assembler Directives

In addition to declarations using the `PUBLIC` and `EXTERN` directives, it is possible to declare macros using the `GLOBAL` directive, which is equivalent to the combination of `PUBLIC` and `EXTERN`.

- `PURGE` *`macro name`* — This directive cancels the loading of the specified macro. It is used when working with the library of macros to avoid a memory shortage.
- `LENGTHOF` — This macro defines the number of data elements. `SIZEOF` defines the data size (both are missing in TASM).

The following are directives for specifying the command set:

- `.8086` — Only commands from the 8086 microprocessor command set are allowed. This directive is used by default.
- `.186` — 186 commands are allowed.
- `.286` and `.286P` — Commands from the i286 processor's command set are allowed. The `P` suffix here and later means that the protected mode commands are allowed.
- `.386` and `.386P` — Stand for allowing the i386 microprocessor's command set.
- `.486` and `.486P` — Commands of the i486 processor are allowed.
- `.586` and `.586P` — This means that Pentium (P5) processor commands are allowed.
- `.686` and `.686P` — Pentium Pro and Pentium II (P6) commands are allowed.
- `.8087` — Commands of the i8087 coprocessor are allowed.
- `.287` — i286 coprocessor commands are allowed.
- `.387` — i387 coprocessor commands are allowed.
- `.MMX` — MMX extension commands are allowed.

The directives for controlling the listing are as follows:

- `NAME` — Specifies the module name.
- `TITLE` — Defines the listing title.

NOTE

By default, both the module name and the listing name match the filename.

- SUBTTL — Defines the listing subtitle.
- PAGE — Defines the size of the listing page: width and height. The PAGE directive without arguments starts a new listing page.
- .LIST — Outputs a listing.
- .XLIST — Does not produce the listing.
- .SALL — Suppresses the printing of macros.
- .SFCOND — Suppresses the printing of conditional blocks with false conditions.
- .LFCOND — Prints conditional blocks with false conditions.
- .CREF — Allows cross-referencing of the listing.
- .XCREF — Suppresses cross-referencing of the listing.

Run-Time Constructs

The constructs in the next two sections are converted to the microprocessor commands in the course of assembling.

Conditional Constructs

A)

```
.IF condition
...
.ENDIF
```

B)

```
.IF condition
...
.ELSE
...
.ENDIF
```

C)

```
.IF condition 1
...
```

```
.ELSEIF condition 2
...
.ELSEIF condition 3
...

...
.ELSE
...
.ENDIF
```

Consider the following fragment containing a conventional construct and the corresponding Assembly code:

```
.IF EAX==12H
   MOV  EAX, 10H
.ELSE
   MOV  EAX, 15H
.ENDIF
```

The preceding fragment is equivalent to the following Assembly code:

```
   CMP  EAX, 12H
   JNE  NO_EQ
   MOV  EAX, 10H
   JMP  EX_BLOK
NO_EQ:
   MOV  EAX, 15H
EX_BLOK:
```

It is rather convenient. However, do not be too enthusiastic about it because, in my opinion, this will carry you from the art of Assembly language programming.

The WHILE Loop

```
.WHILE condition
...

.ENDW
```

For example:

```
WHILE EAX<64H
ADD   EAX, 10H
ENDW
```

For MASM, the following is used:

```
    JMP   L2
L1:
    ADD   EAX, 10H
L2
    CMP   EAX, 64H
    JB    L1
```

For TASM, the following is used:

```
L1:
    CMP   EAX, 64H
    JNB   EXI
    ADD   EAX, 10H
    JMP   L1
EXI:
```

There is a minor differences related to how the two assemblers translate the `.IF` and `.WHILE` directives. TASM32 automatically optimizes the code by adding extra no-operation (`NOP`) commands to align by the quadruple word boundary. This makes the program execution somewhat faster but increases its size. I prefer the MASM attitude.

Developing Programs Equally Translatable in MASM and TASM

Now, consider the problem of writing programs equally translatable by both MASM and TASM. Conditional assembling is suited to this purpose. The most convenient approach is using the `IFDEF` directive and the ability of assemblers to specify symbolic constants. Both ML and TASM32 support the `/D` option, allowing you to specify such constants.

Listing 12.1 demonstrates a program that can be translated by both MASM and TASM. This program is easy. However, carefully studying this example will allow you to create more sophisticated compatible programs.

Listing 12.1. Using conventional assembling to develop a compatible program

```
.586P
; Flat memory model
.MODEL FLAT, STDCALL
; Check whether the MASM symbolic constant is defined
IFDEF MASM
; Work with MASM
 EXTERN      ExitProcess@4:NEAR
```

```
 EXTERN      MessageBoxA@16:NEAR
 includelib c:\masm32\lib\kernel32.lib
 includelib c:\masm32\lib\user32.lib
ELSE
; Work with TASM
 EXTERN     ExitProcess:NEAR
 EXTERN     MessageBoxA:NEAR
 includelib c:\tasm32\lib\import32.lib
 ExitProcess@4 = ExitProcess
 MessageBoxA@16 = MessageBoxA
ENDIF
;--------------------------------------------------
; Data segment
_DATA SEGMENT
 MSG DB "An easy program", 0
    TIT DB "Title", 0
_DATA ENDS
; Code segment
_TEXT SEGMENT
START:
      PUSH  0
      PUSH  OFFSET TIT
      PUSH  OFFSET MSG
      PUSH  0 ; Screen descriptor
      CALL  MessageBoxA@16
;----------------------------------------
     PUSH  0
     CALL ExitProcess@4
_TEXT ENDS
END START
```

To translate the program using MASM, use the following:

```
ML /c /coff /DMASM PROG.ASM
LINK /SUBSYSTEM:WINDOWS PROG.OBJ
```

To translate the same program using TASM, use the following:

```
TASM32 /ml PROG.ASM
TLINK32 -aa PROG.OBJ
```

As you can see, everything is reduced to checking whether the MASM symbolic constant is defined (the `/DMASM` command-line option). Another problem is adding the `@N` suffix. You bypass this problem by using the = operator, with which the names are redefined.

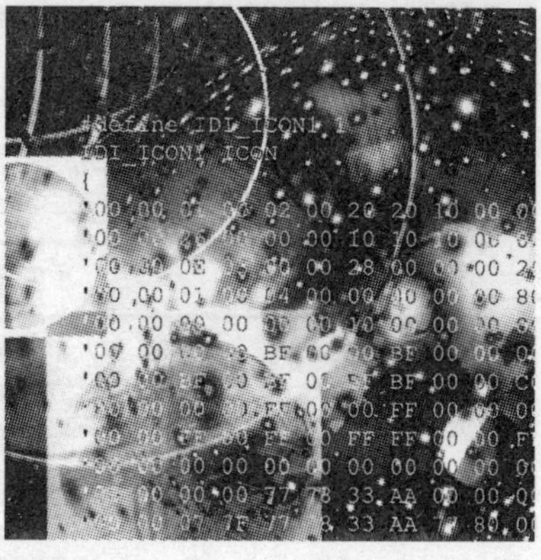

Chapter 13

More about File Management

Because of the importance of the `CreateFile` function, I decided to dedicate a separate chapter to it. Here, I demonstrate the variety of capabilities of this versatile function. I also cover some other application program interface (API) functions related to file management. Besides files, I cover some other input/output devices.

A Detailed Description of the CreateFile Function

Windows operates with the concept of devices. This approach allows it to unify the processes of obtaining and transmitting information, which means that the same API functions are used for data reception and transmission. Table 13.1 lists these devices.

Table 13.1. Main devices for information exchange in the Windows operating system

Device name	Explanation
Pipes	There are two types of pipes: named and anonymous. Named pipes are used for connecting the source and destination through the local area network. Anonymous pipes play the same role within the limits of the same computer.

continues

Table 13.1 *Continued*

Device name	Explanation
Directories	Directories exist as the structural units of file systems. Direct information exchange with a directory can change its attributes (e.g., the file compression attribute for the directory contents).
Communications resources	Mainly, these are devices such as COM and LPT ports, which exchange information with printers, modems, etc.
Console	Text screen and information input/output into the text screen.
Logical	This type includes hard disk partitions and floppy drives. Formatting is the main operation that can cause data exchange.
Mailslots	This allows the transmission of information from several sources to the same destination within the limits of a single computer, a local area network, or domain.
Sockets	Sockets are devices that exchange information between two computers supporting the sockets mechanism.
Files	These devices permanently store large volumes of information.
Physical	These provide access to hard disk structures (e.g., a partition table or structures residing on a partition).

Now, having briefly considered the contents of Table 13.1, it's time to discover the most interesting fact: most of the devices listed in this table can be opened using the `CreateFile` function. Clearly, this function deserves a detailed description and your maximum attention.

In this section, you will consider this function in the file management context. Because the first argument of the `CreateFile` function is the fully qualified filename (the path to the file and its name), it is necessary to briefly consider the rules that must be followed when forming this string parameter.

- For creating a filename, the characters of the current code page with codes larger than 31 must be used.
- The components of the filename are delimited by the `/` and `\` symbols. The name of the file residing on a shared network resource must start with the `\\server\share` prefix. Here, *`server`* is the name of network computer, and *`share`* is the name of the shared network resource (the universal naming convention name).
- The `.` character designates the current directory, and `..` stands for the parent directory. Additionally, the last `.` character in the string separates the filename from the filename extension used by the operating system for recognizing the file type.
- Symbols such as <, >, :, /, |, and \ are invalid for filenames and directory names.

- ❒ Names of devices (e.g., `aux`, `con`, and `prn`) cannot be used as filenames.
- ❒ A fully qualified filename must be represented by a zero-terminated string. The maximum length of such a string is defined by the `MAX_LEN` system constant, which is equal to 260 characters. To use longer strings, it is necessary to employ Unicode encoding and the appropriate version of the `CreateFile` function. In this case, the string must start with the `\\?\` prefix, and the string length can reach 32,000 characters.
- ❒ Functions that use filenames as parameters are insensitive to the case of English characters.
- ❒ Reserved keywords such as `CLOCK$`, `NUL`, `COM1`, and `LPT1` cannot be used as names of files or directories.

NOTE

All devices listed in Table 13.1 are representatives of the kernel objects class. To be more precise, they become kernel objects after they are created using `CreateFile` or any similar function (thus, the `CreateFile` name reflects the essence of the problem). Structures describing objects are stored in the kernel area, which means that they are protected against access by user programs. All such objects are accessed using the descriptor returned when the object is created. Note that the descriptor describes the object only within the limits of the given process.

Now, it is time to consider the parameters accepted by the `CreateFile` function.

- ❒ First parameter — Address of the string containing the filename.
- ❒ Second parameter — Defines how the data will be exchanged with this device. The following values are possible:
  - `0` — It is assumed that there will be no data read or write operations. Only file parameters will be changed (time characteristics, attributes, etc.).
  - `GENERIC_READ = 80000000h` — Data read from the file is expected.
  - `GENERIC_WRITE = 40000000h` — Data write into the file is expected.
  - `GENERIC_READ | GENERIC_WRITE` — This combination allows data read and data write operations.
  - Additionally, this parameter can contain several flags that specify access rights to this file (or to another device). All of these flags are listed in the documentation but are rarely used. For example, the `DELETE = 10000h` value specifies that the file (object) can be deleted.
- ❒ Third parameter — This parameter specifies the type of access to the file. To be more precise, this parameter specifies the desired access, because in practice

the file or object access can be limited because the required object might already be opened by another process. The possible values of this parameter are as follows:

- `0` — Other processes cannot have exclusive access to this file. If the file is already opened by another process, this value of the parameter won't allow you to open the file elsewhere.
- `FILE_SHARE_READ = 1` — This setting enables subsequent open operations on the object to request read access. Otherwise, other processes cannot open the object if they request read access.
- `FILE_SHARE_WRITE = 2` — This setting enables subsequent open operations on the object to request write access. Otherwise, other processes cannot open the object if they request write access.
- `FILE_SHARE_WRITE | FILE_SHARE_READ` — This value allows subsequent open operations on the object to request read and write access. The operation will fail only if another process has already opened this object in exclusive mode.
- `FILE_SHARE_DELETE = 4` — This allows other processes to access the object and delete it.

❒ Fourth parameter — This parameter points to a special structure called `SECURITY_ATTRIBUTES`. This structure allows you to specify security information and determine whether the descriptor returned by the `CreateFile` function must be inherited. Most frequently, this parameter is set to `NULL`. This means that the descriptor is not inherited. Consider the `SECURITY_ATTRIBUTES` structure:

```
SECURITY_ATTRIBUTES STRUC
    L           DD ?
    DESC        DD ?
    INHER       DD ?
SECURITY_ATTRIBUTES ENDS
```

As you can see, the structure includes only three fields. The first field determines the length of the entire structure; in this case, it must be 12 bytes. The second field is the inheritable descriptor. The third field takes the values 0 or 1. If the field value is 1, then all child processes will inherit the descriptor.

❒ Fifth parameter — This parameter defines the behavior of the `CreateFile` function if the file lacks the specified name.

- `CREATE_NEW = 1` — This parameter instructs the system to create a new file if the file with the specified name is missing; otherwise, the function doesn't execute.
- `CREATE_ALWAYS = 2` — This parameter instructs the system to create the file in any case. If the file with the specified name exists, it will be overwritten.

- OPEN_EXISTING = 3 — This setting instructs the system to open the file with the specified name if it exists.
- OPEN_ALWAYS = 4 — This parameter instructs the system to open the file if it exists, or to create a new file if the file with the specified name is missing.
- TRUNCATE_EXISTING = 5 — This parameter instructs the system to open the existing file and reset its size to zero. If the file is missing, the function doesn't execute.

❒ Sixth parameter — This parameter is mainly used for defining the attributes of the file being created (the attribute list was provided in *Chapter 11*). Additionally, here you can specify flags that allow the system to optimize caching algorithms. There are also other flags, the values of which are as follows:

- FILE_FLAG_NO_BUFFERING = 20000000h — The file must be accessed without data buffering.
- FILE_FLAG_SEQUENTIAL_SCAN = 8000000h — If this flag is set, the system assumes that the file is accessed sequentially. Accordingly, the maximum reading rate can be achieved with sequential reading.
- FILE_FLAG_RANDOM_ACCESS = 10000000h — This flag is used for indicating that the system must not read large volumes of redundant data. It should be used if frequent searching in the file is expected.
- FILE_FLAG_WRITE_THROUGH = 80000000h — This flag disables write-through caching when writing into a file. In this case, all changes are written immediately to the disk.
- FILE_FLAG_DELETE_ON_CLOSE = 4000000h — If this flag is set, then the operating system will delete this file after all its descriptors are closed.
- FILE_FLAG_BACKUP_SEMANTICS = 2000000h — This flag is used in backup software.
- FILE_FLAG_POSIX_SEMANTICS = 1000000h — This instructs the system to take into account the case of characters when creating or opening a file.
- FILE_FLAG_OPEN_REPARSE_POINT = 200000h — This flag instructs the system to ignore the presence of the reparse point (see *Chapter 11*).
- FILE_FLAG_OPEN_NO_RECALL = 100000h — If this flag is set, the system doesn't restore the file from remote storage (see *Chapter 11*).
- FILE_FLAG_OVERLAPED = 40000000h — This flag sets asynchronous data exchange with the device. This topic will be covered later in this chapter.

❒ Seventh parameter — This parameter can contain the descriptor of a file already opened. When the file that already exists is opened, the attributes defined by this parameter are used. Usually this parameter is set to NULL.

If the function fails, it returns the INVALID_HANDLE_VALUE = -1.

Other Capabilities of the CreateFile Function

The `CreateFile` function is universal. This is because of the concept of a device adopted in the Windows operating system. In one of examples provided in *Chapter 11* (see Listing 11.4), I used the `CreateFile` function for console output. Now, consider another example that demonstrates the principles of working with mailslots.

Mailslot

This device allows information to be exchanged between processes within the framework of a local area network, not only within a single computer. The only problem is that the mailslot volume doesn't exceed 64 KB. Nevertheless, after considering the mechanism of transmitting data using mailslots, you'll understand that the mailslot size isn't important because under the condition of bidirectional transmission, it is possible to transfer information in sequential blocks.

The main idea of the mailslot mechanism is as follows:

- Every process can create a mailslot using the `CreateMailslot` function. If this function completes successfully, the process gets the mailslot descriptor and the possibility of reading data from it using the `ReadFile` function (as if it were a file). The process that has created the mailslot is called the server.
- After the mailslot is created, any process can connect to it (open the mailslot) using the `CreateFile` function and write a portion of data there using the `WriteFile` function.
- The mailslot is closed when the process that generated it terminates or when all duplicates of the mailslot handle are closed using the `CloseHandle` function.
- When working with the mailslot, the following conventions about the mailslot name should be observed.
  - In general, when creating a mailslot, the `\\.\mailslot\[`*`path`*`]`*`name`* name is used. Here, *`name`* is the mailslot name, and *`path`* is the path that can consist of the names of several directories separated by a slash. Note that these directories have nothing in common with the directories existing on the disk.
  - When a mailslot is opened for reading, the name used when creating it must be used. For example, if the texts mailslot was created — that is, the `\\.\mailslot\texts` full name was used — then the same string must be used when opening the mailslot for reading.
  - If it is necessary to open the mailslot for writing and this mailslot is located on another computer of the local area network, then the following string must be used: `\\`*`ComputerName`*`\mailslot\[`*`path`*`]`*`name`*. Here, *`ComputerName`* is the network name of the required computer.

- If processes that create mailslots operate within the same domain, then it is possible to create a shared mailslot for several processes. For this purpose, all processes must create a mailslot with the same name. If you now open the mailslot for writing using the `CreateFile` function and specify the name in the following format: `\\`*`DomainName`*`\mailslot\[`*`path`*`]`*`name`*, where *`DomainName`* is the name of the domain, then all processes that have created this mailslot will receive messages. In addition, it is also possible to use the `\\*\mailslot\[`*`path`*`]name` for the primary domain.

Thus, after learning the main theory behind mailslots, it is possible to implement practical examples. Listings 13.1 and 13.2 provide the source code of the server software that creates a mailslot and reads messages from there, and the client that sends messages to that mailslot. Note that I have used the results of previous chapters and have written programs that can be translated using both MASM32 and TASM32. Note that starting from this chapter, most programs will be presented in this universal form.

Listing 13.1. The server software (SERVER.ASM) creates a mailslot and waits for messages

```
; Server that creates a mailslot and reads from there
.586P
; Flat memory model
.MODEL FLAT, stdcall
; Constants
STD_OUTPUT_HANDLE       equ -11
MAILSLOT_WAIT_FOREVER   equ -1
; Prototypes of external procedures
IFDEF MASM
        EXTERN  ReadFile@20:NEAR
        EXTERN  CloseHandle@4:NEAR
        EXTERN  lstrlenA@4:NEAR
        EXTERN  WriteConsoleA@20:NEAR
        EXTERN  CreateMailslotA@16:NEAR
        EXTERN  ExitProcess@4:NEAR
        EXTERN  GetStdHandle@4:NEAR
ELSE
        EXTERN  ReadFile:NEAR
        EXTERN  CloseHandle:NEAR
        EXTERN  lstrlenA:NEAR
        EXTERN  WriteConsoleA:NEAR
        EXTERN  CreateMailslotA:NEAR
        EXTERN  GetStdHandle:NEAR
```

```
        EXTERN  ExitProcess:NEAR
        WriteConsoleA@20 = WriteConsoleA
        ReadFile@20 = ReadFile
        lstrlenA@4 = lstrlenA
        CreateMailslotA@16 = CreateMailslotA
        ExitProcess@4  = ExitProcess
        GetStdHandle@4 = GetStdHandle
        CloseHandle@4 =  CloseHandle
ENDIF

; INCLUDELIB directives for the linker
IFDEF MASM
        includelib c:\masm32\lib\user32.lib
        includelib c:\masm32\lib\kernel32.lib
ELSE
        includelib c:\tasm32\lib\import32.lib
ENDIF
;-----------------------------------------------
; Data segment
_DATA SEGMENT
        LENS    DD ? ; String length will be placed here
        PATHM DB "\\.\mailslot\mail1", 0
        BUFER DB 1000 DUP(0)
        H       DD ?
        N       DD ?
        HANDL DD ?
        ERRS DB 'Error!', 0
_DATA ENDS
; Code segment
_TEXT SEGMENT
START:
        PUSH  STD_OUTPUT_HANDLE
        CALL  GetStdHandle@4
        MOV   HANDL, EAX
; Create a mailslot
        PUSH  0
        PUSH  MAILSLOT_WAIT_FOREVER
        PUSH  0
        PUSH  OFFSET PATHM
        CALL  CreateMailslotA@16
        CMP   EAX, -1
        JNZ   CON
        LEA   EAX, ERRS
```

```
        MOV   EDI, 1
        CALL  WRITE
        JMP   EXI
CON:
        MOV   H, EAX
; Read from the mailslot
        PUSH  0
        PUSH  OFFSET N
        PUSH  1000
        PUSH  OFFSET BUFER
        PUSH  H
        CALL  ReadFile@20
; Output the contents
        LEA   EAX, BUFER
        MOV   EDI, 1
        CALL  WRITE
; Close the mailslot
        PUSH  H
        CALL  CloseHandle@4
; Exit the program
EXI:
        PUSH  0
        CALL  ExitProcess@4
; Display the string (terminated with line feed)
; EAX — To the start of the string
; EDI — With or without the line feed
WRITE   PROC
; Get the parameter length
        PUSH  EAX
        PUSH  EAX
        CALL  lstrlenA@4
        MOV   ESI, EAX
        POP   EBX
        CMP   EDI, 1
        JNE   NO_ENT
; Trailing line feed
        MOV   BYTE PTR [EBX+ESI], 13
        MOV   BYTE PTR [EBX+ESI+1], 10
        MOV   BYTE PTR [EBX+ESI+2], 0
        ADD   EAX, 2
NO_ENT:
; String output
        PUSH  0
```

```
        PUSH  OFFSET LENS
        PUSH  EAX
        PUSH  EBX
        PUSH  HANDL
        CALL  WriteConsoleA@20
        RET
        WRITE   ENDP
_TEXT ENDS
END START
```

The SERVER.ASM program creates a mailslot and then calls the `ReadFile` function. Note that when creating the mailslot, the `MAILSLOT_WAIT_FOREVER` parameter was set. This means that the `ReadFile` function will wait infinitely for the data to arrive at the mailslot. The function returns control only after the arrival of the data. The mailslot contents are then displayed on the console.

To translate this program using MASM32, issue the following:

```
ML /c /coff /DMASM server.ASM
LINK /SUBSYSTEM:CONSOLE server.OBJ
```

To translate the same program using TASM32, issue the following:

```
TASM32 /ml server.ASM
TLINK32 -ap server.OBJ
```

Listing 13.2. The client program (CLIENT.ASM) opens the mailslot and writes information there

```
; Client that opens the mailslot and writes information into it
.586P
; Flat memory model
.MODEL FLAT, stdcall
; Constants
STD_OUTPUT_HANDLE  equ -11
GENERIC_WRITE      equ 40000000h
FILE_SHARE_READ    equ 1h
OPEN_EXISTING      equ 3
; Prototypes of external procedures
IFDEF MASM
       EXTERN  WriteFile@20:NEAR
       EXTERN  CreateFileA@28:NEAR
       EXTERN  ExitProcess@4:NEAR
       EXTERN  CloseHandle@4:NEAR
```

```
ELSE
        EXTERN  WriteFile:NEAR
        EXTERN  CreateFileA:NEAR
        EXTERN  ExitProcess:NEAR
        EXTERN  CloseHandle:NEAR
        WriteFile@20 = WriteFile
        CreateFileA@28 = CreateFileA
        ExitProcess@4 = ExitProcess
        CloseHandle@4 =  CloseHandle
ENDIF

; INCLUDELIB directives for the linker
IFDEF MASM
        includelib c:\masm32\lib\user32.lib
        includelib c:\masm32\lib\kernel32.lib
ELSE
        includelib c:\tasm32\lib\import32.lib
ENDIF
;-----------------------------------------------
; Data segment
_DATA SEGMENT
        PATHM DB "\\.\mailslot\mail1", 0
        H  DD ?
        MES DB 'Hello! Server!', 0
        N   DD ?
_DATA ENDS
; Code segment
_TEXT SEGMENT
        START:
        ; Open the mailslot
        PUSH  0                     ; Must be zero
        PUSH  0                     ; File attribute doesn't matter
        PUSH  OPEN_EXISTING         ; How to open
        PUSH  0                     ; Pointer to the security attribute
        PUSH  FILE_SHARE_READ       ; Shared access mode
        PUSH  GENERIC_WRITE         ; Access type
        PUSH  OFFSET PATHM          ; Mailslot name
        CALL  CreateFileA@28
        MOV   H, EAX
        ; Write data to the mailslot
        PUSH  0
        PUSH  OFFSET N
        PUSH  16 ; Message length
```

```
        PUSH   OFFSET MES
        PUSH   H
        CALL   WriteFile@20
        ; Close the mailslot
        PUSH   H
        CALL   CloseHandle@4
        ; Exit
EXI:
        PUSH   0
        CALL   ExitProcess@4
_TEXT ENDS
END START
```

The client program opens the mailslot using the `CreateFile` function. Having received the descriptor, it can send the data to the mailslot. The program sends a zero-terminated string.

To translate this program using MASM32, issue the following commands:

```
ML /c /coff /DMASM client.ASM
LINK /SUBSYSTEM:CONSOLE client.OBJ
```

To translate it using TASM32, use the following:

```
TASM32 /ml client.ASM
TLINK32 -ap client.OBJ
```

The programs in Listings 13.1 and 13.2 are simple. The server program carries out a single data-read operation from the mailslot. There are no difficulties in using the mailslot for permanent data exchange. For this purpose, it is necessary to remember the following:

- The mailslot is released in the course of data read.
- In the course of the write operation, the contents of the mailslot are overwritten.

Principally, the client also can create a mailslot, in which there will be bidirectional data exchange between the client and the server.

Pipes

Pipes provide an efficient method of bidirectional data exchange between processes. There are two types of pipes: anonymous and named. Anonymous pipes will be covered in *Chapter 18* (see Listing 18.3). This type of pipes is convenient for use within the framework of a single application for data exchange between two processes. Named pipes are more powerful. They allow data to be exchanged with applications located on different computers within a local area network. In particular, the Microsoft SQL Server uses named pipes as one of the possible mechanisms of information exchange with clients.

Naturally, before using a named pipe, it is necessary to create it. For this purpose, the `CreateNamePipe` function is used. The process that creates the named pipe is called the server. When creating a named pipe, it is necessary to set several parameters that influence the way, in which this object will operate. The list of these parameters includes the parameter that defines the mode of operation through the pipe. Three modes of operation can be set:

- Bidirectional (duplex) — This method assumes the possibility of bidirectional data exchange: from server to client and from client to server.
- Two unidirectional (simplex) pipes — They assume unidirectional data transmission only.

Generally, the pipe name is represented by the following string: `\\.\pipe\`*`pipename`*. Here, *`pipename`* is the name of the pipe. As with mailslots, for named pipes it is possible to set the mode for infinite waiting. In this case, the `ReadFile` and `WriteFile` functions will complete execution only when data transmission is completed. Having created the pipe, use the `ConnectNamedPipe` function to allow client processes to connect to the pipe — in other words, to switch the server process to the waiting state.

The client process, as with mailslots, can connect to the pipe using the all-embracing `CreateFile` function. To open the pipe, it must use the same structure of the pipe name: `\\.\pipe\`*`pipename`*. Thus, the client process must know the name of the pipe, to which it connects. If this attempt has failed, use the `GetLastError` function to discover the cause of the error. If the function returns the `ERROR_PIPE_BUSY = 231` error code,[i] this means that the pipe is busy serving another process and it is necessary to wait until that process releases the pipe. To set the waiting mode, use the `WaitNamedPipe` function.

Disk Drives

The `CreateFile` function can also open disk devices. To open the first disk of your computer, it is necessary to use the `\\.\PhysicalDrive0` name; to open the C: partition, use the `\\.\C:` name. The most interesting fact here is that after opening the device, you can use the `ReadFile` and `WriteFile` functions.[ii] Additionally, you have the `DeviceIoControl` function at your disposal. The latter function can carry out various operations, including getting statistics about the disk and even formatting the disk.

---

[i] Remember that to discover the cause of the error by its number, it is convenient to use the ERRLOOK.EXE program supplied as part of Microsoft Visual Studio.NET.

[ii] Do not write anything in such a way without carefully studying the disk structure before proceeding.

I won't concentrate attention on this function but, instead, will provide an example illustrating the reading of the Master Boot Record (MBR) of the disk. When the device is opened, the MBR will be located at the starting position of the hypothetical file (Listing 13.3).

Listing 13.3. Reading the disk master boot record and partition table

```
.586P
; Flat memory model
.MODEL FLAT, stdcall
; Constants
        STD_OUTPUT_HANDLE equ -11
        GENERIC_READ      equ 80000000h
        FILE_SHARE_WRITE  equ 2h
        OPEN_EXISTING     equ 3
; Prototypes of external procedures
IFDEF MASM
        EXTERN  GetLastError@0:NEAR
        EXTERN  wsprintfA:NEAR
        EXTERN  lstrlenA@4:NEAR
        EXTERN  ReadFile@20:NEAR
        EXTERN  CreateFileA@28:NEAR
        EXTERN  ExitProcess@4:NEAR
        EXTERN  CloseHandle@4:NEAR
        EXTERN  WriteConsoleA@20:NEAR
        EXTERN  GetStdHandle@4:NEAR
ELSE
        EXTERN  GetLastError:NEAR
        EXTERN  _wsprintfA:NEAR
        EXTERN  GetStdHandle:NEAR
        EXTERN  lstrlenA:NEAR
        EXTERN  ReadFile:NEAR
        EXTERN  CreateFileA:NEAR
        EXTERN  ExitProcess:NEAR
        EXTERN  CloseHandle:NEAR
        EXTERN  WriteConsoleA:NEAR
        GetLastError@0 = GetLastError
        wsprintfA = _wsprintfA
        GetStdHandle@4 = GetStdHandle
        WriteConsoleA@20 = WriteConsoleA
        lstrlenA@4 = lstrlenA
        ReadFile@20 = ReadFile
        CreateFileA@28 = CreateFileA
        ExitProcess@4 = ExitProcess
```

```
        CloseHandle@4 =  CloseHandle
ENDIF

; INCLUDELIB directives for the linker
IFDEF MASM
        includelib c:\masm32\lib\user32.lib
        includelib c:\masm32\lib\kernel32.lib
ELSE
        includelib c:\tasm32\lib\import32.lib
ENDIF
;------------------------------------------------
; Data segment
_DATA SEGMENT
        H            DD 0
        NN           DD 0
        ; Device name (first hard disk)
        PATHM        DB "\\.\PhysicalDrive0", 0
        ALIGN        4  ; Alignment by the double-word boundary
        BUF          DB 512 DUP(0)
        BUF1         DB 24  DUP(0)
        HANDL        DD 0
        LENS         DD 0
        ERRS         DB "Error %u", 0
        SINGL        DB "Signature %x", 0
_DATA ENDS
; Code segment
_TEXT SEGMENT
        START:
        PUSH  STD_OUTPUT_HANDLE
        CALL  GetStdHandle@4
        MOV   HANDL, EAX
        ; Open the physical disk
        PUSH  0               ; Must be zero
        PUSH  0               ; File attribute doesn't matter
        PUSH  OPEN_EXISTING   ; How to open
        PUSH  0               ; Pointer to the security attribute = NULL
        PUSH  FILE_SHARE_WRITE          ; Shared access mode
        PUSH  GENERIC_READ              ; Access type - Read
        PUSH  OFFSET PATHM              ; Device name
        CALL  CreateFileA@28
        CMP   EAX, -1
        JNZ   NO_ERR
ER:
        ; Get error number
```

```
        CALL  GetLastError@0
        ; MOVZX EAX, AX
        PUSH  EAX
        PUSH  OFFSET ERRS
        PUSH  OFFSET BUF1
        CALL  wsprintfA
        ; Output error number
        LEA   EAX, BUF1
        MOV   EDI, 1
        CALL  WRITE
        JMP   EXI
NO_ERR:
        MOV   H, EAX
        ; Reading the partition table
        PUSH  0
        PUSH  OFFSET NN
        PUSH  512
        PUSH  OFFSET BUF
        PUSH  H
        CALL  ReadFile@20
        CMP   EAX, 0
        JZ    ER
        ; Display the partition table signature
        ; Must be aa55
        PUSH  DWORD PTR BUF+510
        PUSH  OFFSET SINGL
        PUSH  OFFSET BUF1
        CALL  wsprintfA
        LEA   EAX, BUF1
        MOV   EDI, 1
        CALL  WRITE
        ; Close the device
        PUSH  H
        CALL  CloseHandle@4
        ; Exit
EXI:
        PUSH  0
        CALL  ExitProcess@4
        ; Display the string terminated by line feed
        ; EAX — To the start of the string
        ; EDI — With or without the line feed
WRITE   PROC
; Get the parameter length
```

```
        PUSH  EAX
        PUSH  EAX
        CALL  lstrlenA@4
        MOV   ESI, EAX
        POP   EBX
        CMP   EDI, 1
        JNE   NO_ENT
        ; The string is terminated with the line feed
        MOV   BYTE PTR [EBX+ESI], 13
        MOV   BYTE PTR [EBX+ESI+1], 10
        MOV   BYTE PTR [EBX+ESI+2], 0
        ADD   EAX, 2
        NO_ENT:
; String output
        PUSH  0
        PUSH  OFFSET LENS
        PUSH  EAX
        PUSH  EBX
        PUSH  HANDL
        CALL  WriteConsoleA@20
        RET
WRITE   ENDP
_TEXT ENDS
END START
```

Now, it is necessary to provide some comments about Listing 13.3.

Note that the starting point of the buffer, into which the sector will be read, must be aligned by the 4-byte boundary. To ensure this, the `ALIGN` directive is used. Such alignment is not needed for reading from a normal file except when you disable data caching (see the description of the `CreateFile` function in the opening section of this chapter).

In this program, I have used the `GetLastError` function for the first time. If an error occurs when you open or read from the device, the program will output the error code to the console. To determine the cause of the error, consult the documentation. You can also try to change the parameters of the `CreateFile` and `ReadFile` functions and view the error codes that will result. In fact, such experimenting is instructive.

To translate this program, issue the following commands using MASM32:

```
ML /c /coff /DMASM prog.ASM
LINK /SUBSYSTEM:CONSOLE prog.OBJ
```

- Issue the following commands using TASM32:

```
TASM32 /ml prog.ASM
TLINK32 -ap prog.OBJ
```

Overview of Other API Functions for File Management

Here, I'll briefly consider some API functions that relate to file management and that I have not covered in detail yet.

- `CreateDirectory` — Using this function, it is possible to create a directory. The function accepts two parameters. The first parameter points to the string containing the name of the directory being created, and the second parameter is the pointer to the security attribute (more details on this attribute will be provided later in this chapter). Usually, the second parameter is assumed to be zero.
- `RemoveDirectory` — This function deletes directories. The only parameter of this function is the address of the string containing the name of the directory to be deleted. The directory must be empty for the function to succeed.
- `SetCurrentDirectory` — This function sets the current directory. The parameter of this function is the address of the string that contains the directory name. Note that every partition can have its own current directory.
- `GetCurrentDirectory` — Using this function, it is possible to get the current directory. The function accepts two parameters. The first parameter must be equal to the buffer length for the current directory string. It is assumed that the string will be zero-terminated. Consequently, the buffer length must take the trailing `0` character into account when the length is computed. The second parameter is the address of the string (buffer), into which the name of the current directory will be placed.
- `DeleteFile` — This function deletes the specified file. The only parameter of this function must contain the address of the string that defines the filename. The function will fail if the file is open or has an attribute that doesn't allow deletion.
- `CopyFile` — This is the function for copying files. The first parameter is the address of the string containing the name of the file being copied. The second parameter points to the string containing the name of the new file. The third parameter defines the function behavior if the file with the specified name already exists in the specified directory. If the value of this parameter is 0, then the existing file will be overwritten. If this parameter has a nonzero value, the function won't overwrite the existing file.
- `MoveFile` — This function moves the file or directory with subdirectories. The first argument of this function is the name of file or directory, and the second argument is the new name of the file or directory.
- `MoveFileEx` — This function moves the file or directory, taking into account the third argument value. The first two arguments are the old name of file or directory

and the new name of the file or directory, respectively. The third argument can take the following values:

- MOVEFILE_REPLACE_EXISTING = 1 — Replaces the existing file.
- MOVEFILE_WRITE_THROUGH = 8 — Guarantees that the function will not return control until the file is flushed from the intermediate buffer to the disk.
- MOVEFILE_COPY_ALLOWED = 2 — Specifies that when the new file is placed to another volume, the movement is carried out using two functions: CopyFile and DeleteFile.
- MOVEFILE_DELAY_UNTIL_REBOOT = 4 — Delays the file movement until the system is rebooted. This requires administrative privileges.

❑ SetFilePointer — This sets the file pointer to an arbitrary position. The first parameter of this function is the descriptor of the opened file. The second parameter is the least significant part (32 bits) of the pointer offset value. The third parameter is the most significant part of the pointer offset. The fourth parameter defines the movement mode and can take the following values:

- FILE_BEGIN = 0 — Counts off the position from the beginning of the file.
- FILE_CURRENT = 1 — Determines the position based on the current position.
- FILE_END = 2 — Determines the pointer position based on the end of the file.

Note that the movement can be carried out toward both the end of the file and the beginning of the file. Thus, the offset is interpreted as a signed 32-bit number.

❑ SetEndOfFile — The function moves the end of the file to the current position. The only argument of this function is the file descriptor. The function can truncate the file or increase its length.

Asynchronous Input and Output

Input and output represent interaction between the process and the specific device, such as a file stored on a disk. The rate of this operation depends more on the performance of the peripheral device and data transmission link rather than on the performance of the central processing unit. The standard method of communicating with a peripheral device supposes that the process will wait for the read or write operation to accomplish on each stage of interaction. This method is called synchronous input/output. It is called synchronous because the process on each stage synchronizes its action with the state of the peripheral device. To increase the system performance when carrying out an input/output operation, asynchronous input/output was implemented.[i] To inform the system about the intention to carry out an asynchronous input/output operation, it is necessary to open the device using the `CreateFile` function and specify the `FILE_FLAG_OVERLAPPED` flag in the sixth parameter. When executing functions such as `ReadFile` and `WriteFile`, the device drive places the input/output request into the queue. The functions then immediately return control to the calling process. Thus, the process can carry out other actions without worrying about the data and whether or not they have been transmitted. The most important point in the entire method is how the driver would inform the process that the data transmission has been completed and with what result.

In the course of asynchronous input/output, the role of parameters of the `ReadFile` and `WriteFile` functions slightly changes. In particular, since both functions immediately return control to the calling process, the fourth parameter ceases to do anything and is usually set to zero. The fifth parameter, on the contrary, starts to play the main role. It must point to the `OVERLAPPED` structure:

```
OVERLAPPED STRUC
        INTERN DD ?
        NBYTE  DD ?
        OFFSL  DD ?
        OFFSH  DD ?
        HEVENT DD ?
OVERLAPPED ENDS
```

Note that the last three fields must be set before carrying out the operation. The fields of this structure are as follows:

- `INTERN` — This field would contain the operation accomplishment status. When the input/output operation is in progress, the value of this field will be set to `STATUS_PENDING = 103h`.
- `NBYTE` — When the operation is completed, this field will contain the number of transmitted bytes.
- `OFFSL` and `OFFSH` — These are the least significant and most significant parts of the pointer position within the file. For devices other than files, this must be set to zero.
- `HEVENT` — This takes its value depending on the method of asynchronous input/output.

It is necessary to bear in mind that the `ReadFile` and `WriteFile` functions return the 0 value in the case of asynchronous input/output. However, sometimes the system might carry out the read/write operation instantly, in which case these functions will

---

[i] To get a proper understanding of this section, you'll need the material presented in *Chapter 15*, which provides an example of parallel asynchronous processing.

return a positive value. If these functions return the 0 value, this doesn't necessarily mean that asynchronous input/output has started successfully. It is possible that some error has occurred. Therefore, it is necessary to call the `GetLastError` function. If it returns the `ERROR_IO_PENDING = 997` value, this will mean that asynchronous process has started successfully. Any other value will serve as an indication that some error has occurred.

Asynchronous input/output is canceled in one of the following cases:

- The `CancelIo` function is executed. The only parameter of this function is the descriptor of the opened device (file). Bear in mind that all asynchronous input/output requests of this thread will be canceled.
- When the device (file) is closed, all requests for asynchronous input/output for this file are canceled.
- If the thread is closed, all its requests are automatically canceled.

There are four mechanisms of informing the process about the termination of the input/output operation.

- Signaling of the kernel object controlling the device[i]
- Signaling of the kernel object controlling events
- Input/output notification
- Use of the input/output termination port

Consider these approaches in more detail.

Signaling of the kernel object controlling the device. In this approach, the `WaitForSingleObject` API function is used (see *Chapter 15*). The function returns control either when the predefined time interval elapses or when a certain kernel object (e.g., an opened file) is switched to a certain state known as signal state. The first argument of this function is the descriptor of the opened device (file), and its second argument is the waiting interval. If the `INFINITE = -1` constant is taken as the value of this parameter, the waiting interval will be infinitely long. The `ReadFile` and `WriteFile` functions set the object to nonsignaled state. When asynchronous input/output is completed, the device driver switches the object to the signaled state, and the `WaitForSingleObject` function returns the control. What is the advantage here, you might ask, since the process continues to wait for the result? Usually, for this method a separate thread is created. The thread that has opened the device might be busy carrying out other tasks. When the process is completed, it is necessary to check the `OVERLAPPED` structure to discover whether there were errors and how many bytes have

---

[i] The kernel is the part of the operating system that runs in the privileged mode. More detailed information on this topic will be provided in *Chapter 24* (see "*Kernel Mode Drivers*").

been transmitted. Before opening the device, this structure must be initialized. In particular, the `HEVENT` field must be initialized with zero.

Signaling of the kernel object controlling events. The preceding method, principally, allows the system to wait for the results of only one input/output operation. There is a more flexible approach, in which the specific event is associated with every input/output operation (`WriteFile` or `ReadFile` function). The event can be created using the `CreateEvent` function (see *Chapter 15*), and its handle must be assigned to the `HEVENT` field of the `OVERLAPPED` structure. To wait for an event, use the `WaitForMultipleObjects` function.

Input/output notification. To use this method, instead of the `ReadFile` and `WriteFile` functions it is necessary to use the `ReadFileEx` and `WriteFileEx` functions. These functions have an additional, sixth parameter that represents the address of the procedure that will be called when asynchronous input/output is completed. This procedure must be created beforehand in your program. Usually, it is called the callback procedure. It has three parameters. The first parameter is the completion code. If its value is 0, this means that asynchronous input/output has completed successfully. If this parameter is equal to `ERROR_HANDLE_EOF = 38`, this means that an attempt was made to read the file beyond its boundary. Provided that the operation has completed successfully, the second parameter will contain the number of read or written bytes. Finally, the third parameter is the address of the `OVERLAPPED` structure that I have already described. It is necessary to bear in mind that the device drive places an appropriate procedure into the queue after the completion of the respective asynchronous input/output operation. To call these procedures, the thread must be switched to the waiting state. To achieve this, use functions such as `SleepEx` and `WaitForSingleObjectEx`. Now, consider the `SleepEx` function in more detail.[i] The first parameter of this function is the number of milliseconds for waiting. The `INFINITE` value of this parameter means that it will wait infinitely. The second parameter can take two values: 0 or 1. If the value of this parameter is 0, then exiting from this function takes place only after the interval specified in the first parameter has elapsed. If this parameter is 1, the function can be exited in two additional ways:

- When the callback function is called
- When this function is placed into the queue

Input/output termination ports. Asynchronous input/output is not often used for file processing. In this case, asynchronous communication between the server and several client applications is considerably more important. The communications mechanism is not of primary importance. Several such mechanisms can be used, including

[i] Later, you will become acquainted with the `Sleep` function, which is simpler than this one.

named pipes, mailslots, or network interaction using the sockets mechanism. Two approaches are possible:

- A single thread waits for the client requests. When a request arrives, the thread processes it. This approach is convenient when client requests are rare. If several client programs access the server simultaneously, a queue is generated. As a result, some clients may have to wait a long time before the server starts processing their queries. This approach is known as sequential processing.
- The server thread waits for the query to arrive. When the query arrives, a new thread is created, which is delegated the responsibility of organizing communications with this client. The first thread continues to wait for new client requests; when they appear, it creates new threads for them. The thread that finishes serving the client is terminated. This approach is called parallel processing. It is significantly more efficient than sequential processing. However, research has shown that when numerous threads run simultaneously, most time is spent on context switching between threads.

The method that uses the input/output termination port is based on the assumption that a limited number of simultaneously running threads serves clients. In other words, this approach is a compromise between the sequential and the parallel approaches. This method also implements another interesting approach: Because a certain time is required for creating individual threads, the entire pool of threads is created. The threads that do not participate in the processing of client requests are in the waiting state.

I will return to considering asynchronous input/output when considering multitasking programming in *Chapter 15.*

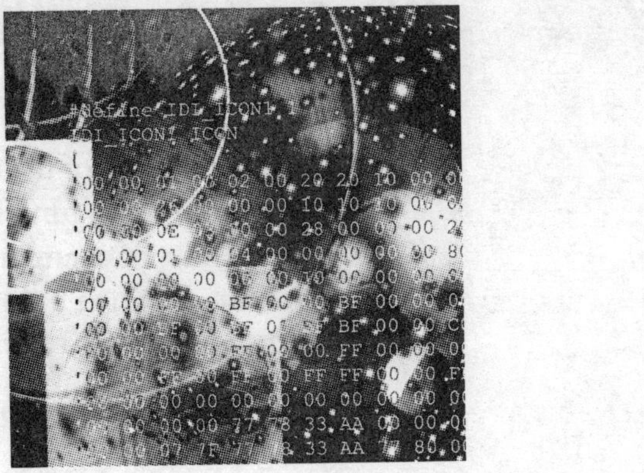

Chapter 14

Examples of Programs Using the Timer

The timer is one of the most powerful instruments provided by the operating system and used to solve various problems. You became acquainted with the timer when considering console applications. There, I used the `timeSetEvent` and `timeKillEvent` functions. These functions are convenient for console applications. In graphic user interface applications, the `SetTimer` and `KillTimer` functions are used more frequently. A feature of the timer created by the `SetTimer` function is that the `WM_TIMER` message, which the system starts to send to the application after execution of the `SetTimer` function, arrives with all other messages. Consequently, the interval between two sequential `WM_TIMER` messages can vary slightly. However, in most cases, this isn't important.

The timer message has another feature. If the system sends the timer message to the application, and the previous message is still waiting in the message queue, the system joins these two messages. Thus, this forced wait doesn't result in the arrival of several timer messages in succession to the application.

The list of tasks that can be carried out using the timer includes the following:

- Tracking the time (seconds counter, watch, etc.) — Periodicity variation is of no importance because, when the message arrives, the time can be tracked by calling the function for getting the system time.
- Implementing multitasking — It is possible to set several timers simultaneously to different functions. As a result, the functions will alternate periodically. More detailed information about multitasking will be provided in *Chapter 15*.

- Periodic refreshing of the displayed information.
- Auto saving — This function is especially useful for editors.
- Setting the rate of changing specific objects displayed on the screen.
- Animation — When a timer message arrives, the graphics displayed on the screen or in the window are refreshed. This creates the animation effect.

Consider how to work with the `SetTimer` function. Here are the parameters of this function:

- First parameter — Descriptor of the window, with which the timer is associated. If this parameter is set to `NULL`, then the second parameter will be ignored.
- Second parameter — Defines the timer identifier.
- Third parameter — Specifies the periodicity interval for the `WM_TIMER` message.
- Fourth parameter — Defines the address of the function, to which the `WM_TIMER` message will arrive. If this parameter is set to `NULL`, the message will arrive to the window function.

If the function has completed successfully, it returns the timer identifier, which, naturally, will match the second parameter if it is other than `NULL`. In the case of failure, the function returns zero.

Thus, the function can be called using the following three methods:

- The window descriptor is specified, and the fourth parameter is set to 0.
- The window descriptor is specified, and the fourth parameter defines the function, to which the `WM_TIMER` message will arrive.
- The window descriptor is set to `NULL`, and the fourth parameter defines the function, to which the `WM_TIMER` message will arrive. Timer identifier in this case will be determined by the value returned by the function.

The function, to which the `WM_TIMER` message arrives, has the following parameters:

- First parameter — Descriptor of the window to which the timer is associated
- Second parameter — The `WM_TIMER` message
- Third parameter — The timer identifier
- Fourth parameter — Time interval in milliseconds that has elapsed since Windows startup

The `KillTimer` function deletes the existing timer. It accepts the following parameters:

- First parameter — Window descriptor
- Second parameter — Timer identifier

The Simplest Example of Using the Timer

The first example to consider is the simplest example of a timer. The timer counts 10 ticks, then closes the window and displays the message box informing the user about the program termination. This program illustrates timer organization on the basis of the window function.

Listing 14.1. The simplest timer

```
// The TIMER.RC file
// Constants
#define WS_SYSMENU          0x00080000L
#define WS_MINIMIZEBOX      0x00020000L
#define WS_MAXIMIZEBOX      0x00010000L

// Style — Button
#define BS_PUSHBUTTON       0x00000000L
// The button must be visible
#define WS_VISIBLE          0x10000000L
// Center the button label
#define BS_CENTER           0x00000300L
// Button style
#define WS_CHILD            0x40000000L
// The possibility of focusing the element
// using the <TAB> key
#define WS_TABSTOP          0x00010000L
#define DS_3DLOOK           0x0004L
// Dialog box definition
DIAL1 DIALOG 0, 0, 240, 120
STYLE WS_SYSMENU | WS_MINIMIZEBOX | WS_MAXIMIZEBOX |DS_3DLOOK
CAPTION "An example of dialog with timer"
FONT 8, "Arial"
{
// Button, identifier 5
 CONTROL "Exit", 5, "button", BS_PUSHBUTTON
 | BS_CENTER | WS_CHILD | WS_VISIBLE | WS_TABSTOP,
 180, 76, 50, 14
}


; The TIMER.INC file
; Constants
```

```
; This message arrives when the window is closed
WM_CLOSE            equ 10h
WM_INITDIALOG       equ 110h
WM_COMMAND          equ 111h
WM_TIMER            equ 113h
; Prototypes of external procedures
IFDEF MASM
   EXTERN         ReleaseDC@8:NEAR
   EXTERN         GetDC@4:NEAR
   EXTERN         TextOutA@20:NEAR
   EXTERN         MessageBoxA@16:NEAR
   EXTERN         ExitProcess@4:NEAR
   EXTERN         GetModuleHandleA@4:NEAR
   EXTERN         DialogBoxParamA@20:NEAR
   EXTERN         EndDialog@8:NEAR
   EXTERN         SendMessageA@16:NEAR
   EXTERN         SetTimer@16:NEAR
   EXTERN         KillTimer@8:NEAR
ELSE
   EXTERN         ReleaseDC:NEAR
   EXTERN         GetDC:NEAR
   EXTERN         TextOutA:NEAR
   EXTERN         MessageBoxA:NEAR
   EXTERN         ExitProcess:NEAR
   EXTERN         GetModuleHandleA:NEAR
   EXTERN         DialogBoxParamA:NEAR
   EXTERN         EndDialog:NEAR
   EXTERN         SendMessageA:NEAR
   EXTERN         SetTimer:NEAR
   EXTERN         KillTimer:NEAR
   ReleaseDC@8 = ReleaseDC
   GetDC@4 = GetDC
   TextOutA@20 = TextOutA
   MessageBoxA@16 = MessageBoxA
   ExitProcess@4 = ExitProcess
   GetModuleHandleA@4 = GetModuleHandleA
   DialogBoxParamA@20 = DialogBoxParamA
   EndDialog@8 = EndDialog
   SendMessageA@16 = SendMessageA
   SetTimer@16 = SetTimer
   KillTimer@8 = KillTimer
ENDIF
; Structures
```

```
; Message structure
MSGSTRUCT STRUC
      MSHWND        DD ?
      MSMESSAGE     DD ?
      MSWPARAM      DD ?
      MSLPARAM      DD ?
      MSTIME        DD ?
      MSPT          DD ?
MSGSTRUCT ENDS

; The TIMER.ASM file
.586P
; Flat memory model
.MODEL FLAT, stdcall
include timer.inc
; INCLUDELIB directives for the linker
IFDEF MASM
; For the LINK.EXE linker
   includelib c:\masm32\lib\user32.lib
   includelib c:\masm32\lib\kernel32.lib
   includelib c:\masm32\lib\gdi32.lib
ELSE
; For the TLINK32.EXE linker
   includelib c:\tasm32\lib\import32.lib
ENDIF
;-------------------------------------------------
; Data segment
_DATA SEGMENT
   MSG      MSGSTRUCT <?>
   HINST    DD 0 ; Application descriptor
   PA       DB "DIAL1", 0
   COUNT    DD 0
   TEXT     DB 0
   CAP      DB 'Message', 0
   MES      DB 'Exit by timer', 0
_DATA ENDS
; Code segment
_TEXT SEGMENT
START:
; Get application descriptor
   PUSH  0
   CALL  GetModuleHandleA@4
   MOV   [HINST], EAX
```

```
;---------------------------------
    PUSH  0
    PUSH  OFFSET WNDPROC
    PUSH  0
    PUSH  OFFSET PA
    PUSH  [HINST]
    CALL  DialogBoxParamA@20
    CMP   EAX, -1
    JNE   KOL
KOL:
;---------------------------------
    PUSH  0
    CALL  ExitProcess@4
;---------------------------------
; Window procedure
; Position of parameters in the stack
; [EBP+014H]           ; LPARAM
; [EBP+10H]            ; WAPARAM
; [EBP+0CH]            ; MES
; [EBP+8]              ; HWND
WNDPROC  PROC
    PUSH  EBP
    MOV   EBP, ESP
    PUSH  EBX
    PUSH  ESI
    PUSH  EDI
;----------------
    CMP   DWORD PTR [EBP+0CH], WM_CLOSE
    JNE   L1
; The reaction to the window closing
L3:
; Delete the timer
    PUSH  1 ; Timer identifier
    PUSH  DWORD PTR [EBP+08H]
    CALL  KillTimer@8
; Close the dialog
    PUSH  0
    PUSH  DWORD PTR [EBP+08H]
    CALL  EndDialog@8
    JMP   FINISH
L1:
    CMP   DWORD PTR [EBP+0CH], WM_INITDIALOG
    JNE   L5
```

```
; The initialization takes place
; Set the timer
      PUSH  0 ; Parameter = NULL
      PUSH  1000 ; Interval of 1 second
      PUSH  1 ; Timer identifier
      PUSH  DWORD PTR [EBP+08H]
      CALL  SetTimer@16
      JMP   FINISH
L5:
      CMP   DWORD PTR [EBP+0CH], WM_COMMAND
      JNE   L2
; Exit button?
      CMP   WORD PTR [EBP+10H], 5
      JNE   FINISH
      JMP   L3
L2:
      CMP   DWORD PTR [EBP+0CH], WM_TIMER
      JNE   FINISH
; Time to exit?
      CMP   COUNT, 9
; Exit without notification
      JA    L3
; Exit through the message
      JE    L4
; The timer message has arrived
; Prepare the text
      MOV   EAX, COUNT
      ADD   EAX, 49
      MOV   TEXT, AL
; Get the context
      PUSH  DWORD PTR [EBP+08H]
      CALL  GetDC@4
; Save the context
      PUSH  EAX
; Display the counter value
      PUSH  1
      PUSH  OFFSET TEXT
      PUSH  10
      PUSH  10
      PUSH  EAX
      CALL  TextOutA@20
  Delete the context
      POP EAX
```

```
        PUSH   EAX
        PUSH   DWORD PTR [EBP+08H]
        CALL   ReleaseDC@8
; Increase the counter
        INC    COUNT
        JMP    FINISH
L4:
        INC COUNT
; The message about exiting from the timer
        PUSH   0
        PUSH   OFFSET CAP
        PUSH   OFFSET MES
        PUSH   DWORD PTR [EBP+08H] ; Window descriptor
        CALL   MessageBoxA@16
        JMP    L3
FINISH:
        POP    EDI
        POP    ESI
        POP    EBX
        POP    EBP
        MOV    EAX, 0
        RET    16
WNDPROC              ENDP
;-------------------------------------------
_TEXT ENDS
END START
```

Now, let me comment on the program provided in Listing 14.1. Timer organization here is simple and obvious. The only thing that can cause some difficulties is leaving the `MessageBox` and simultaneously closing the dialog box. Nevertheless, here everything is simple: the message is displayed when `COUNT=9`, and when the next message arrives, `COUNT` is greater than 9, and the branch that closes the dialog is executed.

To translate this program, issue the following commands using MASM32:

```
ML /c /coff /DMASM timer.asm
RC timer.rc
LINK /SUBSYSTEM:WINDOWS timer.obj timer.res
```

Issue the following commands using TASM32:

```
TASM32 /ml timer.asm
BRCC32 timer.rc
TLINK32 -aa timer.obj,,,,,timer.res
```

The Interaction between Timers

The next program is slightly more difficult than the previous one. Here, two timers are operating. It is possible to say that two tasks are started simultaneously.[i] The first task gets the system time every 0.5 seconds and forms the string for output (STRCOPY). This task has its own function, to which the WM_TIMER message arrives. The second task operates within the framework of the window function. This task displays the data and the time in the edit field of the dialog box at an interval of 1 second. Thus, the two tasks interact to each other using the STRCOPY global variable.

Another important aspect needs to be mentioned related to this program. Because the message that specifies the timer identifier arrives at the timer function, you can implement any number of timers on the basis of a single function.

Listing 14.2. The use of two timers

```
// The TIMER2.RC file
// Constant definitions
#define WS_SYSMENU              0x00080000L
// Elements of the dialog box must be visible
#define WS_VISIBLE              0x10000000L
// Border around the element
#define WS_BORDER               0x00800000L
// Elements can be activated using the <Tab> key
#define WS_TABSTOP              0x00010000L
// Left-align the text in the edit field
#define ES_LEFT                 0x0000L
// Style of all elements of the window
#define WS_CHILD                0x40000000L
// Disable the keyboard input
#define ES_READONLY             0x0800L

#define DS_3DLOOK               0x0004L
// Dialog definition
DIAL1 DIALOG 0, 0, 240, 100
STYLE WS_SYSMENU | DS_3DLOOK
CAPTION "Dialog with the date and clock"
FONT 8, "Arial"
{
 CONTROL "", 1, "edit", ES_LEFT | WS_CHILD
 | WS_VISIBLE | WS_BORDER
```

[i] To be more precise, there are three tasks because the dialog box operates independently.

```
 | WS_TABSTOP | ES_READONLY, 100, 5, 130, 12
}

; The TIMER2.INC file
; Constants
; This message arrives when the window is closed
WM_CLOSE          equ 10h
; This message arrives when the window is created
WM_INITDIALOG     equ 110h
; This message arrives when some event occurs to the window element
WM_COMMAND        equ 111h
; Message from the timer
WM_TIMER          equ 113h
; Message for sending text to the window element
WM_SETTEXT        equ 0Ch
; Prototypes of external procedures
IFDEF MASM
      EXTERN      SendDlgItemMessageA@20:NEAR
      EXTERN      wsprintfA:NEAR
      EXTERN      GetLocalTime@4:NEAR
      EXTERN      ExitProcess@4:NEAR
      EXTERN      GetModuleHandleA@4:NEAR
      EXTERN      DialogBoxParamA@20:NEAR
      EXTERN      EndDialog@8:NEAR
      EXTERN      SetTimer@16:NEAR
      EXTERN      KillTimer@8:NEAR
ELSE
      EXTERN      SendDlgItemMessageA:NEAR
      EXTERN      _wsprintfA:NEAR
      EXTERN      GetLocalTime:NEAR
      EXTERN      ExitProcess:NEAR
      EXTERN      GetModuleHandleA:NEAR
      EXTERN      DialogBoxParamA:NEAR
      EXTERN      EndDialog:NEAR
      EXTERN      SetTimer:NEAR
      EXTERN      KillTimer:NEAR
      SendDlgItemMessageA@20 = SendDlgItemMessageA
      wsprintfA = _wsprintfA
      GetLocalTime@4 = GetLocalTime
      ExitProcess@4 = ExitProcess
      GetModuleHandleA@4 = GetModuleHandleA
      DialogBoxParamA@20 = DialogBoxParamA
      EndDialog@8 = EndDialog
```

```
    SetTimer@16 = SetTimer
    KillTimer@8 = KillTimer
ENDIF
; Structures
; Message structure
MSGSTRUCT STRUC
    MSHWND      DD ?
    MSMESSAGE   DD ?
    MSWPARAM    DD ?
    MSLPARAM    DD ?
    MSTIME      DD ?
    MSPT        DD ?
MSGSTRUCT ENDS
; Date-time data structure
DAT STRUC
    year    DW ?
    month   DW ?
    dayweek DW ?
    day     DW ?
    hour    DW ?
    min     DW ?
    sec     DW ?
    msec    DW ?
DAT ENDS

; The TIMER2.ASM file
.586P
; Flat memory model
.MODEL FLAT, stdcall
include timer2.inc
; INCLUDELIB directives for the linker
IFDEF MASM
; For the LINK.EXE linker
   includelib c:\masm32\lib\user32.lib
   includelib c:\masm32\lib\kernel32.lib
   includelib c:\masm32\lib\gdi32.lib
ELSE
; For the TLINK32.EXE linker
   includelib c:\tasm32\lib\import32.lib
ENDIF
;-------------------------------------------------
; Data segment
_DATA SEGMENT
```

```
    MSG       MSGSTRUCT <?>
    HINST     DD 0 ; Application descriptor
    PA        DB "DIAL1", 0
    TIM       DB "Date %u/%u/%u Time %u:%u:%u", 0
    STRCOPY   DB 50 DUP(?)
    DATA      DAT <0>
_DATA ENDS
; Code segment
_TEXT SEGMENT
START:
; Get application descriptor
    PUSH  0
    CALL  GetModuleHandleA@4
    MOV   [HINST], EAX
; Create a dialog
    PUSH  0
    PUSH  OFFSET WNDPROC
    PUSH  0
    PUSH  OFFSET PA
    PUSH  [HINST]
    CALL  DialogBoxParamA@20
    CMP   EAX, -1
    JNE   KOL
; Error message
KOL:
;-----------------------------------
    PUSH  0
    CALL  ExitProcess@4
;-----------------------------------
; Window procedure
; Position of parameters in the stack
; [EBP+014H]   ; LPARAM
; [EBP+10H]    ; WAPARAM
; [EBP+0CH]    ; MES
; [EBP+8]      ; HWND
WNDPROC     PROC
    PUSH  EBP
    MOV   EBP, ESP
    PUSH  EBX
    PUSH  ESI
    PUSH  EDI
;----------------
    CMP   DWORD PTR [EBP+0CH], WM_CLOSE
```

```
    JNE   L1
; Reaction to window closing
; Delete timer 1
    PUSH  1 ; Timer identifier
    PUSH  DWORD PTR [EBP+08H]
    CALL  KillTimer@8
; Delete timer 2
    PUSH  2 ; Timer identifier
    PUSH  DWORD PTR [EBP+08H]
    CALL  KillTimer@8
; Close the dialog
    PUSH  0
    PUSH  DWORD PTR [EBP+08H]
    CALL  EndDialog@8
    JMP   FINISH
L1:
    CMP   DWORD PTR [EBP+0CH], WM_INITDIALOG
    JNE   L2
; Startup initialization takes place here
; Set timer 1
    PUSH  0 ; Parameter = NULL
    PUSH  1000 ; 1-second interval
    PUSH  1 ; Timer identifier
    PUSH  DWORD PTR [EBP+08H]
    CALL  SetTimer@16
; Set timer 2
    PUSH  OFFSET TIMPROC ; Parameter = NULL
    PUSH  500 ; 0.5-second interval
    PUSH  2 ; Timer identifier
    PUSH  DWORD PTR [EBP+08H]
    CALL  SetTimer@16
    JMP   FINISH
L2:
    CMP   DWORD PTR [EBP+0CH], WM_TIMER
    JNE   FINISH
; Send the string to the window
    PUSH  OFFSET STRCOPY
    PUSH  0
    PUSH  WM_SETTEXT
    PUSH  1 ; Element identifier
    PUSH  DWORD PTR [EBP+08H]
    CALL  SendDlgItemMessageA@20
FINISH:
    POP   EDI
```

```
     POP  ESI
     POP  EBX
     POP  EBP
     MOV  EAX, 0
     RET  16
WNDPROC  ENDP
;------------------------------
; Timer procedure
; Position of parameters in the stack
; [EBP+014H]   ; LPARAM - Interval elapsed since Windows startup
; [EBP+10H]    ; WAPARAM - Timer identifier
; [EBP+0CH]    ; WM_TIMER
; [EBP+8]      ; HWND
TIMPROC      PROC
     PUSH  EBP
     MOV   EBP, ESP
; Get local time
     PUSH  OFFSET DATA
     CALL  GetLocalTime@4
; Get the string for data and time output
     MOVZX EAX, DATA.sec
     PUSH  EAX
     MOVZX EAX, DATA.min
     PUSH  EAX
     MOVZX EAX, DATA.hour
     PUSH  EAX
     MOVZX EAX, DATA.year
     PUSH  EAX
     MOVZX EAX, DATA.month
     PUSH  EAX
     MOVZX EAX, DATA.day
     PUSH  EAX
     PUSH  OFFSET TIM
     PUSH  OFFSET STRCOPY
     CALL  wsprintfA
; Restore the stack
     ADD   ESP, 32
     POP   EBP
     RET   16
TIMPROC      ENDP
_TEXT ENDS
END START
```

To translate this program, proceed as follows for MASM32:

```
ML /c /coff /DMASM timer2.asm
RC timer2.rc
LINK /SUBSYSTEM:WINDOWS timer2.obj timer2.res
```

Proceed as follows for TASM32:

```
TASM32 /ml timer2.asm
BRCC32 timer2.rc
TLINK32 -aa timer2.obj,,,,,timer2.res
```

Fig. 14.1. Result of executing the program presented in Listing 14.2

I would like to draw your attention to one useful function — `GetLocalTime`. Information received using this function (see the `DAT` structure in Listing 14.2) can be easily used for various purposes, including screen output. Similarly, you can use the `SetLocalTime` function to set the current time. To get Greenwich Mean Time (GMT), use the `GetSystemTime` function; accordingly, to set the system time according to GMT, use the `SetSystemTime` function. The argument in all of these function is the previously mentioned structure (or, to be more precise, the pointer to that structure).

Popup Help Windows

In this section, the interesting topic of popup help windows is considered. In visual programming languages, popup help windows are organized by setting appropriate properties for objects located within a container object. Your goal is to develop the mechanism that would allow you to set popup help windows for any window control without using additional libraries. To achieve this, it is necessary to proceed as follows:

- First, it is necessary to notice that a popup help window is simply a window with predefined properties. Here are those properties: `DS_3DLOOK`, `WS_POPUP`, `WS_VISIBLE`, and WS_BORDER. You can experiment by adding or removing the properties. However, there is one property, without which your goal cannot be achieved. This is the WS_POPUP property. Furthermore, the definition of the popup window in the resource file must not contain the CAPTION property.

- The display of the popup help window must not change the situation in the dialog. This means that the popup help call must be modeless by calling the CreateDialogIndirect function. Moreover, it is necessary to make provision for resetting the focus to the dialog box. For this purpose, it is enough to call the SetFocus function when needed (see Listing 14.3).
- Thus, the popup help window is the dialog; consequently, it must have the window function. What should be contained in this function? At the least, it must process the following three events: WM_INITDIALOG, WM_PAINT, and WM_TIMER. Having received the WM_INITDIALOG message, it is necessary to determine the size and position of the popup window. Furthermore, if you assume that the popup window must automatically close after a certain time interval elapses, then it is necessary to set the timer. When the WM_PAINT message is received, it is necessary to output the text into the popup window. If the size of the popup window is set exactly according to the length of the text string that has to be displayed, then the popup window background color will be fully defined by the color of the displayed text. Finally, when the WM_TIMER message arrives, it is necessary to close the popup window.
- As relates to the help string, everything is more or less clear. Now, you must determine where and how this help will be called. The following approach seems preferable to me: In the main dialog, determine the timer whose function would trace the cursor position. Depending on this position, the popup help window will be either called or closed. The timer function must make provision for the following:
  - It must check the cursor position. If the cursor happens to be over the required element, then it is necessary to call the help. At the same time, it is desirable to make sure that popup windows appear with a certain delay. This can be ensured by introducing a counter — call popup help if the counter exceeds a predefined value.
  - When the cursor moves from the area of the required element, the popup help window must be closed.

Listing 14.3 provides a program that demonstrates the described approach. Fig. 14.2 shows a dialog with popup help. Principally, this approach is not the only possible one. After you understand the working principle of this program, you'll be able to invent your own methods of creating popup help windows.

Listing 14.3. Demonstration of popup help windows

```
// The HINT.RC file
// Constant definitions
#define WS_SYSMENU              0x00080000L
// Window elements must be initially visible
#define WS_VISIBLE              0x10000000L
// Border around the element
#define WS_BORDER               0x00800000L
// Elements can be activated using the <Tab> key
#define WS_TABSTOP              0x00010000L
// Text in the help window is left-aligned
#define ES_LEFT                 0x0000L
// Type of all elements of the window
#define WS_CHILD                0x40000000L
// Style — Button
#define BS_PUSHBUTTON           0x00000000L
// Center the button label
#define BS_CENTER               0x00000300L
// Window type — Popup
#define WS_POPUP                0x80000000L
// Windows 95-style dialog
#define DS_3DLOOK               0x0004L
// Dialog box definition
DIAL1 DIALOG 0, 0, 240, 100
STYLE WS_SYSMENU | DS_3DLOOK
CAPTION "Window with popup help"
FONT 8, "Arial"
{
// Edit window, identifier 1
 CONTROL "", 1, "edit", ES_LEFT | WS_CHILD
 | WS_VISIBLE | WS_BORDER
 | WS_TABSTOP , 100, 5, 130, 12
// Button, identifier 2
 CONTROL "Exit", 2, "button", BS_PUSHBUTTON
 | BS_CENTER | WS_CHILD | WS_VISIBLE | WS_TABSTOP,
 180, 76, 50, 14
}

// Help dialog
HINTW DIALOG 0, 0, 240, 8
STYLE DS_3DLOOK | WS_POPUP | WS_VISIBLE | WS_BORDER
FONT 8, "MS Sans Serif"
```

```
{
}

; The HINT.INC file
; Constants
; Help window background color
RED    = 255
GREEN  = 255
BLUE   = 150
RGBB   equ (RED or (GREEN shl 8)) or (BLUE shl 16)
; Foreground color of the popup help window
RED    = 20
GREEN  = 20
BLUE   = 20
RGBT   equ (RED or (GREEN shl 8)) or (BLUE shl 16)
; This message arrives when the window is closed
WM_CLOSE         equ 10h
WM_INITDIALOG    equ 110h
WM_COMMAND       equ 111h
WM_TIMER         equ 113h
WM_SETTEXT       equ 0Ch
WM_COMMAND       equ 111h
WM_PAINT         equ 0Fh
; Prototypes of external procedures
IFDEF MASM
      EXTERN      CreateDialogParamA@20:NEAR
      EXTERN      SetFocus@4:NEAR
      EXTERN      lstrcpyA@8:NEAR
      EXTERN      DestroyWindow@4:NEAR
      EXTERN      lstrlenA@4:NEAR
      EXTERN      GetDlgItem@8:NEAR
      EXTERN      GetCursorPos@4:NEAR
      EXTERN      TextOutA@20:NEAR
      EXTERN      SetBkColor@8:NEAR
      EXTERN      SetTextColor@8:NEAR
      EXTERN      BeginPaint@8:NEAR
      EXTERN      EndPaint@8:NEAR
      EXTERN      GetTextExtentPoint32A@16:NEAR
      EXTERN      MoveWindow@24:NEAR
      EXTERN      GetWindowRect@8:NEAR
      EXTERN      ReleaseDC@8:NEAR
      EXTERN      GetDC@4:NEAR
      EXTERN      SendDlgItemMessageA@20:NEAR
```

```
        EXTERN      ExitProcess@4:NEAR
        EXTERN      GetModuleHandleA@4:NEAR
        EXTERN      DialogBoxParamA@20:NEAR
        EXTERN      EndDialog@8:NEAR
        EXTERN      SetTimer@16:NEAR
        EXTERN      KillTimer@8:NEAR
ELSE
        EXTERN      CreateDialogParamA:NEAR
        EXTERN      SetFocus:NEAR
        EXTERN      lstrcpyA:NEAR
        EXTERN      DestroyWindow:NEAR
        EXTERN      lstrlenA:NEAR
        EXTERN      GetDlgItem:NEAR
        EXTERN      GetCursorPos:NEAR
        EXTERN      TextOutA:NEAR
        EXTERN      SetBkColor:NEAR
        EXTERN      SetTextColor:NEAR
        EXTERN      BeginPaint:NEAR
        EXTERN      EndPaint:NEAR
        EXTERN      GetTextExtentPoint32A:NEAR
        EXTERN      MoveWindow:NEAR
        EXTERN      GetWindowRect:NEAR
        EXTERN      ReleaseDC:NEAR
        EXTERN      GetDC:NEAR
        EXTERN      SendDlgItemMessageA:NEAR
        EXTERN      ExitProcess:NEAR
        EXTERN      GetModuleHandleA:NEAR
        EXTERN      DialogBoxParamA:NEAR
        EXTERN      EndDialog:NEAR
        EXTERN      SetTimer:NEAR
        EXTERN      KillTimer:NEAR
        CreateDialogParamA@20 = CreateDialogParamA
        SetFocus@4 = SetFocus
        lstrcpyA@8 = lstrcpyA
        DestroyWindow@4 = DestroyWindow
        lstrlenA@4 = lstrlenA
        GetDlgItem@8 = GetDlgItem
        GetCursorPos@4 = GetCursorPos
        TextOutA@20 = TextOutA
        SetBkColor@8 = SetBkColor
        SetTextColor@8 = SetTextColor
        BeginPaint@8 = BeginPaint
        EndPaint@8 = EndPaint
```

```
        GetTextExtentPoint32A@16 = GetTextExtentPoint32A
        MoveWindow@24 = MoveWindow
        GetWindowRect@8 = GetWindowRect
        ReleaseDC@8 = ReleaseDC
        GetDC@4 = GetDC
        SendDlgItemMessageA@20 = SendDlgItemMessageA
        ExitProcess@4 = ExitProcess
        GetModuleHandleA@4 = GetModuleHandleA
        DialogBoxParamA@20 = DialogBoxParamA
        EndDialog@8 = EndDialog
        SetTimer@16 = SetTimer
        KillTimer@8 = KillTimer
ENDIF
; Structures
; Message structure
MSGSTRUCT STRUC
        MSHWND          DD ?
        MSMESSAGE       DD ?
        MSWPARAM        DD ?
        MSLPARAM        DD ?
        MSTIME          DD ?
        MSPT            DD ?
MSGSTRUCT ENDS
; Window size stricture
RECT  STRUC
        L  DD ?
        T  DD ?
        R  DD ?
        B  DD ?
RECT  ENDS
; Size structure
SIZ  STRUC
    X DD ?
    Y DD ?
SIZ  ENDS
; Structure for BeginPaint
PAINTSTR STRUC
  hdc     DWORD 0
  fErase DWORD 0
  left    DWORD 0
  top     DWORD 0
  right  DWORD 0
  bottom DWORD 0
```

```
  fRes   DWORD 0
  fIncUp DWORD 0
  Reserv DB 32 dup(0)
PAINTSTR ENDS
; Structure for getting the cursor position
POINT  STRUC
   X DD ?
   Y DD ?
POINT  ENDS

; The HINT.ASM file
.586P
; Flat memory model
.MODEL FLAT, stdcall
include hint.inc
; INCLUDELIB directives for the linker
IFDEF MASM
; For the LINK.EXE linker
     includelib C:\masm32\lib\user32.lib
     includelib C:\masm32\lib\kernel32.lib
     includelib C:\masm32\lib\gdi32.lib
ELSE
; For the TLINK32.EXE linker
     includelib c:\tasm32\lib\import32.lib
ENDIF
;-------------------------------------------------
; Data segment
_DATA SEGMENT
      MSG        MSGSTRUCT <?>
      HINST      DD 0 ; Application descriptor
      PA         DB "DIAL1", 0
      HIN        DB "HINTW", 0
      XX         DD ?
      YY         DD ?
;--------------------------
      R1         RECT  <?>
      R2         RECT  <?>
      S          SIZ   <?>
      PS         PAINTSTR <?>
      PT         POINT  <?>
; Descriptors for popup windows for the first and the second elements
      H1         DD 0
      H2         DD 0
```

```
; Help string
     HINTS      DB 60 DUP(?)
; List of help strings
     HINT1      DB "Edit string", 0
     HINT2      DB "Exit button", 0
; For temporarily storing the device context
     DC         DD ?
; Counter
     P1         DD ?
_DATA ENDS
; Code segment
_TEXT SEGMENT
START:
; Get the application descriptor
     PUSH  0
     CALL  GetModuleHandleA@4
     MOV   [HINST], EAX
;-------------------------------
     PUSH  0
     PUSH  OFFSET WNDPROC
     PUSH  0
     PUSH  OFFSET PA
     PUSH  [HINST]
     CALL  DialogBoxParamA@20
     CMP   EAX, -1
     JNE   KOL
KOL:
;--------------------------------
     PUSH  0
     CALL  ExitProcess@4
;--------------------------------
; Window procedure
; Position of parameters in the stack
; [EBP+014H]  ; LPARAM
; [EBP+10H]   ; WAPARAM
; [EBP+0CH]   ; MES
; [EBP+8]     ; HWND
WNDPROC  PROC
     PUSH  EBP
     MOV   EBP, ESP
     PUSH  EBX
     PUSH  ESI
     PUSH  EDI
```

```
;----------------
      CMP   DWORD PTR [EBP+0CH], WM_CLOSE
      JNE   L1
; The reaction to closing the window
; Delete the timer
L4:
      PUSH  2 ; Timer identifier
      PUSH  DWORD PTR [EBP+08H]
      CALL  KillTimer@8
; Close the dialog
      PUSH  0
      PUSH  DWORD PTR [EBP+08H]
      CALL  EndDialog@8
      JMP   FINISH
L1:
      CMP   DWORD PTR [EBP+0CH], WM_INITDIALOG
      JNE   L2
; Startup initialization
; Set the timer
      PUSH  OFFSET TIMPROC
      PUSH  500 ; 0.5-second interval
      PUSH  2 ; Timer identifier
      PUSH  DWORD PTR [EBP+08H]
      CALL  SetTimer@16
      JMP   FINISH
L2:
      CMP   DWORD PTR [EBP+0CH], WM_COMMAND
      JNE   L3
; Exit button?
      CMP   WORD PTR [EBP+10H], 2
      JNE   L3
      JMP   L4
L3:
FINISH:
      POP   EDI
      POP   ESI
      POP   EBX
      POP   EBP
      MOV   EAX, 0
      RET   16
WNDPROC     ENDP
;-------------------------------------------
; Timer procedure
```

```
; Position of parameters in the stack
; [EBP+014H]   ; LPARAM — Time elapsed since Windows startup
; [EBP+10H]    ; WAPARAM — Timer identifier
; [EBP+0CH]    ; WM_TIMER
; [EBP+8]      ; HWND
TIMPROC  PROC
      PUSH  EBP
      MOV   EBP, ESP
; Get the cursor position
      PUSH  OFFSET PT
      CALL  GetCursorPos@4
; Store the coordinates
      MOV   EAX, PT.X
      MOV   XX, EAX
      MOV   EAX, PT.Y
      MOV   YY, EAX
; Get the elements positions
; Edit window
      PUSH  1
      PUSH  DWORD PTR [EBP+08H]
      CALL  GetDlgItem@8
      PUSH  OFFSET R1
      PUSH  EAX
      CALL  GetWindowRect@8
; Exit button
      PUSH  2
      PUSH  DWORD PTR [EBP+08H]
      CALL  GetDlgItem@8
      PUSH  OFFSET R2
      PUSH  EAX
      CALL  GetWindowRect@8
; Increase the counter
      INC   P1
      MOV   ECX, XX
      MOV   EDX, YY
; Check the conditions
  .IF H1==0 && P1>5
    .IF EDX<=R1.B && EDX>=R1.T && ECX>=R1.L && ECX<=R1.R
; Prepare the string
      PUSH  OFFSET HINT1
      PUSH  OFFSET HINTS
      CALL  lstrcpyA@8
; Create the popup dialog
```

```
        PUSH  0
        PUSH  OFFSET HINT
        PUSH  DWORD PTR [EBP+08H]
        PUSH  OFFSET HIN
        PUSH  [HINST]
        CALL  CreateDialogParamA@20
        MOV   H1, EAX
; Set the focus
        PUSH  DWORD PTR [EBP+08H]
        CALL  SetFocus@4
; Reset the counter to zero
        MOV   P1, 0
        JMP   _END
      .ENDIF
    .ENDIF
    .IF H1!=0
     .IF (EDX>R1.B || EDX<R1.T) || (ECX<R1.L || ECX>R1.R)
; Delete the popup window because of the change of the cursor position
        PUSH  H1
        CALL  DestroyWindow@4
        MOV   H1, 0
        JMP   _END
     .ENDIF
    .ENDIF
    .IF H2==0 && P1>5
     .IF EDX<=R2.B && EDX>=R2.T && ECX>=R2.L && ECX<=R2.R
; Prepare the string
        PUSH  OFFSET HINT2
        PUSH  OFFSET HINTS
        CALL  lstrcpyA@8
; Create the popup dialog
        PUSH  0
        PUSH  OFFSET HINT
        PUSH  DWORD PTR [EBP+08H]
        PUSH  OFFSET HIN
        PUSH  [HINST]
        CALL  CreateDialogParamA@20
        MOV   H2, EAX
; Set the focus
        PUSH  DWORD PTR [EBP+08H]
        CALL  SetFocus@4
; Reset the counter to zero
        MOV   P1, 0
```

```
        JMP   _END
     .ENDIF
    .ENDIF
    .IF H2!=0
     .IF (EDX>R2.B || EDX<R2.T) || (ECX<R2.L || ECX>R2.R)
; Delete the popup window because of the change of the cursor position
        PUSH  H2
        CALL  DestroyWindow@4
        MOV   H2, 0
        JMP   _END
     .ENDIF
    .ENDIF
; Restore the stack
_END:
        POP   EBP
        RET   16
TIMPROC      ENDP
; Window procedure of popup help
HINT PROC
        PUSH  EBP
        MOV   EBP, ESP
        CMP   DWORD PTR [EBP+0CH], WM_INITDIALOG
        JNE   NO_INIT
; Initialization
; Get the context
        PUSH  DWORD PTR [EBP+08H]
        CALL  GetDC@4
        MOV   DC, EAX
; Get the string length
        PUSH  OFFSET HINTS
        CALL  lstrlenA@4
; Get the string length and width
        PUSH  OFFSET S
        PUSH  EAX
        PUSH  OFFSET HINTS
        PUSH  DC
        CALL  GetTextExtentPoint32A@16
; Set the position and the size of the popup window
        PUSH  0
        PUSH  S.Y
        ADD   S.X, 2
        PUSH  S.X
        SUB   YY, 20
```

```
        PUSH  YY
        ADD   XX, 10
        PUSH  XX
        PUSH  DWORD PTR [EBP+08H]
        CALL  MoveWindow@24
; Close the context
        PUSH  DC
        PUSH  DWORD PTR [EBP+08H]
        CALL  ReleaseDC@8
; Set the timer
        PUSH  0
        PUSH  6000 ; 6-second interval
        PUSH  3 ; Timer identifier
        PUSH  DWORD PTR [EBP+08H]
        CALL  SetTimer@16
        JMP   FIN
NO_INIT:
        CMP   DWORD PTR [EBP+0CH], WM_PAINT
        JNE   NO_PAINT
; Redraw the window
; Get the context
        PUSH  OFFSET PS
        PUSH  DWORD PTR [EBP+08H]
        CALL  BeginPaint@8
        MOV   DC, EAX
; Set the foreground and background colors
        PUSH  RGBB
        PUSH  EAX
        CALL  SetBkColor@8
        PUSH  RGBT
        PUSH  DC
        CALL  SetTextColor@8
; Output the text
        PUSH  OFFSET HINTS
        CALL  lstrlenA@4
        PUSH  EAX
        PUSH  OFFSET HINTS
        PUSH  0
        PUSH  0
        PUSH  DC
        CALL  TextOutA@20
; Close the context
        PUSH  OFFSET PS
```

```
        PUSH  DWORD PTR [EBP+08H]
        CALL  EndPaint@8
        JMP   FIN
NO_PAINT:
        CMP   DWORD PTR [EBP+0CH], WM_TIMER
        JNE   FIN
; Process the timer event
; Delete the timer close the dialog
; The popup help window is closed because the
; 6-second timer has expired
        PUSH  3
        PUSH  DWORD PTR [EBP+08H]
        CALL  KillTimer@8
        PUSH  DWORD PTR [EBP+08H]
        CALL  DestroyWindow@4
FIN:
        POP   EBP
        RET   16
HINT ENDP
_TEXT ENDS
END START
```

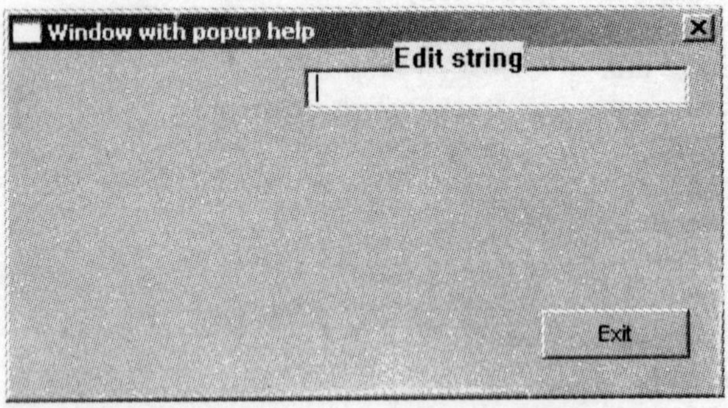

Fig. 14.2. Dialog providing popup help

The program presented in Listing 14.3 requires some comments.

First, note that this program uses conditional run-time constructs. This approach is logical. It is justified by the needs to reduce the program size and improve its readability. Nesting of the conditional constructs and placement of braces are based on the desire to reduce the string length yet preserve program compatibility — the possibility of translating it using both MASM32 and TASM32. As I have already mentioned, these two assemblers differ significantly, especially when speaking about macros.

To translate this program, issue the following commands using MASM32:

```
ML /c /coff /DMASM hint.asm
RC hint.rc
LINK /SUBSYSTEM:WINDOWS hint.obj hint.res
```

To translate this program, issue the following commands using TASM32:

```
TASM32 /ml hint.asm
BRCC32 hint.rc
TLINK32 -aa hint.obj,,,,,hint.res
```

As you probably understand, the timer procedure checks the cursor position every 0.5 seconds. If the cursor is positioned over some element (e.g., edit window or button) and popup help has not been called yet (`H1` or `H2` is different from zero), then popup help is called. At the same time, the value of the counter (`P1`) is taken into account to ensure that the popup help window appears with a certain delay. If the procedure is next called when the cursor is positioned outside the element and the popup window still displayed, it will be closed. However, this mechanism does not account for a cursor that quickly moves from one element to another. In this case, there could be two popup help windows on the screen. The first popup must be closed immediately.

In Listing 14.3, the dialog box has only two elements: the edit window and the button. I wanted to note that popup help can be specified for any element. The position of the popup window in relation to the cursor can be easily regulated. You can change it yourself.

The `GetCursorPos` function places the cursor position in coordinates relative to the screen. No problems will arise here, because the `GetWindowsRec` function also places the position of the window element in absolute coordinates. Before that, you have to determine the window descriptor using the `GetDlgItem` function.

Chapter 15

Multitasking

In the previous chapter, you considered the possibilities of using timers in applied task. Having specified one or more timers, you force the system to call one or more procedures in an automatic mode. Thus, using timers, you can implement multitasking mode within a single process. Furthermore, it was shown that such subtasks could communicate with each other. This is natural, because they share the same address space; consequently, information can be passed through global variables from subtask to subtask. This problem is interesting and complicated. I cover it later in this book. For the moment, consider the multitasking environment in the Windows operating system from the beginning.

Creating a Process

The process is the kernel object (see *Chapter 13*) created by the Windows operating system when loading an executable module. It has the following at its exclusive disposal:

- Virtual memory allocated to it by the operating system.
- Handles of the files opened by it.
- The list of dynamic link libraries (DLLs) loaded by it into its own memory.
- Subprocesses, known as threads, which it has created. Threads execute independently in the memory owned by the process.

I hope that this definition clearly reflects the idea of the process concept. However, for most problems considered in this chapter, an even simpler definition would be sufficient — every executable module (EXE) started in the Windows environment becomes the process.

Now, consider subprocesses. This concept is also simple: Every process can generate other processes within the address space allocated to it. These processes execute independently of each other and of the process that generates them. However, the generating process, if needed, can forcibly terminate (kill) any process it has generated. Such processes are also called threads. Now, it is clear that in the previous chapter I used the timer to create an analogue of threads. However, in the Windows operating system, there are special tools for creating threads.

Now, it is necessary to describe the types of multitasking. In the old 16-bit Windows version, switching between tasks was done only when the task returned control to the operating system. This type of multitasking is called nonpreemptive. In a certain sense, this situation was even worse than that in MS-DOS. There, the elements of multitasking were implemented using so-called terminate-and-stay resident programs. Such programs intercepted interrupts from the timer, the keyboard, or any other device; from time to time, they could gain control in response to events related to those devices.

The situation that existed in the old Windows operating system required the programmer to observe a gentleman's agreement that consisted of avoiding capturing the processor for a long time. The use of timers provided a kind of solution for this problem (as you have seen already). Another solution was the use of the `PeekMessage` function instead of `GetMessage`. The `PeekMessage` function, in contrast to `GetMessage`, returns control immediately, even if there are no messages in the queue.

In 32-bit operating systems of the Windows family (Windows 9*x*, Windows NT, Windows 2000, etc.), the preemptive multitasking is implemented. According to this method, switching between processes and threads is delegated to the operating system. If the process spends too much time on a certain operation, then the cursor over the process window will turn into an hourglass. In this case, other processes will continue to execute, and you'll be able to switch to them. However, access to the window of the current process can be difficult. This problem can be solved using the previously mentioned approach — namely, replacing the `GetMessage` function with the `PeekMessage` function is the waiting loop. However, dividing the process into several threads would be a better solution.

The next few sections will be dedicated to the creation of threads. As relates to the remaining part of this section, it will concentrate on creation of processes. Your application can create processes by starting a specific executable program. These processes will run independently of the main application. At the same time, your application can delete the application that it has started. The process can be created using the `CreateProcess` function. Here is a brief description of parameters accepted by this function:

- First parameter — This specifies the name of the program being started. The name can contain the full path to the program.
- Second parameter — Its value depends on whether or not the first parameter is set to `NULL`. If the first parameter points to a string, then this parameter is interpreted as a startup command line (without the program name). If the first parameter is `NULL`, then this parameter is interpreted as a command line whose first element represents the program name. If the path to the program is not specified, then the `CreateProcess` function searches for the program according to a certain algorithm:
  - Search within the directory, from which the program was started.
  - Search within the current directory.
  - Search in the system directory (which can be obtained by calling the `GetSystemDirectory` function). As a rule, the system directory's name is C:\WINDOWS\SYSTEM or C:\WINDOWS\SYSTEM32.
  - Search in the Windows directory (the actual name can be obtained by calling the `GetWindowsDirectory` function). Usually, this is the C:\WINDOWS directory.
  - Search in directories listed by the `PATH` environment variable.
- Third and fourth parameters — These parameters are used for specifying access attributes of the process being generated. Usually, they are set to zero.
- Fifth parameter — If this parameter is zero, then the process being generated doesn't inherit descriptors of the generating process. If the parameter has a nonzero value, the process being generated inherits descriptors.
- Sixth parameter — This parameter allows you to change the properties of the process being generated. If this parameter is set to zero, then the properties are specified by default. Because this parameter can take a range of values, I won't provide them here. You can find this information in appropriate manuals.
- Seventh parameter — This is a pointer to the buffer that contains environment parameters. If this parameter is set to zero, then the process being generated inherits environment parameters of the generating process.
- Eighth parameter — Specifies the current drive and directory for the process being generated. If this parameter is set to `NULL`, then the process being generated inherits the current drive and directory of the generating process.
- Ninth parameter — This is a pointer to the structure that contains information about the window of the process being created. The fields of this structure will be considered later.

- Tenth parameter — This points to the structure filled when the application is started for execution. Here is this structure:

```
PROCINF STRUC
        HProcess    DD ?    ; Descriptor of the created process
        HThread     DD ?    ; Descriptor of the primary thread
                            ; of the new process
        Idproc      DD ?    ; Identifier of the new process
        IdThr       DD ?    ; Identifier of the primary thread of the
                            ; new process
PROCINF ENDS
```

The main difference between the descriptor (handle) and the identifier lies in that the descriptor is unique only within the limits of a given process and the identifier is the global value. The data area of the current process can be found using an identifier. I assume that you immediately ask the following question: What is the difference between the application descriptor that I get using the `GetModulHandle` function and the values you have just mentioned? Well, the application descriptor and the handle that you obtain using the `GetModulHandle` function are the same value. An application descriptor or module descriptor is a local value, which means that it is in force within the limits of a given process. As a rule, it is equal to the address, by which the module is loaded into the virtual address space. Every module loaded into the memory has a module handle, including DLLs.

Now, consider the structure pointed to by the ninth parameter of the `CreateProcess` function. Here is the structure:

```
STARTUP STRUC
        cb                  DD 0
        lpReserved          DD 0
        lpDesktop           DD 0
        lpTitle             DD 0
        dwX                 DD 0
        dwY                 DD 0
        dwXSize             DD 0
        dwYSize             DD 0
        dwXCountChars       DD 0
        dwYCountChars       DD 0
        dwFillAttribute     DD 0
        dwFlags             DD 0
        wShowWindow         DW 0
        cbReserved2         DW 0
        lpReserved2         DD 0
        hStdInput           DD 0
```

```
    hStdOutput          DD 0
    hStdError           DD 0
STARTUP ENDS
```

The fields of this structure have the following meanings:

- `cb` — The size of this structure in bytes; a mandatory field that must be filled
- `lpReserved` — Reserved; must be zero
- `lpDesktop` — Desktop (and workstation) name; has meaning only for the operating systems from the Windows NT family
- `lpTitle` — Window title for console applications that create their own console; must be zero for all other applications
- `dwX` — X-coordinate of the top left window corner
- `dwY` — Y-coordinate of the top left window corner
- `dwXSize` — Window width
- `dwYSize` — Window height
- `dwXCountChars` — Size of the console buffer (by the X-coordinate)
- `dwYCountChars` — Size of the console buffer (by the Y-coordinate)
- `dwFillAttribute` — Initial color of the text; makes sense only for console applications
- `dwFlags` — Flag of the field values; possible values are listed in Table 15.1

Table 15.1. Possible values of the dwFlags field

Macro value of the flag	Constant value	Explanation
STARTF_USESHOWWINDOW	1h	Enable the `dwShowWindow` field
STARTF_USESIZE	2h	Enable `dwXSize` and `dwYSize`
STARTF_USEPOSITION	4h	Enable `dwX` and `dwY`
STARTF_USECOUNTCHARS	8h	Enable `dwXCountChars` and `dwYCountChars`
STARTF_USEFILLATTRIBUTE	10h	Enable `dwFillAttribute`
STARTF_FORCEONFEEDBACK	40h	Specify that the cursor is in the feedback mode
STARTF_FORCEOFFFEEDBACK	80h	Specify that the cursor feedback mode is off
STARTF_USESTDHANDLES	100h	Enable `kStdInput`

- `wShowWindow` — Defines the window display mode
- `cbReserved2` — Reserved; must be zero
- `hStdInput` — Input descriptor (for the console)
- `hStdOutput` — Output descriptor (for the console)
- `hStdError` — Output descriptor for displaying an error message (for the console)

The example shown in Listing 15.1 demonstrates the procedure of creating a process. The WINWORD.EXE text editor was chosen as a program that generates a process. To check whether this example operates correctly, you'll have to specify the path to the WINWORD.EXE module on your computer (the `PATH` variable). Notice that the application appears on screen in a minimized form, and notice how this is achieved. As you can see, the `CreateProcess` function is much simpler than it seems to be at first glance.

Listing 15.1. Creating a process

```
// The PROCESS.RC file
// Constant definitions
#define WS_SYSMENU          0x00080000L
#define WS_POPUP            0x80000000L
#define DS_3DLOOK           0x0004L

// The menu resource
MENUP MENU
{
 POPUP "&Start Word"
 {
 MENUITEM "&Start", 1
 MENUITEM "&Close", 2
 MENUITEM "E&xit the program", 3
 }
}

// Dialog box definition
DIAL1 DIALOG 0, 0, 240, 120
STYLE WS_POPUP | WS_SYSMENU | DS_3DLOOK
CAPTION "Example of starting the process"
FONT 8, "Arial"
{
}

; The PROCESS.INC file
; Constants
```

```
STARTF_USESHOWWINDOW equ 1h
SW_SHOWMINIMIZED     equ 2
; This message arrives when the window is closed
WM_CLOSE             equ 10h
WM_INITDIALOG        equ 110h
WM_COMMAND           equ 111h
; Prototypes of external procedures
IFDEF MASM
; For MASM
        EXTERN TerminateProcess@8:NEAR
        EXTERN CreateProcessA@40:NEAR
        EXTERN DialogBoxParamA@20:NEAR
        EXTERN EndDialog@8:NEAR
        EXTERN MessageBoxA@16:NEAR
        EXTERN ExitProcess@4:NEAR
        EXTERN GetModuleHandleA@4:NEAR
        EXTERN LoadMenuA@8:NEAR
        EXTERN SetMenu@8:NEAR
        EXTERN TranslateMessage@4:NEAR
ELSE
; For TASM
        EXTERN TerminateProcess:NEAR
        EXTERN CreateProcessA:NEAR
        EXTERN DialogBoxParamA:NEAR
        EXTERN EndDialog:NEAR
        EXTERN MessageBoxA:NEAR
        EXTERN ExitProcess:NEAR
        EXTERN GetModuleHandleA:NEAR
        EXTERN LoadMenuA:NEAR
        EXTERN SetMenu:NEAR
        EXTERN TranslateMessage:NEAR
        TerminateProcess@8 = TerminateProcess
        CreateProcessA@40 = CreateProcessA
        DialogBoxParamA@20 = DialogBoxParamA
        EndDialog@8 = EndDialog
        MessageBoxA@16 = MessageBoxA
        ExitProcess@4 = ExitProcess
        GetModuleHandleA@4 = GetModuleHandleA
        LoadMenuA@8 = LoadMenuA
        SetMenu@8 = SetMenu
        TranslateMessage@4 = TranslateMessage
```

```
ENDIF
; Structures
; Message structure
MSGSTRUCT STRUC
        MSHWND          DD ?
        MSMESSAGE       DD ?
        MSWPARAM        DD ?
        MSLPARAM        DD ?
        MSTIME          DD ?
        MSPT            DD ?
MSGSTRUCT ENDS
; The structure for CreateProcess
STARTUP STRUC
        cb                          DD 0
        lpReserved                  DD 0
        lpDesktop                   DD 0
        lpTitle                     DD 0
        dwX                         DD 0
        dwY                         DD 0
        dwXSize                     DD 0
        dwYSize                     DD 0
        dwXCountChars               DD 0
        dwYCountChars               DD 0
        dwFillAttribute             DD 0
        dwFlags                     DD 0
        wShowWindow                 DW 0
        cbReserved2                 DW 0
        lpReserved2                 DD 0
        hStdInput                   DD 0
        hStdOutput                  DD 0
        hStdError                   DD 0
STARTUP ENDS
; Structure containing information about the process
PROCINF STRUC
        HProcess            DD ?
        HThread             DD ?
        Idproc              DD ?
        IdThr               DD ?
PROCINF ENDS

; The PROCESS.ASM file
.586P
```

```
; Flat memory model
.MODEL FLAT, stdcall
include process.inc
; INCLUDELIB directives for the linker to link libraries
IFDEF MASM
; MASM directives
        includelib c:\masm32\lib\user32.lib
        includelib c:\masm32\lib\kernel32.lib
ELSE
; TASM directives
        includelib c:\tasm32\lib\import32.lib
ENDIF
; Data segment
_DATA SEGMENT
        NEWHWND  DD 0
        MSG      MSGSTRUCT <?>
        STRUP    STARTUP      <?>
        INF      PROCINF <?>
        HINST    DD 0 ; Application handle
        PA       DB "DIAL1", 0
        PMENU    DB "MENUP", 0
        PATH     DB "C:\Program Files\Office\WINWORD.EXE", 0
_DATA ENDS
; Code segment
_TEXT SEGMENT
START:
; Get application descriptor
        PUSH  0
        CALL  GetModuleHandleA@4
        MOV   [HINST], EAX
; Create a modal dialog
        PUSH  0
        PUSH  OFFSET WNDPROC
        PUSH  0
        PUSH  OFFSET PA
        PUSH  [HINST]
        CALL  DialogBoxParamA@20
        PUSH  0
        CALL  ExitProcess@4
;---------------------------------
; Window procedure
; Position of parameters in the stack
```

```
; [EBP+014H]  ; LPARAM
; [EBP+10H]   ; WAPARAM
; [EBP+0CH]   ; MES
; [EBP+8]     ; HWND
WNDPROC PROC
        PUSH  EBP
        MOV   EBP, ESP
        PUSH  EBX
        PUSH  ESI
        PUSH  EDI
; This message arrives when the window is closed
        CMP   DWORD PTR [EBP+0CH], WM_CLOSE
        JNE   L1
; Close the dialog
        JMP   L5
L1:
; The message for window initialization
        CMP   DWORD PTR [EBP+0CH], WM_INITDIALOG
        JNE   L3
; Load the menu
        PUSH  OFFSET PMENU
        PUSH  [HINST]
        CALL  LoadMenuA@8
; Set the menu
        PUSH  EAX
        PUSH  DWORD PTR [EBP+08H]
        CALL  SetMenu@8
        JMP   FINISH
; Check whether some events have happened to the
; menu items in the dialog
L3:
        CMP   DWORD PTR [EBP+0CH], WM_COMMAND
        JNE   FINISH
        CMP   WORD PTR [EBP+10H], 3
        JE    L5
        CMP   WORD PTR [EBP+10H], 2
        JE    L7
        CMP   WORD PTR [EBP+10H], 1
        JE    L6
JMP FINISH
; Close the dialog
L5:
        PUSH  0
```

```
        PUSH  DWORD PTR [EBP+08H]
        CALL  EndDialog@8
        JMP   FINISH
; Start Word
L6:
; Fill the startup structure
; The window must appear in a minimized form
        MOV   STRUP.cb, 68
        MOV   STRUP.lpReserved, 0
        MOV   STRUP.lpDesktop, 0
        MOV   STRUP.lpTitle, 0
        MOV   STRUP.dwFlags, STARTF_USESHOWWINDOW
        MOV   STRUP.cbReserved2, 0
        MOV   STRUP.lpReserved2, 0
        MOV   STRUP.wShowWindow, SW_SHOWMINIMIZED
; Starting the Winword application
        PUSH  OFFSET INF
        PUSH  OFFSET STRUP
        PUSH  0
        PUSH  0
        PUSH  0
        PUSH  0
        PUSH  0
        PUSH  0
        PUSH  OFFSET PATH
        PUSH  0
        CALL  CreateProcessA@40
        JMP   FINISH
; Remove the process from memory
L7:
        PUSH  0 ; Exit code
        PUSH  INF.hProcess
        CALL  TerminateProcess@8
FINISH:
        MOV   EAX, 0
        POP   EDI
        POP   ESI
        POP   EBX
        POP   EBP
        RET   16
WNDPROC    ENDP
_TEXT ENDS
END START
```

To translate the PROCESS.ASM program presented in Listing 15.1, issue the following commands for MASM32:

```
ML /c /coff /DMASM process.asm
RC process.rc
LINK /SUBSYSTEM:WINDOWS process.obj proces.res
```

To translate the PROCESS.ASM program presented in Listing 15.1, issue the following commands for TASM32:

```
TASM32 /ml process.asm
BRCC32 process.rc
TLINK32 -aa process.obj,,,,,process.res
```

I think that the program presented in Listing 15.1 doesn't require any other comment. The window displayed by this program, with the menu, is shown in Fig. 15.1.

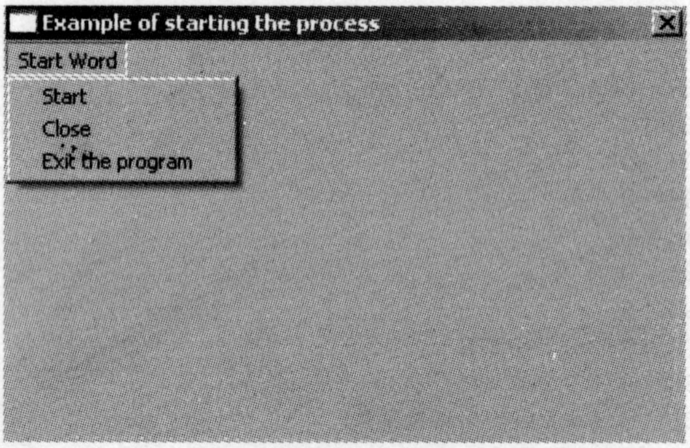

Fig. 15.1. Window of the program that starts WINWORD.EXE and removes it from memory

It is necessary to emphasize how the started process can be unloaded from the memory. Naturally, if you start a module written by someone else, you can hope that the author of that module provided a natural method of exiting that program. In this case, the author of the third-party module bears all the responsibility related to application termination. On the other hand, if you use the `TerminateProcess` function, as was shown in Listing 15.1, then the program may not necessarily terminate correctly. Naturally, the system releases all resources allocated to the process. However, it cannot carry out another component's job. For example, if that program was working with a file, then part of the data might be lost. When using the `TerminateProcess` function, the system doesn't send any notification to the application. As relates to the `ExitProcess` function that I widely use in this book, this is a correct way of terminating a process when writing a program in Assembly language. However, avoid using this function when writing programs in high-level languages. Your application might contain objects, and they will be incorrectly removed from the memory (without executing destructors).

Threads

Now, it is time to consider threads in more detail. First, try to solve the problem from the previous chapter (see Listing 14.2) using the thread.

A thread can be created using the `CreateThread` function. This function accepts the following parameters:

- First parameter — This is a pointer to the structure of the access attributes. It has meaning only for the Windows NT family. As a rule, this parameter is set to `NULL`.
- Second parameter — This is the size of the thread's stack. If this parameter is set to zero, then the default stack size is taken, which is the size of the stack of the parent thread.
- Third parameter — This is a pointer to the thread function. Thread execution starts from the call to this function.
- Fourth parameter — This is the parameter for the thread function.
- Fifth parameter — This flag defines the thread state. If this flag is zero, then thread execution starts immediately. If the flag value is `CREATE_SUSPENDED (4H)`, the thread is in the waiting state and starts after the `ResumeThread` function hasbeen executed.
- Sixth parameter — This is the pointer to the variable, into which the thread handle will be placed.

As already mentioned, thread execution starts from the thread function. Termination of this function naturally terminates the thread (exiting the function using `RET`). The thread can also terminate execution by executing the `ExitThread` function, specifying the exit code. Finally, the generating thread might terminate the operation of the generated thread using the `TerminateThread` function. In Listing 15.2, the generated process cannot terminate its operation and terminates with the application in response to `TerminateThread`. It is necessary to point out that such termination is abnormal and is not recommended for everyday use. This is because when using this type of termination, the system doesn't carry out any actions related to releasing allocated resources (memory blocks, opened files, etc.). Therefore, it is recommended that you build your applications so that the thread would terminate by exiting the thread procedure. Thus, the example in Listing 15.2 demonstrates some of don'ts.

In an ideal situation, the window function takes responsibility for reaction only to events that take place in relation to its elements; all other jobs (e.g., complex computations and file processing) are the responsibility of threads. By the way, a thread can generate other threads, so an entire branched tree may appear as a result.

As I have mentioned already, the program in Listing 15.2 uses a thread to compute the current data and time and display them in the edit window. Note that if such processing is implemented in the window function, you would immediately notice the difference because the window would cease to react to nearly all of your actions.

Listing 15.2. Creating a thread

```
// The TIMER2.RC file
// Constants definitions
#define WS_SYSMENU                0x00080000L
// The window elements must be initially visible
#define WS_VISIBLE                0x10000000L
// Border around the element
#define WS_BORDER                 0x00800000L
// Elements can be activated using the <Tab> key
#define WS_TABSTOP                0x00010000L
// Text in the edit field is left-aligned
#define ES_LEFT                   0x0000L
// Style of all window elements
#define WS_CHILD                  0x40000000L
// Keyboard input is disabled
#define ES_READONLY               0x0800L
// Button style
#define BS_PUSHBUTTON             0x00000000L
// Center the button label
#define BS_CENTER                 0x00000300L

#define DS_3DLOOK                 0x0004L
// Dialog box definition
DIAL1 DIALOG 0, 0, 240, 100
STYLE WS_SYSMENU | DS_3DLOOK
CAPTION "Example of the thread usage"
FONT 8, "Arial"
{
// Edit field, identifier 1
 CONTROL "", 1, "edit", ES_LEFT | WS_CHILD
  | WS_VISIBLE | WS_BORDER
  | WS_TABSTOP | ES_READONLY, 100, 5, 130, 12
// Button, identifier 2
 CONTROL "Exit", 2, "button", BS_PUSHBUTTON
  | BS_CENTER | WS_CHILD | WS_VISIBLE | WS_TABSTOP,
```

```
 180, 76, 50, 14
}

; The TIMER2.INC file
; Constants
; The message arrives when the window is closed
WM_CLOSE       equ 10h
; The message arrives when the window is created
WM_INITDIALOG  equ 110h
; The message arrives when something happens to
; the window elements
WM_COMMAND     equ 111h
; This message sends the text to the window element
WM_SETTEXT     equ 0Ch
; Prototypes of external procedures
IFDEF MASM
; For MASM
        EXTERN      SendMessageA@16:NEAR
        EXTERN      GetDlgItem@8:NEAR
        EXTERN      Sleep@4:NEAR
        EXTERN      TerminateThread@8:NEAR
        EXTERN      CreateThread@24:NEAR
        EXTERN      wsprintfA:NEAR
        EXTERN      GetLocalTime@4:NEAR
        EXTERN      ExitProcess@4:NEAR
        EXTERN      GetModuleHandleA@4:NEAR
        EXTERN      DialogBoxParamA@20:NEAR
        EXTERN      EndDialog@8:NEAR
ELSE
; For TASM
        EXTERN      SendMessageA:NEAR
        EXTERN      GetDlgItem:NEAR
        EXTERN      Sleep:NEAR
        EXTERN      TerminateThread:NEAR
        EXTERN      CreateThread:NEAR
        EXTERN      _wsprintfA:NEAR
        EXTERN      GetLocalTime:NEAR
        EXTERN      ExitProcess:NEAR
        EXTERN      GetModuleHandleA:NEAR
        EXTERN      DialogBoxParamA:NEAR
        EXTERN      EndDialog:NEAR
        SendMessageA@16 = SendMessageA
```

```
        GetDlgItem@8 = GetDlgItem
        Sleep@4 = Sleep
        TerminateThread@8 = TerminateThread
        CreateThread@24 = CreateThread
        wsprintfA = _wsprintfA
        GetLocalTime@4 = GetLocalTime
        ExitProcess@4 = ExitProcess
        GetModuleHandleA@4 = GetModuleHandleA
        DialogBoxParamA@20 = DialogBoxParamA
        EndDialog@8 = EndDialog
ENDIF
; Structures
; Message structure
MSGSTRUCT STRUC
        MSHWND          DD ?
        MSMESSAGE       DD ?
        MSWPARAM        DD ?
        MSLPARAM        DD ?
        MSTIME          DD ?
        MSPT            DD ?
MSGSTRUCT ENDS
; Date-time data structure
DAT STRUC
        year    DW ?
        month   DW ?
        dayweek DW ?
        day     DW ?
        hour    DW ?
        min     DW ?
        sec     DW ?
        msec    DW ?
DAT ENDS

; The TIMER2.ASM file
.586P
; Flat memory model
.MODEL FLAT, stdcall
include thread.inc
; INCLUDELIB directives for the linker to link libraries
IFDEF MASM
; For the LINK.EXE linker
      includelib c:\masm32\lib\user32.lib
```

```
    includelib c:\masm32\lib\kernel32.lib
    includelib c:\masm32\lib\gdi32.lib
ELSE
; For the TLINK32.EXE linker
    includelib c:\tasm32\lib\import32.lib
ENDIF
;---------------------------------------------
; Data segment
_DATA SEGMENT
      MSG     MSGSTRUCT <?>
      HINST   DD 0 ; Application descriptor
      PA      DB "DIAL1", 0
      TIM     DB "Date %u/%u/%u   Time %u:%u:%u", 0
      STRCOPY DB 50 DUP(?)
      DATA    DAT <0>
      HTHR    DD ?
_DATA ENDS
; Code segment
_TEXT SEGMENT
START:
; Get the application descriptor
      PUSH  0
      CALL  GetModuleHandleA@4
      MOV   [HINST], EAX
; Create a dialog
      PUSH  0
      PUSH  OFFSET WNDPROC
      PUSH  0
      PUSH  OFFSET PA
      PUSH  [HINST]
      CALL  DialogBoxParamA@20
      CMP   EAX, -1
      JNE   KOL
; Error message
KOL:
;--------------------------------
      PUSH  0
      CALL  ExitProcess@4
;--------------------------------
; Window procedure
; Position of parameters in the stack
; [EBP+014H]  ; LPARAM
```

```
; [EBP+10H]    ; WAPARAM
; [EBP+0CH]    ; MES
; [EBP+8]      ; HWND
WNDPROC      PROC
        PUSH  EBP
        MOV   EBP, ESP
        PUSH  EBX
        PUSH  ESI
        PUSH  EDI
;----------------
        CMP   DWORD PTR [EBP+0CH], WM_CLOSE
        JNE   L1
L3:
; The reaction to closing the window
; Kill the thread
        PUSH  0
        PUSH  HTHR
        CALL  TerminateThread@8
; Close the dialog
        PUSH  0
        PUSH  DWORD PTR [EBP+08H]
        CALL  EndDialog@8
        JMP   FINISH
L1:
        CMP   DWORD PTR [EBP+0CH], WM_INITDIALOG
        JNE   L2
; Startup initialization
; Get the descriptor of the edit field
        PUSH  1
        PUSH  DWORD PTR [EBP+08H]
        CALL  GetDlgItem@8
; Create a thread
        PUSH  OFFSET HTHR    ; Thread descriptor goes here
        PUSH  0
        PUSH  EAX            ; Parameter
        PUSH  OFFSET GETTIME ; Procedure address
        PUSH  0
        PUSH  0
        CALL  CreateThread@24
        JMP   FINISH
L2:
        CMP   DWORD PTR [EBP+0CH], WM_COMMAND
```

```
        JNE   FINISH
; Exit button?
        CMP   WORD PTR [EBP+10H], 2
        JE    L3
FINISH:
        POP   EDI
        POP   ESI
        POP   EBX
        POP   EBP
        MOV   EAX, 0
        RET   16
WNDPROC    ENDP
; Thread function
; [EBP+8] Parameter = Edit field descriptor
GETTIME PROC
        PUSH  EBP
        MOV   EBP, ESP
LO:
; 1-second delay
        PUSH  1000
        CALL  Sleep@4
; Get local time
        PUSH  OFFSET DATA
        CALL  GetLocalTime@4
; Get the string for data and time output
        MOVZX EAX, DATA.sec
        PUSH  EAX
        MOVZX EAX, DATA.min
        PUSH  EAX
        MOVZX EAX, DATA.hour
        PUSH  EAX
        MOVZX EAX, DATA.year
        PUSH  EAX
        MOVZX EAX, DATA.month
        PUSH  EAX
        MOVZX EAX, DATA.day
        PUSH  EAX
        PUSH  OFFSET TIM
        PUSH  OFFSET STRCOPY
        CALL  wsprintfA
; Send the string to the edit window
        PUSH  OFFSET STRCOPY
```

```
        PUSH  0
        PUSH  WM_SETTEXT
        PUSH  DWORD PTR [EBP+08H]
        CALL  SendMessageA@16
        JMP   LO ; Endless loop
        POP   EBP
        RET  4
GETTIME ENDP
_TEXT ENDS
END START
```

To translate the THREAD.ASM program presented in Listing 15.2, issue the following commands using MASM32:

```
ML /c /coff /DMASM thread.asm
RC thread.rc
LINK /SUBSYSTEM:WINDOWS thread.obj thread.res
```

Issue the following commands using TASM32:

```
TASM32 /ml thread.asm
BRCC32 thread.rc
TLINK32 -aa thread.obj,,,,,thread.res
```

I recommend that you pay attention to a useful function — `Sleep`. This function is frequently used in threads because it frees some processor time.

Interthread Communications

Now, it is time to describe a multithreading program. If threads are not supposed to intercommunicate, the number of started threads doesn't matter. The difficulties arise when the operation of one thread depends on the activities of another thread. Here, different situations are possible. Consider everything in due order.

You have already encountered the situation, in which two parallel processes intercommunicated using global variables. To be more precise, one process was preparing data for another process. Here, there were no difficulties. One process changed the variable contents with the predefined periodicity, and another process read the data from this variable at another periodicity. If the data refresh period is smaller than the data read period, you can be almost sure that the second process will always obtain refreshed data. Sometimes the relationship between the data refresh and the data read period has no meaning, as in this example.

However, it is often impossible to obtain the data periodically. For example, the data may depend on the activity of the third process. How would the second process then know that the data have already been prepared for transmission? At first glance, the problem might be solved by introducing an additional variable. For instance, call this variable `FLAG`. Assume that if `FLAG = 0`, the data are not ready; when `FLAG = 1`, the data are ready. Then, the following easy scheme can be implemented:

```
NO_DAT:
        ...
        CMP  FLAG, 1
        JNE  NO_DAT
        ...  ; Data transmission
        ...
        MOV  FLAG, 0
        ...
```

As you probably guessed, this fragment is intended for the second thread. The first thread also must check the `FLAG` variable and, if `FLAG = 0`, load new data into the variable and set the `FLAG` value to 1. This method is satisfactory when one process waits for another process to accomplish its task. In other words, the data are the result of the operation of that process. For example, suppose that you have started the compiler and another process waits for it to accomplish its operation before it outputs the results of its operation to some device. This situation occurs rather often.

However, what would happen if the data transmission process must be repeated multiple times? As can be easily noticed, this method will also work in a more difficult case. However, it is important to ensure that the second process changes the contents of the `FLAG` variable only after it receives the data and that the first process does the same thing only after it produces the data and loads them into the required variable. If this rule is not observed, collisions might occur. This would happen, for instance, if the second process didn't receive the data and the data were already changed.

This approach can be implemented in a more general case, when two threads (or two processes) must alternately access the same resource. As can be easily seen, this approach assumes that the resource is opened for one or to another process. If the problem is formulated in a different way — the process is either opened or closed for access — some difficulties would arise. A situation is possible, in which both processes would wait for the resource to be opened. In other words, they would continuously check the `FLAG` variable (`CMP FLAG, 1`). It might happen that they would attempt to access the resource simultaneously. Obviously, the need for some "mediator" would arise that would regulate access to the resource. For instance, such a mediator could send a message to one thread first and provide it access to the resource if it waits for its turn to access the resource. Then the same process would be repeated for the second thread.

This scheme is quite good, however, only if the threads access the resource alternately. If this requirement is not satisfied, a serious failure is possible. All considerations provided here aim to demonstrate that the problem of intercommunication among processes and threads and their synchronization is complicated and urgent for multitasking operating systems. Hence, such operating systems must have their own synchronization tools.[i]

NOTE

It should be noticed that continuous polling of a certain variable in a loop can consume a considerable part of the CPU time. Naturally, this is not acceptable for a multitasking operating system.

The remainder of this chapter is dedicated to the synchronization tools of the Windows operating system.

Semaphores

Semaphores are global objects that allow you to synchronize the operation of several processes or threads. From the programmer's point of view, a semaphore is simply a global counter that can be manipulated only using special functions. If this counter is equal to `N`, this means that `N` processes have access to the resource. Consider functions for working with semaphores in more detail.

- `CreateSemaphore` — Creates global object, the semaphore, and returns its descriptor. The function accepts the following parameters:
  - First parameter — The pointer to the structure that defines access attributes. It has meaning only for operating systems of the Windows NT family. Usually, it is assumed to be `NULL`.
  - Second parameter — The initial value of the semaphore counter. It determines how many tasks can initially access the resource.
  - Third parameter — The number of tasks that can simultaneously access the resource.
  - Fourth parameter — Pointer to the string that contains the semaphore name.
- `OpenSemaphore` — Opens the existing semaphore and returns the semaphore descriptor. This function is not used frequently. As a rule, a semaphore is created,

[i] In MS-DOS, which wasn't a multitasking operating system, the problem of coordinating the operation of resident programs was especially urgent. Although the programmers writing such programs have achieved impressive results, concurrent operation of several resident programs often resulted in noticeable conflicts.

and its descriptor is assigned to the global variables and then used in the threads being generated. This function accepts the following parameters:

- First parameter — Defines the desired access level to the semaphore. It can take the following values: `SEMAPHORE_MODIFY_STATE = 2H`, which allows the use of the `ReleaseSemaphore` function; `SYNCHRONIZE = 100000H`, which allows the use of any waiting function (Windows NT family only); and `SEMAPHORE_ALL_ACCESS = 0F0000h + SYNCHRONIZE + 3H`, which specifies all possible access flags to the semaphore.
- Second parameter — Specifies if the process created by the `CreateProcess` function can inherit the handle. If this parameter is set to `TRUE`, then the handle can be inherited; otherwise, the process cannot inherit the handle.
- Third parameter — A pointer to a null-terminated string that names the semaphore to be opened.

❐ `WaitForSingleObject` — Waits for the semaphore to open. If this function competes successfully, which means that access to the requested object is provided, it returns zero. The return value `102h` means that the waiting period has expired. Parameters of this function are as follows:

- First parameter — Semaphore handle.
- Second parameter — Waiting time in milliseconds. If this parameter is equal to `INFINITE = 0FFFFFFFFh`, the waiting time is unlimited.

❐ `ReleaseSemaphore` — Releases the semaphore, thus allowing other processes to gain access to the resource. Parameters of this function are as follows:

- First parameter — Semaphore handle.
- Second parameter — Defines which value must be added to the semaphore counter. Most frequently, this parameter is equal to 1.
- Third parameter — Pointer to the variable, into which the previous counter value must be placed.

Consider the algorithm of working with the semaphore. First, create a semaphore using the `CreateSemaphore` function, and assign its descriptor to the global variable. Before attempting to access the resources, the access to which must be limited, the thread must call the `WaitForSingleObject` function. When access is provided, the function returns 0. Having completed work with the resource, it is necessary to call the `ReleaseSemaphore` function. Thus, the access counter is released by 1, and the `WaitForSingleObject` function, in turn, decreases the counter value. Using semaphores, it is possible to control the number of threads that can simultaneously access the resource. The maximum counter value specifies how many threads can simultaneously access the object. Usually, as I have already mentioned, this value is assumed to be 1.

Events

An event is an object that differs from a semaphore only slightly. Consider the functions for working with events.

- `CreateEvent` — Creates an event object. This function accepts the following parameters:
  - First parameter — This has the same meaning as the first parameter of the `CreateSemaphore` function. Usually, it is set to `NULL`.
  - Second parameter — If this parameter is not equal to zero, then the event can be reset using the `ResetEvent` function. Otherwise, the event is reset if any process tries to access it.
  - Third parameter — If this parameter is zero, then the event is initialized as reset; otherwise, the signal about the appropriate situation is sent immediately.
  - Fourth parameter — This is the pointer to the string containing the event name.
- Waiting for event is carried out the same way as waiting for the semaphore — using the `WaitForSingleObject` function.
- The `OpenEvent` function is similar to the `OpenSemaphore` function. Therefore, I won't concentrate your attention on it.
- `SetEvent` — Sends the signal that the event has occurred. The only parameter of this function is the handle to the event object.

Critical Sections

A critical section allows you to protect certain fragments of the program to ensure that only one thread is executed in this section at a time. Consider the functions for working with critical sections.

- `InitializeCriticalSection` — Creates an object called the critical section. It accepts the only parameter — a pointer to the `CRITICAL_SECTION` structure. The fields of this structure are used only by internal procedures; therefore, their meaning is of no importance for application programmers.

```
CRITICAL_SECTION STRUCT
   DebugInfo      DWORD  ?
   LockCount      LONG   ?
   RecursionCount LONG   ?
   OwningThread   HANDLE ?
   LockSemaphore  HANDLE ?
```

```
    SpinCount       DWORD  ?
  CRITICAL_SECTION ENDS
```

- `EnterCriticalSection` — Enters the critical section. After executing this function, the current thread becomes the owner of the specified critical section. If another thread calls this function, it will enter the waiting state. This function accepts the same parameter as the previous one.
- `LeaveCriticalSection` — Leaves the critical section. After that, the second thread stopped by the `EnterCriticalSection` function will become the owner of the critical section. The `LeaveCriticalSection` function accepts the same parameter as the previous functions.
- `DeleteCriticalSection` — Deletes the critical section object. The parameter of this function is similar to the parameters of the previous functions.

Programmatically, it is possible to determine several critical section objects, with which several threads will operate. When describing critical sections, I intentionally mention only threads. Different processes cannot use this synchronization object.

Now, consider the example illustrating the use of critical section. The idea of the program presented in Listing 15.3 is as follows: Two threads from time to time call the procedure that displays the next character from the string into the window. As a result of such competing operation, the string must be printed. Part of the procedure that outputs the next character is made the critical section; therefore, only one thread at a time outputs data into the window.

Listing 15.3. Synchronizing two threads using a critical section

```
; The THREAD2.INC file
; Constants
; This message arrives when the window is closed
WM_DESTROY              equ 2
; This message arrives when the window is created
WM_CREATE               equ 1
; This message arrives when the left mouse button is clicked
; in the window area
WM_LBUTTONDOWN          equ 201h
; This message arrives when the right mouse button is clicked
; in the window area
WM_RBUTTONDOWN          equ 204h
; Window properties
CS_VREDRAW              equ 1h
CS_HREDRAW              equ 2h
```

```
CS_GLOBALCLASS          equ 4000h
WS_OVERLAPPEDWINDOW     equ 000CF0000H
Stylcl                  equ CS_HREDRAW+CS_VREDRAW+CS_GLOBALCLASS
DX0                     equ 300
DY0                     equ 200
; Color components
RED                     equ 50
GREEN                   equ 50
BLUE                    equ 255
RGBW                    equ (RED or (GREEN shl 8)) or (BLUE shl 16)
RGBT                    equ 255 ; Red
; Standard icon identifier
IDI_APPLICATION         equ 32512
; Cursor identifier
IDC_CROSS               equ 32515
; Display mode — Normal
SW_SHOWNORMAL           equ 1
; Prototypes of external procedures
IFDEF MASM
        EXTERN Sleep@4:NEAR
        EXTERN CreateThread@24:NEAR
        EXTERN InitializeCriticalSection@4:NEAR
        EXTERN EnterCriticalSection@4:NEAR
        EXTERN LeaveCriticalSection@4:NEAR
        EXTERN DeleteCriticalSection@4:NEAR
        EXTERN GetTextExtentPoint32A@16:NEAR
        EXTERN CreateWindowExA@48:NEAR
        EXTERN DefWindowProcA@16:NEAR
        EXTERN DispatchMessageA@4:NEAR
        EXTERN ExitProcess@4:NEAR
        EXTERN GetMessageA@16:NEAR
        EXTERN GetModuleHandleA@4:NEAR
        EXTERN LoadCursorA@8:NEAR
        EXTERN LoadIconA@8:NEAR
        EXTERN PostQuitMessage@4:NEAR
        EXTERN RegisterClassA@4:NEAR
        EXTERN ShowWindow@8:NEAR
        EXTERN TranslateMessage@4:NEAR
        EXTERN UpdateWindow@4:NEAR
        EXTERN TextOutA@20:NEAR
        EXTERN CreateSolidBrush@4:NEAR
        EXTERN SetBkColor@8:NEAR
        EXTERN SetTextColor@8:NEAR
        EXTERN GetDC@4:NEAR
```

```
        EXTERN DeleteDC@4:NEAR
ELSE
        EXTERN Sleep:NEAR
        EXTERN CreateThread:NEAR
        EXTERN InitializeCriticalSection:NEAR
        EXTERN EnterCriticalSection:NEAR
        EXTERN LeaveCriticalSection:NEAR
        EXTERN DeleteCriticalSection:NEAR
        EXTERN GetTextExtentPoint32A:NEAR
        EXTERN CreateWindowExA:NEAR
        EXTERN DefWindowProcA:NEAR
        EXTERN DispatchMessageA:NEAR
        EXTERN ExitProcess:NEAR
        EXTERN GetMessageA:NEAR
        EXTERN GetModuleHandleA:NEAR
        EXTERN LoadCursorA:NEAR
        EXTERN LoadIconA:NEAR
        EXTERN PostQuitMessage:NEAR
        EXTERN RegisterClassA:NEAR
        EXTERN ShowWindow:NEAR
        EXTERN TranslateMessage:NEAR
        EXTERN UpdateWindow:NEAR
        EXTERN TextOutA:NEAR
        EXTERN CreateSolidBrush:NEAR
        EXTERN SetBkColor:NEAR
        EXTERN SetTextColor:NEAR
        EXTERN GetDC:NEAR
        EXTERN DeleteDC:NEAR

        Sleep@4 = Sleep
        CreateThread@24 = CreateThread
        InitializeCriticalSection@4 = InitializeCriticalSection
        EnterCriticalSection@4 = EnterCriticalSection
        LeaveCriticalSection@4 = LeaveCriticalSection
        DeleteCriticalSection@4 = DeleteCriticalSection
        GetTextExtentPoint32A@16 = GetTextExtentPoint32A
        CreateWindowExA@48 = CreateWindowExA
        DefWindowProcA@16 = DefWindowProcA
        DispatchMessageA@4 = DispatchMessageA
        ExitProcess@4 = ExitProcess
        GetMessageA@16 = GetMessageA
        GetModuleHandleA@4 = GetModuleHandleA
        LoadCursorA@8 = LoadCursorA
        LoadIconA@8 = LoadIconA
```

```
        PostQuitMessage@4 = PostQuitMessage
        RegisterClassA@4 = RegisterClassA
        ShowWindow@8 = ShowWindow
        TranslateMessage@4 = TranslateMessage
        UpdateWindow@4 = UpdateWindow
        TextOutA@20 = TextOutA
        CreateSolidBrush@4 = CreateSolidBrush
        SetBkColor@8 = SetBkColor
        SetTextColor@8 = SetTextColor
        GetDC@4 = GetDC
        DeleteDC@4 = DeleteDC
ENDIF
; Structures
; Message structure
MSGSTRUCT STRUC
        MSHWND          DD ?
        MSMESSAGE       DD ?
        MSWPARAM        DD ?
        MSLPARAM        DD ?
        MSTIME          DD ?
        MSPT            DD ?
MSGSTRUCT ENDS
;---------
WNDCLASS STRUC
        CLSSTYLE        DD ?
        CLSLPFNWNDPROC  DD ?
        CLSCBCLSEXTRA   DD ?
        CLSCBWNDEXTRA   DD ?
        CLSHINSTANCE    DD ?
        CLSHICON        DD ?
        CLSHCURSOR      DD ?
        CLSHBRBACKGROUND DD ?
        MENNAME         DD ?
        CLSNAME         DD ?
WNDCLASS ENDS
; Structure for working with the critical section
CRIT STRUC
        DD ?
        DD ?
        DD ?
        DD ?
        DD ?
        DD ?
CRIT ENDS
```

```
; Structure for determining the text length
SIZET STRUC
        X1  DWORD ?
        Y1  DWORD ?
SIZET ENDS

; The THREAD2.ASM file
.586P
; Flat memory model
.MODEL FLAT, stdcall
;-------------------------------------------------
include thread2.inc
; INCLUDELIB directives
IFDEF MASM
        includelib c:\masm32\lib\user32.lib
        includelib c:\masm32\lib\kernel32.lib
        includelib c:\masm32\lib\gdi32.lib
ELSE
        includelib c:\tasm32\lib\import32.lib
ENDIF
;-------------------------------------------------
; Data segment
_DATA SEGMENT
        NEWHWND   DD 0
        MSG       MSGSTRUCT <?>
        WC        WNDCLASS  <?>
        SZT       SIZET   <?>
        HINST     DD 0
        TITLENAME DB 'Output into the window using two threads', 0
        NAM       DB 'CLASS32', 0
        XT        DWORD 30
        YT        DWORD 30
        HW        DD ?
        DC        DD ?
        TEXT      DB 'Text in window is red', 0
        SPA       DB '                          '
                  DB '                          ', 0
        IND       DD 0
        SK        CRIT <?>
        THR1      DD ?
        THR2      DD ?
        FLAG1     DD 0
        FLAG2     DD 0
_DATA ENDS
```

```
; Code segment
_TEXT SEGMENT
START:
; Get the application descriptor
        PUSH  0
        CALL  GetModuleHandleA@4
        MOV   [HINST], EAX
REG_CLASS:
; Fill the window structure
; Style
        MOV   [WC.CLSSTYLE], stylcl
; Message-handling procedure
        MOV   [WC.CLSLPFNWNDPROC],OFFSET WNDPROC
        MOV   [WC.CLSCBCLSEXTRA], 0
        MOV   [WC.CLSCBWNDEXTRA], 0
        MOV   EAX, [HINST]
        MOV   [WC.CLSHINSTANCE], EAX
;---------- Window icon
        PUSH  IDI_APPLICATION
        PUSH  0
        CALL  LoadIconA@8
        MOV   [WC.CLSHICON], EAX
;---------- Window cursor
        PUSH  IDC_CROSS
        PUSH  0
        CALL  LoadCursorA@8
        MOV   [WC.CLSHCURSOR], EAX
;----------
        PUSH  RGBW ; Brush color
        CALL  CreateSolidBrush@4 ; Create a brush
        MOV   [WC.CLSHBRBACKGROUND], EAX
        MOV   DWORD PTR [WC.MENNAME], 0
        MOV   DWORD PTR [WC.CLSNAME], OFFSET NAM
        PUSH  OFFSET WC
        CALL  RegisterClassA@4
; Create a window of the registered class
        PUSH  0
        PUSH  [HINST]
        PUSH  0
        PUSH  0
        PUSH  DY0           ; DY0 - Window height
        PUSH  DX0           ; DX0 - Window width
        PUSH  100           ; Y-coordinate
        PUSH  100           ; X-coordinate
```

```
        PUSH  WS_OVERLAPPEDWINDOW
        PUSH  OFFSET TITLENAME ; Window name
        PUSH  OFFSET NAM     ; Class name
        PUSH  0
        CALL  CreateWindowExA@48
; Check for an error
        CMP   EAX, 0
        JZ    _ERR
        MOV   [NEWHWND], EAX ; Window descriptor
;-----------------------------------
        PUSH  SW_SHOWNORMAL
        PUSH  [NEWHWND]
        CALL  ShowWindow@8 ; Show the newly-created window
;-----------------------------------
        PUSH  [NEWHWND]
        CALL  UpdateWindow@4 ; Redraw the visible part of the window
; Message-processing loop
MSG_LOOP:
        PUSH  0
        PUSH  0
        PUSH  0
        PUSH  OFFSET MSG
        CALL  GetMessageA@16
        CMP   AX, 0
        JE    END_LOOP
        PUSH  OFFSET MSG
        CALL  TranslateMessage@4
        PUSH  OFFSET MSG
        CALL  DispatchMessageA@4
        JMP   MSG_LOOP
END_LOOP:
; Exit the program (close the process)
        PUSH  [MSG.MSWPARAM]
        CALL  ExitProcess@4
_ERR:
        JMP   END_LOOP
;-----------------------------------
; Window procedure
; Position of parameters in the stack
; [EBP+014H]  ; LPARAM
; [EBP+10H]   ; WAPARAM
; [EBP+0CH]   ; MES
; [EBP+8]     ; HWND
WNDPROC    PROC
```

```
        PUSH  EBP
        MOV   EBP, ESP
        PUSH  EBX
        PUSH  ESI
        PUSH  EDI
        CMP   DWORD PTR [EBP+0CH], WM_DESTROY
        JE    WMDESTROY
        CMP   DWORD PTR [EBP+0CH], WM_CREATE
        JE    WMCREATE
        CMP   DWORD PTR [EBP+0CH], WM_LBUTTONDOWN
        JNE   CONTIN
; Check the start flag
        CMP   FLAG1, 0
        JNE   DEFWNDPROC
        MOV   FLAG1, 1
; Initialize pointers
        LEA   EAX, TEXT
        MOV   IND, EAX
        MOV   XT, 30
; Start the first thread
        PUSH  OFFSET THR1
        PUSH  0
        PUSH  EAX
        PUSH  OFFSET THREAD1
        PUSH  0
        PUSH  0
        CALL  CreateThread@24
; Start the second thread
        PUSH  OFFSET THR2
        PUSH  0
        PUSH  EAX
        PUSH  OFFSET THREAD2
        PUSH  0
        PUSH  0
        CALL  CreateThread@24
        JMP   DEFWNDPROC
CONTIN:
        CMP   DWORD PTR [EBP+0CH], WM_RBUTTONDOWN
        JNE   DEFWNDPROC
; Check the start flag
        CMP   FLAG2, 0
        JNE   DEFWNDPROC
        MOV   FLAG2, 1
; Initialize pointers
```

```
        LEA    EAX, SPA
        MOV    IND, EAX
        MOV    XT, 30
; Start the first thread
        PUSH   OFFSET THR1
        PUSH   0
        PUSH   EAX
        PUSH   OFFSET THREAD1
        PUSH   0
        PUSH   0
        CALL   CreateThread@24
; Start the second thread
        PUSH   OFFSET THR2
        PUSH   0
        PUSH   EAX
        PUSH   OFFSET THREAD2
        PUSH   0
        PUSH   0
        CALL   CreateThread@24
        JMP    DEFWNDPROC
WMCREATE:
        MOV    EAX, DWORD PTR [EBP+08H]
; Store the window descriptor in a global variable
        MOV    HW, EAX
; Initialize the critical section
        PUSH   OFFSET SK
        CALL   InitializeCriticalSection@4
        MOV    EAX, 0
        JMP    FINISH
DEFWNDPROC:
        PUSH   DWORD PTR [EBP+14H]
        PUSH   DWORD PTR [EBP+10H]
        PUSH   DWORD PTR [EBP+0CH]
        PUSH   DWORD PTR [EBP+08H]
        CALL   DefWindowProcA@16
        JMP    FINISH
WMDESTROY:
; Delete the critical section
        PUSH   OFFSET SK
        CALL   DeleteCriticalSection@4
        PUSH   0
        CALL   PostQuitMessage@4 ; WM_QUIT
        MOV    EAX, 0
FINISH:
```

```
        POP   EDI
        POP   ESI
        POP   EBX
        POP   EBP
        RET   16
WNDPROC     ENDP
; Output
OUTSTR PROC
; Check whether the text has finished
        MOV   EBX, IND
        CMP   BYTE PTR [EBX], 0
        JNE   NO_0
        RET
NO_0:
; Enter the critical section
        PUSH  OFFSET SK
        CALL  EnterCriticalSection@4
;----------------
        PUSH  HW
        CALL  GetDC@4
        MOV   DC, EAX
;---------------- Background color = Window color
        PUSH  RGBW
        PUSH  EAX
        CALL  SetBkColor@8
;---------------- Text color (red)
        PUSH  RGBT
        PUSH  DC
        CALL  SetTextColor@8
;---------------- Output the text
        PUSH  1
        PUSH  IND
        PUSH  YT
        PUSH  XT
        PUSH  DC
        CALL  TextOutA@20
; Compute the text length in pixels
        PUSH  OFFSET SZT
        PUSH  1
        PUSH  IND
        PUSH  DC
        CALL  GetTextExtentPoint32A@16
; Increase the pointers
        MOV   EAX, SZT.X1
```

```
        ADD   XT, EAX
        INC   IND
;---------------- Close the context
        PUSH  DC
        CALL  DeleteDC@4
; Exit the critical section
        PUSH  OFFSET SK
        CALL  LeaveCriticalSection@4
        RET
OUTSTR ENDP
; First thread
THREAD1 PROC
LO1:
; Check whether the end of the text has been reached
        MOV   EBX, IND
        CMP   BYTE PTR [EBX], 0
        JE    _END1
; Output the next character
        CALL  OUTSTR
; Delay
        PUSH  1000
        CALL  Sleep@4
        JMP   LO1
_END1:
        RET   4
THREAD1 ENDP
; Second thread
THREAD2 PROC
LO2:
; Check whether the end of the text has been reached
        MOV   EBX, IND
        CMP   BYTE PTR [EBX], 0
        JE    _END2
; Output the next character
        CALL  OUTSTR
; Delay
        PUSH  1000
        CALL  Sleep@4
        JMP   LO2
_END2:
        RET   4
THREAD2 ENDP
_TEXT ENDS
END START
```

To translate the THREAD2.ASM program presented in Listing 15.3, issue the following commands using MASM32:

```
ML /c /coff /DMASM thread2.asm
LINK /SUBSYSTEM:WINDOWS thread2.obj
```

Issue the following commands using TASM32:

```
TASM32 /ml thread2.asm
TLINK32 -aa thread2.obj
```

When the user clicks the left mouse button in the window area, the program starts string output. When the user clicks the right mouse button, the displayed string is erased. Flags `FLAG1` and `FLAG2` are introduced to ensure that string output and blank string output could be carried out only once. To slow text output, the delay (`Sleep`) is introduced into the loop for calling the `OUTSTR` procedure in each thread. Note that the letters mainly appear in pairs. This can be explained because when one of the threads outputs a character, the second thread is already waiting for its turn to output a character. Thus, as soon as the first thread leaves the critical section, the second thread immediately outputs the next character. After that, both threads are delayed (the `Sleep` function).

To complete the topic on critical sections, it is necessary to mention that this method of synchronization is the fastest. Drawbacks of this approach include the impossibility of several threads accessing the section simultaneously and the lack of special tools that allow you to count the number of attempts at accessing the resource.

Mutual Exceptions

In this chapter, I did not consider another method of synchronization, which will be covered in detail later in this book. Here, it is only necessary to mention that this method is known as the mutual exception of the mutual exclusion object (mutex). This method of synchronization is not convenient for working with threads. On the other hand, it is more suitable for processes. This synchronization object is created using the `CreateMutex` function. All processes that attempt to create the object that exists already get the descriptor of the existing object created by another process. The most important feature of the mutex object is that only one process can own it. Microsoft's documentation recommends that you use this object to determine whether a specific application has started. This topic will be covered later.

Chapter 16

Creating Dynamic Link Libraries

When I started to work with Windows, the term Dynamic Link Library (DLL) first seemed strange to my ear, because I was accustomed to MS-DOS. In the opinion of those accustomed to the MS-DOS programming paradigm, a library must be bound at the stage of linking. DLLs seemed similar to the concept of overlay. In MS-DOS, overlays were used to utilize random access memory more economically. An overlay manager loaded individual parts of the overlay and unloaded other parts. It allowed impressive economy of the memory. However, overlay could be used only by a single application. DLLs, on the other hand, can be used by several applications simultaneously — hence the term "library."

General Concepts

The use of DLLs is the method of implementing a modular structure at run time. DLLs also simplify the software development process. Instead of recompiling large EXE modules, it is enough to recompile a single DLL. Furthermore, it is possible to simultaneously access a DLL from several executable modules, which makes multitasking more flexible. The most important point is that the structure of a DLL module is practically the same as that of an EXE module. Those who have developed MS-DOS programs must be acquainted with the overlay concept. By its functionality, DLL is similar to overlay;[i] however, its name — dynamic link library — suits it better.

You have already seen how to define the imported functions when creating EXE modules. For this purpose, it is enough to declare these functions as EXTERN. When creating DLLs, you'll have to declare both imported and exported functions.

To proceed further, it is necessary to revisit the concept of linking. I introduced it earlier when describing the linker operation. During translation, the names declared in the program as external (EXTERN) are linked to appropriate names from the declared libraries using the IMPORTLIB directive. This way of linking is known as early, or static, linking. With a DLL, linking takes place at run time. This kind of linking is called late, or dynamic, linking. Dynamic linking can take place automatically at program startup or at any time convenient for the programmer using special application program interface functions. In this case, you are dealing with implicit and explicit linking. These approaches are illustrated in Fig. 16.1. Note also that the use of DLLs allows disk space economy, because the procedure in a library is included only once in contrast to procedures placed into the module from static libraries.[ii]

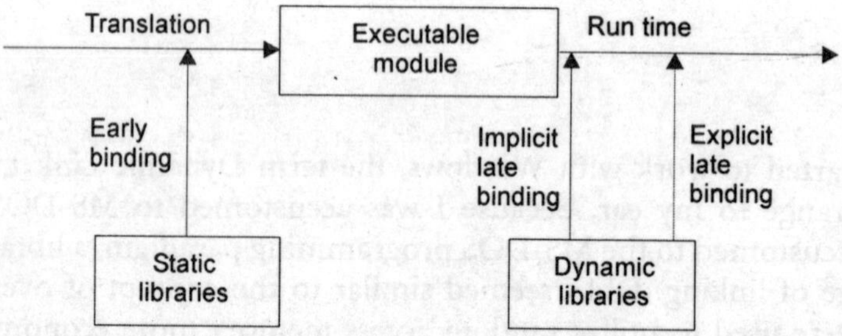

Fig. 16.1. Concept of linking

In the Windows environment, two linking mechanisms are employed: symbolic names and ordinal numbers. In the first case, the function defined in a library is identified by its name; in the latter case, it is identified by its ordinal number, which must be specified in the course of translation. Linking by ordinal number was used in Windows 3.*x*. In my opinion, linking by names is more convenient.

---

[i] Overlay means that different parts are alternately loaded into the overlay memory area.

[ii] Generally, it would be more correct to call the libraries used for Windows programming (such as IMPORT32.LIB and USER32.LIB) import libraries instead of static libraries. These libraries do not contain program code. They only contain information used by translators.

DLLs can also contain resources. For example, font files are DLLs containing only resources. It is necessary to point out that when a DLL is loaded into the address space of your process, it becomes a part of your program. Accordingly, the process data are available from the DLL, and DLL data are available for the process.

In every DLL, it is necessary to define the entry point (entry procedure). By default, it is assumed that the entry point is the label specified after the `END` directive (for example, `END START`). When a DLL is loaded or unloaded, the entry procedure is called automatically. Note that the method of loading the DLL (explicit or implicit) doesn't matter, because the DLL will be unloaded from the memory automatically when the process or thread is closed. Principally, the entry point can be used for startup initialization of variables. Quite often, this procedure remains blank. When this procedure is called, it accepts three parameters:

- First parameter — DLL module identifier
- Second parameter — The reason for the call
- Third parameter — Reserved

Consider the second parameter of the entry procedure in more detail. It can take the following values:

```
DLL_PROCESS_DETACH          equ 0
DLL_PROCESS_ATTACH          equ 1
DLL_THREAD_ATTACH           equ 2
DLL_THREAD_DETACH           equ 3
```

- `DLL_PROCESS_ATTACH` — Informs the program that the DLL has been loaded into the address space of the calling process.
- `DLL_THREAD_ATTACH` — Informs the program that the current process creates a new thread. Such messages are sent to all DLLs loaded by the process for that instance.
- `DLL_PROCESS_DETACH` — Informs the program that the DLL is being unloaded from the address space of the process.
- `DLL_THREAD_DETACH` — Informs the program that a certain thread created by the current process, into whose the address this DLL has been loaded, is going to be closed.

Creating a Dynamic Link Library

Now, it's time to consider some examples that illustrate DLL creation. Listing 16.1 provides an example of the simplest DLL. This DLL isn't doing anything useful. It is just loaded and then unloaded. Its entry procedure — `DLLP1` — is called, and a normal Windows message will be generated. Pay attention to the processes of loading and unloading this library. Also note that the entry procedure must return a nonzero value. The DLLP1 procedure also processes one parameter traditionally passed through the stack.

Listing 16.1. The simplest dynamic link library

```
.586P
; Flat memory model
IFDEF MASM
    .MODEL FLAT, stdcall
ELSE
   .MODEL FLAT
ENDIF
PUBLIC DLLP1
; Constants
; These messages arrive
; when the DLL is opened
DLL_PROCESS_DETACH    equ 0
DLL_PROCESS_ATTACH    equ 1
DLL_THREAD_ATTACH     equ 2
DLL_THREAD_DETACH     equ 3
IFDEF MASM
; MASM
; Prototypes of external procedures
        EXTERN       MessageBoxA@16:NEAR
; INCLUDELIB directives for the linker
        includelib c:\masm32\lib\user32.lib
        includelib c:\masm32\lib\kernel32.lib
ELSE
; TASM
        EXTERN       MessageBoxA:NEAR
        MessageBoxA@16 = MessageBoxA
        includelib c:\tasm32\lib\import32.lib
ENDIF
;-----------------------------------------
; Data segment
_DATA SEGMENT
        TEXT1 DB 'Library's entry point', 0
        TEXT2 DB 'Library's exit point', 0
        MS    DB 'Message from the library', 0
        TEXT  DB 'Calling a procedure from a DLL', 0
_DATA ENDS
; Code segment
_TEXT SEGMENT
; [EBP+10H]    ; Reserved parameter
```

```
; [EBP+0CH]    ; Cause of the call
; [EBP+8]      ; Identifier of the DLL module
DLLENTRY:
        MOV   EAX, DWORD PTR [EBP+0CH]
        CMP   EAX, 0
        JNE   D1
; Closing the library
        PUSH  0
        PUSH  OFFSET MS
        PUSH  OFFSET TEXT2
        PUSH  0
        CALL  MessageBoxA@16
        JMP   _EXIT
D1:
        CMP   EAX, 1
        JNE   _EXIT
; Opening the library
        PUSH  0
        PUSH  OFFSET MS
        PUSH  OFFSET TEXT1
        PUSH  0
        CALL  MessageBoxA@16
_EXIT:
        MOV   EAX, 1
        RET   12
;--------------------
; [EBP+8]    ; Procedure parameter
DLLP1 PROC EXPORT
        PUSH  EBP
        MOV   EBP, ESP
        CMP   DWORD PTR [EBP+8], 1
        JNE   _EX
        PUSH  0
        PUSH  OFFSET MS
        PUSH  OFFSET TEXT
        PUSH  0
        CALL  MessageBoxA@16
_EX:
        POP   EBP
        RET   4
DLLP1 ENDP
_TEXT ENDS
END DLLENTRY
```

The program presented in Listing 16.1 can be translated using both MASM32 and TASM32. This point deserves more careful consideration. First, note that after the name of a procedure called from another module, the `EXPORT` keyword was inserted. This keyword is required for correct translation using MASM. For TASM, this keyword isn't required, but, fortunately, this translator doesn't notice the presence of any keywords after `PROC`. However, TASM requires the `DLLP1` procedure to be defined as `PUBLIC`. Furthermore, for correct translation using TASM, it is necessary to create a DEF file and specify it in the command line for TLINK32. To create DLLs, the `link` linker requires the `/DLL` key to be specified in the `link` command line, and the LINK32 command line requires the `-Tpd` key (the `-Tpe` key is used by default). The `/ENTRY:DLLENTRY` key in the `link` command line can be omitted because the entry point is defined from the `END DLLENTRY` directive.

To translate the DLL from Listing 16.1, issue the following commands for MASM32:

```
ml /c /coff /DMASM dll1.asm
link /subsystem:windows /DLL /ENTRY:DLLENTRY dll1.obj
```

Issue the following commands for TASM32:

```
tasm32 /ml dll1.asm
tlink32 -aa -Tpd dll1.obj,,,,dll1.def
```

The contents of the DLL1.DEF file are as follows:

```
EXPORTS DLLP1
```

Listing 16.2 is the program that loads the DLL shown in Listing 16.1. This is an example of the late linking. First, it is necessary to load the library using the `LoadLibrary` function. Then, it is necessary to determine the procedure address using the `GetProcAddress` function, after which it is possible to call the library. As expected, MASM places `_DLLP1@0` instead of `DLLP1` into the library name. TASM, on the contrary, doesn't change the name. You must take this into account in the program. Also, it is necessary to account for the possibility of errors when calling the `LoadLibrary` and `GetProcAddress` functions. In this respect, consider the following sequence in which the `LoadLibrary` function searches for the library:

1. Search the directory from which the program was started.
2. Search the current directory.
3. Search the system directory (determined using the `GetSystemDirectory` function).
4. Search the Windows directory (determined using the `GetWindowsDirectory` function).
5. Search the directories specified by the `PATH` environment variable.

In the end of the program, the DLL is unloaded from the memory. By the way, this is not necessary because this procedure is carried out automatically when exiting the program.

Listing 16.2. Calling the dynamic link library: Explicit linking

```
.586P
; Flat memory model
.MODEL FLAT, stdcall
; Constants
; Prototypes of external procedures
IFDEF MASM
; MASM
        EXTERN      GetProcAddress@8:NEAR
        EXTERN      LoadLibraryA@4:NEAR
        EXTERN      FreeLibrary@4:NEAR
        EXTERN      ExitProcess@4:NEAR
        EXTERN      MessageBoxA@16:NEAR
; INCLUDELIB directives for the linker
        includelib c:\masm32\lib\user32.lib
        includelib c:\masm32\lib\kernel32.lib
ELSE
; TASM
        EXTERN      GetProcAddress:NEAR
        EXTERN      LoadLibraryA:NEAR
        EXTERN      FreeLibrary:NEAR
        EXTERN      ExitProcess:NEAR
        EXTERN      MessageBoxA:NEAR
; INCLUDELIB directives for the linker
        includelib c:\tasm32\lib\import32.lib
        GetProcAddress@8 = GetProcAddress
        LoadLibraryA@4 = LoadLibraryA
        FreeLibrary@4 = FreeLibrary
        ExitProcess@4 = ExitProcess
        MessageBoxA@16 = MessageBoxA
ENDIF
;---------------------------------------
; Data segment
_DATA SEGMENT
        TXT    DB 'DLL error', 0
        MS     DB 'Message', 0
        LIBR   DB 'DLL1.DLL', 0
        HLIB   DD ?
```

```
IFDEF MASM
        NAMEPROC DB '_DLLP1@0', 0
ELSE
        NAMEPROC DB 'DLLP1', 0
ENDIF
_DATA ENDS
; Code segment
_TEXT SEGMENT
START:
; Load the library
        PUSH  OFFSET LIBR
        CALL  LoadLibraryA@4
        CMP   EAX, 0
        JE    _ERR
        MOV   HLIB, EAX
; Get the procedure address
        PUSH  OFFSET NAMEPROC
        PUSH  HLIB
        CALL  GetProcAddress@8
        CMP   EAX, 0
        JNE   YES_NAME
; Error message
_ERR:
        PUSH  0
        PUSH  OFFSET MS
        PUSH  OFFSET TXT
        PUSH  0
        CALL  MessageBoxA@16
        JMP   _EXIT
YES_NAME:
        PUSH  1 ; Parameter
        CALL  EAX
; Close the library
        PUSH  HLIB
        CALL  FreeLibrary@4
; The library will be closed automatically
; when exiting the program
; Exit
_EXIT:
        PUSH  0
        CALL  ExitProcess@4
_TEXT ENDS
END START
```

The program presented in Listing 16.2 is translated like any other normal program. For MASM32, use the following:

```
ml /c /coff /DMASM dllex.asm
link /subsystem:windows dllex.obj
```

For TASM32, use the following:

```
tasm32 /ml dllex.asm
tlink32 -aa dllex.obj
```

Implicit Linking

Although I have mentioned that, in my opinion, implicit linking is less flexible, it is still necessary to provide an example of implicit linking. Here, consider only the calling program because the called program, naturally, doesn't change. As you can see, the source code of the program became somewhat easier. It is important to note that it is necessary, first, to declare the procedure called from the DLL as external and, second, to link a static library — DLLP1.LIB.

Listing 16.3. Calling the dynamic link library: Implicit linking

```
.586P
; Flat memory model
IFDEF MASM
 .MODEL FLAT, stdcall
ELSE
 .MODEL FLAT
ENDIF
; Constants
; Prototypes of external procedures
includelib dll1.lib
IFDEF MASM
; MASM
      EXTERN      DLLP1@0:NEAR
      EXTERN      ExitProcess@4:NEAR
; INCLUDELIB directives for the linker
      includelib c:\masm32\lib\user32.lib
      includelib c:\masm32\lib\kernel32.lib
ELSE
; INCLUDELIB directives for the linker
      includelib c:\tasm32\lib\import32.lib
      EXTERN      DLLP1:NEAR
```

```
        EXTERN      ExitProcess:NEAR
        DLLP1@0 = DLLP1
        ExitProcess@4 = ExitProcess
ENDIF
;-----------------------------------------------
; Data segment
_DATA SEGMENT
_DATA ENDS
; Code segment
_TEXT SEGMENT
START:
        PUSH  1 ; Parameter
        CALL  DLLP1@0
; Exit
_EXIT:
        PUSH  0
        CALL  ExitProcess@4
_TEXT ENDS
END START
```

You probably want to ask a natural question: Where does the DLLP1.LIB library come from? Everything is clear and straightforward. MASM creates this library automatically, and TASM provides the IMPLIB utility that creates a static library directly from a DLL.

To translate the program from Listing 16.3, issue the following commands for MASM32:

```
ml /c /coff /DMASM dllex.asm
link /subsystem:windows dllex.obj
```

Issue the following commands for TASM32:

```
tasm32 /ml dllex.asm
implib dll1.lib dll1.dll
tlink32 -aa dllex.obj
```

Earlier, it was shown that a possible linking mechanism is determining the procedure address through the ordinal number. Now, consider how this mechanism can be implemented. First, it is necessary to assign some 2-byte number to the procedure that will be called from the DLL. This is achieved by adding the following line into the DEF file: `EXPORTS DLLP1 @1`. Here, the `DLLP1` procedure is mapped to the number 1. You have used DEF files when translating using TASM. When translating with MASM, they can be used the same way (the `/DEF:`*name* for the LINK.EXE program). After that, carry out translation, and the library will be created. Now, when calling the GetProcAddress function, specify the ordinal number (or, to be more precise, the double word whose least significant word contains the ordinal number and whose most significant word is zero) as the parameter. Everything will operate exactly as before, so I don't see any special need to use this approach.

Using Common Address Space

Listing 16.4 provides the code of a DLL and a program calling a procedure from this library. In this program, there isn't anything especially difficult. The main goal of this example is to demonstrate that the primary process and the DLL share the same address space. The process passes addresses of strings located in the data block of the primary process. The procedure, in turn, returns to the primary process the address of the string that resides in the DLLs block of data.

Listing 16.4. Passing parameters between the main module and the dynamic link library

```
; DLL2.ASM
.586P
; Flat memory model
IFDEF MASM
 .MODEL FLAT, stdcall
ELSE
 .MODEL FLAT
ENDIF
PUBLIC DLLP1
; Constants
; Messages that arrive when
; the DLL is opened
DLL_PROCESS_DETACH     equ 0
DLL_PROCESS_ATTACH     equ 1
DLL_THREAD_ATTACH      equ 2
DLL_THREAD_DETACH      equ 3
IFDEF MASM
; MASM
; Prototypes of external procedures
      EXTERN      MessageBoxA@16:NEAR
; INCLUDELIB directives for the linker
      includelib c:\masm32\lib\user32.lib
      includelib c:\masm32\lib\kernel32.lib
ELSE
; TASM
```

```
        EXTERN      MessageBoxA:NEAR
        MessageBoxA@16 = MessageBoxA
        includelib c:\tasm32\lib\import32.lib
ENDIF
;------------------------------------------------
; Data segment
_DATA SEGMENT
        TEXT DB "String in a DLL", 0
_DATA ENDS
; Code segment
_TEXT SEGMENT
; [EBP+10H]     ; Reserved parameter
; [EBP+0CH]     ; Cause of the call
; [EBP+8]       ; DLL module identifier
DLLENTRY:
        MOV   EAX, DWORD PTR [EBP+0CH]
        CMP   EAX, 0
        JNE   D1
; Close the library
        JMP   _EXIT
D1:
        CMP   EAX, 1
        JNE   _EXIT
; Open the library
_EXIT:
        MOV   EAX, 1
        RET   12
;--------------------
; Parameter addresses
; [EBP+8]
; [EBP+0CH]
DLLP1 PROC EXPORT
        PUSH  EBP
        MOV   EBP, ESP
        PUSH  0
        PUSH  DWORD PTR [EBP+0CH]
        PUSH  DWORD PTR [EBP+8]
        PUSH  0
        CALL  MessageBoxA@16
        POP   EBP
        LEA   EAX, TEXT
        RET   8
DLLP1 ENDP
```

```
_TEXT ENDS
END DLLENTRY


; Main module DLLEX2.ASM that calls
; a procedure from the DLL
.586P
; Flat memory model
.MODEL FLAT, stdcall
; Constants
; Prototypes of external procedures
IFDEF MASM
; MASM
        EXTERN      GetProcAddress@8:NEAR
        EXTERN      LoadLibraryA@4:NEAR
        EXTERN      FreeLibrary@4:NEAR
        EXTERN      ExitProcess@4:NEAR
        EXTERN      MessageBoxA@16:NEAR
        includelib c:\masm32\lib\user32.lib
        includelib c:\masm32\lib\kernel32.lib
ELSE
; TASM
        includelib c:\tasm32\lib\import32.lib
        EXTERN      GetProcAddress:NEAR
        EXTERN      LoadLibraryA:NEAR
        EXTERN      FreeLibrary:NEAR
        EXTERN      ExitProcess:NEAR
        EXTERN      MessageBoxA:NEAR
        GetProcAddress@8 = GetProcAddress
        LoadLibraryA@4 = LoadLibraryA
        FreeLibrary@4 = FreeLibrary
        ExitProcess@4 = ExitProcess
        MessageBoxA@16 = MessageBoxA
ENDIF
;-------------------------------------------
; Data segment
_DATA SEGMENT
        TXT  DB 'DLL error', 0
        MS   DB 'Message', 0
        LIBR DB 'DLL2.DLL', 0
        HLIB DD ?
        MS1  DB 'Message from the library', 0
        TEXT DB 'The string is contained in the main module', 0
```

```
IFDEF MASM
        NAMEPROC DB '_DLLP1@0', 0
ELSE
        NAMEPROC DB 'DLLP1', 0
ENDIF
_DATA ENDS
; Code segment
_TEXT SEGMENT
; [EBP+10H]    ; Reserved parameter
; [EBP+0CH]    ; Cause of the call
; [EBP+8]      ; DLL module identifier
START:
; Load the library
        PUSH  OFFSET LIBR
        CALL  LoadLibraryA@4
        CMP   EAX, 0
        JE    _ERR
        MOV   HLIB, EAX
; Get the address
        PUSH  OFFSET NAMEPROC
        PUSH  HLIB
        CALL  GetProcAddress@8
        CMP   EAX, 0
        JNE   YES_NAME
; Error message
_ERR:
        PUSH  0
        PUSH  OFFSET MS
        PUSH  OFFSET TXT
        PUSH  0
        CALL  MessageBoxA@16
        JMP   _EXIT
YES_NAME:
        PUSH  OFFSET MS1
        PUSH  OFFSET TEXT
        CALL  EAX
        PUSH  0
        PUSH  OFFSET MS
        PUSH  EAX
        PUSH  0
        CALL  MessageBoxA@16
; Close the library
        PUSH  HLIB
```

```
        CALL  FreeLibrary@4
; The library is automatically closed
; when exiting the program
; Exit
_EXIT:
        PUSH  0
        CALL  ExitProcess@4
_TEXT ENDS
END START
```

To translate this program, issue the following commands for MASM32:

```
ml /c /coff /DMASM dllex2.asm
link /subsystem:windows dllex2.obj
```

Issue the following commands for TASM32:

```
tasm32 /ml dllex2.asm
tlink32 -aa -Tpd dllex2.obj
```

Next, consider an interesting example (Listing 16.5). The primary process uses the resources of the DLL that it has loaded. I have already mentioned that font files are DLLs. It's convenient, isn't it? The resources can be placed into a DLL, separate from the code, and then can be loaded as needed. The program in Listing 16.5 first loads an icon from the DLL resources and sets it as the window icon. If you right-click the mouse somewhere in the window area, a procedure from the DLL will be called. This procedure will alternately set different icons to the window.

Listing 16.5. Loading resources from the dynamic link library

```
// The DLL3.RC file

// Identifiers
#define IDI_ICON1 3
#define IDI_ICON2 10

// Define icons
IDI_ICON1 ICON "ico1.ico"
IDI_ICON2 ICON "ico2.ico"

; The DLL3.ASM file
.586P
PUBLIC SETIC
; Flat memory model
IFDEF MASM
```

```
 .MODEL FLAT, stdcall
ELSE
 .MODEL FLAT
ENDIF

; Constants
WM_SETICON     equ 80h

IFDEF MASM
; MASM
; Prototypes of external procedures
       EXTERN     LoadIconA@8:NEAR
       EXTERN     PostMessageA@16:NEAR
; INCLUDELIB directives for the linker
       includelib c:\masm32\lib\user32.lib
       includelib c:\masm32\lib\kernel32.lib
ELSE
; TASM
; Prototypes of external procedures
       EXTERN     LoadIconA:NEAR
       EXTERN     PostMessageA:NEAR
; INCLUDELIB directives for the linker
       includelib c:\tasm32\lib\import32.lib
       LoadIconA@8 = LoadIconA
       PostMessageA@16 = PostMessageA
ENDIF
;-----------------------------------------------
; Data segment
_DATA SEGMENT
       PRIZ DB 0
_DATA ENDS
; Code segment
_TEXT SEGMENT
DLLENTRY:
       MOV   EAX, 1
       RET   12
; [EBP+8]
; [EBP+0CH]
SETIC PROC EXPORT
       PUSH  EBP
       MOV   EBP, ESP
; Choose the icon to set
       CMP   PRIZ, 0
```

```
        JZ     IC_1
        MOV    PRIZ, 0
        PUSH   3
        JMP    CONT
IC_1:
        MOV    PRIZ, 1
        PUSH   10
CONT:
; Load the icon from the DLL resources
        PUSH   DWORD PTR [EBP+0CH] ; Identifier
                                   ; of the DLL
        CALL   LoadIconA@8
; Set the window icon
        PUSH   EAX
        PUSH   0
        PUSH   WM_SETICON
        PUSH   DWORD PTR [EBP+08H] ; Window descriptor
        CALL   PostMessageA@16
        POP    EBP
        RET    8
SETIC ENDP
_TEXT ENDS
END DLLENTRY

// The DLLEX3.RC file
// Constant definitions
#define WS_SYSMENU        0x00080000L
#define WS_MINIMIZEBOX    0x00020000L
#define WS_MAXIMIZEBOX    0x00010000L
#define DS_3DLOOK         0x0004L

// Dialog box definition
DIAL1 DIALOG 0, 0, 340, 120
STYLE WS_SYSMENU | WS_MINIMIZEBOX | WS_MAXIMIZEBOX | DS_3DLOOK
CAPTION "Dialog with an icon from DLL resources"
FONT 8, "Arial"
{
}

; Main module DLLEX3.ASM, calling
; the procedure from the DLL
```

```
.586P
; Flat memory model
IFDEF MASM
 .MODEL FLAT, stdcall
ELSE
 .MODEL FLAT
ENDIF
; Constants
; This message arrives when the window is closed
WM_CLOSE         equ 10h
WM_INITDIALOG    equ 110h
WM_SETICON       equ 80h
WM_LBUTTONDOWN   equ 201h
; Prototypes of external procedures
IFDEF MASM
; MASM
        EXTERN      PostMessageA@16:NEAR
        EXTERN      GetProcAddress@8:NEAR
        EXTERN      LoadLibraryA@4:NEAR
        EXTERN      FreeLibrary@4:NEAR
        EXTERN      ExitProcess@4:NEAR
        EXTERN      GetModuleHandleA@4:NEAR
        EXTERN      DialogBoxParamA@20:NEAR
        EXTERN      EndDialog@8:NEAR
        EXTERN      LoadIconA@8:NEAR
; INCLUDELIB directives for the linker
        includelib c:\masm32\lib\user32.lib
        includelib c:\masm32\lib\kernel32.lib
ELSE
; INCLUDELIB directives for the linker
        includelib c:\tasm32\lib\import32.lib
        EXTERN      PostMessageA:NEAR
        EXTERN      GetProcAddress:NEAR
        EXTERN      LoadLibraryA:NEAR
        EXTERN      FreeLibrary:NEAR
        EXTERN      ExitProcess:NEAR
        EXTERN      GetModuleHandleA:NEAR
        EXTERN      DialogBoxParamA:NEAR
        EXTERN      EndDialog:NEAR
        EXTERN      LoadIconA:NEAR
        PostMessageA@16 = PostMessageA
        LoadIconA@8 = LoadIconA
        EndDialog@8 = EndDialog
```

```
        GetModuleHandleA@4 = GetModuleHandleA
        DialogBoxParamA@20 = DialogBoxParamA
        GetProcAddress@8 = GetProcAddress
        LoadLibraryA@4 = LoadLibraryA
        FreeLibrary@4 = FreeLibrary
        ExitProcess@4 = ExitProcess
ENDIF
;-------------------------------------------------
; Data segment
_DATA SEGMENT
        LIBR  DB 'DLL3.DLL', 0
        HLIB  DD ?
        HINST DD ?
        PA          DB "DIAL1", 0
IFDEF MASM
        NAMEPROC DB "_SETIC@0", 0
ELSE
        NAMEPROC DB "SETIC", 0
ENDIF
_DATA ENDS
; Code segment
_TEXT SEGMENT
START:
; Get the application descriptor
        PUSH  0
        CALL  GetModuleHandleA@4
; Create a dialog
        MOV   [HINST], EAX
        PUSH  0
        PUSH  OFFSET WNDPROC
        PUSH  0
        PUSH  OFFSET PA
        PUSH  [HINST]
        CALL  DialogBoxParamA@20
; Exit
_EXIT:
        PUSH  0
        CALL  ExitProcess@4
; Window procedure
; Position of parameters in the stack
; [BP+014H]  ; LPARAM
; [BP+10H]   ; WAPARAM
; [BP+0CH]   ; MES
```

```
; [BP+8]    ; HWND
WNDPROC  PROC
        PUSH  EBP
        MOV   EBP, ESP
        PUSH  EBX
        PUSH  ESI
        PUSH  EDI
;----------------
        CMP   DWORD PTR [EBP+0CH], WM_CLOSE
        JNE   L1
; Close the library
; The library is closed automatically
; when exiting the program
        PUSH  HLIB
        CALL  FreeLibrary@4
        PUSH  0
        PUSH  DWORD PTR [EBP+08H]
        CALL  EndDialog@8
        JMP   FINISH
L1:
        CMP   DWORD PTR [EBP+0CH], WM_INITDIALOG
        JNE   L2
; Load the library
        PUSH  OFFSET LIBR
        CALL  LoadLibraryA@4
        MOV   HLIB, EAX
; Load the icon
        PUSH  3  ; Program identifier
        PUSH  [HLIB] ; Process identifier
        CALL  LoadIconA@8
; Set the icon
        PUSH  EAX
        PUSH  0  ; Icon type (small)
        PUSH  WM_SETICON
        PUSH  DWORD PTR [EBP+08H]
        CALL  PostMessageA@16
        JMP   FINISH
L2:
        CMP   DWORD PTR [EBP+0CH], WM_LBUTTONDOWN
        JNE   FINISH
; Get the address of the DLL procedure
        PUSH  OFFSET NAMEPROC
        PUSH  HLIB
```

```
        CALL   GetProcAddress@8
; Call the procedure with two parameters
        PUSH   [HLIB]
        PUSH   DWORD PTR [EBP+08H]
        CALL   EAX
FINISH:
        POP    EDI
        POP    ESI
        POP    EBX
        POP    EBP
        MOV    EAX, 0
        RET    16
WNDPROC     ENDP
_TEXT ENDS
END START
```

To translate the program from Listing 16.5, issue the following commands for MASM32:

```
ml /c /coff /DMASM dllex3.asm
rc dllex3.rc
link /subsystem:windows dllex3.obj dllex3.res

ml /c /coff /DMASM dll3.asm
rc dll3.rc
link /subsystem:windows /DLL /ENTRY:DLLENTRY dll3.obj dll3.res
```

Issue the following commands for TASM32:

```
tasm32 /ml dllex3.asm
brcc32 dllex3.rc
tlink32 -aa -Tpd dllex3.obj,,,,,dllex3.res

tasm32 /ml dll3.asm
brcc32 dll3.rc
tlink32 -aa -Tpd dll3.obj,,,,dll3.def,dll3.res
```

The contents of the DLL3.DEF file are as follows:

```
EXPORTS SETIC
```

As you have already noticed, the DLL becomes a part of your program and, with the primary process, can use all its capabilities. Thus, for example, using the `GetMessage` and `PeekMessage` functions, it can receive the messages intended for the process. If you need to create a window in the DLL, use the identifier of the program that has called it.

Sharing Memory by Different Processes

Now, it's time to consider how different instances of the same application or different processes use the DLL. If you are acquainted with the principles of Windows operation, then such a formulation may stun you. You might say: Every process has its own address space, in which the DLL is loaded. Naturally, this isn't the most efficient approach; however, it is safe. The use of memory will be covered in detail in *Chapter 19*, but here it is necessary to point out that the application generally can initialize so-called shared memory. I'll return to this problem later and more than once. For the moment, however, consider this problem in relation to DLLs. Consider a practical situation: Suppose that the application loads a DLL and calls a procedure from there, which modifies the data located in that DLL. Now, suppose that the user starts the second instance of the same application. It will also load an instance of the same DLL. It might be desirable to inform the second instance of the application that the DLL data have been changed by the command from the first instance of the same application. Naturally, in this case the data, over which the DLL operates, must be shared. Technically, this is easy to implement. The LINK program has the following option: `/section:` *`name, attributes`*. This allows you to explicitly declare the properties of this section. In this interpretation, the section is simply a segment. Using TLINK32, the same result can be obtained using the DEF file.

The programs presented in Listing 16.6 to illustrate this idea are very simple. Actually, they only demonstrate the use of the shared memory. Before exiting the DLL procedure, the string stored in the shared memory section is modified. The application doesn't terminate its execution. When the next application instance is started, the string modified by the first application instance will be displayed.

Listing 16.6. The use of shared memory in dynamic link libraries

```
; The DLL4.ASM library
.586P
; Flat memory model
IFDEF MASM
   .MODEL FLAT, stdcall
ELSE
   .MODEL FLAT
ENDIF
PUBLIC DLLP1
IFDEF MASM
; MASM
; Prototypes of external procedures
      EXTERN       MessageBoxA@16:NEAR
```

```
; INCLUDELIB directives for the linker
        includelib c:\masm32\lib\user32.lib
        includelib c:\masm32\lib\kernel32.lib
ELSE
; TASM
        EXTERN      MessageBoxA:NEAR
        MessageBoxA@16 = MessageBoxA
        includelib c:\tasm32\lib\import32.lib
ENDIF
;--------------------------------------------------
; Data segment
_DATA SEGMENT
        TEXT DB "String in a DLL", 0
        MS   DB "Message", 0
_DATA ENDS
; Code segment
_TEXT SEGMENT
; [EBP+10H]    ; Reserved parameter
; [EBP+0CH]    ; Cause of call
; [EBP+8]      ; DLL module identifier
DLLENTRY:
        MOV   EAX, 1
        RET   12
;--------------------
; Addresses of parameters
DLLP1 PROC EXPORT
        PUSH  EBP
        MOV   EBP, ESP
        PUSH  0
        PUSH  OFFSET MS
        PUSH  OFFSET TEXT
        PUSH  0
        CALL  MessageBoxA@16
; Modify the string located in the shared memory
        MOV   TEXT, 'O'
        MOV   TEXT+1, 'f'
        POP   EBP
        RET
DLLP1 ENDP
_TEXT ENDS
END DLLENTRY

; The DLLEX4.ASM main module that calls
```

```
; a procedure from the DLL
.586P
; Flat memory model
.MODEL FLAT, stdcall
; Constants
; Prototypes of external procedures
IFDEF MASM
; MASM
        EXTERN      GetProcAddress@8:NEAR
        EXTERN      LoadLibraryA@4:NEAR
        EXTERN      FreeLibrary@4:NEAR
        EXTERN      ExitProcess@4:NEAR
        EXTERN      MessageBoxA@16:NEAR
; INCLUDELIB directives for the linker
        includelib c:\masm32\lib\user32.lib
        includelib c:\masm32\lib\kernel32.lib
ELSE
; INCLUDELIB directives for the linker
        includelib c:\tasm32\lib\import32.lib
        EXTERN      GetProcAddress:NEAR
        EXTERN      LoadLibraryA:NEAR
        EXTERN      FreeLibrary:NEAR
        EXTERN      ExitProcess:NEAR
        EXTERN      MessageBoxA:NEAR
        GetProcAddress@8 = GetProcAddress
        LoadLibraryA@4 = LoadLibraryA
        FreeLibrary@4 = FreeLibrary
        ExitProcess@4 = ExitProcess
        MessageBoxA@16 = MessageBoxA
ENDIF
;--------------------------------------------------
; Data segment
_DATA SEGMENT
        TXT  DB 'DLL error', 0
        MS   DB 'Message', 0
        LIBR DB 'DLL4.DLL', 0
        HLIB DD ?
IFDEF MASM
        NAMEPROC DB '_DLLP1@0', 0
ELSE
        NAMEPROC DB 'DLLP1', 0
ENDIF
_DATA ENDS
; Code segment
```

```
_TEXT SEGMENT
; [EBP+10H]    ; Reserved parameter
; [EBP+0CH]    ; Cause of the call
; [EBP+8]      ; DLL module identifier
START:
; Load the library
        PUSH  OFFSET LIBR
        CALL  LoadLibraryA@4
        CMP   EAX, 0
        JE    _ERR
        MOV   HLIB, EAX
; Get the address
        PUSH  OFFSET NAMEPROC
        PUSH  HLIB
        CALL  GetProcAddress@8
        CMP   EAX, 0
        JNE   YES_NAME
; Error message
_ERR:
        PUSH  0
        PUSH  OFFSET MS
        PUSH  OFFSET TXT
        PUSH  0
        CALL  MessageBoxA@16
        JMP   _EXIT
YES_NAME:
        CALL  EAX
        PUSH  0
        PUSH  OFFSET MS
        PUSH  OFFSET MS
        PUSH  0
        CALL  MessageBoxA@16
; Close the library
; The library is automatically closed
; when exiting the program
        PUSH  OFFSET NAMEPROC
        PUSH  HLIB
        CALL  FreeLibrary@4
; Exit
_EXIT:
        PUSH  0
        CALL  ExitProcess@4
_TEXT ENDS
END START
```

To translate this program, issue the following commands using MASM32:

```
ml /c /coff /DMASM dll4.asm
link /subsystem:windows /DLL /section:.data,SRW dll2.obj
ml /c /coff /DMASM dllex4.asm
link /subsystem:windows dllex4.obj
```

Attributes of the `SECTION` option are `S-SHARED`, `R-READ`, and `W-WRITE`. Issue the following commands using TASM32:

```
tasm32 /ml dll4.asm
tlink32 -aa -Tpd dll4.obj,,,,dll4.def
tasm32 /ml dllex4.asm
tlink32 -aa dllex4.obj
```

The contents of the DEF file are as follows:

```
SECTIONS .DATA SHARED
EXPORTS  DLLP1
```

Chapter 17

Network Programming

This chapter covers a narrow range of a wide programming area called network programming. The main topic that will be covered here is access to the resources of a local area network (LAN). Another aspect of network programming — socket programming — is too vast. Therefore, here, I cover only the basics of this topic.

Network Devices

In application programming, it is often necessary to detect network devices. Principally, this problem can be formulated more generally: How do you determine the type of a specific device? If you have some experience with programming for MS-DOS, you might remember that determining the device type in MS-DOS wasn't a trivial task. Windows simplifies this problem. In this operating system, there is a useful function — `GetDriveType`. The only argument of this function is the string containing the name of the root directory of the device under consideration, for example, A:\ or D:\. The device type is determined by the value returned by this function (see the DRIV.INC file in Listing 17.1). The result of executing this program is shown in Fig. 17.1.

Listing 17.1. A simple example demonstrating how to determine the device type

```
// The DRIV.RC file
// Constant definitions
#define WS_SYSMENU              0x00080000L
#define WS_MINIMIZEBOX          0x00020000L
#define WS_MAXIMIZEBOX          0x00010000L
#define WS_VISIBLE              0x10000000L
#define WS_TABSTOP              0x00010000L
#define WS_VSCROLL              0x00200000L
#define DS_3DLOOK               0x0004L
#define LBS_NOTIFY              0x0001L
#define LBS_SORT                0x0002L
#define LBS_WANTKEYBOARDINPUT 0x0400L

// Identifiers
#define LIST1          101

//Dialog box definition
DIAL1 DIALOG 0, 0, 180, 110
STYLE WS_SYSMENU | WS_MINIMIZEBOX | WS_MAXIMIZEBOX |
DS_3DLOOK
CAPTION "Determining device types"
FONT 8, "Arial"
{
 CONTROL "ListBox1", LIST1, "listbox", WS_VISIBLE |
 WS_TABSTOP | WS_VSCROLL |
  LBS_NOTIFY|LBS_WANTKEYBOARDINPUT,
  16, 16, 100, 75
}

; The DRIV.INC file
; Constants
; Values returned by the GetDriveType function
; Values 0 and 1 can be considered indications
; that the device is missing
DRIVE_REMOVABLE        equ 2 ; Floppy drive
DRIVE_FIXED            equ 3 ; Hard disk drive
DRIVE_REMOTE           equ 4 ; Network disk
DRIVE_CDROM            equ 5 ; CD-ROM drive
DRIVE_RAMDISK          equ 6 ; RAM disk
; This message arrives when the window is closed
WM_CLOSE               equ 10h
```

```
WM_INITDIALOG          equ 110h
WM_COMMAND             equ 111h
LB_ADDSTRING           equ 180h
LB_RESETCONTENT        equ 184h
WM_LBUTTONDOWN         equ 201h
; Prototypes of external procedures
IFDEF MASM
        EXTERN lstrcpyA@8:NEAR
        EXTERN lstrcatA@8:NEAR
        EXTERN GetDriveTypeA@4:NEAR
        EXTERN ExitProcess@4:NEAR
        EXTERN GetModuleHandleA@4:NEAR
        EXTERN DialogBoxParamA@20:NEAR
        EXTERN EndDialog@8:NEAR
        EXTERN SendDlgItemMessageA@20:NEAR
ELSE
        EXTERN lstrcpyA:NEAR
        EXTERN lstrcatA:NEAR
        EXTERN GetDriveTypeA:NEAR
        EXTERN ExitProcess:NEAR
        EXTERN GetModuleHandleA:NEAR
        EXTERN DialogBoxParamA:NEAR
        EXTERN EndDialog:NEAR
        EXTERN SendDlgItemMessageA:NEAR
        lstrcpyA@8 = lstrcpyA
        lstrcatA@8 = lstrcatA
        GetDriveTypeA@4 = GetDriveTypeA
        ExitProcess@4 = ExitProcess
        GetModuleHandleA@4 = GetModuleHandleA
        DialogBoxParamA@20 = DialogBoxParamA
        EndDialog@8 = EndDialog
        SendDlgItemMessageA@20 = SendDlgItemMessageA
ENDIF
; Structures
; Message structure
MSGSTRUCT STRUC
        MSHWND          DD ?
        MSMESSAGE       DD ?
        MSWPARAM        DD ?
        MSLPARAM        DD ?
        MSTIME          DD ?
        MSPT            DD ?
MSGSTRUCT ENDS
```

```
; The DRIV.ASM file
.586P
; Flat memory model
.MODEL FLAT, stdcall
include driv.inc
; INCLUDELIB directives for the linker
IFDEF MASM
        includelib c:\masm32\lib\user32.lib
        includelib c:\masm32\lib\kernel32.lib
ELSE
        includelib c:\tasm32\lib\import32.lib
ENDIF
;-------------------------------------------------
; Data segment
_DATA SEGMENT
        PRIZ   DB 0
        MSG    MSGSTRUCT <?>
        HINST  DD 0 ;Application descriptor
        PA     DB "DIAL1", 0
        ROO    DB "?:\", 0
        BUFER  DB 40 DUP(0)
        TYP0   DB " Device missing", 0
        TYP1   DB " Device missing", 0
        TYP2   DB " Floppy disk", 0
        TYP3   DB " Hard disk", 0
        TYP4   DB " Network disk", 0
        TYP5   DB " CD", 0
        TYP6   DB " RAM drive", 0
        INDEX  DD OFFSET TYP0
               DD OFFSET TYP1
               DD OFFSET TYP2
               DD OFFSET TYP3
               DD OFFSET TYP4
               DD OFFSET TYP5
               DD OFFSET TYP6
_DATA ENDS
; Code segment
_TEXT SEGMENT
START:
; Get the application descriptor
        PUSH   0
        CALL   GetModuleHandleA@4
```

```
        MOV   [HINST], EAX
;--------------------------------
        PUSH  0
        PUSH  OFFSET WNDPROC
        PUSH  0
        PUSH  OFFSET PA
        PUSH  [HINST]
        CALL  DialogBoxParamA@20
        CMP   EAX, -1
        JNE   KOL
; Error message
KOL:
;--------------------------------
        PUSH  0
        CALL  ExitProcess@4
;--------------------------------
; Window procedure
; Position of parameters in the stack
; [BP+014H]  ; LPARAM
; [BP+10H]   ; WAPARAM
; [BP+0CH]   ; MES
; [BP+8]     ; HWND
WNDPROC     PROC
        PUSH  EBP
        MOV   EBP, ESP
        PUSH  EBX
        PUSH  ESI
        PUSH  EDI
;---------------
        CMP   DWORD PTR [EBP+0CH], WM_CLOSE
        JNE   L1
        PUSH  0
        PUSH  DWORD PTR [EBP+08H]
        CALL  EndDialog@8
        JMP   FINISH
L1:
        CMP   DWORD PTR [EBP+0CH], WM_INITDIALOG
        JNE   L2
L4:
; Analyzing the devices and filling the list
        MOV   ECX, 65
LOO:
        PUSH  ECX
```

```
        MOV   ROO, CL
; Determining the device type
        PUSH OFFSET ROO
        CALL GetDriveTypeA@4
; Full list
        CMP   PRIZ, 0
        JZ    _ALL
        CMP   EAX, 2
        JB    L3
_ALL:
; Get the index
        SHL   EAX, 2
        PUSH  EAX
; Create a string for the list
        PUSH  OFFSET ROO
        PUSH  OFFSET BUFER
        CALL  lstrcpyA@8
        POP   EBX
        PUSH  INDEX[EBX]
        PUSH  OFFSET BUFER
        CALL  lstrcatA@8
; Send the string into the list
        PUSH  OFFSET BUFER
        PUSH  0
        PUSH  LB_ADDSTRING
        PUSH  101
        PUSH  DWORD PTR [EBP+08H]
        CALL  SendDlgItemMessageA@20
L3:
; Check whether the loop boundary has been reached
        POP   ECX
        INC   ECX
        CMP   ECX, 91
        JNE   LOO
        JMP   FINISH
L2:
        CMP   DWORD PTR [EBP+0CH], WM_LBUTTONDOWN
        JNE   FINISH
        PUSH  0
        PUSH  0
        PUSH  LB_RESETCONTENT
        PUSH  101
        PUSH  DWORD PTR [EBP+08H]
```

```
        CALL   SendDlgItemMessageA@20
        CMP    PRIZ, 0
        JE     YES_0
        MOV    PRIZ, 0
        JMP    L4
YES_0:
        MOV    PRIZ, 1
        JMP    L4
FINISH:
        MOV    EAX, 0
        POP    EDI
        POP    ESI
        POP    EBX
        POP    EBP
        RET    16
WNDPROC    ENDP
_TEXT ENDS
END START
```

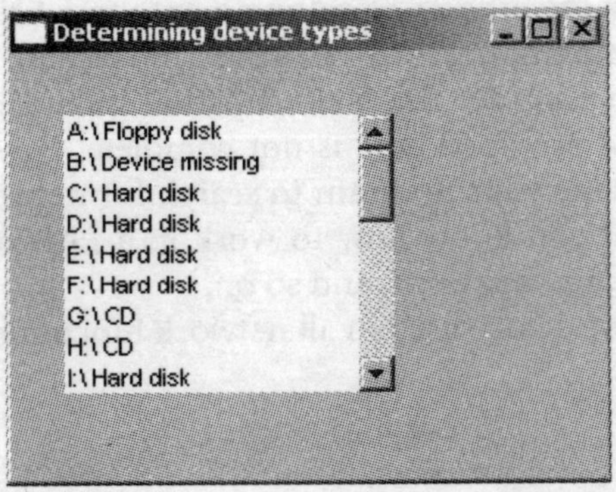

Fig. 17.1. Result of executing the program presented in Listing 17.1

To translate the program presented in Listing 17.1, issue the following commands for MASM32:

```
ml /c /coff /DMASM driv.asm
rc driv.rc
link /subsystem:windows driv.obj driv.res
```

Issue the following commands for TASM32:

```
tasm32 /ml driv.asm
brcc32 driv.rc
tlink32 -aa driv.obj,,,,,driv.res
```

Having determined that a specific device is a network device, you might ask the following: How do I determine the device status? In this case, I interpret the device status as one of the following possible situations: the device is available for reading and writing, the device is read-only, or the device is unavailable. To achieve this, I prefer the following approach: To check the device status, I use the functions `CreateFile` and `GetDiskFreeSpace`. You are already acquainted with the first function. The second function can be used to determine the amount of free disk space. If this device allows you to create a file (the best approach is creating a file with the "delete after closing" attribute, in which case the operating system will automatically delete the file after it is closed) and read information about the device, this means that the device is available for reading and writing. If the device allows you to read information about it but doesn't allow you to create a file, the device is read-only. Finally, if neither of the operations is allowed, the device is unavailable. This approach is simple and straightforward yet efficient.

Searching and Connecting Network Devices

In this section, I cover the aspects of getting access to LAN resources. There are two problems in this context: finding LAN resources and establishing connections to them. First, it is necessary to consider the main function intended for working with a network resource. The list provided here is not complete. However, the functions listed here are enough to enable your program to search for network resources and connect to them. I assume that you know how to work in a LAN and have basic knowledge about network devices, workstations, and so on.

First, consider the structure used in all network functions.

```
NETRESOURCE STRUC
        DwScope          DWORD ?
        DwType           DWORD ?
        DwDisplayType    DWORD ?
        DwUsage          DWORD ?
        LpLocalName      DWORD ?
        LpRemoteName     DWORD ?
        LpComment        DWORD ?
        LpProvider       DWORD ?
NETRESOURCE ENDS
```

Here, the individual elements of the structure are described:

- `DwScope` — Takes one of the following values:
  - `RESOURCE_CONNECTED` — This resource is connected.

- RESOURCE_REMEMBERED — This resource is memorized by the system to automatically establish a connection to it at startup.
- RESOURCE_GLOBALNET — This is a global network resource. You'll probably require only the last value.

❒ DwType — The resource type. The following values are possible:
- RESOURCETYPE_ANY — Any resource
- RESOURCETYPE_DISK — Disk drive
- RESOURCETYPE_PRINT — Network printer

❒ DwDisplayType — This field defines how this resource must be displayed by the network browser depending on its type. The list of types is numerous. For example, the RESOURCEDISPLAYTYPE_SERVER is defined for a network computer, the RESOURCEDISPLAYTYPE_GROUP is used for a group of computers, and so on.

❒ dwUsage — This is most frequently assumed to be zero.

❒ lpLocalName — This is the local name of the device: E:, LPT1:, etc.

❒ lpRemoteName — This is the network name: \\SUPER, \\NDI\EPSON, etc.

❒ lpComment — This string describes the network resource.

❒ LpProvider — This is the provider name. For the moment, assume that it can take one of the two possible values: Microsoft Network and NetWare. Other names are possible.

Now, consider the most popular network application program interface (API) functions:

❒ WNetAddConnection2 — Allows you to connect a network resource (disk or printer) to your computer.
- First parameter — The address of the previously described NETRESOURCE structure. The following fields must be filled: dwType, lpLocalName, lpRemoteName, and lpProvider (usually, NULL). An example of how to fill these fields will be provided later.
- Second parameter — The password required for establishing a connection to the resource. In the case of a blank string, the connection doesn't require a password; if this parameter is set to NULL, then the password associated to the name is taken (this will be described later).
- Third parameter — The username. If this parameter is set to NULL, then the default name will be used.
- Fourth parameter — This parameter defines whether this connection is persistent — in other words, whether the system will further connect to this resource automatically. If this parameter is set to zero, the connection is not persistent.

If the function completes successfully, it returns zero (`NO_ERROR`). The same is true for all functions described in the rest of this section.

- `WNetCancelConnection2` — Disconnects the resource.
  - First parameter — Contains the pointer to the string that contains the resource name. If this is a local name, then the local resource will be disconnected. If the name of a remote resource is specified, all connections to that resource are terminated.
  - Second parameter — Defines whether the system will later connect to this resource automatically. If this value is 0, then the system will reconnect to this resource at the next system startup.
  - Third parameter — If this parameter has a nonzero value, the resource will be disconnected even if there are opened files on the network disk or if the network printer is printing a job sent from your computer.
- `WnetOpenEnum` — Starts the search for network resources. Generally, network resources are organized into a tree-like structure. Therefore, searching for network resources is much alike searching for files using the directory tree.
  - First parameter — The `dwScope` field of the `NETRESOURCE` structure. Usually, it is assumed to be `RESOURCE_GLOBALNET`.
  - Second parameter — The `dwType` field of the `NETRESOURCE` structure. To search for various types of resources, set this value to `RESOURCETYPE_ANY`.
  - Third parameter — The `dwUsage` field of the `NETRESOURCE` structure. Usually, it is set to zero.
  - Fourth parameter — The address of the `NETRESOURCE` structure. If the address is zero (`NULL`), then the search will start from the lowest level (root); otherwise, the search will start from the level defined by the `lpRemoteName` and `lpProvider` fields.
  - Fifth parameter — The pointer to the variable that must receive the descriptor for further search.
- `WnetCloseEnum` — Closes the search. The only parameter of this function is the descriptor received when executing the `WnetOpenEnum` function.
- `WnetEnumResource` — Directly searches for network resources.
  - First parameter — Search descriptor.
  - Second parameter — The pointer to the variable that must contain the maximum number of resources that can be found per search operation. Usually, this variable is assumed to be `0FFFFFFFFH`, which allows you to find all possible resources. If this function completes successfully, the variable will contain the number of found resources.

- Third parameter — The pointer to the array, each element of which represents a NETRESOURCE structure. Obviously, this array must be large enough to hold as much information about the resource as required. Because the structure size is 32 bytes, in a large network the array size must be no less than 32,000 bytes.
- Fourth parameter — The address of the variable that contains the array size. If the array size is too small, the variable will contain the required size.

I'll mention again that this function searches only resources of the current hierarchical level and doesn't search for all resources. Therefore, it is impossible to do without recursion.

- ❑ WNetGetConnection —Allows you to get information about the current connection.
  - First parameter — Address of the local name (A:, C:, LPT2, etc.)
  - Second parameter — Address of the buffer, into which the remote name will be loaded
  - Third parameter — Pointer to the variable that contains the buffer size

To complete this brief overview of the network API function, I'd like to mention again that I have described only the most important network functions. Furthermore, operating systems of the Windows NT family have some specific functions for working with network resources that are missing in Windows 9*x*. By the way, be ready to discover that the behavior of the network API functions will be somewhat different in Windows 9*x*, Windows NT, and Windows 2000. These differences will be emphasized when appropriate.

The program provided in Listing 17.2 demonstrates how to connect network drives. The command-line syntax of this program is as follows: NET *SERVER*\CC Z:. The first parameter is the name of the device being connected, including the name of the network server. The second parameter specifies the drive letter, to which the network disk is to be mapped.

Listing 17.2. An example program that connects to the network resource

```
; The NET program that connects to the network resource
; Usage: NET \\SUPER\\D Z:
.586P
; Flat memory model
.MODEL FLAT, stdcall
; Constants
STD_OUTPUT_HANDLE equ -11
RESOURCETYPE_DISK equ 1h
```

```
; Prototypes of external procedures
IFDEF MASM
    EXTERN  lstrcatA@8:NEAR
    EXTERN  lstrlen@4:NEAR
    EXTERN  GetStdHandle@4:NEAR
    EXTERN  WriteConsoleA@20:NEAR
    EXTERN  ExitProcess@4:NEAR
    EXTERN  GetCommandLineA@0:NEAR
    EXTERN  WNetAddConnection2A@16:NEAR
ELSE
    LOCALS
    EXTERN  lstrcatA:NEAR
    EXTERN  lstrlen:NEAR
    EXTERN  GetStdHandle:NEAR
    EXTERN  WriteConsoleA:NEAR
    EXTERN  ExitProcess:NEAR
    EXTERN  GetCommandLineA:NEAR
    EXTERN  WNetAddConnection2A:NEAR
    lstrcatA@8 = lstrcatA
    lstrlen@4 = lstrlen
    GetStdHandle@4 = GetStdHandle
    WriteConsoleA@20 = WriteConsoleA
    ExitProcess@4 = ExitProcess
    GetCommandLineA@0 = GetCommandLineA
    WNetAddConnection2A@16 = WNetAddConnection2A
ENDIF
; Structures
NETRESOURCE STRUC
    dwScope         DWORD ?
    dwType          DWORD ?
    dwDisplayType   DWORD ?
    dwUsage         DWORD ?
    lpLocalName     DWORD ?
    lpRemoteName    DWORD ?
    lpComment       DWORD ?
    lpProvider      DWORD ?
NETRESOURCE ENDS

; INCLUDELIB directives for the linker
IFDEF MASM
        includelib c:\masm32\lib\user32.lib
        includelib c:\masm32\lib\kernel32.lib
        includelib c:\masm32\lib\mpr.lib
```

```
ELSE
        includelib c:\tasm32\lib\import32.lib
ENDIF
;-----------------------------------------------
; Data segment
_DATA SEGMENT
        BUF1   DB  100 dup(0)
        BUF2   DB  100 dup(0)
        LENS   DWORD ? ; Number of displayed characters
        HANDL  DWORD ?
        NR     NETRESOURCE <0>
        PUSTO  DB 0
        ERR2   DB "Error!", 0
        ERR1   DB "Few parameters!", 0
        ST1    DB "->", 0
_DATA ENDS
; Code segment
_TEXT SEGMENT
START:
; Get the input and output handle
        PUSH  STD_OUTPUT_HANDLE
        CALL  GetStdHandle@4
        MOV   HANDL, EAX
; Get the number of parameters
CALL NUMPAR
        CMP   EAX, 3
        JNB   PAR_OK
        LEA   EBX, ERR1
        CALL  SETMSG
        JMP   _END
PAR_OK:
; Get the parameters
        MOV   EDI, 2
        LEA   EBX, BUF1
        CALL  GETPAR
        MOV   EDI, 3
        LEA   EBX, BUF2
        CALL  GETPAR
; Attempt to establish a connection
; First, fill the NETRESOURCE structure
; For Windows NT, NR.dwType = 0
        MOV   NR.dwType, RESOURCETYPE_DISK
        LEA   EAX, BUF2
```

```
        MOV   NR.lpLocalName, EAX
        LEA   EAX, BUF1
        MOV   NR.lpRemoteName, EAX
        MOV   NR.lpProvider, 0
; Call the function that establishes the connection
        PUSH  0
        PUSH  OFFSET PUSTO
        PUSH  OFFSET PUSTO
        PUSH  OFFSET NR
        CALL  WNetAddConnection2A@16
        CMP   EAX, 0
        JE    _OK
; Error message
        LEA   EBX, ERR2
        CALL  SETMSG
        JMP   _END
_OK:
; Information message about successful connection
        PUSH  OFFSET ST1
        PUSH  OFFSET BUF1
        CALL  lstrcatA@8
        PUSH  OFFSET BUF2
        PUSH  OFFSET BUF1
        CALL  lstrcatA@8
        LEA   EBX, BUF1
        CALL  SETMSG
_END:
        PUSH  0
        CALL  ExitProcess@4
; Determine the number of parameters (->EAX)
NUMPAR PROC
       CALL  GetCommandLineA@0
       MOV   ESI, EAX ; Pointer to the string
       XOR   ECX, ECX ; Counter
       MOV   EDX, 1   ; Flag
@@L1:
       CMP   BYTE PTR [ESI], 0
       JE    @@L4
       CMP   BYTE PTR [ESI], 32
JE @@L3
       ADD   ECX, EDX ; Parameter number
       MOV   EDX, 0
       JMP   @@L2
@@L3:
```

```
        OR    EDX, 1
@@L2:
        INC   ESI
        JMP   @@L1
@@L4:
        MOV   EAX, ECX
        RET
NUMPAR ENDP
; Get the parameter
; EBX — Points to the buffer, in which the parameter will be loaded
; Null-terminated string is loaded into the buffer
; EDI — Parameter number
GETPAR PROC
        CALL  GetCommandLineA@0
        MOV   ESI, EAX ; Pointer to the string
        XOR   ECX, ECX ; Counter
        MOV   EDX, 1   ; Flag
@@L1:
        CMP   BYTE PTR [ESI], 0
        JE    @@L4
        CMP   BYTE PTR [ESI], 32
        JE    @@L3
        ADD   ECX, EDX ; Parameter number
        MOV   EDX, 0
        JMP   @@L2
@@L3:
        OR    EDX, 1
@@L2:
        CMP   ECX, EDI
        JNE   @@L5
        MOV   AL, BYTE PTR [ESI]
        CMP   AL, 32
        JE    @@L5
        MOV   BYTE PTR [EBX], AL
        INC   EBX
@@L5:
        INC   ESI
        JMP   @@L1
@@L4:
        MOV   BYTE PTR [EBX], 0
        RET
GETPAR ENDP
; Message output
; EBX -> string
```

```
SETMSG PROC
        PUSH  EBX
        CALL  lstrlen@4
        PUSH  0
        PUSH  OFFSET LENS
        PUSH  EAX
        PUSH  EBX
        PUSH  HANDL
        CALL  WriteConsoleA@20
        RET
SETMSG ENDP
_TEXT ENDS
END START
```

To translate the program presented in Listing 17.2, issue the following commands for MASM32:

```
ml /c /coff /DMASM net.asm
link /subsystem:console net.obj
```

Issue the following commands for TASM32:

```
tasm32 /ml net.asm
tlink32 -ap net.obj
```

When considering the program presented in Listing 17.2, pay attention to the following:

- Note how local labels are used. MASM recognizes local labels automatically. TASM, on the other hand, requires the local labels to be preceded by the `@@` prefix. Additionally, the `LOCALS` directive must be inserted in the beginning of the program.
- Note one important feature of the `WNetAddConnection2A@16` function. For Windows NT and later operating systems of this family, the `dwType` field of the `NETRESOURCE` structure must contain zero instead of `RESOURCETYPE_DISK`. Unfortunately, there are many other similar differences when working with LAN resources. If you plan to undertake a serious programming task related to working with LAN resources, you'll have to test your program on different computers in various networks.
- Naturally, this program is far from perfect. Therefore, try to improve it. In particular, it would be useful to check whether the local device is network device and, if this is the case, ask permission to establish a persistent connection. In this case, it is necessary to first disconnect the device using the `WNetCancelConnection2` function.
- When it is necessary to connect a network printer, the `dwType` field must be set to `RESOURCETYPE_PRINT`.

The program in Listing 17.3 carries out a recursive search for network resources. It operates in the console mode and displays on the screen provider's name and remote name of the resources found. This program must correctly operate in both Microsoft and Novell networks.

Listing 17.3. Recursive search for network resources in a local area network

```
; The NET1 program that searches for
; network resources
.586P
; Flat memory model
.MODEL FLAT, stdcall
; Constants
STD_OUTPUT_HANDLE  equ -11
RESOURCETYPE_DISK  equ 1h
RESOURCE_GLOBALNET equ 2h
RESOURCETYPE_ANY   equ 0h
; Prototypes of external procedures
IFDEF MASM
        EXTERN  CharToOemA@8:NEAR
        EXTERN  RtlMoveMemory@12:NEAR
        EXTERN  WNetCloseEnum@4:NEAR
        EXTERN  WNetEnumResourceA@16:NEAR
        EXTERN  WNetOpenEnumA@20:NEAR
        EXTERN  lstrcpyA@8:NEAR
        EXTERN  lstrcatA@8:NEAR
        EXTERN  lstrlen@4:NEAR
        EXTERN  GetStdHandle@4:NEAR
        EXTERN  WriteConsoleA@20:NEAR
        EXTERN  ExitProcess@4:NEAR
        EXTERN  GetCommandLineA@0:NEAR
ELSE
        EXTERN  CharToOemA:NEAR
        EXTERN  RtlMoveMemory:NEAR
        EXTERN  WNetCloseEnum:NEAR
        EXTERN  WNetEnumResourceA:NEAR
        EXTERN  WNetOpenEnumA:NEAR
        EXTERN  lstrcpyA:NEAR
        EXTERN  lstrcatA:NEAR
        EXTERN  lstrlen:NEAR
        EXTERN  GetStdHandle:NEAR
        EXTERN  WriteConsoleA:NEAR
```

```
        EXTERN  ExitProcess:NEAR
        EXTERN  GetCommandLineA:NEAR
        CharToOemA@8 = CharToOemA
        RtlMoveMemory@12 = RtlMoveMemory
        WNetCloseEnum@4 = WNetCloseEnum
        WNetEnumResourceA@16 = WNetEnumResourceA
        lstrcpyA@8 = lstrcpyA
        WNetOpenEnumA@20 = WNetOpenEnumA
        lstrcatA@8 = lstrcatA
        lstrlen@4 = lstrlen
        GetStdHandle@4 = GetStdHandle
        WriteConsoleA@20 = WriteConsoleA
        ExitProcess@4 = ExitProcess
        GetCommandLineA@0 = GetCommandLineA
ENDIF
; Structures
NETRESOURCE STRUC
        dwScope        DWORD ?
        dwType         DWORD ?
        dwDisplayType  DWORD ?
        dwUsage        DWORD ?
        lpLocalName    DWORD ?
        lpRemoteName   DWORD ?
        lpComment      DWORD ?
        lpProvider     DWORD ?
NETRESOURCE ENDS

; INCLUDELIB directives for the linker
IFDEF MASM
        includelib c:\masm32\lib\user32.lib
        includelib c:\masm32\lib\kernel32.lib
        includelib c:\masm32\lib\mpr.lib
ELSE
        includelib c:\tasm32\lib\import32.lib
ENDIF
;------------------------------------------------
; Data segment
_DATA SEGMENT
        LENS  DWORD ? ; Number of displayed characters
        HANDL DWORD ?
        NR    NETRESOURCE <0>
        ENT   DB 13, 10, 0
        BUF   DB 100 dup(0)
```

```
_DATA ENDS
; Code segment
_TEXT SEGMENT
START:
; Get the input and output handle
      PUSH   STD_OUTPUT_HANDLE
      CALL   GetStdHandle@4
      MOV    HANDL, EAX
; Start the network search procedure
      PUSH   0
      PUSH   OFFSET NR
      CALL   SEARCH
_END:
      PUSH   0
      CALL   ExitProcess@4
; Search procedure
      PAR1   EQU [EBP+8] ; Pointer to the structure
      PAR2   EQU [EBP+0CH] ; Flag
; Local variables
      HANDLP EQU [EBP-4] ; Search handle
      CC     EQU [EBP-8]
      NB     EQU [EBP-12]
      NR1    EQU [EBP-44] ; Structure
      BUFER  EQU [EBP-144] ; Buffer
      RS     EQU [EBP-32144] ; Array of structures
SEARCH PROC
      PUSH   EBP
      MOV    EBP, ESP
      SUB    ESP, 32144
      CMP    DWORD PTR PAR2, 0
      JNE    SECOND
; NULL at first startup
      XOR    EBX, EBX
      JMP    FIRST
SECOND:
; Startup in the course of recursive search
; First, copy the structure into a local
; variable (this is not required for this program)
      PUSH   32
      PUSH   DWORD PTR PAR1
      LEA    EAX, DWORD PTR NR1
      PUSH   EAX
      CALL   RtlMoveMemory@12
```

```
; In case a recursive search points to a structure
        LEA   EBX, DWORD PTR NR1
FIRST:
; Startup at the first call
        LEA   EAX, HANDLP
        PUSH  EAX
        PUSH  EBX
        PUSH  0
        PUSH  RESOURCETYPE_ANY
        PUSH  RESOURCE_GLOBALNET
        CALL  WNetOpenEnumA@20
        CMP   EAX, 0
        JNE   _EN
; Main search
REPI:
; Starting the WNetEnumResource function
; Size of the array of NETRESOURCE structures
        MOV   DWORD PTR NB, 32000
        LEA   EAX, NB
        PUSH  EAX
        LEA   EAX, RS
        PUSH  EAX
; Get the maximum number of objects
        MOV   DWORD PTR CC, 0FFFFFFFFH
        LEA   EAX, CC
        PUSH  EAX
        PUSH  DWORD PTR HANDLP
        CALL  WNetEnumResourceA@16
        CMP   EAX, 0
        JNE   _CLOSE
; Loop by the resulting array
        MOV   ESI, CC
        SHL   ESI, 5 ; Multiply by 32
        MOV   EDI, 0
LOO:
        CMP   EDI, ESI
        JE    REPI
; Information output
; Provider
        MOV   EBX, DWORD PTR RS[EDI]+28
        CALL  SETMSG
; Remote name
        MOV   EBX, DWORD PTR RS[EDI]+20
```

```
        CALL  SETMSG
; Save the required registers
        PUSH  ESI
        PUSH  EDI
; Recursive call
        PUSH  1
        LEA   EAX, DWORD PTR RS[EDI]
        PUSH  EAX
        CALL  SEARCH
; Restore registers
        POP   EDI
        POP   ESI
        ADD   EDI, 32
        JMP   LOO
;-----------------------------------
        JMP   REPI
;-----------------------------------
_CLOSE:
        PUSH  DWORD PTR HANDLP
        CALL  WNetCloseEnum@4
_EN:
        MOV   ESP, EBP
        POP   EBP
        RET   8
SEARCH ENDP
; Display the message
; EBX -> string
SETMSG PROC
; Copy the text into a separate buffer
        PUSH  EBX
        PUSH  OFFSET BUF
        CALL  lstrcpyA@8
        LEA   EBX, BUF
; Convert for console output
        PUSH  EBX
        PUSH  EBX
        CALL  CharToOemA@8
; Add the line feed
        PUSH  OFFSET ENT
        PUSH  EBX
        CALL  lstrcatA@8
; Determine the string length
        PUSH  EBX
```

```
        CALL  lstrlen@4
; Display the string
        PUSH  0
        PUSH  OFFSET LENS
        PUSH  EAX
        PUSH  EBX
        PUSH  HANDL
        CALL  WriteConsoleA@20
        RET
SETMSG ENDP
_TEXT ENDS
END START
```

To translate the program presented in Listing 17.3, issue the following commands using MASM32:

```
ml /c /coff /DMASM net1.asm
link /subsystem:console /STACK:1000000,1000000 net1.obj
```

Issue the following commands using TASM32:

```
tasm32 /ml net1.asm
tlink32 -ap -S:1000000 -Sc:1000000 net1.obj
```

The program in Listing 17.3 is complicated and requires detailed comments. First, I would like to point out that if you want a proper understanding of network programming (in this context, network programming is interpreted as programming for LANs),[i] it is absolutely necessary to write several programs on your own. The programs presented here will serve as the starting point.

- You encountered local variables when considering file search of the directory tree. This problem is similar; however, it has certain differences. In this case, too many local variables are used. Because of this, I explicitly declared a large volume for the stack (the `STACK` command-line option for MASM and the `S` and `Sc` command-line options for TASM32). By default, the linker sets only 8 KB, which, obviously, is not sufficient.
- The `WnetEnumResource` function requires the array of `NETRESOURCE` structures as one of its parameters. The size of a single structure is 32 bytes. I reserved 1,000 such structures. Isn't this too much, you might ask? To tell the truth, I never encountered

[i] Nowadays, the term network programming is often interpreted as Internet programming or using Internet approaches and methods in a LAN (intranet). However, this chapter describes a relatively narrow range of tasks — those that relate only to LANs.

a LAN with 1,000 workstations. However, I have seen a LAN, in which one of the servers contained about 800 network directories. Honestly, the style of programming that I demonstrate here is not the best possible. A more correct approach would be to first call the `WnetEnumResource` function, then specify a buffer smaller than 32 bytes, in which case the required size will be returned in the variable containing the buffer size. Then, knowing the required size, the program must request the required buffer from the operating system and repeat the call to `WnetEnumResource`. Although this approach is more correct, it is more difficult to implement.

- In a recursive call to the `SEARCH` procedure, the first parameter is the pointer to the element of the array composed of the `NETRESOURCE` structures. I copied the element of this array into the local variable `NR1`. Principally, in this program, such action is not required, and you could immediately use the obtained pointer. However, in more a complicated program, you'll have to do this.
- Note that in the course of information output I copied the string into the buffer that then is used for output. This isn't a fancy code; this is a necessity. Before output, I added the codes 13 and 10 to the string end. Because I output the strings that will be used for further searches, I must use an additional buffer for output.

About TCP/IP Network Protocols

The material of this section looks somewhat strange in this book. However, it will be followed by material related to sockets programming. Therefore, I must provide an elementary introduction related to the topics that you'll certainly encounter if you are going to program sockets.

About the Open Systems Interconnection Model

In the open systems interconnection (OSI) model, networking tools are divided into seven layers. OSI was developed by the International Standard Organization. The OSI model layers are outlined in Table 17.1.

Table 17.1. Open systems interconnection model layers

Layer	Description
Physical	Transmits bits through physical links, such as coaxial cable, twisted pair, or fiber-optic cable. At this layer, physical media characteristics and signal parameters are defined. Sometimes, this layer is called the hardware layer.

continues

Table 17.1 *Continued*

Layer	Description
Data-link	Ensures data frame transmission between any two nodes in networks with typical topology or between two neighboring nodes in networks with arbitrary topology. Data-link layer protocols implement a certain structure of links between computers and the methods of their addressing. Addresses used in the data-link layer protocols in LANs are often called MAC addresses. The data-link layer is divided into two sublayers: • Medium access control (MAC) • Logical link control (LLC)
Network	Ensures data delivery between any two nodes in networks with arbitrary topology. The network layer doesn't ensure reliable data transmission.
Transport	Ensures data transmission between any two network nodes with the required reliability level. To achieve this, the transport layer provides functional capabilities for establishing a connection, packet numbering, buffering and ordering, and taking into account duplicated packets.
Session	Provides the means of controlling communications between interacting parties, determining which of them is active, and synchronizing within the framework of the message exchanging procedure.
Presentation	Deals with the external representation of the data. Various types of data conversion can take place at this layer, including data compression and decompression, encryption, and decryption.
Application	The set of various network services provided to users and applications. Examples of such services are e-mail, terminal services, and file transmission.

More details about the OSI model can be found in an old but comprehensive book by Barry Nance [18], which haven't become obsolete even now.

About the TCP/IP Family

Protocols of the TCP/IP family (TCP/IP stands for Transmission Control Protocol/ Internet Protocol) form a four-layer structure. A schematic representation of this structure is provided in Fig. 17.2.

The TCP/IP family has a long history; nevertheless, these protocols are the most widely used. Among contemporary operating systems, it is impossible to find one that wouldn't support these protocols. Partially, this is because the Internet is built on the basis of TCP/IP.

Application	HTTP, FTP, SMTP, SNMP, telnet
Transport	TCP, UDP
Network	IP, RIP, ARP, ICMP, OSPF
Link	Device drivers

Fig. 17.2. The TCP/IP family

The lowest layer in the TCP/IP stack is not regulated, but it supports all known protocols of the physical and data-link layers of the OSI model.

The next, or third, layer is the internetworking layer. It transmits packets using the transport technology of LANs, transmission networks, communications links, etc. The main protocol of the network layer is IP. IP is the datagram protocol (see the note that follows), which doesn't guarantee the delivery of the packet to the destination node. This layer includes all protocols related to creating and modifying routing tables. These protocols include the Routing Internet Protocol (RIP) and the open shortest path first protocol for collecting the routing information and the Internet control message protocol (ICMP) for internetwork control messages.

NOTE

A datagram is a network packet transmitted independently of other packets without establishing a logical connection.

The second layer is considered the main layer of the TCP/IP stack. Protocols such as TCP and the User Datagram Protocol (UDP)[i] operate at this layer. TCP ensure the transmission of messages between distributed processes, forming virtual connections. UDP ensures the transmission of application packets using the datagram method (similar to IP) and carries out the functions of a link between IP and application processes.

The first layer is the application layer. It includes higher-layer protocols. For example, hypertext transfer protocol allows data transmission in the form of Web pages and the exchange of files between the nodes of a Wide Area Network (WAN).

---

[i] Thus, TCP/IP includes the entire protocol suite, also called protocol stack.

About Internet Protocol Addressing

The possibility of quickly finding the required destination node is the main feature of computer networks. In IP networks, there are three layers of addressing:

- In a LAN, physical or local addressing is based on the network adapter number. These unique 6-byte addresses are assigned by equipment manufacturers. In WANs, local addresses are assigned by the network administrator.
- An IP address comprises 4 bytes. Traditionally, IP addresses are written in a decimal notation (i.e., separating bytes with dots), for example: 137.50.50.83. IP addresses can be assigned manually by a network administrator or automatically by the system. An address consists of two parts — the network address and the host address (more details will be provided later in this chapter). A host may be the member of several networks; therefore, it can have several IP addresses. An IP address is independent of the physical address; therefore, it is not a physical characteristic of a computer. Quite contrary, it is a logical characteristic of a specific host.
- The symbolic address or identifier can consist of several parts separated by dots. Symbolic addresses are assigned by the network administrator. For example, a name such as SERV1.BANK.COM consists of three parts: the domain name COM, the organization name BANK, and the computer name SERV1.

Consider IP addresses in more detail. The address provided earlier as an example (137.50.50.83) can be written in a binary notation:

```
10001001 00110010 00110010 01010011
```

Fig. 17.3 illustrates the existing file classes of IP addresses. As you can see, only the first three classes — A, B, and C — are used to address computers (hosts). The choice of the address class depends on the scale of the network (large, medium, or small).

- Class A networks have addresses ranging from 1 to 126. Zero is not used, and 127 is reserved. Numerous hosts can exist in such networks.
- Class B networks are of a medium size. In such networks, 2 bytes are allocated for the host address. Consequently, an address such as 137.50.50.83 specifies that the computer, to which it is assigned, belongs to a class B network.
- Networks of class C are small networks.
- Class D addresses are special addresses, called multicast addresses. If the packet being transmitted has such an address as its destination, this packet will be delivered to all computers of the destination network. Packets with such an address are called multicast packets.
- Class E is the reserved group of addresses.

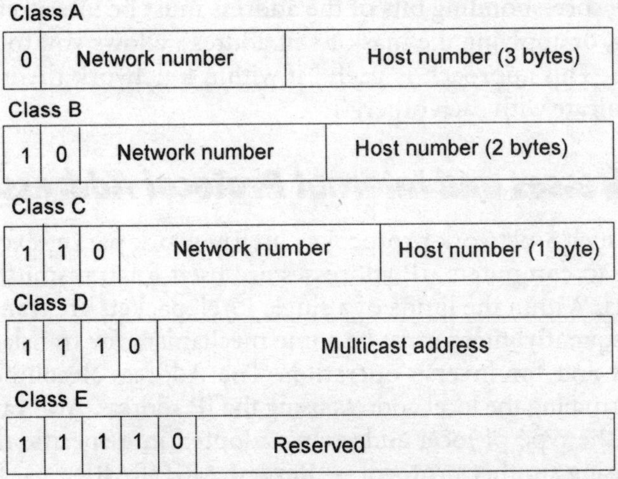

Fig. 17.3. Classes of IP addresses

In addition, there are several special IP addresses:

- An address composed of zeroes is called an undefined address. Such an address designates the address of the host that has generated the packet.
- An address may contain all zeroes except for the host address. By default, it is assumed that the address belongs to the same network as the sender.
- The 255.255.255.255 address is the so-called limited broadcast address. A packet with such an address specified as its destination will be delivered to all hosts of the current network. This broadcast is limited because the packet will never leave the current network.
- If all positions corresponding to the host number of the destination host are filled with ones, the packet with such an address is sent to *all* hosts of the network, the number of which is specified in the destination address.
- The address 127.0.0.1 is the so-called loopback address, which has special meaning. This address is an internal address of the computer or router protocol stack. It is used for testing programs and for organizing the operation of client and server components of the same application installed on the same computer.

Address Masks

Even if you do not know the working principles of TCP/IP, you have probably noticed that when specifying an IP address, the system also prompts you to specify a mask. The mask is the number of the same length as IP address, in which the bits set to one specify that the corresponding bits of the address must be interpreted as a network address. Masking, or applying the mask to an address, allows you to split a network into several subnets. This approach is useful if within a network there are computers that rarely communicate with each other.

Physical Addresses and Internet Protocol Addresses

In contrast to such a network protocol as internetwork packet exchange, IP addresses are not bound to computers. IP addresses are used for transmitting information between networks. Within the limits of a single LAN, packets are transmitted by the local address. Consequently, there must be some mechanism for translating IP addresses to local addresses and for inverse operation. The Address Resolution Protocol (ARP) is used for determining the local address using the IP address. ARP can operate differently depending on the type of local addressing adopted in a specific network. An inverse task is solved using another protocol — Reverse ARP (RARP).

The host that needs to convert an IP address to a local address formulates an ARP request. Note that for different networks the structure of this request might be different. This request is broadcasted within the limits of the current network. All hosts receive this request and compare their IP addresses with the one specified in the request. The host with the matching IP address formulates a reply, in which it specifies its local address and IP address.

In a LAN, local addresses are determined automatically. In WANs, special forwarding tables are used. These tables can be stored on special routers so that requests are sent to the necessary router.

About the Domain Name System Service

The Domain Name System (DNS) ensures automatic mapping of IP addresses to symbolic addresses. DNS is a distributed database. The DNS protocol is an application-layer protocol. It operates with DNS clients and DNS servers. All DNS servers form a logical hierarchical structure. The client requests these servers until the required information (a match) if found.

On the Internet, top-level domains correspond to countries or are assigned by the Internet authorities (e.g., the domain name COM means that the server is owned by a company).

Automatically Assigning Internet Protocol Addresses

Manually assigning IP addresses to network host is a tedious and labor-intensive job. For networks with 50 computers of more, it is recommended that you abandon this approach. To automate the process of assigning IP addresses, a special protocol was developed — the Dynamic Host Configuration Protocol (DHCP). This protocol enables the administrator not only to fully automate the process of address assignment but also to interfere with this process. It is necessary to distinguish between automatic and dynamic address assignment. When automatic address assignment is chosen, a new IP address will be automatically assigned to a computer any time it logs on to the network. When the dynamic assignment mode is used, an IP address may be leased to the computer for a certain time. When dynamic address assignment is used, the number of used addresses can be considerably lower than the number of computers in the network.

Routing

The process of routing is the process of transmitting a packet from the source node to the destination network node. This process involves both routers and individual hosts. Not only routers but also network hosts can have routing tables.

Any record of a routing table must contain at least four fields: the destination network address, the next router address, the output port number, and the distance to the destination network. The latter value can be interpreted in different ways. For example, it might be a time characteristic or the number of nodes, through which the packet must pass. If the routing table contains several records with the same destination network address, then, as a rule, the record with the smallest value of the distance to the destination network is chosen.

The use of such tables assumes the use of so-called single-step routing. Multiple-step routing, when the packet being sent already has information about all routers that it has to pass, is also possible. Such a method is used mainly in debugging situations.

When sending the packet to the next router, ARP is used first because the routing table doesn't contain a local address.

If a host or router detect that this address belongs to the local network, it decides to pass the packet to a specific host, using ARP to determine local address. A routing table also contains records that specify addresses of the network directly connected to this router. Such records contain zeroes in the field specifying the distance to the destination network.

As a rule, a routing table has the `default` record, which contains the address of the default router. If the record with the required address is not found in the routing table, then the packet will be sent to the default router. It is assumed that proceeding this way, the packet will reach the so-called backbone routers that contain all-embracing routing tables.

Three types of routing algorithms are used when composing routing tables:

- Fixed routing — This algorithm is based on manually creating routing tables.
- Simple routing — There are three types of simple routing: flood routing, when the packets are sent in all directions except for the one, from which the packet was

received; event-dependent routing, when the packets is sent to a specific destination network along the route that previously resulted in a successful delivery; and source routing, when the sender places into the packet information about transit routers that must participate in packet delivery to the destination network.

- Adaptive routing — This is the most frequently used type of routing. It is based on routers periodical exchange of information about the network topology, which, by the way, is ever-changing. In this algorithm, not only the network topology but also the bandwidth of specific network sections is taken into account.

Sockets Management

Standard Windows Sockets specification defines the interface in a TCP/IP network, which allows intercommunications between applications. In the simplest interpretation, it is possible to say that two applications in a network interoperate through a socket, to which they are connected. By its properties, a socket is similar to a file descriptor; however, it has specific management and control functions. These functions are stored in a separate DLL. To use these functions in your programs, it is necessary to include the WS2_32.LIB library. When describing sockets, all structures will be described as in the WINDOWS.INC file supplied as part of the MASM32 product.

Now, after considering all essential theoretical aspects, it is time to describe the functions that control sockets, or, to be more precise, the functions that control intercommunications between applications using sockets.

Before using the sockets library, it is necessary to initialize it. The `WSAStartup` function is intended for this purpose. In the case of an error, this function returns a nonzero code. Consider the parameters of this function:

- First parameter — This is a double word, in which the most significant word is not used. The high-order byte of the least significant word specifies the minor version (revision) number, and the most significant byte contains the major part of the library version.
- Second parameter — This parameter is the address of a special structure that gets information on sockets support. Because the contents of this structure (`WSADATA`) are of no particular importance, it is enough to reserve the required number of bytes for it. The structure itself is, briefly, as follows:

```
WSADATA STRUCT
    wVersion          WORD ?
    wHighVersion      WORD ?
    szDescription     BYTE 257 dup (?)
    szSystemStatus    BYTE 129 dup (?)
    iMaxSockets       WORD ?
```

```
    iMaxUdpDg           WORD ?
    lpVendorInfo        DWORD ?
  WSADATA ENDS
```

The next function, `socket`, creates a socket. If this function completes successfully, it returns the socket descriptor. In the case of an error, the function returns –1. This function has three parameters:

- First parameter — Specifies the set of protocols. For TCP/IP, the `AF_INET = 2` constant is used.
- Second parameter — Defines the mode of interaction. Usually, two constants are used: `SOCK_STREAM = 1` for connection-oriented communications and `SOCK_DGRAM = 2` — for connectionless communications.
- Third parameter — Specifies the transport-layer protocol.

To request the server, the `connect` function is used. If this function completes successfully, it returns zero. The function has three parameters:

- First parameter — Must contain a previously created socket.
- Second parameter — Must specify the address of the `socaddr_in` structure containing the address of the server program.
- Third parameter — Gives the structure length.

Consider the previously mentioned `sockaddr_in` structure:

```
sockaddr_in STRUCT
  sin_family     WORD       ?
  sin_port       WORD       ?
  sin_addr       in_addr <>
  sin_zero       BYTE 8 dup (?)
sockaddr_in ENDS
```

As you can see, this structure contains another structure inside of it:

```
in_addr STRUCT
  S_un ADDRESS_UNION <>
in_addr ENDS
```

This structure represents a union:

```
ADDRESS_UNION UNION
    S_un_b S_UN_B <>
    S_un_w S_UN_W <>
    S_addr DWORD ?
ADDRESS_UNION ENDS
```

And finally, this union includes two more structures:

```
S_UN_B STRUCT
  s_b1 BYTE ?
  s_b2 BYTE ?
  s_b3 BYTE ?
  s_b4 BYTE ?
S_UN_B ENDS

S_UN_W STRUCT
  s_w1 WORD ?
  s_w2 WORD ?
S_UN_W ENDS
```

There is nothing difficult here, although these definitions seem too long. However, this seeming complexity only reflects that the `sin_addr` address can be set using three methods. The examples provided later in this chapter will demonstrate the use of these structures.

The `listen` function switches the socket into the listening state, in which it listens for external calls. In the case of success, the function returns zero. Parameters of this function are as follows:

- First parameter — Gives the socket descriptor.
- Second parameter — Defines the maximum length of the incoming calls queue. The standard value is 5.

The `accept` function is used for accepting client requests to establish a connection. Clients send their requests using the `connect` function. The `accept` function must precede the `listen` function, which organizes the queue. This function retrieves the first connection request and returns the descriptor of the socket that will be used for data exchange with the client that requests a connection. If the queue of connection requests is empty, the function switches to the waiting state. Consider the function parameters:

- First parameter — The descriptor of the socket, through which the program receives the request.
- Second parameter — The address of the `sockaddr_in` structure that will receive information about the connection.
- Third parameter — The size of the structure defined by the second parameter.

The `bind` function connects the socket to a communications medium. If this function completes successfully, it returns zero; otherwise, it returns –1. Parameters of this function are as follows:

- First parameter — The descriptor of the socket being bound.
- Second parameter — The pointer to the `sockaddr_in` structure. This structure must be filled beforehand. The `sin_family` field must be equal to `AF_INET = 2`. The `sin_addr.s_addr` field must be set to `INADDR_ANY = 0`. The `port` field must contain the port number, for example, 2000.
- Third parameter — The length of the structure pointed to by the second parameter.

For receiving the data, the `recv` function is used. If data are received successfully, the function returns the number of received bytes. Parameters of this function are as follows:

- First parameter — The socket descriptor.
- Second parameter — The address of the buffer that receives the data.
- Third parameter — The length of the buffer that receives the data.
- Fourth parameter — The reception flag. Most frequently, this parameter is set to zero.

For sending the data, the `send` API function is used. When the function completes successfully, it returns the number of transmitted bytes. The function has the following parameters:

- First parameter — Descriptor of the used socket
- Second parameter — Address of the buffer that receives the data being transmitted
- Third parameter — Buffer length
- Fourth parameter — Flag, which is usually set to zero

The `closesocket` function is used for closing the existing socket. The only parameter of this function is the socket descriptor.

The `shutdown` function is used for urgently closing the socket. The first parameter of this function is the descriptor of the socket that needs to be closed. The second parameter can take the following values: 0 to reset and stop receiving data for reading from this socket, 1 to reset and stop sending the data for transmission, and 2 to reset all.

In addition to the previously listed functions, the functions that follow will be exceptionally useful when working with sockets.

The `gethostname` function is used for receiving the name of the local computer. The first parameter of this function is the buffer, into which this name will be loaded. The second parameter is the buffer length.

The gethostbyname function is used to get information about the remote computer. The only parameter of this function is the pointer to its network name. The function itself returns the pointer to the hostent structure in the case of success and zero in the case of error. Consider the structure returned by this function:

```
hostent STRUCT
  h_name     DWORD    ?
  h_alias    DWORD    ?
  h_addr     WORD     ?
  h_len      WORD     ?
  h_list     DWORD    ?
hostent ENDS
```

The fields of this structure are as follows:

- h_name — The address, by which the official name of the host will be placed.
- h_alias — The pointer to array of additional (alias) names. The names are separated by zero, and the array is terminated by two trailing zeroes.
- h_addr — The type of address, equal to 2 (AF_INET).
- h_len — The length of the host address.
- h_list — The points to the array that contains IP addresses of the host separated by a zero code. The array is terminated by two trailing zeroes. IP address is represented as a sequence of 4 bytes directly following each other.

An Example of Simple Client and Server Applications

In this section, I provide an example that comprises two programs: client and server. Client and server parts of the application communicate using TCP/IP. Program code is presented in Listing 17.4 (server) and Listing 17.5 (client). Note that this is the simplest implementation of a client and server system, which, nevertheless, contains all the main mechanisms of application's communication using sockets. The server waits for the client call and, in response to a client request, sends to it the string that the client displays on the console. The client also sends a message in response to the server, which, in turn, displays it on the console. The server waits in a loop for requests and can reply to ten client requests that directly follow each other. To connect the server, the client must know the network name of the computer, in which the server component of the application runs. Before sending the request, the client determines the server's IP address by its name and displays it on the console.

Listing 17.4. The server component that receives requests from the clients

```
; The SERVER.ASM file
.586P
; Flat memory model
.MODEL FLAT, stdcall
; Constants
STD_OUTPUT_HANDLE equ -11
; Prototypes of external procedures
IFDEF MASM
        EXTERN  shutdown@8:NEAR
        EXTERN  recv@16:NEAR
        EXTERN  send@16:NEAR
        EXTERN  accept@12:NEAR
        EXTERN  listen@8:NEAR
        EXTERN  bind@12:NEAR
        EXTERN  closesocket@4:NEAR
        EXTERN  socket@12:NEAR
        EXTERN  CharToOemA@8:NEAR
        EXTERN  WSAStartup@8:NEAR
        EXTERN  wsprintfA:NEAR
        EXTERN  GetLastError@0:NEAR
        EXTERN  ExitProcess@4:NEAR
        EXTERN  lstrlenA@4:NEAR
        EXTERN  WriteConsoleA@20:NEAR
        EXTERN  GetStdHandle@4:NEAR
ELSE
        EXTERN  shutdown:NEAR
        EXTERN  recv:NEAR
        EXTERN  send:NEAR
        EXTERN  accept:NEAR
        EXTERN  listen:NEAR
        EXTERN  bind:NEAR
        EXTERN  closesocket:NEAR
        EXTERN  socket:NEAR
        EXTERN  CharToOemA:NEAR
        EXTERN  WSAStartup:NEAR
        EXTERN  _wsprintfA:NEAR
        EXTERN  GetLastError:NEAR
        EXTERN  ExitProcess:NEAR
        EXTERN  lstrlenA:NEAR
        EXTERN  WriteConsoleA:NEAR
        EXTERN  GetStdHandle:NEAR
```

```
        shutdown@8 = shutdown
        recv@16 = recv
        send@16 = send
        accept@12 = accept
        listen@8 = listen
        bind@12 = bind
        closesocket@4 = closesocket
        socket@12 = socket
        CharToOemA@8 = CharToOemA
        WSAStartup@8 = WSAStartup
        GetStdHandle@4 = GetStdHandle
        WriteConsoleA@20 = WriteConsoleA
        lstrlenA@4 = lstrlenA
        wsprintfA = _wsprintfA
        GetLastError@0 = GetLastError
        ExitProcess@4 = ExitProcess
ENDIF

; INCLUDELIB directives for the linker
IFDEF MASM
        includelib d:\masm32\lib\user32.lib
        includelib d:\masm32\lib\kernel32.lib
        includelib d:\masm32\lib\ws2_32.lib
ELSE
        includelib c:\tasm32\lib\import32.lib
ENDIF
;-----------------------------------------------

WSADATA STRUCT
        wVersion            WORD        ?
        wHighVersion        WORD        ?
        szDescription       BYTE 257 dup (?)
        szSystemStatus      BYTE 129 dup (?)
        iMaxSockets         WORD        ?
        iMaxUdpDg           WORD        ?
        lpVendorInfo        DWORD       ?
WSADATA ENDS
;-----------------------------------------------
S_UN_B STRUCT
        s_b1 BYTE 0
        s_b2 BYTE 0
        s_b3 BYTE 0
        s_b4 BYTE 0
```

```
S_UN_B ENDS

S_UN_W STRUCT
        s_w1 WORD 0
        s_w2 WORD 0
S_UN_W ENDS  .

ADDRESS_UNION UNION
        s_u_b S_UN_b <>
        s_u_w S_UN_w <>
        s_addr DWORD 0
ADDRESS_UNION ENDS

in_addr STRUCT
        s_un ADDRESS_UNION <>
in_addr ENDS


sockaddr_in STRUCT
        sin_family    WORD      0
        sin_port      WORD      0
        sin_addr      in_addr <>
        sin_zero      BYTE 8 dup (0)
sockaddr_in ENDS

;-------------------------------------------
; Data segment
_DATA SEGMENT
HANDL DD ?
LENS  DD ?
ERRS  DB "Error %u ", 0
;-------------------------------------------
S1    DD ?
S2    DD ?
LEN   DD ?
BUF   DB 100 DUP(0)
BUF1  DB 100 DUP(0)
txt   DB 'Call accepted. Please send acknowledgment.', 0
msg   DB 'The server is down', 0
sin1  sockaddr_in <0>
sin2  sockaddr_in <0>
wsd   WSADATA <0>
len1  DD ?
_DATA ENDS
```

```
; ode segment
_TEXT SEGMENT
START:
; Get the descriptor of the output console
        PUSH  STD_OUTPUT_HANDLE
        CALL  GetStdHandle@4
        MOV   HANDL, EAX
; Activate the sockets library
        PUSH  OFFSET wsd
        MOV   EAX, 0
        MOV   AX, 0202H
        PUSH  EAX
        CALL  WSAStartup@8
        CMP   EAX, 0
        JZ    NO_ER1
        CALL  ERRO
        JMP   EXI
NO_ER1:
; Create a socket
        PUSH  0
        PUSH  1  ; SOCK_STREAM
        PUSH  2  ; AF_INET
        CALL  socket@12
        CMP   EAX, NOT 0
        JNZ   NO_ER2
        CALL  ERRO
        JMP   EXI
NO_ER2:
        MOV    s1, EAX
; Connect a socket
        MOV   sin1.sin_family, 2 ; AF_INET
        MOV   sin1.sin_addr.s_un.s_addr, 0 ; INADDR_ANY
        MOV   sin1.sin_port, 2000 ; Port number
        PUSH  sizeof(sockaddr_in)
        PUSH  OFFSET sin1
        PUSH  s1
        CALL  bind@12
        CMP   EAX, 0
        JZ    NO_ER3
        CALL  ERRO
        JMP   CLOS
NO_ER3:
; Switch the socket to the listening state
        MOV   ESI, 10
```

```
        PUSH  5
        PUSH  s1
        CALL  listen@8
        CMP   EAX, 0
        JZ    NO_ER4
        CALL  ERRO
        JMP   CLOS
NO_ER4:
        MOV   len1, sizeof(sockaddr_in)
; Wait for the client requests
        PUSH  OFFSET len1
        PUSH  OFFSET sin2
        PUSH  s1
        CALL  accept@12
        MOV   s2, EAX
; The request has arrived, now sending the information
        PUSH  0
        PUSH  OFFSET txt
        CALL  lstrlenA@4
        PUSH  EAX
        PUSH  OFFSET txt
        PUSH  s2
        CALL  send@16
; Waiting for response
        PUSH  0
        PUSH  100
        PUSH  OFFSET buf
        PUSH  s2
        CALL  recv@16 ; EAX contains the message length
; First, it is necessary to convert the string
        PUSH  OFFSET buf1
        PUSH  OFFSET buf
        CALL  CharToOemA@8
; Output
        LEA   EAX, BUF1
        MOV   EDI, 1
        CALL  WRITE
; Close the connection
        PUSH  0
        PUSH  s2
        CALL  shutdown@8
; Close the socket
        PUSH  S2
```

```
        CALL   closesocket@4
        DEC    ESI
        JNZ    NO_ER4
; End of the loop
        PUSH   OFFSET buf1
        PUSH   OFFSET msg
        CALL   CharToOemA@8
; Now the conclusion
        LEA    EAX, BUF1
        MOV    EDI, 1
        CALL   WRITE
CLOSE:
        PUSH   S1
        CALL   closesocket@4
EXIT:
; Exiting when all services are terminated
        PUSH   0
        CALL   ExitProcess@4
; Display the string terminated by the line feed
; EAX — To the start of the string
; EDI — With or without the line feed
WRITE   PROC
        PUSH   ESI
; Get the parameter length
        PUSH   EAX
        PUSH   EAX
        CALL   lstrlenA@4
        MOV    ESI, EAX
        POP    EBX
        CMP    EDI, 1
        JNE    NO_ENT
; Line feed in the end
        MOV    BYTE PTR [EBX+ESI], 13
        MOV    BYTE PTR [EBX+ESI+1], 10
        MOV    BYTE PTR [EBX+ESI+2], 0
        ADD    EAX, 2
NO_ENT:
; String output
        PUSH   0
        PUSH   OFFSET LENS
        PUSH   EAX
        PUSH   EBX
        PUSH   HANDL
```

```
        CALL  WriteConsoleA@20
        POP   ESI
        RET
WRITE   ENDP
; The procedure for error code output
ERRO    PROC
        CALL  GetLastError@0
        PUSH  EAX
        PUSH  OFFSET ERRS
        PUSH  OFFSET BUF1
        CALL  wsprintfA
        ADD   ESP, 12
        LEA   EAX, BUF1
        MOV   EDI, 1
        CALL  WRITE
        RET
ERRO    ENDP
_TEXT ENDS
END START
```

To translate the SERVER.ASM (Listing 17.4), issue the following commands for MASM32:

```
ml /c /coff /DMASM server.asm
link /subsystem:console server.obj
```

Issue the following commands for TASM32:

```
tasm32 /ml server.asm
tlink32 -ap server.obj
```

The program presented in Listing 17.4 requires some comments.

- The SERVER.ASM program waits for the client programs to contact it. It listens to port 2000. The waiting is implemented by the `accept` function. This function returns control when a client attempts to connect this server. If the connection was successfully established, the function returns the newly-created socket, through which the server will communicate to the client program.
- The `accept` function has one specific feature. It returns control immediately after receiving a message from the client. This doesn't guarantee yet that the connection has been established; this is especially true for WANs. Consequently, if you build the communications design according to this approach, it is necessary to provide additional features for acknowledging the connection.

- This program implements the simplest method of communication, in which the server can communicate only with one client at a time. To ensure the possibility of simultaneous operation with multiple clients, it is necessary to use another approach: When receiving a message from the client, the server must create a new thread and pass the newly-created socket to it. This thread will further server this client. The main thread will again switch to waiting for new client requests.

Listing 17.5. The client program that calls the server component

```
; The CLIENT.ASM program
.586P
; Flat memory model
.MODEL FLAT, stdcall
; Constants
STD_OUTPUT_HANDLE equu -11
; Prototypes of external procedures
IFDEF MASM
        EXTERN  connect@12:NEAR
        EXTERN  gethostbyname@4:NEAR
        EXTERN  shutdown@8:NEAR
        EXTERN  recv@16:NEAR
        EXTERN  send@16:NEAR
        EXTERN  accept@12:NEAR
        EXTERN  listen@8:NEAR
        EXTERN  bind@12:NEAR
        EXTERN  closesocket@4:NEAR
        EXTERN  socket@12:NEAR
        EXTERN  CharToOemA@8:NEAR
        EXTERN  WSAStartup@8:NEAR
        EXTERN  wsprintfA:NEAR
        EXTERN  GetLastError@0:NEAR
        EXTERN  ExitProcess@4:NEAR
        EXTERN  lstrlenA@4:NEAR
        EXTERN  WriteConsoleA@20:NEAR
        EXTERN  GetStdHandle@4:NEAR
ELSE
        EXTERN  connect:NEAR
        EXTERN  gethostbyname:NEAR
        EXTERN  shutdown:NEAR
        EXTERN  recv:NEAR
        EXTERN  send:NEAR
        EXTERN  accept:NEAR
```

```
        EXTERN  listen:NEAR
        EXTERN  bind:NEAR
        EXTERN  closesocket:NEAR
        EXTERN  socket:NEAR
        EXTERN  CharToOemA:NEAR
        EXTERN  WSAStartup:NEAR
        EXTERN  _wsprintfA:NEAR
        EXTERN  GetLastError:NEAR
        EXTERN  ExitProcess:NEAR
        EXTERN  lstrlenA:NEAR
        EXTERN  WriteConsoleA:NEAR
        EXTERN  GetStdHandle:NEAR
        connect@12 = connect
        gethostbyname@4 = gethostbyname
        shutdown@8 = shutdown
        recv@16 = recv
        send@16 = send
        accept@12 = accept
        listen@8 = listen
        bind@12 = bind
        closesocket@4 = closesocket
        socket@12 = socket
        CharToOemA@8 = CharToOemA
        WSAStartup@8 = WSAStartup
        GetStdHandle@4 = GetStdHandle
        WriteConsoleA@20 = WriteConsoleA
        lstrlenA@4 = lstrlenA
        wsprintfA = _wsprintfA
        GetLastError@0 = GetLastError
        ExitProcess@4 = ExitProcess
ENDIF

; INCLUDELIB directives for the linker
IFDEF MASM
        includelib d:\masm32\lib\user32.lib
        includelib d:\masm32\lib\kernel32.lib
        includelib d:\masm32\lib\ws2_32.lib
ELSE
        includelib c:\tasm32\lib\import32.lib
ENDIF

;-----------------------------------------------
```

```
WSADATA STRUCT
        wVersion              WORD          ?
        wHighVersion          WORD          ?
        szDescription         BYTE 257 dup  (?)
        szSystemStatus        BYTE 129 dup  (?)
        iMaxSockets           WORD          ?
        iMaxUdpDg             WORD          ?
        lpVendorInfo          DWORD         ?
WSADATA ENDS
;-------------------------------------------------
S_UN_B STRUCT
        s_b1 BYTE 0
        s_b2 BYTE 0
        s_b3 BYTE 0
        s_b4 BYTE 0
S_UN_B ENDS

S_UN_W STRUCT
        s_w1 WORD 0
        s_w2 WORD 0
S_UN_W ENDS

ADDRESS_UNION UNION
        s_u_b S_UN_b <>
        s_u_w S_UN_w <>
        s_addr DWORD 0
ADDRESS_UNION ENDS


in_addr STRUCT
        s_un ADDRESS_UNION <>
in_addr ENDS


sockaddr_in STRUCT
        sin_family      WORD        0
        sin_port        WORD        0
        sin_addr        in_addr <>
        sin_zero        BYTE 8 dup (0)
sockaddr_in ENDS

hostent STRUCT
        h_name      DWORD       ?
```

```
        h_alias      DWORD       ?
        h_addr       WORD        ?
        h_len        WORD        ?
        h_list       DWORD       ?
hostent ENDS

;-----------------------------------------------

; Data segment
_DATA SEGMENT
HANDL   DD ?
LENS    DD ?
ERRS    DB "Error %u ", 0
IP      DB "IP address %hu.%hu.%hu.%hu", 0
IPA     DD ?
S1      DD ?
comp    DB "pvjul", 0
txt     DB "Call acknowledged", 0
txt1    DB "Host address", 0
LEN     DD ?
sin2    sockaddr_in <0>
hp      hostent <0>
BUF     DB  100 DUP(0)
BUF1    DB  100 DUP(0)
wsd     WSADATA <0>
_DATA ENDS
; Code segment
_TEXT SEGMENT
START:
; Define the output console handle
        PUSH  STD_OUTPUT_HANDLE
        CALL  GetStdHandle@4
        MOV   HANDL, EAX
; Activate the sockets library
        PUSH  OFFSET wsd
        MOV   EAX, 0
        MOV   AX, 0202H
        PUSH  EAX
        CALL  WSAStartup@8
        CMP   EAX, 0
        JZ    NO_ER1
        CALL  ERRO
        JMP   EXI
```

```
NO_ER1:
; Determine the server address using the host name
        PUSH   OFFSET comp
        CALL   gethostbyname@4
        CMP    EAX, 0
        JNZ    NO_ER2
        CALL   ERRO
        JMP    EXI
NO_ER2:
; Display the address
        MOV    EBX, [EAX+12] ; h_list in the hostent structure
        MOV    EDX, [EBX]
        MOV    EDX, [EDX]
        MOV    IPA, EDX
        SHR    EDX, 24
        AND    EDX, 000000FFH
        PUSH   EDX
        MOV    EDX, IPA
        SHR    EDX, 16
        AND    EDX, 000000FFH
        PUSH   EDX
        MOV    EDX, IPA
        SHR    EDX, 8
        AND    EDX, 000000FFH
        PUSH   EDX
        MOV    EDX, IPA
        AND    EDX, 000000FFH
        PUSH   EDX
        PUSH   OFFSET IP
        PUSH   OFFSET BUF1
        CALL   wsprintfA
        ADD    ESP, 24
        LEA    EAX, BUF1
        MOV    EDI, 1
        CALL   WRITE
        MOV    EDX, IPA
        MOV    sin2.sin_addr.s_un.s_addr, EDX
        MOV    sin2.sin_port, 2000
        MOV    sin2.sin_family, 2 ; AF_INET
; Create a socket
        PUSH   0
        PUSH   1  ; SOCK_STREAM
        PUSH   2  ; AF_INET
```

```
        CALL   socket@12
        CMP    EAX, NOT 0
        JNZ    NO_ER3
        CALL   ERRO
        JMP    EXI
NO_ER3:
        MOV    s1, EAX
; Try to connect the server
        PUSH   sizeof(sockaddr_in)
        PUSH   OFFSET sin2
        PUSH   s1
        CALL   connect@12
        CMP    EAX, 0
        JZ     NO_ER4
        CALL   ERRO
        JMP    CLOS
NO_ER4:
; Wait for information
        PUSH   0
        PUSH   100
        PUSH   OFFSET buf
        PUSH   s1
        CALL   recv@16 ; Message length in EAX
; First, it is necessary to convert the string
        PUSH   OFFSET buf1
        PUSH   OFFSET buf
        CALL   CharToOemA@8
; Output
        LEA    EAX, BUF1
        MOV    EDI, 1
        CALL   WRITE
; Send information
        PUSH   0
        PUSH   OFFSET txt
        CALL   lstrlenA@4
        PUSH   EAX
        PUSH   OFFSET txt
        PUSH   s1
        CALL   send@16
CLOSE:
        PUSH   S1
        CALL   closesocket@4
EXIT:
; Exiting after all services have terminated
```

```
        PUSH  0
        CALL  ExitProcess@4
; Display the string (line feed in the end)
; EAX - To the start of the string
; EDI - With or without the line feed
WRITE   PROC
; Get the parameter length
        PUSH  EAX
        PUSH  EAX
        CALL  lstrlenA@4
        MOV   ESI, EAX
        POP   EBX
        CMP   EDI, 1
        JNE   NO_ENT
; Line feed in the end of the string
        MOV   BYTE PTR [EBX+ESI], 13
        MOV   BYTE PTR [EBX+ESI+1], 10
        MOV   BYTE PTR [EBX+ESI+2], 0
        ADD   EAX, 2
NO_ENT:
; String output
        PUSH  0
        PUSH  OFFSET LENS
        PUSH  EAX
        PUSH  EBX
        PUSH  HANDL
        CALL  WriteConsoleA@20
        RET
WRITE   ENDP
; Display error code
ERRO    PROC
        CALL  GetLastError@0
        PUSH  EAX
        PUSH  OFFSET ERRS
        PUSH  OFFSET BUF1
        CALL  wsprintfA
        ADD   ESP, 12
        LEA   EAX, BUF1
        MOV   EDI, 1
        CALL  WRITE
        RET
ERRO    ENDP
_TEXT ENDS
END START
```

To translate the program presented in Listing 17.5, issue the following commands for MASM32:

```
ml /c /coff /DMASM CLIENT.asm
link /subsystem:console CLIENT.obj
```

Issue the following commands for TASM32:

```
tasm32 /ml CLIENT.asm
tlink32 -ap CLIENT.obj
```

The program presented in Listing 17.5 requires some comments.

- Before trying to access the server, the client must get the IP address of the host that runs the server component of the application. For this purpose, the `gethostbyname` function is used. If this function completes successfully, it returns the pointer to the `hostent` structure that I described earlier. The definition of this structure is placed into the program code, although it doesn't directly use a variable of this type. To make it easier to understand how the IP address is then retrieved, consider the appropriate lines from the program code:

```
MOV  EBX, [EAX+12] ; h_list is in the hostent structure
MOV  EDX, [EBX]
MOV  EDX, [EDX]
MOV  IPA, EDX
```

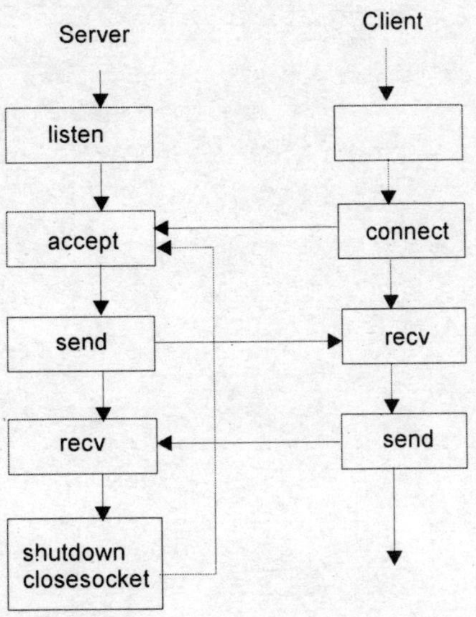

Fig. 17.4. Method of client and server communication (see Listings 17.4 and 17.5)

Note that the `h_list` field resides exactly at 12-byte offset from the starting point of the structure. This field contains the pointer to the string of bytes. This string contains several 4-byte chains, each of which represents an IP address of the host (recall that the host can have several IP addresses). A zero code serves as an indication of the end of this sequence. At the same time, you need to be interested only in the first 4-byte chain; therefore, you read it using the `MOV EDX, [EDX]` command. The least significant byte is the leftmost byte in the IP address.

- ❒ You can modify this program by taking the IP address instead of the host name as a basis. To achieve this, it is necessary to form a double word so that the least significant byte will be the leftmost component of the address and the most significant byte will be the rightmost component. Then, it will be necessary to load this double word into a register (e.g., `EDX`) and execute the following command:

```
MOV  sin2.sin_addr.s_un.s_addr, EDX
```

To conclude the examples of working with sockets, consider Fig. 17.4, which shows a schematic diagram of communications between the SERVER.ASM and CLIENT.ASM programs.

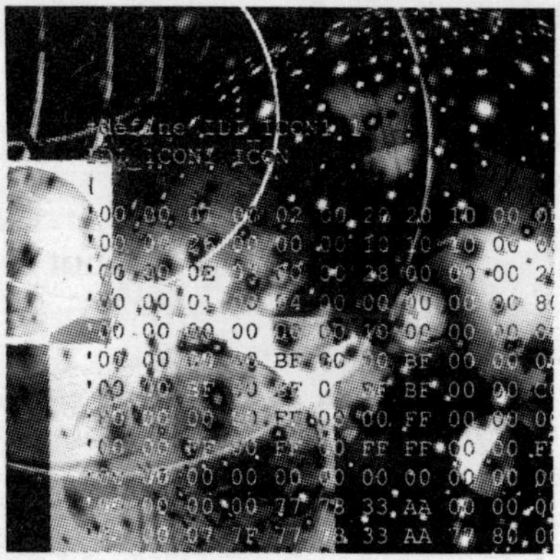

Chapter 18

Solving Some Problems with Windows Programming

This chapter was a compromise for me. There are lots of problems in Windows programming, and my natural desire was to cover them all. However, if I dedicated an entire chapter to every question, the book would soon be too large. Therefore, I decided to devote one chapter to problem-solving aspects and to cover in detail as many interesting problems as I could. This chapter is built on questions that you might ask and answers that I would provide.

Placing an Icon on the System Toolbar

Q. How can I ensure that the icon of the minimized application fits on the system toolbar?

This problem can be solved using the `Shell_NotifyIcon` system function. This solution is so simple that I have to wonder why most programmers employ various libraries for this purpose. The `Shell_NotifyIcon` function accepts the following parameters:

- First parameter — The action that needs to be carried out
  - `NIM_ADD    equ 0h` — Add an icon to the system toolbar
  - `NIM_MODIFY equ 1h` — Delete the icon from the system toolbar
  - `NIM_DELETE equ 2h` — Modify the icon

- Second parameter — The pointer to the structure that contains information required for carrying out the specified action

```
NOTI_ICON STRUC
   cbSize           DWORD ?
   hWnd             DWORD ?
   uID              DWORD ?
   uFlags           DWORD ?
   uCallbackMessage DWORD ?
   hIcon            DWORD ?
   szTip            DB 64 DUP (?)
NOTI_ICON ENDS
```

The elements of the preceding structure are as follows:

- `cbSize` — Structure size.
- `hWnd` — Descriptor of the window, to which the message will be sent (described later).
- `uID` — Icon identifier.
- `uFlags` — Combination of the following flags:
    - `NIF_MESSAGE equ 1h` — Use the `hIcon` field
    - `NIF_ICON    equ 2h` — Use the `uCallbackMessage` field
    - `NIF_TIP     equ 4h` — Use the `szTip` field
- `uCallbackMessage` — Message that arrives to the window identified by the `hWnd` descriptor if some event occurs near the system toolbar icon. The message value must be more than 1024. When this message arrives, `WPARAM` contains the icon identifier and `LPARAM` defines the event that occurred to the icon.
- `hIcon` — Icon handle.
- `SzTip` — Popup help text.

Consider how the entire mechanism operates. If the window is minimized, the `WM_SIZE` message arrives at the window function. In this message, `wParam` must contain the `SIZE_MINIMIZED` value. In this case, it is necessary to use the `Shell_NotifyIcon` function that will place the icon to the system toolbar. Any event related to the mouse when its cursor is located over the icon would cause the `uCallbackMessage` to arrive at the window function. You have defined this message yourself. In this case, the most significant `wParam` word will contain the icon identifier, and the least significant `lParam` word will allow you to define the event type. Listing 18.1 demonstrates how this mechanism operates.

Listing 18.1. The procedure that places an icon on the system toolbar

```
// The TRAY.RC file
// Constant definitions
#define WS_SYSMENU          0x00080000L
#define WS_MINIMIZEBOX      0x00020000L
#define WS_MAXIMIZEBOX      0x00010000L
#define DS_3DLOOK           0x0004L

// Identifiers
#define IDI_ICON1 1

// Define the icon
IDI_ICON1 ICON "ico1.ico"

// Dialog box definition
DIAL1 DIALOG 0, 0, 250, 110
STYLE WS_SYSMENU | WS_MINIMIZEBOX | WS_MAXIMIZEBOX |
DS_3DLOOK
CAPTION "Place the icon on the system toolbar"
FONT 8, "Arial"
{
}

; The TRAY.INC file
; Constants
NIM_ADD             equ 0h ; Add the icon to the system toolbar
NIM_MODIFY          equ 1h ; Remove the icon
NIM_DELETE          equ 2h ; Modify the icon
NIF_MESSAGE         equ 1h ; Use the hIcon field
NIF_ICON            equ 2h ; Use the uCallbackMessage field
NIF_TIP             equ 4h ; Use the szTip field
FLAG                equ NIF_MESSAGE or NIF_ICON or NIF_TIP
SIZE_MINIMIZED      equ 1h
SW_HIDE             equ 0
SW_SHOWNORMAL       equ 1
; This message arrives when the window is closed
WM_CLOSE            equ 10h
WM_INITDIALOG       equ 110h
WM_SIZE             equ 5h
WM_LBUTTONDBLCLK    equ 203h
WM_LBUTTONDOWN      equ 201h
; Prototypes of external procedures
```

```
IFDEF MASM
        EXTERN ShowWindow@8:NEAR
        EXTERN LoadIconA@8:NEAR
        EXTERN lstrcpyA@8:NEAR
        EXTERN Shell_NotifyIconA@8:NEAR
        EXTERN ExitProcess@4:NEAR
        EXTERN GetModuleHandleA@4:NEAR
        EXTERN DialogBoxParamA@20:NEAR
        EXTERN EndDialog@8:NEAR
        EXTERN SendDlgItemMessageA@20:NEAR
ELSE
        EXTERN ShowWindow:NEAR
        EXTERN LoadIconA:NEAR
        EXTERN lstrcpyA:NEAR
        EXTERN Shell_NotifyIconA:NEAR
        EXTERN ExitProcess:NEAR
        EXTERN GetModuleHandleA:NEAR
        EXTERN DialogBoxParamA:NEAR
        EXTERN EndDialog:NEAR
        EXTERN SendDlgItemMessageA:NEAR
        ShowWindow@8 = ShowWindow
        LoadIconA@8 = LoadIconA
        lstrcpyA@8 = lstrcpyA
        Shell_NotifyIconA@8 = Shell_NotifyIconA
        ExitProcess@4 = ExitProcess
        GetModuleHandleA@4 = GetModuleHandleA
        DialogBoxParamA@20 = DialogBoxParamA
        EndDialog@8 = EndDialog
        SendDlgItemMessageA@20 = SendDlgItemMessageA
ENDIF
; Structures
; Message structure
MSGSTRUCT STRUC
        MSHWND          DD ?
        MSMESSAGE       DD ?
        MSWPARAM        DD ?
        MSLPARAM        DD ?
        MSTIME          DD ?
        MSPT            DD ?
MSGSTRUCT ENDS
; Structure for the Shell_NotifyIcon function
NOTI_ICON STRUC
  cbSize                DWORD ?
```

```
  hWnd              DWORD ?
  uID               DWORD ?
  uFlags            DWORD ?
  uCallbackMessage  DWORD ?
  hIcon             DWORD ?
  szTip             DB 64 DUP (?)
NOTI_ICON ENDS

; The TRAY.ASM file
.586P
; Flat memory model
.MODEL FLAT, stdcall
include tray.inc
; INCLUDELIB directives for the linker
IFDEF MASM
       includelib c:\masm32\lib\user32.lib
       includelib c:\masm32\lib\kernel32.lib
       includelib c:\masm32\lib\shell32.lib
ELSE
       includelib c:\tasm32\lib\import32.lib
ENDIF
;-----------------------------------------------
; Data segment
_DATA SEGMENT
       MSG    MSGSTRUCT <?>
       HINST  DD 0 ; Application descriptor
       PA     DB "DIAL1", 0
       NOTI   NOTI_ICON <0>
       TIP    DB "Example of using the function"
              DB "Shell_NotifyIcon", 0
_DATA ENDS
; Code segment
_TEXT SEGMENT
START:
; Get the application handle
       PUSH  0
       CALL  GetModuleHandleA@4
       MOV  [HINST], EAX
;--------------------------------
       PUSH  0
       PUSH  OFFSET WNDPROC
       PUSH  0
       PUSH  OFFSET PA
```

```
        PUSH  [HINST]
        CALL  DialogBoxParamA@20
        CMP   EAX, -1
        JNE   KOL
; Error message
KOL:
;-----------------------------------
        PUSH  0
        CALL  ExitProcess@4
;-----------------------------------
; Window procedure
; Position of parameters in the stack
; [EBP+014H]  ; LPARAM
; [EBP+10H]   ; WAPARAM
; [EBP+0CH]   ; MES
; [EBP+8]     ; HWND
WNDPROC      PROC
        PUSH  EBP
        MOV   EBP, ESP
        PUSH  EBX
        PUSH  ESI
        PUSH  EDI
;-----------------
        CMP   DWORD PTR [EBP+0CH], WM_CLOSE
        JNE   L1
        PUSH  0
        PUSH  DWORD PTR [EBP+08H]
        CALL  EndDialog@8
        JMP   FINISH
L1:
        CMP   DWORD PTR [EBP+0CH], WM_INITDIALOG
        JNE   L2
        JMP   FINISH
L2:
        CMP   DWORD PTR [EBP+0CH], WM_SIZE
        JNE   L3
        CMP   DWORD PTR [EBP+10H], SIZE_MINIMIZED
        JNE   L3
; Here, all work related to setting the icon
; on the system toolbar is carried out
        MOV   NOTI.cbSize, 88
        MOV   EAX, DWORD PTR [EBP+8H]
        MOV   NOTI.hWnd, EAX
```

```
        MOV   NOTI.uFlags, FLAG
        MOV   NOTI.uID, 12 ; Icon identifier
        MOV   NOTI.uCallbackMessage, 2000 ; Message
; Load an icon from the resources
        PUSH  1
        PUSH  [HINST]
        CALL  LoadIconA@8
; Copy the popup help message
        MOV   NOTI.hIcon, EAX
        PUSH  OFFSET TIP
        PUSH  OFFSET NOTI.szTip
        CALL  lstrcpyA@8
; Place the icon
        PUSH  OFFSET NOTI
        PUSH  NIM_ADD
        CALL  Shell_NotifyIconA@8
; Hide the minimized window
        PUSH  SW_HIDE
        PUSH  DWORD PTR [EBP+08H]
        CALL  ShowWindow@8
        JMP   FINISH
L3:
; Message from the toolbar icon?
        CMP   DWORD PTR [EBP+0CH], 2000
        JNE   FINISH
; Identifier of the icon?
        CMP   WORD PTR [EBP+10H], 12
        JNE   FINISH
; What happened? Was it a double click?
        CMP   WORD PTR [EBP+14H], WM_LBUTTONDBLCLK
        JNE   FINISH
; Fill the structure
        MOV   NOTI.cbSize, 88
        MOV   EAX, DWORD PTR [EBP+8H]
        MOV   NOTI.hWnd, EAX
        MOV   NOTI.uFlags, NIF_ICON
        MOV   NOTI.uID, 12 ; Icon identifier
        MOV   NOTI.uCallbackMessage, 1000 ; Message
; Delete the icon
        PUSH  OFFSET NOTI
        PUSH  NIM_DELETE
        CALL  Shell_NotifyIconA@8
; Restore the window
```

```
        PUSH  SW_SHOWNORMAL
        PUSH  DWORD PTR [EBP+08H]
        CALL  ShowWindow@8
FINISH:
        MOV  EAX, 0
        POP  EDI
        POP  ESI
        POP  EBX
        POP  EBP
        RET  16
WNDPROC    ENDP
_TEXT ENDS
END START
```

To translate the program from Listing 18.1, issue the following commands for MASM32:

```
ml /c /coff /DMASM tray.asm
rc tray.rc
link /subsystem:windows tray.obj tray.res
```

Issue the following commands for TASM32:

```
tasm32 /ml tray.asm
brcc32 tray.rc
tlink32 -aa tray.obj,,,,,tray.res
```

In relation to the program from Listing 18.1, I'd like to draw your attention to the `WM_SIZE` message. It's very useful. Assume that you have placed some information in your window. If this window can be resized, you'll have to solve the problem of positioning the information in the window every time it is resized. This message can be used if you carefully redraw and rescale the window output. It is necessary to point out that when the message is sent, the window size has already changed. `WPARAM` contains the flag specifying what has happened to the window, and `LPARAM` gives the new window size (the least significant word is for the width, and the most significant word is for the height).

Processing Files

Q. Are there any additional ways to simplify file processing?

Yes, there are. In particular, these are memory-mapped files. Byte-by-byte reading is not always convenient. Naturally, there is another way of approaching this problem. It is possible to allocate a large enough buffer in memory, to read the file into that buffer, and then to work with that file as with a large array. Memory-mapped files are similar to this; however, in this case, the system carries out most of the job automatically. The most advantageous point here is that the memory-mapped file can be used by several processes. Thus, this mechanism provides another method of interprocess information exchange. However, memory-mapped files have one considerable drawback. After the file is mapped, its size cannot be increased. In this case, the following approach must be used: predict the new file size, and map it to a larger memory area. Actually, the file is not loaded into the memory directly. Instead, it is implemented as mapping to a certain area of the virtual memory (see *Chapter 19*).

NOTE

An interesting fact is that the program loaded into the memory is implemented as a memory-mapped file. Thus, individual parts of the program are loaded into the physical memory only when they are accessed (see *Chapter 19*).

Operations over memory-mapped files are implemented according to the following algorithm:

1. Open or create a file using the `CreateFile` function. This function, as you know, returns the descriptor of the opened file.
2. Create a mapped file using the `CreateFileMapping` function. This function is the one that defines the mapping size. As with the previous function, it also returns the descriptor. However, this time, it is the descriptor of the mapped file.
3. Copy the file or part of it into the mapping area that you have just created using the `MapViewOfFile` function. This function returns the pointer to the starting position of the area where the file will be located. After that, you can do whatever you need with the mapped file.
4. If desired, you can write the memory area into the file using the `FlushViewOfFile` function. Naturally, only that memory area will be flushed to the disk that you reserved when calling the `CreateFileMapping` function. You can save the file to the disk using the well-known `WriteFile` function.
5. Before closing the mapped file, you must invalidate its pointer. This can be achieved using the `UnmapViewOfFile` function.
6. Close both handles. First, close the handle returned by the `CreateFileMapping` function; then, close the handle created by the `CreateFile` function.

As you can see, the algorithm of working with mapped files is easy. Consider the new functions encountered for the first time in this book.

The CreateFileMapping function returns the descriptor of the mapped file.

- First parameter — The descriptor of the opened file.
- Second parameter — The access attribute, usually assumed to be zero.
- Third parameter — Can take any of the following values and must be compatible to the file sharing mode: PAGE_READONLY, PAGE_WRITECOPY, and PAGE_READWRITE. As you can see, this attribute defines the protection of the file being mapped and must not contradict the attribute of the file opened using the CreateFile function.
- Fourth parameter — The most significant part (of the 64-bit value) of the mapped file size.
- Fifth parameter — The least significant part of the mapped file size (the size may not necessarily match the file size). If both parameters are equal to zero, the size is assumed to be equal to the size of the opened file (the first parameter).
- Sixth parameter — The name of the mapped file. Is required only if the mapped file will be used by several processes. In this case, a repeated call to the CreateFileMapping function by other processes with the same name specified would return the descriptor of the existing mapped file instead of creating a new file.

The MapViewOfFile function returns the pointer to the memory area where the mapped file or part of the mapped file resides.

- First parameter — The descriptor returned by the CreateFileMapping function.
- Second parameter — Defines the operation that you are going to carry out. For example, FILE_MAP_READ stands for reading only, and FILE_MAP_WRITE is for reading and writing.
- Third parameter — The most significant part (of the 64-bit value) of the offset in the file, from which the data will begin to be copied into the memory.
- Fourth parameter — The least significant part of the offset in the file, from which data will begin to be copied.
- Fifth parameter — If you want to copy the entire file, set the last three parameters to zero.

The following are the parameters of the FlushViewOfFile function:

- First parameter — Specifies the memory area that has to be flushed into a file.
- Second parameter — Defines the number of bytes to be written.

The UnmapViewOfFile function has one parameter:

- First parameter — Descriptor of the mapped file.

Well, that's all that is required to understand the theory of mapped files. Because this material is simple for programming, I won't provide any examples to illustrate it. I hope that if you were patient enough to read this book to this point, you will easily write you own programs using materials of this section.

Controlling Data in the Edit Field

Q. Is it possible to control information input into the edit field?

Yes, and in *Chapter 10*, you saw how to do this correctly using hotkeys. However, hotkeys can easily block the arrival of certain characters into the edit field. In some cases, it might be required to convert the information being entered on the fly. In this case, the subclasses mechanism can be used. To demonstrate this mechanism, consider the program provided in Listing 3.2. Now, I will modify this program to ensure that it is possible to control the information input.

There isn't anything new in this mechanism. Even in the MS-DOS operating system, it was possible to trap interrupts and build custom procedures into their handling. As a result, the custom procedure was called prior to the previously installed one if a call was made to this interrupt. It also was possible to proceed in a different way: first, to call the existing procedure, and then, to call the custom one. Because it was possible to catch interrupts multiple times, a chain of sequentially executing procedures might appear as a result. I have already compared the calls with the window procedure and the interrupt calls. They are similar, aren't they? For object-oriented programming, this is nothing else but the creation of the parent class.

The foundation of this mechanism is formed by the `SetWindowLong` function, which can change the attributes of the existing window. The parameters of this function are as follows:

- First parameter — The descriptor of the window created by the current process.
- Second parameter — The value that defines what has to be changed. Generally, this is only an offset in a certain memory area. You will be interested only in the value that defines the address of the window procedure. This value is defined by the `DWL_DLGPROC = 4` constant (for the dialog) or by `GWL_WNDPROC = -4` (for a normal window). Hence, this operation can be carried out not only over normal windows but also over dialog boxes.
- Third parameter — The new value of the window attribute.

It is also necessary to mention that this function returns the old attribute value.

I must note that all window elements that you create on a window are also windows with their own window functions. In everyday practice, you usually will be dealing only with messages arriving at the main window procedure.

The next question you might ask is as follows: How do I call the old window procedure? The standard `CALL` command is not suitable in this case. You'll have to use a special function for this purpose — `CallWindowProc`. Parameters of this function are as follows:

- First parameter — The address of the called procedure
- Second parameter — The window descriptor
- Third parameter — The message code
- Fourth parameter — The `WPARAM` parameter
- Fifth parameter — The `LPARAM` parameter

Listing 18.2. The use of subclasses

```
; The EDIT.INC file
; Constants
WM_CHAR                 equ 102h
WM_SETFOCUS             equ 7h
; This message arrives when the window is closed
WM_DESTROY              equ 2
; This message arrives when the window is created
WM_CREATE               equ 1
; This message arrives when something happens to the window elements
WM_COMMAND              equ 111h
; This message allows you to get a string
WM_GETTEXT              equ 0Dh
; The constant for the SetWindowLong function
GWL_WNDPROC             equ -4
; Window properties
CS_VREDRAW              equ 1h
CS_HREDRAW              equ 2h
CS_GLOBALCLASS          equ 4000h
WS_TABSTOP              equ 10000h
WS_SYSMENU              equ 80000h
WS_OVERLAPPEDWINDOW     equ 0+WS_TABSTOP+WS_SYSMENU
STYLE                   equ CS_HREDRAW+CS_VREDRAW+CS_GLOBALCLASS
CS_HREDRAW              equ 2h
BS_DEFPUSHBUTTON        equ 1h
WS_VISIBLE              equ 10000000h
WS_CHILD                equ 40000000h
WS_BORDER               equ 800000h
STYLBTN                 equ WS_CHILD+BS_DEFPUSHBUTTON+WS_VISIBLE+WS_TABSTOP
```

```
STYLEDT                 equ WS_CHILD+WS_VISIBLE+WS_BORDER+WS_TABSTOP
; Standard icon identifier
IDI_APPLICATION         equ 32512
; Cursor identifier
IDC_ARROW               equ 32512
; Window display mode — Normal
SW_SHOWNORMAL           equ 1
; Prototypes of external procedures
IFDEF MASM
      EXTERN      CallWindowProcA@20:NEAR
      EXTERN      SetWindowLongA@12:NEAR
      EXTERN      SetFocus@4:NEAR
      EXTERN      SendMessageA@16:NEAR
      EXTERN      MessageBoxA@16:NEAR
      EXTERN      CreateWindowExA@48:NEAR
      EXTERN      DefWindowProcA@16:NEAR
      EXTERN      DispatchMessageA@4:NEAR
      EXTERN      ExitProcess@4:NEAR
      EXTERN      GetMessageA@16:NEAR
      EXTERN      GetModuleHandleA@4:NEAR
      EXTERN      LoadCursorA@8:NEAR
      EXTERN      LoadIconA@8:NEAR
      EXTERN      PostQuitMessage@4:NEAR
      EXTERN      RegisterClassA@4:NEAR
      EXTERN      ShowWindow@8:NEAR
      EXTERN      TranslateMessage@4:NEAR
      EXTERN      UpdateWindow@4:NEAR
ELSE
      EXTERN      CallWindowProcA:NEAR
      EXTERN      SetWindowLongA:NEAR
      EXTERN      SetFocus:NEAR
      EXTERN      SendMessageA:NEAR
      EXTERN      MessageBoxA:NEAR
      EXTERN      CreateWindowExA:NEAR
      EXTERN      DefWindowProcA:NEAR
      EXTERN      DispatchMessageA:NEAR
      EXTERN      ExitProcess:NEAR
      EXTERN      GetMessageA:NEAR
      EXTERN      GetModuleHandleA:NEAR
      EXTERN      LoadCursorA:NEAR
      EXTERN      LoadIconA:NEAR
      EXTERN      PostQuitMessage:NEAR
      EXTERN      RegisterClassA:NEAR
```

```
        EXTERN      ShowWindow:NEAR
        EXTERN      TranslateMessage:NEAR
        EXTERN      UpdateWindow:NEAR
        CallWindowProcA@20 = CallWindowProcA
        SetWindowLongA@12 = SetWindowLongA
        SetFocus@4 = SetFocus
        SendMessageA@16 = SendMessageA
        MessageBoxA@16 = MessageBoxA
        CreateWindowExA@48 = CreateWindowExA
        DefWindowProcA@16 = DefWindowProcA
        DispatchMessageA@4 = DispatchMessageA
        ExitProcess@4 = ExitProcess
        GetMessageA@16 = GetMessageA
        GetModuleHandleA@4 = GetModuleHandleA
        LoadCursorA@8 = LoadCursorA
        LoadIconA@8 = LoadIconA
        PostQuitMessage@4 = PostQuitMessage
        RegisterClassA@4 = RegisterClassA
        ShowWindow@8 = ShowWindow
        TranslateMessage@4 = TranslateMessage
        UpdateWindow@4 = UpdateWindow
ENDIF
; Structures
; Message structure
MSGSTRUCT STRUC
        MSHWND      DD ?
        MSMESSAGE   DD ?
        MSWPARAM    DD ?
        MSLPARAM    DD ?
        MSTIME      DD ?
        MSPT        DD ?
MSGSTRUCT ENDS
;---- Window class structure
WNDCLASS STRUC
        CLSSTYLE      DD ?
        CLWNDPROC     DD ?
        CLSCBCLSEX    DD ?
        CLSCBWNDEX    DD ?
        CLSHINST      DD ?
        CLSHICON      DD ?
        CLSHCURSOR    DD ?
        CLBKGROUND    DD ?
        CLMENNAME     DD ?
```

```
    CLNAME      DD ?
WNDCLASS ENDS

; The EDIT.ASM file
.586P
; Flat memory model
.MODEL FLAT, stdcall
include editn.inc
; INCLUDELIB directives for the linker
IFDEF MASM
    includelib c:\masm32\lib\user32.lib
    includelib c:\masm32\lib\kernel32.lib
ELSE
    includelib c:\tasm32\lib\import32.lib
ENDIF
;------------------------------------------------
; Data segment
_DATA SEGMENT
    NEWHWND     DD 0
    MSG         MSGSTRUCT <?>
    WC          WNDCLASS  <?>
    HINST       DD    0 ; Application descriptor
    TITLENAME   DB    'Controlling the edit field', 0
    CLASSNAME   DB    'CLASS32', 0
    CPBUT       DB    'Exit', 0 ; Exit
    CPEDT       DB    ' ', 0
    CLSBUTN     DB    'BUTTON', 0
    CLSEDIT     DB    'EDIT', 0
    HWNDBTN     DWORD 0
    HWNDEDT     DWORD 0
    CAP         BYTE 'Message', 0
    MES         BYTE 'Exiting the program', 0
    TEXT        DB 100 DUP(0)
    OLDWND      DD 0
    CHAR        DD ?
_DATA ENDS
; Code segment
_TEXT SEGMENT
START:
; Get the application handle
    PUSH  0
    CALL  GetModuleHandleA@4
    MOV   [HINST], EAX
```

```
REG_CLASS:
; Fill the window structure
; Style
       MOV   [WC.CLSSTYLE], STYLE
; Message-handling procedure
       MOV   [WC.CLWNDPROC], OFFSET WNDPROC
       MOV   [WC.CLSCBCLSEX], 0
       MOV   [WC.CLSCBWNDEX], 0
       MOV   EAX, [HINST]
       MOV   [WC.CLSHINST], EAX
;---------- Window icon
       PUSH  IDI_APPLICATION
       PUSH  0
       CALL  LoadIconA@8
       MOV   [WC.CLSHICON], EAX
;---------- Window cursor
       PUSH  IDC_ARROW
       PUSH  0
       CALL  LoadCursorA@8
       MOV   [WC.CLSHCURSOR], EAX
;----------
       MOV   [WC.CLBKGROUND], 17 ; Window color
       MOV   DWORD PTR [WC.CLMENNAME], 0
       MOV   DWORD PTR [WC.CLNAME], OFFSET CLASSNAME
       PUSH  OFFSET WC
       CALL  RegisterClassA@4
; Create a window of the registered class
       PUSH  0
       PUSH  [HINST]
       PUSH  0
       PUSH  0
       PUSH  150        ; DY - Window height
       PUSH  400        ; DX - Window width
       PUSH  100        ; Y - Coordinate of the top left corner
       PUSH  100        ; X - Coordinate of the top left corner
       PUSH  WS_OVERLAPPEDWINDOW
       PUSH  OFFSET TITLENAME ; Window name
       PUSH  OFFSET CLASSNAME ; Class name
       PUSH  0
       CALL  CreateWindowExA@48
 Check for an error
       CMP   EAX, 0
       JZ    _ERR
```

```
        MOV    [NEWHWND], EAX ; Window descriptor
;----------------------------------
        PUSH   SW_SHOWNORMAL
        PUSH   [NEWHWND]
        CALL   ShowWindow@8 ; Show the newly-created window
;----------------------------------
        PUSH   [NEWHWND]
        CALL   UpdateWindow@4        ; Redraw the visible part
                                     ; of the window, the WM_PAINT message
; Message-processing loop
MSG_LOOP:
        PUSH   0
        PUSH   0
        PUSH   0
        PUSH   OFFSET MSG
        CALL   GetMessageA@16
        CMP    AX, 0
        JE     END_LOOP
        PUSH   OFFSET MSG
        CALL   TranslateMessage@4
        PUSH   OFFSET MSG
        CALL   DispatchMessageA@4
        JMP    MSG_LOOP
END_LOOP:
; Exit the program (close the process)
        PUSH   [MSG.MSWPARAM]
        CALL   ExitProcess@4
_ERR:
        JMP  END_LOOP
;------------------------------------------------
; Window procedure
; Position of parameters in the stack
; [EBP+014H]  ; LPARAM
; [EBP+10H]   ; WAPARAM
; [EBP+0CH]   ; MES
; [EBP+8]     ; HWND
WNDPROC  PROC
        PUSH   EBP
        MOV    EBP, ESP
        PUSH   EBX
        PUSH   ESI
        PUSH   EDI
        CMP    DWORD PTR [EBP+0CH], WM_DESTROY
```

```
        JE      WMDESTROY
        CMP     DWORD PTR [EBP+0CH], WM_CREATE
        JE      WMCREATE
        CMP     DWORD PTR [EBP+0CH], WM_COMMAND
        JE      WMCOMMND
        JMP     DEFWNDPROC
WMCOMMND:
        MOV     EAX, HWNDBTN
        CMP     DWORD PTR [EBP+14H], EAX
        JNE     NODESTROY
        JMP     WMDESTROY
NODESTROY:
        MOV     EAX, 0
        JMP     FINISH
WMCREATE:
; Create the button window
        PUSH    0
        PUSH    [HINST]
        PUSH    0
        PUSH    DWORD PTR [EBP+08H]
        PUSH    20        ; DY
        PUSH    60        ; DX
        PUSH    10        ; Y
        PUSH    10        ; X
        PUSH    STYLBTN
        PUSH    OFFSET CPBUT  ; Window name
        PUSH    OFFSET CLSBUTN ; Class name
        PUSH    0
        CALL    CreateWindowExA@48
        MOV     HWNDBTN, EAX ; Save the button descriptor
; Create the edit field
        PUSH    0
        PUSH    [HINST]
        PUSH    0
        PUSH    DWORD PTR [EBP+08H]
        PUSH    20        ; DY
        PUSH    350       ; DX
        PUSH    50        ; Y
        PUSH    10        ; X
        PUSH    STYLEDT
        PUSH    OFFSET CPEDT   ; Window name
        PUSH    OFFSET CLSEDIT ; Class name
        PUSH    0
```

```
        CALL   CreateWindowExA@48
        MOV    HWNDEDT, EAX
; Set the focus to the edit field
        PUSH   HWNDEDT
        CALL   SetFocus@4
; Set the custom handler procedure
        PUSH   OFFSET WNDEDIT
        PUSH   GWL_WNDPROC
        PUSH   [HWNDEDT]
        CALL   SetWindowLongA@12
        MOV    OLDWND, EAX
        MOV    EAX, 0
        JMP    FINISH
DEFWNDPROC:
        PUSH   DWORD PTR [EBP+14H]
        PUSH   DWORD PTR [EBP+10H]
        PUSH   DWORD PTR [EBP+0CH]
        PUSH   DWORD PTR [EBP+08H]
        CALL   DefWindowProcA@16
        JMP    FINISH
WMDESTROY:
; Get the edited string
        PUSH   OFFSET TEXT
        PUSH   150
        PUSH   WM_GETTEXT
        PUSH   HWNDEDT
        CALL   SendMessageA@16
; Show the edited string
        PUSH   0
        PUSH   OFFSET CAP
        PUSH   OFFSET TEXT
        PUSH   DWORD PTR [EBP+08H] ; Window descriptor
        CALL   MessageBoxA@16
; Go to exit
        PUSH   0
        CALL   PostQuitMessage@4 ; Message WM_QUIT
        MOV    EAX, 0
FINISH:
        POP    EDI
        POP    ESI
        POP    EBX
        POP    EBP
        RET    16
```

```
WNDPROC    ENDP
;-----------------------------------------------
; New message-handling procedure for the edit field
WNDEDIT  PROC
        PUSH  EBP
        MOV   EBP, ESP
        MOV   EAX, DWORD PTR [EBP+10H]
        MOV   CHAR, EAX
        CMP   DWORD PTR [EBP+0CH], WM_CHAR
        JNE   _OLD
; Check the input character
        CMP   AL, 13
        JNE   _OLD
; Send the message about closing the main window
        PUSH  0
        PUSH  0
        PUSH  WM_DESTROY
        PUSH  [NEWHWND]
        CALL  SendMessageA@16
_OLD:
; Call the old procedure
        PUSH  DWORD PTR [EBP+014H]
        PUSH  DWORD PTR [EBP+10H]
        PUSH  DWORD PTR [EBP+0CH]
        PUSH  DWORD PTR [EBP+8H]
        PUSH  [OLDWND]
        CALL  CallWindowProcA@20
FIN:
        POP   EBP
        RET   16
WNDEDIT  ENDP
_TEXT ENDS
END START
```

To translate the program presented in Listing 18.2, issue the following commands for MASM32:

```
ml /c /coff /DMASM editn.asm
link /subsystem:windows editn.obj
```

Issue the following commands for TASM32:

```
tasm32 /ml editn.asm
tlink32 -aa editn.obj
```

When studying the program presented in Listing 18.2, notice that the method provided in this listing allows you to do practically any trick to the edit field. For example, you can block any character by sending the zero code instead of it, or you can replace the sent character with any other one.

Data Exchange between Applications

Q. Are there methods of organizing information exchange between running applications?

I have already described various methods of synchronization and using the shared memory. There is another interesting approach implemented in Windows — anonymous (unnamed) pipes.[i] This approach is the most efficient for organizing information exchange with the console process generated by the current process. Assume that you need your console process started by some application (e.g., some string compiler) to output information to the edit window of the primary process instead of to console. The example of such application is shown in Listing 18.3.

The underlying idea of pipes is easy. When creating a process, it is possible to assign it the appropriate pipe descriptor as the input or the output descriptor. After that, it will be possible to organize information exchange between two processes using the `WriteFile` and `ReadFile` functions.

Listing 18.3. Communications with console process through an anonymous pipe

```
// The PIPE.RC file
// Constant definitions
#define WS_SYSMENU      0x00080000L
#define WS_VISIBLE      0x10000000L
#define WS_TABSTOP      0x00010000L
#define WS_VSCROLL      0x00200000L
#define DS_3DLOOK       0x0004L
#define ES_LEFT         0x0000L
#define WS_CHILD        0x40000000L
#define WS_BORDER       0x00800000L
#define ES_MULTILINE    0x0004L
#define WS_VSCROLL      0x00200000L
#define WS_HSCROLL      0x00100000L


MENUP MENU
```

[i] So-called named pipes are implemented in Windows NT.

```
  POPUP "&Start the program"
  {
  MENUITEM "S&tart", 200
  MENUITEM "E&xit the program", 300
  }
 }

// Dialog box definition
DIAL1 DIALOG 0, 0, 200, 140
STYLE WS_SYSMENU | DS_3DLOOK
CAPTION "Example of PIPE use"
FONT 8, "Arial"
{
 CONTROL "", 101, "edit", ES_LEFT | ES_MULTILINE
 | WS_VISIBLE | WS_BORDER | WS_VSCROLL
 | WS_HSCROLL , 24, 20, 128, 70
}

; The PIPE.INC file
; Constants
SW_HIDE                equ 0
SW_SHOWNORMAL          equ 1
STARTF_USESHOWWINDOW   equ 1h
STARTF_USESTDHANDLES   equ 100h
STARTF_ADD = STARTF_USESHOWWINDOW + STARTF_USESTDHANDLES
; This message arrives when the window is closed
WM_CLOSE               equ 10h
WM_INITDIALOG          equ 110h
WM_COMMAND             equ 111h
EM_REPLACESEL          equ 0C2h
; Prototypes of external procedures
IFDEF MASM
        EXTERN ReadFile@20:NEAR
        EXTERN CloseHandle@4:NEAR
        EXTERN CreatePipe@16:NEAR
        EXTERN SetMenu@8:NEAR
        EXTERN LoadMenuA@8:NEAR
        EXTERN CreateProcessA@40:NEAR
        EXTERN ExitProcess@4:NEAR
        EXTERN GetModuleHandleA@4:NEAR
        EXTERN DialogBoxParamA@20:NEAR
        EXTERN EndDialog@8:NEAR
        EXTERN SendDlgItemMessageA@20:NEAR
```

```
ELSE
        EXTERN ReadFile:NEAR
        EXTERN CloseHandle:NEAR
        EXTERN CreatePipe:NEAR
        EXTERN TerminateProcess:NEAR
        EXTERN WaitForSingleObject:NEAR
        EXTERN SetMenu:NEAR
        EXTERN LoadMenuA:NEAR
        EXTERN CreateProcessA:NEAR
        EXTERN ExitProcess:NEAR
        EXTERN GetModuleHandleA:NEAR
        EXTERN DialogBoxParamA:NEAR
        EXTERN EndDialog:NEAR
        EXTERN SendDlgItemMessageA:NEAR
        ReadFile@20 = ReadFile
        CloseHandle@4 = CloseHandle
        CreatePipe@16 = CreatePipe
        TerminateProcess@8 = TerminateProcess
        WaitForSingleObject@8 = WaitForSingleObject
        SetMenu@8 = SetMenu
        LoadMenuA@8 = LoadMenuA
        CreateProcessA@40 = CreateProcessA
        ExitProcess@4 = ExitProcess
        GetModuleHandleA@4 = GetModuleHandleA
        DialogBoxParamA@20 = DialogBoxParamA
        EndDialog@8 = EndDialog
        SendDlgItemMessageA@20 = SendDlgItemMessageA
ENDIF
; Structures
; Message structure
MSGSTRUCT STRUC
        MSHWND       DD ?
        MSMESSAGE    DD ?
        MSWPARAM     DD ?
        MSLPARAM     DD ?
        MSTIME       DD ?
        MSPT         DD ?
MSGSTRUCT ENDS
; Structure for CreateProcess
STARTUP STRUC
        cb              DD 0
        lpReserved      DD 0
        lpDesktop       DD 0
```

```
        lpTitle          DD 0
        dwX              DD 0
        dwY              DD 0
        dwXSize          DD 0
        dwYSize          DD 0
        dwXCountChars    DD 0
        dwYCountChars    DD 0
        dwFillAttribute  DD 0
        dwFlags          DD 0
        wShowWindow      DW 0
        cbReserved2      DW 0
        lpReserved2      DD 0
        hStdInput        DD 0
        hStdOutput       DD 0
        hStdError        DD 0
STARTUP ENDS
; Structure - Information about the process
PROCINF STRUC
        hProcess         DD ?
        hThread          DD ?
        Idproc           DD ?
        idThr            DD ?
PROCINF ENDS

; The PIPE.ASM file
.586P
; Flat memory model
.MODEL FLAT, stdcall
include pipe.inc
; INCLUDELIB directives for the linker
IFDEF MASM
        includelib c:\masm32\lib\user32.lib
        includelib c:\masm32\lib\kernel32.lib
ELSE
        includelib c:\tasm32\lib\import32.lib
ENDIF
;------------------------------------------------
; Data segment
_DATA SEGMENT
        STRUP    STARTUP   <?>
        INF      PROCINF   <?>
        MSG      MSGSTRUCT <?>
        HINST    DD 0 ; Application descriptor
```

```
     PA        DB "DIAL1", 0
     CMD       DB "c:\tasm32\bin\tlink32.exe", 0
     PMENU     DB "MENUP", 0
     HW        DD ?
     HR        DD ?
     BUFER     DB 3000 DUP(0)
     BYT       DD ?
_DATA ENDS
; Code segment
_TEXT SEGMENT
START:
; Get the application handle
     PUSH  0
     CALL  GetModuleHandleA@4
     MOV   [HINST], EAX
;---------------------------------
     PUSH  0
     PUSH  OFFSET WNDPROC
     PUSH  0
     PUSH  OFFSET PA
     PUSH  [HINST]
     CALL  DialogBoxParamA@20
     CMP   EAX, -1
     JNE   KOL
; Error message
KOL:
;----------------------------------
     PUSH  0
     CALL  ExitProcess@4
;----------------------------------
; Window procedure
; Position of parameters in the stack
; [BP+014H]  ; LPARAM
; [BP+10H]   ; WAPARAM
; [BP+0CH]   ; MES
; [BP+8]     ; HWND
WNDPROC     PROC
     PUSH  EBP
     MOV   EBP, ESP
     PUSH  EBX
     PUSH  ESI
     PUSH  EDI
```

```
        CMP   DWORD PTR [EBP+0CH], WM_CLOSE
        JNE   L1
L3:
        PUSH  0
        PUSH  DWORD PTR [EBP+08H]
        CALL  EndDialog@8
        JMP   FINISH
L1:
        CMP   DWORD PTR [EBP+0CH], WM_INITDIALOG
        JNE   L2
; Load the menu
        PUSH  OFFSET PMENU
        PUSH  [HINST]
        CALL  LoadMenuA@8
; Set the menu
        PUSH  EAX
        PUSH  DWORD PTR [EBP+08H]
        CALL  SetMenu@8
        JMP   FINISH
L2:
        CMP   DWORD PTR [EBP+0CH], WM_COMMAND
        JNE   FINISH
        CMP   WORD PTR [EBP+10H], 300
        JE    L3
        CMP   WORD PTR [EBP+10H], 200
        JNE   FINISH
; Startup here
; PIPE in the beginning
        PUSH  0
        PUSH  0
        PUSH  OFFSET HW
        PUSH  OFFSET HR
        CALL  CreatePipe@16
        MOV   EAX, HW
; Console application starts here
        MOV   STRUP.cb, 68
        MOV   STRUP.lpReserved, 0
        MOV   STRUP.lpDesktop, 0
        MOV   STRUP.lpTitle, 0
        MOV   STRUP.dwFlags, STARTF_ADD
        MOV   STRUP.cbReserved2, 0
        MOV   STRUP.lpReserved2, 0
        MOV   STRUP.wShowWindow, SW_HIDE ; Process window is invisible
```

```
        MOV     STRUP.hStdOutput, EAX
        MOV     STRUP.hStdError, EAX
;--------------------------------
        PUSH    OFFSET INF
        PUSH    OFFSET STRUP
        PUSH    0
        PUSH    0
        PUSH    0
        PUSH    1 ; Inherit descriptors
        PUSH    0
        PUSH    0
        PUSH    OFFSET CMD
        PUSH    0
        CALL    CreateProcessA@40
; Read information
        PUSH    0
        PUSH    OFFSET BYT
        PUSH    3000
        PUSH    OFFSET BUFER
        PUSH    HR
        CALL    ReadFile@20
        PUSH    OFFSET BUFER
        PUSH    0
        PUSH    EM_REPLACESEL
        PUSH    101
        PUSH    DWORD PTR [EBP+08H]
        CALL    SendDlgItemMessageA@20
; Close the handle for writing
        PUSH    HW
        CALL    CloseHandle@4
; Close the handle for reading
        PUSH    HR
        CALL CloseHandle@4
FINISH:
        MOV     EAX, 0
        POP     EDI
        POP     ESI
        POP     EBX
        POP     EBP
        RET     16
WNDPROC     ENDP
_TEXT ENDS
END START
```

To translate the program presented in Listing 18.3, issue the following commands using MASM32:

```
ml /c /coff /DMASM pipe.asm
rc pipe.rc
link /subsystem:windows pipe.obj pipe.res
```

Issue the following commands using TASM32:

```
tasm32 /ml pipe.asm
brcc32 pipe.rc
tlink32 -aa pipe.obj,,,,,pipe.res
```

The program that you just considered requires some comments.

Starting a console application is a complicated task. Therefore, I won't dive into details. In the program in Listing 18.3, this procedure is practically no different from the one used in *Chapter 15* for starting the WINWORD.EXE application. Consider, however, new features implemented in this program. Note that the `EditBox` control plays an interesting role here. This window element plays the role of the output console. To achieve this, set the `ES_MULTILINE` property, which displays the entire text sent to the window using the `EM_REPLACESEL` message. To read the information, a large buffer is used. Principally, it is possible to read the data in smaller portions, checking the number of read bytes as with files.

Preventing an Application from Starting Multiple Times

Q. Is it possible to prevent an application from starting multiple times?

Yes, it is possible. The most frequently used method is to create a mutual exclusion object (mutex). This object is intended for coordinating the interoperation of various processes. To create a mutex, use the `CreateMutex` function. Parameters of this function are briefly outlined as follows:

- First parameter — The pointer to the structure that defines an access attribute. Usually, this parameter is set to `NULL`.
- Second parameter — The priority flag. If this flag has a nonzero value, the process requires immediate access to the object.
- Third parameter — The pointer to the object name.

When the program is started, it creates a mutex. The second parameter of the function must have a nonzero value. When the user makes an attempt to start another copy of the program, the attempt to create a mutex will result in an error, which will cause the program to terminate immediately.

The same result can be achieved using a semaphore or a memory-mapped file. In this case, the task is trivial.

Another approach is based on shared memory. To use this method, define a shared memory area and a variable within it. When the application starts, it checks the variable value and, if it is equal to zero, sets it to one. If the variable is already set to one, then the program must either exit or carry out the actions, for which provision was made just for this case.

All methods described in this section are so easy that there is no need to concentrate special attention on them.

Operations over Groups of Files and Directories

Q. Are there any methods for simplifying operations over groups of files and directories in Windows?

Yes, there is the `SHFileOperation` function that can copy, move, rename, or delete file objects (files and directories, including the nested ones). This function has only one parameter — the pointer to the structure that defines, which operation should be carried out, over which objects, and how. Here is the structure.

```
SH struct
          hwnd                        DWORD ?
          wFunc                       DWORD ?
          pFrom                       DWORD ?
          pTo                         DWORD ?
          fFlags                      DWORD ?
          fAnyOperationsAborted       DWORD ?
          hNameMappings               DWORD ?
          lpszProgressTitle           DWORD ?
SH ENDS
```

Consider the values of the fields of this structure.

- ❒ `hwnd` — Descriptor of the window, into which the operation should be outputted.
- ❒ `wFunc` — Operation code. It can take the following values: `FO_COPY`, `FO_DELETE`, `FO_MOVE`, or `FO_RENAME`. These values are self-evident; therefore, there is no need to clarify them.
- ❒ `pFrom` — Name of the file, directory, or group of files or directories, over which the operation should be carried out. If there are several objects, their names must be separated by symbols with the zero code. It is also possible to distinguish lists, which are separated by two zeros.

- `pTo` — Name or group of object names that must be obtained as a result of the copy operation.
- `fFlags` — Flag that determines the type of operation. It can be formed by combining the following constants:
  - `FOF_ALLOWUNDO` — If possible, save the information required to undo the operation.
  - `FOF_CONFIRMMOUSE` — Not implemented.
  - `FOF_FILESONLY` — If the template is defined, carry out the operation only over files.
  - `FOF_MULTIDESTFILES` — Specifies that `pTo` contains several target files of directories. For example, it is possible to copy into multiple directories. If `pFrom` consists of several files, every file will be copied into its own directory.
  - `FOF_NOCONFIRMATION` — Confirm all requests.
  - `FOF_NOCONFIRMMKDIR` — Do not confirm directory creation if necessary.
  - `FOF_RENAMEONCOLLISION` — Assign new filenames if files with such names already exist in the target directory.
  - `FOF_SILENT` — Do not display the status window.
  - `FOF_SIMPLEPROGRESS` — Display the progress bar but do not display filenames.
  - `FOF_WANTMAPPINGHANDLE` — Fill the mapped file (described later).
- `fAnyOperationsAborted` — Variable whose value makes it possible to determine whether the operation was interrupted after its completion (`!=0` for yes and `=0` for no).
- `hNameMappings` — Descriptor of the memory-mapped file that contains an array consisting of new and old names of the files, over which the operation was carried out.
- `lpszProgressTitle` — Pointer to the header string for the status dialog.

In addition to this function, there is the entire group of functions whose names start with the `SH` prefix. Among them, the `SHGetDesktopFolder` function is the most useful. It displays the dialog for choosing the required desktop folder.

Printing

Q. How do I send the data to the printing device?

This topic is wide; therefore, I recommend that you read another book [12], where it is covered in detail, if you are interested in this topic. As relates to this book, I'll provide the most general algorithm that Windows uses for printing. I hope that it will help you to quickly understand the printing basics.

- Printing is similar to screen output. The same functions, such as `TextOut` or `Ellipse`, are used for this purpose. To accomplish screen output, it is necessary to know the printer context.

- In contrast to screen output, a printer device must be created instead of obtained. To achieve this, use the `CreateDC` function, the second parameter of which is the pointer to the string containing the printer name. The remaining three parameters are usually set to `NULL`.
- The `PrintDLG` function allows the user to choose the printer name in a dialog. This function returns the printer context.
- If you decide to use the `CreateDC` function, you need to get the printer names available in the system. For this purpose, use the `EnumPrinters` function. It provides a powerful tool for detecting not only local but also network printers.
- To start printing a document, call the `StartDoc` function. To terminate printing, use the `EndDoc` function. These two functions enclose the block that carries out printing. Within the limits of that block, it is also possible to paginate the document using the `StartPage` and `EndPage` functions.
- When printing is completed, the printer context must be deleted using the `DeleteDC` function.

Using the Tasklist

Q. Can an application detect, which programs are running?

Yes. The basis for the method of doing so is formed by the `EnumWindows` function, which has the following parameters:

- First parameter — Address of the procedure that will be called automatically if a window is found
- Second parameter — Arbitrary value that will be passed to the procedure

The called procedure itself receives two parameters: the descriptor of the found window and the arbitrary parameter mentioned previously. By the known descriptor, it is possible to determine the unique identifier of the process and the thread that owns the detected window. This is done using the `GetWindowThreadProcessId` function. Knowing this identifier, it is possible, for example, to delete that process from the memory using the `TerminateProcess` function (be very careful).

Listing 18.4 provides an example program that displays the list of running processes; the results are displayed in Fig. 18.1. When considering this example, note how the `GetWindowText` function determining the window header is used. Do not be surprised if the displayed list contains processes whose windows are invisible. Windows can be hidden. Also notice that console applications are listed. This program also determines unique identifiers of the processes.

Listing 18.4. Creating a list of running processes

```
// The PROC.RC file
// Constant definitions
#define WS_SYSMENU          0x00080000L
#define WS_MINIMIZEBOX      0x00020000L
#define WS_VISIBLE          0x10000000L
#define WS_TABSTOP          0x00010000L
#define WS_VSCROLL          0x00200000L
#define WS_HSCROLL          0x00100000L
#define DS_3DLOOK           0x0004L
#define LBS_NOTIFY          0x0001L
#define LBS_SORT            0x0002L

// Identifiers
#define LIST1               101

// Dialog box definition
DIAL1 DIALOG 0, 0, 220, 110
STYLE WS_SYSMENU | WS_MINIMIZEBOX |
DS_3DLOOK
CAPTION "Process list"
FONT 8, "Arial"
{
 CONTROL "ListBox1", LIST1, "listbox", WS_VISIBLE |
 WS_TABSTOP | WS_VSCROLL | WS_HSCROLL |
 LBS_NOTIFY,
 16, 16, 190, 75
}

; The PROC.INC file
; Constants
; Values returned by the GetDiveType function
; The 0 and 1 values can be considered indications
; that the device is missing
DRIVE_REMOVABLE    equ 2 ; Floppy drive
DRIVE_FIXED        equ 3 ; Hard disk
DRIVE_REMOTE       equ 4 ; Network disk
DRIVE_CDROM        equ 5 ; CD-ROM
DRIVE_RAMDISK      equ 6 ; RAM drive
; This message arrives when the window is closed
WM_CLOSE           equ 10h
WM_INITDIALOG      equ 110h
```

```
WM_COMMAND          equ 111h
LB_ADDSTRING        equ 180h
LB_RESETCONTENT     equ 184h
WM_LBUTTONDOWN      equ 201h
; Prototypes of external procedures
IFDEF MASM
       EXTERN wsprintfA:NEAR
       EXTERN GetWindowThreadProcessId@8:NEAR
       EXTERN GetWindowTextA@12:NEAR
       EXTERN EnumWindows@8:NEAR
       EXTERN lstrcatA@8:NEAR
       EXTERN ExitProcess@4:NEAR
       EXTERN GetModuleHandleA@4:NEAR
       EXTERN DialogBoxParamA@20:NEAR
       EXTERN EndDialog@8:NEAR
       EXTERN SendDlgItemMessageA@20:NEAR
ELSE
       EXTERN _wsprintfA:NEAR
       EXTERN GetWindowThreadProcessId:NEAR
       EXTERN GetWindowTextA@12:NEAR
       EXTERN EnumWindows:NEAR
       EXTERN lstrcatA:NEAR
       EXTERN ExitProcess:NEAR
       EXTERN GetModuleHandleA:NEAR
       EXTERN DialogBoxParamA:NEAR
       EXTERN EndDialog:NEAR
       EXTERN SendDlgItemMessageA:NEAR
       wsprintfA = _wsprintfA
       GetWindowThreadProcessId@8 = GetWindowThreadProcessId
       GetWindowTextA@12 = GetWindowTextA
       EnumWindows@8 = EnumWindows
       lstrcatA@8 = lstrcatA
       ExitProcess@4 = ExitProcess
       GetModuleHandleA@4 = GetModuleHandleA
       DialogBoxParamA@20 = DialogBoxParamA
       EndDialog@8 = EndDialog
       SendDlgItemMessageA@20 = SendDlgItemMessageA
ENDIF
; Structures
; Message structure
MSGSTRUCT STRUC
       MSHWND       DD ?
       MSMESSAGE    DD ?
```

```
        MSWPARAM    DD ?
        MSLPARAM    DD ?
        MSTIME      DD ?
        MSPT        DD ?
MSGSTRUCT ENDS

; The PROC.ASM file
.586P
; Flat memory model
.MODEL FLAT, stdcall
include proc.inc
; INCLUDELIB directives for the linker
IFDEF MASM
        includelib c:\masm32\lib\user32.lib
        includelib c:\masm32\lib\kernel32.lib
ELSE
        includelib c:\tasm32\lib\import32.lib
ENDIF
;-----------------------------------------------------
; Data segment
_DATA SEGMENT
        MSG    MSGSTRUCT <?>
        HINST  DD 0 ; Application descriptor
        PA     DB "DIAL1", 0
        BUFER  DB 200 DUP(0)
        BUF    DB 20 DUP(0)
        FORM   DB ";%lu", 0
        IDP    DD ?
        HWN    DD ?
_DATA ENDS
; Code segment
_TEXT SEGMENT
START:
; Get the application descriptor
        PUSH  0
        CALL  GetModuleHandleA@4
        MOV   [HINST], EAX
;-------------------------------
        PUSH  0
        PUSH  OFFSET WNDPROC
        PUSH  0
        PUSH  OFFSET PA
        PUSH  [HINST]
```

```
        CALL  DialogBoxParamA@20
        CMP   EAX, -1
        JNE   KOL
; Error message
KOL:
; -----------------------------------
        PUSH  0
        CALL  ExitProcess@4
; -----------------------------------
; Window procedure
; Position of parameters in the stack
; [EBP+014H]  ; LPARAM
; [EBP+10H]   ; WAPARAM
; [EBP+0CH]   ; MES
; [EBP+8]     ; HWND
WNDPROC  PROC
        PUSH  EBP
        MOV   EBP, ESP
        PUSH  EBX
        PUSH  ESI
        PUSH  EDI
; ----------------
        CMP   DWORD PTR [EBP+0CH], WM_CLOSE
        JNE   L1
        PUSH  0
        PUSH  DWORD PTR [EBP+08H]
        CALL  EndDialog@8
        JMP   FINISH
L1:
        CMP   DWORD PTR [EBP+0CH], WM_INITDIALOG
        JNE   FINISH
; Save the window descriptor
        MOV   EAX, DWORD PTR [EBP+08H]
        MOV   HWN, EAX
; Call the EnumWindows function
        PUSH  1 ; Unused parameter
        PUSH  OFFSET PENUM
        CALL  EnumWindows@8
FINISH:
        MOV   EAX, 0
        POP   EDI
        POP   ESI
        POP   EBX
```

```
        POP    EBP
        RET    16
WNDPROC     ENDP
; Callback procedure when searching for windows
; [EBP+0CH]    ; Parameter
; [EBP+8]      ; Window descriptor
PENUM PROC
        PUSH   EBP
        MOV    EBP, ESP
; Get the window header
        PUSH   200
        PUSH   OFFSET BUFER
        PUSH   DWORD PTR [EBP+8]
        CALL   GetWindowTextA@12
; Get the identifier of the process or thread
; that owns that window
        PUSH   OFFSET IDP
        PUSH   DWORD PTR [EBP+8]
        CALL   GetWindowThreadProcessId@8
; Form a string to be included in the list
        PUSH   OFFSET IDP
        PUSH   OFFSET FORM
        PUSH   OFFSET BUF
        CALL   wsprintfA
        ADD    ESP, 12
        PUSH   OFFSET BUF
        PUSH   OFFSET BUFER
        CALL   lstrcatA@8
; Add the string to the list
        PUSH   OFFSET BUFER
        PUSH   0
        PUSH   LB_ADDSTRING
        PUSH   101
        PUSH   [HWN]
        CALL   SendDlgItemMessageA@20
        POP    EBP
        MOV    EAX, 1
        RET    8
PENUM ENDP
_TEXT ENDS
END START
```

To translate the program presented in Listing 18.4, issue the following commands for MASM32:

```
ml /c /coff /DMASM PROC.asm
rc proc.rc
link /subsystem:windows PROC.obj proc.res
```

Issue the following commands for TASM32:

```
tasm32 /ml proc.asm
brcc32 proc.rc
tlink32 -aa proc.obj,,,,,proc.res
```

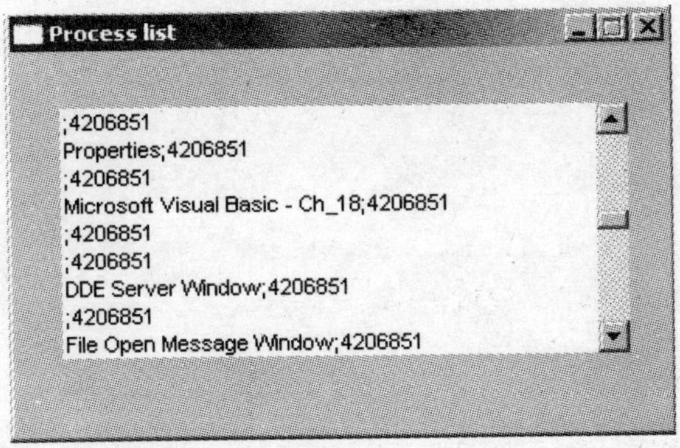

Fig. 18.1. Results of running the application presented in Listing 18.4

PART IV: DEBUGGING, CODE ANALYSIS, AND DRIVER DEVELOPMENT

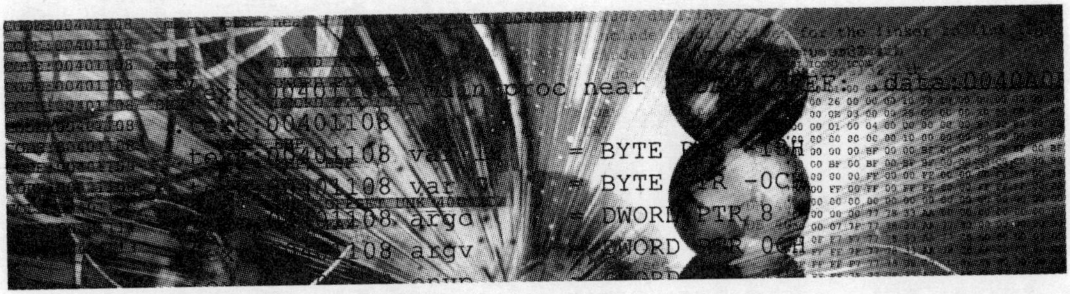

Chapter 19

System Programming in Windows

Most of this chapter concentrates on memory management in Windows. Understanding this material requires you to have some background knowledge of the protected mode of Intel microprocessors. Therefore, I provide the basic information related to this topic. More detailed information about the protected mode can be found in [1, 3, 6, 8, 12]. Materials of this chapter also will be needed in *Chapter 27* when considering kernel-mode drivers.

Page and Segment Addressing

I'll start describing page and segment addressing with a brief historical overview. The Intel[i] family originates from the Intel 8086 microprocessor. Currently, the seventh generation of this family is widely used. Every new generation differed from the previous one programmatically. Mainly, these differences lay in the extension of the command set. However, there were two stages in this evolution that played exceedingly important roles in the development of Intel-based computers. These were the 80286 microprocessor (protected mode) and the 80386 microprocessor (page addressing).

---

[i] I also am referring to Intel-compatible microprocessors from other manufacturers.

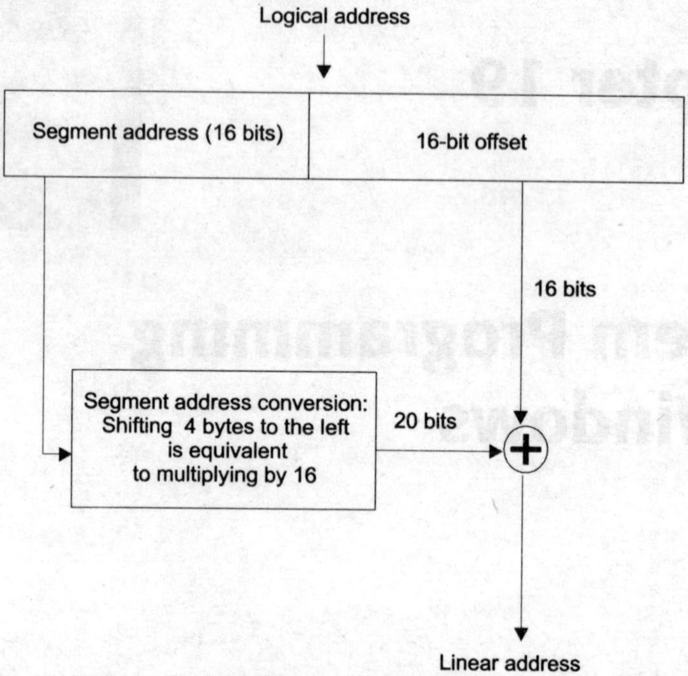

Fig. 19.1. Scheme of converting a logical address to a linear address in real addressing mode

Before the arrival of the 80286 chip, microprocessors were used in so-called real mode of addressing. For programming, logical addresses were used, which consisted of two 16-bit components: segment and offset. The segment address could be stored in one of the four segment registers — CS, DS, SS, or ES. The offset was stored in one of the index registers — DI, SI, BX, BP, or SP.[i] When accessing the memory, the logical address had to be converted: The segment address shifted 4 bytes to the left had to be added to the offset. As a result, a 20-bit address was obtained, which could span about 1 MB of memory[ii] (or, to be more precise, 1087 KB). MS-DOS was initially designed to work in this address space. The resulting 20-bit address was called linear, and it coincided with the physical address of the memory cell. Fig. 19.1 illustrates this mechanism of converting a logical address to a physical address.

Naturally, in the evolution of operating systems, this was a dead end. It was necessary to at least provide the possibility of extending the memory. It would be ideal not

---

[i] In a narrow sense, only the DI and SI registers can be considered index registers.

[ii] Once upon a time, it seemed that 1 MB was a vast amount of memory.

only to extend the memory but also to give all address spaces equal rights. Furthermore, in real mode, the entire memory was available to any running application. Any error (or malicious intent) of the programmer could freeze or even crash the entire system. Introduction of the so-called protected mode provided a way out of this situation.

The greatness of this approach was that at first glance nothing changed. As before, the logical address was formed using segment registers and registers storing the offset. However, segment registers stored a so-called selector instead of the segment address. Part of this selector (13 bits) represented an index in a table called the descriptor table. The index pointed to the descriptor that stored full information about the segment. The size of the descriptor was sufficient for addressing considerably larger memory blocks.

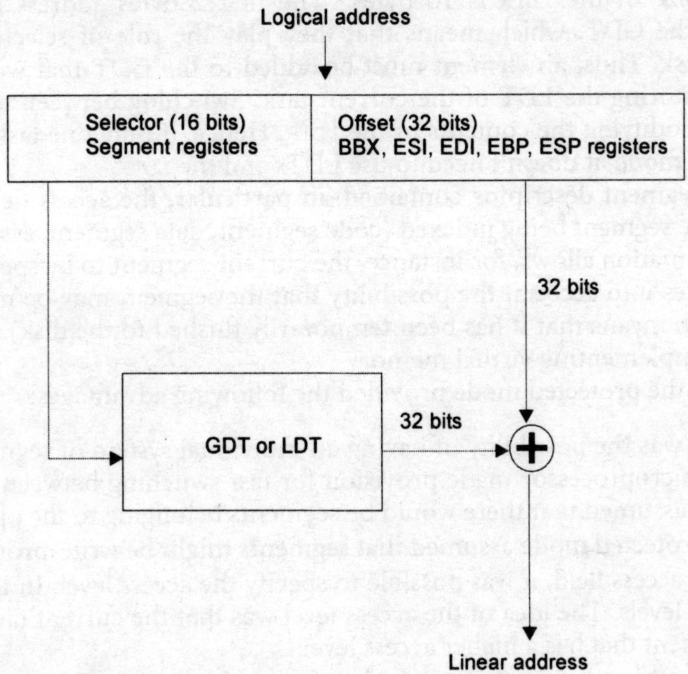

Fig. 19.2. Scheme of converting a local address to a linear address in protected addressing mode

Fig. 19.2 shows a scheme of converting the logical address into the linear address. Here, a 32-bit microprocessor was taken as a basis instead of the 16-bit processor used earlier. The descriptor table, or base address table, could have two types — global (GDT) or local (LDT). The type of the table depended on the second bit of the contents of the segment register. The GDT register (GDTR) pointed at the position of the GDT and its size. It was assumed that the contents of this register must not change after it was loaded. The GDT has to store descriptors of segments taken by the operating system. The address of the LDT was stored in the LDT register (LDTR). It was also assumed that there might be several LDTs — one per running task. Thus, multitasking support was planned at the microprocessor level. The size of the GDTR is 48 bits, with 32 bits for the address of the GDT and 16 bits for its size.

In addition to the GDT, provision was made for another common system table — the Interrupt Descriptor Table (IDT). It contains descriptors of special system objects known as gateways and defines entry points for the interrupt and exception handling procedures. The position of the IDT depends on the contents of the IDT register, the structure of which is similar to the GDTR.

The size of the LDTR is 10 bytes.[i] The first 2 bytes address the LDT indirectly through the GDT, which means that they play the role of selector for each newly-created task. Thus, an element must be added to the GDT that would determine the segment storing the LDT of the current task. Switching between tasks can take place only by modifying the contents of the LDTR. Hence, if only one task is going to run in protected mode, it doesn't need to use LDTs and the LDTR.

The segment descriptor contained, in particular, the access field that defined the type of the segment being indexed (code segment, data segment, system segment, etc.). This information allows, for instance, the current segment to be specified as read-only. It also takes into account the possibility that the segment may be missing from memory (which means that it has been temporarily flushed to the disk). This makes provision for implementing virtual memory.

Thus, the protected mode provided the following advantages:

- There was the possibility of having an individual system of segments for each task. The microprocessor made provision for fast switching between tasks. In addition, it was assumed that there would be segments belonging to the operating system.
- The protected mode assumed that segments might be write-protected.
- In the access field, it was possible to specify the access level. In total, there are four access levels. The idea of the access level was that the current task could not access a segment that has a higher access level.
- Finally, this scheme made provision for implementing virtual memory, the memory formed with the possibility of temporarily storing the segment on disk. With this possibility, the logical address space can be very large.

Consider Fig. 19.2. From this scheme, it follows that the linear address is obtained by conversion. However, in contrast to the 80286 processor, in which it was still possible to equate the linear address to the physical address, for 80386, this is no longer an option.

---

[i] In older models of the Intel microprocessor, this register was only 2 bytes long.

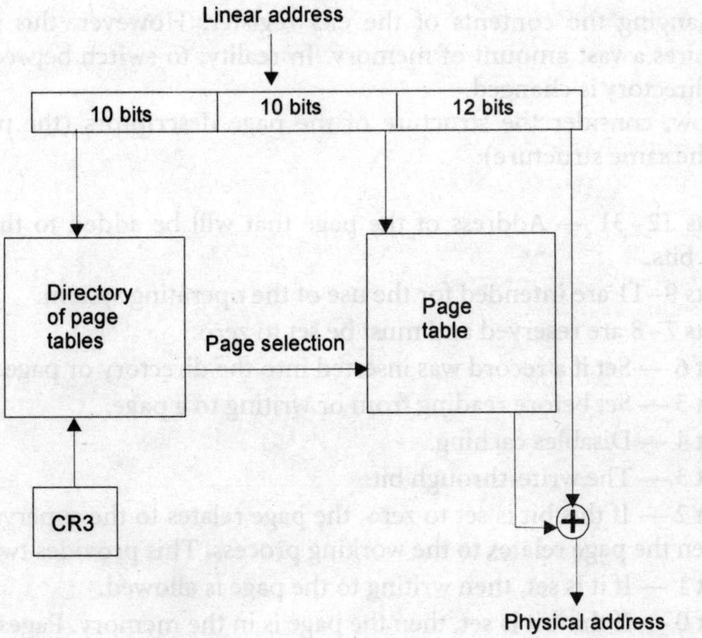

Fig. 19.3. Converting a linear address to a physical address and accounting for page addressing

With the Intel 80386 microprocessor, another mechanism of address conversion appeared — page addressing. To make the page addressing mechanism work, the most significant bit of the CR0 system register must be set to 1.

Consider Fig. 19.3. The linear address obtained using the descriptor conversion (Fig. 19.2) is divided into three parts. The 10 most significant bits are used as an index in the table called the page table directory. The location of the page directory is defined by the contents of the CR3 register. The directory is composed of descriptors, the maximum number of which is 1024. The number of directories can be infinite; however, only the directory pointed by the CR3 register is active.

The next 10 bits of the linear address are intended for indexing the page table, which contains 1024 page descriptors. These descriptors, in turn, specify the physical addresses of the pages. Page size is usually 4 KB. Thus, it is easy to compute the address space that can be spanned by one page table directory. It equals 1024 × 1024 × × 1024 × 4 bytes, or about 4 GB.

The 12 least significant bits define the offset within a page. As can be easily noticed, this makes exactly 4 KB (4095 bytes). Naturally, you probably have guessed that every process must have its own page table directory. You can switch between processes by changing the contents of the CR3 register. However, this is inefficient because it requires a vast amount of memory. In reality, to switch between processes the page table directory is changed.

Now, consider the structure of the page descriptors (the page table descriptors have the same structure):

- Bits 12–31 — Address of the page that will be added to the offset after shifting 12 bits.
- Bits 9–11 are intended for the use of the operating system.
- Bits 7–8 are reserved and must be set to zero.
- Bit 6 — Set if a record was inserted into the directory or page.
- Bit 5 — Set before reading from or writing to a page.
- Bit 4 — Disables caching.
- Bit 3 — The write-through bit.
- Bit 2 — If this bit is set to zero, the page relates to the supervisor; if it is set to one, then the page relates to the working process. This provides two access levels.
- Bit 1 — If it is set, then writing to the page is allowed.
- Bit 0 — If this bit is set, then the page is in the memory. Pages that contain data are flushed to the disk and read when an attempt is made to access them. Pages that contain code are not flushed to the disk. However, they can be swapped from appropriate modules stored on the disk. Therefore, the memory taken by these pages can be used rationally.

Address Space of a Process

In the previous section, I described page and segment addressing. How do these two addressing modes coexist in Windows? As it turns out, everything is simple. Selectors based on addresses of zero are loaded into the segment registers, and the segment size is 4 GB. After this approach is implemented, programmers can forget about the existence of segments and selectors, although this mechanism is still working from the processor's point of view. As for the main mechanism of forming addresses, it is based on page conversions. This memory model became known as the flat memory model. Logical addressing in such a model is defined only by a 32-bit offset. Until now, all the programs presented in this book were written for the flat memory model. At the same time, you assumed that the entire memory area addressed by the 32-bit address was entirely at your disposal. Naturally, you were right; however, this address was the logical address, which also undergoes page conversion; it would be a difficult task to say, into which physical cell it will fall.

Fig. 19.4 shows the logical address space of a process. Pay attention to the shared memory areas (numbers 2, 4, and 5). What does this mean? This means that these memory areas are mapped to the same physical space. Consider these areas in more detail:

- Area 1 — This memory region is blocked. This area is intended for detecting zero pointers. This is especially true for the C language, in which the `malloc` function can return a zero pointer. An attempt to write anything by this address will result in an error message from the operating system.
- Area 2 — This memory area was used in the operating systems of the Windows 9*x* family. In Windows NT and later versions, this area is part of area 3. Address space for MS-DOS and 16-bit applications is allocated in this region.
- Area 3 — This area of the address space, located between the 4 MB and the 2 GB boundaries (in Windows 2000 and later, this area starts at 1 MB), is the process address space. The process takes this area for code and data, including process-specific dynamic link libraries (DLLs). This area is not shared. However, there are some exceptions, which you have encountered already. It is possible to define a shared section, which means that some pages from this logical space will be mapped into the same physical area for different processes.
- Area 4 — This is the reserved memory region used for internal implementation of the operating system.
- Area 5 — This area contains memory-mapped files, system DLLs, and dynamic memory for 16-bit applications. For Windows 2000 and later, this area is included in the sixth area.
- Area 6 — The last part of the address space is allocated for system components. Surprisingly, but in Windows 9*x*, this area is not protected against access by user programs. In operating systems of the Windows NT family, this area is not accessible for executable processes.

To store something in the virtual address space, this space must be mapped to the physical memory. The physical memory page need not be present in RAM. The operating system stores part of the pages in the page file (PAGEFILE.SYS) or in memory-mapped files (see *Chapter 18*). When accessing the address related to the page stored on the disk, the so-called page fault is generated, which loads the page from the disk. So-called free pages participate in this mechanism. The system looks for a free page (which is not occupied by any process) and loads there the data from the page stored on the disk. After that, the page is occupied. If there are no free pages, the system looks for a page that it could flush to disk, frees it, and loads the required data there. Usually, however, the operating system ensures that free pages are available.

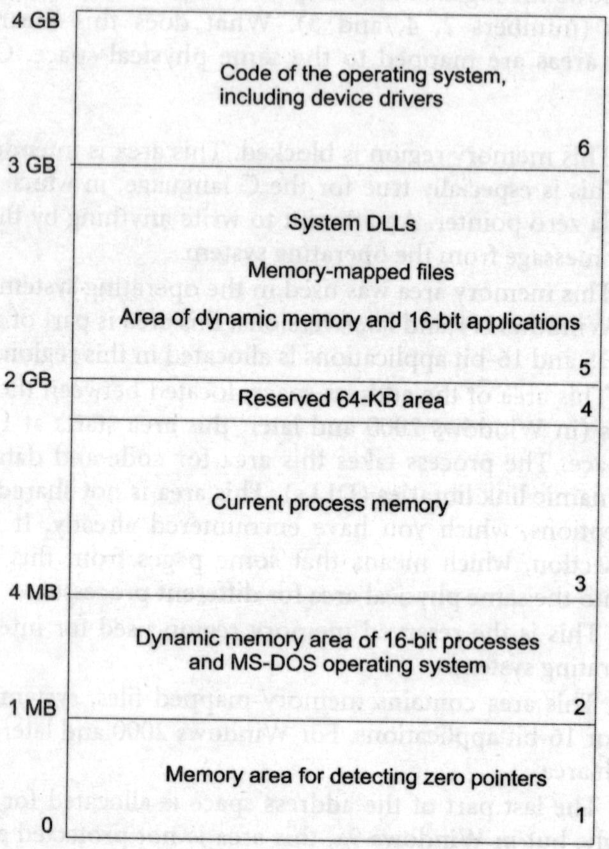

Fig. 19.4. Address space of a process

Memory Management

In this section, several functions allowing you to dynamically allocate and delete memory blocks are covered.

Consider the `GlobalAlloc` function. Another function, `LocalAlloc`, is equivalent to `GlobalAlloc` and has been preserved exclusively for compatibility with older applications. The function has two arguments. The first argument is the flag, which will be covered later. The second argument is the number of the required memory bytes to allocate. If this function completes successfully, it returns the starting address of the block that can be used in further operations. If the system cannot allocate the requested memory block, it returns zero.

Usually, the flag value is set to the GMEM_FIXED constant, which is equal to zero. This means that the memory block is fixed, and the virtual block address will not change, although the physical memory address, to which this block is mapped, can be changed by the system. Combining this flag with the GMEM_ZEROINIT flag automatically fills the allocated block with zeros, which is often convenient. The size of the allocated block can be changed using the GlobalReAlloc function. The first argument of this function is the pointer to the block that needs to be changed, the second argument is the size of the new block, and the third argument is the flag. Note that this function can change the properties of the memory block — for example, make it movable.

Consider the flags of the GlobalAlloc function. If your program works with memory intensely — for example, it frequently allocates and releases the memory — the memory may become fragmented. After all, you do not allow it to move memory blocks. In this case, it is possible to use the GMEM_MOVEABLE flag. Having allocated a block, you can fix it at any time using the GlobalLock function, after which it is possible to work with that block without worrying. The GlobalUnlock function allows you to remove blocking at any time, enabling the system to organize blocks. It is only necessary to bear in mind that, when using the GMEM_MOVEABLE flag, the function returns the handle rather than the address. However, the handle is the argument of the GlobalLock function. As for the GlobalLock function, it returns the address.

An even more exotic approach is possible. This relates to the use of the GMEM_DISCARDABLE flag. This flag is used with the GMEM_MOVEABLE flag. In this case, the system can remove the block from the memory if you have not fixed it beforehand. If the block was removed by the system, then the GlobalLock function will return zero, and you'll have to allocate a block again and load data if necessary.

To delete the memory block, use the GlobalFree function. When a fixed memory block is allocated, the memory block address is the function argument. With a movable memory block, the argument is the descriptor. To release the memory block being deleted, use the GlobalDiscard function.

The GlobalMemoryStatus function deserves special mention. Using this function, it is possible to determine the amount of available memory. The only parameter of this function is the pointer to the structure containing information about the memory. Here is this structure:

```
MEM STRUC
        DwLength           DD ?
        DwMemoryLoad       DD ?
        DwTotalPhys        DD ?
        DwAvailPhys        DD ?
        DwTotalPageFile    DD ?
        DwAvailPageFile    DD ?
        DwTotalVirtual     DD ?
        DwAvailVirtual     DD ?
MEM ENDS
```

The elements of this structure are as follows:

- DwLength — Structure size in bytes
- DwMemoryLoad — Percentage of the used memory
- DwTotalPhys — Total size of the physical memory in bytes
- DwAvailPhys — Size of the available physical memory in bytes
- DwTotalPageFile — Number of physical memory bytes flushed to the disk
- DwAvailPageFile — Number of available memory bytes stored on the disk
- DwTotalVirtual — Total size of the virtual memory
- DwAvailVirtual — Size of the available virtual memory

Listing 19.1 demonstrates the use of the GlobalAlloc function.

Listing 19.1. Dynamical memory allocation

```
; The MEM.ASM file
.586P
; Flat memory model
.MODEL FLAT, stdcall
; Constants
; For console output
STD_OUTPUT_HANDLE  equ -11
GENERIC_READ       equ 80000000h
OPEN_EXISTING       equ 3
IFDEF MASM
; MASM
; Prototypes of external procedures
       EXTERN  GlobalFree@4:NEAR
       EXTERN  GlobalAlloc@8:NEAR
       EXTERN  GetFileSize@8:NEAR
       EXTERN  CloseHandle@4:NEAR
       EXTERN  CreateFileA@28:NEAR
       EXTERN  ReadFile@20:NEAR
       EXTERN  GetStdHandle@4:NEAR
       EXTERN  WriteConsoleA@20:NEAR
       EXTERN  ExitProcess@4:NEAR
       EXTERN  GetCommandLineA@0:NEAR
; INCLUDELIB directives for the linker
       includelib c:\masm32\lib\user32.lib
       includelib c:\masm32\lib\kernel32.lib
ELSE
; TASM
```

```
LOCALS
; Prototypes of external procedures
      EXTERN  GlobalFree:NEAR
      EXTERN  GlobalAlloc:NEAR
      EXTERN  GetFileSize:NEAR
      EXTERN  CloseHandle:NEAR
      EXTERN  CreateFileA:NEAR
      EXTERN  ReadFile:NEAR
      EXTERN  GetStdHandle:NEAR
      EXTERN  WriteConsoleA:NEAR
      EXTERN  ExitProcess:NEAR
      EXTERN  GetCommandLineA:NEAR
      GlobalFree@4 = GlobalFree
      GlobalAlloc@8 = GlobalAlloc
      GetFileSize@8 = GetFileSize
      CloseHandle@4 = CloseHandle
      CreateFileA@28 = CreateFileA
      ReadFile@20 = ReadFile
      GetStdHandle@4 = GetStdHandle
      WriteConsoleA@20 = WriteConsoleA
      ExitProcess@4 = ExitProcess
      GetCommandLineA@0 = GetCommandLineA
; INCLUDELIB directives for the linker
      includelib c:\tasm32\lib\import32.lib
ENDIF
;---------------------------------------------
; Data segment
_DATA SEGMENT
      LENS   DWORD ?
      HANDL  DWORD ? ; Console descriptor
      HF     DWORD ? ; File descriptor
      SIZEH  DWORD ? ; Most significant part of the file length
      SIZEL  DWORD ? ; Least significant part of the file length
      GH     DWORD ? ; Pointer to the memory block
      NUMB   DWORD ?
      BUF    DB 10 DUP(0)
_DATA ENDS
; Code segment
_TEXT SEGMENT
START:
; Get the output handle
      PUSH   STD_OUTPUT_HANDLE
      CALL   GetStdHandle@4
```

```
        MOV   HANDL, EAX
; Get the number of parameters
CALL NUMPAR
        CMP   EAX, 2
        JB    _EXIT
;-------------------------------------
; Get the parameter with the EDI number
        MOV   EDI, 2
        LEA   EBX, BUF
        CALL  GETPAR
; Now, work with the file
; Open as a read-only file
        PUSH  0
        PUSH  0
        PUSH  OPEN_EXISTING
        PUSH  0
        PUSH  0
        PUSH  GENERIC_READ
        PUSH  OFFSET BUF
        CALL  CreateFileA@28
        CMP   EAX, -1
        JE    _EXIT
; Save the file descriptor
        MOV   HF, EAX
; Determine the file size
        PUSH  OFFSET SIZEH
        PUSH  EAX
        CALL  GetFileSize@8
; Save the size, assuming that it
; doesn't exceed 4 GB
        MOV   SIZEL, EAX
; Request the memory for reading the file
        PUSH  EAX
        PUSH  0
        CALL  GlobalAlloc@8
        CMP   EAX, 0
        JE    _CLOSE
; Store the address of the allocated block
        MOV   GH, EAX
; Read the file into the allocated memory
        PUSH  0
        PUSH  OFFSET NUMB
        PUSH  SIZEL
```

```
        PUSH  GH ; Buffer address
        PUSH  HF
        CALL  ReadFile@20
        CMP   EAX, 0
        JE    _FREE
; Output the read data
        PUSH  0
        PUSH  OFFSET LENS
        PUSH  SIZEL
        PUSH  GH
        PUSH  HANDL
        CALL  WriteConsoleA@20
_FREE:
; Release the memory
        PUSH  GH
        CALL  GlobalFree@4
; Close the files
_CLOSE:
        PUSH  HF
        CALL  CloseHandle@4
_EXIT:
; Exit the program
        PUSH  0
        CALL  ExitProcess@4
;-----------------------------------------
; Procedures area
; The procedure for determining the number of parameters in the string
; Determine the number of parameters (->EAX)
NUMPAR PROC
        CALL  GetCommandLineA@0
        MOV   ESI, EAX ; Pointer to the string
        XOR   ECX, ECX ; Counter
        MOV   EDX, 1   ; Flag
@@L1:
        CMP   BYTE PTR [ESI], 0
        JE    @@L4
        CMP   BYTE PTR [ESI], 32
        JE    @@L3
        ADD   ECX, EDX ; Parameter number
        MOV   EDX, 0
        JMP   @@L2
@@L3:
        OR    EDX, 1
```

```
@@L2:
    INC   ESI
    JMP   @@L1
@@L4:
    MOV   EAX, ECX
    RET
NUMPAR ENDP
; Get the parameter from the command line
; EBX — Points to the buffer, in which the parameter will be stored
; Zero-terminated string is placed into the buffer
; EDI — Parameter number
GETPAR PROC
    CALL  GetCommandLineA@0
    MOV   ESI, EAX ; Pointer to the string
    XOR   ECX, ECX ; Counter
    MOV   EDX, 1   ; Flag
@@L1:
    CMP   BYTE PTR [ESI], 0
    JE    @@L4
    CMP   BYTE PTR [ESI], 32
    JE    @@L3
    ADD   ECX, EDX ; Parameter number
    MOV   EDX, 0
    JMP   @@L2
@@L3:
    OR    EDX, 1
@@L2:
    CMP   ECX, EDI
    JNE   @@L5
    MOV   AL, BYTE PTR [ESI]
    MOV   BYTE PTR [EBX], AL
    INC   EBX
@@L5:
    INC   ESI
    JMP   @@L1
@@L4:
    MOV   BYTE PTR [EBX], 0
    RET
GETPAR ENDP
_TEXT ENDS
END START
```

To translate the program presented in Listing 19.1, issue the following commands for MASM32:

```
ML /c /coff /DMASM MEM.ASM
LINK /SUBSYSTEM:CONSOLE MEM.OBJ
```

Issue the following commands for TASM32:

```
TASM32 /ml MEM.ASM
TLINK32 -ap MEM.OBJ
```

Windows also provides a special group of functions for managing virtual memory. The main function of this group is the `VirtualAlloc` function that accepts the following parameters:

- First parameter — This parameter specifies the desired starting address to allocate or reserve. As a rule, it is assumed to be zero, which allows the system to determine, in which part of the address space to allocate the memory.
- Second parameter — This is the region size.
- Third parameter — This parameter can take the following values: `MEM_RESERVE` for reserving a block, `MEM_COMMIT` for reserving a block and passing physical memory to it, `MEM_PHYSICAL` for allocating physical memory, `MEM_RESET` for informing the system that the data in the block will not be needed, and `MEM_TOP_DOWN` for informing the system that the memory must be reserved at the highest possible addresses.
- Fourth parameter — This defines the protection level of the memory region. It can take the following values: `PAGE_READONLY`, `PAGE_READWRITE`, `PAGE_EXECUTE`, or any other constant defined in Windows documentation.

The function returns the virtual address of the allocated region of memory pages.

The main idea of this function is that you can reserve a memory block that is not mapped to the physical memory and then ensure that the entire block or part of it is mapped to the physical memory. After that, the memory block can be used. Note that the function will allocate a memory block that is a multiple of 64 KB with an address that also is a multiple of 64 KB.

Another function, `VirtualFree`, can free blocks allocated using the `VirtualAlloc` function. The fist parameter of this function is the block address. The second parameter is the size of the block to be freed. The third parameter can take one of the following two values: `MEM_DECOMMIT` or `MEM_RELEASE`. In the first case, the block or part of it ceases to be mapped. In the second case, the entire block ceases to be reserved and the second parameter must be zero; if it is not, the function fails.

Hooks

Now, it is time to consider a powerful tool most frequently used for debugging programs. This is the hooks (sometimes called traps) mechanism. The idea of this mechanism is that the programmer can trace the messages both within a single application and within the framework of the entire system by introducing filters. Filters are classified as global (in force within the entire system) or local (in force only within the framework of a single process). Working with filters, it is necessary to bear in mind that they can considerably slow down the operation of the entire system. This is especially true for global filters. From the programming point of view, this mechanism defines a function called by the system if a specific event occurs. It is also possible to describe messages that arrive to the filter function.

Consider some tools for working with filters. The main types of filter messages are as follows:

- `WH_CALLWNDPROC` — The filter is triggered when the `SendMessage` function is called.
- `WH_CALLWNDPROCRET` — The filter is triggered when the `SendMessage` function returns control.
- `WH_CBT` — The message arrives when something happens to the window.
- `WH_DEBUG` — This message is sent before a message is sent to some other filter.
- `WH_GETMESSAGE` — This filter is triggered when the `GetMessage` function receives some message from the queue.
- `WH_JOURNALRECORD` — This message arrives to the filter procedure when the system deletes a message from the queue.
- `WH_JOURNALPLAYBACK` — This message is sent after the arrival of the `WH_JOURNALRECORD` message.
- `WH_KEYBOARD` — This message arrives when keyboard events occur.
- `WH_MOUSE` — This is similar to the previous message but relates to mouse events.
- `WH_MSGFILTER` — This message arrives if user input events have occurred to a dialog box, menu, or scroll bar before these events were handled within this process.
- `WH_SHELL` — This filter is triggered when something happens to the Windows shell.
- `WH_SYSMSGFILTER` — This is similar to the `WH_MSGFILTER` message but relates to the entire system.

The filter is set using the `SetWindowsHookEx` function. Consider the parameters accepted by this function:

- First parameter — This is the filter type. It can take one of the previously listed values.

- Second parameter — This is the address of the filter procedure. If you specify a global filter, this procedure must be located in a DLL. The only exceptions are two types of filters: `WH_JOURNALRECORD` and `WH_JOURNALPLAYBACK`.
- Third parameter — This is the DLL handle, provided that the filter is intended for the entire system. The only exceptions are the two previously mentioned filter types.
- Fourth parameter — This is the thread identifier if you need to trace one of the threads. If the value of this parameter is zero, then a global filter intended for the entire system will be created. In general, the thread can relate to your process or to any other process running in the system.

The `SetWindowsHookEx` function returns the filter descriptor.

The filter function receives three parameters. The first parameter determines the type of event depending on the filter type. The next two parameters are the pointer to the hook procedure and the handle to the DLL containing that procedure. Because there are several types of events for every hook type, I won't list them here. They can be found in Microsoft's documentation.

After completing the operation, the hook must be closed using the `UnhookWindowsHookEx` function, whose only parameter is the handle to the hook that needs to be removed.

In general, a hook is only part of the chain of system calls. Therefore, the programmer must call the `CallNextHookEx` function from the hook procedure. That function will pass the required information along the chain. The first parameter of this function is the handle to the hook. The second, third, and fourth parameters correspond exactly to the three parameters passed to the hook procedure.

Listing 19.2 demonstrates an example of a simple hook that traps all events related to pressing the space bar within the entire system. Note that if the hook is global, the hook procedure must be placed into a DLL.

Listing 19.2. The global hook procedure

```
// The DIAL.RC file for the DLLE.ASM program
// Definitions of constants
#define WS_SYSMENU        0x00080000L
#define WS_MINIMIZEBOX    0x00020000L
#define WS_MAXIMIZEBOX    0x00010000L


// Dialog box definition
DIAL1 DIALOG 0, 0, 240, 120
STYLE WS_SYSMENU | WS_MINIMIZEBOX | WS_MAXIMIZEBOX
```

```
CAPTION "An example of program with a hook"
FONT 8, "Arial"
{
}

; The main module — DLLE.ASM,
; which sets a hook in a DLL
.586P
; Flat memory model
.MODEL FLAT, stdcall
; Constants
; This message arrives when the window is closed
WM_CLOSE        equ 10h
WM_INITDIALOG   equ 110h
WH_KEYBOARD     equ 2
; Message structure
MSGSTRUCT STRUC
        MSHWND      DD ?
        MSMESSAGE   DD ?
        MSWPARAM    DD ?
        MSLPARAM    DD ?
        MSTIME      DD ?
        MSPT        DD ?
MSGSTRUCT ENDS
; Prototypes of external procedures
IFDEF MASM
; MASM
        EXTERN      UnhookWindowsHookEx@4:NEAR
        EXTERN      SetWindowsHookExA@16:NEAR
        EXTERN      EndDialog@8:NEAR
        EXTERN      DialogBoxParamA@20:NEAR
        EXTERN      GetProcAddress@8:NEAR
        EXTERN      LoadLibraryA@4:NEAR
        EXTERN      FreeLibrary@4:NEAR
        EXTERN      ExitProcess@4:NEAR
        EXTERN      MessageBoxA@16:NEAR
; INCLUDELIB directives for the linker
        includelib c:\masm32\lib\user32.lib
        includelib c:\masm32\lib\kernel32.lib

ELSE
        EXTERN      UnhookWindowsHookEx:NEAR
        EXTERN      SetWindowsHookExA:NEAER
        EXTERN      EndDialog:NEAR
```

```
        EXTERN      DialogBoxParamA:NEAR
        EXTERN      GetProcAddress:NEAR
        EXTERN      LoadLibraryA:NEAR
        EXTERN      FreeLibrary:NEAR
        EXTERN      ExitProcess:NEAR
        EXTERN      MessageBoxA:NEAR
        UnhookWindowsHookEx@4 = UnhookWindowsHookEx
        SetWindowsHookExA@16 = SetWindowsHookExA
        EndDialog@8 = EndDialog
        DialogBoxParamA@20 = DialogBoxParamA
        GetProcAddress@8 = GetProcAddress
        LoadLibraryA@4 = LoadLibraryA
        FreeLibrary@4 = FreeLibrary
        ExitProcess@4 = ExitProcess
        MessageBoxA@16 = MessageBoxA
; INCLUDELIB directives for the linker
        includelib c:\tasm32\lib\import32.lib
ENDIF
;-----------------------------------------------
; Data segment
_DATA SEGMENT
        MSG       MSGSTRUCT <?>
        HINST     DD 0 ; Application descriptor
        PA        DB "DIAL1", 0
        LIBR      DB 'DLL2.DLL', 0
        HLIB      DD ?
        APROC     DD ?
        HH        DD ?
        ATOH      DD ?
IFDEF MASM
        NAMEPROC  DB '_HOOK@0', 0
        NAMEPROC1 DB '_TOH@0', 0
ELSE
        NAMEPROC1 DB '_TOH', 0
        NAMEPROC  DB 'HOOK', 0
ENDIF
_DATA ENDS
; Code segment
_TEXT SEGMENT
START:
; Load the DLL
        PUSH  OFFSET LIBR
        CALL  LoadLibraryA@4
```

```
        CMP   EAX, 0
        JE    _EXIT
        MOV   HLIB, EAX
; Get the address of the hook procedure
        PUSH  OFFSET NAMEPROC
        PUSH  HLIB
        CALL  GetProcAddress@8
        CMP   EAX, 0
        JE    _EXIT
        MOV   APROC, EAX
; Get the address of the auxiliary procedure
        PUSH  OFFSET NAMEPROC1
        PUSH  HLIB
        CALL  GetProcAddress@8
        CMP   EAX, 0
        JE    _EXIT
        MOV   ATOH, EAX
; Install the hook
        PUSH  0
        PUSH  HLIB
        PUSH  APROC
        PUSH  WH_KEYBOARD
        CALL  SetWindowsHookExA@16
        MOV   HH, EAX
; Store the hook and pass it to the library
        MOV   EAX, ATOH
        PUSH  HH
        CALL  ATOH
; Open the dialog
        PUSH  0
        PUSH  OFFSET WNDPROC
        PUSH  0
        PUSH  OFFSET PA
        PUSH  [HINST]
        CALL  DialogBoxParamA@20
; Remove the hook
        PUSH  HH
        CALL  UnhookWindowsHookEx@4
; Close the library
; The library will close automatically
; when exiting the program
        PUSH  OFFSET NAMEPROC
        PUSH  HLIB
```

```
        CALL  FreeLibrary@4
; Exit
_EXIT:
        PUSH  0
        CALL  ExitProcess@4
; Window procedure
; Position of parameters in the stack
; [BP+014H]  ; LPARAM
; [BP+10H]   ; WAPARAM
; [BP+0CH]   ; MES
; [BP+8]     ; HWND
WNDPROC   PROC
        PUSH  EBP
        MOV   EBP, ESP
        PUSH  EBX
        PUSH  ESI
        PUSH  EDI
;----------------
        CMP   DWORD PTR [EBP+0CH], WM_CLOSE
        JNE   L1
        PUSH  0
        PUSH  DWORD PTR [EBP+08H]
        CALL  EndDialog@8
        JMP   FINISH
L1:
        CMP   DWORD PTR [EBP+0CH], WM_INITDIALOG
        JNE   FINISH
FINISH:
        POP   EDI
        POP   ESI
        POP   EBX
        POP   EBP
        MOV   EAX, 0
        RET   16
WNDPROC    ENDP
_TEXT ENDS
END START

; The DLL2.ASM DLL
; containing the hook procedure
.586P
; Flat memory model
IFDEF MASM
```

```
   .MODEL FLAT, stdcall
ELSE
   .MODEL FLAT
ENDIF
PUBLIC HOOK, TOH
; Constants
; These messages arrive when
; the DLL is opened
DLL_PROCESS_DETACH    equ 0
DLL_PROCESS_ATTACH    equ 1
DLL_THREAD_ATTACH     equ 2
DLL_THREAD_DETACH     equ 3
IFDEF MASM
; MASM
; Prototypes of external procedures
        EXTERN      CallNextHookEx@16:NEAR
        EXTERN      MessageBoxA@16:NEAR
; INCLUDELIB directives for the linker
        includelib c:\masm32\lib\user32.lib
        includelib c:\masm32\lib\kernel32.lib
ELSE
; TASM
        EXTERN      CallNextHookEx:NEAR
        EXTERN      MessageBoxA:NEAR
        CallNextHookEx@16 = CallNextHookEx
        MessageBoxA@16 = MessageBoxA
        includelib c:\tasm32\lib\import32.lib
ENDIF
;-----------------------------------------------
; Data segment
_DATA SEGMENT
        HDL   DD ?
        HHOOK DD ?
        CAP   DB "Hook message", 0
        MES   DB "Blank key is pressed", 0
_DATA ENDS
; Code segment
_TEXT SEGMENT
; [EBP+10H]    ; Reserved parameter
; [EBP+0CH]    ; Cause of call
; [EBP+8]      ; DLL identifier
DLLENTRY:
        MOV   EAX, DWORD PTR [EBP+0CH]
```

```
        CMP   EAX, 0
        JNE   D1
; Close the library
        JMP   _EXIT
D1:
        CMP   EAX, 1
        JNE   _EXIT
; Open the library
; Store the DLL identifier
        MOV   EDX, DWORD PTR [EBP+08H]
        MOV   HDL, EDX
_EXIT:
        MOV   EAX, 1
        RET   12
;--------------------
TOH PROC EXPORT
        PUSH  EBP
        MOV   EBP, ESP
        MOV   EAX, DWORD PTR [EBP+08H]
        MOV   HHOOK, EAX
        POP   EBP
        RET
TOH ENDP
; Hook procedure
HOOK PROC EXPORT
        PUSH  EBP
        MOV   EBP, ESP
; Send the message along the chain
        PUSH  DWORD PTR [EBP+010H]
        PUSH  DWORD PTR [EBP+0CH]
        PUSH  DWORD PTR [EBP+08H]
        PUSH  HHOOK
        CALL  CallNextHookEx@16
; Check whether the space bar has been pressed
        CMP   DWORD PTR [EBP+0CH], 32
        JNE   _EX
; If yes, then display the message
        PUSH  0          ; MB_OK
        PUSH  OFFSET CAP
        PUSH  OFFSET MES
        PUSH  0 ; In the window
        CALL  MessageBoxA@16
_EX:
```

```
        POP   EBP
        RET
HOOK ENDP
_TEXT ENDS
END DLLENTRY
```

To translate the program in Listing 19.2, issue the following commands for MASM32:

- DLL

```
ml /c /coff /DMASM dll2.asm
link /subsystem:windows /DLL dll2.obj
```

- Main program

```
ml /c /coff /DMASM dllex.asm
rc dial.rc
link /subsystem:windows dllex.obj dial.res
```

Issue the following commands for TASM32:

- DLL

```
TASM32 /ml dll2.asm
Tlink32 /subsystem:windows -aa -Tpd dll2.obj
```

- Main program

```
TASM32 /ml dllex.asm
Brcc32 dial.rc
Tlink32 -aa dllex.obj,,,,,dial.res
```

When considering the program presented in Listing 19.2, note the role of the `TOH` procedure. Also note that the second and the third parameters of the hook procedure exactly correspond the values of similar parameters of the `WM_KEYDOWN` message. By the way, I hope that you understand why two messages are sent when the space bar is pressed — one for pressing the button and one for releasing it.

Chapter 20

Using Assembly Language with High-Level Languages

This chapter concentrates on various aspects of using Assembly language with high-level programming languages. Unfortunately, many contemporary programmers neglect the study of Assembly language or do not know how to use it with high-level languages. Thus, they miss a powerful and flexible programming tool. I would say that every professional programmer, regardless of the chosen programming language, has to master the Assembly language as a second tool. This is similar to a common opinion held by linguists, who say that everyone who chooses to become a professional linguist must master Latin before studying other European languages. Furthermore, the study of Assembly language will bring you joy, so do not miss this opportunity. After all, experiencing the joy of cognizance is a main goal of life. In general, the mating of Assembly language with high-level languages is based on the following foundations: name coordination, parameter coordination, and call coordination. First, it is necessary to consider call coordination.

Call Coordination

In MS-DOS, the called procedure could reside in the same segment as the calling command (in which case the call was classified as NEAR) or in another segment (in which case the call was classified as FAR). The difference between NEAR and FAR calls was that in the first case the call address was formed on the basis of 2 bytes and in the latter case 4 bytes were required. Accordingly, the return from the procedure could be near (RETN), in which case the return address was formed on the basis of 2 bytes popped from the stack, or far (RETF), in which case 4 bytes had to be popped from the stack. Obviously, both the call and the return had to be coordinated. Within the framework of a single program, this usually didn't cause significant difficulties. However, problems could arise when it was necessary to link some external libraries or object modules. If the return into the object module was carried out by RETN, the programmer had to link object modules to join the segment, in which the called procedure resided with segments, from which the call originated. Naturally, the call in this case had to be NEAR. If the return from the procedure was carried out by the RETF, then this procedure must be called by the FAR call. At the same time, the call and the procedure in the course of linking had to fall into different segments. The problem of call coordination was further aggravated because errors were detected at run time, not at the linking time. So-called memory models in the C programming language also resulted from this, and they caused serious headaches for many beginner programmers. By the way, if you look at C libraries for DOS, you'll discover that there was a special library for each memory model. Segmented memory models lead C programmers to another problem — the pointer problem (this, however, is another story). The developers of Turbo Pascal chose another way: They understood that the program should include one data segment and several code segments. When the data couldn't fit within a single segment, the programmer could use the dynamic memory. With the migration to Windows, programmers were given a wonderful gift — the flat memory model. According to this model, all calls are NEAR, which means that they take place within a single vast segment. This eliminates the need to coordinate calls, so I won't return to this problem.

Name Coordination

Coordination of calls, as you have seen, has been removed from the agenda. Name coordination, on the contrary, became more complicated with time. Some of the aspects of this problem are already known to you. The MASM translator adds the @N suffix to names; N is the number of parameters passed to the stack. The Visual C++ compiler does the same thing. Thus, problems arise when it becomes necessary to coordinate two modules written in Assembly language. TASM is a more flexible compiler in this respect, because the @N suffix can be added to any name as needed.

Another problem is the leading underscore character. MASM generates the underscore automatically if the standard call (stdcall) calling convention is specified in the beginning of the program. TASM doesn't do this; consequently, if necessary, this should be done manually, which in my opinion is an advantage. An interesting point is that Borland and Microsoft take different positions in this respect.

Another problem is the coordination of uppercase and lowercase letters. Recall that when assembling a program using TASM, the /ml command-line option is used to distinguish uppercase and lowercase letters. MASM, on the other hand, does this automatically. As you know, the standard for the C programming language initially assumed a difference between uppercase and lowercase characters. Pascal, on the other hand, is not case-sensitive. There is certain logic, because Turbo Pascal and Delphi do not create standard object modules but can link them. When creating dynamic link libraries (DLLs), the names are placed there as they were specified in procedure headers.

Finally, there is the last problem related to the coordination of names — C++ qualifiers. C++ allows so-called overloading. This means that the same name can relate to different functions. In a program, these functions differ in the number of parameters, their types, and the type of the return value. Therefore, the C++ compiler automatically complements the names so that different functions are distinguished when linking. Naturally, Borland and Microsoft add different suffixes to the function names. As usual, they never care to coordinate their positions. However, this problem isn't difficult to overcome. It is only necessary to use the EXTERN modifier for the names expected to be accessed from other C modules. This technique is illustrated in the examples provided later in this chapter.

Parameter Coordination

Table 20.1 lists the main conventions on passing parameters to the procedure. Notice that in all Assembly programs presented in this book, the stdcall type for passing parameters was specified. However, this convention isn't used practically because parameters are passed and retrieved explicitly without the translator's help. When dealing with high-level languages, this must be taken into account. Therefore, the programmer must know how calling conventions work.

Table 20.1. Calling conventions

Convention	Parameter	Clearing the stack	Register
Pascal (the convention adopted in Pascal)	From left to right	Procedure	None.

continues

Table 20.1 *Continued*

Convention	Parameter	Clearing the stack	Register
`Register` (register or fast calling convention)	From left to right	Procedure	Three registers are employed (`EAX`, `EDX`, and `ECX`); if these registers are not sufficient for passing all parameters, then the remaining parameters are passed through the stack.
`Cdecl` (C convention)	From right to left	Calling program	None.
`Stdcall` (standard call)	From right to left	Procedure	None.

This table clearly explains the conventions on calling functions and on passing parameters, so it doesn't need additional clarification.

I'd like to draw your attention to another important aspect — namely, the types of return values. In Assembly language, everything is simple: The value returned in the `EAX` register can be either a number or a pointer to some variable or structure. If the return value has the `WORD` data type, it is passed in the least significant word of the `EAX` register. However, if you are dealing with the C programming language, you should pay attention to the problem of type casting. Type casting can be considered an art or a science, but unfortunately, in this book I can't pay it the attention that it deserves.

A Simple Example of Using Assembly Language with High-Level Languages

In this section, I present a simple module written in Assembly language. This module contains a procedure that copies one string to another string. This module will be linked to different programs, written in the C and Pascal languages, using the following three translators: Borland C++ 5.02, Visual C++ 7.0, and Delphi 7.0.

Borland C++ 5.0

The function that the program calls from the Assembly module is declared using the `extern "C"` and `stdcall` modifiers. Because the module written in Assembly language is translated using TASM, the problem with the underscore character won't arise. The `stdcall` calling type assumes that the stack is cleared in the called procedure. In the Assembly module, the called procedure must be declared using the `PUBLIC` directive.

Listing 20.1. Using a procedure from an external module (built using Borland C++ 5.0)

```
// The COPYC.CPP file
#include <windows.h>
#include <stdio.h>
extern "C" __stdcall COPYSTR(char *, char *);
void main()
{
        char s1[100];
        char *s2="Hello!";
        printf("%s\n", (char *)COPYSTR(s1, s2));
        ExitProcess(0);
}


; The COPY.ASM file
.586P
; This procedure will be called from the external module
PUBLIC COPYSTR
; Flat memory model
.MODEL FLAT, stdcall
_TEXT SEGMENT
; The procedure for copying strings
; Target string [EBP+08H]
; Source string [EBP+0CH]
; Do not account for the target string length
COPYSTR PROC
        PUSH  EBP
        MOV   EBP, ESP
        MOV   ESI, DWORD PTR [EBP+0CH]
        MOV   EDI, DWORD PTR [EBP+08H]
L1:
        MOV   AL, BYTE PTR [ESI]
        MOV   BYTE PTR [EDI], AL
        CMP   AL, 0
        JE    L2
        INC   ESI
        INC   EDI
        JMP   L1
L2:
        MOV   EAX, DWORD PTR [EBP+08H]
```

```
        POP  EBP
        RET  8
COPYSTR ENDP
_TEXT ENDS
END
```

The modules in Listing 20.1 can be translated using one of the following methods:

- First method — Issue the `TASM32 /ml copy.asm` command, then include the COPY.OBJ file into the Borland C++ project.
- Second method — Include the COPY.ASM file into the Borland C++ project; then, the compiler will automatically call the TASM32.EXE translator.
- Third method — Translate all modules from the command line. The batch file named COPY must be prepared beforehand. The contents of this file appear as follows:

  ```
  copyc.cpp
  copy.obj
  ```

  To complete the task, call `bcc32 @copy`.

- Fourth method — In the batch file, include the COPY.ASM file instead of COPY.OBJ.

Visual C++ 7.0

The C++ code didn't change, in contrast to the source code written in Assembly language. The C translator will automatically add the `@8` suffix to the end of the line. In this case, you'll have to abandon customary practice and rely on the MASM translator. To achieve this, you'll have to explicitly specify the parameters in the procedure declaration. After you do this, the translator will carry out part of your job (namely, pass the parameters). In addition, it complements the `COPYSTR` name with the `@8` suffix. I'd like to point out again that when using such a manner of declaration it isn't necessary to explicitly set the `EBP` register and release the stack. The translator will do this automatically.

Listing 20.2. A module written in Assembly language for compiling and linking using Visual C++ 7.0

```
; The PROC.ASM file
.586P
.MODEL FLAT, stdcall
PUBLIC COPYSTR
```

```
; Flat memory model
_TEXT SEGMENT
; Procedure for copying the source string to the target string
; Target string [EBP+08H]
; Source string [EBP+0CH]
; Don't take into account the target string length
; Explicitly specify the parameters
COPYSTR PROC  str1: DWORD, str2: DWORD
        MOV   ESI, str2 ; DWORD PTR [EBP+0CH]
        MOV   EDI, str1 ; DWORD PTR [EBP+08H]
L1:
        MOV   AL, BYTE PTR [ESI]
        MOV   BYTE PTR [EDI], AL
        CMP   AL, 0
        JE    L2
        INC   ESI
        INC   EDI
        JMP   L1
L2:
        MOV   EAX, DWORD PTR [EBP+08H]
RET
COPYSTR ENDP
_TEXT ENDS
END
```

Explicit specification of parameters in the procedure header produces the following results:

- The `@8` suffix is automatically added to the procedure name in the object module (instead of the `@0` suffix).
- The assembler automatically controls the stack.

To translate, take the following steps:

1. Include in the Visual C++ project the object module compiled with ML.EXE.
2. If you want to include the source code, written in Assembly language, into your project, you'll have to specify the translation method for it. To achieve this, specify the ML.EXE command line.

Delphi 7.0

The Delphi translator introduces some minor nuances into the problem. For the code segment, you must choose the name CODE. Because Pascal interprets strings differently than C language does, I had to take an array of symbols instead one of strings. The `writeln` operator, however, is intelligent enough. It has interpreted everything correctly without additional efforts on my part. Note that in this case I used the `stdcall` directive.

Listing 20.3. Using an object module with a Delphi program

```
{The COPYD.PAS program that uses an assembler by linking an object module}
program Project2;
uses
        SysUtils;
{$APPTYPE CONSOLE}
{$L 'copy.OBJ'}
procedure COPYSTR(s1, s2:PChar); stdcall; EXTERNAL;
var
        s1,s2:array[1..30] of char;
begin
        s2[1] := 'H';
        s2[2] := 'e';
        s2[3] := 'l';
        s2[4] := 'l';
        s2[5] := 'o';
        s2[6] := '!';
        s2[7] := char(0);
        COPYSTR(addr(s1[1]), addr(s2[1]));
        writeln(s1);
end.

; The COPY.ASM file
.586P
.MODEL FLAT, stdcall
PUBLIC COPYSTR
; Flat memory model
CODE SEGMENT
; The procedure for copying the source string to the target string
; Target string [EBP+08H]
```

```
; Source string [EBP+0CH]
; Don't account for the target string length
COPYSTR PROC
        PUSH  EBP
        MOV   EBP, ESP
        MOV   ESI, DWORD PTR [EBP+0CH]
        MOV   EDI, DWORD PTR [EBP+08H]
L1:
        MOV   AL, BYTE PTR [ESI]
        MOV   BYTE PTR [EDI], AL
        CMP   AL, 0
        JE    L2
        INC   ESI
        INC   EDI
        JMP   L1
L2:
        MOV   EAX, DWORD PTR [EBP+08H]
        POP   EBP
        RET   8
COPYSTR ENDP
CODE ENDS
END
```

To translate this program, prepare an object module (using TASM32) and specify it in the `{$L COPY.OBJ}` directive. After that, the Delphi translator will do everything automatically.

Passing Parameters through Registers

This section concentrates on another type of call — the fast call, or the register call. According to Table 20.1, this type of call assumes that the first three parameters will be passed in registers (`EAX`, `EDX`, and `ECX`) and that the remaining parameters will be passed through the stack, as was in case with the `stdcall` calling convention. At the same time, if the stack was used, the responsibility for releasing it is delegated to the called procedure. This approach has another nuance. If the fast calling convention is used, the C translator adds the `@` prefix to the names, which must be taken into account in the module written in Assembly language.

Listing 20.4. Using the fast calling convention when calling a procedure

```
// The ADDC.CPP file
#include <windows.h>
#include <stdio.h>
// Declare the external function for adding four integers
extern "C" __fastcall ADDD(DWORD, DWORD, DWORD, DWORD);
void main()
{
 DWORD a, b, c, d;
 a=1; b=2; c=3; d=4;
 printf("%lu\n", (DWORD *)ADDD(a, b, c, d));
 ExitProcess(0);
}

; The ADD.ASM file
.586P
.MODEL FLAT, stdcall
PUBLIC @ADDD
; Flat memory model
_TEXT SEGMENT
; This procedure returns the sum of four parameters
; Parameters are passed through the registers
; The first three parameters are passed in the EAX, EDX, and ECX registers
; The fourth parameter is passed through the stack (e.g., [EPB+08H])
@ADDD PROC
        PUSH  EBP
        MOV   EBP, ESP
        ADD   EAX, ECX
        ADD   EAX, EDX
        ADD   EAX, DWORD PTR [EBP+08H]
        POP   EBP
        RET   4
@ADDD ENDP
_TEXT ENDS
END
```

To translate the modules presented in Listing 20.4, issue the following command:

```
tasm32 /ml add.asm
```

Then, include the ADD.OBJ file in the ADDC project (Borland C++ 5.0)

Application Programming Interface Calls and Resources in Assembly Modules

In this section, I demonstrate that the called procedure written in Assembly language can contain not only auxiliary procedures but also calls to application programming interface (API) functions. Furthermore, it can work with resources. Note that these resources are common for all modules of the project. It is possible to have several resource files. The only thing that you'll have to do is ensuring that the names and the identifiers match.

Listing 20.5. The console application written in C++ calls the graphic user interface-mode procedure (Listing 20.6) defined in an Assembly module

```
#include <windows.h>
#include <stdio.h>
// Declare the external function
extern "C" __stdcall DIAL1();
void main()
{
 DIAL1();
 ExitProcess(0);
}
```

Listing 20.6. Using resources and application program interface calls in the Assembly module

```
// The DIALFORC.RC file
// Definitions of constants
#define WS_SYSMENU      0x00080000L
// Window elements must be initially visible
#define WS_VISIBLE      0x10000000L
// Border around the elements
#define WS_BORDER       0x00800000L
// Elements can be sequentially activated
// by pressing the <Tab> key
#define WS_TABSTOP      0x00010000L
// Text in the edit field is
// aligned to the left side
#define ES_LEFT         0x0000L
// Style of all window elements
#define WS_CHILD        0x40000000L
```

```
// Keyboard input is disabled
#define ES_READONLY    0x0800L

#define DS_3DLOOK     0x0004L
// Dialog box definition
DIAL1 DIALOG 0, 0, 240, 100
STYLE WS_SYSMENU | DS_3DLOOK
CAPTION "An example dialog box with date and time"
FONT 8, "Arial"
{
 CONTROL "", 1, "edit", ES_LEFT | WS_CHILD
 | WS_VISIBLE | WS_BORDER
 | WS_TABSTOP | ES_READONLY, 100, 5, 130, 12
}
```

```
; The DIALFORC.INC file
; Constants
; This message arrives when the window is closed
WM_CLOSE        equ 10h
; This message arrives when the window is created
WM_INITDIALOG   equ 110h
; This message arrives when some event occurs to the window element
WM_COMMAND      equ 111h
; Message from the timer
WM_TIMER        equ 113h
; The message for sending some text to the window element
WM_SETTEXT      equ 0Ch
; Prototypes of external procedures
EXTERN      SendDlgItemMessageA:NEAR
EXTERN      _wsprintfA:NEAR
EXTERN      GetLocalTime:NEAR
EXTERN      ExitProcess:NEAR
EXTERN      GetModuleHandleA:NEAR
EXTERN      DialogBoxParamA:NEAR
EXTERN      EndDialog:NEAR
EXTERN      SetTimer:NEAR
EXTERN      KillTimer:NEAR
; Structures
; Message structure
MSGSTRUCT STRUC
        MSHWND      DD ?
        MSMESSAGE   DD ?
```

```
        MSWPARAM    DD ?
        MSLPARAM    DD ?
        MSTIME      DD ?
        MSPT        DD ?
MSGSTRUCT ENDS
; Date-time data structure
DAT STRUC
        year    DW ?
        month   DW ?
        dayweek DW ?
        day     DW ?
        hour    DW ?
        min     DW ?
        sec     DW ?
        msec    DW ?
DAT ENDS


; The DIALFORC.ASM file
.586P
; Flat memory model
.MODEL FLAT, stdcall
include dialforc.inc
PUBLIC DIAL1
;------------------------------------------------
; Data segment
_DATA SEGMENT
        MSG      MSGSTRUCT <?>
        HINST    DD 0 ; Application descriptor
        PA       DB "DIAL1", 0
        TIM      DB "Date %u/%u/%u   Time %u:%u:%u", 0
        STRCOPY  DB 50 DUP (?)
        DATA     DAT <0>
_DATA ENDS
; Code segment
_TEXT SEGMENT
DIAL1 PROC
        PUSH  EBP
        MOV   EBP, ESP
; Get the application descriptor
        PUSH  0
        CALL  GetModuleHandleA
        MOV   [HINST],  EAX
```

```
; Create a dialog
        PUSH  0
        PUSH  OFFSET WNDPROC
        PUSH  0
        PUSH  OFFSET PA
        PUSH  [HINST]
        CALL  DialogBoxParamA
        CMP   EAX, -1
;-----------------------------------
        POP  EBP
        RET
DIAL1 ENDP
;-----------------------------------
; Window procedure
; Position of parameters in the stack
; [BP+014H]   ; LPARAM
; [BP+10H]    ; WAPARAM
; [BP+0CH]    ; MES
; [BP+8]      ; HWND
WNDPROC        PROC
        PUSH  EBP
        MOV   EBP, ESP
        PUSH  EBX
        PUSH  ESI
        PUSH  EDI
;----------------
        CMP   DWORD PTR [EBP+0CH], WM_CLOSE
        JNE   L1
; Reaction to closing a window
; Delete timer 1
        PUSH  1 ; Timer identifier
        PUSH  DWORD PTR [EBP+08H]
        CALL  KillTimer
; Delete timer 2
        PUSH  2 ; Timer identifier
        PUSH  DWORD PTR [EBP+08H]
        CALL  KillTimer
; Close the dialog
        PUSH  0
        PUSH  DWORD PTR [EBP+08H]
        CALL  EndDialog
        JMP   FINISH
```

```
L1:
        CMP   DWORD PTR [EBP+0CH], WM_INITDIALOG
        JNE   L2
; Startup initialization
; Set timer 1
        PUSH  0    ; Parameter = NULL
        PUSH  1000 ; 1-second interval
        PUSH  1    ; Timer identifier
        PUSH  DWORD PTR [EBP+08H]
        CALL  SetTimer
; Set timer 2
        PUSH  OFFSET TIMPROC ; Parameter = NULL
        PUSH  500            ; 0.5-second interval
        PUSH  2              ; Timer identifier
        PUSH  DWORD PTR [EBP+08H]
        CALL  SetTimer
        JMP   FINISH
L2:
        CMP   DWORD PTR [EBP+0CH], WM_TIMER
        JNE   FINISH
; Send the string to the window
        PUSH  OFFSET STRCOPY
        PUSH  0
        PUSH  WM_SETTEXT
        PUSH  1 ; Element identifier
        PUSH  DWORD PTR [EBP+08H]
        CALL  SendDlgItemMessageA
FINISH:
        POP   EDI
        POP   ESI
        POP   EBX
        POP   EBP
        MOV   EAX, 0
        RET   16
WNDPROC    ENDP
;------------------------------------------
; Timer procedure
; Position of parameters in the stack
; [BP+014H] ; LPARAM - Time elapsed since Windows startup
; [BP+10H]  ; WAPARAM - Timer identifier
; [BP+0CH]  ; WM_TIMER
; [BP+8]    ; HWND
```

```
TIMPROC     PROC
        PUSH  EBP
        MOV   EBP, ESP
; Get the local time
        PUSH  OFFSET DATA
        CALL  GetLocalTime
; Get the string for date and time output
        MOVZX EAX, DATA.sec
        PUSH  EAX
        MOVZX EAX, DATA.min
        PUSH  EAX
        MOVZX EAX, DATA.hour
        PUSH  EAX
        MOVZX EAX, DATA.year
        PUSH  EAX
        MOVZX EAX, DATA.month
        PUSH  EAX
        MOVZX EAX, DATA.day
        PUSH  EAX
        PUSH  OFFSET TIM
        PUSH  OFFSET STRCOPY
        CALL  _wsprintfA
; Restore the stack
        ADD   ESP, 32
        POP   EBP
        RET   16
TIMPROC    ENDP
_TEXT ENDS
END
```

To translate this program, proceed as follows:

- First method — Issue the following commands:

  ```
  tasm32 /ml dialforc.asm
  brcc32 dialforc.rc
  ```

  Then, include the DIALFORC.OBJ and DIALFORC.RES files in the project.

- Second method — This method differs from the previous one in that the DIALFORC.RC file is included in the project instead of the DIALFORC.RES file. Naturally, it is necessary to remove definitions of constants from that file because all required definitions are in the C header files.

Combined Using C and Assembly Code

Here, I present an example of the simplest calculator. For Assembly language, it might be difficult to find libraries with specific procedures. Naturally, you can write everything on your own, but this approach isn't suitable when you are short of time. The method suggested here is simple. The program written in C language (or any other high-level language) is a skeleton. It calls the Assembly procedure, which carries out the main operations. In addition, you can include in the C module those procedures that are easier to write in C language. These procedures will be called from the Assembly code. The example provided in this section illustrates this approach. The C module includes procedures that convert strings into real numbers, carry out requested operations over them, and then convert the result back into a string.

Listing 20.7. A C module for the simplest calculator, which will be combined with the Assembly code in Listing 20.8

```
// CALCC.CPP
#include <windows.h>
#include <stdio.h>

// Call the Assembly procedure
extern "C" __stdcall MAIN1();
// Add
extern "C" __stdcall void sum(char *, char *, char *);
// Subtract
extern "C" __stdcall void su(char *, char *, char *);
// Multiply
extern "C" __stdcall void mu(char *, char *, char *);
// Divide
extern "C" __stdcall void dii(char *, char *, char *);



int WINAPI WinMain (HINSTANCE hThisInst, HINSTANCE hPrevInst,
                    LPSTR lpszArgs, int nWinMode)
{
       MAIN1();
       return 0;
}
extern "C" __stdcall void sum(char * s1, char * s2, char * s)
{
       float f1, f2, f;
```

```
        f1 = atof(s1); f2 = atof(s2);
        f = f1 + f2;
        sprintf(s, "%f", f);
        strcat(s, " +");
        return;
}
extern "C" __stdcall void su(char * s1, char * s2, char * s)
{
        float f1, f2, f;
        f1 = atof(s1); f2 = atof(s2);
        f = f1 - f2;
        sprintf(s, "%f", f);
        strcat(s, " -");
        return;
}
extern "C" __stdcall void mu(char * s1, char * s2, char * s)
{
        float f1, f2, f;
        f1 = atof(s1); f2 = atof(s2);
        f = f1*f2;
        sprintf(s, "%f", f);
        strcat(s, " *");
        return;
}
extern "C" __stdcall void dii(char * s1, char * s2, char * s)
{
        float f1, f2, f;
        f1 = atof(s1); f2 = atof(s2);
        if(f2!=0)
         {
                f = f1/f2;
                sprintf(s, "%f", f);
                strcat(s, " /");
        } else strcpy(s, "Division error");
        return;
}
```

Listing 20.8. Assembly module that must be combined with the C program from Listing 20.7

```
// CALC.RC
// Definitions of constants
// Window styles
```

```
#define WS_SYSMENU          0x00080000L
#define WS_MINIMIZEBOX      0x00020000L
#define DS_3DLOOK           0x0004L
#define ES_LEFT             0x0000L
#define WS_CHILD            0x40000000L
#define WS_VISIBLE          0x10000000L
#define WS_BORDER           0x00800000L
#define WS_TABSTOP          0x00010000L
#define SS_LEFT             0x00000000L
#define BS_PUSHBUTTON       0x00000000L
#define BS_CENTER           0x00000300L
#define DS_LOCALEDIT        0x20L
#define ES_READONLY         0x0800L


// Button identifiers
#define IDC_BUTTON1           101
#define IDC_BUTTON2           102
#define IDC_BUTTON3           103
#define IDC_BUTTON4           104
DIAL1 DIALOG 0, 0, 170, 110
STYLE WS_OVERLAPPED | WS_CAPTION | WS_SYSMENU | WS_MINIMIZEBOX
| DS_3DLOOK
CAPTION "An example of a simple calculator"
FONT 8, "Arial"
{
 CONTROL "", 1, "edit", ES_LEFT | WS_CHILD | WS_VISIBLE
 | WS_BORDER | WS_TABSTOP, 9, 8, 128, 12
 CONTROL "", 2, "edit", ES_LEFT | WS_CHILD | WS_VISIBLE
 | WS_BORDER | WS_TABSTOP, 9, 27, 128, 12
 CONTROL "", 3, "edit", ES_LEFT | WS_CHILD | ES_READONLY
 | WS_VISIBLE | WS_BORDER | WS_TABSTOP, 9, 76, 127, 12
 CONTROL "+", IDC_BUTTON1, "button", BS_PUSHBUTTON
 | BS_CENTER | WS_CHILD | WS_VISIBLE | WS_TABSTOP, 11,
 48, 15, 14
 CONTROL "-", IDC_BUTTON2, "button", BS_PUSHBUTTON
 | BS_CENTER | WS_CHILD | WS_VISIBLE | WS_TABSTOP, 34,
 48, 15, 14
 CONTROL "*", IDC_BUTTON3, "button", BS_PUSHBUTTON
 | BS_CENTER | WS_CHILD | WS_VISIBLE | WS_TABSTOP, 56,
 48, 15, 14
 CONTROL "/", IDC_BUTTON4, "button", BS_PUSHBUTTON
 | BS_CENTER | WS_CHILD | WS_VISIBLE | WS_TABSTOP, 80,
```

```
 48, 15, 14
 }

; CALC.INC
; Constants
; This message arrives when the window is closed
WM_CLOSE        equ 10h
WM_INITDIALOG   equ 110h
WM_COMMAND      equ 111h
WM_GETTEXT      equ 0Dh
WM_SETTEXT      equ 0Ch

; Prototypes of external procedures
EXTERN      ExitProcess:NEAR
EXTERN      GetModuleHandleA:NEAR
EXTERN      DialogBoxParamA:NEAR
EXTERN      EndDialog:NEAR
EXTERN      SendDlgItemMessageA:NEAR
; Structures
; Message structure
MSGSTRUCT STRUC
        MSHWND          DWORD ?
        MSMESSAGE       DWORD ?
        MSWPARAM        DWORD ?
        MSLPARAM        DWORD ?
        MSTIME          DWORD ?
        MSPT            DWORD ?
MSGSTRUCT ENDS

; The CALC.ASM module
.586P
; Flat memory model
.MODEL FLAT, stdcall
include calc.inc
EXTERN sum:NEAR
EXTERN su:NEAR
EXTERN mu:NEAR
EXTERN dii:NEAR
PUBLIC MAIN1
; INCLUDELIB directives for the linker
includelib c:\tasm32\lib\import32.lib
;-----------------------------------------------
; Data segment
```

```
_DATA SEGMENT
        MSG MSGSTRUCT <?>
        HINST DD 0     ; Application descriptor
        PA    DB "DIAL1", 0
        S1    DB 50 DUP(0)
        S2    DB 50 DUP(0)
        S     DB 50 DUP(0)
_DATA ENDS
; Code segment
_TEXT SEGMENT
; The procedure called from the C module
MAIN1 PROC
; Get the application descriptor
        PUSH  0
        CALL  GetModuleHandleA
        MOV  [HINST], EAX
;--------------------------------
        PUSH  0
        PUSH  OFFSET WNDPROC
        PUSH  0
        PUSH  OFFSET PA
        PUSH  [HINST]
        CALL  DialogBoxParamA
;--------------------------------
        RET
MAIN1 ENDP
; Window procedure
; Position of parameters in the stack
; [EBP+014H]  ; LPARAM
; [EBP+10H]   ; WAPARAM
; [EBP+0CH]   ; MES
; [EBP+8]     ; HWND
WNDPROC PROC
        PUSH  EBP
        MOV   EBP, ESP
;--------------------------------
        CMP   DWORD PTR [EBP+0CH], WM_CLOSE
        JNE   L1
        PUSH  0
        PUSH  DWORD PTR [EBP+08H]
        CALL  EndDialog
        MOV   EAX, 1
        JMP   FINISH
```

```
L1:
        CMP   DWORD PTR [EBP+0CH], WM_INITDIALOG
        JNE   L2
; Fill the edit fields if necessary

JMP FINISH
L2:
        CMP   DWORD PTR [EBP+0CH], WM_COMMAND
        JNE   FINISH
        CMP   WORD PTR [EBP+10H], 101
        JNE   NO_SUM
; First addend
        PUSH  OFFSET S1
        PUSH  50
        PUSH  WM_GETTEXT
        PUSH  1
        PUSH  DWORD PTR [EBP+08H]
        CALL  SendDlgItemMessageA
; Second addend
        PUSH  OFFSET S2
        PUSH  50
        PUSH  WM_GETTEXT
        PUSH  2
        PUSH  DWORD PTR [EBP+08H]
        CALL  SendDlgItemMessageA
; Sum
        PUSH  OFFSET S
        PUSH  OFFSET S2
        PUSH  OFFSET S1
        CALL  sum
; Output the sum
        PUSH  OFFSET S
        PUSH  50
        PUSH  WM_SETTEXT
        PUSH  3
        PUSH  DWORD PTR [EBP+08H]
        CALL  SendDlgItemMessageA
        JMP   FINISH
NO_SUM:
        CMP   WORD PTR [EBP+10H], 102
        JNE   NO_SUB
; Minuend
        PUSH  OFFSET S1
```

```
        PUSH  50
        PUSH  WM_GETTEXT
        PUSH  1
        PUSH  DWORD PTR [EBP+08H]
        CALL  SendDlgItemMessageA
; Subtrahend
        PUSH  OFFSET S2
        PUSH  50
        PUSH  WM_GETTEXT
        PUSH  2
        PUSH  DWORD PTR [EBP+08H]
        CALL  SendDlgItemMessageA
; Difference
        PUSH  OFFSET S
        PUSH  OFFSET S2
        PUSH  OFFSET S1
        CALL  su
; Compute the difference
        PUSH  OFFSET S
        PUSH  50
        PUSH  WM_SETTEXT
        PUSH  3
        PUSH  DWORD PTR [EBP+08H]
        CALL  SendDlgItemMessageA
        JMP   FINISH
NO_SUB:
        CMP   WORD PTR [EBP+10H], 103
        JNE   NO_MULT
; First multiplier
        PUSH  OFFSET S1
        PUSH  50
        PUSH  WM_GETTEXT
        PUSH  1
        PUSH  DWORD PTR [EBP+08H]
        CALL  SendDlgItemMessageA
; Second multiplier
        PUSH  OFFSET S2
        PUSH  50
        PUSH  WM_GETTEXT
        PUSH  2
        PUSH  DWORD PTR [EBP+08H]
        CALL  SendDlgItemMessageA
```

```
; Product
        PUSH  OFFSET S
        PUSH  OFFSET S2
        PUSH  OFFSET S1
        CALL  mu
; Output the product
        PUSH  OFFSET S
        PUSH  50
        PUSH  WM_SETTEXT
        PUSH  3
        PUSH  DWORD PTR [EBP+08H]
        CALL SendDlgItemMessageA
        JMP   FINISH
NO_MULT:
        CMP   WORD PTR [EBP+10H], 104
        JNE   FINISH
; Dividend
        PUSH  OFFSET S1
        PUSH  50
        PUSH  WM_GETTEXT
        PUSH  1
        PUSH  DWORD PTR [EBP+08H]
        CALL  SendDlgItemMessageA
; Divisor
        PUSH  OFFSET S2
        PUSH  50
        PUSH  WM_GETTEXT
        PUSH  2
        PUSH  DWORD PTR [EBP+08H]
        CALL  SendDlgItemMessageA
; Division
        PUSH  OFFSET S
        PUSH  OFFSET S2
        PUSH  OFFSET S1
        CALL  dii
; Output the division result
        PUSH  OFFSET S
        PUSH  50
        PUSH  WM_SETTEXT
        PUSH  3
        PUSH  DWORD PTR [EBP+08H]
        CALL  SendDlgItemMessageA
```

```
        JNE    FINISH
FINISH:
        MOV    EAX, 0
        POP    EBP
        RET    16
WNDPROC ENDP
_TEXT ENDS
END
```

To translate this program, issue the following commands:

```
tasm32 /ml calc.asm
brcc32 calc.rc
```

Then, add the CALC.OBJ and CALC.RES files to the CALCC.CPP project (Listing 20.8).

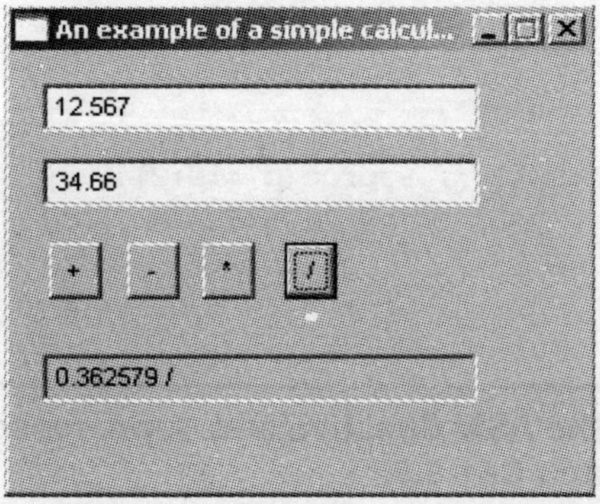

Fig. 20.1. The calculator program (Listings 20.7 and 20.8)

The Inline Assembler

Now, it is time to describe the inline assembler. This is a powerful tool. You should only bear in mind that contemporary inline assemblers often provide limited capabilities in relation to support of new microprocessor commands. This is natural, because the development of a new version of developer tools, such as C++ Builder, requires considerably more time than the development of TASM. In the examples provided in Listings 20.9 and 20.10, coprocessor commands are used.

Listing 20.9. Using the ASM directive and coprocessor commands in a Pascal program

```
program Project2;
{$APPTYPE CONSOLE}
uses
    SysUtils;
var
    d:double;
function soproc(f:double): double;
var res:double;
begin
    asm
        FLD f
        FSIN
        FSTP res
    end;
    soproc:=res;
end;
begin
    d:=-pi;
    while (d<=pi) do
    begin
        writeln(d:10:2, '-', soproc(d):10:2);
        d:=d+0.1;
    end;
end.
```

Listing 20.10. Using the ASM directive and coprocessor commands in a C program (Borland C++ 5.0)

```
#include <windows.h>
#include <stdio.h>
double soproc(double f);
void main()
{
        double w = -3.14;
        while(w<=3.14)
        {
                printf("%f- %f\n", w, soproc(w));
                w = w + 0.1;
        }
        ExitProcess(0);
```

```
}

double soproc(double f)
{
        double d;
        asm
        {
                FLD f
                FSIN
                FSTP d
         }
        return d;
}
```

An Example of Using a Dynamic Link Library

To conclude this chapter, consider an example illustrating how a DLL created in Delphi can be used in an Assembly language program. I recently discovered an algorithm implemented in Delphi, which places a program shortcut on the desktop and simultaneously creates a menu item in the **Start** menu. I am not a great fan of Delphi; however, I was too short of time to implement the same algorithm in C language. Therefore, I simply created a DLL on the basis of the existing Delphi program and now actively use it when creating various Setup utilities.

This example assumes that four parameters are passed to the procedure: two references to the programs and the names of the desktop shortcut and menu item. If desired, you can extend the capabilities of this procedure. If you carefully review the Assembly module, you'll notice that calling this DLL from an Assembly program doesn't have any particular features.

Listing 20.11. A dynamic link library implemented in Delphi

```
library lnk;

uses
        SysUtils,
        Classes,
        Windows,
ShlObj, ActiveX, ComObj, Registry, syncobjs;

procedure setup(prog:PChar; uns: PChar; jar:PChar; menu:PChar); stdcall;
var
```

```
MyObject : IUnknown;
MySLink : IShellLink;
MyPFile : IPersistFile;
FileName : String;
Directory : String;
WFileName : WideString;
MyReg  : TRegIniFile;
ps1, ps2, sn, path, s : string;
nb : dword;
handle : integer;
l : DWORD;
f : text;
begin
        MyObject := CreateComObject(CLSID_ShellLink);
        MySLink := MyObject as IShellLink;
        MyPFile := MyObject as IPersistFile;
        FileName := prog;
        path := ExtractFilePath(FileName);
        with MySLink do
        begin
                SetArguments('');
                SetPath(PChar(FileName));
                SetWorkingDirectory(PChar(ExtractFilePath(FileName)));
        end;
// First, create a desktop shortcut
        MyReg :=
        TRegIniFile.Create('Software\MicroSoft\Windows\CurrentVersion
        \Explorer');
        Directory := MyReg.ReadString('Shell Folders', 'Desktop', '');
        WFileName := Directory+'\';
        WFileName := WFileName+jar;
        WFileName := WFileName+'.lnk';
        MyPFile.Save(PWChar(WFileName), False);
        ps1:=string(WFileName);
        // Create a menu item
        Directory := MyReg.ReadString('Shell Folders', 'Programs', '')+'\';
        Directory := Directory+menu;
        WFileName := Directory+'\';
        WFileName := WFileName+jar;
        WFileName := WFileName+'.lnk';
        CreateDir(Directory);
        ps2 := Directory+'\';
        MyPFile.Save(PWChar(WFileName), False);
//**********************************
        MyObject := CreateComObject(CLSID_ShellLink);
```

```
        MySLink := MyObject as IShellLink;
        MyPFile := MyObject as IPersistFile;
        FileName := uns;
        path := ExtractFilePath(FileName);
        with MySLink do
        begin
                SetArguments('');
                SetPath(PChar(FileName));
                SetWorkingDirectory(PChar(ExtractFilePath(FileName)));
        end;
        WFileName := Directory+'\';
        WFileName := WFileName+'UNFILES.lnk';
        MyPFile.Save(PWChar(WFileName), False);
        MyReg.Free;
// Create a file, in which the information required
// to continue installation will be stored
        sn := path+'perebros.lk';
        AssignFile(f, sn);
        rewrite(f);
        writeln(f, ps1);
        writeln(f, ps2);
        close(f);
end;
//*********************
Procedure DLLMain(r:DWORD);
begin
end;
exports setup;
begin
        DLLProc := @DLLMain;
        DLLMain(dll_Process_Attach);
end.
```

Listing 20.12. How to call the dynamic link library (Listing 20.11) from an Assembly program

```
; The SETUP.ASM file
.586P
; Flat memory model
.MODEL FLAT, stdcall
; Constants
; Prototypes of external procedures
IFDEF MASM
; MASM
```

```
        EXTERN      GetProcAddress@8:NEAR
        EXTERN      LoadLibraryA@4:NEAR
        EXTERN      FreeLibrary@4:NEAR
        EXTERN      ExitProcess@4:NEAR
        EXTERN      MessageBoxA@16:NEAR
        includelib c:\masm32\lib\user32.lib
        includelib c:\masm32\lib\kernel32.lib
ELSE
        includelib c:\tasm32\lib\import32.lib
        EXTERN      GetProcAddress:NEAR
        EXTERN      LoadLibraryA:NEAR
        EXTERN      FreeLibrary:NEAR
        EXTERN      ExitProcess:NEAR
        EXTERN      MessageBoxA:NEAR
        GetProcAddress@8 = GetProcAddress
        LoadLibraryA@4 = LoadLibraryA
        FreeLibrary@4 = FreeLibrary
        ExitProcess@4 = ExitProcess
        MessageBoxA@16 = MessageBoxA
ENDIF
;-----------------------------------------------
; Data segment
_DATA SEGMENT
        TXT    DB 'DLL error', 0
        MS     DB 'Message', 0
        LIBR   DB 'LNK.DLL', 0
        HLIB   DD ?
        PAR1   DB "C:\PROG\FILES.EXE", 0
        PAR2   DB "C:\PROG\UNINST.EXE", 0
        PAR3   DB "Universal search", 0
        PAR4   DB "Universal search program", 0
        NAMEPROC DB 'setup', 0
_DATA ENDS
; Code segment
_TEXT SEGMENT
; [EBP+10H]    ; Reserved parameter
; [EBP+0CH]    ; Cause of the call
; [EBP+8]      ; DLL module identifier
START:
; Load the library
        PUSH  OFFSET LIBR
        CALL  LoadLibraryA@4
        CMP   EAX, 0
        JE    _ERR
        MOV   HLIB, EAX
```

```
; Get the address
        PUSH  OFFSET NAMEPROC
        PUSH  HLIB
        CALL  GetProcAddress@8
        CMP   EAX, 0
        JNE   YES_NAME
; Error message
_ERR:
        PUSH  0
        PUSH  OFFSET MS
        PUSH  OFFSET TXT
        PUSH  0
        CALL  MessageBoxA@16
        JMP   _EXIT
YES_NAME:
        PUSH  OFFSET PAR4
        PUSH  OFFSET PAR3
        PUSH  OFFSET PAR2
        PUSH  OFFSET PAR1
        CALL  EAX
; Close the library
; The library will close automatically
; when exiting the program
        PUSH  HLIB
        CALL  FreeLibrary@4
; Exit
_EXIT:
        PUSH  0
        CALL  ExitProcess@4
_TEXT ENDS
END START
```

To translate this program, issue the following commands using MASM32:

```
ml /c /coff /DMASM setup.asm
link /subsystem:windows setup.obj
```

Issue the following commands using TASM32:

```
tasm32 /ml setup.asm
tlink32 -aa setup.obj
```

To conclude this chapter, I would like to point out that not all possible problems related to using Assembly language with high-level languages have been covered here. However, if you carefully review the examples presented in this chapter, you'll be able to solve most such problems on your own.

Chapter 21

Programming Services

What are services? For what purposes are they used, and how do you program them? All of these topics will be covered in this chapter.

Main Concepts and Control Functions

Services are special applications. Microsoft recommends that programmers implement server applications in the form of services. In the Windows operating system, most functions are delegated to services. A typical example is the Plug and Play service, which tracks all changes in computer hardware configuration and manages device installation and configuration. Another example of a service that runs on computers is the MSSQLSERVER service, which allows calls to the Microsoft SQL Server to be used in applications. The range of services is wide. To view this, start a special application called the Service Control Program (SCP). This program allows you to control the services running on your computer in the interactive mode. To start this application, click the **Start** button and select **Settings | Control Panel** menu options. Then, double-click the **Administrative Tools** icon and start the SCP by double-clicking the **Services** icon.[i] The main window of this application is shown in Fig. 21.1.

---

[i] All material in this chapter relates only to the operating systems of the Windows NT family.

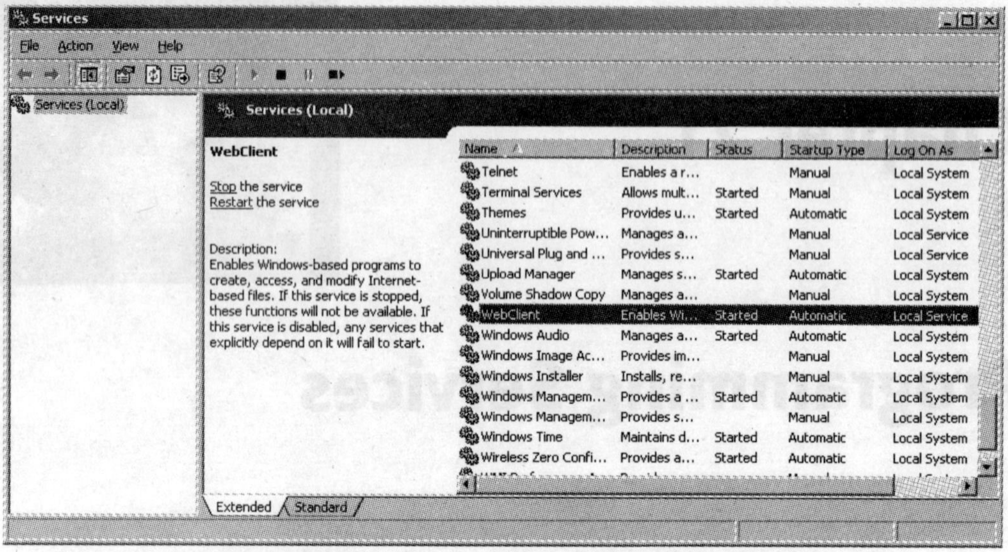

Fig. 21.1. The SCP allows you to control services in Microsoft Windows

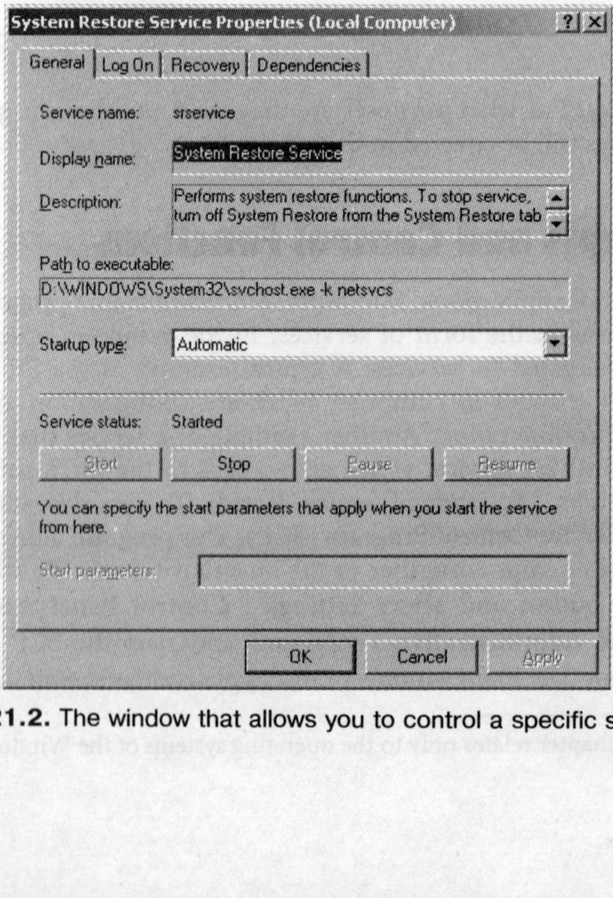

Fig. 21.2. The window that allows you to control a specific service

To control a specific service, select the name of that service from the list and double-click it. The window displaying the properties of that service will open (Fig. 21.2). Note the following four buttons in the service properties window: **Start**, **Stop**, **Pause**, and **Resume**. Using these buttons, you can carry out the following operations over the chosen service:

- Start the service if it is not running.
- Stop a running service; if you want to delete the chosen service, you must stop it first.
- Pause the operation of the running service.
- Resume the execution of the paused service.

The **Startup type** list allows you to change the type of the service startup. The following options are available:

- **Automatic** — This is for automatic startup of the service by the service control manager (SCM). The service will start at the time of the operating system startup before any user logs on to the system.
- **Manual** — This option enables the system administrator to start the service manually when the system is already running. The service can be started manually by clicking the **Start** button in the service properties window or programmatically by calling the `StartService` API function. The latter method of starting services will be covered in more detail later in this chapter.
- **Disabled** — When this option is chosen, the service is disabled.

The system administrator can change the method used by the service to log on to the system. To achieve this, go to the **Log On** tab and choose the appropriate logon options for the service. By default, the `LocalSystem` account is used. Under this account, the service can carry out practically any operation in the system. If you don't want the service to log on under the name of the operating system, you can specify another account and password on this tab.

The **Recovery** tab allows you to define the system reaction if this service fails to start or terminates abnormally. The SCP allows you to specify the actions that the system should carry out in the case of the first, second, and all subsequent failures.

The **Dependencies** tab displays the list of all services that depend on this service, as well as all services, on which this service depends in its turn.

Windows services operate under the control of the SCM. All communications to the service are carried out through the SCM module. This module is implemented by the SERVICE.EXE program that resides in the system directory, starts automatically at system startup, and remains active until system shutdown.

The list of services installed in the system can also be found in the registry. To view this list, start the REGEDIT.EXE program and open the following registry key:

```
HKEY_LOCAL_MACHINE\SYSTEM\CurrentControlSet\Services
```

Fig. 21.3 shows the REGEDIT.EXE window with the list of installed services.

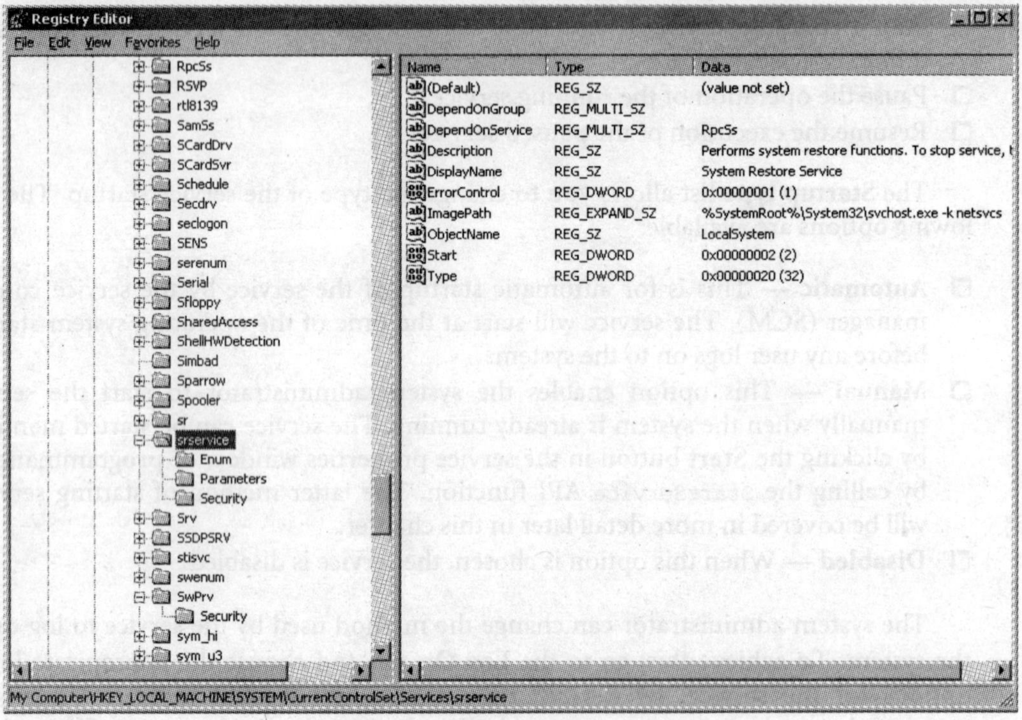

Fig. 21.3. List of services installed in the system and displayed by the REGEDIT.EXE application

NOTE

Do not change anything in the service settings or delete anything from the registry. However, if you are developing a custom service, this approach in some cases may provide the only possibility of debugging your application with minimum expenses.

The Service Structure

Now, it is time to consider the service structure and describe several API functions used for controlling services.

From the operating system's point of view, the service has the standard structure of the executable module. However, it starts in a way different from the standard one and has the following three distinct parts:

- Main function of the process — Its starting point specifies the normal starting address of the program. In the applications that will be presented and described further in this chapter, the starting address is labeled by the `START` label. In the easiest case, only the call to the `StartServiceCtrlDispatcher` function must be placed here. This function registers services and starts the service control dispatcher for controlling all services. No, this is not a misprint — within a single program, there may be several services representing normal functions. Each of these functions will be started by the dispatcher in its own thread. The only parameter of the `StartServiceCtrlDispatcher` function is the address of the array consisting of the following pairs: the service name and its entry point (address). This array must be terminated by two zeros (see the program presented in Listing 21.1).
- Procedures or logical services specified using the `StartServiceCtrlDispatcher` function — These must contain the following three components:
  - The call to the `RegisterServiceCtrlHandler` function registers the command handler procedure for this logical service.
  - The call to the `SetServiceStatus` function sets the service status — `started`.
  - The actions, for which this logical service is intended, must be carried out. As mentioned before, some services are active and running from operating system startup to shutdown, but other services are started only for short periods. A logical service can start any number of threads. After the service carries out its functions and terminates its operation, it again must call the `SetServiceStatus` function to set its status to `stopped`.
- Commands handler — The service control dispatcher communicates with the handler, instructing it, for example, to stop the running service or to send the message on the service status.

Well, that's all that you need to know about the service structure. Now, it is necessary to describe the API functions used for working with services.

The `StartServiceCtrlDispatcher` function was already briefly described. In the next section, an example illustrating its use will be provided.

The `RegisterServiceCtrlHandler` function registers the command handler procedure. It returns the procedure handle. The function receives the following parameters:

- First parameter — This is the address of the logical service name.
- Second parameter — This is the address of the command handler procedure.

The `SetServiceStatus` function sets the service status. It accepts the following parameters:

- First parameter — This is the handle to the command processing procedure.
- Second parameter — This is the pointer to the structure consisting of seven 32-bit fields. These fields, briefly, are as follows:
  - The first field specifies the type of service. The default value is `SERVICE_WIN32_OWN_PROCESS = 10h`, which means that the service will operate as an individual process.
  - The second field defines the state of the service. For example, the value `SERVICE_RUNNING = 4h` means that the service has started.
  - The third field determines, which commands must be processed by the service. There are several constants, which can be combined using the `OR` operation to form the value of this field (see Listing 21.1).
  - The fourth field defines the error code the service uses to report an error that occurs when it is starting or stopping. Usually, this field is assumed to be zero.
  - The fifth field contains a service-specific error code. It is used if the previous field is not set to zero.
  - The sixth field must be periodically incremented when carrying out lengthy operations. In all other cases, it must be zero.
  - The seventh field must contain estimated the time required, in milliseconds, for a pending start, stop, pause, or continue operation. If the value of the second or sixth field doesn't change when the estimated period elapses, the system will assume that an error has occurred.

The preceding functions are required functions, which must be present in the service program. In the simplest case, the command handler will contain only the `SetServiceStatus` function, using which the service status will be determined depending on the received command. The structure of all components of a service will be presented in Listing 21.1.

However, the previously described API functions are not sufficient to make the service operate. To achieve this, the service must already be registered in the services database, which is stored under the `HKEY_LOCAL_MACHINE\SYSTEM\CurrentControlSet\Services` key of the system registry. Only after that can the service start. Often, a separate program is used for registering the service in the services database. This approach is the one chosen for the program presented in Listing 21.1. However, most services are organized so that the operations carried out over the service depend on the command-line parameters.

Consider how the service is registered in the system registry. To achieve this, it is first necessary to open the services database, which is a part of system registry.

The `OpenSCManager` function opens the services database. It accepts several parameters.

- First parameter — This is the name of the network workstation where the database that you want to open is located. If you want to open local registry, this parameter is set to zero.
- Second parameter — This is the address of the services database name. To open the default services database, this parameter must be set to zero.
- Third parameter — This parameter defines the required type of access. Usually, the `SC_MANAGER_ALL_ACCESS = 0F003Fh` constant is used for providing full access.

If the function completes successfully, it returns the database handle. If the database has been opened successfully, then, after carrying out all required operations, it must be closed. For this purpose, use the `CloseServiceHandle` function whose only parameter is the service database handle.

To register the service in the service database, use the `CreateService` API function. This function has the following 13 parameters:

- First parameter — The service database handle (see the description of the `OpenSCManager` function).
- Second parameter — This is the address of the string that contains the name of one of the logical services, by which it will be possible to access that service. Thus, for each logical service it is necessary to call the `CreateService` function. The service will appear in the system registry under this name. This name also allows the service to be accessed programmatically.
- Third parameter — This defines the so-called display name.
- Fourth parameter — Possible type of access to the service. In the example provided later in this chapter, the `SERVICE_ALL_ACCESS = 0F01FFH` (full access) value is used.
- Fifth parameter — Type of service. In the example provided in this chapter, the `SERVICE_WIN32_OWN_PROCESS = 10H` constant is used.
- Sixth parameter — Service startup type. In the example provided in this chapter, the `SERVICE_DEMAND_START = 3` constant is used, which means that the service can be started on demand. It is also possible to use other constants, for example, `SERVICE_BOOT_START = 0`, which means that the service must be started at system startup.

- Seventh parameter — This defines the level of reaction to possible errors. The default value is `SERVICE_ERROR_NORMAL = 1`.
- Eighth parameter — This is the pointer to the string that contains the name of the service program. The name must specify the full path (e.g., D:\masm32\BIN\mt.exe). The EXE filename extension is not necessary.
- Ninth parameter — There are several groups of services in the operating system. These groups are loaded in a predefined order. If your service must be loaded only after specific services, it is necessary to specify the address of the service group name, to which your service will belong. The list of service group names can be found in Windows documentation. If loading order is not important, this parameter is set to zero.
- Tenth parameter — It always must be zero because it is used only for drivers (see *Chapter 27* for more details).
- 11th parameter — This defines services or groups of services, on which your service depends. It must point to the array composed of names of services and service groups. This array must be terminated by two zeros.
- 12th parameter — This parameter specifies the user account name, which must be used for starting the service. By default, this parameter is assumed to be zero, because it is supposed that the service will start as `LocalSystem`.
- 13th parameter — The password of the account used by the service to log on to the system (see parameter 12). If the 12th parameter is set to zero, the 13th parameter must also be set to zero.

Now, consider the procedures required to start the service programmatically. Note that the service must previously be registered using the `CreateService` function. The order of operations is as follows:

1. Open the services database using the `OpenSCManager` function.
2. Open the service using the `OpenService` function.
3. Start the service using the `StartService` function.
4. Close the services database.

Now, consider some functions not described yet. The `OpenService` function accepts three parameters:

- First parameter — The handle to the services database.
- Second parameter — This parameter defines the name of the service to be opened. This name must correspond to the name, under which the service was previously registered in the system registry.
- Third parameter — This parameter defines the level of access to the service. Usually, the `SC_MANAGER_ALL_ACCESS` value is used (for removing the service, the `DELETE` constant can be used).

The `StartService`, like the previous function, also accepts three parameters. The first parameter is the handle returned by the `OpenService` function. The second and third parameters are parameters passed to the service. Usually, these values are assumed to be zero, which means that this feature is not used.

Finally, it is necessary to consider another important aspect of service programming — how to programmatically delete the service from the system registry. To achieve this, it is necessary to carry out the following operations.

1. Open the services database.
2. Open the required service.
3. If this service is started, it must be stopped before deletion. This can be achieved using the `ControlService` function. If the service is not running, nothing bad will happen.
4. Delete the service from the registry using the `DeleteService` function.
5. Close the services database.

Now, it is time to describe functions that have not been covered yet. The `ControlService` function has three parameters:

- First parameter — The handle to the service.
- Second parameter — The command sent to the service. This command will be passed to the command handler. For example, to stop the service, it is necessary to set this parameter to `SERVICE_CONTROL_STOP = 1`.
- Third parameter — The address of the string containing the internal service name.

The `DeleteService` function accepts only one parameter — the handle to the previously opened service.

A Sample Service

Well, now the most interesting part of the chapter begins — naturally, these are the examples. For clarity, I have divided the task into four subtasks: writing the service program, registering the service in the system registry, starting the service, and stopping the service and removing it from the registry. The SERV.EXE program presented in Listing 21.1 cannot be started in a normal way. If you try, you'll fail. The structure of this program requires it to be previously registered in the system registry using the SETSERV.EXE program shown in Listing 21.2. After that, the service can be started for execution using the STSERV.EXE program presented in Listing 21.3. The same result can be achieved using the standard **Services** console in the standard **Administrative Tools** window. Finally, the service can be deleted using the DELSERV.EXE program (Listing 21.4) whether it is running or not.

Listing 21.1. The simplest service (SERV.EXE)

```
.586P
; Flat memory model
.MODEL FLAT, stdcall
; Constants
 SERVICE_CONTROL_STOP             equ 1h
 SERVICE_CONTROL_SHUTDOWN         equ 5h
 SERVICE_CONTROL_INTERROGATE      equ 4h
 SERVICE_CONTROL_CONTINUE         equ 3h
 SERVICE_START_PENDING            equ 2h
 ERROR_SERVICE_SPECIFIC_ERROR     equ 1066
 SERVICE_RUNNING                  equ 4h
 MB_SERVICE_NOTIFICATION          equ 200000h

 CRST EQU SERVICE_CONTROL_STOP OR \
 SERVICE_CONTROL_SHUTDOWN OR \
 SERVICE_CONTROL_CONTINUE
 SERVICE_WIN32_OWN_PROCESS        equ 00000010h
 ; Prototypes of external procedures
 IFDEF MASM
       EXTERN  Sleep@4:NEAR
       EXTERN  SetServiceStatus@8:NEAR
       EXTERN  RegisterServiceCtrlHandlerA@8:NEAR
       EXTERN  StartServiceCtrlDispatcherA@4:NEAR
       EXTERN  ExitProcess@4:NEAR
       EXTERN  MessageBoxA@16:NEAR
 ELSE
       EXTERN  Sleep:NEAR
       EXTERN  SetServiceStatus:NEAR
       EXTERN  RegisterServiceCtrlHandlerA:NEAR
       EXTERN  StartServiceCtrlDispatcherA:NEAR
       EXTERN  ExitProcess:NEAR
       EXTERN  MessageBoxA:NEAR
       Sleep@4 = Sleep
       SetServiceStatus@8 = SetServiceStatus
       MessageBoxA@16 = MessageBoxA
       RegisterServiceCtrlHandlerA@8 = RegisterServiceCtrlHandlerA
       StartServiceCtrlDispatcherA@4=StartServiceCtrlDispatcherA
       ExitProcess@4 = ExitProcess
 ENDIF

 ; INCLUDELIB directives for the linker
```

```
IFDEF MASM
        includelib d:\masm32\lib\user32.lib
        includelib d:\masm32\lib\kernel32.lib
        includelib d:\masm32\lib\advapi32.lib
ELSE
        includelib c:\tasm32\lib\import32.lib
ENDIF
;-----------------------------------------------

SSTATUS STRUC
        STYPE    DD ?
        SSTATE   DD ?
        SACCEPT  DD ?
        SEXCODE  DD ?
        SEXSCOD  DD ?
        SCHEKPO  DD ?
        SWAITHI  DD ?
SSTATUS ENDS

; Data segment
_DATA SEGMENT
        SNAME   DB  "MyService", 0
        DTS     DD  OFFSET SNAME, OFFSET WINSERV, 0, 0
        SRS     SSTATUS <0>
        H1      DD  ?
_DATA ENDS
; Code segment
_TEXT SEGMENT
START:
; Service registration
        PUSH  OFFSET DTS
        CALL  StartServiceCtrlDispatcherA@4
; Exit after the service has stopped
        PUSH  0
        CALL  ExitProcess@4
; The service
WINSERV PROC
; Fill the structure
        MOV   SRS.STYPE, SERVICE_WIN32_OWN_PROCESS
        MOV   SRS.SSTATE, SERVICE_RUNNING ; SERVICE_START_PENDING
        MOV   SRS.SACCEPT, CRST
        MOV   SRS.SEXCODE, 0 ; ERROR_SERVICE_SPECIFIC_ERROR
        MOV   SRS.SEXSCOD, 0
```

```
        MOV   SRS.SCHEKPO, 0
        MOV   SRS.SWAITHI, 1
; Register the command-handling function
        PUSH  OFFSET HANDLER
        PUSH  OFFSET SNAME
        CALL RegisterServiceCtrlHandlerA@8
; Set the status
        MOV   H1, EAX
        PUSH  OFFSET SRS
        PUSH  H1
        CALL  SetServiceStatus@8
; Main function of this service starts here
        PUSH  200000
        CALL  Sleep@4
; Set the status
        MOV   SRS.SSTATE, SERVICE_CONTROL_STOP
        PUSH  OFFSET SRS
        PUSH  H1
        CALL  SetServiceStatus@8
        RET   8
WINSERV ENDP
; Interrupt handler
; [EBP+08H] — The only parameter
HANDLER PROC
        PUSH  EBP
        MOV   EBP, ESP
        INC   SRS.SCHEKPO
        MOV   EAX, DWORD PTR [EBP+08H]
        CMP   EAX, SERVICE_CONTROL_STOP
        JNZ   NO_STOP
        MOV   SRS.SSTATE, SERVICE_CONTROL_STOP
        JMP   _SET
NO_STOP:
        CMP   EAX, SERVICE_CONTROL_SHUTDOWN
        JNZ   NO_SHUTDOWN
        MOV   SRS.SSTATE, SERVICE_CONTROL_STOP
        JMP   _SET
NO_SHUTDOWN:
        CMP   EAX, SERVICE_CONTROL_CONTINUE
        JNZ   NO_CONTINUE
        MOV   SRS.SSTATE, SERVICE_CONTROL_CONTINUE
        JMP   _SET
NO_CONTINUE:
        CMP   EAX, SERVICE_CONTROL_INTERROGATE
```

```
; Set the service status
_SET:
        PUSH  OFFSET SRS
        PUSH  H1
        CALL  SetServiceStatus@8
; The message included for debugging
; The MB_SERVICE_NOTIFICATION constant is required
        PUSH  0 OR MB_SERVICE_NOTIFICATION
        PUSH  OFFSET SNAME
        PUSH  OFFSET SNAME
        PUSH  0
        CALL  MessageBoxA@16
;------------------------------
        MOV   ESP, EBP
        POP   EBP
        RET   4
HANDLER ENDP
_TEXT ENDS
END START
```

The program presented in Listing 21.1 requires some comments.

- Pay attention to the program structure. As already mentioned, it contains the main function (the `START` label), the logical service (in this program, there is only one such service — `WINSERV`), and the command handler called `HANDLER`.
- For simplicity, I used the `Sleep` function with a long delay as the executable process. When the STSERV program starts for execution, this function is started. Principally, this service doesn't need to be stopped forcibly, because after the termination of the `Sleep` function it will stop automatically.
- The `WINSERV` function is terminated by `RET 8`. This means that two parameters are sent to the function but are never processed (see the description of `StartService`).
- From the Assembly language programmer's point of view, the structure of the `HANDLER` procedure is simple. Principally, this handler is needed only for processing the `SERVICE_CONTROL_STOP` command.
- For debugging purposes, I have placed the `MessageBox` function into the command handler. This aspect is quite interesting. The message must appear in relation to a specific desktop. Because of this, I used the `MB_SERVICE_NOTIFICATION` constant intended for displaying the messages from the service. This message will appear even if no user is logged on to the computer.
- The `RET 4` command that terminates the handler means that only one parameter — the command to the service — is accepted in the course of the call.

To translate this program, issue the following commands for MASM32:

```
ML /c /coff /DMASM serv.asm
LINK /SUBSYSTEM:CONSOLE serv.obj
```

Issue the following commands for TASM32:

```
TASM32 /ml serv.asm
TLINK32 -ap serv.obj
```

Listing 21.2. The program that installs the service (SETSERV.EXE)

```
.586P
; Flat memory model
.MODEL FLAT, stdcall
; Constants
STD_OUTPUT_HANDLE           equ -11
SC_MANAGER_ALL_ACCESS       equ 0F003Fh
SERVICE_ALL_ACCESS          equ 0F01FFH
SERVICE_WIN32_OWN_PROCESS   equ 00000010h
SERVICE_DEMAND_START        equ 00000003h
SERVICE_ERROR_NORMAL        equ 00000001h
; Prototypes of external procedures
IFDEF MASM
       EXTERN  CreateServiceA@52:NEAR
       EXTERN  CloseServiceHandle@4:NEAR
       EXTERN  OpenSCManagerA@12:NEAR
       EXTERN  wsprintfA:NEAR
       EXTERN  GetLastError@0:NEAR
       EXTERN  StartServiceCtrlDispatcherA@4:NEAR
       EXTERN  ExitProcess@4:NEAR
       EXTERN  lstrlenA@4:NEAR
       EXTERN  WriteConsoleA@20:NEAR
       EXTERN  GetStdHandle@4:NEAR
ELSE
       EXTERN  CreateServiceA:NEAR
       EXTERN  CloseServiceHandle:NEAR
       EXTERN  OpenSCManagerA:NEAR
       EXTERN  _wsprintfA:NEAR
       EXTERN  GetLastError:NEAR
       EXTERN  StartServiceCtrlDispatcherA:NEAR
       EXTERN  ExitProcess:NEAR
       EXTERN  MessageBoxA:NEAR
       EXTERN  lstrlenA:NEAR
```

```
        EXTERN  WriteConsoleA:NEAR
        EXTERN  GetStdHandle:NEAR
        CreateServiceA@52 = CreateServiceA
        CloseServiceHandle@4 = CloseServiceHandle
        OpenSCManagerA@12 = OpenSCManagerA
        GetStdHandle@4 = GetStdHandle
        WriteConsoleA@20 = WriteConsoleA
        lstrlenA@4 = lstrlenA
        wsprintfA = _wsprintfA
        GetLastError@0 = GetLastError
        StartServiceCtrlDispatcherA@4 = StartServiceCtrlDispatcherA
        ExitProcess@4 = ExitProcess
ENDIF

; INCLUDELIB directives for the linker
IFDEF MASM
        includelib d:\masm32\lib\user32.lib
        includelib d:\masm32\lib\kernel32.lib
        includelib d:\masm32\lib\advapi32.lib
ELSE
        includelib c:\tasm32\lib\import32.lib
ENDIF
;-----------------------------------------------


; Data segment
_DATA SEGMENT
    H1      DD ?
    H2      DD ?
    ALIGN   4
    SNAME1  DB  "MyService", 0
    ALIGN   4
    NM      DB "D:\masm32\BIN\serv.exe", 0
    LENS    DD 0
    HANDL   DD 0
    BUF1    DB 512 DUP(0)
    ERRS    DB "Error %u ", 0
_DATA ENDS
; Code segment
_TEXT SEGMENT
START:
; Define the output console handle
        PUSH   STD_OUTPUT_HANDLE
```

```
        CALL  GetStdHandle@4
        MOV   HANDL, EAX
; Open the services database
        PUSH  SC_MANAGER_ALL_ACCESS
        PUSH  0
        PUSH  0
        CALL  OpenSCManagerA@12
        CMP   EAX, 0
        JNZ   NO_ERR
        CALL  ERROB
        JMP   EXI
NO_ERR:
        MOV   H1, EAX
; Identifier received; now, create the service
        PUSH  0
        PUSH  0
        PUSH  0
        PUSH  0
        PUSH  0
        PUSH  OFFSET NM
        PUSH  SERVICE_ERROR_NORMAL
        PUSH  SERVICE_DEMAND_START
        PUSH  SERVICE_WIN32_OWN_PROCESS
        PUSH  SERVICE_ALL_ACCESS
        PUSH  OFFSET SNAME1
        PUSH  OFFSET SNAME1
        PUSH  H1
        CALL  CreateServiceA@52
        CMP   EAX, 0
        JNZ   CLOS
        MOV   H2, EAX
        CALL  ERROB
        JMP   CLOS1
; Error-handling block
ERROB:
        CALL  GetLastError@0
        PUSH  EAX
        PUSH  OFFSET ERRS
        PUSH  OFFSET BUF1
        CALL  wsprintfA
        ADD   ESP, 12
        LEA   EAX, BUF1
        MOV   EDI, 1
```

```
        CALL  WRITE
        RET
CLOSE1:
; Close the service
        PUSH  H2
        CALL  CloseServiceHandle@4
CLOSE:
; Close the services database
        PUSH  H1
        CALL  CloseServiceHandle@4
EXI:
; Exit after all services terminate
        PUSH  0
        CALL  ExitProcess@4
; Output the string (line feed in the end)
; EAX — To the start of the string
; EDI — With or without the line feed
WRITE   PROC
; Get the parameter length
        PUSH  EAX
        PUSH  EAX
        CALL  lstrlenA@4
        MOV   ESI, EAX
        POP   EBX
        CMP   EDI, 1
        JNE   NO_ENT
; Line feed in the end
        MOV   BYTE PTR [EBX+ESI], 13
        MOV   BYTE PTR [EBX+ESI+1], 10
        MOV   BYTE PTR [EBX+ESI+2], 0
        ADD   EAX, 2
NO_ENT:
; String output
        PUSH  0
        PUSH  OFFSET LENS
        PUSH  EAX
        PUSH  EBX
        PUSH  HANDL
        CALL  WriteConsoleA@20
        RET
WRITE   ENDP
_TEXT ENDS
END START
```

When considering the program presented in Listing 21.2 (SETSERV.EXE), pay attention to the following aspects:

- This program registers the SERV.EXE service in the system registry using the `CreateService` API function.
- Note that here you handle all possible errors when using this function and, if an error has occurred, you output the error code to the console.

To translate this program, issue the following commands for MASM32:

```
ML /c /coff /DMASM setserv.asm
LINK /SUBSYSTEM:CONSOLE setserv.obj
```

Issue the following commands for TASM32:

```
TASM32 /ml setserv.asm
TLINK32 -ap setserv.obj
```

Listing 21.3. The program that starts the service (STSERV.EXE)

```
.586P
; Flat memory model
.MODEL FLAT, stdcall
; Constants
DELETE                          equ 10000h
STD_OUTPUT_HANDLE               equ -11
SC_MANAGER_ALL_ACCESS           equ 0F003Fh
SERVICE_ALL_ACCESS              equ 0F01FFH
SERVICE_WIN32_OWN_PROCESS       equ 00000010h
SERVICE_DEMAND_START            equ 00000003h
SERVICE_ERROR_NORMAL            equ 00000001h
SERVICE_CONTROL_STOP            equ 1h
; Prototypes of external procedures
IFDEF MASM
        EXTERN  StartServiceA@12:NEAR
        EXTERN  OpenServiceA@12:NEAR
        EXTERN  CloseServiceHandle@4:NEAR
        EXTERN  OpenSCManagerA@12:NEAR
        EXTERN  wsprintfA:NEAR
        EXTERN  GetLastError@0:NEAR
        EXTERN  ExitProcess@4:NEAR
        EXTERN  lstrlenA@4:NEAR
        EXTERN  WriteConsoleA@20:NEAR
        EXTERN  GetStdHandle@4:NEAR
```

```
ELSE
        EXTERN  StartServiceA:NEAR
        EXTERN  OpenServiceA:NEAR
        EXTERN  CloseServiceHandle:NEAR
        EXTERN  OpenSCManagerA:NEAR
        EXTERN  _wsprintfA:NEAR
        EXTERN  GetLastError:NEAR
        EXTERN  ExitProcess:NEAR
        EXTERN  lstrlenA:NEAR
        EXTERN  WriteConsoleA:NEAR
        EXTERN  GetStdHandle:NEAR
        StartServiceA@12 = StartServiceA
        OpenServiceA@12 = OpenServiceA
        CloseServiceHandle@4 = CloseServiceHandle
        OpenSCManagerA@12 = OpenSCManagerA
        GetStdHandle@4 = GetStdHandle
        WriteConsoleA@20 = WriteConsoleA
        lstrlenA@4 = lstrlenA
        wsprintfA = _wsprintfA
        GetLastError@0 = GetLastError
        ExitProcess@4 = ExitProcess
ENDIF

; INCLUDELIB directives for the linker
IFDEF MASM
        includelib d:\masm32\lib\user32.lib
        includelib d:\masm32\lib\kernel32.lib
        includelib d:\masm32\lib\advapi32.lib
ELSE
        includelib c:\tasm32\lib\import32.lib
ENDIF
;-----------------------------------------------

SSTATUS STRUC
        STYPE    DD ?
        SSTATE   DD ?
        SACCEPT  DD ?
        SEXCODE  DD ?
        SEXSCOD  DD ?
        SCHEKPO  DD ?
        SWAITHI  DD ?
SSTATUS ENDS
```

```
; Data segment
_DATA SEGMENT
    SRS      SSTATUS <?>
    H1       DD ?
    H2       DD ?
    ALIGN    4
    SNAME1   DB  "MyService", 0
    ALIGN    4
    LENS     DD 0
    HANDL    DD 0
    BUF1     DB 512 DUP(0)
    ERRS     DB "Error %u ", 0
_DATA ENDS
; Code segment
_TEXT SEGMENT
START:
        PUSH  STD_OUTPUT_HANDLE
        CALL  GetStdHandle@4
        MOV   HANDL, EAX
;------------------------
        PUSH  SC_MANAGER_ALL_ACCESS
        PUSH  0
        PUSH  0
        CALL  OpenSCManagerA@12
        CMP   EAX, 0
        JNZ   NO_ERR1
        CALL  ERROB
        JMP   EXI
NO_ERR1:
        MOV   H1, EAX
; Identifier received
        PUSH  SC_MANAGER_ALL_ACCESS ; DELETE
        PUSH  OFFSET SNAME1
        PUSH  H1
        CALL  OpenServiceA@12
        CMP   EAX, 0
        JNZ   NO_ERR2
        CALL  ERROB
        JMP   CLOSE
NO_ERR2:
        MOV   H2, EAX
; Service identifier received
; Send the command for starting the service
```

```
        PUSH  0
        PUSH  0
        PUSH  H2
        CALL  StartServiceA@12
        CMP   EAX, 0
        JNZ   CLOSE1
        CALL  ERROB
        JMP   CLOS1
; Error-handling block
ERROB:
        CALL  GetLastError@0
        PUSH  EAX
        PUSH  OFFSET ERRS
        PUSH  OFFSET BUF1
        CALL  wsprintfA
        ADD   ESP, 12
        LEA   EAX, BUF1
        MOV   EDI, 1
        CALL  WRITE
        RET

CLOSE1:
; Close the service
        PUSH  H2
        CALL  CloseServiceHandle@4
; Close the services database
CLOSE:
        PUSH  H1
        CALL  CloseServiceHandle@4
EXI:
; Exit
        PUSH  0
        CALL  ExitProcess@4
; Output the string (line feed in the end)
; EAX — To the start of the string
; EDI — With or without line feed
WRITE   PROC
; Get the parameter length
        PUSH  EAX
        PUSH  EAX
        CALL  lstrlenA@4
        MOV   ESI, EAX
        POP   EBX
```

```
        CMP   EDI, 1
        JNE   NO_ENT
; Line feed in the end
        MOV   BYTE PTR [EBX+ESI], 13
        MOV   BYTE PTR [EBX+ESI+1], 10
        MOV   BYTE PTR [EBX+ESI+2], 0
        ADD   EAX, 2
NO_ENT:
; String output
        PUSH  0
        PUSH  OFFSET LENS
        PUSH  EAX
        PUSH  EBX
        PUSH  HANDL
        CALL  WriteConsoleA@20
        RET
WRITE   ENDP
_TEXT ENDS
END START
```

The STSERV.EXE program presented in Listing 21.3 starts the service with the name `MyService` for execution. The start is carried out using the `StartService` API function.

To translate this program, issue the following commands for MASM32:

```
ML /c /coff /DMASM stserv.asm
LINK /SUBSYSTEM:CONSOLE stserv.obj
```

Issue the following commands for TASM32:

```
TASM32 /ml stserv.asm
TLINK32 -ap stserv.obj
```

Listing 21.4. The program that deletes the service (DELSERV.EXE)

```
.586P
; Flat memory model
.MODEL FLAT, stdcall
; Constants
DELETE                      equ 10000h
STD_OUTPUT_HANDLE           equ -11
SC_MANAGER_ALL_ACCESS       equ 0F003Fh
SERVICE_ALL_ACCESS          equ 0F01FFH
SERVICE_WIN32_OWN_PROCESS   equ 00000010h
```

```
SERVICE_DEMAND_START        equ 00000003h
SERVICE_ERROR_NORMAL        equ 00000001h
SERVICE_CONTROL_STOP        equ 1h
; Prototypes of external procedures
IFDEF MASM
        EXTERN  ControlService@12:NEAR
        EXTERN  DeleteService@4:NEAR
        EXTERN  OpenServiceA@12:NEAR
        EXTERN  CloseServiceHandle@4:NEAR
        EXTERN  OpenSCManagerA@12:NEAR
        EXTERN  wsprintfA:NEAR
        EXTERN  GetLastError@0:NEAR
        EXTERN  ExitProcess@4:NEAR
        EXTERN  lstrlenA@4:NEAR
        EXTERN  WriteConsoleA@20:NEAR
        EXTERN  GetStdHandle@4:NEAR
ELSE
        EXTERN  ControlService:NEAR
        EXTERN  DeleteService:NEAR
        EXTERN  OpenServiceA:NEAR
        EXTERN  CloseServiceHandle:NEAR
        EXTERN  OpenSCManagerA:NEAR
        EXTERN  _wsprintfA:NEAR
        EXTERN  GetLastError:NEAR
        EXTERN  ExitProcess:NEAR
        EXTERN  lstrlenA:NEAR
        EXTERN  WriteConsoleA:NEAR
        EXTERN  GetStdHandle:NEAR
        ControlService@12 = ControlService
        DeleteService@4 = DeleteService
        OpenServiceA@12 = OpenServiceA
        CloseServiceHandle@4 = CloseServiceHandle
        OpenSCManagerA@12 = OpenSCManagerA
        GetStdHandle@4 = GetStdHandle
        WriteConsoleA@20 = WriteConsoleA
        lstrlenA@4 = lstrlenA
        wsprintfA = _wsprintfA
        GetLastError@0 = GetLastError
        StartServiceCtrlDispatcherA@4 = StartServiceCtrlDispatcherA
        MessageBoxA@16 = MessageBoxA
        ExitProcess@4 = ExitProcess
ENDIF
```

```
; INCLUDELIB directives for the linker
IFDEF MASM
        includelib d:\masm32\lib\user32.lib
        includelib d:\masm32\lib\kernel32.lib
        includelib d:\masm32\lib\advapi32.lib
ELSE
        includelib c:\tasm32\lib\import32.lib
ENDIF
;------------------------------------------------

SSTATUS STRUC
        STYPE    DD ?
        SSTATE   DD ?
        SACCEPT  DD ?
        SEXCODE  DD ?
        SEXSCOD  DD ?
        SCHEKPO  DD ?
        SWAITHI  DD ?
SSTATUS ENDS

; Data segment
_DATA SEGMENT
    SRS     SSTATUS <?>
    H1      DD ?
    H2      DD ?
    ALIGN   4
    SNAME1  DB  "MyService", 0
    ALIGN   4
    LENS    DD 0
    HANDL   DD 0
    BUF1    DB 512 DUP(0)
    ERRS    DB "Error %u ", 0
_DATA ENDS
; Code segment
_TEXT SEGMENT
START:
        PUSH  STD_OUTPUT_HANDLE
        CALL  GetStdHandle@4
        MOV   HANDL, EAX
; Open the services database
        PUSH  SC_MANAGER_ALL_ACCESS
        PUSH  0
        PUSH  0
```

```
        CALL  OpenSCManagerA@12
        CMP   EAX, 0
        JNZ   Z1
        CALL  ERROB
        JMP   EXI
Z1:
        MOV   H1, EAX
; Identifier has been received; open the service
        PUSH  SC_MANAGER_ALL_ACCESS ; DELETE
        PUSH  OFFSET SNAME1
        PUSH  H1
        CALL  OpenServiceA@12
        CMP   EAX, 0
        JNZ   Z2
        CALL  ERROB
        JMP   CLOSE
Z2:
        MOV   H2, EAX
; Send the stop command
        PUSH  OFFSET SRS
        PUSH  SERVICE_CONTROL_STOP
        PUSH  H2
        CALL  ControlService@12
        CMP   EAX, 0
        JNZ   Z3
        CALL  ERROB
Z3:
; Delete the service
        PUSH  H2
        CALL  DeleteService@4
        CMP   EAX, 0
        JNZ   CLOSE
        CALL  ERROB
        JMP   CLOSE1
; Error-handling block
ERROB:
        CALL  GetLastError@0
        PUSH  EAX
        PUSH  OFFSET ERRS
        PUSH  OFFSET BUF1
        CALL  wsprintfA
        ADD   ESP, 12
        LEA   EAX, BUF1
```

```
        MOV   EDI, 1
        CALL  WRITE
        RET
CLOSE1:
; Close the service
        PUSH  H2
        CALL  CloseServiceHandle@4
CLOSE:
; Close the services database
        PUSH  H1
        CALL  CloseServiceHandle@4
EXI:
; Exit when all services stop
        PUSH  0
        CALL  ExitProcess@4
; Output the string (line feed in the end)
; EAX — To the start of the string
; EDI — With or without the line feed
WRITE   PROC
; Get the parameter length
        PUSH  EAX
        PUSH  EAX
        CALL  lstrlenA@4
        MOV   ESI, EAX
        POP   EBX
        CMP   EDI, 1
        JNE   NO_ENT
; Line feed in the end
        MOV   BYTE PTR [EBX+ESI], 13
        MOV   BYTE PTR [EBX+ESI+1], 10
        MOV   BYTE PTR [EBX+ESI+2], 0
        ADD   EAX, 2
NO_ENT:
; String output
        PUSH  0
        PUSH  OFFSET LENS
        PUSH  EAX
        PUSH  EBX
        PUSH  HANDL
        CALL  WriteConsoleA@20
        RET
WRITE   ENDP
_TEXT ENDS
END START
```

To translate this program, issue the following commands for MASM32:

```
ML /c /coff /DMASM delserv.asm
LINK /SUBSYSTEM:CONSOLE delserv.obj
```

Issue the following commands for TASM32:

```
TASM32 /ml delserv.asm
TLINK32 -ap delserv.obj
```

This program requires some comments.

This example shows how it is possible to delete the service even if it is running. This can be achieved if the service makes provision for a reaction to the stop command. Principally, everything is self-evident. However, note that even if an error occurs when executing the `ControlService` API function, everything will continue to execute in due order. The point is that this command sends the stop command to the service. However, if the service is registered in the services database but is not running, then the function will return error code 1062, which means that the service has been stopped already.

Chapter 22

Overview of Debuggers and Disassemblers

Do you remember the DEBUG.EXE program? As far as I know, it is still present in Windows XP. Unfortunately, Microsoft no longer supports it and it is practically useless. But do you remember how many things are related to it? That was the time of a legend.

This chapter describes many debuggers and disassemblers. It does not describe the three most famous ones, which deserve separate chapters and, accordingly, will be covered in the next two chapters.

Microsoft Utilities

EDIDBIN.EXE

This program has a promising name. Nevertheless, it hardly deserves to be called an editor. Its main goal is to convert object files in the OMF format into the COFF format. In addition, this utility allows for changing some other attributes of executable and object modules. If you specify the name of the object module in its command line, then, if that module is in the OMF format, it will be converted into the COFF format.

Consider the command-line options of this program. They can be applied to both executable and object modules.

- `/BIND` — Allows you to specify the paths to dynamic link libraries (DLLs) that use this executable module. For example: `EDITBIN /BIND:PATH=c:\edit;d:\dll EDIT.EXE`.
- `/HEAP` — Specifies the heap size in bytes. For example: `EDITBIN /HEAP:100000,100000` (see the LINK.EXE options).
- `/LARGEADDRESSAWARE` — Specifies that the application operates with addresses larger than 2 GB.
- `/NOLOGO` — Suppresses the output of information about the program.
- `/REBASE` — Sets the module's base address. By default, the base address for an executable module is equal to 400000H, and for DLLs, it is 10000000H.
- `/RELEASE` — Sets the checksum in the header of the executable module.
- `/SECTION` — Changes the attributes of the sections of the executable module. The full format of this option is as follows:

```
/SECTION:name[=newname][,attributes][,alignment]
```

Table 22.1. Attribute values

Attribute	Value	Attribute	Value
C	Code	O	Link information
D	Discardable	P	Paged virtual memory
E	Executable	R	Read
I	Initialized data	S	Shared
K	Cached virtual memory	U	Uninitialized data
M	Link remove	w	Write

Table 22.2. The value of the alignment option

Option	Alignment (in bytes)	Option	Alignment (in bytes)
1	1	p	16
2	2	t	32
4	4	s	64
8	8	x	No alignment

- /STACK — Changes the value required for the executable module's stack. For example: EDITBIN /STACK:10000,10000 EDIT.EXE.
- /SUBSYSTEM — Redefines the subsystem, in which this program operates. For example, if the program has been translated with the /SUBSYSTEM:WINDOWS option, this setting can be changed without recompiling: EDITBIN /SUBSYSTEM:CONSOLE EDIT.EXE.
- /SWAPRUN — Sets the "move to swap file" attribute for the executable module.
- /VERSION — Sets the version for the executable module.
- /WS (/WS:AGGRESSIVE) — Sets the AGGRESSIVE attribute, which is used by operating systems of the Windows NT family.

This utility is useful for quickly changing attributes of executable and object modules.

DUMPBIN.EXE

This program is mainly used for the investigation of executable and object modules in the COFF format. It outputs information to the current console. The command-line options of this program are as follows:

- /ALL — Outputs all available information about the module except the Assembly code.
- /ARCH — Outputs information about the .arch section of the module header.
- /ARCHIVEMEMBERS — Outputs minimal information about the elements of the object library.
- /DEPENDENTS — Outputs the names of DLLs, from which the module imports functions.
- /DIRECTIVES — Outputs the contents of the .drectve section created by the compiler (only for object modules).
- /DISASM — Disassembles the contents of module sections using symbolic information (if present).
- /EXPORTS — Outputs the names exported by the module.
- /HEADER — Outputs headers of the module and all its sections. In the case of an object library, it outputs the headers of all object modules that make up that library.
- /IMPORTS — Outputs the names imported by this module.
- /LINENUMBERS — Outputs the line numbers of the object module (if it contains numbered lines).

- `/LINKERMEMBER[:{1|2}]` — Outputs all names defined as `public` in the object library.
  - `/LINKERMEMBER:1` — Outputs in the order, in which object modules follow each other in the library.
  - `/LINKERMEMBER:2` — First outputs the offset and the index of object modules, then outputs an alphabetically sorted list of names for each module.
  - `/LINKERMEMBER` — Combines options 1 and 2.
- `/OUT` — Specifies the data that should be output to the file (i.e., `/OUT:ED.TXT`) instead of to a console.
- `/PDATA` — Outputs the contents of exception tables.
- `/RAWDATA` — Outputs the dump of each file section. This option has the following variants: `/RAWDATA:BYTE`, `/RAWDATA:SHORTS`, `/RAWDATA:LONGS`, `/RAWDATA:NONE`, and `/RAWDATA:, number`. Here, `number` defines the length of the output strings.
- `/SUMMARY` — Outputs minimal information about sections.
- `/SYMBOLS` — Outputs the symbols table of the COFF file.

This program is a powerful disassembling tool. Suppose that the program name is PROG.ASM. Translate this program as follows:

```
ml  /c /coff /Zi /Zd prog.asm
link /debug /subsystem:windows prog.obj
```

In this case, in addition to the executable module PROG.EXE, another file, PROG.PDB, will appear. This file will contain the debug information. Now, issue the command `DUMPBIN /DISASM /OUT:PROG.TXT PROG.EXE`. As a result, you'll get the disassembled code, practically identical to the source code of the program. Part of this code is presented in Listing 22.1.

Listing 22.1. Fragment of the disassembled code

```
_START:
0040101C: 6A00          PUSH   0
0040101E: E843020000    CALL   _GetModuleHandleA@4
00401023: A344404000    MOV    [00404044],eax
00401028: C7051C404000 MOV    DWORD PTR DS:[40401Ch], 4003h
    03400000
00401032: C70520404000 MOV    DWORD PTR DS:[404020h], offset @ILT+0(_WNDPROC@0)
    05104000
0040103C: C70524404000 MOV    DWORD PTR DS:[404024h], 0
    00000000
00401046: C70528404000 MOV    DWORD PTR DS:[404028h], 0
```

```
            00000000
00401050: A144404000    MOV   EAX, [00404044]
00401055: A32C404000    MOV   [0040402C], EAX
0040105A: 68007F0000    PUSH  7F00h
0040105F: 6A00          PUSH  0
00401061: E8D6010000    CALL  _LoadIconA@8
00401066: A330404000    MOV   [00404030], EAX
0040106B: 68037F0000    PUSH  7F03h
00401070: 6A00          PUSH  0
00401072: E8BF010000    CALL  _LoadCursorA@8
```

As you can see, this is a transparent code that is practically no different from normal code written in Assembly language. Near the end of the file, interesting information can be found. Here is the fragment:

```
_LoadIconA@8:
0040123C: FF2510514000 JMP DWORD PTR [__IMP__LoadIconA@8]
```

When a function is called, for example, `_LoadIconA@8`, the jump is carried out to the address of the following command:

```
JMP DWORD PTR [__IMP__LoadIconA@8].
```

Because of this, you can declare `_imp__LoadIconA@8` instead of `LoadIcon@8`, which will somewhat improve the performance of your program. I didn't mention this possibility before because of two reasons:

- The performance gain achieved using this approach is minimal.
- TASM32 does everything in a slightly different manner. This topic is covered in more detail later in this chapter.

Utilities from Other Developers

DUMPPE.EXE

This program was briefly mentioned in *Chapter 1*. In many respects, it is similar to the DUMPBIN.EXE utility; however, it has limited functionality in comparison to it.

HIEW.EXE

This program is widely known among programmers in the hacker world. Its name is an abbreviation of the phrase "hacker's view." The main tasks carried out by this program are viewing and editing executable modules. There are three possible modes of work in this program: binary, text, and assembly. There are tons of good disassembling programs; however, the programs similar to this one are few.

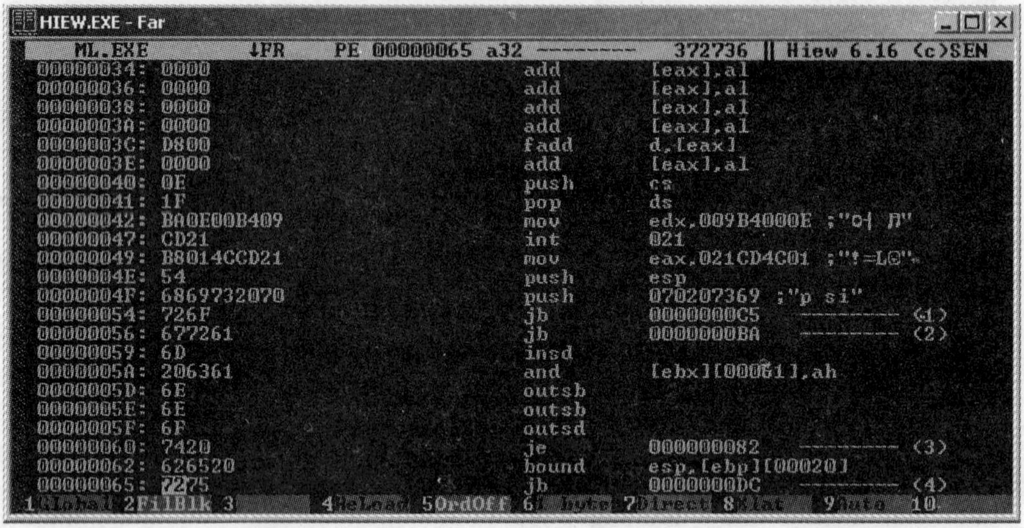

Fig. 22.1. HIEW.EXE program at work

The interface of this program makes you recall the interfaces found in FAR Manager or Norton Commander (see Fig. 22.1). All commands are issued by functional keys (including combinations with the <Alt> and <Ctrl> keys). For example, by pressing <F4>, you can choose the mode of displaying the file: text, assembly, or binary. By pressing <F3>, you switch to the editing mode (provided that you are viewing the file in binary or assembly modes). If you switch to the assembly view and press <F2> after <F3>, you'll be able to edit machine commands in symbolic form. I will not describe the commands of this program in detail because they are simple and obvious, and the list of available commands can be obtained by pressing <F1>. Therefore, I'll demonstrate a practical example of using this program. For clarity, I will use a simple console application.

Listing 22.2 presents a simple console application that outputs a text string to the console.

Listing 22.2. A simple console application

```
.586P
; Flat memory model
.MODEL FLAT, stdcall
```

```
; Constants
STD_OUTPUT_HANDLE       equ -11
INVALID_HANDLE_VALUE  equ -1
; Prototypes of external procedures
EXTERN  GetStdHandle@4:NEAR
EXTERN  WriteConsoleA@20:NEAR
EXTERN  ExitProcess@4:NEAR
; INCLUDELIB directives for the linker
includelib c:\masm32\lib\user32.lib
includelib c:\masm32\lib\kernel32.lib
;-----------------------------------------------
; Data segment
_DATA SEGMENT
      BUF   DB  "Output string", 0
      LENS  DWORD ? ; Number of characters for output
      HANDL DWORD ?
_DATA ENDS
; Code segment
_TEXT SEGMENT
START:
; Get the HANDLE output handle
        PUSH  STD_OUTPUT_HANDLE
        CALL  GetStdHandle@4
        CMP   EAX, INVALID_HANDLE_VALUE
        JNE   _EX
        MOV   HANDL, EAX
; String output
        PUSH  0
        PUSH  OFFSET LENS
        PUSH  17
        PUSH  OFFSET BUF
        PUSH  HANDL
        CALL  WriteConsoleA@20
_EX:
        PUSH  0
        CALL  ExitProcess@4
_TEXT ENDS
END START
```

The program in Listing 22.2 is easy. Now imagine that in the course of debugging, you accidentally changed a single command: you inserted `JNE` instead of `JE`. As a result, the program ceased to operate after translation. Is it possible to correct it without using the Assembly code? Of course, this is possible. To achieve this goal, it is necessary to disassemble the program, locate the error, and then use the HIEW.EXE program. It is possible to use only the HIEW program because it disassembles correctly. However, to illustrate the approach, I will carry out the task in two stages.

Disassemble the module using the DUMPBIN.EXE program. The disassembled code of this program is presented in Listing 22.3.

Listing 22.3. Disassembled code of the program in Listing 22.2

```
Dump of file cons1.exe

File Type: EXECUTABLE IMAGE

 00401000: 6AF5          PUSH    0F5h
 00401002: E82B000000    CALL    00401032
 00401007: 83F8FF        CMP     EAX, 0FFh
 0040100A: 751E          JNE     0040102A
 0040100C: A316304000    MOV     [00403016], EAX
 00401011: 6A00          PUSH    0
 00401013: 6812304000    PUSH    403012h
 00401018: 6A11          PUSH    11h
 0040101A: 6800304000    PUSH    403000h
 0040101F: FF3516304000  PUSH    DWORD PTR DS:[00403016h]
 00401025: E80E000000    CALL    00401038
 0040102A: 6A00          PUSH    0
 0040102C: E80D000000    CALL    0040103E
 00401031: CC            INT     3
 00401032: FF2508204000  JMP     DWORD PTR DS:[00402008h]
 00401038: FF2500204000  JMP     DWORD PTR DS:[00402000h]
 0040103E: FF2504204000  JMP     DWORD PTR DS:[00402004h]
```

By the disassembled code, it is easy to locate the error. By the way, the `CMP EAX, 0FFh` command must naturally be interpreted as `CMP EAX, 0FFFFFFFFh`. Memorize the required code, `83F8FF`, and start HIEW.EXE, then press <F7> to search for the required combination. After that, press <F3>; then press <F2> and replace `JNE` with `JE`. Having completed this, press <F9> to save the change. As a result, you'll correct the program without needing to recompile and rebuild it.

DEWIN.EXE

This program operates in the command-line mode; however, it has several advantages in comparison to DUMPBIN.EXE. Its main advantage is the recognition of high-level languages. In addition, it provides the possibility of writing scripts using the built-in macro language.

IDA Pro

This is one of the most powerful disassemblers. Its functional capabilities are so rich that most programmers consider it a universal and almighty tool. When working with the text of the program being disassembled, it is possible to rename labels and procedures and to provide custom comments so that the disassembled text finally becomes easily readable and understandable. The corrected program text is saved in a special database and is recovered at the next startup. The main window of the IDA Pro disassembler is shown in Fig. 22.2. This illustration shows the disassembled code of the EDIT.EXE program (see Listing 3.2 in *Chapter 3*). By the way, notice the `offset WNDPROC` reference. The `WNDPROC` name was assigned in the course of analyzing the code of this program.

Now, consider some features of this disassembler:

- It can rename procedures and labels in a program. Naturally, in the course of disassembling, IDA Pro gives internal names to all procedures and labels. You can replace them with custom names to make the program text more understandable. All changes introduced into the text will be stored in special database and can be recovered after restart.
- It recognizes library and application program interface functions (see Fig. 22.2). The disassembler not only recognizes these functions but also comments their parameters.
- Using the context menu or double-clicking the mouse on the `JMP` or `CALL` commands, it is possible to jump to the specified location within a program and continue to execute the jumps any number of times. To return any number of steps back, use the arrow button on the toolbar.
- Using key combinations such as <Shift>+<Insert>, the <Insert> key, and commands from the **Edit** menu, it is possible to insert a comment in any location within a program. Like custom label names, comments are saved in the program database. However, the most advantageous feature is that it is possible to insert the address of a specific program line or label name into the text of the comment. If you double-click that address or label, you'll automatically jump to the required location.

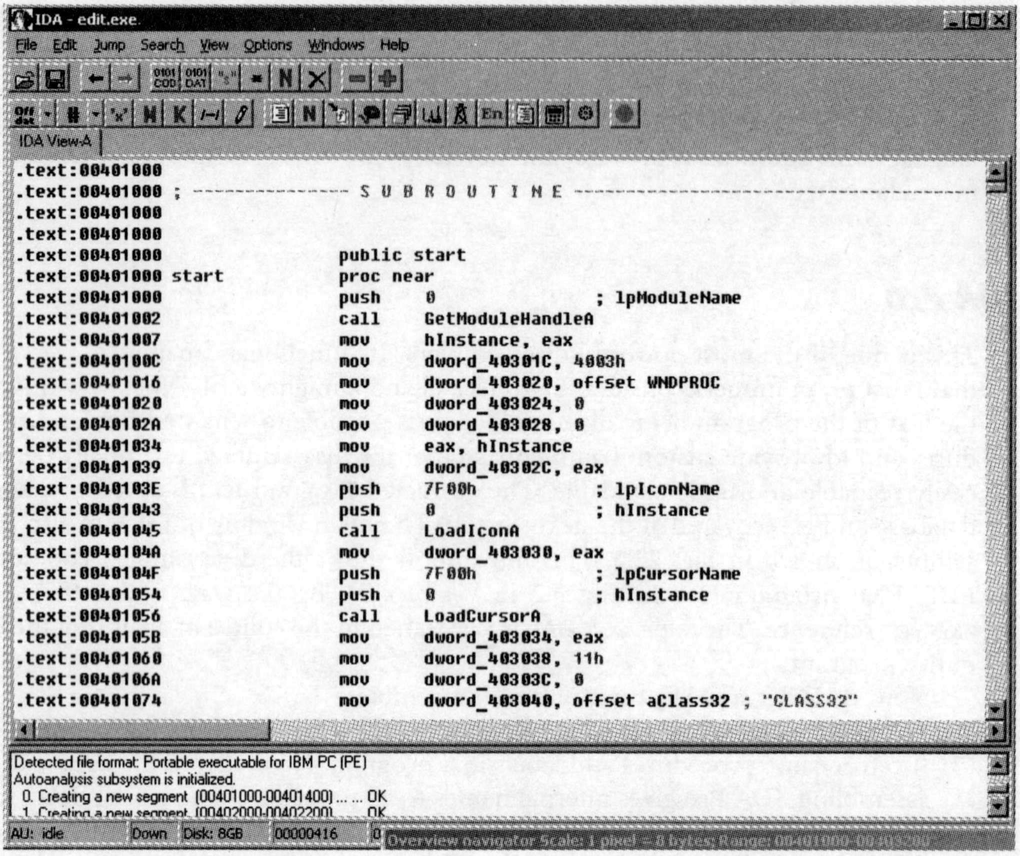

Fig. 22.2. Program disassembling using the IDA Pro disassembler

- This disassembler can expand and collapse procedures. By pressing the <-> key on the numeric keypad, it is possible to collapse the procedure. Pressing the <+> key expands the collapsed procedure. Presenting procedures in collapsed form allows you to represent the program code in more compact and readable form.
- IDA Pro correctly recognizes both code and data. Fig. 22.3 shows the disassembled part of the EDIT.EXE program containing data.

IDA Pro also allows you to create and execute batch files. The language of IDA Pro batch files is close to the C programming language. Because of the limited volume of this book, I will not cover this language in detail. Nevertheless, I will provide an example batch file demonstrating this capability of IDA Pro.

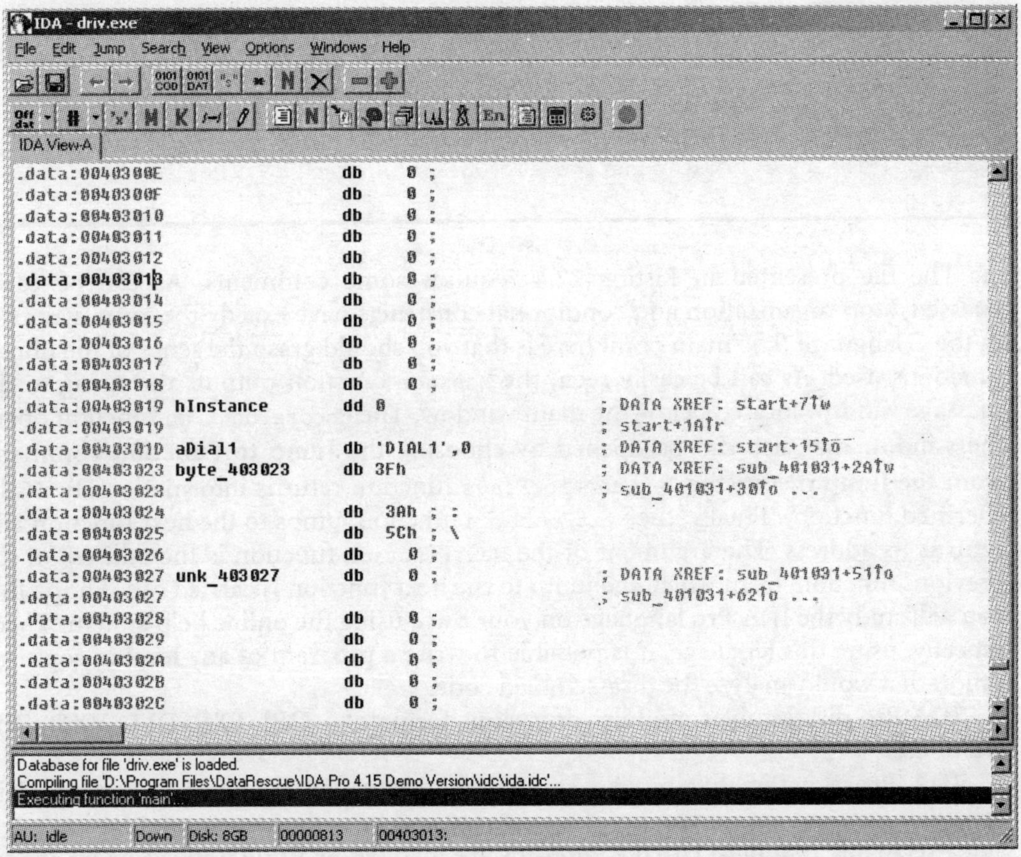

Fig. 22.3. Program fragment containing data disassembled using IDA Pro

Listing 22.4. An IDA Pro batch file

```
//
// This example shows how to get a list of functions.
//
#include <idc.idc>
static main() {
auto ea, x;

for (ea = NextFunction(0); ea != BADADDR; ea = NextFunction(ea) ) {
 Message("Function at %08lX:%s", ea, GetFunctionName(ea));
 x = GetFunctionFlags(ea);
```

```
  if ( x & FUNC_NORET ) Message(" Noret");
  if ( x & FUNC_FAR ) Message(" Far");
  Message("\n");
 }
 ea = ChooseFunction("Please choose a function");
 Message("The user chose function at %08lX\n", ea);
}
```

The file presented in Listing 22.4 requires some comments. As can be easily guessed, loop organization and conditional constructs have exactly the same syntax as in the C language. The main point here is that you should grasp the sense of the library functions used. As can be easily seen, the `Message` function outputs the string to the message window located below the main window. The `ChooseFunction` function opens the window that also can be opened by choosing the **Jump to Function** command from the **Jump** menu (the `GetFunctionFlags` function returns information about the specified function). Finally, the `NextFunction` function jumps to the next function and returns its address. The argument of the `NextFunction` function is the address of the previous function, from which the jump to the next function is carried out. I hope that you will study the IDA Pro language on your own, using the online help system. Theoretically, using this language, it is possible to write a program of any level of sophistication that would analyze the disassembled code.

IDA Pro disassembles modules of various formats — OBJ, EXE, DLL, VXD, ZIP, NLM, etc.

IDA Pro functionality can be considerably extended by using various plug-in modules. Plug-ins are written in C++ language and have the structure of typical portable executable modules. Usually, plug-ins are invoked by using hotkeys or by choosing the **Edit | Plugins** menu commands. Plug-ins must be located in a special plug-ins directory with the configuration file that specifies these modules.

Another advantage of this disassembler is that it creates an Assembly file that makes it possible to work in the text mode.

Chapter 23

Introduction to Turbo Debugger

Borland Turbo Debugger is a powerful tool for debugging programs. It was developed in the time of MS-DOS and mainly is oriented toward Borland's implementations of most programming languages. The most important point is that this debugger allows program debugging both at the level of disassembled microprocessor commands and at the symbolic level (i.e., using the source code of the program being debugged). In the latter case, for successful debugging it is necessary to include the debug information in the executable module at compile time.

For example, consider the program from Listing 17.1 in *Chapter 17*. This program displays the window containing the list of available disks and drives (both local and network, if there are any). To include the debug information in this module, add the `/zi` command-line option when assembling the program with TASM32. At build time, add the `-v` option to the TLINK32.EXE command-line options. In this case, all information required for symbolic debugging will be saved in the executable module.

It is important to bear in mind that more than the executable module and the debug information that it contains are required for symbolic debugging. In addition to this, you'll need the program's source code. The executable module stores the information that allows you to compare machine codes and the source code of the program. Fig. 23.1 shows the debugger window with the loaded debug information of the DRIV.ASM program (see Listing 17.1 in *Chapter 17*). The debugger allows you to execute the program step by step (more details on the modes of program execution are provided later in this chapter), simultaneously viewing the source code of the program being debugged and its disassembled listing. By walking through the program, you'll be able to view the results of executing each step.

Fig. 23.1 shows the three most frequently used debugger windows: the window containing the source code, the Central Processing Unit (CPU) window that displays the disassembled text, and even the current information about registers and flags, which is especially important when debugging GUI applications.

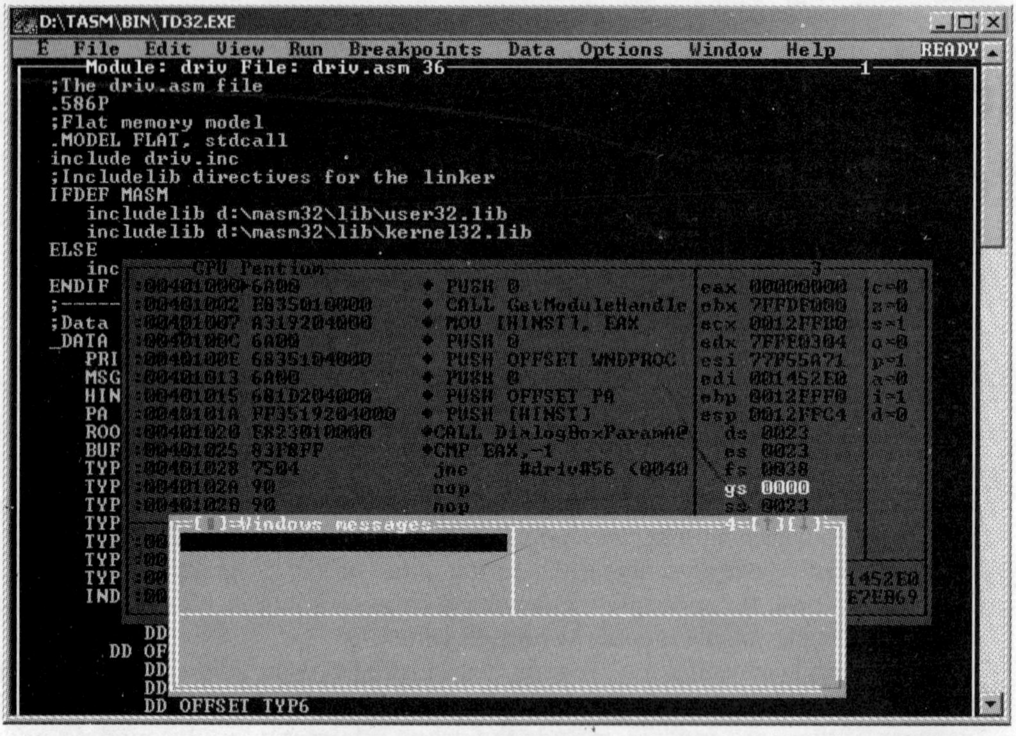

Fig. 23.1. Turbo Debugger windows

Consider the debugger commands and its functional capabilities:

- Starting the application being debugged — This can be achieved by pressing <F9> or selecting the **RUN** command from the **RUN** menu. The program executes until it accomplishes its tasks, provided that the breakpoint on a specific line of code is not set in the **CPU** window. To set a breakpoint, press <F2>. By opening the **Watch** window (**View | Watches**), you'll be able to specify the settings to track the changes of the variables, which are of interest to you. In this case, the breakpoints will also prove to be useful.

- Executing the program up to the line where the cursor is positioned — To execute a command, press <F4> or select the appropriate menu item. The meaning of this command is that if you are interested in some program fragment, you can execute the program up to a specific line and review the result. This is similar to breakpoints but is more responsive. Furthermore, by pressing <Alt>+<F9>, you can execute the program up to a specific address.
- Executing an individual command — This is achieved by pressing <F7>. If the cursor is in the source code window, then the operator of a specific programming language will be executed. If the cursor is in the **CPU** window, then the appropriate CPU instruction will be executed.
- Executing a command by walking through the procedure — This command is executed when the user presses <F8>. It differs from the previous command in that it doesn't enter the procedure but that all instructions in the procedure are executed automatically (within a single step).
- Executing the procedure — If the cursor is positioned on the command for calling a procedure, then it is possible to execute that procedure by pressing <Alt>+<F8>.
- Delaying the execution — It is also possible to instruct the debugger to execute the program with a certain delay after each command. This is achieved by choosing the **Animate** command from the **Run** menu.

When executing any of the previously listed commands, it is also possible to specify command-line options. This can be achieved by choosing the **Run | Arguments...** commands.

Now, consider the most important windows of this debugger, some of which I have already mentioned. To display a specific debugger window, choose an appropriate command from the **View** menu.

To display the program text, choose the **Module** command of the **View** menu. The program must be translated with the options ensuring that the debug information is saved in the executable module. Unfortunately, this is only true for the modules compiled using Borland products: C++, Delphi, and Turbo Assembler. Debugging information of other developers cannot be recognized by Turbo Debugger. Later in this chapter, I provide an example illustrating the debugging of a program written in Borland C++.

If Turbo Debugger doesn't recognize the debug information in the executable module, you will have to use the **CPU** window in the course of debugging. This window is divided into five parts (these are shown in Fig. 23.2):

- Microprocessor instructions
- Data segment
- Stack segment
- Registers state
- Main flags

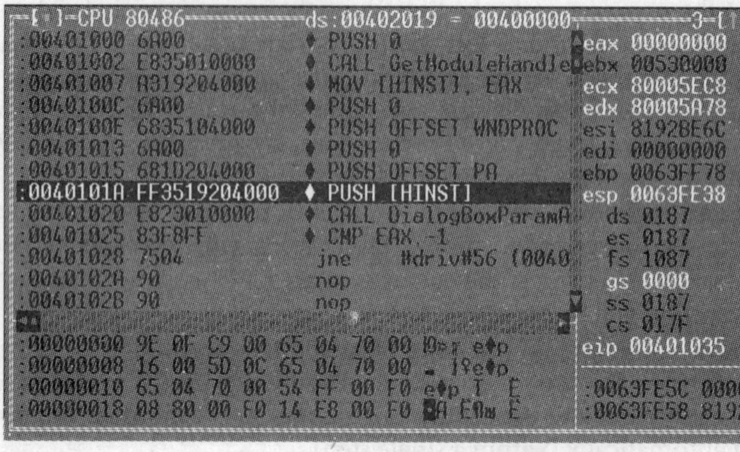

Fig. 23.2. Turbo Debugger **CPU** window

Other windows of Turbo Debugger are as follows:

- Window for watching variables — This window is opened by selecting **View | Watches**. By clicking the right mouse button, you can add to this window variables whose values you want to watch. When the program is executed step by step or with breakpoints, it is possible to control the values of variables at each step.
- Stack window — This window shows the state of the stack. The first called function will be at the bottom of the stack.
- Breakpoints window — This window contains information about all breakpoints set within the program. It is possible to add new breakpoints.
- Log window — This window stores information about all events that take place in the debugger.
- Variables window — This window displays variables available in the current context.
- Files window — In this window, you can view the binary file and correct it when necessary.
- Memory display window — This window allows you to view the memory contents line by line.
- Coprocessor window — This window displays the current coprocessor state.
- Execution history window — This window displays the history of program execution.
- Hierarchy window — This window displays the hierarchical tree of all objects and all class types used in the current module. An example window displaying the hierarchy of object classes is shown in Fig. 23.3.
- Threads window — This window displays information about all threads running in the process being debugged.

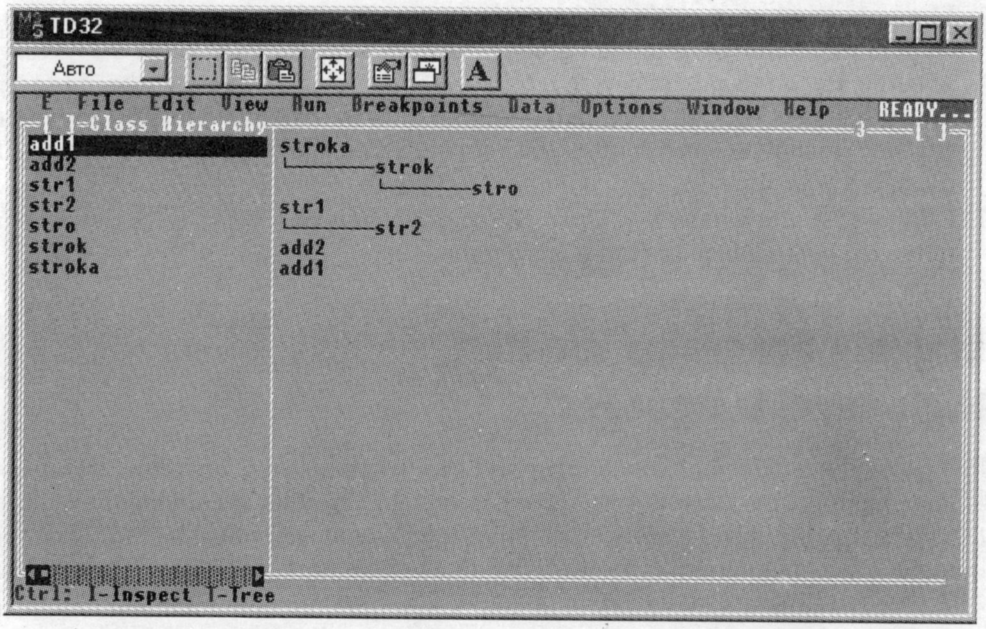

Fig. 23.3. Turbo Debugger window displaying class hierarchy

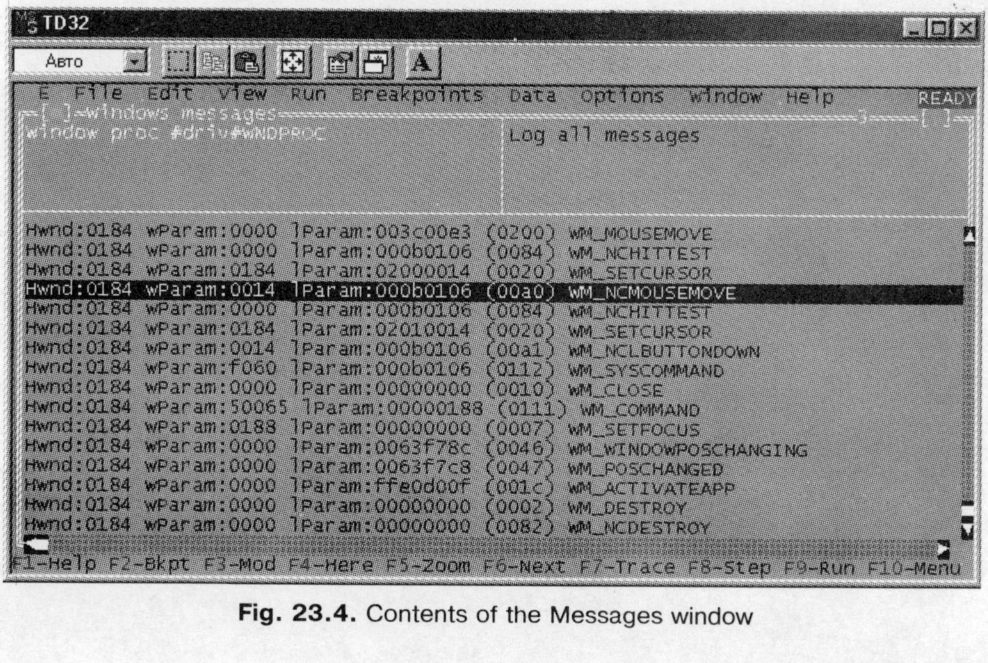

Fig. 23.4. Contents of the Messages window

- Messages window — Using this window, it is possible to trace all messages received by the current window. Fig. 23.4 provides an example of using the messages window. Here, it is possible to select the class of messages to be traced or to specify individual messages for tracing. In addition to tracing, it is possible to specify another reaction — interrupt execution (i.e., to set the breakpoint to the specific message).
- Clipboard buffer window — Using this window, it is possible to trace the contents of the clipboard when executing a program.

Debugging Programs Written in High-Level Languages

Now, it is time describe debugging programs written using high-level languages. If the debug information was saved in the executable module at compile time, Turbo Debugger will be able to work with high-level language. Consider, for example, a simple console program demonstrating the bubble sort algorithm. The program is presented in Listing 23.1.

Listing 23.1. A simple console application

```
#include <windows.h>
#include <stdio.h>
void sort(DWORD a[], DWORD );
void main()
{
        DWORD a[10];
        DWORD j, p, k, r;
        randomize();
        for(j=0; j<10; j++) a[j]=random(10);
// Sorting
        {
        for(k=9; k>1; k--)
                {
                r=0;
                        for(j=0; j<k; j++)
                                {
                                        if(a[j]>a[j+1]){p=a[j+1];
                                        a[j+1]=a[j];
                                        a[j]=p;
                                        r=1; };
```

```
            }
            if(r==0)break;
      }
      for(j=0; j<10; j++) printf("%lu\n", a[j]);
      ExitProcess(0);
}
```

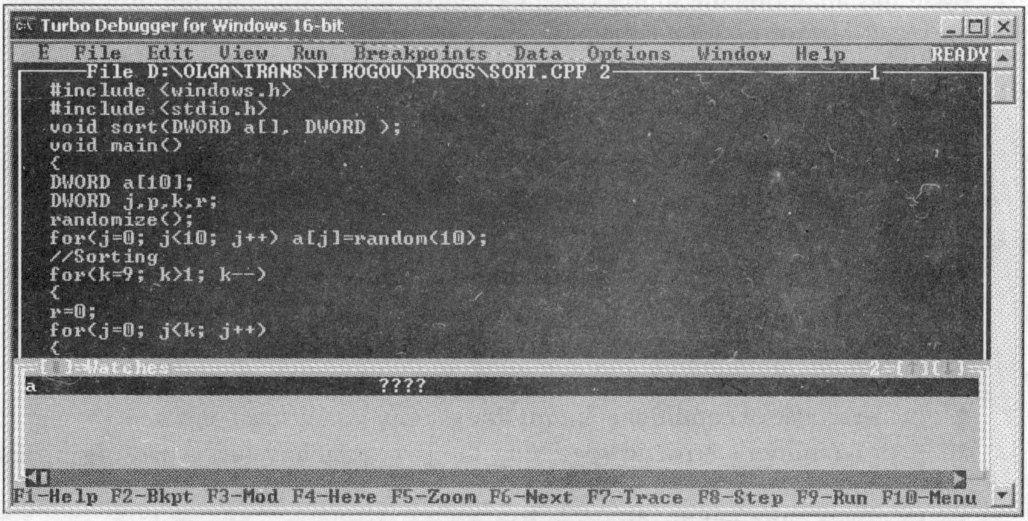

Fig. 23.5. Program from Listing 23.1 in the debugger window

Fig. 23.5 shows the Turbo Debugger window with the program from Listing 23.1 loaded. In the lower part of the main window, the **Watches** window resides. This window traces the values of elements of the array `a[]`. If you switch to the CPU window, you'll see how the bubble sort algorithm implemented in C language is converted into Assembly code.

Debugging Technique

Debugging a program that contains debugging information is the main goal of Turbo Debugger. Although this debugger disassembles the program and it is possible to view the disassembled code in the CPU window, such disassemblers as W32Dasm and IDA Pro are considerably more powerful in this respect than Turbo Debugger. The Ice debugger, which works in ring 0, also is more convenient for analyzing executable modules. Turbo Debugger takes its place among various debugging tools because it debugs at the source code level. In this section, I will cover several aspects of debugging techniques.

Generally, the debugging process can be divided into four stages:

1. Error detection — Errors in programs are detected in the course of program testing and practical use.
2. Error localization — Most frequently, this stage is the most difficult and labor-intensive. This is the stage, in which debuggers are useful. Professional programmers know that it is sometimes difficult to locate errors in sophisticated algorithms by simply analyzing the source code. Of course, it is possible to output intermediate results; however, for a large program, you might need too many output operations. A good debugger is indispensable in such cases because it allows the variable values to be traced at every step.
3. Determination of the error cause — Apart from algorithmic errors, consider the most typical Assembly errors:
   - Error in the order of operands. For example: `MOV EAX, EBX` instead of `MOV EBX, EAX`.
   - Stack overflow when using recursive algorithms or a too-deep nesting level of procedure calls.
   - Corruption of the contents of some registers when calling procedures.
   - A stack that is not cleared when exiting a procedure.
   - Incorrect use of conditional jumps, for example, `JA` instead of `JNA`.
   - A programmer's error in specifying the last variable values when organizing loops.
   - Incorrect setting of the direction flag.
   - Errors related to incorrectly determining the boundaries of variables and arrays. Such errors often cause the corruption of other variables.
   - Incorrect type casting of operands. For example, the programmer might load `MOV AL, BL`, then use `EAX` and forget to reset to zero the most significant bytes of the `EAX` register.
4. Error correction — If the detected error is simple and obvious, it won't be difficult to correct it. By the way, you have probably already guessed that Turbo Debugger doesn't allow you to correct executable modules. However, situations are possible, in which a specific program section (or procedure) produces an erroneous value but you are short of time to properly locate the error because the program section under consideration is too complicated. Sometimes, the incorrect value of the output information occurs only if input parameters take a rare combination of values. In this case, an easy technique can be applied: insert several lines of code that check output information and correct it if needed between the detected program section and the remaining part of the program. This technique is useful when debugging someone else's large program if it is impossible to understand the logic of the algorithm (especially an erroneous one).

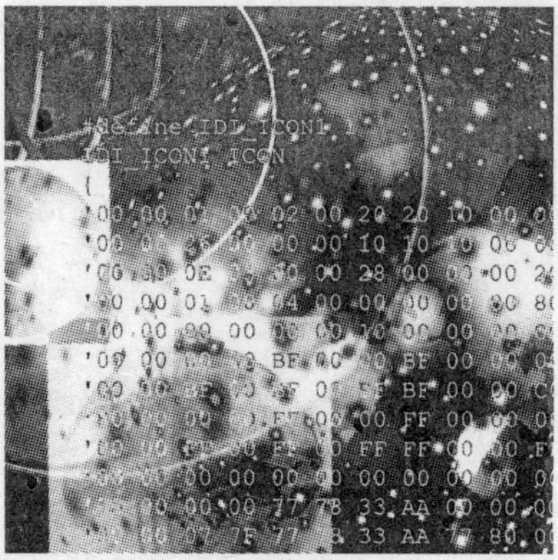

Chapter 24

Working with the W32Dasm Disassembler and SoftIce Debugger

In this chapter, I cover my two favorite tools for analyzing programs.

W32Dasm Debugger

The W32Dasm is a symbiosis of a powerful disassembler and a debugger. For the moment, version 8.93 of this program is the most widespread. It can work not only with PE modules but also with DOS, NE, and LE modules. In this chapter, I cover methods of working with this program in as much detail as possible.

Getting Started

The program window is shown in Fig. 24.1. The menu is supplemented by the toolbar whose elements are activated depending on the situation.

As already mentioned, this program is a combined disassembler and debugger. This is reflected by the presence of two menu items: **Disassembler** and **Debugger**. Accordingly, there are individual settings for debugger and disassembler. For disassembler, there are only three options related to the analysis of cross-references in conditional jumps, unconditional jumps, and procedure calls. By default, all three options are set. Disabling these options is undesirable, because it reduces the informative value of the disassembled code. However, you might wish to disable these options when disassembling large programs to speed up the code analysis.

Debugger options are greater in number; however, they all are self-evident. The debugger options window is shown in Fig. 24.2. All these options relate to specific features of loading processes, threads, and dynamic link libraries (DLLs).

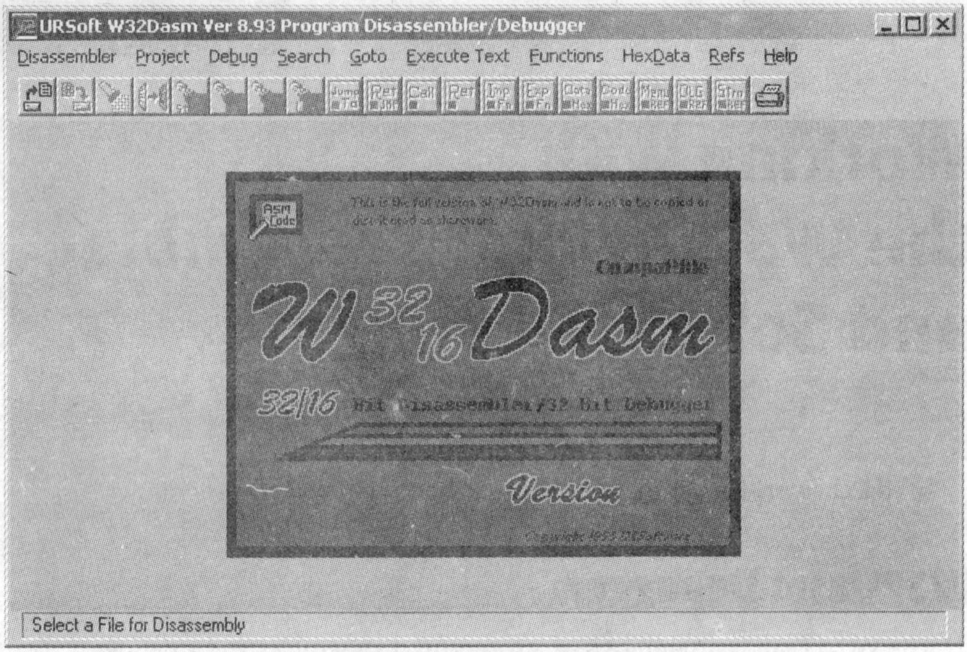

Fig. 24.1. W32Dasm window

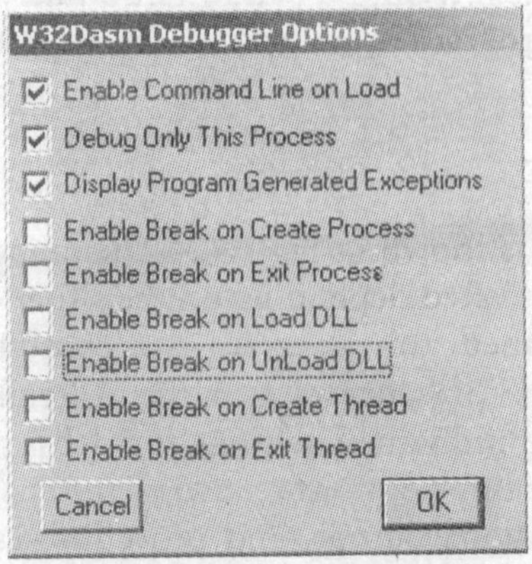

Fig. 24.2. Debugger options

To begin working with the executable module, choose the required file from the **Disassembler | Open File...** menu. After that, the program will analyze the module and output the disassembled text with comprehensive information about the module's sections.[i] W32Dasm correctly recognizes Application Programming Interface (API) functions and comments them (Fig. 24.3).

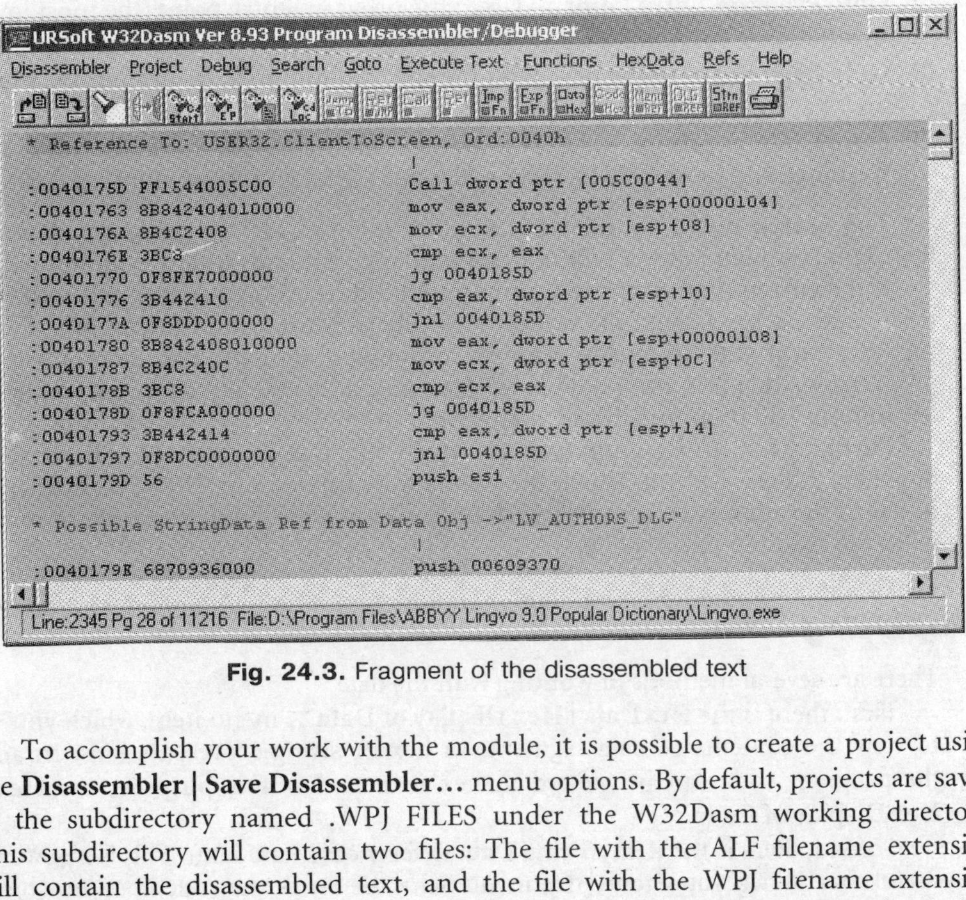

Fig. 24.3. Fragment of the disassembled text

To accomplish your work with the module, it is possible to create a project using the **Disassembler | Save Disassembler...** menu options. By default, projects are saved in the subdirectory named .WPJ FILES under the W32Dasm working directory. This subdirectory will contain two files: The file with the ALF filename extension will contain the disassembled text, and the file with the WPJ filename extension will contain the project. When you need to restart your work, you can open the project instead of the file. This is accomplished by choosing the **Project | Open...** menu commands.

[i] Although W32Dasm works with modules of different types, only PE modules are considered here.

Navigating the Disassembled Text

When navigating the disassembled text, the current line is highlighted. Jumps and procedure calls are specially highlighted. Navigation is further simplified by the **Goto** menu command:

- **Goto Code Start** — Go to the start of the listing.
- **Goto Program Entry Point** — Go to the program entry point (the most important menu item).
- **Goto Page** — Go to the page with the specified number; by default, the number of lines per page is assumed to be 50.
- **Goto Code Location** — Jump to the specified address; if the address is missing, the range and proximity to other addresses are taken into account.

The **Search** menu command is another method of navigating the disassembled text. This command doesn't differ from similar commands found in other programs.

If the current line contains a jump or procedure call, you can jump to the appropriate address by clicking the respective toolbar button. You can continue navigating this way until you detect the required program fragment. The most advantageous point here is that it is also possible to move in the inverse direction. All required toolbar buttons will be automatically highlighted.

Furthermore, those addresses, to which the jump is carried out, contain lists of source addresses, from which the jumps were carried out. If you highlight the line, in which the address is located, and double-click it with the right mouse button, you'll go to the required line of code.

Displaying Data

There are several methods of working with the data.

First, there is the **HexData | Hex Display of Data...** menu item, which you can use to view the contents of data segments in hex or string representations. In addition, the program code can be viewed in hex format. For this purpose, use **HexData | Hex Display of Code....**

Second, there is the **Refs | String Data References** menu item. This is a powerful and useful tool. When you choose this menu item, the list of the code lines, to which there are references from the program text, will appear. This list includes everything that the disassembler could detect when analyzing the program. By selecting the required line, you can double-click it and jump to the required program location. If this line is referred to from several locations, you can continue double-clicking to visit all required locations. Fig. 24.4 displays the window containing references to string data types.

As you can see from Fig. 24.4, it is possible to copy either the selected string or all strings into the clipboard.

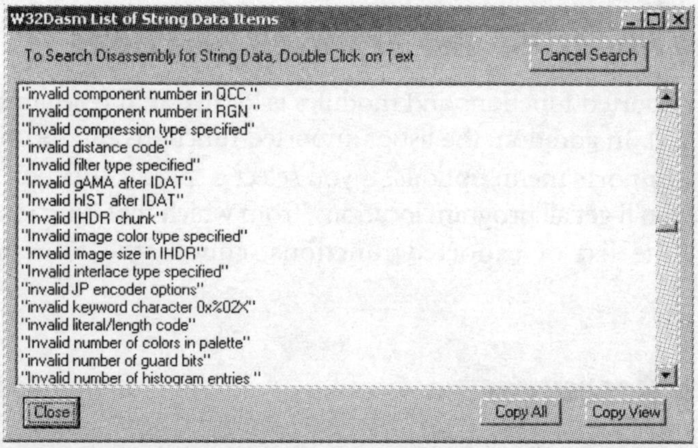

Fig. 24.4. Window displaying references to strings

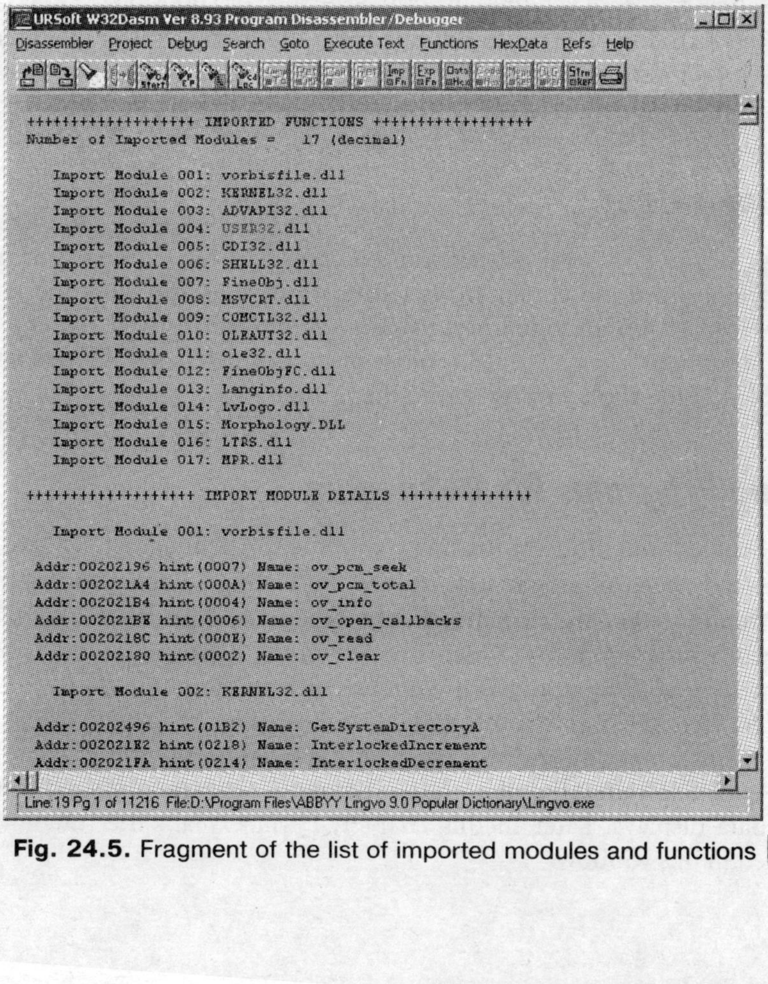

Fig. 24.5. Fragment of the list of imported modules and functions

Outputting Imported and Exported Functions

The list of imported functions and modules is located in the beginning of the disassembled text (Fig. 24.5). In addition, the list of imported functions can be obtained by choosing the **Functions | Imports** menu options. If you select a specific function from the list and double-click it, you'll get all program locations, from which that function is called.

To get the list of exported functions, choose the **Functions | Exports** menu commands.

Displaying Resources

Resources (or, to be more precise, two main resources — menu and dialog) are also described in the beginning of the disassembled text. It is possible to work with the list of resources in special windows that can be opened by choosing the **Refs | Menu References** and **Refs | Dialog references** options from the menu. String resources can be viewed in the previously mentioned window for viewing string references (see Fig. 24.4). Unfortunately, this version of the program doesn't recognize other types of resources.

Text Operations

Strings of the disassembled text can be copied to the clipboard or printed. To select the string, move the cursor to its leftmost position and click the left mouse button. To select a group of code lines, use the <Shift> key as well. To copy or print the selected fragment, click a special toolbar button, which is highlighted when the fragment is copied to the clipboard or sent to the printer.

Loading Programs for Debugging

There are two methods of loading a module for debugging. To load the module that has already been disassembled, choose the **Debug | Load Process** menu commands. The **Debug | Attach to an Active Process** menu options allow you to attach and debug the process loaded into the memory. When the debugger loads, two windows appear on the screen. The first one is the information window (Fig. 24.6).

The second window is the control window (Fig. 24.7).

The information window contains several list boxes: contents of the CPU registers, processor flag values, breakpoints, contents of segment registers, base addresses, and two data displays. Later in this chapter, I will explain the functions of the buttons located in this window.

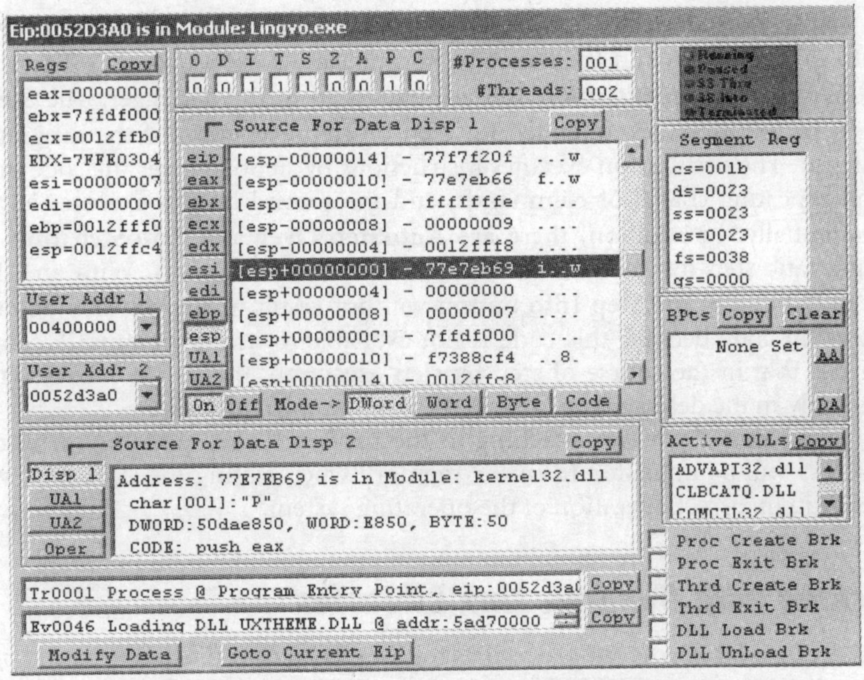

Fig. 24.6. First information window of the debugger

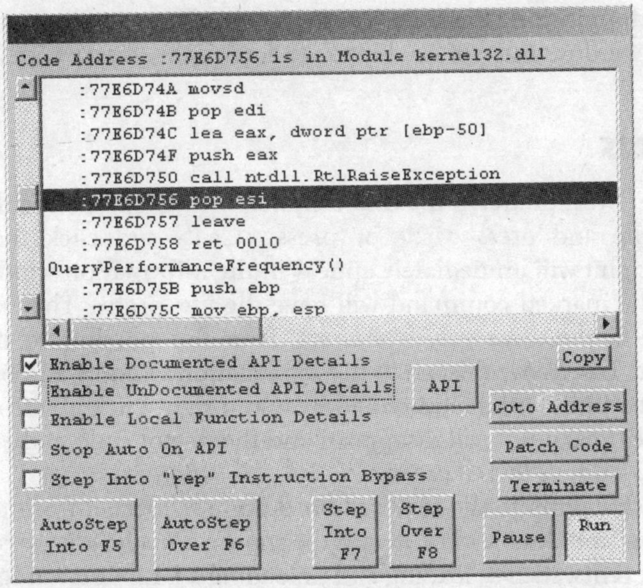

Fig. 24.7. Control window of the debugger

Now, consider the control window. The **Run** button starts the program loaded into the debugger, and the **Pause** button pauses its execution. The **Terminate** button stops the program execution and removes it from the debugger. The **Step Over** and **Step Into** buttons are intended for step-by-step execution of the program being debugged. The first button executes instructions by stepping over the code of procedures and repeating chains of commands, and the second button executes all instructions sequentially. In addition, there are **AutoStep Over** and **AutoStep Into** buttons for automatic step-by-step execution of the debugged program. With an API function, even the use of the **Step Into** button will not result in step-by-step execution of the function code because this code is not available to user programs. A convenient feature is that in the course of step-by-step execution, the cursor moves synchronously not only in the debugger but also in the disassembler window.

Note that if you are attaching to the process loaded into the memory, then this process will be unloaded from the memory when exiting the debugger, which might result in incorrect operation of the operating system.

Working with Dynamic Link Libraries

To debug a DLL, you can proceed as follows: Load into the debugger the program that accesses the required DLL. Then, view the list of used DLLs. To work with this DLL, you might be required to start the program and execute one of its functions. After you double-click the required library, you'll get its disassembled code in the disassembler window and will be able to work with the library code.

Breakpoints

You can set breakpoints in the disassembled listing. To achieve this, go to the required line of code and press <F2> or press <Ctrl> and click the left mouse button. The breakpoint will immediately appear in the information window and in the control window; the marked command will have the `BP*` prefix. The existing breakpoint can be deleted in the same way it was set. It is also possible to deactivate the existing breakpoint. To achieve this, go to the information window and open the list of existing breakpoints. Choose the required address and right-click it with the mouse. The asterisk near the breakpoint will disappear, and the line of code in the disassembler window will change from yellow to green.

To quickly jump to the required breakpoint, choose it from the list in the information window and double-click it with the mouse. Finally, it is possible to set breakpoints to specific events, such as loading and unloading a DLL or creating and deleting a thread. These goals are achieved by setting an appropriate flag in the information window.

Modifying Code, Data, and Registers

The debugger allows you to modify the code that you loaded previously. To do so, click the **Patch Code** button in the control window (Fig. 24.8). It is important to note that only the code loaded into the debugger is modified, not the disassembled text. Having found the required location in the code being debugged, you can modify this code and immediately test the result of modification by running the program. If your modification was correct, you can proceed with modifying the module.

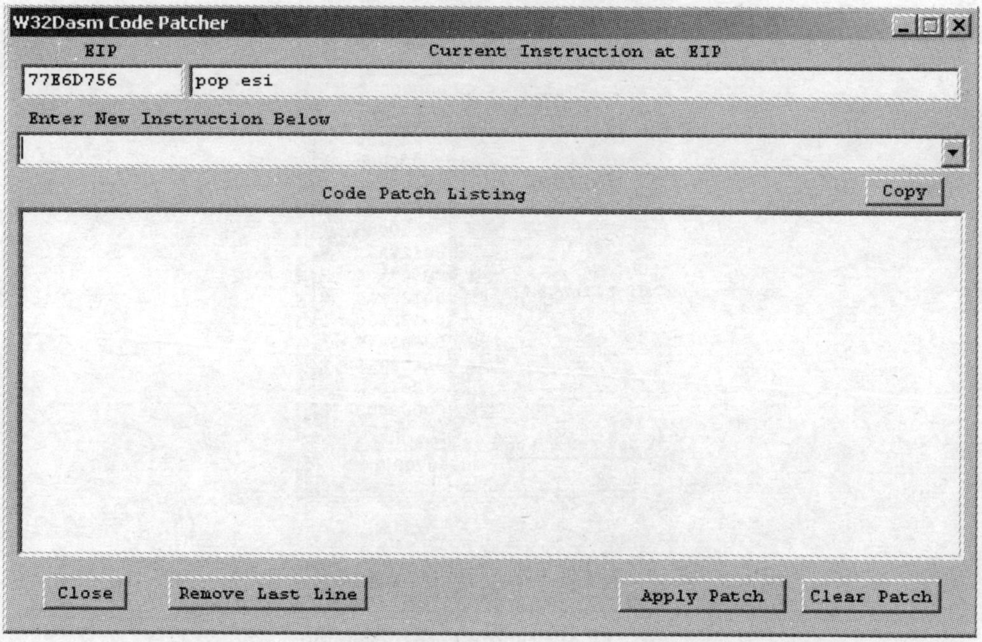

Fig. 24.8. Window for modifying the code being debugged

To modify the registers and memory cells of an executable process, there is a special toolbar button — the **Modify Data** button on the toolbar of the information window. This window is shown in Fig. 24.9. At first glance, it might seem that this window is cluttered with elements; however, after you carefully study this window, you'll discover that there isn't anything redundant here. The top part of the window displays the current values of the main processor flags, which you can change. To modify the content of a register or memory cell, first set the modifier value using **Enter Value**. Then choose the required register and click the button next to it. To restore the previous value, click the **R** button to the left of the register field chosen. To change the content of the memory cell, first write the cell address to the **Mem Lock** field and then use the **Mem** button. Other operations that can be carried out in this window are self-evident.

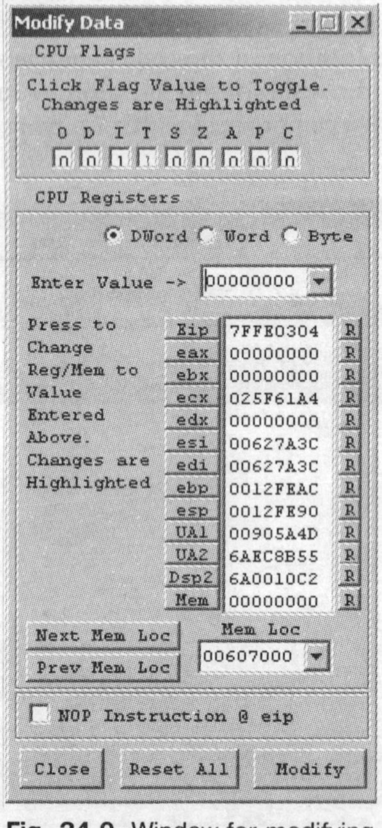

Fig. 24.9. Window for modifying the contents of registers and memory cells

Additional Abilities for Working with an Application Programming Interface

The debugger allows you to output additional information about executed API functions. To use this functionality, proceed as follows: Go to the control window and set the following flags: **Enable Documented API Detail** and **Stop Auto On API**. Then, press <F5> to start the program execution. Every time the program passes an API function, it will stop and the screen will display information about the specific function.

Searching for the Required Locations in a Program

Quite often, it is necessary to find a location within the disassembled code that corresponds to a specific location within the executable program. The most efficient way of achieving this goal is as follows: Load the required module into the debugger. Then, start it for execution, step to the required position, and click the **Terminate** button. As a result, the highlighted string in the disassembled code will be at the required position. You should only bear in mind that some programs introduce modifications that remain in force. For instance, the hotkeys can be classified as such modifications.

The use of the W32Dasm will be covered in more detail later in this book.

The SoftIce Debugger

SoftIce (v. 4.05),[i] sometimes referred to as simply Ice, is intended for use under Windows 9*x* or Windows NT. The debugger includes the kernel-mode debugger; in addition, SoftIce has a symbolic loader for loading executable modules into the debugger. The loader allows you to read the debug information for Microsoft and Borland products.

Debugging using SoftIce provides the following capabilities:

- Symbolic and normal debugging of 32-bit applications
- Debugging drivers for Windows NT and Windows 9*x*, debugging 16-bit MS-DOS and Windows applications, and debugging system programs
- Setting breakpoints to the commands located by a specific address
- Setting breakpoints to read and write operations to or from memory and to input and output ports
- Setting breakpoints to Windows messages
- Setting conditional breakpoints, which are triggered if a specific condition is satisfied
- Getting internal information about the operating system
- Using the debugger on a remote computer

SoftIce implementations for Windows 9*x* and Windows NT are different. In the first case, it is implemented as a virtual extended driver started from AUTOEXEC.BAT (the WINICE.EXE program). In Windows NT, it is the kernel-mode driver NTICE.SYS.

---

[i] For Windows 2000 or later Windows versions, it is necessary to use SoftIce version 4.2.7.

Installation

Installation of the product is straightforward. The main problem that you'll have to solve during the installation is correctly choosing the video adapter and mouse. As a rule, it is recommended that you choose the standard video graphics array adapter. In this case, there won't be any problems with the video subsystem. SoftIce also assumes that the mouse will be used for controlling the debugging process. However, the mouse isn't required; you can work with SoftIce without it.

After you complete the installation and reboot the system, you'll probably need to customize the settings in the WINICE.DAT file. General recommendations related to this task are as follows:

- The `PHYSMB=32` line specifies the amount in MB of RAM physically installed on your computer. Edit this string by specifying the actual memory available on your computer.
- The `INIT=` string defines the interface settings. I prefer the settings specified by the following string: `INIT="SET FONT 1; SET ORIGIN 30 30; LINES 65; WIDTH 90; WR; WF; WD 4; WL; WC 30; X;"`. You can specify the parameters according to your preferences. You can also change the settings on the fly in the debugger window.
- In the end of the file, there are commented strings that look as follows: `; EXP=c: \windows\system\kernel32.dll`. Uncomment them to enable the debugger to recognize the imported functions from standard DLLs.
- In Windows 9*x*, SoftIce adds the following string to the end of the AUTOEXEC.BAT file: C:\ICE\WINICE.EXE. If desired, you can comment it out.

Loading a Program for Debugging

SoftIce provides a special program called LOADER32.EXE for loading programs into the debugger. It is used for loading 32-bit applications. For loading 16-bit applications, the utilities located in the UTIL16 subdirectory are used.

Consider the LOADER32.EXE program. The loader looks as shown in Fig. 24.10. The sequence of actions that must be carried out to load a program into the debugger is as follows: Open the module, translate the module by converting the debug information into an NMS file, then load the module. If the debugger has correctly interpreted the debug information, the program text will appear in the debugger window; otherwise, you'll have to work with the disassembled code. After loading the module, you'll be able to customize the module startup in the debugger using the **Module | Setting** menu options (Fig. 24.11). The procedure is straightforward; therefore, I will not cover the options of this window in detail.

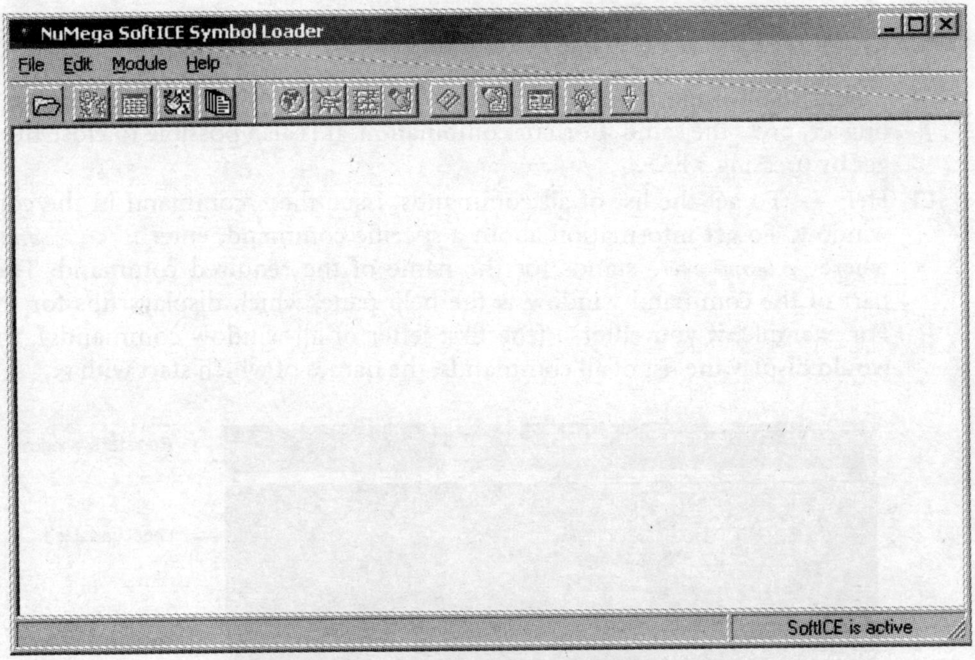

Fig. 24.10. SoftIce loader (LOADER32.EXE)

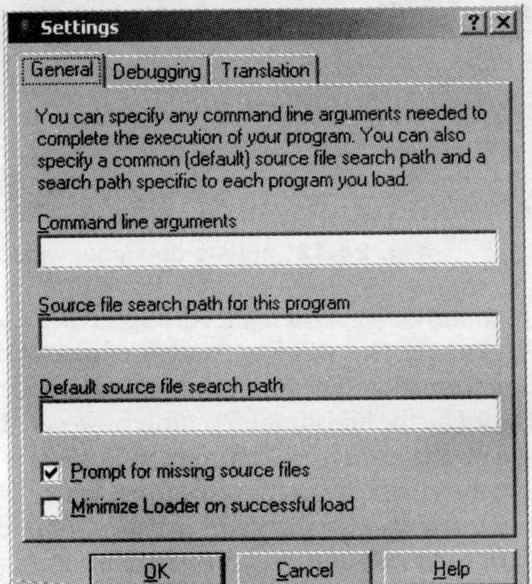

Fig. 24.11. Module startup customization window in SoftIce

Overview of the Debugger Commands

- Calling the debugger — To call the debugger, press <Ctrl>+<D>. To close the debugger, press the same shortcut combination. It is also possible to close the debugger by pressing <F5>.
- Help — To get the list of all commands, issue the `h` command in the command window. To get information about a specific command, enter `h` <*command_name*>, where *command_name* stands for the name of the required command. The lower part of the command window is the help pane, which displays tips for the user. For example, if you enter `w` (the first letter of all window commands), the pane would display the list of all commands, the names of which start with `w`.

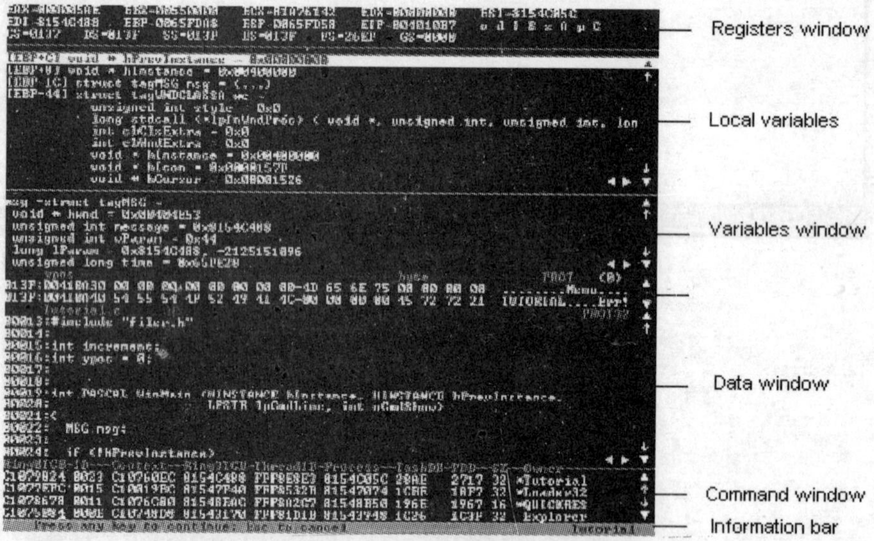

Fig. 24.12. SoftIce debugger window

- Working with windows — When the debugger is called, its window appears on the screen (Fig. 24.12.). This window consists of several panes, each intended for displaying specific information. The number of panes and the size of the initially displayed window are defined by the initialization setting; however, this can be changed as needed while working with the debugger. The command pane is intended for entering commands. Usually, the cursor is positioned in this pane. Every pane has its mnemonic designation, for example, `c` is the code pane, `d` is the data pane, `r` is the registers pane, `f` is the coprocessor pane, `w` is the variable watching pane, `s` is the stack pane, `l` is the local variables pane, and `x` is the Pentium III registers pane. The <Alt>+<*window_mnemonic*> command allows the user to switch to certain windows.

The task of detecting whether such switching is possible for a specific window is easy. To switch back, it is sufficient to issue the same command. If a specific window is missing, it can be created by issuing one of the commands, in which `w` is the first character, followed by the mnemonic designation of the required window. For example, if the data window is missing, you can issue the `wd` command to create it. The same command will remove the data window from the list of displayed windows. Window height is specified by the command parameter, for example: `wc 20`. I recommend that you memorize some other useful commands: <Ctrl>+<↑> or <↓> to scroll the code window, <Alt>+<↑> or <↓> to scroll the data window, and <Alt>+<Ctrl>+<↑>, <↓>, <←>, or <→> to move the debugger window over the screen.

- Viewing code and data — One of available methods of navigating and viewing the program is already known to you: you can scroll in the code window using <Ctrl>+<↑> or <↓>. To scroll in the data window, <Alt> is used instead of <Ctrl>. However, the most convenient method is to use the `U` command. The general format of this command is as follows: `U [address [length]] | [name]`. In this command, *address* is the address, either directly specified or defined through a register; *length* is the number of bytes for output, and *name* instructs the debugger to scroll the window until the specified name is encountered. For example: `u ebx -20` is the output instructions starting from the address after byte 20 and to the address `CS:EBX`. The `u` command without parameters outputs codes starting from `CS:EIP`. If l is specified as the second parameter, the information is output to the command window. The `D` command for the data window operates in a similar way. This command has the following format: `D [address], [length]`. For example, this could be `d 100, 100` or `d eax`. Assume that you have encountered the command `MOV EAX, [EBX-10]`. You can view the data area, from which the `EAX` value is taken, by issuing the following command: `d ebx-10`.
- Viewing and modifying registers — Switching to the registers window, as already mentioned, can be achieved by using the <Alt>+<r> shortcut. When you are in the registers window, you can change the register contents. The same result can be obtained by executing the `R` command from the command line. Commands such as `r reg=value` are also possible. For example: `r eax=10`. The `-d` option allows you to output register contents into the command window. The `r ecx` command moves the cursor to the required register, and the `r fl` command moves the cursor to the flags register. The command that appears as `r fl=o+a-p` will set the `o` and `a` flags and will reset the `p` flag.
- Code tracing — Hotkeys for this functionality are as follows: <F8> allows you to step into procedure, <F10> allows you to step over the procedure, and <F7> allows you to execute instructions to the current command (if you are in the code window). Pressing the <F7> key is the equivalent of using the `HERE` command. The < F12> key executes the code until the RET command is encountered (equivalent to the `P` command with the `RET` parameter). <F11> allows you to return to the last executed `CALL` command.

When working in the command line, you can use the `T` command, which has the following format: `T [=address] [count]`. Here *address* is the address, from which the execution starts, and *count* is the number of steps.

- Breakpoints — This is the most powerful and flexible debugging tool of the SoftIce program. Breakpoints can be classified in the following categories:
  - Standard breakpoints — The list of existing breakpoints can be viewed using the `BL` command. Each breakpoint is mapped to a number, which you'll see in the list. To delete a specific breakpoint or breakpoints from the list, use the `BC <number or list>` command. If you need to delete all breakpoints, use the `BC *` command. When working in the code window, you can add a breakpoint by pressing the <F9> key. The breakpoint will be set on the current line of code, and the line will be highlighted. Repeated pressing of the <F9> key will remove the breakpoint from the current line. The `BD` command deactivates the breakpoint but doesn't delete it from the list. The `BE` command reactivates the disabled breakpoint. It is also possible to add a breakpoint using the `bpx address` command.
  - Breakpoints at API functions — For example, the `bpx MessageBoxA` command will set a breakpoint to any call of this function. To check whether the debugger recognizes the functions of this group, execute the `exp MessageBox` command. The appropriate list will be displayed in the command window.
  - Conditional breakpoints — The `bpx` command uses the following syntax: `BPX [address] [if expression] [do "command1; command2.."]`. Thus, the breakpoint will be triggered only if the condition has been satisfied. When this happens, the specified sequence of the debugger commands will be executed. For example, the following expression is possible: `BPX eip if eax=10 do "db bx"`.
  - Breakpoints on specific messages — To set a breakpoint on a message, use the `bmsg` command. To succeed, you'll need to know the window handle. To get this information, use the `hwnd` command, which would provide the list of windows, their descriptors, and the addresses of their procedures. For example, the command `BMSG 0b0f wm_destroywindow` instructs the debugger to set a breakpoint to the `WM_DESTROYWINDOW` message arriving to the window with the handle `0b0fh`. Because these messages are integer numbers, it is possible to specify the ranges of messages using the blank character as a delimiter. Furthermore, the breakpoint can be supplemented by a condition (`if`) and a set of commands (`do`).
- Other commands — SoftIce has a range of about 200 commands. You can find their descriptions in the documentation supplied with the product. To quickly get information about a specific command, execute the `h` command or press <F1>. Most impressive is the number of commands for getting system information. I hope that you'll work with this information on your own.

Examples illustrating the practical use of W32Dasm and SoftIce will be provided in later chapters.

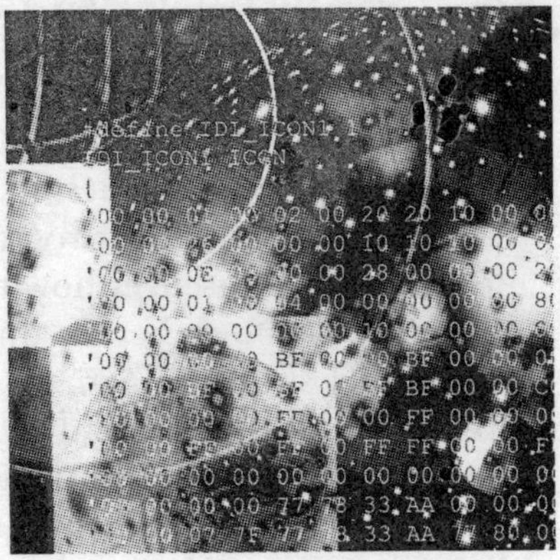

Chapter 25

Code Analysis Basics

Most executable modules are written in high-level programming languages and do not contain debug information. However, even in this case, it is sometimes necessary to analyze their code. To speed up the procedure of code analysis, the programmer has to know, or at least have reference information about, standard Assembly language structures corresponding to specific structures of high-level programming languages. Naturally, it is necessary to point out that in this chapter I mainly describe 32-bit applications.

Variables and Constants

Contemporary compilers optimize the source code quite efficiently; therefore, sometimes it is difficult to determine which variable is used and where. Mainly, this is because the compiler uses registers for storing variables whenever possible. As a rule, the compiler would start using memory only when there are no available registers.

To illustrate this situation, I have taken an easy console application written on Borland C++. The source code of this application takes about 15 lines of code. The EXE file, however, is more than 50 KB. The size of executable files isn't any wonder, though. Another point is more interesting in this respect: Only one disassembler has correctly solved the problem of determining the entry point — the `_main` label.

As you have probably guessed, this was IDA Pro. Naturally, all disassemblers have correctly disassembled the program section that carries out the job; however, only IDA Pro was able to discover how the jump to that section of code is carried out. The most advantageous point here is that it has also correctly recognized the `_printf` function. Listing 25.1 shows a fragment of the disassembled program corresponding to the `main` procedure. The source code was written in C language, and disassembling was carried out using IDA Pro. The debugger doesn't provide any clear possibilities of quickly finding this fragment. Hence, the usefulness of the combined use of the debugger and disassembler is obvious.

Listing 25.1. The main function of a console application

```
CODE:00401108   _main  proc near ; DATA XREF: DATA:0040B044
CODE:00401108
CODE:00401108   argc        = DWORD PTR 8
CODE:00401108   ARGV        = DWORD PTR 0CH
CODE:00401108   ENVP        = DWORD PTR 10H
CODE:00401108
CODE:00401108          PUSH  EBP
CODE:00401109          MOV   EBP, ESP
CODE:0040110B          PUSH  EBX
CODE:0040110C          MOV   EDX, OFFSET UNK_40D42C
CODE:00401111          XOR   EAX, EAX
CODE:00401113
CODE:00401113 LOC_401113: ; CODE XREF: _MAIN+22
CODE:00401113          MOV   ECX, 1FH
CODE:00401118          SUB   ECX, EAX
CODE:0040111A          MOV   EBX, DS:OFF_40B074
CODE:00401120          MOV   CL, [EBX+ECX]
CODE:00401123          MOV   [EDX+EAX], CL
CODE:00401126          INC   EAX
CODE:00401127          CMP   EAX, 21H
CODE:0040112A          JL    SHORT LOC_401113
CODE:0040112C          MOV   BYTE PTR [EDX+20H], 0
CODE:00401130          PUSH  EDX        ; CHAR
CODE:00401131          PUSH  OFFSET AS ;  __VA_ARGS
CODE:00401136          CALL  _PRINTF
CODE:0040113B          ADD   ESP, 8
CODE:0040113E          POP   EBX
CODE:0040113F          POP   EBP
CODE:00401140          RETN
CODE:00401140 _MAIN       ENDP
```

Now consider the way the programmer might determine which program written in C language was the source of the fragment under consideration. To begin with, consider the standard structures. This fragment contains only one standard structure, namely, the loop. The key command in the loop organization appears as follows:

```
CODE:0040112A JL SHORT LOC_401113
```

Obviously, the `inc eax` command increments the loop variable. Thus, the `EAX` register stores some variable that plays the role of the loop parameter. I suggest that you call this variable `i`. This assumption is confirmed by the presence of the `XOR EAX, EAX` command before the loop start. Naturally, this command is equivalent to `i=0`. The `INC EAX` stands for `i++`. Now, try to discover other variables. Pay attention to the following command:

```
CODE:0040110C  MOV EDX, OFFSET UNK_40D42C
```

This command deserves special attention because some address is loaded into the `EDX` register. Trace how the `EDX` register will be used further. Note the presence of the following command:

```
CODE:00401123  MOV [EDX+EAX], CL
```

Other commands using the `EDX` register are missing in the loop; with the presence of the preceding command, this drives the code analyzer to assume that `EDX` plays the role of the pointer to an array, string, or record. This assumption must be confirmed or refuted at the next step. At this step, pay attention to the following two commands:

```
CODE:0040112C          MOV  BYTE PTR [EDX+20H], 0
```

and

```
CODE:00401130          PUSH  EDX      ; CHAR
```

The first command assures the programmer that `EDX` points to a string, because it is the string that is terminated by the `0` character. The second command passes the second parameter to the `printf` function. Based on this information, and on the comment supplied by IDA Pro (the debugger correctly interpreted this code and did it quickly), it is possible to conclude that `EDX` is a pointer to some string. Note that this conclusion was drawn without reviewing the data block, which would certainly speed up the investigation. I suggest that you designate this pointer `s1`. In this relationship, the `[EDX+EAX]` expression can be interpreted as `s1[i]` or as `*(s1+i)`.

Now consider the following command:

```
CODE:0040111A     MOV  EBX, DS:OFF_40B074
```

It means that the `EBX` register also points to some string (I'll designate it `s2`). All further lines of code, which move characters from `s2` to `s1`, confirm this assumption. This deserves more detailed coverage.

What is the meaning of the following sequence of commands?

```
CODE:00401113          MOV  ECX, 1FH
CODE:00401118          SUB  ECX, EAX
```

Only one answer is possible: at every loop iteration, ECX will contain numbers from 1FH (31) to 0 (1FH will be the last value of the EAX register, that is, of the i variable, participating in the SUB ECX, EAX command). Because the MOV CX, 1FH command also participates in forming the content of the ECX register, it would be logical to assume that the ECX register, before moving characters from string to string, would always contain the 1FH-i (or 31-i) number. The [EBX+ECX] expression will then be equivalent to s2[31-i] or *(s2+31-i).

As a result, it is possible to conclude that the following commands:

```
CODE:00401120          MOV  CL, [EBX+ECX]
CODE:00401123          MOV  [EDX+EAX], CL
```

Can be replaced by the following expression: s1[i] = s2[31-i].

Now, you are prepared to consider the entire fragment:

```
CODE:00401111          XOR  EAX, EAX
CODE:00401113
CODE:00401113 LOC_401113: ; CODE XREF: _MAIN+22
CODE:00401113          MOV  ECX, 1FH
CODE:00401118          SUB  ECX, EAX
CODE:0040111A          MOV  EBX, DS:OFF_40B074
CODE:00401120          MOV  CL, [EBX+ECX]
CODE:00401123          MOV  [EDX+EAX], CL
CODE:00401126          INC  EAX
CODE:00401127          CMP  EAX, 21H
CODE:0040112A          JL   SHORT LOC_401113
```

For example, I hope that I'd be right if I wrote the following code fragment in C language:

```
i=0;
do {
    s1[i]=s2[31-i];
    i++;
} while(i>0x20)
```

Everything seems OK except the presence of the following string in the loop:

```
CODE:0040111A   MOV EBX, DS:OFF_40B074
```

Why is it in the loop instead of before the loop? This was done at the compiler's discretion. Note that this mustn't necessarily be the DO loop. In this case, the number of loop iterations is specified explicitly, and it is possible to make one conditional jump in the end of the loop. In other words, the previously provided structure could also be the result of optimization of the WHILE loop.

It is also possible to ask another question: Where are the s1 and s2 strings stored? This can be discovered quickly and easily. The main procedure is the standard one; consequently, if the strings in question were local variables, there would be an area in the stack reserved for them using commands such as SUB ESP, N (or ADD ESP, -N). Thus, if there are no such commands, s1 and s2 are global variables. The interesting point is that other variables, which are local ones, are stored in registers in accordance to the principle stating that variables must be stored in registers whenever possible.[i]

Thus, the result of the code analysis can be presented in Listing 25.2.

Listing 25.2. The final form of the C program reconstructed on the basis of the disassembled code

```
char s1[32];
char * s2="abcdefghigklmnopqrstuvwxyz";
void main()
{
    int i;
    i=0;
    do {
          s1[i]=s2[31-i];
           i++;
        } while(i>32);
          s1[32]=0;
          printf("%s\n", s1);
}
```

To conclude this example, I'll point out that variable s1 is not initialized and variable s2 receives an initial value. Initialized variables are stored in the DATA section, and uninitialized ones are in the BSS section (for the Borland C++ compiler).

Contemporary compilers allow the use of 64-bit integers. The Assembly code in this case becomes more complicated; however, these complications are not too considerable. It is necessary to bear in mind that the 64-bit variable is stored in two adjacent 32-bit blocks. The most significant part of such a variable has the higher address. To manipulate such a variable, a couple of registers are used as a rule — EDX:EAX for most

[i] In classical C language, to instruct the compiler to store variables in registers, they should be declared as register.

significant and least significant parts, respectively. Therefore, suppose that you encounter the following strings:

```
MOV    DWORD PTR [adr], EAX
MOV    DWORD PTR [adr+4], EDX
```

In this case, you can assume that you are dealing with a 64-bit variable.

C Control Structures

In this section, I cover some classical control structures of the C programming language and their conversion into Assembly language in the course of translation.

Conditional Constructs

The following is an incomplete conditional construct:

```
if(simple condition)
      {
            .
            .
            .
      }
```

If the condition is simple, such as `i == 1`, it is replaced by the following sequence of commands:

```
      CMP    EAX, 1
      JNZ    L1
      .
      .
      .
L1:
```

A complete conditional construct looks as follows:

```
if(simple condition)
{
      .
      .
      .
} else
{
      .
      .
      .
```

```
}

        CMP   EAX, 1
        JNZ   L1
        .
        .
        .
        JMP   L2
L1:
        .
        .
        .
L2:
```

Nested Conditional Constructs

Everything is self-evident in the following code:

```
        CMP   EAX, 1
        JNZ   L1
        CMP   EBX, 2
        JNZ   L1
        .
        .
        .
L1:
```

Naturally, this Assembly construct is equivalent to one aggregate condition connected by the AND operator. The OR operator is replaced by a conditional check in the ELSE block.

The Switch Operator

The switch operator is widely used in window functions. Sound knowledge of its Assembly structure will allow you to easily find such constructs in the disassembled code, such as follows:

```
switch(i)
{
 case 1:
        .
        .
        .
```

```
break;
case 3:
    .
    .
    .
break;
case 5:
    .
    .
    .
break;
}
```

Here is the Assembly code corresponding to this construct:

```
      DEC   EAX
      JZ    L1
      SUB   EAX, 2
      JZ    L2
      SUB   EAX, 2
      JZ    L3
      JMP   L4
L1:
      .
      .
      .
      JMP   L4
L2:
      .
      .
      .
      JMP   L4
L3:
      .
      .
      .
L4:
```

As you can see, this is an interesting structure. Such an approach allows better optimization when checking a large number of conditions.

In reality, the `switch` operator can be encoded in another way. Here is the alternative variant of representing the `switch` operator:

```
CMP   EAX, 10
JE    1
```

```
CMP   EAX, 5
JE    2
CMP   EAX, 11
JE    3
...
```

Loops

In this chapter, I have already mentioned loop organization using the C programming language. I'd only like to mention the two widely used structures.

The first structure is as follows:

```
L1:
        .
        .
        .
        CMP   EAX, 10
        JL    L1
```

The second structure is as follows:

```
L2:
        CMP   EAX, 10
        JA    L1
        .
        .
        .
        JMP   L2
L1:
```

The first structure corresponds to the following fragment:

```
int i;
...
do {
...
    }
while (i < 10);
```

Or, in Pascal, it corresponds to the following:

```
var i: integer;
...
repeat
...
until (i>=10);
```

The second structure corresponds to the following fragment:

```
unsigned int i;
...
while (i <= 10) {
...
}
```

Or, in Pascal, it corresponds to the following:

```
var i:integer;
...

while (i<=10) do
begin
...
end;
```

The first structure can be slightly modified and can appear as follows:

```
        JMP    L2
L1:
        ...
        CMP    EAX, 10
L2:
        JL     L1
```

Thus, the `DO` loop converts into the `WHILE` loop.

I didn't mention the monster of the `FOR` loop, but, in the C language, it is principally the same as `WHILE` loop.

Local Variables

Usually, you'll work with local variables. Local variables are stored in predefined segments. Thus, a really good disassembler would easily localize them if the references to them are recognized correctly. With local variables, the task often becomes more complicated. This is especially true for records and arrays. A good disassembler will considerably simplify your problem. For example, consider the fragment in Listing 25.3 disassembled using IDA Pro.

Listing 25.3. Two local arrays in a program disassembled using IDA Pro

```
CODE:00401108 _main proc near ; DATA XREF: DATA:0040B044
CODE:00401108
CODE:00401108 var_54     = DWORD PTR -54h
```

```
CODE:00401108 VAR_28     = BYTE PTR -28H
CODE:00401108 ARGC       = DWORD PTR 8
CODE:00401108 ARGV       = DWORD PTR 0CH
CODE:00401108 ENVP       = DWORD PTR 10H
CODE:00401108
CODE:00401108            PUSH  EBP
CODE:00401109            MOV   EBP, ESP
CODE:0040110B            ADD   ESP, 0FFFFFFACH
CODE:0040110E            PUSH  EBX
CODE:0040110F            XOR   EBX, EBX
```

Carefully look at the fragment from Listing 25.3. As you can see, the debugger has correctly recognized everything. Two variables, `var_54` and `var_28`, are `DWORD` arrays. The first array is allocated `28h` bytes (e.g., 40 bytes or 10 array elements), and the second variable is allocated `54h-28h=2CH=44` (or 11 array elements). Consequently, 84 bytes are reserved for local variables. And what is the meaning of the `ADD ESP, 0FFFFFFACH` command? It's hard to deceive a qualified code analyzer! Here, `0-0FFFFFFACH = 54H` is equal to 84 in decimal notation. This means that the memory space for storing local variables is allocated in the first place.

As relates to arrays, it should be mentioned that C language initially made provision for two methods of accessing array elements: using indexes and using pointers. In other words, it is possible to write both `a[i]=10` and `*(a+i)=10`. At the same time, the second approach proved to be more efficient. Naturally, now it is possible to use both approaches. However, Borland C++ 5.0 and Microsoft C++ 6.0 produce the same Assembly code for both variants. This is encouraging because it means that compilers are being improved. By the way, comparing the Assembly code produced by different compilers would be instructive. I won't concentrate on this topic here; however, even a superficial comparison of the Borland C++ 5.0 and Microsoft Visual C++ 7.0 compilers has shown that Microsoft's development tools optimize the code more efficiently.

Now, it is necessary to return to the code fragment provided in Listing 25.3. Consider how the beginning of the `main` function appears in the W32Dasm.

Listing 25.4. The code fragment from Listing 25.3 in W32Dasm

```
:00401108 55         PUSH  EBP
:00401109 8BEC       MOV   EBP, ESP
:0040110B 83C4AC     ADD   ESP, FFFFFFAC
:0040110E 53         PUSH  EBX
:0040110F 33DB       XOR   EBX, EBX
```

As you can see, W32Dasm is less informative. On the basis of the fragment presented in Listing 25.4, it is only possible to conclude that local variables are allocated 84 bytes. The structure of local variables can be clarified by analyzing the code presented later.

When analyzing the code generated by Visual C++ 7.0, you'll find that local variables are not always recognizable. This translator has a powerful code optimizer. In some cases, it simply omits local variables, frequently without using the `ESP` register. The variable either gets transformed into a constant or is stored in a register. Naturally, this optimizes the resulting code. For example, consider the following fragment of some function:

```
...
int b=10;
...
c=c+b;
```

The `b` variable is local. If it isn't used anywhere except this fragment, then, principally, it is a constant. Therefore, the translator doesn't reserve stack memory for it. Instead of this, it generates a command such as `ADD EAX, 10`, assuming that the `c` variable is stored in the `EAX` register. In the next section, I provide an example illustrating such a behavior of the Visual C++ translator.

Functions and Procedures

Functions and procedures are easily identified. You already know the structure of calls and the internal parts of procedures. It only remains to recall some basic concepts.

A procedure call appears as follows:

```
PUSH  par1
PUSH  par2
PUSH  par3
CALL  232343
```

Everything is straightforward here. The main goal is recognizing parameters and the order, in which they are placed into the stack. You should also bear in mind that there is a special protocol for passing data through registers (see *Chapter 20*). For example, when using the `fastcall` convention, the first three parameters are loaded into the `EAX`, `ECX`, and `EDX` registers, and other parameters (if there are any) are loaded into the stack in a standard way. The procedure call might be followed by the `ADD ESP, N` command for clearing the stack.

The internal part of the procedure was considered many times (see *Chapters 2* and *20*). I hope that you are now capable of recognizing it; therefore, I won't draw your attention to this topic. However, bear in mind that the presence of local variables doesn't automatically mean that they will be allocated a place in the stack and will use the `EBP` register.

For the purposes of optimization, the translator can either replace it with a constant expression or store it in a general-purpose register. For accessing parameters, the ESP register will be used. To explain this statement with a practical example, consider a simple C function:

```
int func(int a, int b)
{
        int i;
        i = a + b + 0 x 1234;
        return i;
}
```

Translate it using Visual C++, and you'll get a surprising result:

```
:00401000 8B442408          MOV EAX, DWORD PTR [ESP+08]
:00401004 8B4C2404          MOV ECX, DWORD PTR [ESP+04]
:00401008 8D840134120000    LEA EAX, DWORD PTR [ECX+EAX+00001234]
:0040100F C3                RET
```

As you can see, the local variable is not reserved, and the EBP register is not used. However, everything is theoretically correct. Why do you need to reserve the memory for storing a variable if you can do without it and use only registers?

Finally, don't forget that functions return the result either through the EAX register or through the EDX:EAX pair (for 64-bit variables). All this information will enable you to quickly understand the goal of a specific function.

Code Optimization

In the previous few sections, I tried to explain to you how to restore the program source code on the basis of the disassembled listing. Now, you can evaluate and conclude whether I have succeeded when accomplishing this task. This can be achieved by comparing the restored code to the source code. You'll immediately notice that I mistakenly used the DO loop instead of the WHILE loop, which was used in the source code. However, if you compile and build the resulting program, it will work in the same way as the original one. The difference between the texts of the two programs (both are simple) is because the code is optimized by the translator. Because of this optimization, it is principally impossible to restore the source code using the executable code. However, it is still possible to get the program code that correctly describes the program's algorithm. This means that code analysis allows you to understand the idea of the program and what operations it executes. This is the main problem solved in this chapter.

Now, consider a small and trivial C program.

Listing 25.5. A small C program

```
void main ()
{
        int i;
        char a[10];
        char b[11];
        for(i=0; i<10; i++)
        {
                a[i] = 'a';
                *(b+i) = 'a';
                printf("%c %c\n", a[i], b[i]);
        }
        ExitProcess(0);
}
```

Now, consider the Assembly code of this program obtained using Borland C++ 5.0.

Listing 25.6. Disassembled code of the program in Listing 25.5 compiled using Borland C++ 5.0

```
.text:00401108 _main proc near ; DATA XREF: .data:0040A0B8
.text:00401108
.text:00401108 var_18      = BYTE PTR -18H
.text:00401108 var_C       = BYTE PTR -0CH
.text:00401108 argc        = DWORD PTR 8
.text:00401108 argv        = DWORD PTR 0CH
.text:00401108 envp        = DWORD PTR 10H
.text:00401108
.text:00401108             PUSH  EBP
.text:00401109             MOV   EBP, ESP
.text:0040110B             ADD   ESP, 0FFFFFFE8H
.text:0040110E             PUSH  EBX
.text:0040110F             XOR   EBX, EBX
.text:00401111
.text:00401111 loc_401111: ; CODE XREF: _main+30
.text:00401111             MOV   [EBP+EBX+VAR_C], 61H
.text:00401116             MOV   [EBP+EBX+VAR_18], 61H
.text:0040111B             MOVSX EAX, [EBP+EBX+VAR_18]
.text:00401120             PUSH  EAX
.text:00401121             Movsx EDX, [EBP+EBX+VAR_C]
.text:00401126             PUSH  EDX         ; CHAR
```

```
.text:00401127          PUSH    OFFSET ACC ; __VA_ARGS
.text:0040112C          CALL    _PRINTF
.text:00401131          ADD     ESP, 0CH,
.text:00401134          INC     EBX
.text:00401135          CMP     EBX, 0AH
.text:00401138          Jl      Short Loc_401111
.text:0040113A          PUSH    0 ; uExitCode
.text:0040113C          CALL    ExitProcess
.text:00401141          POP     EBX
.text:00401142          MOV     ESP, EBP
.text:00401144          POP     EBP
.text:00401145          RETN
.text:00401145 _main        ENDP
```

By the way, the `ExitProcess(0)` function was introduced into the program text for a quick search of the required fragments in a debugger or in the disassembled code. Even with the naked eye, you'll notice that there was no optimization. Using this text, it doesn't make it difficult to restore the original C program. Now, consider the code optimized by Visual C++ 7.0.

Listing 25.7. Disassembled code of the program from Listing 25.5 compiled using Visual C++ 7.0

```
.text:00401000 sub_401000 proc near ; CODE XREF: start+AF
.text:00401000          PUSH ESI
.text:00401001          MOV ESI, 0AH
.text:00401006
.text:00401006 loc_401006: ; CODE XREF: sub_401000+18
.text:00401006          PUSH    61H
.text:00401008          PUSH    61H
.text:0040100A          PUSH    OFFSET ACC ; "%C %C\N"
.text:0040100F          CALL    SUB_401030 ; PRINTF
.text:00401014          ADD     ESP, 0CH
.text:00401017          DEC     ESI
.text:00401018          JNZ     SHORT LOC_401006
.text:0040101A          PUSH    0  ; uExitCode
.text:0040101C          CALL    DS:ExitProcess
.text:00401022          POP     ESI
.text:00401023          RETN
.text:00401023 sub_401000    ENDP
```

I guess that the code presented in Listing 25.7 will surprise you. But what's surprising here? Consider the code of the original C program. Two arrays of characters specified in the source code are not needed. The Visual C++ compiler immediately noticed this and modified the code so that it became impossible to restore the original code despite all efforts. Naturally, the optimization became possible only because these arrays are used in a limited area.

Now, it is time to consider some methods of optimization that might be useful when writing programs in Assembly language.

Speed versus Size

When dealing with the CPU, the topic of speed versus size is important. For example, the `MOV EAX, EBX` command executes faster than `XCHG EAX, EBX`; however, its code is longer. Being aware of this feature, you can either set the size of your program or make it execute faster. For example, such operations as `MUL` are often replaced by other commands, such as `SHL`, and `DIV` operations are commonly replaced by `SHR`. Doing so can considerably increase the program's performance but increase its size. The interesting point is that arithmetical operations can also be carried out using the `LEA` command. Contemporary translators actively use this feature. Thus, the `MUL` command isn't encountered in the translated code as frequently as it might seem at first glance (based on the program's source code). Generally, it is a good practice to investigate properties of specific commands because you'll discover lots of interesting facts. For example, unsigned modulo-4 division is carried out as follows: `AND EAX, 0003h` — an original approach, isn't it?

Optimizing Conditional Jumps

As you'll detect, there are some reserves. For example, the conditional check can be organized to minimize the number of jumps. This will make the program fragment under consideration run faster. Assume that you have the following code fragment:

```
...
        CMP  EAX, 100
        JB   L1

        Fragment 1

        JMP  L2
L1:

        Fragment 2

L2:
```

You know, however, that the EAX register most often contains the values smaller than 100. Consequently, this fragment can be replaced by the following:

```
...
        CMP   EAX, 100
        JNB   L1

        Fragment 2

        JMP   L2
L1:

        Fragment 1

L2:
```

Optimizing Procedure Calls

Consider the following code fragment:

```
P1 PROC
        .
        .
        .
        CALL  P2
        RET
P1 ENDP
        .
        .
        .
P2 PROC
        .
        .
        .
        RET
P2 ENDP
```

This fragment can be replaced by a more efficient one. This approach can often be encountered when viewing program code using a debugger:

```
P1 PROC
        .
        .
        .
        JMP   P2
```

```
P1 ENDP
    .
    .
    .
P2 PROC
    .
    .
    .
      RET
P2 ENDP
```

The code becomes shorter and faster; however, it becomes less understandable. To conclude this description of optimization techniques, I'd like to recommend that you read a book [12], in which you'll find more information on this topic.

Object-Oriented Programming

Object-oriented programming considerably complicates the resulting executable code. Consider one small example. Listing 25.8 contains an easy C++ program.

Listing 25.8. A simple C++ program using objects

```
#include <windows.h>
#include <stdio.h>
class string {
      public:
      char c[200];
      char g[100];
      string() {strcpy(c, "Hello"); strcpy(g, "Hello");}
      int strcp();
};
 string::stri()
{
 strcpy(c, g);
 return 0;
}
 main()
{
 string * s = new string;
 s->strcp();
 printf("%s\n", s->c);
 delete s;
}
```

Listing 25.9 contains the disassembled code of the main procedure. Disassembling was done with IDA Pro.

Listing 25.9. Disassembled code of the main procedure in Listing 25.8

```
CODE:00401122 _main proc near ; DATA XREF: DATA:0040C044
CODE:00401122
CODE:00401122 var_28     = DWORD PTR -28H
CODE:00401122 var_18     = WORD PTR -18H
CODE:00401122 dest       = DWORD PTR -4
CODE:00401122 argc       = DWORD PTR 8
CODE:00401122 argv       = DWORD PTR 0CH
CODE:00401122 envp       = DWORD PTR 10H
CODE:00401122
CODE:00401122          PUSH  EBP
CODE:00401123          MOV   EBP, ESP
CODE:00401125          ADD   ESP, 0FFFFFFD8H
CODE:00401128          PUSH  EBX
CODE:00401129          MOV   EAX, OFFSET STRU_40C084
CODE:0040112E          CALL  @__INITEXCEPTBLOCKLDTC
CODE:00401133          PUSH  12CH
CODE:00401138          CALL  UNKNOWN_LIBNAME_8
CODE:0040113D          POP   ECX
CODE:0040113E          MOV   [EBP+DEST], EAX
CODE:00401141          TEST  EAX, EAX
CODE:00401143          JZ    SHORT LOC_40117D
CODE:00401145          MOV   [EBP+VAR_18], 14H
CODE:0040114B          PUSH  OFFSET aHello ; SRC
CODE:00401150          PUSH  [EBP+DEST]    ; DEST
CODE:00401153          CALL  _STRCPY
CODE:00401158          ADD   ESP, 8
CODE:0040115B          PUSH  OFFSET aHello_0 ; SRC
CODE:00401160          MOV   EDX, [EBP+DEST]
CODE:00401163          ADD   EDX, 0C8H
CODE:00401169          PUSH  EDX          ; DEST
CODE:0040116A          CALL  _STRCPY
CODE:0040116F          ADD   ESP, 8
CODE:00401172          MOV   [EBP+VAR_18], 8
CODE:00401178          MOV   EBX, [EBP+DEST]
CODE:0040117B          JMP   SHORT LOC_401180
CODE:0040117D ;-------------------------------------
CODE:0040117D
```

```
CODE:0040117D LOC_40117D:     ; CODE XREF: _MAIN+21
CODE:0040117D             MOV   EBX, [EBP+DEST]
CODE:00401180
CODE:00401180 LOC_401180:   ; CODE XREF:  _MAIN+59
CODE:00401180             PUSH  EBX        ; DEST
CODE:00401181             CALL  SUB_401108
CODE:00401186             POP   ECX
CODE:00401187             PUSH  EBX        ; CHAR
CODE:00401188             PUSH  OFFSET AS ;  __VA_ARGS
CODE:0040118D             CALL  _PRINTF
CODE:00401192             ADD   ESP, 8
CODE:00401195             PUSH  EBX        ; BLOCK
CODE:00401196             CALL  @$BDELE$QPV ; OPERATOR DELETE(VOID *)
CODE:0040119B             POP   ECX
CODE:0040119C             MOV   EAX, [EBP+VAR_28]
CODE:0040119F             MOV   LARGE FS:0, EAX
CODE:004011A5             XOR   EAX, EAX
CODE:004011A7             POP   EBX
CODE:004011A8             MOV   ESP, EBP
CODE:004011AA             POP   EBP
CODE:004011AB             RETN
CODE:004011AB _MAIN          ENDP
```

As you can see, the disassembled code is sophisticated. Note that because of the limited volume of this book I won't provide detailed analysis of this code; in this case, it would be necessary to include an analysis of the library functions. However, some key facts deserve special attention:

- The `NEW` operator is reduced to the execution of a library procedure, `unknown_libname_8`. The latter allocates memory for the properties of the object instance (300 bytes).
- The constructor is stored and executed directly in the program body. This is because the constructor is defined in the class text. For experimental purposes, try to place the constructor text into a separate function. You'll see that the constructor will be called from `main` like any normal function.
- The `@__InitExceptBlockLDTC` procedure is inserted by the translator for exception handling. You can remove the information needed for exception handling, which will reduce the size of the executable code. However, you won't be able of using exception-handling operators such as `try` or `catch`.
- When calling some method, at least one parameter — the pointer to the object instance — is always placed into the stack.

Now, consider the fragment, disassembled using IDA Pro, of the same C++ program. This time the program was compiled using the -x option, which for Borland C++ means that exception handling is not supported. As you can see, the program text is considerably simpler in Listing 25.10.

Listing 25.10. Disassembled code of the main function from Listing 25.8 using the -x Borland C++ option

```
.text:00401122 _main proc near ; DATA XREF: .data:0040B0C8
.text:00401122
.text:00401122 argc        = dword ptr 8
.text:00401122 argv        = dword ptr 0Ch
.text:00401122 envp        = dword ptr 10h
.text:00401122
.text:00401122             PUSH   EBP
.text:00401123             MOV    EBP, ESP
.text:00401125             PUSH   EBX
.text:00401126             PUSH   12CH
.text:0040112B             CALL   UNKNOWN_LIBNAME_8
.text:00401130             POP    ECX
.text:00401131             MOV    EBX, EAX
.text:00401133             TEST   EAX, EAX
.text:00401135             JZ     SHORT LOC_40115D
.text:00401137             PUSH   OFFSET aHello ; SRC
.text:0040113C             PUSH   EBX        ; DEST
.text:0040113D             CALL   _STRCPY
.text:00401142             ADD    ESP, 8
.text:00401145             PUSH   OFFSET aHello_0 ; src
.text:0040114A             LEA    EDX, [EBX+0C8H]
.text:00401150             PUSH   EDX        ; DEST
.text:00401151             CALL   _STRCPY
.text:00401156             ADD    ESP, 8
.text:00401159             MOV    ECX, EBX
.text:0040115B             JMP    SHORT LOC_40115F
.text:0040115D ;-----------------------------------------
.text:0040115D
.text:0040115D loc_40115D: ; CODE XREF: _main+13
.text:0040115D             MOV     ECX, EBX
.text:0040115F
.text:0040115F loc_40115F: ; CODE XREF: _main+39
.text:0040115F             MOV     EBX, ECX
```

```
.text:00401161          PUSH  EBX        ; DEST
.text:00401162          CALL  SUB_401108
.text:00401167          POP   ECX
.text:00401168          PUSH  EBX        ; CHAR
.text:00401169          PUSH  OFFSET aS ; __va_args
.text:0040116E          CALL  _PRINTF
.text:00401173          ADD   ESP, 8
.text:00401176          PUSH  EBX       ; handle
.text:00401177          CALL  __RTL_CLOSE
.text:0040117C          POP   ECX
.text:0040117D          XOR   EAX, EAX
.text:0040117F          POP   EBX
.text:00401180          POP   EBP
.text:00401181          RETN
.text:00401181 _main       ENDP
```

Chapter 26

Correcting Executable Modules

It is necessary to bear in mind that the correction of executable modules is a difficult task, which requires practical skills and theoretical knowledge. It is impossible to cope with this task without knowing Assembly language. However, I hope that you won't experience difficulties if you have read my book up to this chapter. After all, everything must be OK with your knowledge of the Assembly language! In the *Preface*, I already substantiated the necessity of investigating and correcting the code of executable modules. I think that both security specialists and hackers are needed in society. In this book, I provide only the required minimum information related to the correction of executable modules.

A Practical Example of Correcting Executable Module

Now, consider a simple[i] example illustrating how to accomplish a job of this type. The problem considered in this section is simple, and it is possible to solve it using only W32Dasm.

---

[i] Simple in relation to the possible problems that might arise when correcting executable modules.

The program under consideration is called All Screen 95 Pro. As its name implies, it allows you to capture screenshots of various windows or specific parts of the screen. I downloaded its shareware release from the Internet. This program has been written in Delphi; however, as you'll see, the task can be accomplished even without knowing the development tool, which was used for writing the program. After you start this program, the screen shown in Fig. 26.1 will appear. When you get closely acquainted with this topic, you'll discover that most frequently, it is necessary to locate the program fragment that corresponds to a specific visual effect, such as opening or closing a window or outputting text.

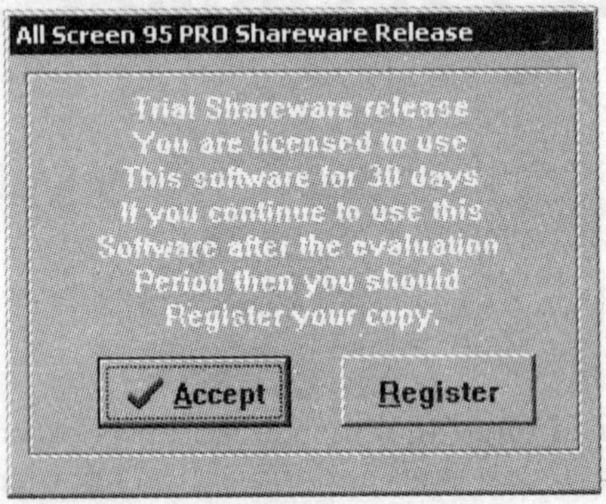

Fig. 26.1. Window that appears when the All Screen program is started

After you click the **Accept** button, there is a delay of approximately six seconds. Then, the program operates normally.

After you start the program 15 times, it displays the window informing that the trial version has expired, and exits.

Thus, you need to solve the following two problems:

- Eliminate the irritating delay.
- Correct the program so that it runs correctly no matter how many times you run it.

The window informing the user on the delay is a blunder by the programmer who developed its protection mechanism. The window and its contents can be hidden in the resources. However, when a new record appears in the same window, it becomes the program code. Thus, run W32Dasm and load the All Screen 95 PRO program there. Open the string data reference window and look for the `Shareware Delay` string there and double-click it. After closing the window, you'll move to the required location within the program. This fragment is presented in Listing 26.1.

Listing 26.1. The code fragment responsible for the delay

```
* Referenced by an (U)nconditional or (C)onditional Jump at Address:
|:004420BC(C)
|
:00442123 33D2          XOR   EDX, EDX
:00442125 8B83B0010000  MOV   EAX, DWORD PTR [EBX+000001B0]
:0044212B E8541DFDFF    CALL  00413E84
:00442130 33D2          XOR   EDX, EDX
:00442132 8B83B4010000  MOV   EAX, DWORD PTR [EBX+000001B4]
:00442138 E8471DFDFF    CALL  00413E84
:0044213D 33D2          XOR   EDX, EDX
:0044213F 8B83B8010000  MOV   EAX, DWORD PTR [EBX+000001B8]
:00442145 E83A1DFDFF    CALL  00413E84
:0044214A BA50000000    MOV   EDX, 00000050
:0044214F 8B83BC010000  MOV   EAX, DWORD ptr [ebx+000001BC]
:00442155 E8D618FDFF    CALL  00413A30

* Possible StringData Ref from Code Obj ->"Shareware Delay"
|
:0044215A BAA8214400    MOV   EDX, 004421A8
:0044215F 8B83BC010000  MOV   EAX, DWORD PTR [EBX+000001BC]
:00442165 E8EE1DFDFF    CALL  00413F58
:0044216A 33D2          XOR   EDX, EDX
:0044216C 8B83C0010000  MOV   EAX, DWORD PTR [EBX+000001C0]
:00442172 E80D1DFDFF    CALL  00413E84
:00442177 33D2          XOR   EDX, EDX
:00442179 8B83C4010000  MOV   EAX, DWORD PTR [EBX+000001C4]
:0044217F E8001DFDFF    CALL  00413E84
:00442184 33D2          XOR   EDX, EDX
:00442186 8B83C8010000  MOV   EAX, DWORD PTR [EBX+000001C8]
:0044218C E8F31CFDFF    CALL  00413E84
:00442191 8B83CC010000  MOV   EAX, DWORD PTR [EBX+000001CC]
:00442197 E8E8D4FFFF    CALL  0043F684
:0044219C 5B            POP   EBX
:0044219D C3            RET
```

I intentionally included more lines of code in the listing, among them several starting strings. You see the entire delaying procedure in Listing 26.1. Guessing the meaning of every `CALL` command is senseless, although you can discover, for example, that `CALL 00413E84` removes a string from the screen.

To eliminate the delay, it is enough to disable this fragment of code. The easiest way of doing so is inserting the `pop ebx / ret` commands into its start. Any hex editor, such as HIEW, is suitable for this task. As a result, the delay will be eliminated.

Now, you can tackle the second problem by removing the limitation on the number of times the user can start the program. In one glance at this window, it becomes clear that it is formed in the program. Consequently, to solve this problem, you can try to locate the text displayed on the screen in the program code.

Listing 26.2. The code fragment that checks the number of times the program was started

```
:00443326 8BC0              MOV   EAX, EAX
:00443328 53                PUSH  EBX
:00443329 8BD8              MOV   EBX, EAX
:0044332B 803DEC56440001    CMP   BYTE PTR [004456EC], 01
:00443332 7546              JNE   0044337A
:00443334 A124564400        MOV   EAX, DWORD PTR [00445624]
:00443339 E84E2CFEFF        CALL  00425F8C
:0044333E A1D8564400        MOV   EAX, DWORD PTR [004456D8]
:00443343 E87816FEFF        CALL  004249C0
:00443348 FF05F0564400      INC   DWORD PTR [004456F0]
:0044334E C605EC56440000    MOV   BYTE PTR [004456EC], 00
:00443355 833DF05644000F    CMP   DWORD PTR [004456F0], 0000000F
:0044335C 7E1C              JLE   0044337A
:0044335E 6A00              PUSH  00000000
:00443360 668B0DB0334400    MOV   CX, WORD PTR [004433B0]
:00443367 B202              MOV   DL, 02

* Possible StringData Ref from Code Obj ->"This Software Has Been Used Over"
|
:00443369 B8BC334400        MOV   EAX, 004433BC
:0044336E E8BDAEFEFF        CALL  0042E230
:00443373 8BC3              MOV   EAX, EBX
:00443375 E84214FEFF        CALL  004247BC

* Referenced by an (U)nconditional or (C)onditional Jump at Addresses:
|:00443332(C), :0044335C(C)
|
:0044337A 33D2              XOR   EDX, EDX
:0044337C 8B83F4010000      MOV   EAX, DWORD PTR [EBX+000001F4]
:00443382 E8A52DFFFF        CALL  0043612C
:00443387 33D2              XOR   EDX, EDX
```

```
:00443389 8B83F8010000  MOV   EAX, DWORD PTR [EBX+000001F8]
:0044338F E8982DFFFF    CALL  0043612C
:00443394 33D2          XOR   EDX, EDX
:00443396 8B83FC010000  MOV   EAX, DWORD PTR [EBX+000001FC]
:0044339C E88B2DFFFF    CALL  0043612C
:004433A1 33D2          XOR   EDX, EDX
:004433A3 8B8314020000  MOV   EAX, DWORD PTR [EBX+00000214]
:004433A9 E87E2DFFFF    CALL  0043612C
:004433AE 5B            POP   EBX
:004433AF C3            RET
```

This time, I included the entire fragment in the listing. Using the cross-reference to the required string, you can easily locate the suspicious command:

```
CMP DWORD PTR [004456F0], 0000000F
JLE 0044337A
```

Recall that the programs ceases to operate after it has been run exactly 15 times. The simplest way of eliminating this situation is to fill the program fragment from `0044335E` to `00443375` with the `NOP (90)` commands using HIEW.

Searching for the Window Procedure

Most operations in Windows programs are executed in windows. Window behavior is defined by its function. To change the program behavior, you often need to find the required window function to edit it.

To demonstrate this technique, I have chosen the FILES.EXE program. This program is useful for searching information in a local area network. For example, choose one of the dialogs of this program and try to find its window function. Let it be the "Network computer name" window.

First, use the W32Dasm program. The step-by-step searching procedure is as follows:

1. Load the FILES.EXE program.
2. Choose the **Debug | Load Process** menu options to start the debugger.
3. Press <F9> to start the program and go to the required window.
4. Now is the crucial moment. Click the **Terminate Process** button to open the disassembler window.
5. Scroll the code upward, and you'll locate the call to the `DialogBoxParam` API function. Listing 26.3 shows the required code fragment.

Listing 26.3. The code fragment containing the call to the DialogBoxParam function

```
* Referenced by an (U)nconditional or (C)onditional Jump at Address:
|:004156BE(C)
|
:004156CA FF7508          PUSH  [EBP+08]
:004156CD E8369EFFFF      CALL  0040F508
:004156D2 59              POP   ECX
:004156D3 6A00            PUSH  00000000
:004156D5 68019C4000      PUSH  00409C01
:004156DA FF7508          PUSH  [EBP+08]

* Possible StringData Ref from Data Obj ->"DIAL3000"
|
:004156DD 6896904300      PUSH  00439096
:004156E2 FF3548CA4300    PUSH  DWORD PTR [0043CA48]

* Reference To: USER32.DialogBoxParamA, Ord:0000h
|
:004156E8 E85F0D0200      CALL  0043644C
:004156ED 8A153C324D00    MOV   DL, BYTE PTR [004D323C]
```

Recall the arguments of the `DialogBoxParam` function. The fourth parameter is the address of the window procedure. Thus, you'll discover that the window procedure is located by the address `00409C01`. Go to that address (Listing 26.4).

Listing 26.4. The beginning of the window function

```
:00409C01 55              PUSH  EBP
:00409C02 8BEC            MOV   EBP, ESP
:00409C04 8B450C          MOV   EAX, DWORD PTR [EBP+0C]
:00409C07 2D10010000      SUB   EAX, 00000110
:00409C0C 7413            JE    00409C21
:00409C0E 48              DEC   EAX
:00409C0F 0F84EB000000    JE    00409D00
:00409C15 2D01020000      SUB   EAX, 00000201
:00409C1A 7444            JE    00409C60
:00409C1C E969010000      JMP   00409D8A
```

Look at Fig 26.4 to make sure that this code starts some function. To make sure that this function is the one that you require, it is necessary to introduce some changes and check the result.

Now, try to achieve the same goal using the SoftIce debugger:

1. Use LOADER32.EXE to load the FILES.EXE program into the SoftIce debugger.
2. Press <Ctrl>+<D> to start the program.
3. Open all dialogs except the last one.
4. Before opening the last dialog, enter the debugger and set a breakpoint to the `DialogBoxParamA` function: `BPX DialogBoxParamA`.
5. Return to the program that you need to change, and open the required dialog. The debugger will start automatically because of the breakpoint.
6. Press <F11>, and you'll be returned to the breakpoint either immediately or after closing the dialog (once again, you'll be returned to the debugger).
7. View the call to the `DialogBoxParam` function, and you'll easily find the address of the window procedure. Naturally, it will be the same as the address found using the W32Dasm debugger (see Listing 26.3).

To continue the use of the SoftIce debugger, I'll mention that there is another way of finding the window function. This method consists in using the `HWND` command to locate the handles of opened windows. After that, set a breakpoint to the content of the first parameter, which must be equal to the window handle. For example, this can be done using the following command:

```
BPX EIP IF(EBP+8==N)
```

Here, `N` is the window handle that you located earlier. After that, it only remains to carry out some operation in the window; this will cause a message to be sent to its window function.

Chapter 27

Driver Structure and Development

This chapter concentrates on the basics of driver development for the Windows operating system. The first part of this chapter covers virtual device drivers (VxDs). I do not agree with the common opinion that obsolete materials are not worthy of being considered in contemporary books on computing. On the contrary, in practically all other branches of science, historical information is considered an important part of the knowledge accumulated in a specific area. The student must know how the discipline evolved and must understand the logic of its evolution. Therefore, I didn't exclude the chapter about 16-bit programming, and I preserved material about VxDs. The second part of this chapter concentrates on kernel-mode drivers. This material is important for programmers and has preserved its urgency.

Furthermore, it is important to mention that this chapter is oriented toward MASM32.

Virtual Device Drivers

The "x" character in the VxD abbreviation means "any type of device." Although a new type of driver has been introduced in addition to VxD, the use of VxDs remains important because many users all over the world continue to work with Windows 98 and Windows Millennium Edition. In this chapter, in contrast to my normal practice,

I extensively use macro definitions contained in the INC files supplied with Microsoft's Windows Driver Development Kit (DDK). Using this approach allows me to provide all the material in one chapter.

To develop VxDs, you'll need files such as VMM.INC, SHELL.INC, and VCOND.INC, which are supplied with the Windows DDK.

At Windows startup, the WIN.COM program loads the VMM32.VXD driver (VMM stands for Virtual Machine Manager). This driver, in turn, initializes other VxDs. Then, VMM switches the processor to the protected mode and initializes the system virtual machine. In addition, VMM provides services to other VxDs. When the user starts an MS-DOS application, a separate virtual machine is allocated to that application so that the DOS application has the illusion of running on an individual computer. When the user starts normal 32-bit applications, they operate within the framework of the system virtual machine. Applications that run on different virtual machines are unaware of the existence of other virtual machines. The most important goal of virtual drivers is to ensure shared access to the hardware without conflicts for all concurrently running virtual machines. Another task that virtual drivers must carry out is organizing communications between the system virtual machine and other virtual machines running on the same computer.

Note that in Windows, there are also so-called standard drivers that have the DRV filename extension, are characterized by the Dynamic Link Library (DLL) structure, and export API functions for working with some peripheral devices (e.g., a video adapter). These drivers get access to peripheral devices through VxDs. Because VxDs operate in ring 0, they can access any memory region and use input and output ports to directly access peripheral devices.

All virtual drivers are divided into two classes — static and dynamic. Static drivers are loaded at system startup and remain in the memory until system shutdown. Static drivers existed even in Windows 3.*x*. Dynamic drivers can be loaded and unloaded as needed by the system. Mainly, they are used for serving Plug-and-Play devices and are loaded by the configuration manager. A dynamic virtual driver can also be loaded from a normal application using standard functions for working with files.

There are three mechanisms that can be used by virtual drivers for intercommunication:

1. *Control messages* — The VMM sends these messages to virtual drivers. Drivers also can exchange information using such messages. This mechanism is similar to the way applications use Windows messages to communicate with each other and with the operating system.
2. *Callback functions* — The virtual driver can allow another driver to use the callback function.
3. *Virtual drivers and VMM* — These can export specific functions for calling them from other virtual drivers. To call the function, it is necessary to know the number of the virtual driver exporting this function and the number of this function.

The format of virtual drivers is the Linear Executable (LE) format. This format supports the presence of both 16-bit and 32-bit code. This is urgent for static VxDs, which are initialized in a real (unprivileged) mode. In Windows NT, drivers are loaded in the protected mode. Therefore, this format is not used in this operating system.

Code and data in the LE format file are placed in segments. The following list briefly describes possible classes of segments:

- `LCODE` — The code or data contained within that code couldn't be paged to the disk.
- `PCODE` — The code can be temporarily paged to the disk.
- `PDATE` — Similar to the previous class, in this case the class is related to data.
- `ICODE` — The segment stores the initialization code. After initialization, the segment is removed from the memory.
- `DBOCODE` — This is used for starting the driver under the control of the debugger.
- `SCODE` — Static code or data. These always remain in the memory, even if the driver is unloaded.
- `RCODE` — This contains 16-bit code for real-mode initialization.
- `16ICODE` — This is 16-bit code for protected-mode initialization.
- `MCODE` — This contains message strings.

The preceding classes of segments are not specified directly in the program text. Segments and classes are declared in a DEF file. The VMM.INC file contains a vast number of macro definitions, and you can't do without them. However, this allows me to describe all of this material within one chapter.

The Project Description

Consider the contents of the DEF file (Listing 27.1). This listing contains segments for every possible case. Naturally, you do not need to use all segments defined here. Thus, this file can be used for creating practically any virtual driver. Segments belonging to the same class will be joined into the same segment after compiling and building. Only the first string specifying the driver name must be changed. Note that the driver name must be specified in uppercase letters. In addition, in the first line, it is possible to specify the driver type. By default, it is assumed that this is a static driver. If you specify a string such as `VXD VXD1 DYNAMIC`, the compiler would create a dynamic virtual driver.

Listing 27.1. The VXD.DEF file used for compiling and building a virtual driver

```
VXD VXD1
SEGMENTS
_LPTEXT   CLASS 'LCODE'   PRELOAD NONDISCARDABLE
_LTEXT    CLASS 'LCODE'   PRELOAD NONDISCARDABLE
```

```
_LDATA      CLASS 'LCODE'   PRELOAD NONDISCARDABLE
_TEXT       CLASS 'LCODE'   PRELOAD NONDISCARDABLE
_DATA       CLASS 'LCODE'   PRELOAD NONDISCARDABLE
CONST       CLASS 'LCODE'   PRELOAD NONDISCARDABLE
_TLS        CLASS 'LCODE'   PRELOAD NONDISCARDABLE
_BSS        CLASS 'LCODE'   PRELOAD NONDISCARDABLE
_LMGTABLE   CLASS 'MCODE'   PRELOAD NONDISCARDABLE IOPL
_LMSGDATA   CLASS 'MCODE'   PRELOAD NONDISCARDABLE IOPL
_IMSGTABLE  CLASS 'MCODE'   PRELOAD DISCARDABLE IOPL
_IMSGDATA   CLASS 'MCODE'   PRELOAD DISCARDABLE IOPL
_ITEXT      CLASS 'ICODE'   DISCARDABLE
_IDATA      CLASS 'ICODE'   DISCARDABLE
_PTEXT      CLASS 'PCODE'   NONDISCARDABLE
_PMSGTABLE  CLASS 'MCODE'   NONDISCARDABLE IOPL
_PMSGDATA   CLASS 'MCODE'   NONDISCARDABLE IOPL
_PDATA      CLASS 'PDATA'   NONDISCARDABLE SHARED
_STEXT      CLASS 'SCODE'   RESIDENT
_SDATA      CLASS 'SCODE'   RESIDENT
_DBOSTART   CLASS 'DBOCODE' PRELOAD NONDISCARDABLE CONFORMING
_DBOCODE    CLASS 'DBOCODE' PRELOAD NONDISCARDABLE CONFORMING
_DBODATA    CLASS 'DBOCODE' PRELOAD NONDISCARDABLE CONFORMING
_16ICODE    CLASS '16ICODE' PRELOAD DISCARDABLE
_RCODE      CLASS 'RCODE'
EXPORTS
  VXD1_DDB @1
```

In the end of this file, the only exported variable — the Device Description Block (DDB) — is specified. This block is defined in the VMM.INC file. It contains 22 fields and provides information about the virtual driver.

The VMM.INC file defines macro names for all segments listed previously. For example, for the `_LTEXT` segment, the `VxD_LOCKED_CODE_SEG` name is specified, and the `_RCODE` segment has the `VxD_REAL_INIT_SEG` name. Listings provided in this chapter actively use these macro names.

Now, consider the translation of virtual drivers. To produce a virtual driver, issue the following commands:

```
ml /coff /c /Cx /DMASM6 /DBLD_COFF /DIS_32 vxd1.asm
link /vxd /def:vxd.def vxd1.obj
```

Constants such as `MASM6`, `BLD_COF`, `IS_32` are used by conditional translation operators specified in the VMM.INC and VCOND.INC files. Note that if you are using the DEF file in the form specified in Listing 27.1, then warning messages informing you that specific sections are missing might appear in the course of compiling. These warnings can be ignored.

To carry out some actions, you'll often need to use macro definitions from the VMM.INC file. Therefore, it is necessary to become acquainted with the most frequently used ones.

The most important is the `Declare_Virtual_Device` macro. It fills the DDB structure, thus simplifying the programmer's task. The general format of this macro is as follows (the structure of the macro can be found in the VMM.INC file):

```
Declare_Virtual_Device Name, MajorVer, MinorVer, CtrlProc, DeviceID,
InitOrder, V86Proc, PMProc, RefData
```

Consider the macro parameters:

- `Name` — The virtual driver name. This name must match the name specified in the DEF file.
- `MajorVer`, `MinorVer` — Major and minor version numbers of the driver.
- `CtrlProc` — The name of the driver's control procedure. This procedure receives and processes the messages arriving at the driver. The procedure name consists of two parts: the driver name and `Control` suffix. For example, if the driver name is `VXD1`, then the procedure will have the following name: `VXD1_Control`.
- `DeviceID` — The 16-bit unique identifier of the virtual driver. It must be specified if the virtual driver must provide services to other drivers. In addition, this identifier might be needed if your driver is intended to operate in real mode.
- `InitOrder` — The driver's loading order. This is an ordinal number. Drivers with lower ordinal numbers are the first to be loaded. This parameter is meaningful only for static drivers.
- `V86Proc`, `PMProc` — Addresses of functions that the driver will export for MS-DOS and standard Windows applications. If the driver won't export functions, these parameters should be omitted.
- `Ref_Data` — The reference to the data used by the input/output supervisor. As a rule, this parameter is omitted.

To define the control procedure, use the `Begin_control_dispatch` and `End_control_dispatch` macros. This can be done as follows:

```
Begin_control_dispatch VXD1
Control_Dispatch message, function
End_control_dispatch VXD1
```

The `Control_Dispatch` macro defines, which messages must be processed by which functions. For example:

```
Begin_control_dispatch VXD1
Control_Dispatch INIT_COMPLETE, INIT
End_control_dispatch VXD1
```

Thus, you have all the required information to build the simplest driver. To be more precise, this will be the skeleton of the future driver. For the moment, you don't even need to clearly understand how it will work.

Listing 27.2. A virtual driver's "skeleton"

```
.586P
include vmm.inc
include vcond.inc
DECLARE_VIRTUAL_DEVICE VXD1, 1, 0, VXD1_Control, \
UNDEFINED_DEVICE_ID, UNDEFINED_INIT_ORDER

Begin_control_dispatch VXD1
Control_Dispatch INIT_COMPLETE, INIT
End_control_dispatch VXD1

VxD_LOCKED_CODE_SEG
BeginProc INIT
EndProc INIT
VxD_LOCKED_CODE_ENDS

end
```

Now, translate the driver provided in Listing 27.2 according to the algorithm described earlier. Do not forget to add the `/MAP` command-line option. As a result, the VXD1.MAP file will appear in your working directory in addition to the VXD1.VXD file. The contents of this file are shown in Listing 27.3.

Listing 27.3. The contents of the VXD1.MAP file

```
VXD1

 Timestamp is 3bb5ad7a (Sat Sep 29 17:16:10 2001)

 Preferred load address is 00400000
```

```
 Start     Length   Name          Class
 0001:00000000 00000050H _LDATA         CODE
 0001:00000050 00000007H _LTEXT         CODE

Address    Publics by Value Rva+Base  Lib:Object

0001:00000000 VXD1_DDB        00401000  vxd1.obj
0001:00000050 VXD1_Control    00401050 f vxd1.obj
0001:00000057 INIT            00401057 f vxd1.obj

entry point at     0000:00000000

Static symbols
```

When viewing the MAP file, note that there are two segments defined there: `_LDATA` and `_LTEXT`. Both segments relate to the same class.

To conclude this listing, I'd like to mention that instead of the standard `name proc/name endp` combination, the `BeginProc` and `EndProc` macros are used here. Definitions of these macros are provided in the VMM.INC file.

Virtual drivers can provide services to other drivers. In other words, virtual drivers export their functions. The call to an exported function is a 6-byte value, shown as follows:

```
int 20h
DD 00110002H
```

Here, `11H` is the virtual driver identifier, and `02H` is the service number (the index in the table of services). However, I won't write the call in this form. Instead, I'll use the `VMMCall` and `VxDCall` macros. The first macro is intended for calling VMM services, and the second macro is used for calling services of other virtual drivers.

A Sample Driver

Now you have all the information required for writing a simple but usable static driver. The text of this driver is provided in Listing 27.3. After the listing, I provide comments about this driver and cover the basic principles of building static virtual drivers.

Listing 27.3. A sample static virtual driver

```
.586P

include vmm.inc
include shell.inc
include vcond.inc
```

```
; Fill the DDB structure
DECLARE_VIRTUAL_DEVICE VXD2, 1, 0, VXD2_Control, \
UNDEFINED_DEVICE_ID, UNDEFINED_INIT_ORDER

; Declare the received messages
; and the procedures to process them
Begin_control_dispatch VXD2
  Control_Dispatch Create_VM, OnVMCreate
  Control_Dispatch VM_Terminate2, OnVMClose
End_control_dispatch VXD2

; Segment for storing messages
VxD_PAGEABLE_DATA_SEG
  MsgTitle db "Message from a VXD driver", 0
  VMCreated db "Creating a virtual machine", 0
  VMDestroyed db "Destroying a virtual machine", 0
  VMFocus db "Changing a virtual machine focus"
VxD_PAGEABLE_DATA_ENDS

; Segment containing code
VxD_PAGEABLE_CODE_SEG

; Procedure that reacts to virtual machine creation
BeginProc OnVMCreate
; Your code goes here

        MOV   ECX, OFFSET VMCreated
        CALL  MES
        RET
EndProc OnVMCreate

; Procedure that reacts to the closing of a virtual machine
BeginProc OnVMClose
; Your code goes here

        MOV   ECX, OFFSET VMDestroyed
        CALL  MES
        RET
EndProc OnVMClose

; Procedure that outputs a message
MES PROC
```

```
; Get the system virtual machine handle
        VMMCall Get_sys_vm_handle
; The handle is returned in EBX,
; and the message flag is returned in EAX
        MOV    EAX, MB_OK
; Message header address
        MOV    EDI, OFFSET MsgTitle
; Address of the CallBack function, NULL in this case
        XOR    ESI, ESI
; Reference to the CallBack function data
        XOR    EDX, EDX
; VxD service function — message window
        VxDCall SHELL_Message
MES ENDP
VxD_PAGEABLE_CODE_ENDS

end
```

As already mentioned, a static driver is loaded at system startup and remains in memory until system shutdown. The most convenient way of loading such a driver is inserting a string such as `device=driver_name` into the `[386enh]` section of the SYSTEM.INI file. You can also use the system registry by including the following value entry there:

```
HKEY_LOCAL_MACHINE\System\CurrentControlSet\Services\VxD\key\
StaticVxD=pathname
```

However, the first approach is more convenient because, in case of error, your VxD can be easily disabled by editing the SYSTEM.INI file under MS-DOS.

When installing VxDs, VMM sends the following messages to the drivers:

- `SysCriticalInit` — This message is sent when switching to the protected mode but before enabling interrupts.
- `Device_Init` — This message is sent after enabling interrupts. This message is used most frequently by virtual drivers for startup initialization.
- `Init_Complete` — This is the last message sent to virtual drivers at system startup.

  Having received the message and carried out all required tasks, the driver must reset the carry flag and return control to the operating system.

Before unloading, static virtual drivers also must receive several messages.

- `System_Exit2` — This message is sent before the system shutdown. The microprocessor at that time is still in the protected mode.

- `Sys_Critical_Exit2` — This is the next message sent to virtual drivers before system shutdown.
- `Device_Reboot_Notify2` — This message informs virtual drivers that the system is going to shut down. However, interrupts are still available.
- `Crit_Reboot_Notify2` — This is similar to the previous message, but interrupts are no longer available.

Now, consider the program provided in Listing 27.3. This driver outputs the message about activation of the virtual machine (e.g., the creation of a console or startup of an MS-DOS application) and its deactivation. The following two service functions were used in this driver: get the handle to the system virtual machine and output the message. Consider these functions in more detail:

- `Get_sys_vm_handle` — Get the handle to the system virtual machine. The handle is returned in the `EBX` register.
- `SHELL_Message` — Output the message. Parameters are stored in the following registers:
  - `EBX` — The handle to the virtual machine
  - `EAX` — The message flag (e.g., `MB_OK`)
  - `ECX` — The 32-bit address of the message string
  - `EDI` — The 32-bit address of the header string
  - `ESI` — The address of the function that reacts to user input (if such a function is missing, this parameter is equal to zero)
  - `EDX` — The address of the data to be sent to the function

Finally, when exiting, the driver must clear the carry flag. In this case, this operation depends on the correct execution of the `SHELL_Message` function.

Dynamic Virtual Drivers

In this section, I cover dynamic virtual drivers. There are three methods of loading such drivers:

- Place a driver into the \SYSTEM\IOSUBSYS directory. Drivers residing in this directory are loaded by the input/output manager.
- Use the `VxDLDR` service. This service function can be called only from virtual drivers.
- Use the `CreateFile` function.

The latter method of loading dynamic drivers is the one I will explain in detail now. The sequence of steps that you need to carry out to complete this task is as follows:

1. Open the driver using the `CreateFile` function. In the case of success, the function returns the identifier that will then be used when calling the functions exported by this driver.
2. Use the dynamic driver function by calling the `DeviceIoControl` API function.
3. Close the driver by calling the `CloseHandle` function; the driver will then be automatically unloaded from the memory.

Now, consider the program that loads a dynamic driver. This program is shown in Listing 27.4. It loads the MSG.VXD driver and calls its service number 3.

Listing 27.4. The program that loads, uses, then unloads the virtual driver from the memory

```
; The FILES1.ASM file
.586P
; Flat memory model
.MODEL FLAT, stdcall
; Constants
STD_INPUT_HANDLE equ -10
FILE_FLAG_DELETE_ON_CLOSE   equ 4000000h
; Prototypes of external procedures
EXTERN  GetStdHandle@4:NEAR
EXTERN  ExitProcess@4:NEAR
EXTERN  GetCommandLineA@0:NEAR
EXTERN  CreateFileA@28:NEAR
EXTERN  CloseHandle@4:NEAR
EXTERN  MessageBoxA@16:NEAR
EXTERN  ReadConsoleA@20:NEAR
EXTERN  DeviceIoControl@32:NEAR
;
;-------------------------------------------------
; INCLUDELIB directives for the linker
includelib c:\masm32\lib\user32.lib
includelib c:\masm32\lib\kernel32.lib
;-------------------------------------------------
;
; Data segment
_DATA SEGMENT
HANDL DWORD ?
```

```
HFILE DWORD ?
BUF  DB "\\.\msg.vxd", 0
        CAP  DB "Message box", 0
        MES DB "Error loading the driver", 0
        BUFER DB 20 DUP(0)
        LENS DWORD ? ; Number of characters for output
        MES1 DB "Service call OK!", 0
_DATA ENDS
; Code segment
_TEXT SEGMENT
START:
; Get the output handle
        PUSH  STD_INPUT_HANDLE
        CALL  GetStdHandle@4
        MOV   HANDL, EAX
; Open the file
        PUSH  0
        PUSH  FILE_FLAG_DELETE_ON_CLOSE
        PUSH  0
        PUSH  0
        PUSH  0
        PUSH  0
        PUSH  OFFSET BUF
        CALL  CreateFileA@28
        CMP   EAX, -1
        JE    _ERR
        MOV   HFILE, EAX
; Call the VxD service
        PUSH  0
        PUSH  0
        PUSH  0
        PUSH  0
        PUSH  18
        PUSH  OFFSET MES1
        PUSH  3 ; Service number
        PUSH  HFILE
        CALL  DeviceIoControl@32
; Wait for the <ENTER> key
        PUSH  0
        PUSH  OFFSET LENS
        PUSH  200
        PUSH  OFFSET BUFER
        PUSH  HANDL
```

```
        CALL  ReadConsoleA@20
; Close and unload the driver
        PUSH  HFILE
        CALL  CloseHandle@4
_EXIT:
; Program termination
        PUSH  0
        CALL  ExitProcess@4
_ERR:
        PUSH  0 ; MB_OK
        PUSH  OFFSET CAP
        PUSH  OFFSET MES
        PUSH  0 ; Window handle
        CALL  MessageBoxA@16
        JMP   _EXIT
_TEXT ENDS
END START
```

The program presented in Listing 27.4 requires some comments. The most important role is delegated to the `DeviceIoControl` function. Here are the parameters of this function:

- First parameter — The descriptor of the driver obtained using the `CreateFile` function
- Second parameter — The number of the required operation
- Third parameter — The address of the data for the driver
- Fourth parameter — The data length
- Fifth parameter — The buffer, in which the driver will store its data
- Sixth parameter — The buffer length
- Seventh parameter — The address of the variable that will store the number of bytes loaded into the buffer by the driver
- Eighth parameter — The address of the `OVERLAPPED` structure

As you can see, when calling the function, you pass the pointer to the `MES1` string.

I hope that you won't experience any difficulties understanding how the driver loading program operates. Now, it is time to consider the driver. This driver carries out a simple function. When its service is called, this driver displays a message on the screen. At the same time, the message text is passed by the calling program. When calling the `DeviceIoControl` function with the driver handle, the `w32_deviceIoControl` message is delivered to the driver. The `EBX` register contains the virtual machine handle, and `ESI` points to the structure, the contents of which will be covered in detail later in this section. It is necessary to bear in mind that when the driver is unloaded, the same message arrives to it, which also needs to be processed. Now, consider the structure referenced by the `ESI` register.

```
DIOCParams          STRUC
        Internal1           DD          ?
        VMHandle            DD          ?
        Internal2           DD          ?
        dwIoControlCode     DD          ?
        lpvInBuffer         DD          ?
        cbInBuffer          DD          ?
        lpvOutBuffer        DD          ?
        cbOutBuffer         DD          ?
        lpcbBytesReturned   DD          ?
        lpoOverlapped       DD          ?
        hDevice             DD          ?
        tagProcess          DD          ?
DIOCParams                  ENDS
```

The fields of this structure are as follows.

- `Internal1` — The pointer to the `Client_Reg_Struc` structure that defines the registers of the calling application (see Listing 27.6. and the comments about it)
- `VMHandle` — The virtual machine handle
- `Internal2` — The pointer to the DDB
- `dwIoControlCode` — The number of the required operation
- `lpvInBuffer` — The pointer to the buffer containing information about the calling program
- `cbInBuffer` — The number of bytes sent in the buffer
- `lpvOutBuffer` — The pointer to the buffer, in which the driver can store the information for the calling program
- `cbOutBuffer` — The number of bytes in the buffer
- `lpcbBytesReturned` — The number of bytes to be returned
- `lpoOverlapped` — The pointer to the `Overlapped` structure
- `hDevice` — The driver handle returned by the `CreateFile` function
- `tagProcess` — The process tag

Listing 27.5. An example dynamic driver

```
.586P
include vmm.inc
include vcond.inc
include vwin32.inc
```

```
include shell.inc

DECLARE_VIRTUAL_DEVICE MSG, 1, 0, MSG_Control,\
 UNDEFINED_DEVICE_ID, UNDEFINED_INIT_ORDER

Begin_control_dispatch MSG
; The w32_DeviceIoControl message
; will be processed by the PROC1 procedure
Control_Dispatch w32_DeviceIoControl, PROC1
End_control_dispatch MSG

; Data segment
VxD_PAGEABLE_DATA_SEG
      CAP1  DB "Message box", 0
      MES1  DB 50 DUP(0)
VxD_PAGEABLE_DATA_ENDS

; Code segment
VxD_PAGEABLE_CODE_SEG
BeginProc PROC1
      CMP   DWORD PTR [ESI]+12, DIOC_Open
      JNE   L1
      XOR   EAX, EAX
      JMP   _EXIT
L1:
      CMP   DWORD PTR [ESI]+12, 3
      JNZ   _EXIT
; String length
      MOV   EDI, DWORD PTR [ESI]+16
      VMMCall _lstrlen,<EDI>
; Copy to buffer
      INC   EAX ; Length
      VMMCall _lstrcpyn, <OFFSET MES1, EDI, EAX>
; Call the SHELL_Message function
      MOV   ECX, OFFSET MES1 ; DWORD PTR [ESI]+14
      MOV   EDI, OFFSET CAP1
      MOV   EAX, MB_OK+MB_ICONEXCLAMATION
      VMMCall Get_Sys_VM_Handle
; Address of the CallBack function, NULL in this case
      XOR   ESI, ESI
; Reference to the data for the CallBack function
      XOR   EDX, EDX
      VxDCall SHELL_Message
```

```
        XOR    EAX, EAX
_EXIT:
        RET
EndProc PROC1
VxD_PAGEABLE_CODE_ENDS

end
```

The program in Listing 27.5 requires some comments.

As I pointed out earlier, when the driver loads, it receives the `w32_DeviceIoControl` message, and the `ESI` register points to the message structure. The `dwIoControlCode` field will contain the `DIOC_Open` number, which is equal to zero. The `dwIoControlCode` field is located by the offset `ESI+12`. After making sure that this location contains zero, the driver returns control after resetting `EAX` to zero (this is required).

When calling the driver from the program, you use number 3. After making sure that the `dwIoControlCode` field contains 3, the driver must carry out the actions expected by the program.

The task of this driver is to display a message containing the string received from the calling program. The string address and its length are specified. To demonstrate some functions of a VxD service, you define the string length again and copy it into the buffer prepared in the driver body.

Finally, it is necessary to output the message and return the control after resetting the `EAX` register to zero.

It is time to provide a listing and some comments about the `Client_Reg_Struc` structure.

Listing 27.6. The structure containing the values of registers of the calling application

```
Client_Reg_Struc STRUC
        Client_EDI      DD ?
        Client_ESI      DD ?
        Client_EBP      DD ?
        Client_res0     DD ?
        Client_EBX      DD ?
        Client_EDX      DD ?
        Client_ECX      DD ?
        Client_EAX      DD ?
        Client_Error    DD ?
        Client_EIP      DD ?
        Client_CS       DW ?
```

```
        Client_res1             DW ?
        Client_EFlags           DD ?
        Client_ESP              DD ?
        Client_SS               DW ?
        Client_res2             DW ?
        Client_ES               DW ?
        Client_res3             DW ?
        Client_DS               DW ?
        Client_res4             DW ?
        Client_FS               DW ?
        Client_res5             DW ?
        Client_GS               DW ?
        Client_res6             DW ?
        Client_Alt_EIP          DD ?
        Client_Alt_CS           DW ?
        Client_res7             DW ?
        Client_Alt_EFlags       DD ?
        Client_Alt_ESP          DD ?
        Client_Alt_SS           DW ?
        Client_res8             DW ?
        Client_Alt_ES           DW ?
        Client_res9             DW ?
        Client_Alt_DS           DW ?
        Client_res10            DW ?
        Client_Alt_FS           DW ?
        Client_res11            DW ?
        Client_Alt_GS           DW ?
        Client_res12            DW ?
Client_Reg_Struc ENDS
```

The structure in Listing 27.6 contains three types of fields:

- `Client_resX` — Reserved fields
- `Client_XXX` — Registers of the program started within a virtual machine
- `Client_Alt_XXX` — Registers of a 32-bit program started in the system virtual machine

At this point, the description of virtual drivers comes to a logical end.

Basic Concepts of Kernel-Mode Drivers

The material that covered in this section is generally considered difficult. Therefore, before you study it, I recommend that you achieve a proper understanding of page addressing (*Chapter 19*) and services programming (*Chapter 21*). When describing kernel-mode drivers, I will actively use material provided in these chapters.

Kernel-mode drivers that can operate only under operating systems of the Windows NT family should not be confused with Win32 Driver Model (WDM) drivers. WDM drivers can run under Windows 98, Windows 2000, and Windows XP because they are compatible at the level of binary code. This type of driver will not be covered here.

The Kernel and Memory Structure

First, it is necessary to define the operating system kernel. The kernel is part of the operating system stored in RAM. The kernel must be protected against any attempts at infringement (malicious or not) by application programs. It is impossible to ensure absolute kernel protection without hardware support. The protected mode of Intel processors provides such a support. In *Chapter 19*, I described the protected mode in relation to memory management. I hope that you have acquired basic knowledge about the protected mode. Review Fig. 19.4, which illustrates the address space of a process. The use of the paging mechanism allows you to achieve a wonderful effect — the address space significantly exceeds the real size of the physical memory. At the same time, the actual memory page might be stored in the so-called paging file instead of physical memory. This is an interesting effect; however, the limited space in this book prevents me from considering it in detail.

Intel processors simultaneously use two mechanisms of forming memory addresses. These are segment and page mechanisms. The page mechanism operates at a lower level. When it comes to protection, segment-level protection has higher priority than page-level protection. In other words, if a specific segment is assigned the highest privilege, this privilege will be in force regardless of the privilege levels set for the page level. On the other hand, if protection level 3 is set for the segment, then everything depends on the privilege level set for specific pages. There are only two privilege levels for pages — 0 and 3. In Windows, the so-called flat memory model is adopted. The selector that points to the segment descriptor starting at address 0 is loaded into segment registers. Because the offset within a segment is defined by a 32-bit value, this allows an address space of 4 GB. No other segments are assumed to exist in the system. This means that there is only one vast segment. Well, then, where is the protection? The answer is straightforward — the protection is implemented at the page level. Return to Fig. 19.4, where you'll see the memory region occupied by the operating system (to be more precise, occupied by its kernel, according to the definition provided earlier in this chapter). These pages are protected against access by normal executable modules, although they reside in the same address space. Also note that page memory organization allows you to protect the program code. Pages containing the program code are marked as read-only. In parallel to this, all mechanisms of segment addressing, such as gateways and interrupts, are operating, because they cannot be implemented at the page level. These operations are hidden from a normal program, which sees only the flat address space.

How is multitasking implemented? Here, the page table mechanism comes into action (see Fig. 19.3). The CR3 register contains the address of the page table directory. Every task has its individual directory of page tables. Thus, switching between tasks can be implemented by changing the contents of the CR3 register. The directory contents define the mapping of the virtual address space to physical resources of the computer. The most important point is that the operating system kernel is mapped to the address space of every task. The goal is to consider legal mechanisms that allow the driver (e.g., some software module) to start in the kernel mode and communicate to applications that have lower privileges. Kernel-mode drivers have great power over the operating system and the entire computer. First, they can directly access peripheral devices through input and output ports. Second, such drivers can directly call the operating system kernel code. These capabilities imply greater responsibility, because even the slightest error can crash the entire operating system, causing the "blue screen of death" to appear. This topic is the most interesting because now you are approaching the inner sanctum of the Windows operating system.

Controlling Drivers

However surprising this might seem, kernel-mode drivers are controlled according to the same method used for controlling services. In *Chapter 21*, I explained in detail how to proceed to install, configure, start, stop, and remove services. Kernel-mode drivers are controlled in exactly the same way. Thus, the programs presented in *Chapter 21* can be used practically without changes. Recall that the program in Listing 21.1 represents the service text. Naturally, it won't be needed here. The program in Listing 21.2 carries out service installation, the program in Listing 21.3 starts the service, and the program in Listing 21.4 stops the service and deletes it from the system. Among these programs, only the program in Listing 21.2 requires considerable changes. These modifications relate to the CreateService function call. The following is the fragment illustrating how to use the CreateService function to install a kernel-mode driver:

```
PUSH  0
PUSH  0
PUSH  0
PUSH  0
```

```
PUSH  0
PUSH  OFFSET NM
PUSH  SERVICE_ERROR_NORMAL
PUSH  SERVICE_DEMAND_START
PUSH  SERVICE_KERNEL_DRIVER
PUSH  SERVICE_START + DELETE ; Instead of SERVICE_ALL_ACCESS
PUSH  OFFSET SNAME1
PUSH  OFFSET SNAME1
PUSH  H1
CALL  CreateServiceA@52
```

Also, I have changed some parameters. The list of constants that I used is as follows:

```
DELETE                 equ 10000h
SERVICE_START          equ 10h
SERVICE_KERNEL_DRIVER  equ 00000001h
```

Pay attention to the fifth parameter from the end. It specifies the service type, which in this case is `SERVICE_KERNEL_DRIVER`. This means that the program informs the service control manager that this program isn't a normal service but is a kernel-mode driver.

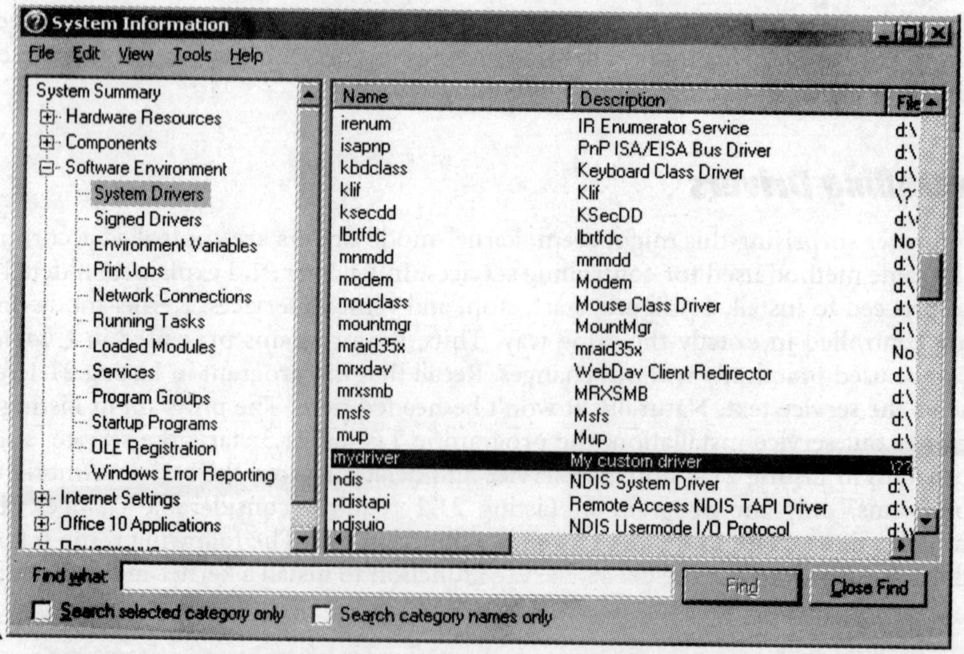

Fig. 27.1. Console of the MSINFO32.EXE program allows you to view the list of drivers installed in the system

NOTE

The service control program allowing you to control services in the interactive dialog mode is useless here. All manipulations with drivers can only be done programmatically. As relates to the system registry, all data related to drivers are stored under the same registry key as the service-related data:

`HKEY_LOCAL_MACHINE\SYSTEM\CurrentControlSet\Services`

Accordingly, if you delete all references to a specific driver from the registry, you'll remove that driver from the system. Nevertheless, you can view the list of drivers installed in the system using the MSINFO32.EXE program. If your driver has been correctly installed, you'll find it in the list displayed by this program. Fig. 27.1 shows the console window of this program. Unfortunately, this program doesn't provide any capabilities except viewing the list of installed drivers.

An Example of a Simple Kernel-Mode Driver

The goal of this section is to show you how to write the simplest kernel-mode driver, which would demonstrate the main capabilities of programs granted the highest privileges. I have chosen sound playback. To observe the purity of the experiment, I'll first try to reproduce the sound playback algorithm in a simple console application.

Listing 27.7. Attempting to play sound by accessing input and output ports in a console program

```
.586P
; Flat memory model
.MODEL FLAT, stdcall
EXTERN  ExitProcess@4:NEAR
;-------------------------------------------
; INCLUDELIB directives for the linker
includelib d:\masm32\lib\kernel32.lib
;-------------------------------------------
; Data segment
_DATA SEGMENT
_DATA ENDS
; Code segment
_TEXT SEGMENT
START:
; Setting the write mode
        CLI
        MOV   AL, 10110110B
        OUT   43H, AL
```

```
        IN    AL, 61H
; Allow communication with the timer
        OR    AL, 3
        OUT   61H, AL
        MOV   AX, 1200
; Set the sound frequency
; The timer is triggered immediately
; after sending the counter value
        OUT   42H, AL
        MOV   AL, AH
        OUT   42H, AL
        STI
        MOV   ECX, 0FFFFFFH
; Delay
LOO:
        LOOP  LOO
; Detach the channel from the speaker, which means stop sound playback
        CLI
        IN    AL, 61H
        AND   AL, 11111100B
        OUT   61H, AL
        STI
;-------------------------------
        PUSH  0
        CALL  ExitProcess@4
_TEXT ENDS
END START
```

You can compile this console application in the usual way. It seems OK at first glance; however, when you start it, an error message will appear. Why does this happen? This program starts in ring 3, and the operating system informs you that you cannot execute a privileged input/output command in this ring. Well, this is the first part of experiment. The goal of the second part of this experiment is to demonstrate that the kernel-mode driver can play back sound using the method provided in Listing 27.7.

However, at this point it is necessary to provide some comments related to low-level operations with the speaker. Sound generation is based on communication between the system timer chip and the speaker. The timer chip counts pulses received from the system clock. After a predefined number of pulses (this number can be specified programmatically), it produces an output signal. When these signals are sent to the speaker input, the speaker produces a sound. The tone of this signal depends on the frequency of signals supplied to the speaker input. Generally, this is all that relates to the basic idea of sound generation in the standard IBM PC configuration. Now, consider this process in more detail.

The timer chip has three channels — timer 0, timer 1, and timer 2. The timer 0 channel is responsible for the system clock. The signal from this channel generates the timer interrupt. The procedure pointed to by the interrupt vector number 8 is carried out 18.2 times per second. This procedure modifies the memory area, in which the current time is stored. The special latch register stores the number of synch pulses, after which the signal from timer must cause the timer interrupt. By decreasing this number (through the channel port), it is possible to make the system clock run faster. The address of the channel 0 port is `40H`.

The timer 1 channel is responsible for time regeneration. The port address of this channel is `41H`. Principally, the number of memory regeneration cycles per second can be reduced, which would improve performance. However, this is possible only within certain limits, because the probability of memory failure grows with an increased regeneration interval.

As a rule, the timer 2 channel is used for working with the speaker, although the signals from this channel can be used for other purposes. The address of the port of this channel is `42H`. The idea of sound generation is simple. A counter value (some number) is sent to port `42H`. The value of this counter immediately starts to decrease. When a 0 value is reached, a signal is supplied to the speaker, after which the entire process is repeated. The greater the counter value, the lower the signal frequency, and consequently, the lower the tone.

The timer 2 channel communicates to the speaker through port `61H`. If bit 1 of this port is set to 1, then channel 2 sends signals to the speaker. In addition, to enable the sending of signals from the system clock to channel 2, bit 0 of this port must be set to 1 (which corresponds to the high level of the signal).

To program channels, it is necessary to first set port `43H`. Bit values of this port are outlined in Table 27.1.

Table 27.1. The bits of port 43H

Bit	Value
0	0 indicates binary data; 1 indicates data in binary coded decimal format.
1 – 3	The mode number; as a rule, mode 3 is used.
4 – 5	The type of operation: • 00 — Pass the counter value to the latch. • 01 — Read or write the most significant byte only. • 10 — Read or write the least significant byte only. • 11 — Read or write the most significant byte then the least significant byte.
6 – 7	The number of the programmable timer channel (0 – 2).

Note how the CLI and STI commands are used. They enable and disable processor interrupts. Disabling interrupts before working with input and output ports is natural, because interrupts are highly undesirable when an input or an output operation is in progress.

Well, everything is clear with sound generation. Now, it is possible to demonstrate that the previously-described method of sound playback can be implemented in the kernel-mode driver, because the kernel mode allows direct access to the input and output ports.

Listing 27.8. A simple kernel-mode driver that plays back a short sound signal

```
; A simple kernel-mode driver
; that plays a short sound signal
.586P
.MODEL FLAT, stdcall
INCLUDE KERN.INC
includelib d:\masm32\lib\hal.lib
_TEXT SEGMENT
; DWORD PTR [EBP+0CH] ; Points to DRIVER_OBJECT
; DWORD PTR [EBP+08H] ; Points to UNICODE_STRING
ENTRY PROC ; Entry point
PUSH EBP
        MOV   EBP, ESP ; Now, EBP points to the top of the stack
        PUSH  EBX
        PUSH  ESI
        PUSH  EDI
; Specify the frequency
        MOV   EDX, 1200
; Set the write mode
        CLI
        MOV   AL, 10110110B
        OUT   43H, AL
        IN    AL, 61H
; Allow communication to the timer
        OR    AL, 3
        OUT   61H, AL
; Set the sound frequency
; The timer is triggered immediately
; after supplying the counter
```

```
        MOV   EAX, EDX
        OUT   42H, AL
        MOV   AL, AH
        OUT   42H, AL
        MOV   ECX, 0FFFFFFH
        STI
; Delay
LOO:
        LOOP LOO
; Detach the channel from the speaker (i.e., stop the sound)
        CLI
        IN    AL, 61H
        AND   AL, 11111100B
        OUT   61H, AL
        STI
; Set the exit code
        MOV   EAX, STATUS_DEVICE_CONFIGURATION_ERROR
        POP   EDI
        POP   ESI
        POP   EBX
        POP   EBP
        RET   8
ENTRY ENDP
_TEXT ENDS
END ENTRY
```

The program in Listing 27.8 requires some comments.

Kernel-mode drivers cannot use the same API functions as normal unprivileged programs. Instead, a kernel-mode driver must use functions available from the kernel. Therefore, such drivers must use other libraries. These libraries are supplied as part of the Microsoft Windows DDK. This program includes one such library, HAL.LIB, although it doesn't use any of its functions. Unfortunately, information about kernel functions is available only from the DDK documentation or from third-party developers. Furthermore, this information often is incomplete.

In addition to libraries, DDK includes INC files containing many definitions of types, structures, constants, and function prototypes. Placing this information into the program is senseless. I have created a custom INC file (KERN.INC) on the basis of several INC files supplied with Windows DDK. This file contains definitions of the main structures and types. The complete listing of this file is provided in Listing 27.9. I also included this file in the program, although it uses only one constant from this file — `STATUS_DEVICE_CONFIGURATION_ERROR`.

- The entry point of this driver is the `ENTRY` procedure. This procedure starts when the `StartService` function is executed. Programs in Listings 21.2, 21.3, and 21.4, and the modifications that you need to introduce there to ensure that these programs serve the kernel-mode driver, were described earlier. As a result, the driver will execute the code that accesses input and output ports, and a short sound signal will be produced. The procedure will then return the `STATUS_DEVICE_CONFIGURATION_ERROR` value. This method is a standard technique that ensures that the system, after executing the procedure, unloads the driver from the memory (although it remains in the driver database).

The entry point procedure has two parameters that were not used until now. The first parameter points to the `DRIVER_OBJECT` structure. This structure can be found in Listing 27.9. This structure is a complicated one because it references other structures, which, in turn, refer to other structures. However, for the goals of this program, the only important thing is that this structure describes the object being created — a kernel-mode driver object. The fields of this structure set the properties of the kernel object being created. The second parameter of the entry point procedure is the Unicode string. This string specifies the name of the registry key where the initialization parameters of the kernel-mode driver are stored.

Listing 27.9. The KERN.INC file used by the driver in Listing 27.8

```
; The KERN.INC file

PVOID                   typedef       PTR
PIRP                    typedef       PTR _IRP
NTSTATUS                typedef       DWORD
PKEVENT                 typedef       PTR KEVENT
PIO_STATUS_BLOCK        typedef       PTR IO_STATUS_BLOCK
BOOLEAN                 typedef       BYTE
PCHAR                   typedef       PTR BYTE
PWSTR                   typedef       PTR WORD
KPROCESSOR_MODE         typedef       BYTE
CHAR                    typedef       BYTE
WCHAR                   typedef       WORD
DEVICE_TYPE             typedef       DWORD
IO_TYPE_DEVICE_QUEUE    equ           14h
KSPIN_LOCK              typedef       DWORD
IO_TYPE_DPC             equ           13h
PDWORD                  typedef       PTR DWORD
PSECURITY_DESCRIPTOR    typedef       PTR
```

```
MAXIMUM_VOLUME_LABEL_LENGTH  equu       (32 * sizeof(WCHAR))

; Constants defining the request type
IRP_MJ_CREATE                         equ  0
IRP_MJ_CREATE_NAMED_PIPE              equ  1
IRP_MJ_CLOSE                          equ  2
IRP_MJ_READ                           equ  3
IRP_MJ_WRITE                          equ  4
IRP_MJ_QUERY_INFORMATION              equ  5
IRP_MJ_SET_INFORMATION                equ  6
IRP_MJ_QUERY_EA                       equ  7
IRP_MJ_SET_EA                         equ  8
IRP_MJ_FLUSH_BUFFERS                  equ  9
IRP_MJ_QUERY_VOLUME_INFORMATION       equ  0Ah
IRP_MJ_SET_VOLUME_INFORMATION         equ  0Bh
IRP_MJ_DIRECTORY_CONTROL              equ  0Ch
IRP_MJ_FILE_SYSTEM_CONTROL            equ  0Dh
IRP_MJ_DEVICE_CONTROL                 equ  0Eh
IRP_MJ_INTERNAL_DEVICE_CONTROL        equ  0Fh
IRP_MJ_SHUTDOWN                       equ  10h
IRP_MJ_LOCK_CONTROL                   equ  11h
IRP_MJ_CLEANUP                        equ  12h
IRP_MJ_CREATE_MAILSLOT                equ  13h
IRP_MJ_QUERY_SECURITY                 equ  14h
IRP_MJ_SET_SECURITY                   equ  15h
IRP_MJ_POWER                          equ  16h
IRP_MJ_SYSTEM_CONTROL                 equ  17h
IRP_MJ_DEVICE_CHANGE                  equ  18h
IRP_MJ_QUERY_QUOTA                    equ  19h
IRP_MJ_SET_QUOTA                      equ  1Ah
IRP_MJ_PNP                            equ  1Bh
IRP_MJ_PNP_POWER                      equ  IRP_MJ_PNP
IRP_MJ_MAXIMUM_FUNCTION               equ  1Bh

VPB STRUCT
  fwType              WORD   IO_TYPE_VPB
  cbSize              WORD   ?
  Flags               WORD   ?
  VolumeLabelLength   WORD   ?
  DeviceObject        PVOID  ?
  RealDevice          PVOID  ?
  SerialNumber        DWORD  ?
  ReferenceCount      DWORD  ?
```

```
 VolumeLabel   WORD (MAXIMUM_VOLUME_LABEL_LENGTH/(sizeof WCHAR)) dup(?)
VPB ENDS
PVPB  typedef        PTR VPB

UNICODE_STRING STRUCT
     woLength        WORD  ?
     MaximumLength   WORD  ?
     Buffer          PWSTR ?
UNICODE_STRING ENDS

SECTION_OBJECT_POINTERS STRUCT
       DataSectionObject      PVOID ?
       SharedCacheMap         PVOID ?
       ImageSectionObject     PVOID ?
SECTION_OBJECT_POINTERS ENDS

PSECTION_OBJECT_POINTERS typedef PTR SECTION_OBJECT_POINTERS


IO_COMPLETION_CONTEXT STRUCT
       Port  PVOID ?
       Key   PVOID ?
IO_COMPLETION_CONTEXT ENDS

PIO_COMPLETION_CONTEXT typedef PTR IO_COMPLETION_CONTEXT

LARGE_INTEGER UNION
    struct
        LowPart    DWORD ?
        HighPart   DWORD ?
    ends
    struct u
        LowPart    DWORD ?
        HighPart   DWORD ?
    ends
        QuadPart    QWORD ?
LARGE_INTEGER ENDS

LIST_ENTRY STRUCT
       Flink        PVOID ?
       Blink        PVOID ?
LIST_ENTRY ENDS
```

```
KDPC STRUCT
        woType              WORD   IO_TYPE_DPC
        Number              BYTE   ?
        Importance          BYTE   ?
        DpcListEntry        LIST_ENTRY <>
        DeferredRoutine     PVOID  ?
        DeferredContext     PVOID  ?
        SystemArgument1     PVOID  ?
        SystemArgument2     PVOID  ?
        pdwLock             PDWORD ?
KDPC ENDS

KDEVICE_QUEUE STRUCT
        fwType            WORD  IO_TYPE_DEVICE_QUEUE
        cbSize            WORD  ?
        DeviceListHead    LIST_ENTRY <>
        ksLock            KSPIN_LOCK ?
        Busy              BOOLEAN ?
        db                3 dup (?)
KDEVICE_QUEUE ENDS

KDEVICE_QUEUE_ENTRY STRUCT ; sizeof = 10h
        DeviceListEntry  LIST_ENTRY <>
        SortKey          DWORD ?
        Inserted         BOOLEAN ?
        Db          3 dup(?)
KDEVICE_QUEUE_ENTRY ENDS

WAIT_CONTEXT_BLOCK STRUCT
        WaitQueueEntry          KDEVICE_QUEUE_ENTRY <>
        DeviceRoutine           PVOID ?
        DeviceContext           PVOID ?
        NumberOfMapRegisters    DWORD ?
        DeviceObject            PVOID ?
        CurrentIrp              PVOID ?
        BufferChainingDpc       PVOID ?
WAIT_CONTEXT_BLOCK ENDS

DISPATCHER_HEADER STRUCT
        byType          BYTE ?
        Absolute        BYTE ?
```

```
        cbSize          BYTE   ?
        Inserted        BYTE   ?
        SignalState     DWORD ?
        WaitListHead    LIST_ENTRY <>
DISPATCHER_HEADER ENDS


KEVENT STRUCT
        Header   DISPATCHER_HEADER  <>
KEVENT ENDS

FILE_OBJECT STRUCT
        fwType                  WORD IO_TYPE_FILE
        cbSize                  WORD  ?
        DeviceObject            PVOID ?
        Vpb                     PVOID ?
        FsContext               PVOID ?
        FsContext2              PVOID ?
        SectionObjectPointer    PSECTION_OBJECT_POINTERS ?
        PrivateCacheMap         PVOID ?
        FinalStatus             NTSTATUS ?
        RelatedFileObject       PVOID ?
        LockOperation           BOOLEAN ?
        DeletePending           BOOLEAN ?
        ReadAccess              BOOLEAN ?
        WriteAccess             BOOLEAN ?
        DeleteAccess            BOOLEAN ?
        SharedRead              BOOLEAN ?
        SharedWrite             BOOLEAN ?
        SharedDelete            BOOLEAN ?
        Flags                   DWORD ?
        FileName                UNICODE_STRING <>
        CurrentByteOffset       LARGE_INTEGER <>
        Waiters                 DWORD ?
        Busy                    DWORD ?
        LastLock                PVOID ?
        kevLock                 EVENT <>
        Event                   KEVENT <>
        CompletionContext       PIO_COMPLETION_CONTEXT ?
FILE_OBJECT ENDS

PFILE_OBJECT typedef PTR FILE_OBJECT
```

```
IO_STATUS_BLOCK STRUCT
       Status          NTSTATUS ?
       Information     DWORD    ?
IO_STATUS_BLOCK ENDS

STATUS_DEVICE_CONFIGURATION_ERROR equ 00C0000182h
STATUS_SUCCESS equ 0

IO_STATUS_BLOCK STRUCT
       Status          NTSTATUS ?
       Information      DWORD   ?
IO_STATUS_BLOCK ENDS

KAPC STRUCT
       fwType                 WORD   IO_TYPE_APC
       cbSize                 WORD   ?
       Spare0                 DWORD  ?
       Thread                 PVOID  ?
       ApcListEntry           LIST_ENTRY <>
       KernelRoutine          PVOID  ?
       RundownRoutine         PVOID  ?
       NormalRoutine          PVOID  ?
       NormalContext          PVOID  ?
       ; The following two fields must be together
       SystemArgument1        PVOID  ?
       SystemArgument2        PVOID  ?
       ApcStateIndex          CHAR   ?
       ApcMode                KPROCESSOR_MODE ?
       Inserted               BOOLEAN ?
       db                     ?
KAPC ENDS

_IRP STRUCT
       fwType                  WORD  ?
       cbSize                  WORD  ?
       MdlAddress              PVOID ?
       Flags                   DWORD ?
       UNION AssociatedIrp
               MasterIrp       PVOID ?
               IrpCount        DWORD ?
               SystemBuffer    PVOID ?
       ENDS
```

```
ThreadListEntry     LIST_ENTRY <>
IoStatus            IO_STATUS_BLOCK <>
RequestorMode       BYTE ?
PendingReturned     BYTE ?
StackCount          BYTE ?
CurrentLocation     BYTE ?
Cancel              BYTE ?
CancelIrql          BYTE ?
ApcEnvironment      BYTE ?
AllocationFlags     BYTE ?
UserIosb            PIO_STATUS_BLOCK ?
UserEvent           PKEVENT ?
UNION Overlay
        STRUCT AsynchronousParameters
                UserApcRoutine  PVOID ?
                UserApcContext  PVOID ?
        ENDS
AllocationSize          LARGE_INTEGER   <>     .
ENDS

CancelRoutine          PVOID  ?
UserBuffer             PVOID  ?

UNION Tail
    STRUCT Overlay
          UNION
                DeviceQueueEntry  KDEVICE_QUEUE_ENTRY <>
                STRUCT
                   DriverContext  PVOID  4 dup(?)
                ENDS
          ENDS
                Thread                      PVOID  ?

                AuxiliaryBuffer             PCHAR  ?
                STRUCT
                        ListEntry           LIST_ENTRY  <>
                UNION
                        PacketType          DWORD  ?
                ENDS
        ENDS
        OriginalFileObject        PFILE_OBJECT  ?
        ENDS
```

```
            Apc                     KAPC <>
            CompletionKey           PVOID ?
        ENDS

 _IRP ENDS

 DEVICE_OBJECT STRUCT
        fwType              WORD  IO_TYPE_DEVICE
        cbSize              WORD  ?
        ReferenceCount      DWORD ?
        DriverObject        PVOID ?
        NextDevice          PVOID ?
        AttachedDevice      PVOID ?
        PDEVICE_OBJECT
        CurrentIrp          PIRP  ?
        Timer               PVOID ?
        Flags               DWORD ?
        Characteristics     DWORD ?
        Vpb                 PVPB  ?
        DeviceExtension     PVOID ?
        DeviceType          DEVICE_TYPE ?
        StackSize           CHAR  ?
        db                  3 dup (?)
        UNION Queue
                ListEntry           LIST_ENTRY <>
                Wcb                 WAIT_CONTEXT_BLOCK <>
        ENDS
        AlignmentRequirement        DWORD ?
        DeviceQueue                 KDEVICE_QUEUE  <>
        Dpc                         KDPC  <>
        ActiveThreadCount           DWORD ?
        SecurityDescriptor          PSECURITY_DESCRIPTOR ?
        DeviceLock                  KEVENT <>
        SectorSize                  WORD   ?
        Spare1                      WORD   ?
        DeviceObjectExtension       PVOID  ?        PDEVOBJ_EXTENSION
        Reserved                    PVOID  ?
 DEVICE_OBJECT ENDS

 PDEVICE_OBJECT     typedef PTR DEVICE_OBJECT
 PDRIVER_EXTENSION  typedef PTR DRIVER_EXTENSION
 PUNICODE_STRING    typedef PTR UNICODE_STRING
```

```
DRIVER_OBJECT STRUCT ; sizeof = 0A8h
        fwType            WORD               IO_TYPE_DRIVER
        cbSize            WORD               ?
        DeviceObject      PDEVICE_OBJECT     ?
        Flags             DWORD              ?
        DriverStart       PVOID              ?
        DriverSize        DWORD              ?
        DriverSection     PVOID              ?
        DriverExtension   PDRIVER_EXTENSION ?
        DriverName        UNICODE_STRING    <>
        HardwareDatabase  PUNICODE_STRING    ?
        FastIoDispatch    PVOID              ?
        DriverInit        PVOID              ?
        DriverStartIo     PVOID              ?
        DriverUnload      PVOID              ?
        MajorFunction     PVOID   (IRP_MJ_MAXIMUM_FUNCTION + 1) dup (?)
DRIVER_OBJECT ENDS

IO_STACK_LOCATION STRUCT
        MajorFunction       BYTE  ?
        MinorFunction       BYTE  ?
        Flags               BYTE  ?
        Control             BYTE  ?
        union Parameters
                struct Create
                        SecurityContext   PVOID  ?
                        Options           DWORD  ?
                        FileAttributes    WORD   ?
                        ShareAccess       WORD   ?
                        EaLength          DWORD  ?
                ends
                struct Read
                        dwLength          DWORD          ?
                        Key               DWORD          ?
                        ByteOffset        LARGE_INTEGER <>
                ends
                struct Write
                        dwLength          DWORD          ?
                        Key               DWORD          ?
                        ByteOffset        LARGE_INTEGER <>
                ends

                struct QueryFile
```

```
                    dwLength                DWORD  ?
                    FileInformationClass    DWORD  ?
                ends

    struct DeviceIoControl
                OutputBufferLength          DWORD  ?
                InputBufferLength           DWORD  ?
                IoControlCode               DWORD  ?
                Type3InputBuffer            PVOID  ?
    ends
    struct ReadWriteConfig
                WhichSpace              DWORD  ?
                Buffer                  PVOID  ?
                dwOffset                DWORD  ?
                wdLength                DWORD  ?
    ends

                struct SetLock
                bLock       BOOLEAN  ?
                db          3 dup (?)
                ends


                struct Others
                    Argument1           PVOID  ?
                    Argument2           PVOID  ?
                    Argument3           PVOID  ?
                    Argument4           PVOID  ?
                ends

        ends

        DeviceObject            PDEVICE_OBJECT  ?
        FileObject              PFILE_OBJECT    ?
        CompletionRoutine       PVOID           ?
        Context                 PVOID           ?
IO_STACK_LOCATION ENDS
```

To translate the driver provided in Listing 27.8, issue the following commands:

```
ml /c /coff sound.asm
link /driver /base:0x1000 /subsystem:native sound.obj
```

As you can see, the command line of the ML.EXE program uses the standard parameters. As relates to the command-line parameters of the LINK.EXE program, they are different from the usual ones. The `/driver` parameter specifies that the linker should create the driver. The `/base:0x1000` option informs the linker that the driver will be loaded by address `1000H`. Finally, the `/subsystem:native` option is the standard subsystem value for a Windows NT driver.

To stimulate your interest in investigating kernel-mode drivers, and to gain some practical skills, I recommend that you rewrite this driver using two interesting kernel functions. The first of these functions is `READ_PORT_UCHAR`. This function has only one parameter (see the `READ_PORT_UCHAR@4` prototype). This is the address of the input/output port. This function practically replaces the `IN` microprocessor command. The second function is `WRITE_PORT_UCHAR`. It accepts two parameters. The first parameter is the number of the input/output port, and the second parameter is the operand, from which the data will be supplied to the port. Both functions are defined in the HAL.LIB library. As usual, their prototypes must be defined at the beginning of your program. The resulting driver must produce the same result as the use of standard `IN` and `OUT` commands of the Intel microprocessor. Why is such duplication needed? This is needed for compatibility so that the operating system will work with the microprocessor of another family.

NOTE

A sound signal is convenient for debugging drivers. Other ways of informing you how a specific function was executed are not as easy to implement.

Kernel-Mode Drivers and Devices

The goal of this section is to show you how to develop another kernel-mode driver that creates a device that can be accessed using standard file input and output.

First, consider the program that runs in the user mode and needs to access a device created by a kernel-mode driver (Listing 27.10). This is the fourth program for controlling drivers. The first three programs that install, start, and remove drivers were described earlier. In practice, they are similar to the programs for controlling services (see *Chapter 21*). A device created and served by a kernel-mode driver is opened using the `CreateFile` function. Pay attention to the device name: `'\\.\SLN'`. In case of success, the program sends the data to the driver through this device. This is achieved using the `DeviceIoControl` function. If this function executes successfully, the program receives the data from the driver. For checking, the `MessageBox` function is used, which outputs these data. To close the device, the standard `CloseHandle` function is used. This function is used for closing most kernel objects.

Listing 27.10. The program that opens the device created by the driver in Listing 27.11

```
.586P
; Flat memory model
.MODEL FLAT, stdcall

DTP    equ 8000H
ACCESS equ 0H
OPER   equ 800H
MBUF   equ 0H
; The command passed to the driver
CMD   equ (DTP SHL 16) OR (ACCESS SHL 14) OR (OPER SHL 2) OR MBUF

GENERIC_READ    equ 80000000h
GENERIC_WRITE   equ 40000000h
GEN = GENERIC_READ or GENERIC_WRITE
SHARE = 0
OPEN_EXISTING     equ 3
STD_OUTPUT_HANDLE equ -11

EXTERN  CloseHandle@4:NEAR
EXTERN  CreateFileA@28:NEAR
EXTERN  ExitProcess@4:NEAR
EXTERN  MessageBoxA@16:NEAR
EXTERN  MessageBoxW@16:NEAR
EXTERN  wsprintfA:NEAR
EXTERN  GetLastError@0:NEAR
EXTERN  lstrlenA@4:NEAR
EXTERN  WriteConsoleA@20:NEAR
EXTERN  GetStdHandle@4:NEAR
EXTERN  DeviceIoControl@32:NEAR
;-----------------------------------------------
; INCLUDELIB directives for the linker
includelib d:\masm32\lib\kernel32.lib
includelib d:\masm32\lib\user32.lib
;-----------------------------------------------

; Data segment
_DATA SEGMENT
```

```
; Device name
        PATH    DB '\\.\SLN', 0
        H1      DD ?
        HANDL   DD ?
        LENS    DD ?
        BUF1    DB 512 DUP (0)
        ERRS    DB "Error %u ", 0
        BUFIN   DB "For Mydriver", 88 DUP (0)
        BUFOUT  DB 100 DUP(0)
        BYTES   DD 0
_DATA ENDS
; Code segment
_TEXT SEGMENT
START:
        PUSH  STD_OUTPUT_HANDLE
        CALL  GetStdHandle@4
        MOV   HANDL, EAX
; Open the device
        PUSH  0
        PUSH  0
        PUSH  OPEN_EXISTING
        PUSH  0
        PUSH  0
        PUSH  GEN
        PUSH  OFFSET PATH
        CALL  CreateFileA@28
        CMP   EAX, -1
        JNZ   NOER
        CALL  ERROB
        JMP   EXI
NOER:
; Pass the command and data to the driver
; in the BUFIN buffer
        MOV   H1, EAX
        PUSH  0
        PUSH  OFFSET BYTES
        PUSH  100
        PUSH  OFFSET BUFOUT
        PUSH  100
        PUSH  OFFSET BUFIN
        PUSH  CMD
        PUSH  H1
        CALL  DeviceIoControl@32
```

```
        CMP   EAX, 0
        JZ    CLOS
        CMP   BYTES, 0
        JZ    CLOS
; Output the contents of the returned buffer
        PUSH  0
        PUSH  OFFSET BUFOUT
        PUSH  OFFSET BUFOUT
        PUSH  0 ; Screen handle
        CALL  MessageBoxA@16

CLOS:
        PUSH  H1
        CALL  CloseHandle@4
EXI:
        PUSH  0
        CALL  ExitProcess@4
ERROB:
        CALL  GetLastError@0
        PUSH  EAX
        PUSH  OFFSET ERRS
        PUSH  OFFSET BUF1
        CALL  wsprintfA
        ADD   ESP, 12
        LEA   EAX, BUF1
        MOV   EDI, 1
        CALL  WRITE
        RET
; Output the string (line feed in the end)
; EAX - To the start of the string
; EDI - With or without line feed
WRITE PROC
; Get the parameter length
        PUSH  EAX
        PUSH  EAX
        CALL  lstrlenA@4
        MOV   ESI, EAX
        POP   EBX
        CMP   EDI, 1
        JNE   NO_ENT
; Line feed in the end
        MOV   BYTE PTR [EBX+ESI], 13
        MOV   BYTE PTR [EBX+ESI+1], 10
```

```
        MOV   BYTE PTR [EBX+ESI+2], 0
        ADD   EAX, 2
NO_ENT:
; String output
        PUSH  0
        PUSH  OFFSET LENS
        PUSH  EAX
        PUSH  EBX
        PUSH  HANDL
        CALL  WriteConsoleA@20
        RET
WRITE   ENDP

_TEXT ENDS
END START
```

To translate the program, issue the following commands:

```
ml /c /coff prog.asm
link /subsystem:console prog.obj
```

The program presented in Listing 27.10 requires some comments.

The `DeviceIoControl` function was already covered in this chapter. However, I would like to draw your attention to the second parameter of this function. This parameter contains the control code passed to the driver. Individual devices have specific sets of control codes. When creating a custom control code, it is necessary to bear in mind that it must be created according to strictly defined rules. These rules are as follows: Bits 0–1 define whether the input or output is buffered. The 0 value corresponds to the standard buffered input or output; other values define input or output without buffering. Bits 3–13 define the command that the driver must execute. The values `0–7FFH` are reserved, and other values can be used at programmer's discretion. Bits 14–15 define the requested access rights. The 0 value specifies the maximum possible access level. The 1 and 2 values correspond to read and write access, respectively. Bits 16–31 define the device type. Here programmers at their discretion can use the values ranging from `8000H` to `0FFFFH`. For example, I have formed a custom `CMD` command (see Listing 27.10).

Debugging kernel-mode drivers is a difficult task. In the course of this work, it is impossible to avoid the infamous blue screen of death. The programs that communicate with the driver being debugged are also involved in the debugging process. Error handling plays an extremely important role here. This program handles and outputs possible errors of the `CreateFile` function. To determine the cause of the error, use the ERRLOOKUP.EXE program that I mentioned earlier in this book. The `MessageBox` function also plays the role of the debugging mechanism — not only for this program but also for the driver, to which it communicates.

Now, consider the text of the driver presented in Listing 27.11. Similar to the simplest driver described in the previous section, this driver has the entry point procedure. This procedure carries out the following tasks:

- Create a device.
- Create a symbolic link to the device. This name is the one used as a device name in the `CreateFile` function.
- Define the procedure for unloading the driver. This procedure is called before deleting the driver. At this point, it is necessary to release or delete all resources allocated by the driver.
- Define the callback procedures. In this program, three such procedures are defined: the procedure called when opening the device (`CreateFile`), the procedure called when closing the device (`CloseHandle`), and the procedure called when sending a control code to the device.

As mentioned earlier, the functions that execute in the kernel mode operate with Unicode strings. In particular, this means that you will have to deal with the following structures:

```
UNICODE_STRING STRUCT
        woLength            WORD    ?
        MaximumLength       WORD    ?
        Buffer              PWSTR   ?

UNICODE_STRING ENDS
```

Here, `woLength` is the length of the Unicode string in bytes, `MaximumLength` is the length in bytes of the buffer containing the string, and `Buffer` is the address of the buffer (`PWSTR` stands for `PTR WORD`). To fill this structure using the Unicode string prepared beforehand, the `_RtlInitUnicodeString` function is used.[i]

Listing 27.11. The kernel-mode driver for creating a device that processes several requests

```
; An example of a kernel-mode driver
; that creates a device
.586P
.MODEL FLAT
```

[i] As already mentioned, it is impossible to use normal API functions at the kernel level. Instead, it is necessary to use special kernel functions that can be used only within the kernel.

```
INCLUDE KERN.INC

EXTERN _RtlInitUnicodeString@8:NEAR
EXTERN _IoCreateDevice@28:NEAR
EXTERN _IoCreateSymbolicLink@8:NEAR
EXTERN _IoDeleteSymbolicLink@4:NEAR
EXTERN _IoDeleteDevice@4:NEAR
EXTERN @IofCompleteRequest@8:NEAR

DTP    equ 8000H
ACCESS equ 0H
OPER   equ 800H
MBUF   equ 0H
; The command processed by the driver
CMD    equ (DTP SHL 16) OR (ACCESS SHL 14) OR (OPER SHL 2) OR MBUF

includelib d:\masm32\lib\ntoskrnl.lib

_DATA SEGMENT
; Device name
       DNAME DW "\", "D", "e", "v", "i", "c", "e", "\", "D", "e", "v", 0
; Reference to the name
       LNAME DW "\", "?", "?", "\", "S", "L", "N", 0
; UNICODE_STRING structures for storing names
       DEVN  UNICODE_STRING  <?>
       SLNKN UNICODE_STRING  <?>
; The structure used for creating a device
       PD DEVICE_OBJECT <?>
; Other variables
       MES DB "From depth", 0
       MES1 DB "For Mydriver", 0
_DATA ENDS

_TEXT SEGMENT

; Driver entry point procedure
; DWORD PTR [EBP+08H] - Pointer to the DRIVER_OBJECT structure
; DWORD PTR [EBP+12] - Pointer to the UNICODE_STRING structure
_ENTRY PROC ; Driver entry point
       PUSH  EBP
       MOV   EBP, ESP ; Now EBP points to the stack top
       PUSH  EBX
       PUSH  ESI
```

```
        PUSH    EDI
; Define the device name
        PUSH    OFFSET LNAME
        PUSH    OFFSET SLNKN
        CALL    _RtlInitUnicodeString@8
; Define the symbolic link to the device name
        PUSH    OFFSET DNAME
        PUSH    OFFSET DEVN
        CALL    _RtlInitUnicodeString@8
; Create a device
        PUSH    OFFSET PD
        PUSH    0
        PUSH    0
        PUSH    22H ; FILE_DEVICE_UNKNOWN
        PUSH    OFFSET DEVN
        PUSH    0
        PUSH    DWORD PTR [EBP+08H]
        CALL    _IoCreateDevice@28
        CMP     EAX, 0
        JZ      OK
        MOV     EAX, STATUS_DEVICE_CONFIGURATION_ERROR
        JMP     EXI
OK:
; Create the symbolic link to the device
        PUSH    OFFSET DEVN
        PUSH    OFFSET SLNKN
        CALL    _IoCreateSymbolicLink@8
; EAX points to the DRIVER_OBJECT structure
        MOV     EAX, DWORD PTR [EBP+08H]
        ASSUME EAX:PTR DRIVER_OBJECT
; Define the procedure for unloading the driver
        MOV     [EAX].DriverUnload, OFFSET DELDRIVER
; Define the callback procedures
; Open the device
        MOV     [EAX].MajorFunction[IRP_MJ_CREATE*4], OFFSET CR_FILE
; Close the device
        MOV     [EAX].MajorFunction[IRP_MJ_CLOSE*4], OFFSET CL_FILE
; Control the device
        MOV     [EAX].MajorFunction[IRP_MJ_DEVICE_CONTROL*4], OFFSET CTL_DEV
        ASSUME EAX:NOTHING
; Set the exit code
        MOV     EAX, STATUS_SUCCESS
EXI:
        POP     EDI
```

```
        POP    ESI
        POP    EBX
        POP    EBP
        RET    8
_ENTRY ENDP
; The procedure called when deleting the driver
; DWORD PTR [EBP+08H] — Pointer to the DRIVER_OBJECT structure
DELDRIVER PROC
        PUSH   EBP
        MOV    EBP, ESP ; Now EBP points to the stack top
; Delete the symbolic link
        PUSH   OFFSET SLNKN
        CALL   _IoDeleteSymbolicLink@4
; Delete the device
        MOV    EAX, DWORD PTR [EBP+08H]
        ASSUME EAX:PTR DRIVER_OBJECT
        PUSH   [EAX].DeviceObject
        CALL   _IoDeleteDevice@4
        POP    EBP
        RET    4
DELDRIVER ENDP
; The procedure called when executing the CreateFile function
; DWORD PTR [EBP+08H] — Pointer to the DEVICE_OBJECT structure
; DWORD PTR [EBP+12] — Pointer to the IRP structure
CR_FILE PROC
        PUSH   EBP
        MOV    EBP, ESP
        MOV    EAX, DWORD PTR [EBP+12]
        ASSUME EAX:PTR _IRP
        MOV    [EAX].IoStatus.Status, STATUS_SUCCESS
        MOV    [EAX].IoStatus.Information, 0
        ASSUME EAX:NOTHING
; Completing the input/output operation
; The call in fastcall format
        MOV    ECX, DWORD PTR [EBP+12]
        XOR    EDX, EDX
        CALL   @IofCompleteRequest@8
        MOV    EAX, STATUS_SUCCESS
        POP    EBP
        RET    8
CR_FILE ENDP
; The procedure called when executing the CloseHandle function
; DWORD PTR [EBP+08H] — Pointer to the DEVICE_OBJECT structure
; DWORD PTR [EBP+12] — Pointer to the IRP structure
```

```
CL_FILE PROC
        PUSH   EBP
        MOV    EBP, ESP
        MOV    EAX, DWORD PTR [EBP+12]
        ASSUME EAX:PTR _IRP
        MOV    [EAX].IoStatus.Status, STATUS_SUCCESS
        AND    [EAX].IoStatus.Information, 0
        ASSUME EAX:NOTHING
; Completing the input/output operation
; The call in the fastcall format
        MOV    ECX, DWORD PTR [EBP+12]
        XOR    EDX, EDX
        CALL   @IofCompleteRequest@8
        MOV    EAX, STATUS_SUCCESS
        POP    EBP
        RET    8
CL_FILE ENDP
; The procedure called when executing the ControlService function
; DWORD PTR [EBP+08H] — The pointer to the DEVICE_OBJECT structure
; DWORD PTR [EBP+12] — The pointer to the IRP structure
CTL_DEV PROC
        PUSH   EBP
        MOV    EBP, ESP
        PUSH   EBX
; EAX will point to the IRP structure
        MOV    EAX, DWORD PTR [EBP+12]
        ASSUME EAX:PTR _IRP
; EDI will point to the IO_STACK_LOCATION structure,
; which must contain the command sent to the driver
        MOV    EDI, [EAX].Tail.Overlay.CurrentStackLocation
        ASSUME EDI:PTR IO_STACK_LOCATION
        CMP    [EDI].Parameters.DeviceIoControl.IoControlCode, CMD
        JNZ    NO_CMD
; The command
        MOV    ESI, [EAX].AssociatedIrp.SystemBuffer
; Now, check the delivered message
        PUSH   ESI
        PUSH   OFFSET MES1
        CALL   CMPSTR
        CMP    EBX, 1
        JZ     NO_CMD
; Copy the string passed from the driver into the buffer
        PUSH   OFFSET MES
        PUSH   ESI
```

```
        CALL    COPYSTR
; The string length will also be passed into the application program
        PUSH    OFFSET MES
        CALL    LENSTR
        MOV     [EAX].IoStatus.Status, STATUS_SUCCESS
        MOV     [EAX].IoStatus.Information, EBX
NO_CMD:
        ASSUME EDI:NOTHING
        ASSUME EAX:NOTHING
; Complete the input/output operation
; The call in the fastcall format
        MOV     ECX, DWORD PTR [EBP+12]
        XOR     EDX, EDX
        CALL    @IofCompleteRequest@8
        MOV     EAX, STATUS_SUCCESS
        POP     EBX
        POP     EBP
        RET     8
CTL_DEV ENDP
; The procedure that copies the source string to the target string
; The target string [EBP+08H] is the first parameter
; The source string [EBP+0CH] is the second parameter
; Do not take into account the target string length
COPYSTR PROC
        PUSH    EBP
        MOV     EBP, ESP
        PUSH    ESI
        PUSH    EDI
        PUSH    EAX
        MOV     ESI, DWORD PTR [EBP+0CH]
        MOV     EDI, DWORD PTR [EBP+08H]
L1:
        MOV     AL, BYTE PTR [ESI]
        MOV     BYTE PTR [EDI], AL
        CMP     AL, 0
        JE      L2
        INC     ESI
        INC     EDI
        JMP     L1
L2:
        POP     EAX
        POP     EDI
        POP     ESI
        POP     EBP
```

```
        RET   8
COPYSTR ENDP
; The function for getting the string length
; [EBP+08H] — Pointer to the string
; EBX — Sting length
LENSTR PROC
        PUSH  EBP
        MOV   EBP, ESP
        PUSH  ESI
        MOV   ESI, DWORD PTR [EBP+8]
        XOR   EBX, EBX
LBL1:
        CMP   BYTE PTR [ESI], 0
        JZ    LBL2
        INC   EBX
        INC   ESI
        JMP   LBL1
LBL2:
        POP   ESI
        POP   EBP
        RET   4
LENSTR ENDP
; The procedure for comparing two strings
; [EBP+08H] — First parameter
; [EBP+012] — Second parameter
; EBX = 0 if strings are equal, and EBX = 1 if strings are not equal
CMPSTR  PROC
        PUSH  EBP
        MOV   EBP, ESP
        PUSH  ESI
        PUSH  EDI
        PUSH  EAX
        MOV   ESI, DWORD PTR [EBP+012]
        MOV   EDI, DWORD PTR [EBP+08H]
L1:
        MOV   AL, BYTE PTR [ESI]
        MOV   EBX, 1
        CMP   BYTE PTR [EDI], AL
        JNZ   EXI
        XOR   EBX, EBX
        CMP   AL, 0
        JZ    EXI
        INC   ESI
        INC   EDI
```

```
        JMP     L1
EXI:
        POP     EAX
        POP     EDI
        POP     ESI
        POP     EBP
        RET     8
CMPSTR ENDP
_TEXT ENDS
END _ENTRY
```

To translate the driver, issue the following commands:

```
ML /c /coff driver.asm
link /driver /base:0x1000 /subsystem:native driver.obj
```

The program in Listing 27.11 requires some comments.

Note that the listing doesn't contain the `STDCALL` directive. This is not an error. The name of the `@IofCompleteRequest` function must not have the underscore prefix in the object module. As relates to other functions, their names must have this prefix. This is why you must explicitly specify this prefix in the names of functions and omit the `STDCALL` directive. The `@IofCompleteRequest` function notifies the program that the request has been processed. This function is called in the `fastcall` format. Two parameters of this function are loaded into the `ECX` and `EDX` registers.

This listing uses pointers to some structures described in Listing 27.9. Here they are:

- `device_object` — The structure that describes the device created by the driver. Note that in the `DELDRIVER` procedure, you get the pointer to this structure from the `driver_object (DeviceObject)` structure.
- `driver_object` — The structure describing the driver object. In particular, this structure includes the `MajorFunction` array. This array contains the pointers to procedures for handling requests. Each element of this array is responsible for a specific request. Element numbers are defined by numeric constants defined in header files.
- `_IRP` — This structure contains information about the request to the driver (IRP stands for Input/output Request Packet). In particular, this structure will include the pointer to the `IO_STACK_LOCATION` structure containing the code of the command that arrived at the driver with the request (see the `CTL_DEV` text).

Pay attention to the following three procedures: `CMPSTR` (compare two strings), `LENSTR` (string length), and `COPYSTR` (copy source string to target string). These procedures have appeared in this code because of the impossibility of using standard API functions at the kernel level.

Bibliography

1. Abel, Peter. IBM PC Assembly Language and Programming. Pearson Education; 5th edition (January 15, 2001). ISBN: 013030655X.
2. Pietrek, Matt. Windows 95 System Programming Secrets. John Wiley & Sons; Book & Disk edition (November 1, 1995). ASIN: 1568843186.
3. Brey, Barry B. The Intel Microprocessors. Prentice Hall; 6th edition (August 15, 2002). ISBN: 0130607142.
4. Schildt, Herbert. Schildt's Advanced Windows 95 Programming in C and C++. McGraw-Hill Osborne Media (February 1, 1996). ASIN: 0078821746.
5. Brumm, Penn and Brumm, Don. 80386 Macro Assembler and Toolkit. McGraw-Hill (May 1, 1989). ASIN: 083060247X.
6. Kauler, Barry. Windows Assembly Language and Systems Programming. CMP Books (July 1, 1997). ISBN: 087930474X.
7. Johnson, Marcus. Assembly Language: For Real Programmers Only! Prentice Hall Computer Books; Book & Disk edition (April 1, 1993). ASIN: 0672484706.
8. Morse, Stephen, Isaacson, Eric, and Albert, Douglas J. 80386/387 Architecture. John Wiley & Sons (August 1, 1987). ASIN: 0471853526.
9. Strauss, Edmund. Inside 80286. Prentice Hall Computer Books (1986). ASIN: 0893035823.
10. Petzold, Charles. Programming Windows. Microsoft Press; 5th Book & CD-ROM edition (November 11, 1998). ISBN: 157231995X.
11. Duntemann, Jeff. Assembly Language Step-by-Step: Programming with DOS and Linux. Wiley; 2nd edition (May 24, 2000). ISBN: 0471375233.
12. Duncan, Ray. Power Programming with Microsoft Macro Assembler Microsoft Press; Book & Disk edition (September 1, 1991). ASIN: 1556152566.

13. Richter, Jeffrey. Advanced Windows. Microsoft Press; 3rd Book & CD-ROM edition (February 1, 1997). ASIN: 1572315482.
14. Hart, Johnson M. Win32 System Programming: A Windows 2000 Application Developer's Guide. Addison-Wesley Publishing; 2nd Book & CD-ROM edition (September 29, 2000) ISBN: 0201703106.
15. Richter, Jeffrey and Clark, Jason D. Programming Server-Side Applications for Microsoft Windows 2000. Microsoft Press; Book & CD-ROM edition (March 1, 2000). ASIN: 0735607532.
16. Appleman, Dan. Dan Appleman's Visual Basic Programmer's Guide to the Win32 API. SAMS; Book & CD-ROM edition (February 1999) ISBN: 0672315904.
17. Jones, Anthony and Ohlund, James. Network Programming for Microsoft Windows. Microsoft Press; 2nd Book & CD-ROM edition (February 13, 2002). ASIN: 0735615799.
18. Nance, Barry. Network Programming in C. Que; Set edition (May 1, 1990). ASIN: 0880225696.

Index

1

A

E

F

G

H

I

N

O

P

Q

R

S

X

Z

ISBN	TITLE	AUTHOR	PRICE	PAGES
8170087503	**Cisco IP Routing Protocols: Troubleshooting Techniques**	V. Anand, K. Chakrabarty	Rs. 295.00	409

DATABASES

ISBN	TITLE	AUTHOR	PRICE	PAGES
8170087147	**DBMS-Complete Practical Approach**	Sharad Maheshwari, Ruchin Jain	Rs. 230.00	530
8170082404	**Learn to Program Visual Basic-Examples**	John Smiley	Rs. 295.00	500
8170082412	**Learn to Program Visual Basic-Databases**	John Smiley	Rs. 325.00	670
8170082420	**Learn to Program Visual Basic-Objects**	John Smiley	Rs. 325.00	700
817008475X	**IT Resources-Access 2002 VBA Programming Access**	Michele Amelot	Rs. 195.00	424
8170084512	**The Power of Oracle 9i**	Rajiv Parida, Vinod Sharma	Rs. 475.00	1100

DOEACC 'O' LEVEL

ISBN	TITLE	AUTHOR	PRICE	PAGES
8170088089	**DOEACC 'O' Level Model Test Papers**	Ramesh Bangia	Rs. 175.00	296
8170085640	**Programming and Problem Solving Through "C" Language**	Harsha Priya, R. Ranjeet	Rs. 95.00	306
8170084474	**IT Tools and Applications**	Ramesh Bangia	Rs. 145.00	392
8170085594	**Business Systems**	Ramesh Bangia	Rs. 175.00	452
8170085454	**Internet & Web Design**	Ramesh Bangia	Rs. 120.00	321

ELECTRONIC COMMERCE

ISBN	TITLE	AUTHOR	PRICE	PAGES
8170085497	**Electronic Commerce**	Pete Loshin, John Vacca	Rs. 295.00	472
817008119X	**E-Commerce**	Mamta Bhusry	Rs. 95.00	215
8170083524	**Marketing in The Cyber Age**	Kurt Rohner	Rs. 295.00	250

HARDWARE/EMBEDDED SYSTEMS

ISBN	TITLE	AUTHOR	PRICE	PAGES
8170087473	**Essentials Electronics for PC Technicians**	John W. Farber	Rs. 295.00	546
8170086264	**Grid Computing: A Practical Guide to Technology and Applications**	Ahmar Abbas	Rs. 295.00	408
8170088186	**CD Cracking Uncovered Protection Against Unsanctioned CD Copy**	Kris Kaspersky	Rs. 295.00	422
8170083435	**Practical Linux Programming: Device Drivers, Embedded Systems**	Ashfaq A. Khan	Rs. 295.00	420

ISBN	TITLE	AUTHOR	PRICE	PAGES
8170083575	**TCP/IP Application Layer Protocols for Embedded Systems**	M. Tim Jones	Rs. 295.00	350
	INTERNET			
8170083206	**The Internet Hand Book for Writers, Students & Teachers**	Mary McGuire, Linda Stillborne	Rs. 195.00	288
8170084776	**Way in-Internet Getting Started**	Elizabeth Bramire	Rs. 95.00	165
	KEEPING AHEAD SERIES			
8170084652	**Keeping Ahead Exchange 2002 Server**	Philippe Levesque	Rs. 145.00	285
8170084660	**Keeping Ahead Windows 2000 Professional**	Jose Dardoigne	Rs. 175.00	388
8170084679	**Keeping Ahead Windows 2000 Server**	Philippe Mathon	Rs. 175.00	360
8170084687	**Keeping Ahead Linux Administration Kernel Version 2.0 to 2.2**	Bruno Guerin	Rs. 125.00	240
8170084695	**Keeping Ahead Using Linux Kernel Version 2.0 to 2.2**	Bruno Guerin	Rs. 125.00	258
8170084709	**Keeping Ahead Java 2**	Benjamin Aumaille	Rs. 145.00	284
8170084717	**Keeping Ahead SQL Server 7**	Joelle Mosset	Rs. 145.00	329
8170084725	**Keeping Ahead Java Script and VB Script**	Benjamin Aumaille	Rs. 145.00	313
8170084733	**Keeping Ahead C++ Programming Language**	Bruno Dubois	Rs. 125.00	234
8170084741	**Keeping Ahead TCP/IP in the NT Environment**	Bruno Ferec	Rs. 125.00	230
	MCSE			
817008489X	**MCSE-Administering SQL Server 7.0**	Jerome Gabillaud	Rs. 295.00	580
8170084903	**MCSE-Networking Essentials**	Jose Dordoigne	Rs. 245.00	453
8170084911	**MCSE-Windows 2000 Professional**	Jose Dordoigne	Rs. 325.00	665
817008492X	**MCSE-Windows 2000 Server**	Philippe Mathon	Rs. 345.00	712
	MULTIMEDIA AND ANIMATION			
8170088208	**3 DS Max 6 Animation with Character Studio 4 and Plug-Ins**	Boris Kulagin, Dmitry Morozov	Rs. 175.00	216
8170088216	**Adobe Audition: Soundtracks for Digital Video**	Roman Petelin, Yury Petelin	Rs. 195.00	278

ISBN	TITLE	AUTHOR	PRICE	PAGES
8170086205	**Building A Digital Human**	Karl Brilliant	Rs. 295.00	380
8170086213	**Making Digital Videos**	Ben Long	Rs. 295.00	284
8170087171	**Illustrating with Macromedia Flash TM MX 2004**	Robert Firbaugh	Rs. 245.00	366
8170082439	**Multimedia Basics-Technology (Vol. I)**	Andreas Holzinger	Rs. 195.00	285
8170082447	**Multimedia Basics-Learning (Vol. II)**	Andreas Holzinger	Rs. 195.00	300
8170082455	**Multimedia Basics-Design (Vol. III)**	Andreas Holzinger	Rs. 195.00	280
8170083532	**Maya Feature Creature Creations**	Todd Palamar	Rs. 295.00	450
8170083540	**Sound Forge Power**	Scott R. Garrigus	Rs. 195.00	250
8170086116	**Multimedia and Web Technology**	Ramesh Bangia	Rs. 295.00	706

NETWORKING

ISBN	TITLE	AUTHOR	PRICE	PAGES
817008721X	**Networking Essentials**	Jose Dordoigne	Rs. 195.00	453
8170087023	**Computer Networks**	Ajit Kumar Singh	Rs. 95.00	181
817008203X	**Telecom & Networking Glossary**	Robert Mastin	Rs. 300.00	250
8170082048	**Data Networking Made Easy**	Karen Patten	Rs. 360.00	350
8170082056	**Digital Convergence**	Andy Covell	Rs. 300.00	250

OFFICE AUTOMATION

ISBN	TITLE	AUTHOR	PRICE	PAGES
8170088003	**Desk Top Publishing**	Dinesh Maidasani	Rs. 125.00	210
8170087805	**Learning Computer Programming, MS Office and Internet & Web Tech.**	Dinesh Maidasani	Rs. 95.00	318
8170087686	**MS Word 2000 Thumb-Rules and Details**	Snigdha Banerjee	Rs. 175.00	390

ON YOUR SIDE SERIES

ISBN	TITLE	AUTHOR	PRICE	PAGES
8170084830	**On your side-Powerpoint 2002**	Andrew Blackburn	Rs. 145.00	282
8170084849	**On your side-Excel 2002**	Adrienne Tommy	Rs. 125.00	275
8170084857	**On your side-Word 2002**	Adrienne Tommy	Rs. 125.00	289
8170084865	**On your side-Access 2002**	Adrienne Tommy	Rs. 125.00	303
8170084873	**On your side-Frontpage 2002**	Andrew Blackburn	Rs. 95.00	220
8170084881	**On your side-Windows XP**	Adrienne Tommy	Rs. 125.00	310

OPERATING SYSTEMS

ISBN	TITLE	AUTHOR	PRICE	PAGES
8170087236	**Linux-A Practical Approach**	B. Mohamed Ibrahim	Rs. 95.00	187
8170083427	**The MS-Windows XP Professional Handbook**	Louis Columbus	Rs. 295.00	330
8170084784	**Way in-Windows XP Home Edition**	Andrew Blackburn	Rs. 95.00	183

ISBN	TITLE	AUTHOR	PRICE	PAGES
8170086221	**Cyber Rookies—Operating System Fundamentals**	D. Irtegov	Rs. 295.00	498

PROGRAMMING

ISBN	TITLE	AUTHOR	PRICE	PAGES
8170087791	**The Art of Programming Through Flowcharts & Algorithms**	Anil Bikas Chaudhuri	Rs. 95.00	160
8170086248	**Preventative Programming Techniques**	Brian Hawkins	Rs. 295.00	322
8170083443	**Learning Computer Programming : It's not about Languages**	Mary Farrell	Rs. 295.00	375
8170086256	**Object-Oriented Programming From Problem Solving to Java**	Jose M. Garrido	Rs. 295.00	360
8170088038	**Assembly Language Programming for Intel Processors Family**	Vasile Lungu	Rs. 295.00	577
8170088178	**The Assembly Programming Master Book**	Vlad Pirogov	Rs. 395.00	726

PROGRAMMING - C#, C, C++

ISBN	TITLE	AUTHOR	PRICE	PAGES
8170083702	**The Power of C#**	Rajiv Parida	Rs. 295.00	592
8170085632	**Mastering Graphics Programming in 'C'**	Sudhir Dawra	Rs. 145.00	286
8170087074	**Mastering C Programs**	J.B. Dixit	Rs. 195.00	434
8170081262	**Programming in C**	J.B. Dixit	Rs. 245.00	505
8170087619	**Unix and C Programming**	Ashok Arora, Shefali Bansal	Rs. 295.00	606
8170086140	**Data Structure for 'C' Programming, 2nd Edition**	Ajay Kumar	Rs. 145.00	290
8170081270	**Programming in C++**	J.B. Dixit	Rs. 260.00	601
8170088194	**Hackish C++ Pranks & Tricks**	Michael Flenov	Rs. 245.00	326
8170082889	**Basics of C++ Programming**	Nishant Kundalia	Rs. 95.00	168
8170083648	**Mastering C++ Programs**	J.B. Dixit	Rs. 295.00	614
817008623X	**Cyber Rookies—C++ Programming Fundamentals**	Chuck Easttom	Rs. 295.00	417

SECURITY

ISBN	TITLE	AUTHOR	PRICE	PAGES
8170083419	**Computer Forensics : Computer Crime Scene Investigation**	John Vacca	Rs. 445.00	600
8170083494	**Firewall Architecture for the Enterprise**	Norbert Pohlmann, Tim Crothers	Rs. 295.00	480
8170086272	**Net Spies**	Andrew Gauntlett	Rs. 195.00	210

ISBN	TITLE	AUTHOR	PRICE	PAGES
	SOFTWARE ENGINEERING AND TECHNOLOGY			
817008718X	**Human Aspects of Software Engineering**	James E. Tomayko, Orit Hazzar	Rs. 195.00	338
8170087899	**Management Information Systems**	Avdhesh Gupta, Anurag Malik	Rs. 175.00	362
8170087953	**Human Computer Interaction**	Rajendra Ranjan Kumar	Rs. 95.00	210
8170088097	**System Analysis and Design**	Preeti Gupta	Rs. 125.00	192
817008802X	**Autocad 2005 for Engineers**	Ionel Simion	Rs. 175.00	271
8170088054	**Digital Signal Processing Fundamentals**	Ashfaq A. Khan	Rs. 295.00	391
817008363X	**Practical Project Management**	Ivan Bayross	Rs. 195.00	342
	STRAIGHT TO THE POINT SERIES			
8170084601	**STTP : Word 2002**	Corinne Hervo	Rs. 45.00	154
817008461X	**STTP : Excel 2002**	Corinne Hervo	Rs. 45.00	153
8170084628	**STTP : Dreamweaver 4**	Corinne Hervo	Rs. 45.00	135
8170084636	**STTP : Flash 5**	Corinne Hervo	Rs. 45.00	126
8170084644	**STTP : Photoshop 6**	Corinne Hervo	Rs. 45.00	152
8170084482	**STTP : MS Office 2000**	Ramesh Bangia	Rs. 95.00	300
8170086108	**STTP : MS Office 2003**	Ramesh Bangia	Rs. 145.00	288
8170087651	**STTP : MS Word 2003**	Ramesh Bangia	Rs. 60.00	150
8170088011	**STTP : Photoshop CS**	Firewall Media	Rs. 60.00	150
8170088143	**STTP : MS Excel 2003**	Firewall Media	Rs. 60.00	150
8170088151	**STTP : Coreldraw 12**	Firewall Media	Rs. 60.00	150
	STUDIO FACTORY			
8170084792	**Studio Factory-Photoshop 6**	Christophe Aubry	Rs. 175.00	364
8170084806	**Studio Factory-Flash 5**	Sami Ben Yahiya	Rs. 145.00	314
8170084814	**Studio Factory-Dreamweaver Ultradev 4**	Philippe Chatellier	Rs. 95.00	240
8170084822	**Studio Factory-Dreamweaver 4**	Christophe Aubry	Rs. 175.00	373
8170087627	**Studio Factory-Flash MX**	Arnaud Blanche	Rs. 145.00	337
8170087643	**Studio Factory-Dreamweaver MX**	Christophe Aubry	Rs. 195.00	407
817008766X	**Studio Factory-Photoshop 7**	Cyril Guerin	Rs. 175.00	390
	WEB TECHNOLOGY			
8170087163	**Web Design with Macromedia Studio MX 2004**	Eric Hunley	Rs. 295.00	558

Please write for a free color Firewall Media Catalog for details on the above books.

ISBN	TITLE	AUTHOR	PRICE	PAGES
8170083400	**Professional Web Design (Techniques and Templates)**	Clint Eccher	Rs. 295.00	425
8170088046	**HTML, XHTML, CSS and XML**	Teodoru Gugoiu	Rs. 195.00	355
8170083583	**FrontPage 2000 for Visual Learners**	Chris Charuhas	Rs. 95.00	200
8170083591	**HTML & Java Script for Visual Learners**	Chris Charuhas	Rs. 95.00	200
8170083605	**The Visual Learner's Guide to Managing Web Projects**	Chris Charuhas	Rs. 95.00	130
8170083613	**Dreamweaver 4 for Visual Learners**	Chris Charuhas	Rs. 95.00	200
8170084768	**IT Resource-Implementing XML: Managing and Formatting Data**	Johhny Brochard	Rs. 125.00	279
8170085470	**Design Your Web World**	Sunil Jalota	Rs. 45.00	103

ORDER FORM

LAXMI PUBLICATIONS (P) LTD.

7/19, Ansari Road, Daryaganj, New Delhi-110002
Phones : 23262368, 23262370 ; *Faxes* : 011-2325 25 72, 2326 22 79
Email : colaxmi@hotmail.com
Website : www.laxmipublications.com

Please send me the following books by V.P.P. I have sent Rs. .... by M.O./Draft on Date ....

☐ ____________________
☐ ____________________
☐ ____________________
☐ ____________________
☐ ____________________
☐ ____________________
☐ ____________________

(Please use separate sheet if you need more books)

Fill in this coupon in BLOCK letters only.

Name ____________________

Address ____________________

____

P.O. ____________ Distt. ____________

State ____________ Pin Code ☐☐☐☐☐☐

Phone ____________ Email ____________

Please do not refuse to accept the V.P.P. Honour it and write to us if there is any complaint. We shall set right your complaint, if any.

Our books are available at all leading bookshops.

Please mention Name of Books, clearly.

It is necessary to send Rs. 50.00 per book as an advance. Without advance order will not be sent.

Terms and Conditions for the supply of Books by V.P. Parcels to Students

1. Mention your name, address and nearest post office, with Pin Code No., in capital block letters for quick compliance of your order.
2. You can also send complete payment in advance by Money Order.
3. V.P. Parcels are detained by the Postal Authorities for only 5 days. Hence the same should be honoured on receiving intimation to avoid legal action against the defaulter.
4. Half Postage free.
5. All disputes will be settled in Delhi Courts only.
6. V.P. Parcels are not accepted for stations served by A.P.O. 56 and A.P.O. 99. While ordering for our Books from these stations, please ascertain and send the amount in full, in advance, on receipt of which, the books will be sent by registered post.
7. (*i*) V.P.P. Orders should be accompanied with advance of Rs. 50.00 per book. Without advance, ordered book(s) will not be sent.

   (*ii*) While sending advance by money order, please write your requirements on the last part of money order (space for communication). On its reverse side write your complete name and address.

   (*iii*) **Please note that the upper part of the money order form here you have written your address, remains with post office. So it is necessary to write your address again on last part of the M.O. form.**
8. Order placed will not be cancelled.
9. For books which are not supplied to you due to their being out of stock, please write again after 30 days with 25% advance.
10. Requests for our Books from students who did not honour their previous order will not be considered unless they send us full advance payment plus the postage charges for the returned parcel.
11. Prices are subject to change without notice.

Please write your letters to :

LAXMI PUBLICATIONS (P) LTD.

7/19, Ansari Road, Daryaganj, New Delhi-110002
Phones : 23262368, 23262370 ; *Faxes* : 011-2325 25 72, 2326 22 79
Email : colaxmi@hotmail.com
Website : www.laxmipublications.com